SURVIVING AMONG STRANGERS

STRANGERS' SURVIVAL STRATEGIES

REV EMMANUEL OGHENE

Surviving Among Strangers
Strangers' Survival Strategies

Copyright © 2017 by Rev Emmanuel Oghene.

Paperback ISBN: 978-1-952982-19-4
Ebook ISBN: 978-1-952982-20-0

All rights reserved. No part in this book may be produced and transmitted in any form or by any means, electronic, or mechanical, including photocopying, recording, or by any information storage and retrieval system, without permission in writing from the copyright owner.

The views expressed in this work are solely those of the author and do not necessarily reflect the views of the publisher hereby disclaims any responsibility for them.

Unless otherwise indicated, scriptures are from Today's English Version (TEV), New International Version (NIV), New Century Version (NCV), Amplified Bible (AMP), New Living Translation (NLT), The Living Bible (TLB), Contemporary English Bible (CEV), New American Standard Bible (NASB) and Easy-to-Read-Version (ERV)

Published by Golden Ink Media Services   09/11/2020

Golden Ink Media Services
(302) 703-7235
support@goldeninkmediaservices@gmail.com

TABLE OF CONTENTS

Dedication ix

Appreciation xi

Introduction xiii

Chapter 1   The Arrival, Readying, Rise, and
             Reign (TARRR) 1

Chapter 2   Surviving Among Resentful
             Natives (SARN) 30

Chapter 3   Do Not Get Carried Away 72

Chapter 4   Scandalous Surviving Strategies
             Among Strangers (SSSAS) 160

Chapter 5   Form and Fan Favorable Friendship 177

Chapter 6   Prepare to Pay Appropriately 234

Chapter 7   God's Help Plus/Hard Work Plus 275

Chapter 8   Wishes Don't Better Beggars 301

Chapter 9	Tolerance's Tortuous Trap	342
Chapter 10	The Obnoxiousness of Overstay	411
Chapter 11	Be Focused	432
Chapter 12	Mind Your Business	501
Chapter 13	Reduce Friction with Your Native Neigbhors	537
Chapter 14	Strategic Purchase of Loyalty	576
Chapter 15	Rewarding Self-integration	606
Chapter 16	Self-saving Secrecy	629
Chapter 17	Migrants' Investment Mindset (MIM)	639
Chapter 18	Ignoring the Inevitables	645
Chapter 19	Needfulness Nullifies Negativity	672
Chapter 20	Engage in Legitimate Endeavours	695
Chapter 21	Work for the Good of the Land	716
Chapter 22	United Voice/Front	737
Chapter 23	Maintaining Self-saving Spirituality (MSS)	764
Chapter 24	Functional Facts	776
Chapter 25	Natives Right to Suspect/Resent Strangers (NRSRS)	797
Chapter 26	Migration Motive/Reasons for Migration	809

Chapter 27 Youthful Adventure/Peer Pressure 854

Chapter 28 Notorious Nativity Nature/Mentality

or Monstrous Nativity Mindset.....................866

Chapter 29 Home-based Immigrants or Native

Stranger/Strangers at Home 889

Chapter 30 Do Not Flaunt Your Success and Affluence...913

Chapter 31 The Victimization of Natives 949

Chapter 32 Magnificent Migration Management 990

Author's Other Published Titles..1005

Dedication

Donald J Trump

The Forty-fifth President of the United States of America

APPRECIATION

My greatest gratitude goes to the Lord who, during the final phase of this work, proved beyond all doubts that this is His project. He made see and hear cases that confirmed what the Holy Spirit had imputed into my heart to note for each chapter to prove that nothing has changed about bible stories and contemporary experiences. My special thanks to my many encouragers too numerous to mention here.

Introduction

A stranger, migrant or immigrant is tactically, a squatter in his or her land of sojourn. A stranger and squatter is someone whose rights are limited wherever he lives. Perhaps, his rights are at the discretion of the natives and hosts. This is illustrated in a story of a teacher in the days when "Teachers' Grade III" was highly regarded in Nigerian educational system. This teacher came up with some signs to indicate to his wife the extent to which any visiting relative or friend should be taken care of.

He was the first to acquire western education among members of his extended family and lived in an urban center. This made the relatives to visit and stay with him frequently because of which he was spending a lot of his income on hosting visitors. So, he came up with the idea of using his fingers to demonstrate to his wife how well the visitor should be treated. He would tell the wife to cook meals badly so that the visitors would not like to stay long. If he gesticulated with a finger while telling the wife something like "this relative you are looking at is very important to me, make sure you feed him very well, and pointed a finger, it means she should not give him enough food, if he pointed two fingers, it meant she should give average size food but if he used three fingers while demonstrating, it meant the person should be well fed. Though he did not mind hosting some of the visiting relatives, but some were becoming a nuisance, so he would dictate who should be well fed.

Feeding some well and others poorly meant that while those who were well-fed would talk well of the wife and their brother, those underfed would say otherwise and that would help him still have some of the relatives liking him and others not liking him as much. One key point in the story of this teacher is that both friends and relatives who visited him were at his mercy and that of his wife who determined what measure of comfort they enjoy during their visiting-stay. Whoever did not like the treatment meted out to him or her, would have to leave quickly or go elsewhere. This is the reality of life as no one could tell them, "Mr. and Mrs., you cannot treat me this way". If you abhor the way you are being treated, then do not prolong your stay and never return again. It is like the subject of the house owner and his or her tenant; anyhow, it is the tenant who would have to leave the house for the owner. You either abide by the rules of the Romans to enjoy your stay with them or you relocate elsewhere promptly.

1

THE ARRIVAL, READYING, RISE, AND REIGN (TARRR)

Genesis 24:1-67 confirms that during Eliezer's transnational border travel to get a wife for Isaac he and Abraham who sent him agreed that he needed God's help to be successful. Ezra 8:21-23 and 31-32 confirm that to ensure personal protection and safety the priest and scholar of God's commandments provoked spiritual support through fasting and prayers. His objective was to ensure that he and members of his entourage arrived Jerusalem safely as planned. It was a transnational border travel and they were relocating to the land of Judah permanently. Ezra's generation of Jews might have been born away from their ancestral land of Judah but were returning home to make their own contribution to the development of their native land. The fact that he was religious did not make him assume that God of Israel would give them journey mercies that would guarantee their safe travel automatically or without their making personal self-sacrifice by way of abstinence from food and drinks for three days. In addition to all the preparations that they made to return to Jerusalem they did not forget to take measures to ensure that they got home safely. He recognized that no amount of planning and good motive that they had while leaving Suza, if they did not get to Jerusalem safely because of attacks along the way, they would fail to achieve their aims and objective for going to Jerusalem.

Nehemiah 2:9 confirms that when Nehemiah was returning, he got military protection from his boss, the Persian Emperor. He did not take his security for granted. He did not assume that because God had given him favour with his boss to grant all his material requests God would automatically provide protection. Ezra's and Nehemiah's cases teach us that whether migrating outside native land of birth, return home after a long time or born abroad and returning home, the subject of safe arrival at the destination should not be trivialized. There are people who returned home to contribute to the development of their ancestral land who were killed by hoodlums shortly after arriving home. There are others who died in plane crash while traveling home to visit loved ones or resettle after many years of sojourn in a foreign land. No one should be so excited to relocate to the extent of disregarding personal safety.

Generally, all travels have their inherent dangers. Joseph's journey to Egypt nearly cost his life because of his older brothers' envy engineered threats. The fact that God meant Paul to preach to the Gentiles meant that his journey to Rome was a monumental God's plan instigated migration to where he should accomplish the real reason God sent him through his parents to live on earth. Despite the fact that God authored the journey, his life was threatened, and they had to fast (go on without food and water or any other drink) for 14 days before they could survive the threat to their lives. Judges 19:1-30 recounts the story of a Levite whose wife was raped while they travelled from her parents' home to their home. It can be called 'travel's traditional travails' or 'travellers' traditional travails'.

Every travel or migration has inherent troubles just like traveling through this world or planet earth from creation to eternity has its own troubles and tribulations.

Arriving destination safely is the first success or victory that the traveler or migrant whether away or back home achieves or must strive to achieve. The first victory Jacob won was getting to Laban's place which was where he had in mind when he left home. Genesis 11:27-30 and 12:1-9 confirm that when Abraham left his original hometown or locality, he, his father, and other family members went with him and their ultimate destination was Canaan however, his father could not get there. In fact, other family members like Nahor and his household members did not get to Canaan. Only Abraham and his wife and their nephew Lot got to the destination of Canaan. It is like candidates admitted studying over a period to obtain a certain certificate by the end of it. Usually, some would fall by way side, it is exceedingly rare for all the students who registered for the programme to follow through till the very end and graduate successfully. Surviving the hazards of the travel route by any means of travel is the starting point of success wherever one migrates to settle either briefly or for long.

Exodus 1:8-22 can be interpreted to partly mean that the more the Egyptians oppressed the Israelites the more the Israelites increased numerically. Also, the more the Israelites increased the angrier the king of Egypt became with the Israelites. Genesis 15:12-21, Exodus 1:11-12 and Acts 7:17 can be said to mean that part of the reason God took the Israelites to live in Egypt for 430 years was to enable them increase numerically enough to form an independent nation upon their departure. This strongly suggests that even God-sponsored strangers' or migrants' success, progress and prosperity offend natives naturally. It is like the way that amateurs' success offends established professionals a great deal. Genesis 26:1-6 and 12-23 confirms that God-sponsored Isaac's prosperity in Gerar offended the native Philistines hosts a great deal. They could not help persecuting Isaac for daring to prosper in their land while they did not do as well because of ravaging famine.

One of the reasons that could make God-sponsored prosperity violate non-beneficiaries is that it could subjugate them to the beneficiary. In this respect, I Chronicles 4:9-10 confirms that it made Jabez become greater than his siblings and relatives. Genesis 30:25-43 and 31:1-16 say it made Jacob richer than his uncle turned employer and father-in-law, Laban to the envy of Laban and his sons. It made the Pharisees hate Jesus. David was considered an amateur when he killed Goliath and it never went down well with King Saul who felt humiliated that the professional he could not defeat as a professional warrior was defeated by an underrated amateur like David. I Kings 13:1-32 can be interpreted to mean that the old prophet at Bethel took exception to a younger and unknown prophet from Judah coming over to his Bethel base to deliver God's message to the king of Israel rather than God using him (the old prophet) to deliver His message to King Jeroboam of Israel. Genesis 37:1-36 can be interpreted to mean that the revelation that Joseph would become greater offended his older brothers. Verses 3 and 10-11 confirm that even their father who claimed to love him berated him for it. It can be called "How God's Help Hurts" or "God's Help's Unintended Hurt."

Amos 1:1 and 7:10-17 can be interpreted to mean that Amaziah, the substantive or presiding priest of Bethel threatened the life of Prophet Amos who was a farmer transformed into a prophet and coming over to Bethel to give a message to the Israelites. Amaziah meant that it is unacceptable for an amateur like Amos to come over from his agricultural field of endeavour to do God's work that Amaziah believed to be his exclusive right to do. Numbers 3:1-49, 4:1-49, 6:22-27, 8:5-26, 16:41-50, 17:1-13 and 18:1-7, Deuteronomy 10:8, I Chronicles 15:7-15 and II Chronicles 26:15-23 confirm that the priests who descended from Aaron leading worship at the Temple in Jerusalem and who believed that they were the chief custodians of the religious life of the Israelites as a nation invoked God's power to deal decisively with King Uzziah for daring to cross from his exclusive royal rights into the rights and responsibilities territory of Aaronite priests.

Genesis 21:25-26 and 26:16-22 say the same way that the Philistines persecuted Abraham by blocking the wells he dug so also they persecuted Isaac by blocking the new wells that he dug and his father's dug wells that he tried to resuscitate. This is even though Genesis 20:1-18, 21:22-34, 26:26-29 confirm that –

(1) the Philistines were very much aware that God was with or sponsored and protected Abraham and his covenant son and God ordained and ordered heir or chief inheritor, Isaac.

(2) the Philistines' King Abimelech had ordered them not to do anything whatsoever to oppress and offend Abraham and Isaac. That sounds like migrants' prospering beside their native neighbours have been an offence for quite a while.

(3) Genesis 26:7-11 and 16-25 says the same King Abimelech who once told his palace officials and fellow Philistine subjects never to do anything to hurt Isaac later led his officials and native subjects to afflict the same Isaac

because they could not live with the realization that Isaac prospered greatly while they did not.

Verses 26-33 say it was only after Isaac had gone to settle outside of their land that the same Abimelech went to seek peace agreement with Isaac because according to him, it was undeniable that God's presence was with Isaac. But he never thought it was enough reason to ask Isaac to return to his domain. Matthew 1:17 confirms that from Abraham to Jesus there were 42 generations and we can add whatever is the estimated number of generations since Jesus died on the cross, rose from the dead and ascended to heaven. That sounds like natives' resentment for migrants for diverse reasons have been around since human record led by the Sacred Books now known as the Holy Bible began. We shall not at this point delve into the subject of the role of God's reaction to mankind's attempt to build the tower of Babel reported in Genesis 11:1-9 has played in this matter.

Something else is the fact that God's plan and its implementation offends non-direct beneficiaries nearly always. For instance,

God's plan for Joseph offended his older brothers just like that of David offended his boss, King Saul. That of Jesus offended the Pharisees just as Laban can be said to have reacted negatively to that of Jacob. Genesis 26:1-34 says the Philistines were not happy with Isaac's God of Israel-sponsored prosperity during famine while he lived among them. We have taken the examples of Jacob and his uncle, Joseph and his older brothers, David and Saul as well as Jesus and the Pharisees to affirm that this fact have nothing to with whether one lives among strangers or his own people, it is just natural that people would resent God-sponsored extraordinary help to anyone, anywhere and at anytime.

The case of Apostate Saul of Tarsus turned Apostle Paul is very striking. As long as he worked against the core reason God sent him to live, his fellow Jews and their religious rulers approved of him and his nefarious activities however from the point when he found out God's original plans and set out to live accordingly the same Jews and their religious rulers sought to kill him. It means that he was safer while doing the wrong thing and gravely endangered when he began to do the right thing. That is how crooked this world is. The world's most endangered species are those who have found out and determined to vigorously pursue God's plan for their lives. The day Jesus was baptized, and heaven voiced the affirmation of His mandatory mission on earth was the beginning of His real troubles spearheaded by Satan who recruited the traditional Jewish religious rulers to front for him. One of the fundamental reasons is because Satan, God's archenemy is the prince or ruler of this present world.

Genesis 46:8-27, Exodus 1:1-7 and Acts 7:9-14 confirm that when the Israelites entered Egypt they were only 75 persons in total only for Exodus 12:37, Numbers 1:20-46 and 11:21 to confirm that by the time they were leaving there were not less than 600,000 men of war. This outgoing figure did not take account of members of the tribe of Levi as well as the women and children of the other tribes which must have been more in number. Numbers 4:34-48 confirms that the able-bodied men excluding women and children of the tribe of Levi were 8,580. The harsher King Saul treated David the greater David became in the sense that once he forced David out of his army of Israel, I Samuel 21:1-4 confirms that the first batch of 400 men who believed that David was worthy of serving under as their leader joined David. They took their families to become David's followers as different from the soldiers who I Samuel 18:13 confirms that Saul appointed David to serve as their commander earlier. I Samuel 23:1-5 and 13 and 30:1-6, 9 and 21-25 say not long after the number of David's followers increased to 600 men. Then, I Samuel 27:1-12 and I Chronicles 12:1-22 confirm that several thousands of Israel's warriors deserted King Saul to go and join David and his earlier followers while David was living in Ziklag among the Philistines during Saul's final 16 months before I Samuel 29:1-11, 31:1-13 and I Chronicles 10:1-14 say Saul died during what became his final battle against the Philistines.

This point to the subject of Persecution Piloted Progress and Promotion or Promotional Persecution like the Israelites experienced in Egypt, Genesis 37:1-36, 39:1-23 and 41:1-57 say of Joseph among his older brothers and in Egypt or David in the hands of his predecessor, King Saul. The more Saul persecuted David the higher David's profile rose. The first mistake Saul made in his relationship with David was to despise David when he was going into battle with the Philistines at the valley of Elah in the territory of Judah. I Samuel 16:1-23 confirms that (1) Samuel had anointed David as the next king of Israel after Saul and (2) Saul had engaged David to serve as his personal musician and apparently one of his armour bearers. However, I Samuel 17:1-58 confirms that when Saul was leading the Israelite warriors to battle the Philistines at the valley of Elah for reasons best known to him, he left David behind in the palace while David's three eldest brothers went with Saul and other Israelites to this battle.

On hindsight we can postulate that apparently God knew that Saul was about to face humiliation from the Philistines in battle at the valley of Elah and stage-managed David to be available at Saul's beck and call so He could use David to save Saul and the army of Israel from that embarrassment. But unfortunately, Saul did not understand and left David behind in his palace while going to this battle that turned out to be one of the most embarrassing battles that Saul ever led the army of Israel to fight during his 40-year reign. I Samuel 17:1-58 includes the fact that it took David's father sending him to the battlefield to save Saul and the army of Israel from the humiliation of the Philistine warriors.

I Samuel 17:55-58 says when Saul saw David going out to kill Goliath he asked his COAS, Abner to find out who's son David was despite the fact that I Samuel 16:14-23 confirms that he had appointed David as his personal musician and battlefield armour bearer a little earlier. It means that when Saul appointed David earlier, he did not take personal note of David. That is a reflection of what I John 2:16 calls 'pride of life' because his consciousness of the position of the king of Israel that he occupied did not allow him to regard David. It must be the reason that despite appointing David as his armour bearer he did not think that David was worth taking to the battle against the Philistines at the valley of Elah. It is the reason it took Jesse sending David to check on the wellbeing of his three eldest brothers for David to learn of Goliath and volunteered to confront and crush Goliath.

Ecclesiastes 9:13-16 says the powerfuls of this world do not regard the poor even when the poor have the wisdom that could save the rich and powerfuls who rule society from their enemies. Saul and his experienced warriors were useless to the defeat of the Philistines in I Samuel 17:1-58 meanwhile David who was useful was the very person who Saul failed to take along even when David was at his beck and call to do his bidding. The way Saul treated David in this instance or respect can be said to be similar to the way Daniel 5:1-31 says King Nebuchadnezzar's son and successor, Belshazzar treated Daniel to Belshazzar's regret. The presence of David in his palace as one of his palace servants had not registered in Saul's subconscious until David killed Goliath. However, the fact that the Goliath he could not kill in battle for 40 days and nights was killed by David within few hours of learning about how Goliath had been mesmerizing Saul and other Israelites incensed Saul's envy and jealousy. It fits the concept of "Disregarding the Relevant Remnant to Embrace the Irrelevant Majority" or "Majoring in the Meaningless and Minoring in the Meaningful". One of Satan's strategies to shortchange a man is to manipulate him to prefer the meaningless/useless because they are in the majority and by so doing the man disregards the meaningful and useful because they are in the minority. Numbers 13 and 14 confirm that it created problems for the Israelites at Kadesh Barnea when they believed the evil report of 84% of Moses' spies and rejected the good faith in God of Israel-based report of 16% (made up of Joshua and Caleb). The Israelites must have thought that because 84% of the spies said the same thing then their report should be believed and adopted for implementation rather than what they considered as minority report. The voice of the majority is not always the voice of God. The lone voice of Jeremiah was the real prophetic voice of God in his generation of the Jews, all other priests and prophets who countered his voice were not speaking for their God who is also the God of the universe. I Kings 22:1-40 and I Chronicles 18:1-34 confirm that Prophet Micaiah was the only authentic voice of God to King Ahab though Ahab believed his preferred precarious prophets to his own peril. Jesus was the authentic voice of God while the High Priests, Pharisees and Sadducees were not.

If Saul had taken David along to that battle earlier, David would have killed Goliath the very first day and the delay that made very obvious of the fact that Saul could no longer lead the army of Israel to victory would have been avoided. The embarrassment of David achieving what Saul could not achieve was greater by reason of the bigger window of the opportunity that Saul and other Israelite warriors had and yet could not. The Israelites beginning with Saul knew that it was God who helped David to defeat the Philistines in the battle and II Samuel 3:6-20 confirms that Saul's cousin and COAS, Abner attested to this fact. Saul refused to accept his blame for failing to recognize God's prior solution provision in David against the Philistines.

On David's part, he did not insist that Saul must take him to that battle as Saul's newly appointed battlefield armour bearer. He accepted Saul's decision to leave him behind and decided to occupy himself with going back to tend his father's flock at the grazing fields of Bethlehem since that was what he did earlier before his elevation to serve in Saul's palace. He waited for God's appointed time for him to prove his military skills and God's extraordinary presence in his life to the entire nation of Israel. The fact that he was ignored by Saul initially did not stop God from making him relevant to the envy of Saul.

It is helpful to ask God for help to prosper amidst the persecution by all those who feel shortchanged or less favoured by God's plan for you. There is a slight difference between God's plan in one's favour and overcoming the attendant persecutions by the angered. Saul could have been sad that God helped David to achieve what he could not without taking it out on David. If that were the case, David would need to ask God to continue to help him to achieve or lead the defeat of enemies of Israel like I Samuel 18:30 says:

> 30 The Philistine armies would come and fight, but in every battle David was more successful than any of Saul's other officers. As a result David became very famous. (TEV)

This means that after the killing of Goliath, God continued to help David to lead the defeat of the Philistines and as a result David became even more popular. It established the fact that David was a capable warrior. In any case, there was a time in the past when Saul was the 'war-winning and greatest warrior' darling of the nation of Israel. It ceased when God withdrew his support from Saul and his greatest warrior credentials, or rating began to nose-dive. However, even though David continued to lead the defeat of Israel's enemies, he had to get God's help to survive Saul's home-based threats to his life. He needed God's protection outside of battles against external enemies. There is the subject of recognizing when the honeymoon of the greatest is over. The first sign that Saul's ability to lead the defeat of the enemies of the Israelites was when I Samuel 13:1-23, 14:1-53 and 17:1-58 confirm that the last time he fought the Philistines before David defeated them by killing Goliath it was his son, Jonathan who did it for him. He should have known that it was time for him to depend on the younger generation to sustain him on the throne before he could live up to his responsibilities as king of Israel and remain their war-winning ruler warrior. It means that David's killing of Goliath was the second sign that sealed Saul's fate that his celebration as the capable ruler of Israel was over for good.

I Samuel 23:14 confirms that God provided the spiritual protection he needed from Saul's threats. As a result, he continued to prosper despite Saul's threat and this really got

Saul madder at him. There are two types of God-provided spiritual protection as well as support to any man or a group of people. For instance, in the case of Samuel, I Samuel 16:1-13 says Samuel formally asked for God's protection solution to Saul's likely angry reaction to the news of his having gone to anoint David as his replacement as king of Israel. Then, I Samuel 19:18-24 can be interpreted to mean that without Samuel formally asking for God's protection God provided protection for Samuel when Saul tried to go and capture David who had gone to hide at Samuel's home at Ramah in the territory of the tribe of Ephraim. Samuel was offering sacrifices on the day that Saul made four different attempts to invade Samuel's home that failed because of what can be interpreted to be God's direct intervention from heaven.

This is significant because it seems that whenever Samuel is offering sacrifices or engaged in any religious ritual, God's presence is made available to him in an unprecedented manner. This is confirmed by the fact that I Samuel 3:1-18 says the first time he heard God's voice clearly was while sleeping at God's worship centre at Shiloh. Then, I Samuel 3:19-23 confirms that so long as he was there, he heard God's message and passed it on to the Israelites who complied accordingly. Also, whatever he said on God's behalf, God established it. Next, I Samuel 7:1-14 confirms that the day he would bring down heaven's help to enable the Israelites defeat their enemies in battle, all he did was to offer sacrifices. I Samuel 9:1-27 says on the day he would meet Saul for the very first time, it was during a religious festival at his hometown of Ramah because he had relocated his operation headquarters from Shiloh to Ramah. These strongly suggests that for Samuel, offering of sacrifices or engaging in God of Israel pleasing religious ritual automatically invoked God's powerful presence to achieve whatever Samuel needed in the immediate.

In the case of David, I Samuel 23:14 can be safely interpreted to mean that God provided protection to David as God deemed fit. This is different from when I Samuel 23:6-13 says David formally asked God for guidance which provided the basis for him, accompanied by his men of war, to escape from Saul's reach in the town of Keilah. Therefore, we can say that there is volunteered protection provision as different from requested protection provision by God from heaven. There is volunteered protection provision and prosperity provision. It is like what is called solicited and unsolicited employment application in personnel management and administration. To make Joseph great in Egypt, God volunteered prosperity to make his Egyptian bosses to regard and promote him. Joseph did not have to fast and pray before God prospered him wherever he worked in Egypt.

Meanwhile, Genesis 28:10-22 confirms that Jacob's prosperity in Laban's employment was the combination of God's promise to be with Jacob wherever he went as well as in response to Jacob's vow at Bethel where he over-nighted that if God prospered him during his stay at Laban's place he would pay God the tithe of a tenth of his total earnings upon his return to the land of Canaan. Meanwhile, there is no record that Esau asked God's help formally before he prospered back home in Canaan rather the only link we can say that he had with God was taking good care of their father, Isaac who was God's covenant carrier beyond Abraham, God's covenant friend. Technically speaking, the first battle David fought against Saul was that of despising in the sense that when he arrived Saul's palace, Saul never regarded him as someone worthy of his attention until God used the killing of Goliath to give David victory over Saul's consciousness in that regard. However, it opened the new door of envy and jealousy engineered battle of threat to David's life because he felt that David had stolen the attention of the Israelites from him as well as warming up to become king of Israel after him.

I Samuel 18:6-12, 19:1-24, 20:1-42, 21:1-15, 22:1-23, 23:7-14 and 27:1-12 can be said to mean that in addition to God's spiritual protection of David from Saul's threats, David took personal measures to escape Saul's threats by way of asking God's guidance to escape. This means that he did not remain where Saul could catch up with him just because God had installed a spiritual barrier that made it impossible for Saul to catch up with and kill him. David played his part in his search for God's protection to enable him to outlive Saul so he could return to become king of Israel afterwards. I Samuel 16:1-13 and 19:18-24 can be interpreted to mean that in addition to God's protection, Samuel took practical measures to protect himself from been killed by Saul for lending support to David becoming Saul's successor at the expense of any of Saul's sons.

Samuel's anointing of David did not cause any problems for David until Saul found out that God had chosen David to replace any of his sons as his successor. This means that if others do not know about God's plans the chief beneficiary could be relatively safe. Until Joseph's brothers noticed that their father preferred him, they let him be. Until they learnt that God meant him to be greater than them, they did not threaten his life. Sometimes it is better when people do not find out God's plan for your life and it is implemented to their shock so that they would be too intimidated to attempt any threat. Because Joseph's brothers knew too soon about God's plans to make him their ruler, they tried to kill him but when he had become the most powerful official in Egypt, they were too afraid to dare him a second time.

Genesis 45:4-13 and Psalm 105:16-18 confirm that God orchestrated Joseph's sojourn in Egypt to serve as a precursor for his father and the rest of his family's entry into Egypt just as

Genesis 15:12-17 confirms that God had revealed to Abraham nearly 500 years earlier. Genesis 37:1-36, 39:1-23, 40:1-23, 41:1-57 and 47:13-26, Psalm 105:16-24 and Acts 7:9-15 confirm that Joseph arrived in Egypt as a slave where he learnt resource management first, at the home of Potiphar, his first Egyptian master and next at the royal prisons. The experiences he garnered at Potiphar's home and royal prisons were used to manage the economy of Egypt for Pharaoh. Much as God meant him to live great in his adult life in Egypt, he did not become great on the very first day, month or year he arrived Egypt. God knew that Joseph lacked the experience to manage the economy of Egypt on the very day that he arrived Egypt so He let him garner some experience before creating the circumstances that warranted Joseph's emergence as the Prime Minister of Egypt. God did not want Joseph to bring disgrace to His name by reason of poor performance if he became the head of Empire's administration immediately he arrived in Egypt. He wanted everyone in Egypt to know that He was Joseph's chief sponsor to the position of greatness but at the same time, he did not want Joseph to perform poorly because of lack of experience.

The earlier years in the strange land are meant to prepare the enabling environment for the migrant to flourish. They are meant for him to adapt to the lifestyle and ways of doing things in the new location. The preparatory years are not wasted at all. They are the foundation building period for the life that the migrant would enjoy later. When David returned to the land of Judah after Saul's death, he was not made the king of Israel immediately as God meant rather, he was first made the king of the tribal kingdom of Judah at Hebron. It was not until seven and a half years later before he was made the king of Israel in addition to Judah, the same size of the kingdom that Saul had ruled over during his 40-year reign. II Samuel 5:1-3 and I Chronicles 11:1-3 confirm that when David was made king of Israel in addition to Judah it was rooted in I Samuel 16:1-13 detailed anointing by Samuel as God ordered ever before I Samuel 16:14-23 says David went to serve in Saul's palace as musician and armour bearer and I Samuel 17:1-58 confirms that David killed Goliath. Genesis 15:12-17, Exodus 3 – 15, I Samuel 12:6 and 8, Psalm 77:20, 99:6 and 105:26, Micah 6:4, Acts 7:35 and Hebrews 11:24-27 confirm that God used Moses assisted by Aaron to lead their generation of Israelites out of Egypt. However, Deuteronomy 7:1 and 22 and 8:1-10 confirm that the same God who used Moses to lead the Israelites from Egypt to take over the land of Canaan told them the reason their taking over of the entire land would be a gradual process. Much as it is yours, the possession process would be gradual though sure.

Samuel was a micro migrant when he was taken from his hometown of Ramah to live with Eli as a child at the place of worship at Shiloh. Even when the original plan before he was conceived was that he would replace Hophni and Phinehas as their father, Eli's successor, I Samuel 1:1-28, 2:1-21 and 3:1-21 confirm that there at Shiloh Eli prepared him to hear and relate God's message to the Israelites and offer sacrifices to God as and when necessary. I Samuel 3:19-21, 4:1-22, 5:1-12, 6:1-21 and 7:1 strongly suggest that Samuel remained at Shiloh from where he led the Israelites for nearly two decades immediately following Eli's death. Then, I Samuel 7:2-17 can be said to confirm that afterwards he relocated back to his hometown of Ramah and ruled Israel from there.

I Samuel 16:1-23 can be interpreted to mean that David was another micro migrant after Samuel when he was seconded from working for his father as chief herdsman in Bethlehem to become personal musician and armour bearer to King Saul in Gibeah. Then, I Samuel 27:1-12 can be interpreted to mean that Saul's persecution forced him to become a macro or transnational border migrant when he crossed from the territory of Israel to hide with the king of the Philistines for the 16 months just before Saul died fighting the Philistines. After the death of Saul, II Samuel 1:1-27 and 2:1-7 confirm that David sought and got God's guidance to return to the land of Judah where the leaders of Hebron made him king over their tribal kingdom of Judah.

Genesis 31:38-42 confirms that it took Jacob a total of 20 years of hard work in Haran to earn enough to take back to Canaan to live wealthy and enjoy some sense of fulfillment. Genesis 29:1-30 and 30:25-36 and 31:1-2 and 38-42 can be said to suggest that it was not until 14 years stay before Jacob got the confidence to negotiate for the right amount of wages that he deserved from his employer as a migrant in Haran.

Genesis 29:14-15 says Jacob could not ask for any wages during the first month of his stay in Haran until the employer asked him to name his wages. Daniel 1:1-21 confirms that Daniel, Shadrach, Meshach and Abednego (DSMA) spent their first three years in Babylon to prepare before they could gain the personal recognition of the king of Babylon who they were to work with for the many decades that they spent away from Judah in Babylon.

Ezekiel 1 – 4 can be safely interpreted to mean that Ezekiel was packaged to become a priest in the temple as a young man descended from the priestly lineage of Israel. However, because he was carried away alongside other Jews to live as captives in Babylon, God took him through a packaging or reorientation process to transit from a priest to let him serve as a prophet among the Jewish captive.

2

SURVIVING AMONG RESENTFUL NATIVES (SARN)

There is a dig-dong cat and mouse dealership between natives and migrants nearly inevitably. I Samuel 20:1-43, 21:1-15 and 27:1-12 confirm that King Saul's threats forced David to relocate to Gath of the Philistines, the hometown of Goliath who he killed to become famous and established as the greatest warrior in Israel and as a reward he was appointed officer in Saul's army of Israel. I Samuel 29:1-11 says most of the Philistines did not trust David's acclaimed loyalty to them and his chief host, King Achish of the Philistines with his throne in Goliath's hometown of Gath. I Samuel 27:1-12 can be interpreted to mean that David stage-managed his loyalty to Achish in order to survive throughout the 16 months he lived among them, prior to when Saul died and he returned to the land of Israel where he was made king over the tribal kingdom of Judah in their headquarter of Hebron. This means that David found a Philistine native among the resentful Philistines who liked him enough to accommodate him. Also, the loving and accommodating Philistine was an influential personality among them.

Genesis 33:18-20 and 34:1-31 say when Jacob arrived to settle in Shechem he paid the full price for the estate he occupied with his wealth. While there his only daughter, Dinah was raped by the heir-prince of Shechem who determined to marry Dinah afterwards. However, Genesis 34:23 says part of the heart-hidden heinous and regrettable reason that the men of Shechem agreed to adopt the circumcision custom of Jacob and his sons was that they would scheme to rob Jacob of the wealth that he brought along to settle in their territory. Also significant is the fact that verses 30-31 say Jacob's sons claimed that they would not tolerate any form of insult from the Shechemites just because they were migrants in Shechem. This means that natives would not let migrants insult them in their land just as migrants would not let natives insult them – that is nothing short of endless tug of war.

The punishment that Jacob's sons implemented for the rape of Dinah was more than the offence committed. Meanwhile, the Shechemites were plotting to swindle Jacob and his family of the wealth he brought along to live among them in addition to raping his daughter. Then, there is the subject of verses 13-24 implying that the king and men of Shechem gave concession to Jacob's sons' proposal to adopt their circumcision custom because they had an ulterior motive that was injurious to Jacob and his family. Meanwhile, verses 25-29 confirm that Jacob's sons agreed that Shechemites' heir-prince could marry their only sister but had an ulterior motive that was dastardly detrimental to the Shechemites. This gives enough ground to say that it is nearly natural for natives and migrants to deal deceptively with themselves.

Genesis 29:1-24 and 30:25-43 confirm that just as Laban cheated Jacob so also Jacob cheated Laban during the 20 years that Jacob lived with and worked for Laban in Laban's hometown of Padan-Aram in retaliation. I Samuel 17:1-58 tells the story of David's killing of Goliath the Philistines' unbeaten champion warrior. I Samuel 18:24-27 and 30 and 19:8 confirm other times that David did not hide his dastard disdain for the Philistines after the killing of Goliath. I Samuel 21:10-15 says when next David came in contact with Goliath's King Achish he feigned insanity which prompted Achish to ordered his officials to get David out of his sight. However, shockingly, I Samuel 27:1-12 says the same Achish decided to appoint David to seemingly replace Goliath and David dealt deceptively with Achish throughout the 16 months that he lived in Achish's domain and feigned loyal service to Achish. I Samuel 29:1-11 says unlike Achish, the other Philistine leaders were not fooled by David's acclaimed loyalty to Abimelech. They were able to see through David's deception and told Achish to stop deceiving himself that David was genuinely loyal to the wellbeing of the Philistines. They understood that David merely used them to survive Saul. David's stay among the Philistines is very striking in the sense that I Samuel 24:1-22, 26:1-25 and 27:1-12 confirm that while he spared the life of Saul who wanted him dead on two occasions he killed the Philistines who contributed to save his life from Saul by giving him a safe place to live until Saul died.

Jacob and Laban's deceptive dealings with one another like Jacob's sons and the Shechemites' deceptive dealings as well as David's deceptive dealings with Achish typify the ever feigned faithfulness or laughable loyalty between natives and migrants in any generation. Deception is lie-laundering. The Shechemites were no longer satisfied with the full price that Jacob paid them for the estate that he occupied among them. They wanted more from the wealth that Jacob brought with him from Haran to settle among them. That sounds like greed guided deceptive dealings. It amounts to desiring more than the legitimate requirement from the migrant. **Tasking the migrant more than necessary; letting in the migrant for benefit sake only or sole benefit reason or factor.** I Samuel 27:5-12 conclude in verse 12 that the heart-hidden reason Achish hosted David in his domain was that he had hoped that David would serve him all his life or till death. He did not know or care about God's plan that David would become king of Israel after the death of Saul.

He never let David know that he expected David to remain his loyal warrior until David's dying day. In the same way, David did not let Achish know that he was harming his Philistine subjects and kinsmen rather than the Israelites as Achish had hoped that David would do since he protected David from Saul's threats. Natives and migrants hardly deal honestly and helpfully with themselves since the time of Abraham's sojourn among the Canaanites.

Ezra 4:11-16 says there are persons who just do not like the Jews because the Jews do not join others to do things in the same way. Such persons do not care the reason the Jews behave differently from all other's inhabitants of the earth. It amounts to having a biased opinion of the Jews. They are treated with suspicion nearly always. Esther 2:20 and 3:1-23 can be summed up to mean that Mordecai taught that understanding to the younger generation of Jews so that they would know how to conduct themselves among others wherever they live. It is impossible to be fair to a people that you are biased against already. Genesis 39:1-19 can be said to mean that it is when people want to be mischievous that they would emphasize the background of the stranger. Until Joseph turned down her amoral advances Potiphar's wife did not refer to him derogatorily as Potiphar's Hebrew slave. All the while that their household was getting extraordinary prosperity because of Joseph it was laughter all the way but once Joseph refused to do her bidding, she did not care about Joseph's reasons for turning down her ridiculous request. It can be called "man's monstrous mindset". If you deny man his heart desire, he will not care to consider the reason for the denial rather he would seek the destruction of the persons who dared to deny him what he craves.

For Joseph to be relevant according to God's will and promise revealed through dreams when he was only a boy of 17 years, the powerful ruler of Egypt whose nobles cannot question his authority and decision had to like and appoint him to the powerful position of Prime Minister. Even though God can do whatever He likes, He did not use just any unrespectable Egyptian to help Joseph but the most powerful Egyptian to establish His planned purpose for the life of Joseph. This means that if Joseph had detested Pharaoh, it would have been difficult to enter the planned greatness God meant for him to enjoy in his adult life. Even though Egyptians despised Hebrews and Joseph was the first Hebrew they met, they accepted him because their most powerful kinsman, Pharaoh, made him their ruler. It would have been regrettable if Joseph refused to keep the rewarding relationship he was privileged to strike with Pharaoh. This is part of the reason Genesis 47:13-26 confirms that Joseph went out of his way to enslave the Egyptians to Pharaoh even though it was not part of what Genesis 41:1-44 indicates as the terms of reference he was given when he was appointed as the Prime Minister. He understood that if he sustained the harmonious relationship with his benefactor, he would continue to rule over the very people who would have resented and disrespected him while living in Egypt. Genesis 41:37-44, 53-57, 45:4-9 and 47:13-26 tell how Joseph decided to show appreciation to God and his God-sent earthly benefactor, Pharaoh. There is also the subject of the powerfulness in the host community using the willing strangers to pursue their unholy heart-hidden desires. Pharaoh let Joseph have whatever he wanted so long as he enriched him at the expense of his subjects. God enabled competence catapulted Joseph, David, DSMA and Nehemiah in their lifetime.

In the same vein, Genesis 45:9-11, 16-20, 46:31-34 and 47:1-6 strongly suggest that in order to survive among naturally resentful hosts or natives, Joseph told his brothers to request to live in the region of Goshen because he had heard that when his boss and benefactor, Pharaoh learnt about the presence of his relatives, he had said he would not mind assigning them Goshen as their exclusive residential neighbourhood as Joseph preferred rather than have them live right in the midst of the Egyptians who abhorred Hebrews. It is important to note that Joseph did not say since he was living around the palace, his relatives should be accorded the same respect and be allowed to live beside him. This means that Joseph wisely agreed to the decision of his boss that while he lived in the official quarters allotted to him in the palace area, his relatives should live far away where the boss thought was suitable for them by reason of their Hebrew background. Joseph did not say so long as he remained the highest official in the kingdom of Egypt; it was his right to be allowed to decide where was best for his relatives without the approval of his benefactor and boss.

As powerful as he was in the kingdom, he accepted that his authority and actions remained subject to his Egyptian boss who made him great in the strange land of Egypt. This is what would make a stranger continue to enjoy the support and protection of his God-assigned benefactor in the strange land. The fact that God made that benefactor to favour him does not mean that he should disregard his opinion on any matter. Since his heart is right enough for God to use him to help the stranger, the onus is on the stranger to take indigenous benefactor seriously enough to do his or her bidding on any issue unless God says otherwise. Nevertheless, it is important to point out that usually, any person whose heart God found amenable enough to help you in a strange land would do it always. The phrase 'would do it always' means that he or she would always follow God's promptings to tell you to do the things that would not cause crisis during your stay in the land. Such an individual can be called "Individual's God-ordained/ordered Seasonal/Location Benefactor/Beneficiary.

Consider the examples of David and Jonathan as well as Barnabas and Paul. I Samuel 17:1-58 and 18:1-5 confirm that one of the main fallouts from David's killing of Goliath was that King Saul's eldest son and preferred successor, Jonathan practically fell in love with David, not as his bedmate but genuine soul-mate in the matter of pursuit of God's planned purpose for them as members of the generation that should succeed Saul's generation of Israelites. It was a friendship fabricated in heaven and delivered to them on earth for optimal enjoyment. I Samuel 19:1-24 and 20:1-43 recount that Jonathan did whatever was humanly possible to prevail on his father to resist the pressure of envy and jealousy to continue to seek to kill David. When he saw that persuasion was not doing the trick he even confronted his father over the issue to the extent that his father threatened his own life too. Finally, I Samuel 23:15-18 confirms that he confessed the spiritual reason he was hell-bent on defying his father to support his friend, David to be the fact that apparently God meant him to serve as David's second-in-command on the throne of Israel as Joseph was to Pharaoh on the throne of Egypt.

I Samuel 15:1-30, 16:13-14, 18:12 and 28-29 and 20:13b can be safely interpreted to mean that apart from Samuel and Saul himself, Jonathan was the third person to understand that God had abandoned Saul and shifted His support to David as the next ruler of Israel. He told David that God's presence and support for his father had become past tense while that of David was the present tense of their generation. It was like he noticed that David was not conscious of that vital fact so he reminded David during their private discussion in I Samuel 20:13. From the point that Jonathan liked David until he died his fondness for David was as strong as the Rock of Gibraltar and constant as the northern star. Once he understood that it was a waste of time trying to convince his father to stop seeking to kill David, he was honest enough to let go of David from his father's royal service. He did not stir up sentiment that David remained in his father's service because he knew that his father needed David more than ever before.

Acts 9:1-31 confirms in verses 26-28 that Barnabas was the first respected believer to come to Paul's support when the body of believers resented him initially upon his conversion because of his previous persecution of believers' record. Acts 9:29-31 and 11:19-26 confirm that after Paul withdrew from the group of Christians because of his ferocious preaching, it was this same Barnabas who went after him to his hometown of Tarsus to fish him out and bring him back to join the mainstream of Christians to take his rightful place to preach the Gospel of salvation symbolized by Jesus. Finally, when God would reveal the real reason that Barnabas and Paul seemed to have a natural bond of cordial relationship, Acts 13:1-3 says God indicated that actually He had meant them to work together as apostolic partners to the Gentiles in their lifetime. Barnabas was 'Paul's comrade in the council of Paul's resenters' just like Jonathan and Michal were David's own comrades in the household of Saul that resented David. Among the council of any migrant's resenters there are persons that God had planted in their midst to provide succor for the migrant. It can be called "My Man in their Midst", "My Man Among Them", "My Benefactor Among Them", "My Benefactor Among the Beasts", "My Benefactor Among the Animals", "My God Appointed Benefactors Among the Animals who suppose that they are honorable humans" or

"My Man in the Midst of the Monstrous Enemies". John 3:1-21, 7:40-52 and 19:38-40 can be said to mean that Nicodemus and Joseph of Arimathea was to Jesus amongst the Pharisees or Jesus haters and archenemies.

There is no doubt about the fact that Daniel was a powerful noble in the palace of Babylon for a long time or throughout the time he lived there. Lending credence to this fact, Daniel 1:17-21, 2:46-49 say:

> 17 God gave the four young men knowledge and skill in literature and philosophy. In addition, he gave Daniel skill in interpreting visions and dreams. 18 At the end of the three years set by the king, Ashpenaz took all the young men to Nebuchadnezzar. 19 The king talked with them all, and Daniel, Hananiah, Mishael, and Azariah impressed him more than any of the others. So they became members of the king's court. 20 No matter what question the king asked or what problem he raised, these four knew ten times more

than any fortuneteller or magician in his whole kingdom. 21 Daniel remained at the royal court until Cyrus, the emperor of Persia, conquered Babylonia.

46 Then King Nebuchadnezzar bowed to the ground and gave orders for sacrifices and offerings to be made to Daniel. 47 The king said, "Your God is the greatest of all gods, the Lord over kings, and the one who reveals mysteries. I know this because you have been able to explain this mystery." 48 Then he gave Daniel a high position, presented him with many splendid gifts, put him in charge of the province of Babylon, and made him the head of all the royal advisers. 49 At Daniel's request the king put Shadrach, Meshach, and Abednego in charge of the affairs of the province of Babylon; Daniel, however, remained at the royal court. (TEV)

Interestingly, Daniel 4:22-33 says when the same King Nebuchadnezzar who had bowed low to show reverence for Daniel had to be told the mind of God for him, Daniel presented it respectfully, rather than speak arrogantly to Nebuchadnezzar. He still addressed him as "Your Majesty" and pleaded with him to heed his counsel so that the revealed misfortune would not happen to him. This suggests that Daniel understood that irrespective of his greatness in Babylon, he was still a stranger and therefore, could not afford to be rude to his boss who was a native just because God had magnified him in the presence of his boss, the nobles and subjects. This means that in the height of his God-given greatness, he did not lose focus of his immediate status of a stranger in Babylon. He never had problems with the natives and Daniel 6:1-28 says when some of his noble colleagues attacked him unjustly, they suffered for so doing.

God's plan for any individual has limit wherever he or she lives. Daniel understood that God's plan for him in Babylon which God first made known during the reign of Daniel's ancestor, King Hezekiah of Judah in Jerusalem was not necessarily to become the king of Babylon rather to serve as an official in Babylonian palace. II Kings 20:1-19 and Isaiah 38:1-8 and 39:1-8 confirm in II Kings 20:17-18 and Isaiah 39:5-7 that God meant Daniel to be a palace official in Babylon rather than king like I Kings 19:15-18 and II Kings 2:1-22, 8:7-15 and 9:1-13 say God meant Hazael to transform from a palace official to become the king of Syria and Jehu to transform from an army officer to become the king of Israel while Elisha was to transform from being an agriculturist into the leading prophet of Israel.

Daniel 5:1-28 can be interpreted to mean that remaining within known God's limit is part of the reason that Daniel did not seek to become the king of Babylon after making known to palace officials the fact that God had terminated the rule and reign of Belshazzar. Rather, Daniel agreed to continue to serve as high official under Darius who murdered and replaced Belshazzar as the king of Babylon the day following Daniel's revelation that God's personnel department in heaven had terminated Belshazzar's rule and reign over Babylon after his father the great King Nebuchadnezzar. Daniel's case is very striking when we remember that Daniel 2 confirms that Nebuchadnezzar once bowed low to worship at the feet of Daniel. It made Daniel seem greater than Nebuchadnezzar yet it did not puff up Daniel to seek to replace Nebuchadnezzar or his son as king of Babylon apparently because he understood that occupying the throne of Babylon was never part of God's plan for him during his stay as a high official in palace of Babylon. As a result, Daniel can be said to have restrained himself to live within his God allowed limit in the palace of Babylon just as John 6:1-15 can be said to mean that Jesus did not accept the throne of Israel that the Jews offered Him because He understood that God never meant Him to serve as the king of the Jews in the manner and moment that the Jews offered it to Him after feeding them with both the word of life as well as natural food.

Living within God-set limit is important because exceeding such limits creates problems for the individual and everyone else who are inalienably associated with them. If Jesus had accepted to be the king of the Jews as the Jews demanded, He would have upset God the Father's plan for Him to go to Satan's headquarters to dispossess Satan of the power of death and the key of hell. I Samuel 16:1-13, 18:6-12 and 20:27-33, II Samuel 2:1-32, 3:1-39, 4:1-12 and 5:1-3 and I Chronicles 11:1-3 can be interpreted to mean that Abner, Ishbosheth, Baanah and Rechab died when and how they did mostly because they chose to exceed God's set limits for King Saul's dynasty and themselves after Saul's death. Isaiah 40:3, Matthew 3:1-12 and 14:1-12, Mark 1:1-8 and 6:14-29. Luke 3:1-18 and 9:7-9 and John 1:19-28 can be said to mean that John the Baptist died the way that he is known to have because he exceeded God-set limit for him as a prophet of God. God never meant him to preach against city dwellers in the city but to preach to any of them that left the city and came to him in his God-assigned preaching and prophetic headquarters in the wilderness. The only assignment that heaven meant him to do in the city was to baptize his converts at the River Jordan rather than seek to condemn Herod for taking his brother, Philip's wife, Herodias. He tried to correct a pair of incorrigibles that God never meant him to make to repent of their evil or immoral ways.

Based on Romans 1:24-32 with special reference to verses 24, 18 and 31-32, they were the pair with reprobate hearts who God had left to please themselves until they would be punished in eternity. It is like the way that I Samuel 2:12-17 and 22-36, 3:1-18 and 4:1-22 can be said to mean that that God left Eli's Hophni and Phinehas to please themselves until He pulled off the plug of His patience and turned on the switch of divine punishment on them finally using the Philistines. Satan needs salvation more than anyone else but Jesus never wasted His precious time trying to persuade Satan to mend his wicked ways. The Pharisees needed to change their ways, but Jesus never wasted His precious time trying to convince them to change their ways. Jesus understood that reprobates are irredeemable and therefore better left alone.

Let us take note of something else highly significant in the story of Daniel, Shadrach, Meshach, and Abednego (DSMA) during their stay in Babylon. One would have thought that when Nebuchadnezzar recognized the help of the God of the Jews to Daniel in Daniel 1:1-21, 2:1-49, 3:1-30 and 4:1-37, he would have opted to join them to serve their God of Israel, maker of the universe. But Nebuchadnezzar continued to serve the gods of his ancestors. Also, when he invented his own statue for his subjects to worship, Shadrach, Meshach and Abednego refused to join others to worship it and the contest ended with Nebuchadnezzar acknowledging their God of all gods but he still did not find it enough reason to join them to worship their God at the expense of his ancestors' gods. Interestingly, there is no record that DSMA went further to mock Nebuchadnezzar for failing to take the step of discarding the worship of his native gods.

As strangers in Babylon, it was enough that they lived their lives in such a way that their hosts recognized that they had a relationship with the God of all gods but what they decided to do with the information was left to them. If DSMA had tried to compel Nebuchadnezzar to join them and their fellow Jews to worship the God of all gods, they would have seen the bad side of the same Nebuchadnezzar who regarded highly and rewarded them according to their excellent performances as nobles in his palace.

Genesis 13:1-13, 14:1-24 and 19:1-29 say when Lot tried to correct natives of his host community they told him that as long as he was a stranger he could not possibly tell them what to do. This is even though Genesis 14:1-16 and 21-24 confirm that his hosts were saved from their captors by his uncle, Abraham because of Lot. Also, Genesis 19:1-3 confirms that Lot had become one of their city leaders who presided over disputes or the city gate judges. Again, this is in addition to the fact that Genesis 19:14 confirms that he was set to let his two daughters to intermarry with two of their young men. Genesis 41:45-46 and 53-57 says even when the Egyptians knew that their king had given Joseph what we can call sweeping powers of royal authority to rule over them on his behalf, when it was time to really comply with whatever Joseph instructed the Egyptians went back to their kinsman and king, Pharaoh who appointed Joseph nine years earlier to reconfirm if he still wanted them to obey his directives. They meant that if not for one of them, who they regard highly because he is their king by the title of Pharaoh, they can never take instructions from a stranger in their own land.

Without a respectable native's support, it would be difficult for any stranger in position of authority to get the natives to obey his legitimate authority-based instructions to the natives. The fact that Genesis 41:45-46 and 50-52 says Joseph had become an Egyptian by marriage and in fact, had two sons who are natives by reason of their mother who was from an influential Egyptian family did not make the Egyptians to think that they did not need to ask their king for clarification, before obeying Joseph. This was around the 9th year since Joseph had been made their most powerful noble and royal palace official. Genesis 41:46b says when he was first appointed, he left the palace and he toured the entire nation to familiarize himself with the citizens and their localities. Then, he supervised all the storage facilities that were built in the different parts of the nation. Again, Genesis 41:47-48 confirms that he travelled the length and breadth of the nation buying up their excess grains during the seven years of surplus.

During the seven years of the bumper harvest the Egyptians had no reason to clarify from the king if they should obey Joseph because they had abundance harvest and the only relationship or contact they had with Joseph was buying off their excess produce. But when their seven-year bumper harvest leftovers were exhausted and they needed help from the royal treasury to stay alive, that was when Joseph began to dish out what they regarded un-Egyptian decrees that the Egyptians must give up part of their farmlands and its yield to get the help that they needed desperately from the royal treasury. The policy was too strange, bizarre, and dumbfounding so they went to their kinsman, the king to prevail on his appointed official to rescind the policy or they would not comply. It was when Pharaoh approved that they returned to comply with whatever Joseph's new economic policy was that they obeyed.

The other point is that strangers should resist the temptation to introduce strange ideas to the natives of their host communities. He made the Egyptians to pay exorbitant prices for the grains he bought from them earlier at give away prices just like the foreigners who come from abroad to buy from the royal treasury that Joseph controlled on the behalf of the king. Genesis 41:47-49 confirms that Joseph bought up all the excess grain during the seven years of bumper harvest and surpluses of grain. The people must have sold to him at give away prices. Then, Genesis 41:53-54 says there was no food in any other country except

Egypt or the ones that Joseph mopped up and stored for his boss. Genesis 41:55-57 says as a result, the Egyptians went to their king to help them while people from other nations came over to Egypt to buy grain. Genesis 42:25-28 and 43:12 and 15 confirm that the foreigners paid with money just as Genesis 47:13-15 confirms that initially the Egyptians paid with money – most likely part of the money that Joseph paid them to buy up their excess produce during the earlier years of surplus. Then, Genesis 47:13-26 says:

> 13 The famine was so severe that there was no food anywhere, and the people of Egypt and Canaan became weak with hunger. 14 As they bought grain, Joseph collected all the money and took it to the palace. 15 When all the money in Egypt and Canaan was spent, the Egyptians came to Joseph and said, "Give us food! Don't let us die. Do something! Our money is all gone." 16 Joseph answered, "Bring your livestock; I will give you food in exchange for it if your money is all gone." 17 So they brought their

livestock to Joseph, and he gave them food in exchange for their horses, sheep, goats, cattle, and donkeys. That year he supplied them with food in exchange for all their livestock. 18 The following year they came to him and said, "We will not hide the fact from you, sir, that our money is all gone and our livestock belongs to you. There is nothing left to give you except our bodies and our lands. 19 Don't let us die. Do something! Don't let our fields be deserted. Buy us and our land in exchange for food. We will be the king's slaves, and he will own our land. Give us grain to keep us alive and seed so that we can plant our fields." 20 Joseph bought all the land in Egypt for the king. Every Egyptian was forced to sell his land, because the famine was so severe; and all the land became the king's property. 21 Joseph made slaves of the people from one end of Egypt to the other. 22 The only land he did not buy was the land that belonged to the priests. They did not have to sell their lands, because the king gave them an allowance to live on. 23 Joseph said to the people, "You see, I have now bought you and your lands for the king. Here is seed for you to sow in your fields. 24 At the time of harvest you must give one-fifth to the king. You can use the rest for seed and for food for yourselves and your families." 25 They answered, "You have saved our lives; you have been good to us, sir, and we will be the king's slaves." 26 So Joseph made it a law for the land of Egypt that one-fifth of the harvest should belong to the king. This law still remains in force today. Only the lands of the priests did not become the king's property. (TEV)

First, when the priests were exempted from paying for the grains that they got from the royal treasury it was noted. Yet, there is no record that the stored grains were sold to the Egyptians who grew them at a lesser price to the ones sold to persons who came from abroad to buy. This means that the Egyptians were treated the same way as non-Egyptians in Joseph's economic policy. It did not matter to Pharaoh most likely because as verse 14 puts it all the money that he got from selling the grains he took to his boss, Pharaoh's bank in the palace. Whenever your kinsman is supporting a stranger who is treating you unfairly you can be rest assured that your kinsman is benefiting personally from the unfair treatment that you are experiencing at home in the hands of a stranger-turned native by reason of long stay and marriage to one of your natives.

Second, this is slavery in exchange for staying alive or afloat or 'saved to serve as slave'. Joshua 9:1-27 confirms that during Joshua's leadership dispensation, the Gibeonites accepted to live and be treated in like manner by the Israelites. Verses 22-27 confirm that the Gibeonites did not mind. Pharaoh used Joseph to treat his Egyptian kinsmen worse than he treated Joseph's kinsmen or relatives. Also, the non-Egyptians who Genesis 41:53-57 says visited to buy grains were not enslaved. He made slaves of his vulnerable kinsmen or his fellow Egyptians. Pharaoh and Joseph fit the description of Vulnerables' Villain. Exodus 17:8-16 says the Amalekites treated the Israelites in like manner and God could not forgive the Amalekites for so doing. It can be likened to what Genesis 25:29-34 confirms that Jacob did to Esau. Jacob could not afford to give a meal to his starving twin brother for brotherhood's sake. It is slavery in exchange for salvation – accept to remain a slave or starve to death. Proverbs 17:17, 18:24, Amos 2:9-12 and Obadiah 1:10-18 say:

> 17 Friends always show their love. What are relatives for if not to share trouble?

> 24 Some friendships do not last, but some friends are more loyal than brothers.

> 9 "And yet, my people, it was for your sake that I totally destroyed the Amorites, who were as tall as cedar trees and as strong as oaks. 10 I brought you out of Egypt, led you through the desert for forty years, and gave you the land of the Amorites to be your own. 11 I chose some of your sons to be prophets and some of your young men to be Nazirites. Isn't this true, people of Israel? I, the Lord, have spoken. 12 But you made the Nazirites

drink wine, and ordered the prophets not to speak my message.

10 "Because you robbed and killed your relatives, the descendants of Jacob, you will be destroyed and dishonored forever. 11 You stood aside on that day when enemies broke down their gates. You were as bad as those strangers who carried off Jerusalem's wealth and divided it among themselves. 12 You should not have gloated over the misfortune of your relatives in Judah. You should not have been glad on the day of their ruin. You should not have laughed at them in their distress. 13 You should not have entered the city of my people to gloat over their suffering and to seize their riches on the day of their disaster. 14 You should not have stood at the crossroads to catch those trying to escape. You should not have handed them over to the enemy on the day of their distress. 15 "The day is near when I, the Lord, will judge all nations. Edom, what you have

done will be done to you. You will get back what you have given. 16 My people have drunk a bitter cup of punishment on my sacred hill. But all the surrounding nations will drink a still more bitter cup of punishment; they will drink it all and vanish away. 17 "But on Mount Zion some will escape, and it will be a sacred place. The people of Jacob will possess the land that is theirs by right. 18 The people of Jacob and of Joseph will be like fire; they will destroy the people of Esau as fire burns stubble. No descendant of Esau will survive. I, the Lord, have spoken. (TEV)

Even friends are meant to support one another to survive distressful circumstance but as it turned out, Pharaoh decided to turn his back on his kinsmen in their worst moments. It should be said that it matters to God because Amos 2:9-12 and Obadiah 1:10-18 above confirm that Pharaoh should not have watched his own people suffer when he could have done something much better to help them. Because of personal gain of increased riches and control over the economic life of the people, Pharaoh jettisoned the age-long universal concept of brotherhood bond that is meant to be of help on the day of trouble. Pharaoh and Joseph's solution to the economic predicament of the Egyptians is slavery in exchange for salvation. Joseph took advantage of the vulnerable Egyptians to enrich his boss and benefactor.

Someone could say the Egyptians offered to be the king's slaves as long as they were helped to stay alive. They were under duress to remain alive and since Joseph did not say he had gotten the king's approval to give them grain without paying for it, they had to make a proposition to Joseph. They knew that since the famine got severe and forced them to seek his help, all he wanted was to get something from them before he would give them food to live on. The claim in verse 14 that he paid all the money that he got from the Egyptians as well as foreigners into the royal safe in the palace meant that he enriched his boss to repay him for been his God-sent benefactor. Genesis 41:1-32 says he claimed that it was God that gave the two dreams to Pharaoh and the meaning of the dreams to him (Joseph) to tell the king. Whether the solution that he gave to the king on how to solve the problem that would result from the fulfillment of the dreams was also from God or based on Joseph's own wisdom based on his experience of the management of resources in Potiphar's household or the royal prisons we are not told. Perhaps, his father, Jacob had told him about his personal experience during the 20 years that he lived and worked in his father-in-law, Laban's household business.

Genesis 29:1-30, 30:25-42 and 31:1-16 confirm that while Jacob saved his income, Laban squandered his bumper profits during the 20 years. The story says as a result, when Jacob had become very wealthy and eager to withdraw his services and return to Canaan Laban became desperate. Joseph might have understood from the story of his father's experience with his maternal grand father and paternal grand uncle that during surplus season the reaper should save at least 20% of his income to sustain him during the period of scarcity that would necessarily follow. If that is what happened it means that the information that God gave through dreams about imminent season of surplus followed by season of scarcity, Joseph and Pharaoh hijacked it to benefit themselves at the expense of the people who were ignorant of the looming season of scarcity. God did not say it would be their chance to make slaves of the Egyptians. God gave the king the information so he would plan to help his own people without making slaves of them.

Genesis 15:12-17 and Exodus 1:1-21 and 3:7-10 say the enslavement that would happen and He would allow for a reason was the Egyptians making slaves of the Israelites rather than Joseph enslaving the Egyptians to Pharaoh. Therefore, we can call the slavery that Joseph and Pharaoh perpetuated on the Egyptians as man-made and perhaps, most importantly, God had no aims and objectives to achieve with it. Again, God never provided the Egyptians the grace with which to live with it like I Corinthians 10:13 says God do not allow anyone to be tempted more than he can cope with. Pharaoh and Joseph managed the famine in such a way that the Egyptians were forced to trade off their dignity and sense of self-worth. This is a proof that like I Kings 4:1-19 and 27-28, Ecclesiastes 5:8-9, Ezekiel 22:23-28 and Zephaniah 1:9 can be said to mean that rulers and their lieutenants do not have the interest of the populace at heart. Whatever God reveals to them they deploy as a tool to exploit the populace. They use privilege information to make mince meat of the ignorant populace. Even the man who had suffered oppression with the rest of the larger populace, once he is opportune to join the ruler's leadership council, he would join the ruler and his other lieutenants, to make life a living hell for the larger populace. Privilege migrants join or collaborate with native rulers to oppress the under-privileged. Joseph's treatment of the starving Egyptians under the supervision of his benefactor Pharaoh typifies this tortuous truth of life. Sometimes the thought that rulership in any form is more of a curse than blessing cannot be suppressed. At least the sons of men have turned rulership which God meant originally for the benefit of humankind into a source of sorrow and regret.

When Genesis 45:16-20 says in verse 18 that the best land in Egypt belonged to the king to offer to whom ever he liked, it means that he had the best land in the territory of Egypt even before he found reason to appoint Joseph as his deputy and Prime Minister. The point is that if he already had the best land what else does he need the worst estates or the non-best or non-choice land if there is such a thing that belonged to the people for? Why does he want to control the entire land in the nation? It is like when I Kings 3:3-14, 4:1-19 and 21 and 10:14-29 and II Chronicles 9:13-28 say Solomon deliberately appointed governors for the sole purpose of extorting from his subjects that God had made him richer than. That is part of what can be called the ridiculousness of the rich. What makes a man to seek to collect the little that his neighbour has to add to his own abundance? It must be something beyond the blessed boundary of sanity. It is part of what God indicted David of over the collection of Uriah's wife. As the sitting king, David could afford as many young girls as he liked yet, II Samuel 11:1-27 and 12:1-23 confirm that it is the only one owned by one of his finest officers by the name of Uriah that he coveted to the extent of killing Uriah in order to have her for keeps. Whoever tries to indulge such sickened souls by claiming that it is the regular human natural vice of greed should not forget that it is an unforgivable version of greed. One of my late father's philosophy was if you want to be rich associate with the rich because they are the ones who have some amount of money to spare to implement projects in which you could render your services to earn part of the money. But these regrettable rich people say the reverse is the case or in addition to getting from their fellow rich they must also get from the poor to add to what they already have.

Someone might say what about it after wards, Matthew 25:28-30 and Luke 19:24-26 confirm Jesus' claim that the one with little or nothing would be dispossessed to add to the one who already have. Much as Jesus said so, we should not forget that Jesus meant that the man with little or nothing was been punished meanwhile, I Chronicles 14:1-2 and 18:14, Nehemiah 5:14-18, Proverbs 20:28, 29:4 and 14, 31:1-9 and Jeremiah 22:3 and 13-17, 21:11-12, 23:1-2 and 4-6 confirm that God's fundamental plan and purpose for the ruler is to use his lieutenants to benefit the populace not otherwise. It can be summed up as Rulers' God-assigned Rewarding Role and Responsibility.

What David and Solomon did might not have mattered except that II Samuel 11-20 and I Kings 12:1-21 confirm that it had grave consequences during David's lifetime as well as after Solomon's death. The Yoruba people would say when people have become over filled they would begin to look for what is not missing in their lives that would ruin them eventually. Deuteronomy 8:7-11 and 32:11 can be said to lend credence to this fact when it says the Israelites forgot God after becoming prosperous like I Kings 11:1-42 surmise that Solomon did. Sometimes they would simply say he or she is looking or searching for what is not missing in his or her life. Pharaoh was already considered greater than the regular Egyptians so what point was he trying to prove by watching the official who he appointed make slaves of his subjects and he saw nothing wrong with it?

The other point worthy of note is that just because you got away with something or a concept that popped up in your head does not mean that the concept is proper. Isaiah 10:1-2 says there are unjust laws making or not every law made by rulers are just. Any law that enslaves the vulnerable to the powerfuls cannot be said to be just. There are powerfuls precarious practices or POP which means Powerfuls' Obnoxious or Objectionable Practices. The implementation of injurious ideas may prosper the implementer in the immediate but may precipitate long term consequences. David succeeded in using his COAS, Joab and the Ammonites to kill Uriah to make it seem that he took

Uriah's wife only after his death during the battle against the Ammonites but II Samuel 11 – 18 confirms that as a result his daughter was raped, his two sons died violently, several thousands of Israel's warriors died along with one of them, he lost his throne in Jerusalem for a while. In addition, he passed on to his descendants, violent death until the end of the age. Solomon had his way living off his subjects and fellow Israelites, but it became one of the reasons the kingdom broke up after his death because his son and successor would not agree to reduce Solomon's burden on the people.

That the Egyptians failed to save their excess harvest throughout the seven years of bumper harvest and had to ask for supplies to live on during scarcity was enough humiliation, yet Pharaoh and Joseph chose to add the pains of slavery. Pharaoh may have succeeded in making slaves of the Israelites initially however they regretted it greatly by the time God empowered and sent Moses to lead the freedom of the Israelites by force. Abner may have succeeded in sustaining Saul's dynasty for seven and a half years after Saul's death, but it cut short Abner's and Ishbosheth's lives. Ishbosheth's murderers succeeded in murdering him but it led to their death when they expected reward. Exodus 17:8-16, Deuteronomy 25:17-19 and I Samuel 15:2-9 say God could not afford to forgive the Amalekites who chose to attack vulnerable persons because they were easy prey.

Genesis 31:1-16 can be said to mean that Laban regretted robbing his two daughters – Leah and Rachel of their dues later. This means that he could and did rob them successfully did not make him to have the last laugh over his daughters and their cousin turned husband, Jacob. Sarah regretted the implementation of the idea of converting her Egyptian maid into her husband's concubine. The candid counsel is "Don't just because you can in the immediate" rather consider the long-term implications. I Samuel 24:1-22 and 26:1-25 can be said to mean that David did not kill Saul just because he could or had the chance. He did not heed his men's counsel to kill Saul. He must have thought that since he was God's anointed through Samuel just like Saul was once anointed through Samuel, if he killed Saul – a God's anointed, it might sow the seed that its fruits could lead to his been killed by someone later on. He understood that God expects that His anointed is spared of his deserved punishment for the sake of His holy name attached to the life of such an anointed individual. II Samuel 16:5-14 confirms that David did not grant approval for Shimei to be killed while Absalom's rebellion supported by the all-wise Ahithophel still raged. In fact, like he refused to grant permission for his henchmen to murder Saul, II Samuel 16:5-14 and 19:15-23 confirm that he refused to grant the requested approval to kill Shimei twice – before the killing of Absalom which signaled the end of Absalom's rebellion. Much as David was offended enough to want Shimei punished with death, he suspended Shimei's deserved punishment until much later. His immediate concern was quashing Absalom's rebellion despite Ahithophel's support to enable him to return to rule in Jerusalem. II Samuel 19:15-23 and I Kings 2:1-12 and 36-45 tell how David achieved his aim of killing Shimei for insulting him while Absalom's rebellion raged without causing personal pains to himself. Sarah regretted converting her maid into her husband's concubine just as Naomi regretted her household's relocation to Moab. It is profitable to (1) consider the long term implication of any idea before implementing it, (2) since God knows the end from the beginning and in fact, determines the course of history clarify with him before implementing any idea.

3

DO NOT GET CARRIED AWAY

A Preacher would say he does not believe in the idea of 'remember the son or child of who you are wherever you are and in whatever you do' because he believes that it is part of the mindset and cautionary measures that hinders youngsters from adventures that could give them the desired break in their effort to amount to respectable personalities that their parents could not attain in their younger years. There is no doubt that sometimes excessive caution cages an individual's progression into remarkable prosperity. Yet, there is the other side of excessive craving for additional success or victories that often put the successfuls into serious troubles which leads to their losing all that they had gathered through achievement up to date.

Most times, strangers get into troubles in their land of sojourn because they get carried away with the success they have recorded in some areas and try to deploy the same clout to delve into issues God never meant them to resolve. We can claim that God sent DSMA to the palace of Nebuchadnezzar to enable Nebuchadnezzar realize that above the gods of his native land, He as the God of all gods does exist so that on the dreadful Day of Judgment, Nebuchadnezzar would not say he would have served Him if he had known. Once DSMA had lived in such a way that Nebuchadnezzar recognized the God of heaven and earth, it was not part of God's assignment for them to make Nebuchadnezzar accept to join them to worship Him. Any attempt to compel Nebuchadnezzar to join them would have led to regret for the four of them.

Haman was one man who got carried away as one of the high officials in the Persian royal palace in Suza. Upon learning or confirming that Mordecai was disobeying their boss' command that he (Haman) be respected and honoured rather than report the disobedience to their boss and let their boss decide what punishment that Mordecai deserved, Haman chose to punish

Mordecai personally. There is no provision in the king's order that Haman should take it upon himself to punish any palace official who failed to show respect to Haman as the Emperor commanded. It was like –

(1) Haman concluded that if he drew Mordecai's disrespect and disobedience to the king's attention, the king is not likely to do anything tangible to punish Mordecai to his (Haman's) satisfaction,

(2) Haman had been looking for a chance to avenge the destruction of his ancestors by the Israelites in I Samuel 15:2-33 or

(3) The king did not have personal reason to hate and punish Mordecai and his fellow Jews like he as a descendant of Agag whom Samuel killed in the palace of King Saul of Israel in Gibeah had personal reason to do.

(4) He did not want the king to find reason to forgive Mordecai and as a result he would miss the chance to punish the Jews which was what happened eventually.

It is as a result that Esther 3:1-15 confirms in verses 8-11 that when asking the king's approval to sign the decree to exterminate Mordecai and his fellow Jews, Haman did not specify that the Jews were the target of his draconian decree. Haman believed that the king trusted him so much that he could make the king to approve for him to do whatever he liked to whoever he liked in the empire without any repercussion. Verses 1-6 say though only one Jew offended yet, he determined to punish all Jews. Equally shocking is the fact that once he got the deadly decree approved, he announced that he did not think it worthwhile for him to spend his time and effort to find out how the Jews were preparing for the doomsday that he had set for them. Even if he learnt that they were plotting to puncture his plot against them (to do something to save themselves), Haman did not think it was worthwhile for him to react to it or do anything further to waste their self-saving efforts. I Corinthians 10:12 says whoever thinks he is safe or double sure of himself should take heed lest he fall when he least expects like Luke 22:31-34, 39-62 confirms that over confidence made Peter to deny Jesus when he least expected. Furthermore, Esther 5:1-14 says when he was invited for an exclusive feast with the king by Queen Esther, he saw it as a sign that he was the best thing that ever happened to the kingdom. It propped up his prideful gauge to determine to hang Mordecai before the original doomsday that he had set against Mordecai and his fellow Jews.

How Haman Hanged Himself means that he confirmed the day the Jews who included Mordecai lack spiritual defense and protection or most vulnerable yet, he decided to prepare a 75 fit gallows to hang Mordecai before the day that Mordecai should be most vulnerable. It means that he decided to attack or try to kill Mordecai on a day that Mordecai was not vulnerable or not an easy prey to kill without resistance from the spiritual realm and repercussion. It was pride that made Haman forget that the day he chose to hang Mordecai was not a day that Mordecai is vulnerable to be killed cheaply. Also, Esther 5:9-13 confirms that he confessed to his wife and friends that he cannot be happy so long as he still saw Mordecai alive and well in the royal palace. He meant that his status in the palace must be crowned with the knowledge that he had a last laugh over Mordecai. It should be noted that Haman was just not eager to enrich his boss and benefactor by adding money to the treasury rather he was eager to use his position of Prime Minister to prove a point that no other appointed official in the palace could dare him as the highest appointed official in the Emperor's palace. He wanted to prove that whoever dared him dies. He wanted to impress his wife and friends but ended up screwing up himself. That was never part of the reason the Emperor appointed him as his deputy. Meanwhile, he did all of this without the full knowledge of the Emperor. Using delegated authority for the wrong aim and objective usually backfires.

Again, Esther 6:1-11 says when the king talked about honouring a man he rushed to conclude that he must be that man deserving the Emperor's planned honour. That is the mindset of a man who believes that (1) nothing good should happen to anyone near him and (2) he is the only one that deserves the goodies of this life while everyone else should have and live with all the bad things that happen in this world. When an individual's conduct suggests that he does not regard the concept of "Live and let others live" the Urhobos would ask "Are you the only human being?" They mean why acting so selfishly or without regard for the need for others to live as well. Even God never meant life to be so rosy for one man while all others wallow in sorrow. That is why Ecclesiastes 3:1-8 says God has apportioned time for both joy and sadness while Ecclesiastes 7:4 and 14 says it is stupid to think of only happiness. Then, Proverbs 29:8 says people with no regard for others can throw a whole city into turmoil by their beastly attitude and actions. Again, II Corinthians 8:13-14 can be said to mean that God meant members of the same generation to prosper at different times in their lifetime. Though they were members of the same generation, Samuel, Kish, and Jesse did not become relevant and respected at the same time. While Samuel had been famous since they were young, Kish became famous when his son, Saul was chosen to be king when they had become old and Samuel's sons were rejected as his successor to the leadership office of Israel. It was much later that Jesse became famous when his youngest son, David killed Goliath, an achievement which made David famous and by implication, Jesse.

There are two other significant points about Haman's misadventure during the short period that he served as the Prime

Minister of the Persian Empire. First, the achievement that earned him the promotion to the office of the Prime Minister of the Persian Empire was never given like Genesis 41:1-46 gives the reason for Joseph's promotion to similar position by the king of Egypt. Genesis 39:1-6 and 21-23 gives the reason Joseph was promoted by Potiphar and the prison superintendent. I Samuel 17:1-58 and 18:1-5 recount the reason David became an officer in the army of Israel is well known. Daniel 1:1-21 details the reason DSMA were promoted in the Babylonian Empire's palace. Yet, the position Haman got undeservingly he decided to use to hurt whoever he resented.

Second, Haman was not contented with the respect and honour of all other nobles. He seemed to have believed that the king's order that he be shown respect by all the other palace officials was his non-negotiable entitlement that he could never give up a fraction of it. Haman coveted complete compliance with the king's directive that he believed that he was the chief beneficiary. Greed for complete compliance consumes is one of the cardinal points here. God never ordained complete compliance otherwise everyone would have accepted Jesus in His lifetime, in which case, He would not have been killed the way they did. Matthew 13:53-58, Mark 6:1-6 and Luke 4:16-30 confirm that even the natives of His supposed hometown of Nazareth did not accept Him. In fact, John 7:1-5 concludes with the shocking fact that not even His younger brothers believed in Him. Meanwhile, John 2:1-11 confirms that the miracle of converting water into wine at the wedding in Cana of Galilee made His disciples to believe in Him. Luke 5:1-11 says the catching of many fishes was enough to convince Peter, James, and John to desert their fishing profession and John and James's father, Zebedee to become Jesus' fulltime disciples.

John 7:5's claim that Jesus' younger brothers did not believe in Him is a very serious matter because, what else did they expect from their eldest sibling before they will regard and determine to spend their lives supporting what He was doing? Dearly beloved, if it were possible, if you find Jesus' younger siblings ask them what they were thinking because their claim and attitude in John 7:1-5 is very illogical. They claimed that Jesus had something to offer to the great and the mighty in Jerusalem yet, they would not join the others to accept the same Jesus that the great and the mighty would regard and respect.

Haman did not realize that the king gave the order for king's personal convenience. The aim was for the king's benefit rather than to massage Haman's personal ego. It was never meant to make Haman feel more important than other palace officials. That is why he should have reported Mordecai's disobedience to the king to deal with as the king considered appropriate. If the king ordered 156 palace officials to show you respect and 155 complied, if you are wise and humble, should you not be content with that 99.9% compliance?

He should have treated Mordecai's refusal to respect him as their king ordered as the tithe that he needed to pay to enjoy the position of the Prime Minister of the Empire. Because of insisting on adding the 0.01% to the 99.9% he ended up losing everything because of loquacious lack of contentment and commonsense. In fact, the concept of the payment of ten percent tithe says Haman should have expected that at least 15 palace officials would disobey that directive and he should not be bitter and determine to compel them to comply. Not even God gets 100% of what He deserves all the time or in fact, at any point in time.

Satan and his fallen angels chose to disobey God making God not to have the complete loyalty of the angels in heaven. Going by Matthew 7:13-14 and Luke 13:23-24's claim that only a few would be saved, it means that only a few would obey God's command till the end of the age to deserve God's salvation in eternity. Matthew 25:1-13 recounts the parable of the ten virgins that depicts the fact that only a half of the people who claim to believe in God of Israel through Jesus Christ would be saved by the end of the age. Matthew 24:40-41 and Luke 17:34-35 lend further credence to this fact. This is apart from the fact that Matthew 7:13-14 and Luke 13:24 confirm that Jesus affirmed that few people would seek to get to heaven. It suggests that among the few seeking heaven only half of them would make it which lend credence to the claim that when it matters the most, one would be taken and the other would be left behind.

I Kings 14:7-8 confirms that God made David's loyalty to Him as the yardstick with which to measure all subsequent kings of Israel and Judah's loyalty to Him. However, II Samuel 11:1-27 and 12:1-23 and I Kings 15:5 can be interpreted to mean that there was an instance when David practically erred or offended God enough to punish David and even his descendants with violent death. That mistake did not stop God from speaking highly of David long after his death.

Imagine the experience of David when he ruled over 8% of the kingdom of Saul after Saul's death even though God meant him to rule over the entire nation immediately after Saul's death. For seven and a half years immediately following Saul's death, Abner stopped David from controlling the other 92% or eleven tribes while David ruled over only his native tribe of Judah from Hebron. David endured Abner-led resistance until circumstances not orchestrated by David forced Abner to determine to let David rule over the remaining 92% of the nation of Israel. During those seven and a half years, David desired to rule over the other tribes but cautioned himself to wait until when God would instigate the handing over of the control of the other tribes. This means that David was content with what became available to him meanwhile until the full measure that God meant for him originally was delivered.

There is the concept of 'ignore the inevitable otherwise regret'. Because Haman refused to ignore Mordecai's insolence, he suffered by way of loosing his life, his sons, the exalted primisterial position and the respect of all the other palace officials while Mordecai gained everything at his expense. In his absence, his wife, daughters, and friends were at the mercy of Mordecai and the Jews. Not even Jesus got 100% loyalty from His twelve disciples. Judas Iscariot was not loyal to Jesus yet, Jesus practically ignored him throughout the three and a half years that the apostolic disciples worked under Him on fulltime basis. Jesus knew that it was best to ignore Judas Iscariot rather than waste His time trying to compel Judas to be loyal and honest like the other eleven disciples. In fact, Jesus never tried to replace Judas Iscariot. Jesus waited till the last minute to deal with Judas by not rescuing him from the consequences of his actions. David tolerated Joab and Shimei until his last moment when he told Solomon to punish them with death for him.

There are persons and things that if you do not agree to live with would cost you what God gave you to enjoy. Part of the troubles across the globe is caused by those who believe that they must make every nation to conform to their self-styled image of good governance which is impossible.

One of the core cause of the problem that the Israelites had with God during their famous journey from Egypt to settle in Canaan is the subject of insisting that they must enjoy the very meals and pleasures that they were used to while in Egypt. They were not willing to sacrifice anything during their travel time. They were not willing to endure the inevitable sacrifices of any basic travel is the meaning. God wanted them to learn prioritization based on the prevailing circumstances. He wanted them to be matured in their value system – understand that been freed from oppression was more important in the immediate. When a man decides not to live with the inevitables of his current circumstances, he is doomed. Like Haman, the generation of Israelites who did not get their priorities right or refused to live with the inevitables of their travel through the desert ended their lives abruptly. If Haman had endured Mordecai, he would have enjoyed the position of the Prime Minister of the Persian Empire for much longer.

II Samuel 16:5-14 and 19:18-23 and I Kings 2:8-9 and 36-46 can be said to mean that David handled Shimei's resentment during Absalom's rebellion profitably. He knew that he would punish Shimei with death for daring to insult him while Absalom's rebellion raged but he suppressed his determination to get Shimei killed because he understood that quelling Absalom's rebellion was more expedient. Even when his nephews including his COAS pressured him to grant them approval to kill Shimei while Absalom remained a threat, he shut them down and let Shimei be. He went further to deceive Shimei in God's name that he had forgiven him for the offence committed against him during Absalom's brief reign. However, shortly before he died and during his very final directives to his son and successor, Solomon, he instructed that Shimei must be punished with death for insulting him during Absalom's rebellion.

How David went about punishing someone that he adjudged to have offended him can be considered a classic example of grandmaster maturity. He was even more matured in his dealing with Joab in this respect. Joab offended by killing Abner against David's approval. He began reacting to it by cursing Joab and his descendants and forcing Joab to openly mourn for Abner obviously against Joab's wishes. Then, Joab went a step further to disregard David's decision and pleas to kill Amasa and Absalom. He even reprimanded David after killing Absalom at the very moment that David was mourning for Absalom. As a result, II Samuel 3:6-39 and 5:1-5, I Kings 2:1-12 and I Chronicles 3:4 and 29:27 can be interpreted to mean that 33 years after Abner's murder David instructed Solomon to kill Joab for the murder of Abner as well as Amasa. For face-saving reasons, David did not add the killing of Absalom despite his pleas for his life to be saved to the reason that Joab must be killed.

This means that David endured Joab's punishment for the murder of Abner for 33 years during which period he used Joab to lead and win many wars that David did not play active part in which II Samuel 11:1-27 and 12:26-31 and I Chronicles 20:1-3 confirm that Uriah's death was stage-managed by Joab in compliance with David's directive. That is even a superior maturity in the matter of enduring the presence of intolerable personalities around you until such a time that they can be punished without any repercussion. This is important because Haman's experience with Mordecai is practically that he could not succeed in punishing Mordecai for the offence that Mordecai committed without repercussion. This means that it is not enough to determine to punish a subordinate, the superior must be wise enough to implement the punishment in such a way that it does not spill over to cause the superior personal pains like Haman experienced.

The other thing worthy of mention is the subject of curtailing abominable advisers like I Samuel 24:1-22 and 26:1-25 and II Samuel 16:5-14 confirm that David did to resist the urging of his lieutenants to spare Saul's life successfully because he honoured God in Saul's life even before he became king of Israel and afterwards. Again, II Samuel 16:5-14 confirms that David was able to stop Joab and Abishai from getting his approval to kill Shimei while Absalom's rebellion was still raging. There is the concept of "Annihilation by Advisers" or "Annihilated by Advisers" like II Samuel 10:1-19 and I Chronicles 19:1-19 say the king of Ammon by the name of Hanun caused problem for himself and his subjects because he let his advisers mislead him. Jeremiah 38:1-28 emphasize in verses 21-22 that King Zedekiah of Judah was misled and overruled by his friends/advisers and that it is as a result that Jeremiah 39:1-10 confirms that he was captured and carried captive to Babylon by King Nebuchadnezzar and his army commander, Nebuzaradan.

I Samuel 15:1-35 can be interpreted to mean that King Saul was another man who God made great but let his appointed officials make him offend God and Samuel who God had used to make him king of Israel. I Samuel 8 – 11 recounts how God had used Samuel to make Saul king of Israel when Saul least expected. I Samuel 15 opens with the fact that Samuel reminded Saul of this fact before relaying God's directive to Saul yet Saul chose to disobey God and Samuel to heed the curious counsel or abominable advice of his officials and officers for whatever reasons best known to Saul only. Of course, the regrettable reason he gave was that he was afraid of his officials hence he heeded their counsel that negated God's directive through Samuel. Only Saul can explain why he was afraid of his appointed officials more than God who made him king of Israel, the position that gave him the authority to appoint those officials and officers. However, by so doing, Saul lost his last chance to retain God's support to remain king of Israel and extend his dynasty beyond his lifetime through any of his sons. As a result, Kings Saul of Israel and Zedekiah of Judah can be said to have let their lieutenants literally liquidate them making them unworthy rulers in that respect. It is an abomination for anyone to let his appointed officials liquidate him through curious counsel. The persons that they made great made them to offend the person who made them great. It is as unbelievable as it is unforgivable. The made should not have the capacity to unmake its maker, all things being equal, but all things never seemed to have been equal for Saul and Zedekiah. The maker should have the capacity to unmake the made but not the other way round. It is profitable to have the capacity to muzzle misleading voices always.

II Kings 5:1-15 confirms that it was Syrian COAS by the name of Naaman was helped by his maid and personal aides to get his healing from God of Israel through Prophet Elisha. His domestic lieutenants contributed their quota to his getting the help that he needed. Spouse and lieutenants should be a blessing rather than a curse. The reason God approved the appointment of lieutenants for Moses as the man He appointed to lead the Israelites during Moses' final 40 years was for them to help him lead the Israelites rather than add to the burden of the job. It is the reason his father-in-law advised him to appoint judges to deputize for him. Any lieutenant that causes problems for the leader should be punished severely.

This is important because Esther 5:1-14 and 6:1-13 can be interpreted to mean that Haman was misled by his wife and friends. It was only after he began to suffer defeat and shame in the hands of Mordecai that they reminded him that as long as Mordecai was a Jew he would not prevail, meanwhile, they taught him to build a gallows where he could hang Mordecai. Since they knew that he could never prevail against Mordecai because of his Jewish background, why did they counsel him to hang Mordecai? In fact, Haman's first bad advisers were the palace officials who drew his attention to the disrespect of Mordecai. If only he had been able to disregard their motivation to punish Mordecai. This is important because Haman was eventually hanged in that same gallows while Mordecai was promoted to replace him as the Prime Minister of the Empire. Daniel 6:1-28 tells how King Darius was misled into threatening Daniel's life against his wishes. He was so angry that he had been tricked to sign a decree against Daniel that he ordered the massacre of the officials and their families for trying to use him kill Daniel. II Chronicles 24:15-23 says it was the advisers who caused problems for King Joash of Judah after the death of his benefactor, the priest Jehoiada. I Kings 12:1-16 confirms that the advisers contributed to the break-up of the kingdom of Israel and Judah that Rehoboam was supposed to have inherited from his father, Solomon.

Acts 9:15-16, 22:21, 23:11 and 26:17 and Galatians 1:15-16 and 2:8-10 confirm that Apostle Paul was ordained and ordered by God to preach the Gospel of Jesus Christ alongside Barnabas to the Gentiles. Yet, quoting the same Paul, I Corinthians 3:4-9 and II Corinthians 10:13-16 say he understood or recognized and restrained himself to do the work of God of preaching to the Gentiles within the limits and localities that God had set for him. He will not and did not do the aspect of the assignment of preaching the Gospel that God had assigned to some other persons. One of the greatest assignments any man can do during his stay on earth is to do God-assigned responsibilities and duties. Yet, it is not every God's work that is assigned to an individual. God assigns specific tasks to individuals to do for Him during his or her stay on earth. Paul meant that he would never allow overzealousness to push him to go beyond what he has recognized as his God assigned limits in the work of preaching the Gospel of Salvation that Jesus symbolizes.

Beyond knowing that he was meant by God to work among the Gentiles and remaining within God-set limits for him while working among the Gentiles, Paul did something else that is very profound as an active apostle. Acts 18:1-4 and 20:33-34 and I Corinthians 4:12 and 9:3-15 say he never asked the Gentiles to support him monetarily and materially rather he worked as a tent-maker to sustain himself in the earlier years of taking the Gospel to them. I Corinthians 9:11-12 and 23 confirms his confession that he did it for two reasons; so that he would not be an obstacle to the Gentiles – so that they will not think that he came to preach to them because he merely wanted to collect their resources to live on rather than in order for the Gentiles to share in the blessings of the Gospel. But when he thought that the Gentiles were matured enough to shoulder the responsibility of providing for him as they were under obligation to do, II Corinthians 8:1-15 and 9:1-14 and Philippians 4:10-19 say he began to write to the Gentile believers to provide for his needs as appropriate. That means that he conducted himself decently among the Gentiles who God sent him primarily to preach the Gospel to. He knew when they were matured enough to tell them to live up to their responsibility to provide for the person God sent to benefit them. That is a classic example of commendable cautious character and conduct while carrying out God-assigned duties and responsibilities. He did not use the Holy Scriptures that talks about fending for the prophets and priests to flog them like a whip to force them to give when they were still like suckling babies in the matter of understanding of the Gospel of Jesus Christ. It can be called operating within laudable limits, blessed balance or the balance that blesses.

If balance blesses and it does, then the opposite or in-balance injures. Paul engaged in what can be tagged 'consider and conduct within laudable limits' which means that he considered the likely negative impact that could result from making the Gentiles to support him from the very first time that he started working among them and decided not to talk about it until the Gentiles had become receptive to the Gospel. He understood that it was strange to them. As for his team mates, Peter, John, James and some others who God meant to work among the Jews, it was not a problem because the Mosaic Law that they were very familiar with had commanded that the worshippers must provide for the needs of the priests working for their benefit in the place of worship. It was part and parcel of the life of the Jews.

What Acts 4:32-47 and 5:1-11 say Peter and other leading apostles did among the Jews when the rich sold their estates and brought it to the apostles' feet to share equally among the believers, Paul could never have done such a thing among the Gentiles who were just learning about the Way of the Lord. Paul understood what was safe to be done among the Gentiles that God sent him to preach the Gospel to per time. In fact, before he started writing to the Corinthian Christians to supply his needs, their fellow Gentile Christians from Macedonia had decided to support him of their own volition. It was part of what he used as an example in his writing to the Corinthians that Gentile believers like them were already living up to their expectation or responsibility. In this respect, CYC means Conduct Yourself Commendably or Cautiously while CYA means Conduct Yourself Admirably and CYAA means Conduct Yourself Appropriately and Admirably. CCC is Commendable Conduct's Contribution which means that commendable character and conduct contribute to acceptance and applaud.

It is helpful to recognize that human error margin is greatly limited, and it is profitable to remain within rescue limits. Genesis 13:1-13, 14:1-16, 18:20-33 and 19:1-38 tell the emotional gory tales of Lot travails in Sodom. Genesis 12:5-9 confirms that he was the only relative that Abraham took along to Canaan apart from of course, Sarah who Abraham married though she was his younger half-sister. Genesis 13:1-13 says after Lot became wealthy alongside Abraham, he did not think that it was important for him to prevail on his servants to stop striving inappropriately over space with his uncle and benefactor, Abraham's servants. Genesis 36:1-8 says Esau never allowed contest for space to even commence before he left their family house for Jacob and his household and possession to have for keeps while he relocated to his own new space in the hill-country of Edom.

DSMA are among the sanest souls who never forgot themselves to dispense with their Jewish traditions that they held very dearly in a foreign land. Daniel 1:1-21 says when they arrived in Babylon and were chosen to be at the palace of their king, they held on to their Jewish beliefs to the extent of disobeying the king without creating a scene even when they were captives. They did not turn their determination to hold on to their native traditions into activism. They did not make any showmanship of it under the guise that they wanted their fellow Jews to do likewise to protect their national identity in the foreign land that they had found themselves. Whatever they determined to do as show of loyalty to their native traditions they did discretely without attracting or incurring the wrath of the king of their host nation. There is no doubt that Daniel 3 and 6 say their self-appointed detractors resented them for it and reported them to their bosses but it was well known that they did not get into trouble because they were nasty or did not behave appropriately.

II Kings 20:12-18 and Isaiah 39:1-7 confirm in verses 18 and 7 respectively that in fact, the presence of DSMA in the presence of the king of Babylon had been determined and made known by God since the time of their ancestor, King Hezekiah of Judah who ruled in Jerusalem. This means that DSMA did not think and act as if since God planned their stay in the palace of Babylon, they would do whatever they liked and get away with it. They respected the authority of the king of Babylon who God allowed to carry them captive to Babylon. They must have been aware of the account of Jeremiah 27:4-8 in which God counseled that they submit to and serve the king of Babylon because it was His will even before they were carried away from Babylon. Activism activate avoidable attacks is a truism. The aims and objectives of most activism is attention attraction to the activists more than the acclaimed cause. They can be said to typify the God ordained and ordered yet orderly, the orderly God ordained and ordered great or the obedient God ordained great. They did not use their God enabled greatness to misbehave like Solomon can be said to have done.

DSMA stood for what they believed very strongly in without attracting unnecessary and unprofitable attention. The fact that they were able to conceal their refusal to obey the king of Babylon to eat the food that the king approved for them for three years means that surely, they were disciplined and highly discrete individuals. They never forgot themselves to boast about it to someone who reported their disobedience to someone who in-turn reported it to the king. Perhaps, it was easier for them to conduct themselves in a very matured manner or competently in the palace of Babylon because they were born and bred in the palace of Judah in Jerusalem. They knew how to comport one's self as an official in the palace of the king of the nation before they arrived in the palace of Babylon. That is like bringing their wealth of experience at home to bear in the foreign land that God sent them to live.

Ezra 7:1-11 confirms that Ezra descended from the Aaronite High Priest lineage of Israel. The priests were supposed to lead worship of God of Israel in the temple in Jerusalem. However, Ezra was not in Jerusalem to lead worship in the temple, yet he devoted his time to the study of the mosaic laws during his stay outside Jerusalem and Judah. He was so knowledgeable in the Mosaic Laws that he could not go unnoticed by the king of the country where he lived. This means that like DSMA, he did not forget his Jewish heritage just because he was living away from home. It means that Ezra held on to what can be described as the priestly heritage of his ancestors like Joseph told his brothers to tell his boss the king of Egypt that they were shepherds like their ancestors had always been. They remained faithful to their national heritage wherever they were. Mordecai knew that non-Jews do not fancy them and told Esther to conceal her Jewish heritage among strangers as much as possible. Mordecai did not deceive himself and his household members. He told them who they were and peoples' perception of them and the solution to surviving among natural resenters and haters.

Also important is the fact that he kept an eye on her even when she had become the reigning queen of the empire. That is looking out for one another in a strange land. Anyone who lies to himself is his own greatest enemy. If people do not like or despise you, devise a way to survive among them without creating any scene or attracting avoidable attention to yourself. Joseph taught that one of the ways to survive resenters is to live apart from them to avoid constant conflict while Mordecai's version of solution is to conceal your real national identity for as long as possible. DSMA says conceal your heritage instigated practices from the prying eyes of natives or any other who could resent you for it.

Haman and Mordecai were Amalekites and Jew respectively, who found themselves serving as officials in the Persian Empire palace. They carried over their inherited nationality hatred for one another in the foreign land that they found themselves. It was not a matter of a native against a migrant but two migrants of different nationalities determining to continue or resume ancient battles. They could not tolerate themselves and they used their chief host to torture themselves. While Haman got the king's approval to attempt to destroy Mordecai and his fellow Jews, Mordecai got the same king to kill Haman and promote Mordecai to replace Haman as the prime minister of the empire. Haman could have ignored Mordecai's disrespect to concentrate on using his position to work for the good of the empire which was the reason the emperor made him the prime minister and help his fellow Amalekites as much as reasonably possible.

Migrants should be conscious of people's opinion of them like Mordecai counseled Esther about her Jewish background and it turned out that he was right. Then, most importantly like I Peter 3:16 implies, they should let their character and conduct prove them wrong where they hate you and prove them right where they think highly of your background. The Egyptians had a preconceived view of the Hebrews before Joseph or his family arrived in Egypt. He made his brothers to join him to serve the king of Egypt. The story of Joseph in Egyptian palace, DSMA in Babylonian palace, and Ezra, Esther, Mordecai, Nehemiah in the Persian Empire can be interpreted to mean that they were skilled enough to serve the king of the nations where they were migrants because Proverbs 22:29 says if a man is good at his chosen profession he would be considered fit to work for the king.

Daniel 6:1-4 says he lived in such a way that his detractors could not find any regular misdemeanour to frame him. The fact that Daniel was good at what he did as well as strived to stay out of trouble did not keep him out of trouble. His determined/unrepentant and fanatical/frantic fault-finding detractors thought that he was doing too well for their comfort – his success, progress and prosperity was their greatest source of sadness and sorrow. That is a classic example of condemnable caustic cause for concern. All hardworking and successful humans have such perpetual protestant persecutors. In the case of Daniel, they were his royal palace colleagues. They did not care that he had saved their lives earlier when Daniel 2:1-49 says in their boss' moment of madness he insisted that they either reminded him of his dream as well as told the meaning or they would be killed. It was Daniel who came to their rescue to escape been killed unjustly as it seemed. Later, they forgot about all that and determined to kill Daniel unjustly. The injustice that Nebuchadnezzar did to them they determined to do the same to Daniel who had saved them from Nebuchadnezzar. That was the human reason their new boss, Darius could not spare them and ensured that they and their family members were killed in place of Daniel.

The full story of their plot against Daniel as reported in Daniel 6:1-28 is very striking. Verses 1-4 can be said to mean that even when they did not find anything incriminating, they did not back down and left Daniel alone. They insisted on harming him to the extent that they concocted some strange fault to accuse him of. It helps us to understand Mordecai's self-saving survival strategy to Esther that she hid her national which is ancestral nativity-identity for as long as possible. Daniel might have understood like Mordecai that most other nationals hated the Jews. It is as a result that he did not act without caution at any time to give the Jewish-hate fundamentalists the excuse that they desperately desired to deal dastardly with the Jews.

Daniel 3:1-25 says it was some Babylonians who reported the disobedience of SMA to King Nebuchadnezzar. The

Babylonians could not comprehend that Jews who were captives in their nation's palace could have the courage to disobey their great king. The Today's English Version says in verse 8 that the Babylonian officials saw the disobedience of SMA as an opportunity to denounce as well as report them to their kinsman, King Nebuchadnezzar. That suggests that the Babylonian officials had been looking for an opportunity, basis or chance to find fault with SMA, perhaps, because they had been sad that Nebuchadnezzar found the reason of merit to elevate SMA to position of authority and respectability as Daniel 1:1-21 and 2:1-49 confirm that until they found reason to disobey Nebuchadnezzar. Also, their accusers must have believed that they should have disregarded whatever reason that they had to obey Nebuchadnezzar's command because Nebuchadnezzar disregarded the fact that they were captives in Babylon to promote them on merit. John 12:31, 14:30 and 16:11 and Revelation 12:10 give the impression that Satan who is also known as the prince of this world is the accuser of God's beloved, Abraham's covenant descendants both physical and spiritual descendants.

Before we continue, this is a point that needs stressing. Migrants should realize that even when they merit promotion or an award or some natives are fair and just enough to let them have anything worthwhile as they deserved, there are other natives who would take offence that the migrant is getting the best of everything in their homestead. In any case, even if you are at home there would be kinsmen who would take offence that you are getting all the good even if it is on merit. No matter where one lives and what one gets on merit there would be persons who would downplay the merit reason for getting promotion to attack the promotion beneficiary. That is just part of life.

David was an Israelite when Saul attacked him for getting the reward that the women of Israel believed that he deserved for killing Goliath. I Samuel 17:1-58 and 18:1-30 is a mixed bag of reactions to David's reward for the killing of Goliath. While most Israelites, including Saul's eldest son and biological heir, Jonathan were happy with David, Saul and a few of his die-hard loyalists were sad that the killing of Goliath made David to become nearly more famous than Saul. I Samuel 23:1-12 can be said to mean that even though David risked his life to save the people of Keilah from the oppression of the Philistines they still determined to hand him over to Saul to kill.

I Samuel 23:14-29 says while God and Jonathan did not want David hurt by Saul, verse 19 says some people from Ziph travelled from their city to Saul's hometown and seat of his regime at Gibeah to report the presence of David in their town so that Saul could come over to capture and kill David. If David was not a warrior and easy to capture or behead without any strong resistance, the natives of Ziph might have beheaded and taken his head to Saul in order to get a reward like II Samuel 4:1-12 says Baanah and Rechab beheaded Ishbosheth and took his head to David with the hope of getting David's favour after Joab had murdered Abner. In fact, I Samuel 25:2-38 strongly suggests that while Nabal took sides with Saul, his wife, Abigail and employees took sides with David. Nabal was from David's tribe of Judah while Saul was from the tribe of Benjamin. Saul's die-hard supporters frequently reported David's whereabouts to Saul so that Saul could go there to try to kill David. I Samuel 17:1-58, 18:6-12 and 19:1-6 can be said to mean that even Saul was happy with David for helping to kill Goliath initially. It was when he thought deeply over the rating of the women of Israel that he became angry with and began plotting David's death because of envy and jealousy. Good deeds provoke both positive and negative reaction naturally wherever and whenever.

Mordecai and Haman's conflict are slightly different in the sense that both of them were not native Persians when they clashed. Mordecai was a Jews and Haman an Amalekite. That is, Mordecai and Haman were both migrants working in the palace of the Persian Empire. That is another angle to the subject of attacks in a foreign land or on migrants. There are fellow migrants who have age long reasons to resent you as a migrant. Exodus 17:8-16 says without been provoked the Amalekites attacked the Israelites also known as Jews in the wilderness while the Israelites were on their way to settle as a full-fledged nation in Canaan after God had forced the Egyptians to let go of the Israelites. Numbers 24:7, Deuteronomy 25:17-19 and I Samuel 15:2-9 can be interpreted to mean that because of the unwarranted attack on the Israelites by the Amalekites during Moses' leadership dispensation, God put an eternal enmity between the Israelites and the Amalekites. God decreed that as a result the Amalekites are no longer fit to inhabit the earth that He created. Also, until the Amalekites are completely wiped out of the surface of the earth wherever they dwell beside the Israelites, He would ensure that the Israelites lived as superiors to the Amalekites. This can be said to be the heart-hidden reason that Esther 3:1-6 says Mordecai insisted that as long as he was a Jew he could never bow low to show respect to Haman in obedience to the command of their overall boss, the Emperor of Persia. In response, it is the reason verse 6 says when Haman learnt that disobedient and despiteful Mordecai was a Jew he determined to use his position of Prime Minister that made him accountable only to the Emperor to wipe out not just Mordecai but his fellow Jews wherever they lived in the Persian Empire.

The other significant point is that it means that whether in Daniel 3, 6 or Esther 3 – that is, whether under Kings Nebuchadnezzar, Darius or Ahasuerus, the Jews were been watched by their enemies constantly. Their enemies were always looking for the slightest excuse to undo them. Daniel 6:1-28 can be interpreted to mean that it is as a result that Daniel made sure that as much as humanly possible, he would not give opportunity to his damnable detractors to hurt him because of where he hailed from to find any fault in him. His effort to remain faultless might not have stopped them but at least it was abundantly clear that they crossed the line of decency into their own damnation. It must have been a considerable amount of self-discipline and sacrifice to keep such a clean slate of faultlessness for many decades. As tough as it might have been, he knew that he needed it to be a step ahead of his lifelong sworn detractors that had made up their minds that there is nothing he could do to appease them that would actually appease them and let him alone to enjoy his life without watching his back constantly.

The near natural emanating candid counsel is that migrants must take after Daniel or Mordecai to make concerted efforts to mind their character and conduct because of those constantly watching any of their moves to find fault to finish them. Daniel and the others did not wait to give room for their detractors to have tangible reason to deal with them before lamenting that they were been persecuted on account of their Jewish background, they did not deceive themselves that just because they were employed at the highest office in the land, it means that they have fully integrated into the Babylonian or Persian Empire so no one would hunt them down again. They kept themselves legally pure so to speak, so that their age long fault-finding detractors would not find any legal blemish to spot and use to destroy them like they love to do since their history began. Their detractors did not care to find out from them why they determined never to worship Nebuchadnezzar's statue. Mordecai's colleagues did not care to ask the reason for reiterating that as long as he was a Jew and Haman was an Amalekite, he could never regard Haman as the Emperor commanded. Their core concern was that SMA or Mordecai either joined them to comply with the king's command or they are punished severely.

The case of Mordecai is very striking in a sense. When Mordecai saved the life of the Emperor, none of his palace colleagues reminded or counseled the Emperor to reward Mordecai appropriately. But when he refused to join them to honour Haman they did not hesitate to point it out to Haman. The story says their reason for drawing Haman's attention to Mordecai's disdain for him was to see if Haman would tolerate it. It means that they expected Haman to do something to punish Mordecai. They meant that if they had the authority, they would have punished Mordecai themselves. Esther 2:21-23 and 6:1-11 confirm that until whenever Emperor Xerxes remembered to reward Mordecai for saving his (Xerxes) life Mordecai's palace official colleagues never thought it worth devoting their time and effort to convince Xerxes to reward Mordecai. In fact, appointing Haman as Prime Minister and next-in-command to Xerxes after Mordecai saved the king's life amounted to denying Mordecai his dues because of Haman. Yet, none of the palace officials saw it from that angle. There is no record that Haman got the position of the Prime Minister on merit like we can safely claim that Genesis 41:1-57 says of Joseph in Egypt, Daniel 1:1-21 and 2:1-46 say of DSMA in Nebuchadnezzar's Babylonian Empire or Genesis 39:1-23 says of Joseph in Potiphar's household or royal prison in Egypt.

When the Hebrews, Israelites or Jews were few they were despised for being shepherds – their legitimate means of livelihood. They were not thieves but livestock farmers, yet it was enough reason to resent them. Then, Exodus 1:1-23 says their generation of Moses was hated for increasing numerically which was considered enough reason to make slaves of them. Verses 8-21 say when enslavement did not achieve the desired aims and objective of reducing their population growth, their enemies resorted to killing their male babies. When their God saved them from these oppressors, the Amalekites converted themselves into their new haters for the singular reason that they were weak and vulnerable from the tiredness of traveling through the desert. God considered it to be so horrendous that He swore that He would punish them some day. Then, Numbers 22-25 confirms that there was the Midianites and Moabites who spent huge amount of money to hire Balaam to lace them with a curse. They spent heavily to ensure this fact even when Deuteronomy 2:8-24 can be said to mean that God commanded, and the Israelites obeyed never to offend the Midianites and Moabites in the least manner. There are people who are determined to pay any amount to get certain persons afflicted, even if their own family members are starving to death they would still prefer to borrow to fund the affliction of their perceived enemies rather than provide for their starving families.

There is the subject of Greatness-galvanized Pride and Arrogance or Elevation-engineered Pride and Arrogance. When someone insignificant become great, mighty, and respected they nearly or naturally always become vulnerable to pride, arrogance and disobedient to their benefactor. I Kings 16:1-4 says God was disappointed that after making Nadab king of Israel he became proud and disobedient to Him. I Samuel 9:15-22, 10:17-27 and 15:24-30 say the same Saul who said he thought that he was too insignificant to be king of Israel turned round to demand that Samuel who God used to make him king showed him respect. He insisted on getting respect from Samuel to the extent that he tore Samuel's dress. He was so shy on the day that he was anointed publicly that he went into hiding and it took God revealing where he was hiding before he could be found. Curiously, the same Saul who wanted Samuel to show him respect dreaded his own appointed officials enough to disobey God's instruction through Samuel. I Samuel 18:17-19, 24:14 and 26:20, II Samuel 18:1-3, 19:26-27 and 21:15-21 and I Chronicles 14:1-2 and 18:14 strongly suggest that David is one of the few in Bible history who was seemingly insignificant before God made him great and remembered to protect the poor and weak from the strong and powerful of society. Then, Job 1:1-5 and 21 and 29:1-11 confirm Job's conviction that God of Israel made him affluent and influential. Job 29:12-17 and 31:13-32 can be said to mean that it is as a result that he ensured that he dealt fairly with all humans and particularly kind to the poor, weak, homeless, orphans and widows.

Genesis 37:1-36, 39:1-23, 41:50-52 and 42:20-22 confirm that Joseph was saddened by the fact that he was oppressed during his vulnerable years. Then, Genesis 45:4-9 confirms that he was elated to occupy the position of second-in-command to the king of the same Egypt where he had been a slave and a prisoner in the previous years. Yet, someone who had personal experience of the pains of sufferings of slavery and imprisonment, Genesis 47:13-26 confirms that some years down the line he too made slaves of vulnerable people who needed his help to stay alive. He got carried away with the greatness and glamour of the position that he occupied to the extent that he forgot the feelings of the pains of heartaches of vulnerability and did to others the same awful things that was done to him as a younger man.

Furthermore, Genesis 41:39-41, 46, 55, 45:9-10, 12-13, 48:5-7 and 50:22-26 say:

> 39 The king said to Joseph, ... 40 I will put you in charge of my country, and all my people will obey your orders. Your authority will be second only to mine. 41 I now appoint you governor over all Egypt." ···. Joseph was thirty years old when he began to serve the king of Egypt...
>
> 55 When the <u>Egyptians</u> began to be hungry, they <u>cried out to the king for food</u>. So <u>he ordered them to go to Joseph and do what he told them</u>.
>
> 9 "... tell him that this is what his son Joseph says: 'God has made me ruler of all Egypt; come to me without delay. 10 You can live in the region of Goshen, where you can be near me—you, your children, your grandchildren, your sheep, your goats, your cattle, and everything else that you have. 12... I am really Joseph. 13 Tell my father

how powerful I am here in Egypt and tell him about everything that you have seen..."

5 Jacob continued, "Joseph, your two sons, who were born to you in Egypt before I came here, belong to me; Ephraim and Manasseh are just as much my sons as Reuben and Simeon. 6 If you have any more sons, they will not be considered mine; the inheritance they get will come through Ephraim and Manasseh. 7 I am doing this because of your mother Rachel. To my great sorrow she died in the land of Canaan, not far from Ephrath, as I was returning from Mesopotamia. I buried her there beside the road to Ephrath." (... known as Bethlehem.)

22 Joseph continued to live in Egypt with his father's family; he was 110 years old when he died. 23 He lived to see Ephraim's children and grandchildren. He also lived to receive the children of Machir son of Manasseh into the

family. 24 He said to his brothers, "I am about to die, but God will certainly take care of you and lead you out of this land to the land he solemnly promised to Abraham, Isaac, and Jacob." 25 Then Joseph asked his people to make a vow. "Promise me," he said, "that when God leads you to that land, you will take my body with you." 26 So Joseph died in Egypt at the age of 110. They embalmed his body and put it in a coffin. (TEV)

This means that though Joseph was highly elated that he was appointed the Prime Minister of Egypt at the age of 30 which would make many at that age to run riot with pleasure and extravagant lifestyle yet, he did not follow in the footsteps of the prodigal son who Luke 16:11-16 says collected all his inheritance while his father was still alive and blew it all up on prodigality in a far away country. The prodigal son got carried away with the availability of abundance in the time of his youthful exuberance/delinquency which he never worked for but only got merely because he was the son of a wealthy man. Genesis 48:5-7 and 50:22-24 above confirm that despite the fact that Joseph's father encouraged him to have more than his two sons who were born before his father and relatives joined him in Egypt, he never complied with that counsel. On the one hand, Joseph did not follow in the footsteps of Shebna who Isaiah 22:15-19 says spent his royal privileges on his high taste without helping the needy. On the other hand, he did not over pamper his relatives until they overwhelmed him or made him to offend his boss and benefactor like Isaiah 22:20-25 strongly suggests that Eliakim did to his own downfall. As elated as he was, he was rewardingly cautious.

Genesis 41:37-44 and 53-57 can be interpreted to mean that Pharaoh enforced his imposition of Joseph on his palace officials and subjects when the subjects went to ask him to talk to Joseph on their behalf, he told them to return to do Joseph's bidding. It helps to explain why Genesis 41:1-44 and 47:13-26, Ecclesiastes 5:8-9 can be understood to mean that Joseph exceeded his terms of reference to enslave the Egyptian subjects to Pharaoh. This means that Joseph cared a great deal about maintaining a cordial relationship with his boss and benefactor throughout the 90 years that he spent as the Prime Minister of Egypt.

This is very important and would have made God envious because He did not get similar loyalty from most of those He made king. II Samuel 7:1-17, I Kings 2:13-15 and 11:1-10 and I Chronicles 17:1-15, 22:1-10, 28:1-21 and 29:1-25 say after God ensured that Solomon was made king at the expense of his eldest surviving brother, Adonijah who enjoyed more support from the Israelites, he turned round to disobey and disregard God's caution. Similarly, I Kings 11:28-41, 12:1-33, 13:1-10, 33-35 and 14 confirm that after God made Jeroboam king of Israel, he turned his back on God. Again, I Kings 16:1-3 says after God elevated Nadab from a commoner to become king of Israel, he turned his back on God. II Chronicles 12:1 confirms that after God established Rehoboam as king of Judah, he turned his back on God. There is the concept of like Solomon like his successors – Solomon's disobedience constrained God to share his throne between his son, Rehoboam and one of his officials, Jeroboam son of Nebat. However, coincidentally, Rehoboam and Jeroboam disobeyed God just as Solomon had done.

Furthermore, II Chronicles 22:10-12, 23:1-15 and 24:1-22 confirm that after the priest Jehoiada and his wife, Jehosheba who was Joash's paternal aunt risked their lives to make him king of Judah in Jerusalem, he turned an ingrate by killing their son, Prophet Zechariah who God sent to correct him or prevail on him to refrain from any act of ungodliness at the urging of his palace officials. I Samuel 9-11, 13 and 15 say after God used Samuel to single-handedly make Saul king of Israel, chapter 15:30-31 says he demanded that Samuel should show him respect in the presence of his officials and officers in his palace. Chapter 15:2-11 says God lamented to Samuel that Saul no longer obeyed His directives. The Good News Bible Translation says God said that Saul had turned away from Him and as a result regretted making him king of Israel. Joseph did not give God and Pharaoh any reason to regret over making him the Prime Minister of Egypt. Jeremiah 35:1-19 says God wished that Abraham's descendants, the Israelites obeyed His commands like the Rechabites continued to obey their ancestor, Jonadab. God must have wished that Saul, Solomon, Nadab, Jeroboam and Rehoboam had followed in Joseph's footsteps rather than the way they turned their backs on Him after making them great. I Kings 14:7-8 quotes God telling Jeroboam that He had wished that Jeroboam had followed in David's footsteps to do only what He approved. All benefactors beginning with God have an expectation from their beneficiaries. Beneficiaries have a responsibility to ensure that they continue to act in a way that makes their benefactors to remain happy with them. They must care for their benefactors regularly.

Genesis 43:32, 45:9-11, 16-20, 46:31-35 and 47:1-6 say because Joseph understood that the Egyptians despised his Hebrew relatives he requested and got the approval of his boss to keep them in the secluded part of Egypt, Goshen where they would not have frequent interaction with the Egyptians. This was meant to avoid frequent conflict. Also, he did not help them outside his boss' approval. This case is very crucial because God authored the Israelites' stay in Egypt yet, Joseph took necessary steps to ensure that there was not much conflict between them and their hosts, the Egyptians. God did not blame Joseph for so doing as a sign of lack of faith in His ability to make the Egyptians to respect his relatives like they respected him. God had played His part by constraining Pharaoh to appoint him to the office of the Prime Minister. God had made his boss to approve that he provides for them from the royal treasury. The aspect that Joseph and his relatives needed to play was to avoid regular clashes with the Egyptians and Joseph as their leader took up the challenge and made strategic arrangement to avoid the conflict.

Joseph understood that if the Egyptians had conflict with his fellow Hebrews who the Egyptians despised naturally, the resulting conflict would get to the hearing of his boss and if it becomes too frequent his boss might be compelled to do something to please his fellow Egyptians who Genesis 42:32 confirms resented his Hebrew relatives. He understood that the fact that his boss approved that his relatives lived freely in the land of Egypt and even employed them to look after his own flock would not change the mindset of an average Egyptian to regard his relatives automatically. As leader of his generation of the covenant descendants of Abraham in Egypt he thought ahead and put policies in place to help his relatives and covenant descendants of Abraham live in such a way that they would not create avoidable problems for him to contend with.

It is very important to note that if Joseph had devoted considerable part of his time and effort to prodigal pleasure like most powerful and prominent personalities do, he would not have been able to focus on ensuring that his fellow migrant kinsmen in Egypt avoided constant conflict with the natives as he was able to achieve as long as he lived and ruled in Egypt. He did not rely on his authority and cordial relationship with his boss and benefactor who was an Egyptian to compel the Egyptians to tolerate his migrant kinsmen. Rather, he found or devised a non-confrontational way to prevent any conflict in his lifetime. Joseph provided mankind with what we can call the fundamentals of harmonious relationship between natives and migrants.

Now, it is important to note that Goshen was part of the Royal Reserved Area owned by Pharaoh and protected from the citizens' encroachment. Since Pharaoh liked Joseph a lot, he would not trouble Joseph's parents and relatives while living in Goshen and because the Egyptians were not allowed to go to the king's reserved lands, they would not have needed to go to Goshen and clash with them. Also, Pharaoh engaged them as his chief shepherds. It meant that just as Joseph was working for him, his relatives were working for him as well and as the king's employees the Egyptians would not like to offend them in any way. Genesis 15:12-14, Psalms 105:16-25 says:

> 12 When the sun was going down, Abram fell into a deep sleep, and fear and terror came over him. 13 The Lord said to him, "Your descendants will be strangers in a foreign land; they will be slaves there and will be treated cruelly for four hundred years. 14 But I will punish the nation that enslaves them, and when they leave that foreign land, they will take great wealth with them.
>
> 16 The Lord sent famine to their country and took away all their food. 17 But he sent a man ahead of them, Joseph, who had been sold as a slave. 18 His feet were kept in chains, and an iron collar was around his neck, 19 until what he had predicted came true. The word of the Lord proved him right. 20 Then the king of Egypt had

him released; the ruler of nations set him free. 21 He put him in charge of his government and made him ruler over all the land, 22 with power over the king's officials and authority to instruct his advisers. 23 Then Jacob went to Egypt and settled in that country. 24 The Lord gave many children to his people and made them stronger than their enemies. 25 He made the Egyptians hate his people and treat his servants with deceit. (TEV)

This means that God used Joseph to lead Abraham's descendants into Egypt and therefore, it is important to note that Joseph's appointment to the newly created office of the Prime Minister of the kingdom of Egypt was part of God's agenda to lead the covenant descendants of Abraham to Egypt as the foreign nation that He indicated to Abraham much earlier. Therefore, Joseph was not made Prime Minister just because God wanted to give him the opportunity to enjoy life but to lead what we can call part of the fulfillment of the promise that He had made to his ancestor, Abraham. This means that the destiny of his generation of Abraham's descendants hung on his shoulder like a burden or yoke that he must not fail them by trivializing the position by converting it into his chance to live prodigally.

Genesis 45:4-11 can be said to confirm in verses 8-9 that Joseph was highly elated about his highest official status in the palace of Egypt yet it can be safely said it did not make him to forget that as the leader of the Israelites or Hebrews he must take the precaution necessary to prevent avoidable friction between his people who were strangers and their native hosts. This means that in addition to the ruler's legislation protecting migrants typified by Genesis 45:16-20 and 47:1-12-reiterated Pharaoh's order in favour of Joseph's parents, brothers and their families that migrants' leaders must make conscious efforts to reduce friction between migrants and native or reduce natives' hostilities towards migrants. Joseph did not use his authority to force natives to accept his migrant relatives rather he managed his relatives in a way to reduce constant contact that fuels conflict.

It is a fact of life that frequency fosters or fuels fighting. If siblings live side-by-side they would soon begin to find fault with one another inevitably. Genesis 13:1-18 says though Abraham and Lot were relatives – uncle and nephew respectively, because they shared a common space their servants soon clashed over space and it took Abraham's wise initiative for them to separate to reduce the tension between them. It was increase in wealth that triggered the tension between them. That means that prosperity promotes tension. If prosperity promoted tension between relatives who grew up with the same custom and traditions or way of life one can only imagine the gravity of the tension that it would cause between natives and migrants with different backgrounds.

The claim that after the death of Joseph the Israelites were oppressed can be interpreted to mean that it was partly because in the absence of Joseph the Israelites could not continue to organize themselves in the way that Joseph did to reduce their daily contact with the Egyptians. Exodus 1:6-10 says:

> 6 In the course of time Joseph, his brothers, and all the rest of that generation died, 7 but their descendants, the Israelites, had many children and

became so numerous and strong that Egypt was filled with them. 8 Then, a new king, who knew nothing about Joseph, came to power in Egypt. 9 He said to his people, "These Israelites are so numerous and strong that they are a threat to us. 10 In case of war they might join our enemies in order to fight against us, and might escape from the country. We must find some way to keep them from becoming even more numerous."
(TEV)

First, if Joseph were still alive, he would have found the solution of relocating the Israelites to new areas that is, creating new satellite towns for his fellow Hebrews to further reduce their daily contact with the Egyptians. Goshen was a new area that the Egyptians never inhabited that was wisely allocated to the Hebrews to reduce their contact with the Egyptians. Genesis 45:1-28, 46:1-5 and 26-34 and 47:1-6 confirm that Joseph's extended family made up of father, siblings and their families, servants and possessions settling in Goshen to avoid their constant contact with the Egyptians was Joseph's idea which he stage-managed his boss to approve and his father and relatives accepted accordingly. It could be that once Pharaoh learnt that Joseph would prefer his father and relatives to live in Goshen, he understood that Joseph chose that exclusive area for them in order to avoid the potential conflict that could arise if the Hebrews had frequent contact with his fellow Egyptians. It is as a result that he readily approved for Joseph to settle them there.

Second, it can be claimed that as a result of astronomical numerical increase, the space in Goshen became inadequate and as a result the Israelites spread throughout Egypt and began to have daily contact with the Egyptians which stoked the flame of the age long resentment that the Egyptians had against the Israelites or Hebrews. This was after the Israelites must have spent more than 300 years in Egypt. It means that even after 300 years of integration the age long resentment was still raw and real as ever. The generation of the Hebrews who entered Egypt while Joseph was Prime Minister had all died which means that the generation that was been oppressed were born and bred in Egypt.

Despite being a generation of Egypt-born Israelites, the native Egyptians could not get over the inherited mindset that the Hebrews were not part of them and do not deserve equal treatment. This is even though Exodus 2:1-10 confirms that the native Egyptians planned to make Moses, an Israelite their king some day. However,

(1) the day they found out that Moses was determined to ensure fair treatment of the Israelites as equal to native Egyptians they stopped the plan to make him their king and went a step further to try to kill him.

(2) it means that their plan or heart-hidden plan or hope was that when Moses became their king eventually, he would continue the policy of oppressing the Israelites even when he was one of them. They meant that he must not follow in Joseph's footsteps to work for the wellbeing of his fellow Israelites.

(3) the Egyptians meant that it was only for the sake of expediency that they adopted Moses as their heir-prince rather than because they had started considering the Hebrews as been their equal or deserving their respect.

From generation to generation, Joseph's solution to the reduction of conflict between natives and migrants remain relevant and rewarding.

Daniel 2:41-43 says it is impossible for iron and clay to mix successfully. Exodus 12:37-38 and Numbers 11:4-6 confirm that some Egyptians left Egypt with the Israelites when God used Moses to free the Israelites from Egyptian bondage eventually. It means that much as most Egyptian natives despised the Israelites there were a handful of Egyptians who liked the Israelites enough to relocate from Egypt along with them even when they did not know that God was using Moses to lead the Israelites. This means that much as some natives would not mind having migrants live among them yet still, there would always be natives who would not accept migrants no matter how long the migrants have lived among them or even if they are the fourth generation of migrants in their country.

This is what government must understand and find solution to beyond just believing that criminalization of resentment of migrants is the one-piece-meal solution. There should be regular engagement of hard-line migrant-resenters to pull down their strong wall of resistance and resentment of migrants. It is a resentment and resistance based on mindset and any mindset battle can only be won by persistent persuasion more than the brute of force that criminalization represents. Proverbs 25:15 and Luke 18:1-8 can be said to mean that patient persuasion coverts 'no' into 'yes' over time. It can be likened to when Romans 10:17 says faith comes from hearing the message or constant persuasion convinces over time. It can be summed up as 'repetition repels resentment' or 'repetition removes or reduces resentment'.

A wise parent would not brutalize his children for resenting a stranger that he has decided to house rather he or she would educate the children on the need and benefit of housing such a stranger – explain to them the real reason for the decision to house and help the stranger and continue to remind them such reason(s) until the children embraces the idea of accepting the stranger. It would be outrageous to use the tool of punishment to force your children to accept a stranger that they cannot find enough reason to accept. One of the cardinal purposes and benefit of history is to learn from the events of the past to better the present and future. One key point from the cases of the Israelites led by Joseph and Moses in Egypt is the fact that the challenge of making natives to tolerate migrants have been in existence since human history began by the case of the Holy Bible. Some natives would like some migrants while other natives would not. The nation's leaders would tell the subject natives to tolerate migrants, yet some natives would still disregard their kinsmen ruler's directives to continue to resent migrants. However, the key point is that it would help to learn from Joseph's practices that reduced the friction between the native Egyptians and his fellow Hebrews so long as he lived.

Exodus 2:15-24 and 3:1-2 and Acts 7:23-30 can be safely interpreted to mean that Jethro's family members can be said to have accepted his decision to accommodate total stranger, an Egyptian by the name of Moses because by hosting Moses, first, he found a husband for one of his seven daughters and together they populated Jethro's household with two sons. Jethro's other grandchildren got two cousins from Moses to share their lives with. Second, Moses rendered service to Jethro's family business. This means that Moses contributed to the economy of Jethro's household. Other members of the household benefited from Moses' presence in some ways. It can be said that it was partly as a result that Moses spent 40 years without any incident of resentment by any member of Jethro's household. If any member of the family considered hurting Moses, he or she would remember that whatever he or she did to hurt Moses would hurt one of them, his wife, Zipporah and the two sons she bore him.

Migration managers should spend on preventive persuasion more than punitive and/or punitive preventive punishment. If some palace officials had consciously reminded the new king of Egypt what they had benefited from Joseph in the past perhaps, he would not have pursued the policy of the oppression of the

Israelites the way he did because he did not remember the contribution of one of the Israelites to the sustenance of the Egyptian economy in the past. This means that part of the reason the Egyptians tolerated Joseph's generation of Israelites was because of what they considered as immense benefit from Joseph during the years of famine. It means that natives understand the reason to tolerate the presence of strangers more when they can see what they are benefiting from such strangers. Therefore, constant reminder of natives of the benefits from migrants is very profitable in reducing tension between natives and migrants. It is called "For Benefits' Sake", "Tolerate for Benefits' Sake", "Endure for Benefits' Sake" or "Endure Them to Enjoy Their Contributions".

There is the subject of "Rulers' Regrettable Role" in what can be called the mismanagement of migration matters. Once Pharaoh said Joseph's kinsmen could settle in the land of Egypt, he did not visit that subject to evaluate the level of compliance until he and Joseph died. Of course, because he was the king, he was presumptuously confident that his order in favour of Joseph's father and relatives living freely in his domain was automatically binding on his subjects and Egyptian kinsmen. For as long as there was no report of any Egyptian attacking Joseph's people brought to his attention, he concluded that his kinsmen had joined him to embrace Joseph's people. It was an assumption that was far from the reality on the ground. There is no doubt that there was no conflict, but he did not know that it was Joseph who took measures that prevented the potential conflict that his order was meant to achieve.

There is huge gulf between legislation and conviction to comply with the legislation by those expected to comply with the legislation. For as long as the people are not convinced of the need to comply with the legislation, they would find a way not to comply and continue to evade due punishment. That is why convincing to induce compliance is important. Genesis 20:1-18 and 21:22-26 can be interpreted to mean that King Abimelech's officials did not comply with his order to let Abraham be remain in his domain without been troubled by any of the natives, the Philistines. Genesis 21:25-26 and 26:1-27 confirm that just as they blocked Abraham's dug wells so also, they blocked that of his son, Isaac later. It means that the ruler's legislation does not convince even some of the ruler's officials to comply with his order to accept migrants automatically. When rulers assume that the relevant legislation that they have put in place is enough to protect migrants, it suggests that the rulers are not in touch with the reality on the ground in their domain.

There is what we can call "This is (Not Necessarily) Your Chance". I Samuel 24:1-22 and 26:1-25 confirm that David's initial followers who can be said to have formed the bedrock of his die-hard loyalists later on said to him that God had given him the chance to kill King Saul and take revenge but he refused to consider it as his chance to avenge and rather spared Saul's life. I Samuel 24:16-20 and 26:21 confirm that even Saul was overwhelmed that David could spare his life at such an opportunity. Much earlier, Genesis 30:25-43 says when Jacob had the chance, he swindled his uncle turned father-in-law and employer as well as host, Laban as much as Laban had swindled him earlier. II Samuel 2:12-32 and 3:20-30 confirm that when Abner came to Hebron to make peace with David and hand over the eleven other tribes of Israel to David's control in addition to the tribe of Judah, Joab saw it as his chance to avenge the killing of his youngest brother, Asahel whom Abner was forced to kill during battle for supremacy between forces loyal to Saul and those loyal to David as king of the kingdom of the tribe of Judah.

Acts 23:12-35 says the Jews determined to use the chance of taking Paul to the Emperor to kill him but it was leaked to the army commander who ensured that Paul was sent to the emperor safely. Esther 3-9 says Queen Esther used the chance of the special banquet that she hosted for the Emperor and Prime Minister Haman to convince the Emperor to kill Haman who had plotted the massacre of the Jews which should have included Esther and her relatives which included Mordecai. We can go on and on about the subject of chance made available to man to express his heart-hidden desire. Man must strive to ensure that he does not use his God-given privilege to do wrong or act in a way that would cause pain to persons that God meant to use him to help as long as he enjoys the position of privilege.

We are very familiar with the infamous story of Solomon using the chance of sitting on the throne of his father over Israel in

Jerusalem, the prosperity and wisdom which God gave him and the magnitude of attention and attraction it brought to him across the world to live prodigally. It led to his marrying 'only' 700 wives and keeping additional 300 concubines to match his status, as we would have said it way back in secondary school. Such level of marital affinity is perfect to give such an individual the title of the highest or greatest amoral and sensual maniac who ever lived. Someone might argue that his father sowed the seed for this considering that II Samuel 5:1-13 and I Chronicles 11:1-9 and 14:1-3 confirm that after David had become king of Israel and Judah combined and moved his throne from Hebron to Jerusalem, he went ahead to marry more wives and got more concubines. He did it as if it was part of God's will for him to use the marriage of more women as part of the mark of his celebration of the privilege that God gave him to rule over the nation of Israel after King Saul. Much as God did not blame him for taking more wives at this point yet it seemed to have become the practice or habit for a king to marry many wives to prove that he is capable of fending for more wives and children than any other man in his kingdom. However, curiously, I

Samuel 14:49-50a and II Samuel 21:1-14 confirm that David's predecessors, Eli, Samuel, and Saul seem to have married only one wife. Only Saul was reported to have had a concubine. Eli and Samuel had only two sons each while Saul had a total of six sons and two daughters including the two sons born him by his concubine.

Some women are not keen about their husbands becoming explosively wealthy because they think that generally, men assume that great wealth is enough reason or excuse to have as many women as possible for intimate relationship. Also, wealth makes more women to seek intimate relationship with such men so they and the children they have for such a man could share in his wealth. I Samuel 25:2-44 suggests that Abigail exploited her first encounter with David to sow the seed of the relationship that led to her becoming one of David's wives shortly afterwards upon the death of her husband which she cannot absolve herself of.

The immediate interest is the fact that Joseph did not get carried away with the excitement of the privilege that the position of the Prime Minister provided for him. With regards to the fact that he was very conscious of his privileged position and status in Egypt, Genesis 45:9-13 that we read earlier confirms that he was thrilled with the position of the Prime Minister and therefore, it is very important to note that Genesis 43:16-34 confirms that he went home for his lunch break just as there is no record that he engaged in any feasting that we know that rulers of nations engage in regularly even when most of it leads to regret. This means that he concentrated on his job to ensure that he did not do anything untoward that could lead to his losing the position and put his relatives whom God meant to use him to support and sustain during this period in trouble. Therefore, strangers in a foreign land like Joseph should use whatever privileged position that God gives them to achieve God's reason for giving it to them rather than fall prey to vices normally associated with occupants of such exalted positions. As we know their story as long as Joseph was alive and remained the Prime Minister of Egypt, his kinsmen, the people of God and descendants of Abraham, Isaac and Jacob and for whose sake Genesis 45:4-5 and Psalm 105:16-19 confirm that God sent Joseph to Egypt to become ruler under their king, Pharaoh did not have any reason to regret until after the death of Joseph when their sorrows took roots.

In the same vein, it means that if Joseph had engaged in some untoward practices and lost that exalted position, the sufferings of his people would have started even before his death. If the wealthy man whom God is using to sustain his extended family gets involved intimately with a lady who causes him losses to the extent that he becomes poor, he is not the only one who would suffer rather his dependant relatives would suffer along with him. This is the more reason why whoever is like the umbrella-like provider for his family members must always act cautiously so that his misfortune would not only be irreversible but also not affect several others around him. This is the reason that II Samuel 18:1-3 and 21:15-19 can be said to imply that David's henchmen said he should not take risks that could cost his life because he provided the unseen covering of God for them to live under as respectable persons on earth. At one point, they claimed that he was worth more than ten thousand of them in their estimation.

Genesis 12:1-3 and Amos 6:1 can be said to mean that there are prime personalities because God of Israel helps them to be a source of help to their fellow humans during their stay on earth. After God used Samuel to make Saul king of Israel, the position gave Saul the authoritative capacity to make his paternal cousin, Abner the chief of army staff of the army of Israel. Furthermore in this respect, I Samuel 16:14-23 and 18:1-30 confirm that God stopped supporting Saul and began to sponsor David in Saul's stead and I Samuel 20:13 confirms that Saul's son and preferred heir, Jonathan attested to the fact that God chose to sponsor David like He had done for his father in the past. As a result, I Chronicles 12:1-22 confirms that while Saul was still sitting king of Israel or towards the end of his reign when some of his officers found out, they deserted him to join David despite the fact that David was still hiding from Saul's threats in the land of the Philistines. The officers who left Saul to join David confessed in I Chronicles 12:16-18 that the reason they did was because they had realized that God was with David which implied that they had realized that God was no longer with Saul as in the past or before David emerged into prominence.

Again, II Kings 18:18 and Isaiah 22:15-25 and 36:1-3 and 11 tell the story of Eliakim son of Hilkiah, a high official in the palace of Judah in Jerusalem during the reign of King Hezekiah. Much as God helped Eliakim to be promoted to become the most powerful official in the palace of Judah in Jerusalem like Genesis 41:37-46 and 45:4-13 and Psalm 105:16-23 confirm of Joseph son of Jacob in Egypt, when Eliakim got into trouble and lost the position, his family members who depended on him suffered as well because Eliakim was their only source of sustenance. Then, Daniel 4:1-37 tells the story of the great King Nebuchadnezzar. Verses 10-12 says many people enjoyed life under the greatness that God apportioned to Nebuchadnezzar as the greatest king on earth until he was punished with the loss of the throne for seven years during which he lived among animals in the wild.

GEEPP means God Empowerment/Elevation Purpose and Plan. Jeremiah 25:1-14 and 27:1-11 tell why God made Nebuchadnezzar the greatest king on earth in his generation. God's reason for making David king of Israel was to establish His plan that David's tribe of Judah would provide royal rulership for the Israelites as God's chosen people on earth. Also, to defeat the neighbouring enemies of Israel so that Solomon would lead the building of the Temple which was part of the reason that He chose Abraham and his covenant descendants to be His special people on earth.

PAPP means Pride/Arrogance Producing Process – Daniel 2:1-49, 3:1-29 and 4:1-37 can be interpreted to mean that it was when Nebuchadnezzar found out that there was a spiritual support for his greatness and that he would remain the greatest ever ruler on earth that he grew proud to the extent that he could not restrain himself to heed God's warning to humble himself. This led to his seven years stay in the wild. II Chronicles 26:15-23 tells how God's enabled greatness stirred pride in King Josiah to the extent that God could not tolerate him, and he was punished as God deemed fit.

There are things that anyone made great by God should not do for the sake of remaining alive and in position to continue to provide covering for all others. In this respect, King Saul's deserters meant that they desired to enjoy God's covering through

David rather than remain with Saul who no longer enjoyed similar God-provided covering. Man needs God's protective and prospering covering to prosper and remain alive to enjoy the prosperity. Isaiah 22:15-25 can be interpreted to mean that God elevated Eliakim to provide respect, relevance, and support for his family members. Also, Daniel 4:20-37 can be said to mean that King Nebuchadnezzar provided such spiritual covering for many during his reign as God decided. Dearly beloved, what do you think happened to all those enjoying refuge under the spiritual shadow that God used Nebuchadnezzar to provide for them during the seven years that he was out of the throne? Such persons would have suffered all sorts of affliction in his absence and in fact, some of such persons would have died before he returned to the throne with greater honour. Part of what happened was that Nebuchadnezzar did not consider the fate of those God assigned to depend on his greatness when he went ahead to misbehave to the extent that God could not overlook his misconduct and decided to punish him appropriately. He was single-handedly responsible for the misfortune of those persons who should continue to depend on him during those seven years that he had to stay away from the throne of Babylon.

'For their sake' is one of the most serious matters that parents and particularly aged parents should discuss with or remind their children of, whenever they can discuss. The children should be made to realize the need for them to operate cautiously wherever they are practicing their career to earn a living and share part of it with the parents who now look up to them. The children should realize that if anything untoward happens to them it would have a ripple effect on the parents, younger ones and other family members who look up to them for support in diverse forms. Since Romans 10:17 says faith in God cometh by hearing the word of God, regular reminder would help the children who are in their hyper-active years to remain cautious and act and react moderately to be able to keep their status by the help that God adds to their marvellous moderate behaviour.

David's men said they are better dead than to remain alive without David. There is no doubt that David died eventually but for as long as they could contribute to preserve his life they did. They believed that he was an integral part of who they needed for them to enjoy comfort and convenience. Sensible persons protect whatever they consider a need and that is what they did. Even when they understood that he stage-managed the death of their colleague, Uriah, they never thought that it was enough reason to lead rebellion against him. When Absalom led rebellion and determined to kill him, they risked their lives to crush the rebellion. While Nebuchadnezzar did not heed Daniel's counsel, David heed the counsel of his henchmen. This is the reason many rulers that some regard as despots remain in power because they have henchmen who are determined to sustain them in power because their wellbeing depends on such rulers.

There are parents and even relatives who do not need the income earned by their successful child and relative who operates in a strange land but the fulfillment that one of their own is successful where he is living is worth more than any amount of money such a person would send back home. His greatness is a pleasant plus for the family name. It would be part of the reason non-family members would respect the family members wherever they are identified as been related to the successful and highly placed individual. Even if you are at home, if you get carried away, you will suffer like Laban who squandered the increased profit he made during the twenty years Jacob worked in his family business. It was because he had squandered that extra windfall that he became desperate when Jacob withdrew his services finally. If he had reinvested the windfall profits during the period, he would not have become jittery when Jacob determined to withdraw his services and return home with his savings.

Daniel did not try to use his position to ensure the return of the Jews to Jerusalem before God's appointed time. Then, there is the story of Eliakim son of Hilkiah who God elevated to replace one Sheba as the manager of the royal household during the reign of King Hezekiah of Judah in Jerusalem. In this respect, II Kings 18:18, Isaiah 22:15-25 and 36:1-3 say:

> 18 Then they sent for King Hezekiah, and three of his officials went out to meet them: Eliakim son of Hilkiah, who was in charge of the palace;

Shebna, the court secretary; and Joah son of Asaph, who was in charge of the records.

15 The Sovereign LORD Almighty told me to go to Shebna, the manager of the royal household, and say to him, 16 "Who do you think you are? What right have you to carve a tomb for yourself out of the rocky hillside? 17 You may be important, but the LORD will pick you up and throw you away. 18 He will pick you up like a ball and throw you into a much larger country. You will die there beside the chariots you were so proud of. You are a disgrace to your master's household. 19 The LORD will remove you from office and bring you down from your high position." 20 The LORD said to Shebna, "When that happens, I will send for my servant Eliakim son of Hilkiah. 21 I will put your official robe and belt on him and give him all the authority you have had. He will be like a father to the people of Jerusalem and Judah. 22 I will give him complete authority

under the king, the descendant of David. He will have the keys of office; what he opens, no one will shut, and what he shuts, no one will open. 23 I will fasten him firmly in place like a peg, and he will be a source of honour to his whole family. 24 "But all his relatives and dependants will become a burden to him. They will hang on him like pots and bowls hanging from a peg! 25 When that happens, the peg that was firmly fastened will work loose and fall. And that will be the end of everything that was hanging on it." The LORD has spoken.

1 In the fourteenth year that Hezekiah was king of Judah, Sennacherib, the emperor of Assyria, attacked the fortified cities of Judah and captured them. 2 Then he ordered his chief official to go from Lachish to Jerusalem with a large military force to demand that King Hezekiah surrender. The official occupied the road where the cloth makers work, by the ditch that brings water from

the upper pool. 3 Three Judeans came out to meet him: the official in charge of the palace, Eliakim son of Hilkiah; the court secretary, Shebna; and the official in charge of the records, Joah son of Asaph. (TEV)

This is nothing short of 'self-ensnaring extremism' on the part of Eliakim. Anything one does without consideration for caution against injurious impact is extremism. He is not the first person to work for the good of his relatives, Esther 10:1-3 confirms what Mordecai as Prime Minister of the Persian Empire under Emperor Ahasuerus did for his fellow Jews but he did not jeopardize his occupation of the office. Esther 4:1-17 can be interpreted to mean that when Queen Esther thought that her determination to use her position of the reigning queen to help her fellow Jews, she asked the Jews to join her to fast alongside herself and her royal maids to ensure that she helped them without any colossal consequence on her part. It was extremism that destroyed Saul as king of Israel when I Samuel 15:1-35 confirms in verse 24 that he chose to disobey God because he was afraid of his army officers. I Samuel 28:17-19 confirms that it was the reason God concluded that he deserved to lose the throne of Israel. He heeded the counsel of his officers and officials beyond laudable limit.

Then, I Samuel 28:1-25, 31:1-12 and I Chronicles 10:1-14 say because he went beyond God-set boundaries to seek God's help to hopefully lead the defeat of the enemies of Israel because as sitting king it was his responsibility to do so, God engineered his death along with his three sons the day following his going to seek God's guidance through a witch. God desires that man seeks His guidance but there are means through which such guidance should never be sought no matter how desperate the individual is. Joshua 9:1-27 and II Samuel 21:1-14 can be interpreted to mean that because of Saul's extremist zeal for the Israelites he violated a peace agreement made in God's name between the Gibeonites and Israelites to destroy the Gibeonites. The consequences were that long after his death and during the reign of King David, the nation of Israel suffered a three-year long famine. To appease the Gibeonites for the unwarranted attack by King Saul, his seven male descendants made of up of two sons and five grandsons were slaughtered. That is just an individual's extremist attitude's ensnarement experience (IEAEE).

It is saddening to be able to infer that in practical terms, kindness conquered Eliakim is the meaning of the above passage. He was a victim of kindness and the concept of charity which also means kindness begins at home despite the fact that God admonishes that we should be kind to others as much as it lies within our power to do so. The "Ever Ensnaring Extremism" means that the consequence of extremism does not respect whether you are holy and righteous or not. The iconoclastic aspect of the case of Eliakim above is the fact that he did not survive the consequence of extremism just because it was God who helped him get a higher position in the palace of Hezekiah.

The way Isaiah 22:15-25 is presented suggest that it had not happened when God was talking about it. If so, why would God know how Eliakim would misuse the position of authority and honour that He was about to give to him, and He did not guide Eliakim to avert it. Could it be that based on what God knows about how Eliakim behaved towards the wellbeing of his relatives God knew that no matter the efforts He would make to caution Eliakim against hurting himself by way of losing the position in his desperation to work for the wellbeing of his relatives would make Eliakim to heed and prevent the self-inflicted misfortune. The man who was unkind to the needy, whether family members or non-family members named Shebna lost the position of authority and honour yet, the man who determined to be kind to the needy equally lost it because of 'incautious', untamed, reckless and extreme kindness. In most cases, anything done recklessly wrecks and ruins and therefore, reels out regrettable. It is for the sake of care, concern, and kindness sickened souls like Eliakim that Proverbs 25:16-17, 27, 29:19, 21, 30:7-9 and Ecclesiastes 7:16-18 say:

> 16 Never eat more honey than you need; too much may make you vomit. 17 Don't visit your neighhour too often; he may get tired of you and come to hate you. 27 Too much honey is bad for you, and so is trying to win too much praise.

19 You cannot correct servants just by talking to them. They may understand you, but they will pay no attention. 21 If you give your servants everything they want from childhood on, some day they will take over everything you own.

7 I ask you, God, to let me have two things before I die: 8 keep me from lying, and let me be neither rich nor poor. So give me only as much food as I need. 9 If I have more, I might say that I do not need you. But if I am poor, I might steal and bring disgrace on my God.

16 So <u>don't be too good</u> or <u>too wise</u>—why kill yourself 17 but <u>don't be too wicked</u> or <u>too foolish</u>, either—<u>why die before you have to</u>? 18 <u>Avoid both extremes</u>. If you have reverence for God, you will be successful anyway. (TEV)

This means that being too good or too evil causes premature death or extremism exterminates the extremist anyhow. Extremism has both sides – good and evil no matter what you are doing. Excess wisdom causes premature death just like extreme foolishness. Extremism ensnares and even exterminates. The extremely good would be grounded by it just as the extremely bad would be buried by it. The solution is to avoid extremism or live moderately. In addition, Ecclesiastes 10:8-9 can be said to mean that whether you do legitimate or illegitimate job, you will still get hurt. There is no aspect of life that the subject of avoidance of extremism is not advisable. If these wisdoms had been written by David, Solomon or Moses it would mean that they were very much available for Eliakim to learn from, but he failed to embrace and live by them and, as a result, suffered for helping to sustain his relatives beyond advisable limits. Caustic kindness is not only when the kind uses the privilege of helping to abuse the beneficiary rather this case is pointing out the fact that the kind could undo himself and suffer. Perhaps, one of the most critical point is the fact that because Eliakim failed to be cautious in the course of helping his relatives, when he fell from that position of authority as a result, the help that he had made his relatives to become so addicted to that they would not do anything to support themselves by themselves stopped. Therefore, he is not the only one who suffered but those depending on him did along with him.

Therefore, it would have been better if he had restrained himself to support them cautiously so that he could keep the position for as long as he lived. According to the passage above, extremism can cause a man's premature death, it can cause shame or make a man proud and arrogant and God resists the proud. In one word, extremism on both sides of good and evil is fraught with pains, aches, sadness, and sorrows. Revelations 2:7, 11, 17 and 29 and 3:6, 13 and 22 say let those who have ears hear what the spirit of God is saying to the churches and it should have added that those that make up what Hebrews 12:23 calls the church of the firstborn and who Exodus 32:32, Psalm 69:28, Isaiah 34:16, Philippians 4:3 and Revelations 3:5, 13:8 and 17:8 say their names had been written in the book of living from the foundations of the earth.

4

Scandalous Surviving Strategies Among Strangers (SSSAS)

The great King David can be described as one of the most dangerous, delicate, and deadliest anointed men of God that ever lived. This is in addition to the fact that he was the greatest individual who ever ruled over his nation in recorded history because he had the privilege of God promising him an eternal dynasty. Survival streak is one very controversial topic in human affairs. It is about the extent to which one can go in his or her desperation to survive. Someone could say Naomi and Ruth did not think anything absurd about Ruth becoming one of the wives of Boaz as long as it gave them the opportunity to have Boaz provide for them from his wealth. It can be called 'personal survival streak and sensibilities, morality and reasonability'.

The extent to which some consider morality in the sense of not hurting others in their desperation to survive personally differs from person to person. Some would say, "Whether it is your hard-earned money or another person's money, what is important is that you have money to spend when you need to". Some others would talk about OPM which is 'other people's money' in your care which can be reframed as MOPM which is managing other people's money in your care marvelously. There might be divergence of opinion between the haves and the have-nots in this matter. It is not right to make others sorrow because you must survive or cannot convert or turn other people's mistake and misfortune into your miracle.

Laban swindled his daughters and their husband, Jacob to fund his lavish lifestyle. Genesis 29:21-30 says he swindled Jacob to host seven days' feasting to celebrate the wedding of his older daughter, Leah to Jacob and another seven days' feasting to celebrate the wedding of his younger daughter, Rachel to the same Jacob simply because Jacob was inexperienced in negotiating for a wife. He hid under the guise of tradition which Jacob was not knowledgeable about to force Leah on Jacob against Jacob and Rachel's mutual wishes. In order to maximize God's prospering presence in Jacob's life, Laban forced Jacob to marry his two daughters without caring about the fact that as marital rivals, the girls who grew up as siblings would be at one another's throat for the rest of their lives. He did not care about the joy and happiness of his daughters so long as it increased his wealth to enjoy life with. Anyone with such attitude to life fits an example of the concept of TPP – Tortuous Profit Pirates. SPP could mean Shameless Profit Pursuers and SSPP could mean Soul Sickening Profit Pursuers. Laban saw nothing wrong with profiting at the expense of his supposed loved ones. CCAAC means commission for comfort and convenience at any cost while AAC is At Any Cost.

There is the subject of host's hurting habits – the host could hurt himself or his guest/visitors like Laban hurt Jacob before it turned round to hurt Laban. Genesis 29:21-30 give the impression that he held a great feast for 14 consecutive days to celebrate the wedding of his two daughters to Jacob. There is a relentless battle between the host and the sojourner such as the one that Genesis 29-31 say was between Laban and Jacob, Genesis 33:18-20 and 34:1-31 (22-24) say of the Shechemites and Jacob, Exodus 1:1-22, 2:1-15 and 5:1-19 say of the Egyptians and Israelites, Genesis 20:1-18 and 21:22-34 say about the Philistines and Abraham as well as Genesis 26:1-33 says raged between the Philistines and Isaac. Initially, there was no animosity between Laban and Jacob until profit maximization triggered it.

The subject of personal survival at the ensnaring expense of others is very serious and abominable. I Kings 4:7 and 21-29 as well as 12:1-4 and 13-17 confirm that it was because Solomon somewhat made an art out of extorting from his subjects to sustain his prodigal lifestyle that led to the break-up of his kingdom after his death because his son and successor, King Rehoboam said he would not stop extorting from the people. The story says Solomon was armed with God given wisdom just as the Israelites were prosperous when Solomon made life miserable for the people by claiming their possessions from them to sustain his own life. This means that whenever someone takes from others to sustain themselves those losing their possession are saddened.

About David's scandalous survival strategy, profit prompted precariousness or sustenance spurred sickening style during the sixteen months that he spent in the land of the Philistines before King Saul's death, which freed him to return to the land of Israel to become king first over his tribe of Judah in Hebron, I Samuel 27:1-12 says:

> 1 But David thought to himself, "One of these days I will be destroyed by the hand of Saul. The best thing I can do is to escape to the land of the Philistines. Then Saul will give up searching for me anywhere in Israel, and I will slip out of his hand." 2 So David and the six hundred men with him left and went over to Achish son of Maoch king of Gath. 3 David and his men settled in Gath with Achish. Each man had his family with him, and David had his two wives: Ahinoam of Jezreel and Abigail of Carmel, the widow of

Nabal. 4 When Saul was told that David had fled to Gath, he no longer searched for him. 5 Then David said to Achish, "If I have found favor in your eyes, let a place be assigned to me in one of the country towns, that I may live there. Why should your servant live in the royal city with you?" 6 So on that day Achish gave him Ziklag, and it has belonged to the kings of Judah ever since. 7 David lived in Philistine territory a year and four months. 8 Now David and his men went up and raided the Geshurites, the Girzites and the Amalekites. (From ancient times these peoples had lived in the land extending to Shur and Egypt.) 9 Whenever David attacked an area, he did not leave a man or woman alive, but took sheep and cattle, donkeys and camels, and clothes. Then he returned to Achish. 10 When Achish asked, "Where did you go raiding today?" David would say, "Against the Negev of Judah" or "Against the Negev of Jerahmeel" or "Against the Negev of the Kenites." 11 He did not leave a man or woman alive to be brought to Gath, for he thought, "They might inform on us and say, 'This is what David did.'" And such was his practice as long as he lived in Philistine territory. 12 Achish trusted David and said to himself, "He has become so odious to his people, the Israelites, that he will be my servant forever." (NIV)

DBA might mean different things to different people but here is means Despite Being Anointed. It is a case of between status and survival. I Samuel 30:1-5 and 18-20 confirms that David's 600 warriors had their own wives and children as well. This simply means that for David to survive among the Philistines with his heavy duty dependants, he resorted to what can safely be described as inappropriate and untoward tactics. He started by asking his chief host to let him live away from the vicinity of the locals. It is most likely that Ziklag was a forest when David arrived there, which means that he had to make the environment habitable. We see him returning to pledge his continued loyalty to Achish even when it was not true. Then, he covered the evil he did to survive, and his track was foolproof. He was a professional warrior, so killing fellow humans to make a living was his stock in trade. It is called, "Battle-borne Blessing Profession and Professionals". But in the moral sense, any professional who is constrained to resort to inappropriate practices to survive in a strange land must ensure that he covers his track well because if he was ever caught, he will not escape the punishment. I Samuel 29:1-11 can be said to mean that the claim of other Philistines can be interpreted correctly to mean that Achish was not wise by trusting David but as long as there was no proof, David could not be punished appropriately.

There is also the subject of Despite Being Authorized like when Exodus 1:15-22 confirms that Shiphrah and Puah honored God to spare the lives of newly born Israelite boys despite Pharaoh's order to kill them. I Samuel 22:16-19 tells how King Saul's bodyguards disregarded Saul's order or authorization to honor God of their ancestors. I Kings 2:8-9 and 36-46 confirms that much as David had authorized Solomon to kill Shimei, Solomon did not immediately rather he waited for Shimei to breach the agreement that Shimei reached with him to remain in Jerusalem. II Kings 1:1-17 says the captain of the third group sent by King Ahaziah of Israel to arrest Prophet Elijah conducted himself in a way to save his life and that of his men unlike his two predecessors.

Despite Being Available can be said to describe the situation in which I Samuel 16:1-13 says despite being readily present God disregarded David's older brothers to chose him who was conspicuously absent on the day He sent Samuel to Bethlehem to anoint David as Saul's replacement or successor at the expense of any of Saul's four sons. Then, Despite Being Absent would mean that even though David was absent, God chose him among the sons of his father to be king. CIA mean Chosen-In-Absentia or IHA means Indicated in His Absence – God indicated to Samuel that David was His choice for Saul's replacement on the day Samuel went to anoint one of Jesse's sons appropriately. Despite Being Angry/Annoyed describes the fact that David endure Joab and Shimei despite being angry with them enough to want them punished with death.

David killed two groups of people to get what to live on in I Samuel 27:1-12 above. The first group was those who have wealth that he needed. The second group was those who may not have anything or much wealth but could escape and go to inform the king of the havoc that David was causing among the Philistines away from the king's purview. Genesis 14:1-16 says it was someone who escaped from Sodom that went to alert Abraham about the misfortune that had befallen Lot and his hosts. This was the kind of thing that David prevented. David later killed Uriah to both have his wife as well as cover up the atrocity that he committed with her that resulted in pregnancy. While David killed to survive among strangers later, Genesis 37:1-36, 39:1-23, 40:1-23, 41:13-26 can be interpreted to mean that earlier, Joseph made slaves of his hosts in order to repay his chief host, boss benefactor, Pharaoh the king of Egypt. Genesis 47:13-26 confirms that he exploited the Egyptians in their most vulnerable period to enrich Pharaoh. Ironically, Zephaniah 1:8-9 and John 10:10 say:

> 8 "On that day of slaughter," says the Lord, "I will punish the officials, the king's sons, and all

who practice foreign customs. 9 I will punish all who worship like pagans and <u>who steal and kill in order to fill their master's house with loot</u>.

10 The thief comes only in order to steal, kill, and destroy. I have come in order that you might have life—life in all its fullness. (TEV)

It can be claimed that all those who steal, and kill are Satan's disciples. This is part of the concept of "For Stomach's Sake". Some prostitute to get what to live on. Others lie from both sides of their mouth to have something to live on. Some afflict their supposed loved ones as a result. Even God's anointed did in I Samuel 27:1-12 that we read earlier. Apparently, even the priest Abiathar shared in the product of violence. This is equivalent of 'scandalous survival strategy'. Esther 3:1-11 says the Prime Minister of the Persian Empire, Haman assured his boss, King Xerxes who appointed him to the office of Prime Minister that he would enrich his royal treasury greatly if Xerxes gave him approval to kill the Jews. The passage can be interpreted to mean that increasing the revenue in the royal treasury was enough reason for Xerxes to approve the request without asking further clarifications such as the offence of the citizens of the empire ear-marked for annihilation or even their background. It was easy for Haman to know the curious carrot of idea that he could tender/dangle in words or proposal that would stir up the king to quickly approve his request to waste the lives of some of the citizens of the empire without any clarifications because Numbers 24:7, I Samuel 15:7-9 and 32 and Esther 3:1 can be said to confirm that Haman was a descendant of the ruling house of the Amalekites. He understood the workings of the heart of kings and he was right. Though he was not operating in the palace of his native Amalek, he knew that all rulers think the same way when it comes to adding revenue to the royal treasury for them to control. There is nothing, no matter how awful, that rulers cannot do to

(1) get more income,

(2) retain their position,

(3) remain alive to continue in their position.

They can give up any of their loved ones to remain alive to continue in their position. This case points to the fact that rulers are so greedy for resources/revenue that they would approve any request that would enrich them no matter how dastardly it afflicts his subjects. It typifies the curious concept of "Rulers' Ridiculous/Regrettable Revenue Drive Desperation or Rulers' Injurious Greed for Revenue/Resources". They are not different from anyone who can kill his parents, children, or any supposed loved ones to either become rich or obtain their ambitions. They prefer and love lieutenants who do not mind killing some of their subjects to increase their national wealth that is in their control.

As sad as it was that David had to resort to what can be described as morally inappropriate survival strategies in a strange land, let us understand that it is a pointer to the fact that sometimes situations would arise that one cannot help but do some inappropriate things to survive wherever one lives. Along this line, I Kings 8:46, II Chronicles 6:36, Job 14:4, Psalm 143:2, Proverbs 20:9, Ecclesiastes 7:20, Isaiah 64:6, Matthew 19:17, Mark 10:18, Luke 18:19 and John 8:7-8 there is no one that does not sin. Genesis 12:10-23 and 20:1-18 confirm that for the sake of personal survival in the strange land that God led him to live, Abraham lied twice about the fact that Sarah was his wife in addition to being his younger half-sister. As if he was determined to follow in the footsteps of his father, Genesis 26:1-9 confirms that Isaac lied about his marital relationship with his wife, Rebecca when he went to live among the Philistines where God led him to live during famine.

It is striking that God did not think that just because Abraham and Isaac were His beloved men that lived on earth, the writers of the Bible should not indicate the fact that they lied at some points for us to read so we would not rush to conclude that it was because they were perfect human beings that He chose them for what can be called covenanted friendship with eternal relevance. God instituted favorable friendship fraternity without regard for the lie they told for the sake of personal survival. It is not unlikely that part of God's reason for noting the faults of Abraham, Isaac, Jacob, David and many others is to help us avoid the trap of 'scandalous sanctimonious sense of godliness and holiness' by apostles of 'holier than thou' believers in God through Christ Jesus of Nazareth.

There are 'holier than thou' pontiffs in Christendom from long time immemorial. Every good man has his grievous aspect inevitably and worst still, Isaiah 64:6 includes the fact that the best of our human righteousness is comparable to a filthy rag in the sight of God or in the measuring standard of God's expected righteousness from man. Man is perpetually imperfect before God and this makes invoking the righteousness of Jesus in our favour in our relationship with God vital and helpful. Quoting Jesus, Matthew 19:17, Mark 14:18 and Luke 18:19 confirm that only God of Israel is without sin. John 8:1-12 tells how Jesus shamed the Pharisees who tried to behave as if they were without any sin in them. It can be described as the Pharisees' Sacrilegious Sanctimony.

Genesis 12:10-13, 20:11 and 26:6-7 say Isaac engaged in fear-fueled lying just like his father had done even before he was born. They did not see anything wrong about telling lies to have their host communities to treat them well as well as not harm them. Also important is the fact that strangers do not trust their hosts. They are not sure if they will not harm them because of what they have brought along to their land to live with. Abraham's claim that he desired that the Egyptians treat him well because of Sarah means that strangers love their host communities to treat them kindly. Also, strangers can go to any length to have their hosts to treat them kindly. Exodus 22:21 and 23:9, Leviticus 19:33-34, Deuteronomy 24:17-18 and 27:19, Matthew 18:21-35 confirm that God of Israel admonishes that natives should be kind and fair to strangers partly because every native had been a stranger and oppressed sometimes in the past before God set him free from their oppressors.

It is important to note that I Kings 8:46 and II Chronicles 6:36 say there is no one that does not sin during his stay on the earth. I John 1:8 says if anyone claims that he or she is not a sinner, such an individual is not telling the truth. Proverbs 20:9 says no one can honestly say that his conscience is clear and that he has got rid of his sin. Despite the fact that I Samuel 13:14, 15:28 and 28:17, II Samuel 7:15, I Kings 14:7-8, I Chronicles 17:13 and Acts 13:21-22 confirm that God declared that David was a man after His heart, I Kings 15:5 says he was guilty of killing Uriah the Hittite according to the record of heaven during the 70 years that II Samuel 5:4-5, I Kings 2:11 and I Chronicles 3:4 and 29:26-28 confirm that he lived and spent the last forty as king of Judah and Israel. Ecclesiastes 7:20 says there is no one that does not do evil and I would add that, at one point or the other.

5

Form and Fan Favorable Friendship

Genesis 12:1-9, 15:1-21 and 22:1-19 confirm that one of the fundamentals of God's relationship with Abraham and his covenant descendants through Isaac, Jacob and the Israelites is that God meant to give the land of Canaan to him and his descendants. Leviticus 18:21-29, II Samuel 7:23-24, II Kings 16:3, 17:8 and 21:2, I Chronicles 17:21-22 and II Chronicles 28:2-3 and 33:2 can be said to mean that the reason God gave the land of the Canaanites to the Israelites was that the Canaanites chose to worship other gods rather than the maker of the universe.

Genesis 12:10-20 and 20:1-18 say Abraham lied to the kings of Egypt and of the Philistines that Sarah was not his wife because he feared that they were ungodly and wicked enough to kill him to have his wife. Yet, Genesis 14:1-16 can be interpreted to mean that despite believing that the Egyptians and Philistines are evil he still found some of the Amorites to be good enough to befriend and make alliance with. No matter how terrible the people or natives are, God will still find some to be nice to the stranger wherever He leads him to live. Even when Genesis 24:1-10 can be said to mean that Abraham did not find any of his Canaanite allies good enough to get his daughter to be Isaac's wife, he cultivated and sustained good relationship with them.

Genesis 14:1-24 confirms that it was the friends that he made from among the Canaanites who lent him support when he had to fight a battle to save his nephew, Lot. It is very important to note that verses 18-20 confirm that God's personally assigned High Priest to Abraham by the name of Melchizedek met Abraham on his return from the rescue of Lot and there is no record that Melchizedek castigated Abraham for asking the support of some Canaanites who God had told him would lose their land to Abraham and his covenant descendants. In fact, what Melchizedek did suggest hailing Abraham's intervention to save Lot. Also important to note is the fact that verses 20b-24 confirm that just as Abraham paid appropriate tithe to God so also he ensured that the reward that his Canaanite allies deserved were given to them.

This highlights the importance of impressive rewarding interpersonal relationship management skills and the broad concept of "Rewarding the Rewarding", "Refreshing the Rewarding", "Recognizing and Repaying the Rewarding", "Reciprocal Reward" or "Rewarding Reciprocity". Abraham understood his boundaries in his relationship with his friends. He knew that he should not and under no circumstances must he force his personal principles, policy, and practices on his friends just because they are his friends who chose to be loyal to him. His personal belief is that he could not collect any personal reward from a man he helped to free from his captors. Abraham was content with the fact that it is on record that he was able to rescue his nephew from the trouble of captivity that he found himself. But he knew that his allies must get their dues so that the contribution of his allies in the rescue of his nephew would not have gone unrewarded. He was glad that they readily answered his call for their assistance without hesitation.

The other implied point is the subject of giving God's dues to Him as that of his human helpers to them appropriately. He did not forget the key contributors to his successful victory over the enemies he attacked. He recognized and rewarded everyone who deserved to be rewarded. Matthew 1:17 and 22:21, Mark 12:17 and Luke 20:25 can be interpreted to mean that 42 generations after Abraham, Jesus reiterated the same fact by implication when He said give God's dues to Him as well as the Emperor's dues to him. Ensuring that everyone gets their dues always would contribute to make the world a better place than it is presently. Abraham did not cajole his allies to show greater loyalty to him by forfeiting their entitlements from the war loot like he had decided to do. Forced forfeiture fractures fraternity means when friends are forced to forfeit their dues it reduces their loyalty to the forceful friend. Just as you decided what to do with your dues let others get their dues and decide what to do with it of their own volition.

Abraham did not rationalize that he never formally prayed to God for help before he set out to confront and conquer the enemies and that as a result he did not think that God helped him and deserved any tithe from the loot. He just believed that without God's support, his allies help alone could not have given him the victory in that battle. He believed very strongly that God's support made it possible for him and his friends to defeat the enemies and as a result must give God His dues just like his allies must get theirs. Reward for every ounce of assistance rendered refreshes relationship because it proves sense of appreciation. II Samuel 7:1-29 and I Chronicles 17:1-27 can be said to mean that it boosted the personal relationship that existed between God and David. This can be summed up as "Sharing cheers up", "Reward Refreshes Relationship" or "Remembering to Reward Assistance Refreshes and Rewards Relationship".

I Samuel 30:20-25 says David insisted that his strong warriors must share their war loot with those who were too weak to participate in any battle. The practice would make the non-participants in the current battle to feel that their contribution in the past is recognized though they were not fit to participate in the previous battle. David understood that everyone cannot be fit for every battle at the same time therefore, those who participated in a battle must share with those who could not, so that when those that participated in the previous but could not participate in the next battle would share with those who participated. It is a comradeship culture of ensuring that comrades do not suffer because of immediate precarious predicament. It is part of the commendable culture of 'live and let others live heartily beside you' – kind of 'help for help'. II Corinthians 8:13-15 can be said to lend credence to this profitable practice.

Proverbs 17:17 and 18:24 say a true friend sticks at all times and since these friends went to war with Abraham, they should be considered dependable and therefore, fantastically faithful/fruitful friends. Reliable friends are rewarding and highly fruitful because dependability and sustaining support in times of trouble is part of the fantastic fruits of friendship. If all friends are dependable and give fantastic support always, this world would have been a much better place for all humans.

The claim that "one with God is the majority" partly means that God's support makes an individual to overwhelm most people who lack His support at the same level and time. We talk of unequal level because the fact that any man is alive means it is because of God's support. Yet there are persons who enjoy greater level of God's support when under the attack of or are contending with their fellow men. In fact, the claim in Genesis 12:1-3 that God's plan is to bless Abraham in order to bless the rest of mankind means that while God is his benefactor, he would be the God-assigned and sent benefactor to his fellow man. Since Acts 20:35 says it is better to give than to receive, it means that Abraham was destined to enjoy God's favour and help above his fellow humans.

If an individual enjoying God's support is in the majority then many people lacking God's support are as weak and in minority compared to the individual who enjoys God's support enormously Daniel 6:1-21 recounts the case of Daniel against his notorious noble neighbours who died along with their household members as their punishment for threatening his life. II Samuel 2:1-42 and 3:1 say while David's smaller supporters/loyalists prevailed, that of Saul's loyalists led by Abner continued to suffer defeat. It is the reason Judges 7:1-25 and 8:1-29 confirm that Gideon and his 300 warriors defeated Midian's larger army. It is part of what David's die-hard loyalists meant in II Samuel 18:1-3 when they claimed that he was worth more than ten thousand of them put together. It is what Daniel meant when he remarked in Daniel 5:18-19 that God of Israel gave Nebuchadnezzar the authority of life and death over his fellow humans during his reign and rule over the earth in his lifetime.

Despite the fact that Abraham enjoyed God's support considerably, Genesis 14:1-16 can be interpreted to mean that he deemed it necessary to have and maintain a personal standing army of 318 warriors and he went a step further to make friends with persons who were strong enough to accompany him to the only war that he is known to have fought in his lifetime. He did not think that because he had enough resources to keep a personal army, it was enough reason to disregard the importance of equally strong persons for friends. That they were strong enough for battle is important because there are all sorts of friends–the capable and the incapable. It is not advisable to keep only weak persons as friends just because you support them or are a lot concerned about the weak and the vulnerable of the society. No matter the magnitude of your concern for the needy, you still need capable friends amid your passion to support the weak.

Abraham can be said to have exemplified the concept of "God's Help Plus", "Heavenly Help Plus" or "Spiritual Help Plus" which means the necessary addition of human help to God's help from His home in heaven. I Samuel 22:1-4 and I Chronicles 12:1-22 confirm that in addition to God's help that was obvious to all and sundry David accepted the human help offered by those who believed very strongly that God was with and helping him greatly. I Samuel 16:1-13, II Samuel 2:1-32, 3:1 and 6-21 and 5:1-3 and I Chronicles 11:1-3 can be interpreted to mean that much as God had used Samuel to indicate that David would be king by going to Bethlehem to anoint David, he could not become king of Israel as God meant until Abner and other leading citizens of Israel made their contribution sometimes after Samuel's death. In addition to God's help, Jesus got disciples to support Him just as Luke 8:1-3 confirms that He did not reject the supplies of some women who supported Him and His fulltime disciples with material and monetary gifts.

With regards to David surviving Saul to become the king of Israel as God of Israel meant, first, I Samuel 23:14 and 25-28 says God protected David from the spiritual realm. Second, I Samuel 18:6-11 and 19:9-10 say David dodged Saul's attempts on his life. Third, I Samuel 19:1-6 and 20:1-43 say David accepted Jonathan's assistance to escape Saul's threats to his life. Four, I Samuel 19:11-18 means that David accepted his wife, Michal's help to escape her father, Saul's threats. Five, I Samuel 19:18-24 confirms that David sought refuge with Samuel at Ramah from Saul's threats. Six, I Samuel 21:1-10 says David sought the help of the priest Ahimelech and lied to Ahimelech that he was on assignment for King Saul when he was running away from Saul. Seven, I Samuel 21:10-15 says he feigned insanity before King Achish of the Philistines. Eight, I Samuel 23:6-13 says he asked God's guidance to escape Saul's threats when Saul tried to capture him at Keilah. Nine, I Samuel 23:15-24 says David went to hide in different caves and wilderness from Saul. Ten, I Samuel 22:1-4 says he relocated his parents and relatives outside of Saul's reach so that Saul would not hurt them to get to him. Eleven, I Samuel 27:1-12 says David took the initiative to go and hide among the Philistines. Twelve, I Samuel 30:1-30 says much as David wanted to defeat the Amalekite raiders, he would not set out to attack them until he had secured God's assured help. In that battle, verses 9-20 can be said to mean that he needed two thirds of his 600 warriors to prevail and it was only the capable 400 that he took to the battle and God used them to defeat the Amalekites just like Judges 7:1-25 confirms that God supported Gideon and 300 warriors for a battle that 32,000 Israelite warriors volunteered for initially.

God's spiritual help still need human complementary component. God never meant His help to anyone on earth to be exclusive of the human component. The same God, who was with Moses, let Moses have human helpers during the 40 years he led the Israelites. Numbers 27:15-23 can be interpreted to mean that much as God chose Joshua to be Moses' successor, God gave the impression that Joshua needed Moses' approval by way of Moses placing his hands on Joshua's head in the presence of the Israelites in order to encourage the Israelites to accept

Joshua as his authentic successor. This is logically necessary because Moses' two sons were very much available. If he did not make Joshua's succession public it was very possible for member of Moses' tribe of Levi to want Moses' sons to succeed him since it was Aaron's sons who took over from him as the High Priest or religious leader of the nation after the death of Aaron. Moreover, Joshua would need the High Priest, Eleazar. Deuteronomy 34:9 can be said to mean that until Moses placed his hands-on Joshua's head, Joshua did not receive the wisdom that he needed to lead the Israelites as Moses' successor.

In addition to Moses' and Eleazar's God-instructed contributions towards Joshua's success, Deuteronomy 31:23 and Joshua 1:1-9 confirm that God gave Joshua personal assurances of His unfailing support like He had supported Moses which Joshua witnessed firsthand. Interestingly, Joshua 1:7-8 says God still added that in addition to everything else, Joshua still needed to study and meditate on His word as written for them by Moses. Deuteronomy 31:7-8 says Moses added his own words of encouragement to that of God to Joshua. Then, Joshua 7:6

and Judges 2:7 confirm that there were leaders who served as Joshua's lieutenants.

II Samuel 18:1-16 and 21:15-22 can be interpreted to mean that David might have died in battle despite God's support at some point in his life if not for the support of his die-hard warriors. It is as if God meant that just as we maintain cordial relationship with Him, we should do likewise with our fellow humans with whom we inhabit the earth. We need Him just as we need our fellow humans during the number of months and years that Genesis 6:3, Job 14:5, Psalm 39:4, 90:10 and 139:16 and Acts 17:26 confirm that He had assigned to us to live on earth.

Just as man needs his fellow man's help in addition to God's help so also man need God's help in addition to his fellow man's help to survive on earth successfully. It is like the relationship between employer and employee – they both need one another just as both cannot do without their clients or customers. God needs a man and a woman to procreate the next generation of mankind to sustain the earth that He created. God needs man to establish achieve His aims and objectives on earth while man needs God's help to survive on earth. If it were possible for Jesus to achieve God's plans on earth without Peter and other apostolic disciples, He would not have recruited them to serve as His fulltime disciples. Yet, without His continued support from heaven, Peter, other disciples and successive persons who believe in God of Israel through Jesus Christ such as Apostle Paul and all men of God till date would not be able to function effectively on God's behalf. When God chose Aaron and his sons to serve as the HP to lead the religious life of the Israelites, the same God designated their Levite kinsmen to assist then necessarily. Just as the now famous Levitical priests could not usurp the role of Aaronite priests so also the Aaronite priests could not usurp the role of the Levites. If the Aaronite priests despised their Levite supporters and the Levites decided to embark on industrial action or strike/walkout the Aaronite priests would not be able to perform their duties effectively.

In life, there are those you need as well as those who need you. Among colleagues, there are those you need and those who need you. In the family, there are those you need and those who need you. In Isaac's household, Esau needed Isaac's favour to prosper as a result he spent part of his earnings to fend for Isaac to get what he needed from Isaac to enjoy life with. He did not need the presence of his mother and brother because the only mission they had to his life was to ruin him. In the story of Joseph in Potiphar's household, Potiphar realized that he needed Joseph more than any other servant in his household to prosper. In prison, Genesis 40:1-23 and 41:1-46 can be interpreted to meant that Joseph needed Pharaoh's wine steward to get out of prison more than he needed Pharaoh's chief baker because the chief baker was never destined to live longer to be in the position to help Joseph get out of prison.

There is when people need you and when you need others. I Samuel 22:1-4 can be said to mean that David's men needed him to give meaning to their lives earlier while II Samuel 18:1-3 and 21:15-22 strongly suggest that David needed them to remain alive or not be killed by enemies in battle much later. I Samuel 16:1-23, 17:1-58, 18:1-30 and 21:10-15 can be said to mean that Saul made David popular throughout the nation of Israel and beyond while Saul needed David to defeat the Philistines later. This means that towards the end of Saul's rule, while David needed Saul to register him in the subconscious of the Israelites as the next king of Israel-in-waiting, Saul needed David to lead the defeat of the enemies of the Israelites. Paul made Silas and Timothy popular, yet Paul found out later that he could not do without their support. Peter and the other apostolic disciples of Jesus needed Jesus to give meaning to their lives yet, Jesus needed them to continue the work of ministry that He pioneered and had to leave behind for them as He returned to be at the right hand of God the Father in heaven.

II Corinthians 8:13-14 says God meant that the rich should share their wealth or surplus with the needy so that when the table of fortune turns 360° the poor turned prosperous should support the prosperous turned poor. I Timothy 5:4 can be said to imply that children should fend for the parents who tended them when they were younger. This means that there is when children need their parents and parents turn round to need the children they once supported. Ruth 1:1-22, 2:1-23, 3:1-18 and 4:1-22 confirm that while Ruth needed Naomi to remain glued to the commonwealth of Israelites, Naomi needed Ruth to be happy in her old age. Naomi guided Ruth to be happily married to Boaz while the child Ruth bore Boaz gave Naomi hope for a better end. II Kings 4:8-37 and 8:1-6 confirm how Prophet Elisha and the rich woman of Shunem benefited themselves mutually. I Kings 17:1-24 can be said to mean that the Prophet Elijah and the widow of Zarephath benefited from one another mutually as God can be said to have ordered.

Judges 7:1-8 says while Gideon needed only 300 out of the 32,000 who volunteered to accompany him into battle to lead the defeat of the Midianites by God's help, the other 31, 700 volunteers needed Gideon and the 300 capable volunteers to fight and win that war on behalf of the nation as the men of the age of war in their generation of Israelites. Gideon needed to defeat the Midianites to emerge as the ruler of Israel for the rest of his lifetime. God said he could not do it alone though he was the one that God sent His angel to commission. Then, God said Gideon needed the 300 men and his personal assistant or weapon of war carrier. If Gideon had made the mistake of regarding the 31,700 more than the 300 men just because the 31,700 were more in number, he would have lost that battle.

I Samuel 16:1-23 give the impression that David had become one of Saul's armour bearer before the battle in which David killed Goliath to lead the defeat of the Philistines. However, I Samuel 17:1-58 can be safely interpreted to mean that for some reasons, Saul did not use David as his armour bearer in that battle. I Samuel 17:12-22 says as a result David was freed to return home to Bethlehem to continue to look after his father's flock as he did before he was anointed by Samuel and appointed to serve Saul in his palace at Gibeah. It was during one of those visits to Bethlehem that his father, Jesse asked him to go and check on the wellbeing of his three oldest brothers who had gone with Saul and other Israeli's men of war to the battle against the Philistines. This was when David heard of Goliath's boast and determined to confront and defeat him. Saul and Israel's men of war that he was leading against the Philistines had spent 40 days and nights before David arrived the battlefield to run errand for his father. This means that Saul took those that he did not need to defeat the Philistines to the battlefield and left the only man that he needed to defeat them behind in his palace.

I Samuel 15:1-35 can be safely interpreted to mean that because Saul forgot that he needed God and Samuel to remain king of Israel whereas his appointed officials needed his favour to remain respected and honoured in Israel, but he made the mistake of disregarding God's directive through Samuel to obey the suggestion of his officials. His acclaimed reason in verse 24 was that he was afraid of his palace officials and army officers who gave him the suggestion that contradicted God's command. He forgot that until God used Samuel to make him king of Israel, a position which gave him the privilege to appoint those officials and officers, the Israelites did not regard him. It is a very painful case or experience of Saul to note particularly because I Samuel 27:1-12 and I Chronicles 12:1-22 confirm that during the last 16 months of Saul's rule and before he died, some of his officers and men deserted him and went to join David. Meanwhile, I Chronicles 12:16-18 says according to these officers and men, it was because they had realized that God had abandoned Saul and was with David. God's desertion of him was not in doubt and in fact, I Samuel 18:12, 15 and 28-29 confirm that even Saul was very much aware of this fact.

I Samuel 15:2-28 and 28:17-19 can be said to confirm that the reason God rejected Saul's rule and terminated his dynasty was because he chose to please his officials in disobedience to His command to destroy the Amalekites completely. This is the real trouble and heart wrenching point and realization in the rejection of Saul by God. What if some of the officers who later deserted him to be with David were among the officers who convinced him to disobey God? It would mean that the officials and officers that he appointed helped to destroy him and abandoned him when they found out the person that God chose to replace him because he heeded their curious counsel to disobey God. It means that he displeased the person that he needed the most to please those who needed him to remain relevant and respected in their lifetime. Those who needed him did not lose anything because they merely migrated to join his replacement so that they could continue to enjoy the recognition and respect of the people of Israel as warriors worthy to be appointed officers by whoever was their sitting king.

In the same vein, once Barnabas broke up with Paul who he needed to remain relevant in the work of ministry to the

Gentiles and replaced Paul with John Mark who needed him and Paul to be relevant in the work of ministry, not much was heard about Barnabas' apostolic endeavours again. As a result, to remain relevant and respected, John Mark deserted Barnabas and returned to join Paul even though it was on his account that Barnabas broke up with Paul. Meanwhile, Acts 9:1-31, 11:1-26 and 13:1-3 can be said to mean that earlier Paul needed Barnabas to be accepted into the fold of believers in Jesus' spearheaded spiritual salvation. It means that God meant that after Barnabas would have helped Paul to be accepted by Christians, He would use Paul to make Barnabas remain in the limelight among Christians until Barnabas' death. It is important to confirm from God who you need among those who need you currently so that you deal wisely with everyone around you at any point time.

The fact that God approved, or at least, did not stop Abraham from keeping these strong persons as friends even when God said that He would punish the Canaanites means that God understood that the person He is helping through life still have need of the friendship and occasional support of capable humans around him. It must be the reason that Exodus 34:11-13, Deuteronomy 7:1-6, II Samuel 5:11-12, I Kings 5:1, I Chronicles 14:1-2 and II Chronicles 3:6 can be interpreted to mean that though God forbade the Israelite from making alliance with any of the nations in Canaan land, He still allowed David to keep harmonious relationship with King Hiram of Tyre who contributed to the building of David's palace in Jerusalem just as I Kings 5:1-11 and II Chronicles 2:1-16 confirm that he contributed to the building of the Temple by Solomon after the death of David.

I Kings 9:14 confirms that King Hiram gave Solomon more than 4000 kilogrammes of gold at some point in their relationship. I Kings 9:26-28, 10:11-12 and II Chronicles 8:17-18 and 9:10-11 confirm that as part of the continuation of David's friendship with Hiram, Solomon did massive business with Hiram. I Kings 9:10-11a confirms that King Hiram provided Solomon with all the cedar and pine as well as all the gold that Solomon needed to build the temple and his palace in Jerusalem. That is before I Kings 9:14 confirms that he gave Solomon another 4000 kilogrammes of gold. This means that just as Hiram helped

David to build his palace so also, he helped Solomon to build his palace and the Temple in Jerusalem which is the real reason that God sent Solomon to live on earth.

It is very striking to note that the Hiram that God would use to help Solomon to build the temple had been his father's friend even before his mother became one of David's wives. That is how God prepares everything that we need to accomplish the reason He sent us to live on earth long before we arrive to live. Also, it means that Solomon did not need the alliance that he made with the other kings including the king of Egypt because there is no record that the kings that he married their daughters contributed anything to the building of Temple for the worship of the God of his ancestors/Israel and his personal palace both in Jerusalem. Meanwhile he did not marry any of Hiram's daughters to share the palace that Hiram contributed to its building.

We have to say it like this for the sake of Christians who think they do not need their fellow man because they enjoy God's support. It is easier for God to encourage a friend to help one in response to our prayers than use a complete stranger even when Proverbs 21:1 says the heart of the great and mighty including kings, are at God's control. II Samuel 23:8-39 and I Chronicles 11:10-42 confirm that much as God made David king of Israel, He assigned some individuals to support and sustain his regime, rule, and reign because such human supporters were inevitable and indispensable. As a result, it is important to reiterate that it is profitable to keep other friends who are strong so that they would be able to help in your time of trouble. Jesus had Peter, John, and James. Paul had Barnabas and later Silas, Timothy, and John Mark to assist while he worked amongst the Gentiles.

There is no doubt that friendship costs, anyhow, there must have been what Abraham sacrificed to keep these capable friends who came to his aid when he needed to rescue Lot from his captors. There is nothing beneficial that do not cost, and someone must pay the price. Abraham paid the price of maintaining the friendship until the day he needed their help and they gleefully rendered it without complain. Genesis 13:1-14 and 14:1-16 can be interpreted to mean that Lot could not keep capable friends to save him from being carried captive along with the natives of Sodom. He failed to learn the importance of keeping capable friends to rely on to save one's self from attackers from Abraham. What did he do with his wealth while his uncle spent part of his to keep a standing army as well as strong allies? Lot represents regrettable relatives who never care to plan for their self-sustenance rather they leave their personal life's responsibilities for their reasonable and caring rich relatives to bear for them so long as they live. Rather, Abraham had to mobilize his own friends to join him to rescue Lot and the captured Sodomites.

Despite living beside Abraham from childhood until he became wealthy enough adult to claim his independence from Abraham, he could not cultivate personal relationship with the God of Abraham and as a result, Genesis 18:16-17 and 20-33 and 19:1-29 say when God would save Lot and his family from the destruction of Sodom and Gomorrah, it was only on account of Abraham rather than Lot's personal right standing in God's sight. It means that if not that Lot's death would hurt Abraham's feelings God would not have spared Lot and his family while destroying Sodom and Gomorrah where Lot left Abraham behind in Canaan to live. Abraham was the prototype of a man's rewarding relationship with God for Lot to observe and chose to emulate to ask for similar relationship with God, but he failed to make such right and rewarding choice. Lot belonged to the class of persons that not even the best teaching aids can help them to grasp what they are been taught. No number of good examples around them would make them determine to be good.

One other aspect of that story means that throughout the time that Lot spent with Abraham, he never learnt anything rewarding in this respect. He never understood the reason his uncle was making and sustaining friendship with his fellow wealthy men as well as keeping a standing army. Abraham had slaves who worked to increase his wealth just as he kept others as warriors, and this was the only battle that they fought for Abraham, but he kept them. This is significant because sometimes people complain that too much money or national resources is being spent on the army and in keeping military relationships that never benefit for two or even three decades. It is the practice because the day that you will need their services and support, it would be disastrous not to have them like Judges

18:1-31 confirms that the nation of Laish suffered because they had no friendship with any neighbouring nations.

Joshua 9:1-27 tells the story of the Gibeonites who sought friendship with the Israelites during Joshua's leadership dispensation. They even lied to secure that friendship and when there was an attack from their former allies, Joshua 10:1-43 says they asked Joshua and his army of Israel for help which they got. Joshua 10:1-7 can be said to mean that while asking for the help, they implied to Joshua that the key reason they made alliance with Israel was partly to protect them from their enemies. The Israelites were supposed to be strangers to the Gibeonites. The reason the Gibeonites sought alliance with the Israelites was because they had heard how God had helped the Israelites to defeat other nations beginning with Egypt.

Talking about keeping weak friends, we know that when Job had his problems, most of the people he helped could not sustain him because they were all needy and had nothing to offer him in his time of trouble. It is not completely beneficial to help only the weak around because there is limit to what they can do to help when your time of trouble comes, and everyone has his or her God-assigned time of troubles. II Samuel 15 – 18:1-16 can be said to imply that when David had to abdicate the throne of Israel in Jerusalem, there were all sorts of persons who showed concern for his plight. Some could not do more than cry as he left Jerusalem. Some followed him out of Jerusalem just as he used some to deceive the rebel leader to his own destruction. Yet, II Samuel 17:27-29 confirms that one Barzillai, a wealthy man and some others supplied his needs during the period he lived outside Jerusalem. If he did not have such a wealthy loyalist, his standard of living outside the palace would have fallen beyond unacceptable standard for a king. Luke 7:1-10 confirms that it was not the Jews who enjoyed the synagogue the Roman officer built for them who were able to repay him. Acts 9:36-42 and 10:1-6 can be interpreted to meant that it was not the poor that Dorcas and Cornelius helped who repaid them.

There is something common to the story of Jacob's sojourn in Laban's place and that of his son, Joseph's sojourn in Egypt in the matter of keeping capable friends to help in the day of trouble in a strange land. They both lacked faithful and helpful friends in their lifetime. Let us not make the mistake of thinking that the man who mentioned Joseph to Pharaoh was a friend of his because it was only when his boss, Pharaoh needed help that he remembered that he left Joseph behind in prison. Genesis 40:12-15 and 20-23 and 41:1-14 confirm that the wine steward forgot about Joseph and his request to be helped to get out of prison until he needed Joseph's help once again to interpret his boss' dreams. If the need for Joseph's help never arose, he would not have done anything to repay Joseph for interpreting his dream earlier. There is no record that he ever visited Joseph in prison once he left to resume his service to the king. He can be said to have followed in Lot's footsteps as there is no record that Lot ever visited Abraham once he had relocated to Sodom. Not even when Abraham hosted a great feast to celebrate Isaac's weaning did, he consider it worthwhile to return to share the joy of the conception and birth of Isaac with them. This is even though Isaac was supposed to be his cousin and Abraham his lifelong benefactor uncle.

The extent to which the consciousness of the fact that God was with them made Jacob and Joseph to care less about making friends to support themselves is another matter. Curiously, there is no record that Isaac made friends for himself like his father Abraham did. He did not think it was necessary to renew his father's friendship with the sons of his father's friends despite the fact that we are admonished to sustain the relationship between our father's or parents with their friends even in the absence of our parents. Children are allowed to make their own friends in addition to keeping those of their parents when Proverbs 27:10 says no wise son should neglect his friends as well as his father's friends because 'a friend nearby is better than a brother or sibling far away on one's day of trouble'. Amos 1:9-10 can be interpreted to mean that the subject of loyalty is so important to God that He does not hesitate to punish whoever is not loyal to a friend. In the case of Jacob, Genesis 31:38-42 says:

> 38 "I have been with you for twenty years now. Your sheep and goats have not miscarried, nor have I eaten rams from your flocks. 39 I did not bring you animals torn by wild beasts; I bore the loss myself. And you demanded payment from me for whatever was stolen by day or night. 40

This was my situation: The heat consumed me in the daytime and the cold at night, and sleep fled from my eyes. 41 It was like this for the twenty years I was in your household. I worked for you fourteen years for your two daughters and six years for your flocks, and you changed my wages ten times. 42 If the God of my father, the God of Abraham and the Fear of Isaac, had not been with me, you would surely have sent me away empty-handed. But God has seen my hardship and the toil of my hands, and last night he rebuked you." 43 Laban answered Jacob, "The women are my daughters, the children are my children, and the flocks are my flocks. All you see is mine. Yet what can I do today about these daughters of mine, or about the children they have borne? 44 Come now, let's make a covenant, you and I, and let it serve as a witness between us." (NIV)

This suggests that Jacob was so busy that he did not have time to make friends with any man in Haran or Padan-Aram.

This thought can be taken further to say because he had no dependable friend among the natives, he could not find anyone to support him to stop Laban's cheating throughout his stay. If God had not helped him from heaven, he would not have returned to Canaan with anything tangible. It means that Jacob placed the burden of what friends should have done for him on God in addition to God's role from heaven in his life. Persons who have relationship with God alone make God to have to send His support from heaven as well as do the aspect that the earthly friends of such persons should have done for them. If Jacob was sharing part of his income with another native despite the fact that Laban was robbing him, that benefiting native would have told him the many lies and tricks that Laban was using and how he can counter and stop him. Jacob had extremely poor interpersonal relationship. Probably he never learnt of how his grandfather, Abraham survived in Canaan in this respect.

Jacob's case teaches us that if one fails to make reliable friends one would suffer some pains that such friendship could have helped to prevent even when one has God's backing. As we can see, despite God's prospering presence in Jacob's life, Laban still succeeded in making life miserable for him. In the case of Joseph, like his father, his job was the only thing he focused on in Egypt and as a result, when his master's wife lied against him, there was no friend among his fellow servants who could say he was double sure that Joseph could not have done such an awful thing. The madam put pressure on him for some time before she resorted to blackmail to make her husband and his boss punish him. Throughout the time she was asking him for an illicit affair, Joseph did not have a trusted friend to confide in so that if it ever comes into the open the friend would testify in his favour. Now, we often say that God passed Joseph through slavery and prison to the palace of Egypt to rule but part of the truth is that Joseph left some lapses that helped his enemy or detractor to send him to jail.

One of the understandings that make this matter of having trusted allies imperative is the fact that much as God dissuades us from putting our trust in fellow man or any other god, we see that God of Israel has allies in whatever He does. When He would commence creation of man, Genesis 1:26 confirms that

He said "let us make man in our own image" which means that He was talking to persons or beings we could tag as His allies whom He was sure would not object to His ideas and their implementation. When He made angels, it was with the aim of having allies in the form of emissaries to implement His ideas as and when necessary. When He made man and placed him on the earth that He had made, it was to enable Him to have an ally to establish His plan on earth. This is the reason God expects individuals to have allies wherever he or she lives. There is no doubt that it is most likely that God guided Abraham to choose his allies in Canaan like God guided Jesus to choose His apostolic disciples after intense all-night long prayers alone.

We must ask God to guide us to make allies wherever we live so that as God sends His version of help from heaven there would be earthly allies to supply their necessary version of help as well to complete the dose of help that we need to accomplish and by so doing, enjoy the benefits of such help as we truly desire. It is "Getting necessary God and Man's Help to be Happy" on earth. Take for instance, the fact that God can do all things did not make Him send angels to deliver Jesus on earth as mankind's Messiah. He contracted humans in the person of Mary the relative of Elizabeth and her husband, Joseph who supported Mary to raise Jesus until He came of age and left home to pursue and accomplish the purpose that He was sent to accomplish on earth. Luke 1:26-45 confirms that angel Gabriel played his relevant part in the announcement of the imminent conception and birth of Jesus. Matthew 1:18-25, 2:13-15, 19-23 confirms that other angels played their part in appearing to Joseph more than once. Luke 2:1-20 confirms that some other angels appeared to shepherd to confirm that Jesus the messiah had been born. God understood that Mary could not raise the child Jesus alone so enlisted Joseph to support her. God established the concept of friendship to benefit mankind just as He established the concept of marriage to make man enjoy his stay on earth. Persons who do not make friend out of their spouse often have tales of woe to tell in their marriage just as persons who do not find a friend in their siblings and relatives do not usually have pleasant stories to tell about family relationships.

Genesis 11:27-31 says Abraham, Nahor and Sarah were siblings while Lot and Milcah were siblings, the children of Abraham, Nahor and Sarah's fourth sibling, Haran. This makes Lot and Milcah nephew and niece to Abraham, Nahor and Sarah. Also, while Abraham married Sarah Nahor married Milcah. Haran died before their father, Terah. Genesis 12:1-9 confirms that Abraham left Nahor, his wife, Milcah and their family which included their son Bethuel behind in Haran taking Sarah and Lot along to settle in Canaan. Then, Genesis 14:1-16 confirms that when Abraham had need for assistance to rescue Lot, rather than send back to Haran for Nahor to come over to help it was his Canaanite neighbours and friends that he contacted to come help him to go rescue Lot. This agrees with Proverbs 17:11, 18:24 and 27:10 that say:

> 17 Friends always show their love. What are relatives for if not to share trouble?

> 24 Some friendships do not last, but some friends are more loyal than brothers.

10 Do not forget your friends or your father's friends. If you are in trouble, don't ask a relative for help; a nearby neighbor can help you more than relatives who are far away. (TEV)

Also, Acts 23:12-22 confirms in verse 16 that Paul had a nephew or Paul's sister's son who God used to save his life at a point. Even though this nephew of his did not opt to join him in his God-given apostolic work but opted to work with the likes of Silas, Timothy, Epaphroditus, etc who were not his relatives. Everyone needs partners beyond relatives to achieve God assigned tasks. However, Genesis 24:1-67 can be said to mean that when it was time to get a wife for his God-indicated preferred heir, Isaac, Abraham sent back to his relatives rather than get a wife from among his Canaanite allies. There is when you need family members and when you need friends therefore, everyone should strive to sustain rewarding relationship with relatives and friends as much as humanly possible at all time. Abraham knew when to seek family members' assistance as well as when to seek friends' assistance. Neither offend family to please friends nor offend friends to please family members is a beneficial counsel or policy.

There was no time that Joseph kept rewarding friends in Egypt. Even with the members of his wife's family who were Egyptians there was nothing significant that is recorded that he did for them as his in-laws. There is no record that he appointed any member of his wife's family to head or supervise any of the storage facilities he built all over Egypt during the years of surplus and scarcity. As the Prime Minister of Egypt, there is nothing wrong if he appointed his wife's relatives to positions of authority. If he claimed that there was no trustworthy individual among his wife's relatives, it would amount to displaying hurting 'holier than thou' attitude and he had forgotten that his older brothers conspired to sell him into Egypt as a slave earlier. He can be described as righteous but ruthless considering that he did not use the privilege of his office to enrich himself or the vulnerability of the women to have as many as he could as wives or concubines. Some scandalous persons might have gone to the ensnaring extent of marrying mother and daughter or daughters-in-law because they were desperate to get his support to survive the famine.

There is no record that he abrogated the obnoxious subjects' enslavement to their ruler's decree during the period that such subjects are most vulnerable even when the acclaimed circumstances of famine had abated or ended. The failure to abrogate the draconian decree even when the famine that he claimed necessitated it had abated gives us room to believe that he merely hid under the famine forced emergency to make slave of the Egyptians to his benefactor, boss and chief host, Pharaoh the king of Egypt. Again, he and Pharaoh were conspirators in oppressing the Egyptians. The reason is that when God revealed the imminent economic boom and doom the reason was for the Egyptians to prepare in advance to reduce the injurious impact. The idea that Joseph proposed was not the only option possible. He said the king should store the excess grains during the first seven years of surplus to sustain the people during the following seven years of scarcity or famine. The people are the ones farming the land to produce the grains. Therefore, he could have as well said the king should appoint an official to the position of minister of agriculture and cooperative societies who would pass the information to the farming population that the bumper harvest would be for only seven years and afterwards there would be seven years of famine. Therefore, the people should organize themselves into cooperative societies to store their excess produce. If the people had been informed about Pharaoh's dreams and its meaning and what they could do to reduce the painful impact on them but failed to act on it for their own benefit then it would have been their fault but for the king and Joseph to conceal it and take advantage of the information to make slaves of the Egyptians suggest that Pharaoh and Joseph had a sinister motive from the very beginning.

Someone might say Joseph could not have bypassed Pharaoh to inform the Egyptians of Pharaoh's dreams and its meaning and solution. But his fault was giving only an option to the king as the solution. He should have told Pharaoh the other possible way to implement the solution by involving the farming population directly to store their excess produce by themselves. They should have asked the people to expand their barns or storage facilities rather than the king engaging in the business venture of buying excess produce off the subjects over a period of seven years and reselling the same products back to them when they were starving nationwide. Nehemiah 5:14-18 says it is bad governance for the king to allow his lieutenants to oppress the subjects during his reign. Deuteronomy 17:14-20 says in verse 17b that the king should not be greedy for gain to the extent of getting involved in money making ventures. This means that ruling over the people by ensuring that the rights of the poor are protected should be his primary concern and a fulltime job.

The subject of nationwide is very crucial because it means that the entire population could not support one another. Relatives could not help relatives just as friends could not help friends, neighbours could not help neighbours. If the people had been allowed to store their excess produce personally during the season of bumper harvest, even if some did not believe and store their excess produce they could be supported by their relatives, friends or neighbours who complied and stored. But the king and Joseph conspired and made the king the owner of the only reservoir of grains in the nation. Joseph and the king left the business of administration of justice, ensuring fairness and prevention of oppression of the poor by the rich and powerful to focus on profiting on the vulnerable citizens. Before the famine, the king had only royal authority and control over the subjects. However, he used Joseph to manage the famine in such a way that he added the exercise of economic authority and control over the people. It is an unfair advantage over vulnerable subjects. The king should not control the means of livelihood of the subjects.

It makes sense to conclude from Genesis 41:53-57 that it was when he introduced the decree that was strange to the traditions and practices of the Egyptians that they went to their king who was their kinsman to ask that he prevailed on this stranger from Canaan. Rather than help his people as they requested or pleaded or both with him, the passage says the king told them to return to obey whatever directives he gave to them. My constant argument when people in authority say such annoying things is that 'for crying out loud, if what your subordinate instructed was proper and acceptable, would the complainant came to you to complain or ask you to speak to your subordinate over his complaint?' The complainant came to ask your intervention because your subordinate or accredited agent is doing something untoward with the privilege of authority that you delegated to him to act on your behalf. The proper thing to do is not to say the complainant should return to comply with whatever he said should be done. It is either you are a lazy superior who sees your responsibility as a burden that you shifted to your subordinate or as it can be inferred from Ecclesiastes 5:8-9 and Zephaniah 1:9b you instructed your subordinate to do the tortuous things that the people consider too strangely and inappropriate to endure and expect you to stop your subordinate from doing because you are benefiting personally from the precarious policy's implementation.

The proper thing to do is to hear the complainant out and then cross-check if there is any variation with your specific instructions. If there are variations between the complainant's claims and the instructions you gave to your subordinates then, cross-check with your subordinate in the absence of the complainant and after hearing his own side get back to the complainant. Otherwise, over time the people would conclude that you are the one using your subordinates to oppress the people and some day, when you least expect they would revolt against you and your subordinates altogether. And you would be the greatest loser because everyone would heap the blame on you for not been able to tame the excesses of your subordinates. It is suicidal for any leader or superior not to hear any form of complainants about his subordinates because once the lieutenants and subordinates know that their superior does not care enough to hear how they are acting on his behalf, they would begin to abuse the privilege giving them by their superior. That is only normal with subordinates.

There is nothing seriously surprising with the reaction of their king considering the fact that Jeremiah 17:9 says the heart of man is desperately wicked and none can fathom it. Our focus will not permit us to delve in details on the subject of whether the king had been looking for a way of proving that he was superior to the subjects by claiming part of their land and resources and therefore, was most glad when Joseph could exploit the rare opportunity that the famine provided. If so, then Pharaoh must have been most glad that he chose Joseph to rule over Egypt on his behalf. In which case, whenever he claimed that Joseph was the best individual who had ever occupied the position of next in command to him, he meant that Joseph was the first official who helped him lord himself over his subjects. It is not likely that when he was taking over the throne of his ancestors, he promised to subjugate them by way of claiming ownership of the land that the subjects inherited from their ancestors and part of the proceed of their land. Considering the way that –

(a) Genesis 41:37-58 and 47:13-26 confirm that Pharaoh appointed and let Joseph to subjugate his subjects,

(b) I Kings 4:1-19, 23-24 and 26-27 claims that Solomon appointed governors for the sole purpose of extorting from his subjects to sustain his prodigality even though he was richer than his subjects,

(c) I Kings 12:1-17 confirms that the Israelites were very unhappy with Solomon's burdensomeness throughout his reign and rule over them,

(d) Nehemiah 5:14-18 says Governor Nehemiah's predecessors let their appointed officials to oppress the Jews,

(e) Esther 3:1-11 confirms that King Xerxes approved that his newly appointed Prime Minister, Haman could exterminate some of his subjects who turned out to be the Jews as long as Haman increased revenue of his royal treasury, and

(f) Ecclesiastes 5:8-9 confirms that the norm is for rulers let their appointed officials extort from the populace because he get his own percentage of share from the proceeds of such extortion, we can safely conclude without any controversy that when rulers appoint officials to supervise their subject's affairs they mean in their hearts that such officials have their implied approval to subjugate their subjects to his slavish control.

Proverbs 14:20 says the rich man, and we can include occupiers of powerful positions, are among those that get many friends because of what others could benefit from them. However, despite Joseph's exalted position of Prime Minister, there is no record that he took delight in any of the Egyptians who came to beg for grains to favour so that they could be his friends. He dealt with them officially rather than use his position to help and make such beneficiaries his personal dependable friends among the Egyptians whom God ordained him to live with. Let us remember that Joseph's own descendants were among the Israelites that were oppressed, yet there was no Egyptian who considered that their matriarch, Joseph's wife was an Egyptian. Her relatives did not think it was important for them to restrain their fellow Egyptians from oppressing their cousins born to Joseph.

It is like the contrasting story of the man whom Matthew 9:1-8, Mark 2:1-12 and Luke 5:17-26 say his friends broke through the roof of the house where Jesus was, to lower him down into the presence of Jesus to heal whereas John 5:1-18 says there was another man who told Jesus shortly before he was healed at the pool of Bethzartha or Bethesda that there was no one to help him. Jesus said both took ill because of their sins in which case He forgave them to heal them. But the man at the pool of Bethzartha or Bethesda should tell everyone why his friends abandoned him while another person's friends supported him until they could get Jesus to help him or until they constrained Jesus to help him.

For the friendless man, Jesus had to go out of His way to meet him where he was lying helpless to help him whereas for the other man, his friends went as far as committing the offence of breaking through the roof of another man's house in order to get him to Jesus' presence to help him recover as if they had concluded that Jesus must help their friend 'by force by fire' as they say it in Nigerian Christians' circle. By force by fire means by any means possible, including force. It means that the desperate individual would fast and pray persistently until something tangibly good and delightful happens to him.

Matthew 9:1-2, Mark 2:1-5, Luke 5:17-20 and John 5:1-9 can be interpreted to mean that while Jesus healed the man at the pool of Bethesda because he had suffered enough for the sins he committed to deserve being crippled, Jesus healed the man who was lowered through the broken roof into His presence because of the faith of the four friends who brought him into His presence. The faith and effort of the four friends made up for the remaining number of years that he deserved to suffer. It highlights the importance of friendship – friends who have the necessary resources both spiritual and physical required to make up for the deficiency of the individual.

Furthermore, consider the case of Jacob's escape from Shechem when Genesis 34:1-31 and 35:1-21 say he was afraid that the friends or allies of the Shechemites might attack and destroy him and his household members. Since Genesis 35:5 says that it was because God sent fear on the surrounding nations that prevented them from attacking him, then it makes sense to agree that they could have attacked Jacob and his family to avenge the death of the Shechemites. Therefore, as much as that was possible, it is equally true that at such a time, Jacob was not sure of any ally or friend around who could come to his aid if he was attacked and we know that it means that upon settling in Shechem, he continued in his usual lifestyle of never making friends with anyone around him.

We should not be surprised at all, because if Jacob could not befriend his only brother and father, it is understandable that he could never go out of his individualized enclave or conclave to befriend an outsider away from home. Part of the reason Genesis 26:34-35 says while his twin brother and only sibling got two wives in the locality where they were born and bred in Canaan and that Jacob did not get one, not even a single female friend, is that he was not a friendly personality; there was no parent in Canaan who thought that he should marry their daughter even though he was the son of a rich man. There is no record that their father had a personal family friend who could have presented Jacob a lady to marry or befriend as any young man is attracted to any available young woman in his sight. He could not attract any young girl because he was a classic example of a recluse and injurious introvert.

Much as one cannot afford to make every person his friend, it is absurd for anyone and particularly someone living in a strange land not to have a single dependable friend there. God had used the case of Abraham to set an example for his covenant descendants to follow in the matter of fruitful friendship, but

Jacob failed in this respect to his own detriment. I am not too sure of what it is in some other parts of the world but I know that pastoral duties has brought me in contact with particularly mothers, who make a mountain out of the molehill of issue of their daughters or sons who they claim have never attracted or have any man or lady around them for a personal relationship. This will help us to appreciate what was wrong with the way that Isaac and Jacob lived in this matter. By the time Abraham sent Eliezer to get Rebecca to become Isaac's wife, there is no record that Isaac had any female friend or that by the time Rebecca manipulated Isaac to send Jacob to her brother, Laban's place to get a wife, Jacob had any female friend or fan or both.

In a typical South west Nigerian Yoruba family, the mother of such a man would be worried to death that some enemies might have used some spiritual veil to cover the natural attraction of the opposite sex to their son. This is made worse by the fact that his twin brother had already taken two wives when they attained the age of forty. The core Christian women would have proclaimed seven days of fasting and prayers for the entire family for God to intervene and remove the evil covering that enemies have placed over the life of their son and sibling that makes the opposite sex to avoid him or her. Let us not consider the desirability of such level of concern for the inability of their son or daughter to attract the opposite sex for a rewarding relationship between a man and a woman.

Apparently because Jacob gave necessary time and attention to bring up Joseph, he failed to teach him about the usefulness of friendship. But it is even wrong for anyone to expect Jacob to emphasize the importance of friendship to personal survival in life particularly in a foreign land to Joseph or anyone he was teaching such things because as they say "no one can give what he or she does not have personally". An immoral person cannot teach morality to his child or anyone to embrace and live accordingly. You can only give what you have. The other problem that most parents have is insincerity and shame. They cannot tell their children what they did wrong that increased their sorrows or sowed the seed for their sorrows in the past or even present. Jacob had never gone out of his way to befriend anyone for any reason and could not admit it to Joseph, so he avoided that aspect while teaching Joseph how to live as a child.

He could not admit that he failed to keep friends who could have benefited him throughout the years that he spent in Haran and Shechem.

Jeremiah 38:1-13 and 39:15-18 confirm that when Jeremiah should have died in the dried but muddy well which he was put by the nobles of Judah in Jerusalem like the one that Genesis 37 says Joseph was thrown in by those that can be rightly called his brotherhood of wickedness, it was a foreigner who served in the palace of the king of Judah in Jerusalem who spoke to the king to order Jeremiah's evacuation from the well. There is no record that God formally prompted this man to speak in favour of Jeremiah to spare his life at this point. If Jeremiah had refused to befriend this man just because he was not a Jew like himself, Jeremiah's fellow Jews would have killed him because the persons that ensured that he was thrown inside the well were his fellow Jews. This is a prophet whom God said He had ordained to serve as a prophet before he was conceived by his mother yet, he had a foreigner as a trusted friend in his own nation and benefited greatly from so doing. Therefore, it is absurd and amounts to personal punitive practice for someone who is living among strangers to despise the need for a trusted friend among them. If Jeremiah did not keep good relationship with this man, the man would not have been passionate about saving him from the well. Jeremiah 39:15-18 confirms that because of the way Ebedmelech helped Jeremiah, God took note in heaven and decided to reward him because he lived up to the tenets of friendship in God's sight. This is not to say that trusted friends cannot fail on the day of trouble. Judges 4:12-24 says:

> 12 When they told Sisera that Barak son of Abinoam had gone up to Mount Tabor, 13 Sisera gathered together his nine hundred iron chariots and all the men with him, from Harosheth Haggoyim to the Kishon River. 14 Then Deborah said to Barak, "Go! This is the day the Lord has given Sisera into your hands. Has not the Lord gone ahead of you?" So Barak went down Mount Tabor, followed by ten thousand men. 15 At Barak's advance, the Lord routed Sisera and all his chariots and army by the sword, and Sisera abandoned his chariot and fled on foot. 16 But

Barak pursued the chariots and army as far as Harosheth Haggoyim. All the troops of Sisera fell by the sword; not a man was left. 17 Sisera, however, fled on foot to the tent of Jael, the wife of Heber the Kenite, because there were friendly relations between Jabin king of Hazor and the clan of Heber the Kenite. 18 Jael went out to meet Sisera and said to him, "Come, my lord, come right in. Don't be afraid." So he entered her tent, and she put a covering over him. 19 "I'm thirsty," he said. "Please give me some water." She opened a skin of milk, gave him a drink, and covered him up. 20 "Stand in the doorway of the tent," he told her. "If someone comes by and asks you, 'Is anyone here?' say 'No.'" 21 But Jael, Heber's wife, picked up a tent peg and a hammer and went quietly to him while he lay fast asleep, exhausted. She drove the peg through his temple into the ground, and he died. 22 Barak came by in pursuit of Sisera, and Jael went out to meet him. "Come," she said, "I will show you the man you're looking for." So he went in with her, and there lay Sisera with the tent peg through his temple — dead. 23 On that day God subdued Jabin, the Canaanite king, before the Israelites. 24 And the hand of the Israelites grew stronger and stronger against Jabin, the Canaanite king, until they destroyed him. (NIV)

We see the army commander of the Canaanite kingdom of Hazor, Sisera sought safety with a supposed family friend on the day of what turned out to be the worst battle for Sisera but was betrayed by the friend's wife. But at least he had a friend whose wife chose to betray him when he needed her help the most. It is still better that it was a trusted friend who turned tortuous on the worst day. But to disregard God's established concept of rewarding friendship because Sisera was betrayed by a supposed trusted friend is more disastrous. We cannot be as wise as God who deemed it fit to establish the idea of friendship for our benefit. The whole idea of Abrahamic covenant is based on the friendship God initiated with Abraham. The benefits of the friendship are eternal to whoever embraces God's friendship with Abraham.

God instituted friendship to benefit mankind fundamentally. Part of the spiritual angle to the above story is the fact that God chose to reverse the benefits of the concept of friendship in the case of Sisera to achieve His desired purpose. As the God of heaven and the universe, He has the prerogative to decide what to do with anything including what He meant to benefit mankind originally. This means that He can deploy what He meant to help man to undo man for reasons best known to Him in the immediate.

6

PREPARE TO PAY APPROPRIATELY

Genesis 12:1-9 and 14:14-18 confirm that God assured Abraham that He would give the land of Canaan to him and his descendants forever. Genesis 15:6 confirms that Abraham believed God's promise and as a result God accepted him. Then, Genesis 23:1-20 can be interpreted to mean that despite knowing that God meant him and his descendants to own the land of Canaan when he needed a parcel of land for family burial ground, Abraham insisted and paid the full amount for what became his family burial ground when it was needed for his wife even when his allies among the Canaanites who owned the land that he needed for family burial ground said that their harmonious relationship was worth more than the value of the estate. This means that

Abraham did not circumvent the human angle to the ownership of the land just because God had promised to give it to him and his descendants.

The allies were not aware of any such promise by God to him and he was not ready to tell them about it. In that sense, he paid up to protect what he considered as the vital information about his sojourn in Canaan. Genesis 15:12-16 confirms in verse 13 that God had told Abraham even before Isaac was born that it would be much later before God would help his descendants to claim the land from the Canaanites. This means that Abraham was aware that until it is God's appointed time to finally hand over the land to him through his descendants, he must pay for any inch of the land that he needed in Canaan. It means that he understood what God said and his limits on the land of Canaan during his lifetime. CCII means Commendable Concealment of Important Information while CCVI means Commendable Concealment of Vital Information. Having the required amount to pay for the family burial ground meant that he did not waste the wealth that he accumulated from God's blessing on him. He had enough savings from which to pay for whatever he considered important to him.

Also, II Samuel 24:18-25 and I Chronicles 21:18-26 say even when David was the sitting king of Israel, he insisted on paying the full price for the estate of a Jebusite named Araunah that he needed for the site of the Temple. It is important to note that II Samuel 5:6-12 and I Chronicles 14:1-2 confirm that David had taken over the city of Jerusalem from the original inhabitants, the Jebusites and that in fact, Araunah from whom he bought the piece of land was a Jebusite whom David and his warriors did not force out of the city when they took it over. Despite this fact, David still insisted on paying for the land. This means that David treated a conquered subject just as I Chronicles 14:1-2 and 18:14 say he ensured that his fellow Israelites were treated fairly by the powerfuls of his domain.

Now, Abraham and David are significant individuals in the Christian faith because while tracing the genealogy of Jesus as mankind's Messiah, Matthew 1:17 confirms that from Abraham to David there were 14 generations and from David to Jesus

Christ of Nazareth the Messiah, there were 28 generations. That suggests that the examples that the three of them left for Christians to follow is important. Now, the example that Abraham and David gave us to follow is that we should not desire free gifts particularly among strangers. Unfortunately however, there are many things we do as Christians that are not in tandem with the examples of those who can be summed up as the 'heroes of faith' left behind for us to follow according to the Bible account of the way they lived their lives. While David said that the reason he must pay the full amount for the land that he needed for the temple is that he did not want to give any gift that did not cost him some amount, Abraham did not provide the reason he determined to pay for the property he needed. His failure to give specific reason gives room for us to speculate. Some Christians would depend on Isaiah 61:6 and 66:12 to say that God of Israel or the Jews promised to give us the wealth of the Gentiles but here we see Abraham and David whom God approved of the way they lived while on earth rejecting gift from supposed Gentiles and paid for what they needed from them.

First, Genesis 14:1-24 says Abraham the famous father of the Christian faith rejected his deserved reward for the singular reason that he did not want to leave any room for a Gentile to take credit for his prosperity. The case of Abraham is very striking because Genesis 14:17-24 confirms in verse 20 that Abraham paid due tithe to God's High Priest, yet he would not take anything for himself. It means that Abraham gave his share of gain to the man he helped after payment of ten percent tithe. Genesis 14:24 confirms that Abraham ensured that his allies who had supported him to help the king of Sodom was paid their deserved reward as well. This means that Abraham settled everyone else except himself. How can the descendants of a man who was never covetous be covetous and not realize that they are doing something wrong yet continue to shout from the rooftop that they are the descendants of such a contented man? It is absurd. It amounts to being Solomon's disheartening disciples – while his father treated the Israelites fairly he did the exact opposite despite the fact that he was the one who formally asked God for the wisdom to rule over the Israelites wisely or properly. God and his father did much to make his life and reign easy for him, but he turned round to do the exact opposite of what his father did. While his father ensured that he pleased God and was kind to the Israelites Solomon displeased God and oppressed the Israelites later in his reign. Though God made him richer than his subjects he still extorted from them to sustain his prodigal lifestyle. It is Solomon's sickening style to take from persons who are not as rich to sustain one's lust for pleasure.

Second, II Kings 5:1-27 confirms that Prophet Elisha rejected the great gifts that the Syrian General, Naaman offered him after he followed Elisha's instructions to be cleansed of his skin disease. Acts 8:9-24 confirms that Apostle Peter damned a magician by the name of Simon who wanted to pay money to get the Holy Spirit. Everything the heroes of the Christian faith rejected is what contemporary Christians crave greedily yet, contemporary Christians continue to claim to be confident that they are going to the same heaven as these heroes of faith. It is like a student who is not studying but hoping to graduate and practice his desired profession upon graduation. How does he hope to be able to cope with the demands of the profession upon leaving school? It is one thing to leave school and another to earn the qualifications to practice successfully. There are different ways to leave school including dropping out or being told that because of failure to meet graduation requirements the certificate cannot be issued but what they call certificate of attendance would be issued which does not give the attendee the school authority's formal approval to practice.

This is not the instance to highlight the fact that Genesis 15:14b and Exodus 3:21-22, 11:2 and 12:35-36 include the fact that God asked the generation of Israelites that left Egypt to collect precious items from their Egyptian neighbours to take along with them to Canaan when they were leaving Egypt after spending 430 years. Abraham decided of his own volition to pay the full amount to buy a piece of land for his family's burial ground or vault. Contemporary Christians disregard Jesus' cautioning against condemnable covetousness, Mark 7:20-23 and Luke 12:15 quote Jesus as saying covetousness is one of the evils that defiles a man while Romans 1:28-32 confirms in verse 29 that covetousness is one of the indices of a corrupted mind, persons who God have given up on and no longer interested in rescuing from eternal damnation. It is deducible from II Corinthians 9:5 that it is best to let people give to God or because of God willingly rather than be forced to do so by any means no matter how subtle. People should give to God because they are personally convinced rather than because they are made to give against their wish.

II Corinthians 8:1-4 and Romans 15:26-17a confirm that the Macedonia Christians gave to support fellow Christians as well as Paul's personal needs of their own volition or without anyone putting unnecessary pressure on them. Philippians 4:15 confirms that the Philippi Christians did likewise while Paul was working among other Christians. Then, Ephesians 5:3-4 says like sexual immorality, covetousness or greed should not be mentioned among any Christian. No Christian should be found guilty of greed is the point while Colossians 3:5 admonishes that a true Christian should be dead to earthly and carnal desires including greed to have what others had inappropriately.

The grievousness of greed or covetousness is getting what belong to others against their wish and to their hurt. You can desire and determine to own a car like your neighbour but such pursuit must not lead to your dispossessing your neighbour of his own car so that he suffers the inconveniences of not owning a car while you enjoy his. You may decide not to help your neighbour to keep his car or valuable, but God expects that you must never make any conscious effort to convert his valuable into yours. If he gives it to you after getting a replacement you could have it but to get his and thereby leave him with nothing is not allowed by God. I Thessalonians 2:5 can be interpreted to mean that (1) it is possible to use flattery talk to conceal greed to defraud one's hearers as a Christian preacher, (2) it should not be done by genuine God-ordained and ordered Bible preachers because God judges everyone's heart-hidden motive for whatever he does and says. Furthermore, I Timothy 6:6-10, Hebrews 13:5 and II Peter 2:1-4 say:

> 6 yet true godliness with contentment is itself great wealth. 7 After all, we brought nothing with us when we came into the world, and we can't take anything with us when we leave it. 8 So if we have enough food and clothing, let us be

content. 9 But people who long to be rich fall into temptations and are trapped by many foolish and harmful desires that plunge them into ruin and destruction. 10 For the love of money is the root or all kinds of evil. And some people, craving money, have wandered from the true faith and pierced. (NLT)

5 Keep your lives free from the love of money, and be satisfied with what you have. For God has said, "I will never leave you; I will never abandon you."

1 False prophets appeared in the past among the people, and in the same way false teachers will appear among you. They will bring in destructive, untrue doctrines, and will deny the Master who redeemed them, and so they will bring upon themselves sudden destruction. 2 Even so, many will follow their immoral ways; and because of the Way of truth. 3 In their greed these false teachers will make a profit out of telling you made-up

stories. For a long time now their Judge has been ready, and their Destroyer has been wide awake! 4 God did not spare the angels who sinned, but threw them into hell, where they are kept chained in darkness, waiting for the Day of Judgement. (TEV)

These passages emphasize the fact that greed has consequences and to forewarn us to desist from all forms of greed. Also important is the fact that God never meant relationship with Him to be solely to enrich man materially and monetarily. It is not the central theme of man's relationship with Him. In fact, Ecclesiastes 12:13 says the most important reason He made the earth and man to live in it is for man to devote his time and effort to worship Him and do His bidding while on earth. It makes it a religious abomination for any man to use his religious activities mostly to enrich himself and worst still, at the expense of others or persons not as rich as himself. Since Matthew 6:25-33, Luke 12:22-31 and Hebrews 13:5 include the fact that God is able to provide adequately for the needs of anyone who trusts in Him, men of God should be the first to give example in this respect, that is, God's ability to provide adequately for whoever trusts in Him rather than transfer the responsibility to do so to their hearers by urging them to give to the men of God while their hearers wait for God to supply their needs.

Much as Luke 8:1-3 confirms that Jesus accepted support from some women, Matthew 14:13-21 and 15:32-39, Mark 6:30-44 and 8:1-10, Luke 9:10-17 and John 6:1-14 confirm that the same Jesus taught as well as fed His hearers who were hungry. He was not the owner of the little supplies that He used to feed the several thousands, but He deployed God's power at His disposal to multiply the little supplies on two occasions. This means that He showed greater faith in God's ability to provide for the needs of persons who looked up to Him than His hearers. There is no doubt that Luke 6:38 confirms that Jesus admonished giving and Mark 12:41-44 and Luke 21:1-4 say He noted the worth of what worshippers gave during a service yet, He never encouraged focusing on riches.

II Samuel 24:1-25 and I Chronicles 21:1-30 and 22:1 confirm that God led David to the land owned by Araunah to build an altar because it would be the site of the Temple which God had approved for David to build through his successor to the throne of Israel. Araunah offered it to David for free but David insisted and paid the full amount for it. If David were a Christian of this generation, he would say it was God who touched the heart of Araunah to give it for free. The material and monetary greedy breed of contemporary Christian leaders and their faulty followers act as if they believe that the more they are able to get freebies from others the more the proof that they enjoy God's favour than their peers who do not live on freebies. They seem to prefer that God make others to fend for them than for God to help them to earn their living and be respected for it. God of Israel never meant His chosen people to be perpetual freebies fans – it is as a result that once the Israelites entered Canaan, He stopped feeding them with the manna freebies. God meant that (1) free food or sustenance in the form of manna was meant to be a temporary form of sustenance. (2) The permanent means of sustenance was for them to work hard by way of growing their own food just like their ancestors, Abraham and Isaac were known to have earned their own living for as long as they lived in Canaan. (3) There is no record that God made the Canaanites or Philistines to provide for Abraham and Isaac therefore, it would be ridiculous for persons who claim to be their descendants by any means to delight in freebies rather than getting God's help to be self-sufficient.

If God were comfortable with us living off others, He would not have counseled against covetousness in the first place. King Solomon was one of the most covetous souls who ever lived even though He was greatly beloved by God of Israel and his ancestors and father, the great King David. I Kings 4:7-19 and 11:1-9 can be safely interpreted to mean that just as he coveted the wealth of his subjects who were not as rich as himself so also he coveted the gods of other nations though their gods were not as great and powerful as the God of his ancestors and father who sent him to live as the king of Israel after his father. This unprecedented greed of his, pitched him against God and his subjects and led to both God and his subjects rejecting his rule over the subjects forever. His descendants suffered the consequences of his greed when God and his fellow Israelites would not allow his descendants to rule over them on God's behalf as God had promised his father before he was born. Contemporary Christians have no regard for admonition in I Thessalonians 4:11-12 which says that it is important for a Christian to aim to live a quiet life, mind his own business, and earn his own living rather than depend on others for personal need. It goes further to add that this is important because these three things contribute immensely to earning the respect of everyone including non-Christians.

Unfortunately, contemporary Christians do not regard the warning against covetousness when they greedily collect the treasure of others for their personal benefit. Let us consider this issue of David realistically. I Chronicles 21:18-30, 22:1, Proverbs 19:17, 28:27, Luke 6:38 and Acts 20:35 say:

> 18 The angel of the Lord told Gad to command David to go and build an altar to the Lord at Araunah's threshing place. 19 David obeyed the Lord's command and went, as Gad had told him to. 20 There at the threshing place Araunah and his four sons were threshing wheat, and when

they saw the angel, the sons ran and hid. 21 As soon as Araunah saw King David approaching, he left the threshing place and bowed low, with his face touching the ground. 22 David said to him, "Sell me your threshing place, so that I can build an altar to the Lord, to stop the epidemic. I'll give you the full price." 23 "Take it, Your Majesty," Araunah said, "and do whatever you wish. Here are these oxen to burn as an offering on the altar, and here are the threshing boards to use as fuel, and wheat to give as an offering. I give it all to you." 24 But the king answered, "No, I will pay you the full price. I will not give as an offering to the Lord something that belongs to you, something that costs me nothing." 25 And he paid Araunah six hundred gold coins for the threshing place. 26 He built an altar to the Lord there and offered burnt offerings and fellowship offerings. He prayed, and the Lord answered him by sending fire from heaven to burn the sacrifices on the altar. 27 The Lord told the angel to put his sword away, and the angel obeyed. 28 David saw by this that the Lord had answered his prayer, so he offered sacrifices on the altar at Araunah's threshing place. 29 The Tent of the Lord's presence which Moses had made in the wilderness, and the altar on which sacrifices were burned were still at the place of worship at Gibeon at this time; 30 but David was not able to go there to worship God, because he was afraid of the sword of the Lord's angel.

1 So David said, "This is where the Temple of the Lord God will be. Here is the altar where the people of Israel are to offer burnt offerings."

17 When you give to the poor, it is like lending to the Lord, and the Lord will pay you back.

27 Give to the poor and you will never be in need. If you close your eyes to the poor, many people will curse you.

> 38 Give to others, and God will give to you. Indeed, you will receive a full measure, a generous helping, poured into your hands—all that you can hold. The measure you use for others is the one that God will use for you."
>
> 35 I have shown you in all things that by working hard in this way we must help the weak, remembering the words that the Lord Jesus himself said, 'There is more happiness in giving than in receiving.'" (TEV)

Poor David, he was ignorant of member of this generation when he shouted to high heavens that over his dead body would he offer to God what does not cost him any personal sacrifice. He did not foresee that this current generation would get what others own and keep 90% to themselves and give God miserable 10% which would include all the tithes and offering put together. He did not know that this generation would think that something must be seriously wrong with him to reject freebies and save the wealth that God helped him to earn from the many wars that he fought and won by God's help. After all, there is no indication that God said he must pay for the site of the temple from his personal pocket or that he coerced Araunah to give it up. If the man revered God enough to give up the estate of his own freewill why should he reject it? What kind of precarious point was David trying to prove by his insistence that he must pay for what Araunah was eager to give up without being paid?

This is where the subject of personal values becomes particularly important. After payment for the site of the temple, I Chronicles 28:1-21 and 29:1-9 confirm that David went a step further to give more towards the building of the Temple. This is even though he was very much aware that he would not be taking credit for the building of the Temple. FFFF means Frustrating Freebies Faithful Fans of this wearisome world. David could have said that since God decided that Solomon should take credit for the building of the temple that he (David) conceived its idea, God should help Solomon to sort out everything about the building of the Temple.

Even the animals for David's intended sacrifice to God was volunteered by Araunah, the landowner yet David insisted on paying for everything that Araunah had to offer. David mentioned that God led him to build an altar on the land and the God factor might have made Araunah give more than David requested possibly so that he would share in the blessing or reward which God would give David for obeying the commandment and yet David said 'no way', he was adamant about paying the full amount.

Someone could say that it was because David, as the sitting king of Israel, had become wealthy by this time and did not want it to be on record that he could not afford to pay for the land God desired for him to build an altar. Someone could say that it was because he did not want a heathen to contribute to the gift he wanted to give to God. Another could say that it was because he understood the message of 'it is better to give than to receive and the giver is superior to the getter' and he did not want to give spiritual basis for a heathen to seem to be superior to him by reason of collecting a gift from him. Even if these were some of his heart-hidden reasons, why are Christians not following in his example? Why do contemporary Christians cheapen themselves by preferring to remain perpetual getters than givers? Why do we not strive to follow in Jesus' example when Matthew 14:13-21 and 15:32-38, Mark 6:30-44 and 8:1-10, Luke 9:10-11 and John 6:1-14, 7:25-26, 30-32 and 45-46 confirm that in addition to teaching deep truths about God's expectations from us and performing outstanding miracles by God's power and help, He went even a step further to feed His hearers rather than collect money and materials from them? The Jewish religious rulers who had no sound knowledge of God's message to teach collected money and material things from the worshippers and that is what we are repeating. Meanwhile, we parade ourselves as Jesus' followers not the disciples of the Pharisees.

Nonetheless, let us consider another practical or even carnal economic aspect of the above passage. This man was using this piece of land as a threshing place and because of his respect for David and reverence for God of the universe who sent him to live on earth in his generation, he decided on the spur of the moment, even when he never expected the great King David to visit him, to give up the land. David might have thought that it was not the best thing to collect his threshing floor and his animals to offer and leave him and his children with no land and animals to provide for them. Supposing this was the only asset Araunah and his family members depended on, if David had collected it for God and himself, this man would not have had anything else to live on and they would have starved, possibly, to death. This is not the point to claim that God would compensate them. We engaged in what can be called the most cantercarious and condemnable covetousness of all times or since history began. It is commercial cannibalization, religious reeled commercial cannibalization.

Even if it is because Araunah believed that God would compensate him, it means that David too believed that God would compensate whoever gave his asset for God to use for this purpose and it is as a result that David decided that he would prefer God to reward him rather than Araunah who was not Abraham's descendant like himself. Luke 5:1-11 can be said to lend credence to the fact that if one gives his asset to God to use to achieve His purpose, God will reward such an individual.

After Peter loaned his fishing boat to Jesus to use as the platform and pulpit to preach to a large crowd, Jesus rewarded him. The reward captivated Peter, John and James to the extent that they left their fishing profession to become Jesus' fulltime followers. Why ask a man with less faith in God to exercise the faith of giving up his only means of livelihood while you who claim to have greater faith in God would not give more than the man with less faith? After all, Luke 12:48 says "to whom much is given much is expected or required".

Apparently, the last thing that Araunah expected was for David to visit his place of business and the shock made him claim to be willing to give up everything without considering the economic implications that he must face as the head of his household who should provide for the other members of the family. There is no record that God told David that He prompted the man to surrender his estate and business at this point and therefore, should not have rejected it. God did not say anything about David's reaction to Araunah's offer as if to say David's action here was right and should be written for us to note and follow as a perfect example in our dealings with persons who are not necessarily richer than us or not even as wealthy as we are. The General Overseers of churches who collect from their members who do not have a tenth of what the General Overseers have personally is a case in point.

It is the spirit of Solomon as sitting king of Israel whom God had made richer than all his subjects even possibly put together, yet I Kings 4:1-19, 22-23 and 27-28 says he appointed officials for the sole purpose of collecting the resources that he needed for his daily sustenance from his subjects to fund his prodigal and loquacious lascivious lifestyle as long as he reigned. Curiously, on the contrary, I Chronicles 14:1-2 and 18:14 can be interpreted to mean that his father had given the example of ensuring that the subjects were never oppressed by anyone. Since his father never did anything to oppress or let anyone else oppress them, he could not claim to have learnt it from or followed in his footsteps. But that is what we do daily; we do the very things that Jesus never set as an example for us to follow in his lifetime.

It is very sad to say here that General Overseers, Senior Pastors and other Christian leaders are the very or part of the reason that some persons from Christian homes do not like and love God enough to dedicate their lives to serve Him. There are families that the reason the wife and children are not enjoying moderate standard of living that their husband and father could afford from his regular income is because the church pastor deploy diverse methods to collect their income for themselves and church projects. Such things make the woman and the children of the household to think that all that God and His sent pastors do is to collect all the resources they should have lived on and be comfortable in life. Pastors might not like this exposure but those church members who are suffering because their household is overburdened with giving everything to church projects and providing for the man of God know the punitive impact that such action is having on them.

What use is getting all income of a man for church projects and yourself while his wife and children resent God and His assigned men as a result? We know that when David paid the full amount for the estate, Araunah would be able to buy another piece of land where he would continue his business and his children would have something valuable to inherit from him. All things being equal, they would not be constrained to resent David and God because their father's only asset was claimed from them because their father offered and David collected without payment, not considering that it was important for Araunah to continue to work in order to provide for his own family and subsequently leave something for the children to inherit and live on after him.

Araunah was not an Israelite so David could have claimed that getting his means of livelihood for God's planned Temple was God's own way of transferring the wealth of the Gentiles to the Jews which agrees with God's promise to Jews that Genesis 15:13-14, Exodus 3:21-22, 11:2 and 12:35-36, Psalm 1-5:37 and Isaiah 61:6b reiterate. David could have thought that it was the continuation of God adding to his wealth beyond the loot he got from the many battles that God helped him to win. This means that David did not think that because Araunah was not a Jew he should be left impoverished just because God chose his estate and business location to be the site of the temple of worship that he conceived. If God indicate someone's estate as the place that He had designated for His project that He meant you to lead its building ask God to give you the required resources to pay the owner for the value so that claiming his valuable would not leave him and his family poorer and as a result they would begin to speak ill of God of all gods that you claim to represent to them and other members of your generation.

II Samuel 5:6-10 and I Chronicles 11:4-9 confirm that David led the army of Israel to take over Jerusalem from the control of the Jebusites, Araunah's kinsmen. It means that ordinarily, Araunah like his fellow Jebusites were subject to David and his fellow Israelites yet David paid Araunah for what he needed for God's use. It means that David did not use his vantage position or royal authority to dispossess Araunah of his valuable. Let us remember that I Chronicles 14:1-2 and 18:14 confirm that part of the reason David ensured that the poor or weak Israelites were treated fairly was because he believed that God made him king in order that he would work for the wellbeing of his fellow Israelites. Yet, it can be claimed that his treatment of Araunah means that just as he ensured that the Israelites were not oppressed so also, he too tried as much as it is humanly possible never to oppress non-Israelites. He did not give his fellow Israelites the impression that it was proper to dispossess conquered victims of their valuables. There is no doubt that it would be easier for David or any Israelite to convince Araunah and his household members to join them to worship their God of Israel than it would have been if David had failed to pay Araunah his dues. There is no record that David asked Abiathar to use the ephod to confirm from God if he should treat the Israelites and non-Israelites in his domain fairly before he knew that it was the right thing to do. There is no record that he learnt it from his father while he grew up. Meanwhile, his son and successor, Solomon who knew that he treated the Israelites' fairly refused to follow in his footsteps to treat the Israelites fairly. He made life miserable for both Israelites and non-Israelites in his domain except his non-Israelite wives. This is part of the reason that the claim that an individual did evil because he observed his parents do it while growing up is one of the most injurious indulgences in human history.

Abraham and David did not extend the tentacles of their faith in God of all gods to get what belonged to others without paying the full amount for the value. They did not portray God of

Israel as an oppressor who cannot afford to pay for what He needs for His special people. Abraham and David proved to their non-God of Israel worshipping neighbours that their God of Israel can enrich them enough to be able to afford whatever they needed to do the will of God. No matter how eloquent any bible preacher can convince his hearers, it would be hard for the persons supplying him freebies to accept that he is representing a God who can supply all human needs – his freebies' supplier will never take him serious as long as he continues to live on his freebies. How can you be representing a wealthy God, yet you are still living off someone who does not have close relationship with that acclaimed wealthy God? David proved to Araunah that his God is not only able to help conquer and control their city of Jerusalem but also able to provide him the resources to pay for whatever he needed to both please God as well as live laudably. Genesis 33:18-20 confirms that when Jacob went to settle in Shechem upon his return from Laban's place where he had spent 20 years he had enough to pay for the estate that he built his home for him and his household members to live in. He did not seek God's special intervention to constrain the

Shechemites to let him use part of their land without paying for it.

Someone could argue that Jesus used someone's home to hold the last supper with His disciples or rode on someone's donkey during the famous triumphant entry into Jerusalem. Such persons should not forget that Jesus never dispossessed the original owners of their valuables. It was a one-off usage after which He left the treasures for their owners. Joseph of Arimathaea who gave up his graveyard to bury Jesus did so of his own volition as a disciple of Jesus. Joseph was not a heathen who was cajoled to give up the gravesite that he had prepared for himself. Like Roman 15:26-27a and II Corinthians 8:3c-4 and 11:9 confirm that the Macedonia Christians supported God's work as well as the Apostle Paul of their own volition so also Matthew 27:57 and 60, Mark 15:42-46, Luke 23:50-53 and John 19:38-42 confirm that Joseph of Arimathaea and Nicodemus voluntarily spent their own resources to give Jesus the befitting burial possible in agreement with what Isaiah 53:9 says God's planned much earlier.

Again, abhor free benefits because the subsequent generation(s) of those who gave you the special privilege of free benefits might insist on getting back what you enjoyed in the past. To afford your needs and wants, you have to work hard to earn enough to do so. You must not be given to frivolities that natives could afford. When non-natives are made to pay more tax than natives in contemporary society it is partly a show of this principle that strangers cannot enjoy equal rights with natives. As a result, any stranger who fails to work extra hard might not have anything left for him or her.

Genesis 27:41-46 and 28:1-5 confirm that the real reason or indicated reason that led Jacob to Laban's place was for Jacob to be protected from Esau's threats as well as marry one of Jacob's cousins, Laban's daughters. Genesis 28:10-22 confirms in verses 20-21 that it was on the way to Laban's place that Jacob used the opportunity of his encounter with God's angel in his dreams at Bethel to make a verbal vow to God that if God prospered him at Laban's place and brought him back to Canaan safely, he would pay a tithe of ten percent of all earnings to God. This means that Jacob had idea of what he wanted for himself before he arrived at Laban's place. We can claim that he had his own reason or heart-hidden reason in addition to his mother and father's counseled and approved reason/mandate for him. He knew that he would like to return to Canaan as the land of his birth with wealth someday. This was the first time that Jacob proved that he had a mind of his own and that he believed that he could ask and get God's help to get his heart desire.

Genesis 31:38-42 says to enable him save enough from his earnings while working for Laban he did not just work hard rather he toiled day and night without taking any holiday. It means that while Laban and his sons did not devote all their time to hard work like him, he did not follow in the footsteps of his employer and his sons who were natives of Haran where he lived as a migrant employee. If you live responsibly even your employer and boss would be indicted at the end if your employer had been living irresponsibly. When the employee becomes richer than the employer over a period it means that the employer had been squandering his profits while the employee had been saving his earnings. That was what made Laban desperate when

Jacob was leaving Laban's business with greater wealth – it is an unintended implied unacceptable and unbearable indictment.

Jacob was wise enough not to follow in his uncle's footsteps to squander his share of profits or income. During the time that he lived with and worked for his uncle, he was aware that he would some day return to his hometown of Canaan and that it would be very shameful if he returned a poor man while his twin brother, Esau was richer. He knew that Esau had always been a hard worker and great earner. So, he saved most of his income. By the time he was ready to return he had become richer than his uncle to the extent that his uncle and his sons who were Jacob's cousins envied him. Genesis 29:15-30, 31:1-3, 14-16 say:

> 15 Laban said to Jacob, "You shouldn't work for me for nothing just because you are my relative. How much pay do you want?" 16 Laban had two daughters; the older was named Leah, and the younger Rachel. 17 Leah had lovely eyes, but Rachel was shapely and beautiful. 18 Jacob was in love with Rachel, so he said, "I will work seven

years for you, if you will let me marry Rachel." 19 Laban answered, "I would rather give her to you than to anyone else; stay here with me." 20 Jacob worked seven years so that he could have Rachel, and the time seemed like only a few days to him, because he loved her. 21 Then Jacob said to Laban, "The time is up; let me marry your daughter." 22 So Laban gave a wedding feast and invited everyone. 23 But that night, instead of Rachel, he took Leah to Jacob, and Jacob had intercourse with her. (24 Laban gave his slave woman Zilpah to his daughter Leah as her maid.) 25 Not until the next morning did Jacob discover that it was Leah. He went to Laban and said, "Why did you do this to me? I worked to get Rachel. Why have you tricked me?" 26 Laban answered, "It is not the custom here to give the younger daughter in marriage before the older. 27 Wait until the week's marriage celebrations are over, and I will give you Rachel, if you will work for me another seven years." 28 Jacob agreed, and when the week of marriage celebrations was over, Laban gave him his daughter Rachel as his wife. (29 Laban gave his slave woman Bilhah to his daughter Rachel as her maid.) 30 Jacob had intercourse with Rachel also, and he loved her more than Leah. Then he worked for Laban another seven years.

1 Jacob heard that Laban's sons were saying, "Jacob has taken everything that belonged to our father. He got all his wealth from what our father owned." 2 He also saw that Laban was no longer as friendly as he had been earlier. 3 Then the Lord said to him, "Go back to the land of your fathers and to your relatives. I will be with you." 14 Rachel and Leah answered Jacob, "There is nothing left for us to inherit from our father. 15 He treats us like foreigners. He sold us, and now he has spent all the money he was paid for us. 16 All this wealth which God has taken from

our father belongs to us and to our children. Do whatever God has told you." (TEV)

Laban felt humiliated that his employer and younger man had become richer than he was. Imagine his sons backbiting that Jacob had taken all their father's wealth hence he was richer than him. There is no doubt that it is their right to inherit their father but why were they watching when their father was squandering his income and funding fourteen days feasting because his daughters got married? It is most likely that the wedding that John 2:1-12 reports that Jesus attended and performed His first miracle ever must have been a one-day affair. Even Joseph's wedding that the king of Egypt arranged, there is no mention in Genesis 41:45-46 or anywhere else in the Holy Bible that Pharaoh hosted a seven-day feasting to celebrate it for Joseph as his second-in-command. They chose to stay at home waiting for their cousin to work hard and earn for their father to spend on them in the immediate and inherit the leftover upon the death of their father. That is remarkably interesting. They were waiting to inherit the wealth that they did not contribute to its accumulation even when they had the chance to make their own contribution. It amounts to 'wasting while waiting unknowingly'. Even if they were to inherit anything, they will never have the experience to sustain and increase the wealth for themselves and pass it on to their own children and their father's grandchildren. Such persons are inglorious/injurious inheritors. Curiously and coincidentally, Jacob had been a 'stay home' son in Canaan wile Esau went out to get busy before Jacob relocated to Laban's place before he chose to go out of the house to work hard to pay for the bride price of his wives and fend for his family. What Jacob did at home in Canaan, his maternal cousins did at their own hometown of Haran. Apparently, Jacob had learnt from Esau that it is the man who goes out to work hard that prospers or earns enough to share with others and that their father would have blessed Esau at his expense as a result.

Before we continue, the reason we said Laban's sons were backbiting is that Genesis 31:1 above says that Jacob heard them rather than they confronted Jacob to say that he was stealing their father's share of profit and that it is as a result that he had become richer than their father. Jacob heard their claims meant that they were making the claim to the hearing of some other persons who reported it to his wives who in turn reported it to Jacob. Laban's sons assumed that their father's wealth would be passed on to them naturally without any hassles. They did not think that it was necessary to join Jacob to look after their father's wealth. If they had, their regular presence would have made it difficult for Jacob to short-change their father and by extension they who should inherit their father were short-changed. If they were physically present wherever their father's flock were while Jacob was working for their father, there would have been no room for Jacob to play all the tricks that Genesis 30:25-43 recounts that Jacob employed to become richer than their father.

This means that just as Laban's feasting short-changed his sons and daughters so also Jacob's tricks short-changed his sons. Only his daughters and their children benefited from the wealth that accrued to Jacob through his Genesis 30:25-43-detailed equivalent of buccaneer breeding methods and tactics. Of course, Laban's sons short-changed themselves when they left Jacob alone to manage their father's flock without monitoring his activities on daily basis. They should have taken turns to stay where Jacob was working on their father's flock to ensure that he never had the slightest chance to short-change them. Genesis 31:38-42 gives the impression in verses 39 and 40 that Jacob worked both day and night to increase Laban's flock – what else were Laban's sons doing day and night that prevented them to watch over Jacob's activities day and night? Verses 38-41 include the fact that Laban treated Jacob harshly throughout the 20 years that he served as Laban's business manager. Laban or his sons should have known that Jacob would find a way to get even with Laban. Since Laban confirmed in Genesis 30:23 that he found out by divination that his business prospered because of Jacob's presence as his business manager, did he and his sons not go a step further to clarify by divination if Jacob would deal honestly with them while managing his flock in the grazing fields in their absence. But of course, they did not believe that they were ill-treating Jacob, or he could have the courage to get even with them. That is nothing short of taking your fellow man for granted by believing that you could treat someone shabbily and get away with it.

Jacob can be said to have purposed and planned for refreshing return to Canaan. It can also be called "I Shall Return Rejoicing". Acts 1:10-11 confirms that Jesus would return the same way that He was taken up to heaven. This concept can be said to be applicable to Samuel whose mother took to Shiloh as a child to be with Eli as priest-in-training, a position that he held until Eli died along with his two sons and daughters-in-law. Samuel remained in Shiloh for a long time before he relocated to his hometown of Ramah where he continued to operate from as the sole administrator of the kingdom of Israel. This means that Samuel returned to Ramah to rule and reign over all Israel. Jacob gave a good account of himself by the end of his 20-year sojourn in the land of Haran.

Nehemiah and Ezra as well as Mordecai and Esther equally gave a good account of themselves where they lived away from their homeland. Nehemiah and Ezra returned gloriously to make their contributions to their ancestors' land of birth. They were recognized by the king of the country where they were migrants and got the support of the king to return home to make tangible contributions to the wellbeing of their kinsmen. Mordecai and Esther attained position of authority in the foreign land and used their privileged position to work for the wellbeing of their kinsmen. DSMA gave creditable account of themselves during their stay in the Babylonian palace. They proved that it is possible to be captain in captivity by determination and God's help as well as the fact that captivity is not enough reason to not live great, mighty, and powerful.

7

God's Help Plus/ Hard Work Plus

The procurement of God's prospering presence to enhance success in all endeavours is both helpful and needful whether at home or abroad. Genesis 25:19-24 and Romans 9:10-13 can be said to mean that before Jacob was born God had chosen him to be greater than his twin brother, Esau. Genesis 25:29-34 and Hebrews 12:16-17 confirm that Jacob had shortchanged Esau spiritually over birth-right long before the subject of stealing blessing that prompted going away to Laban's home ever happened. Also, Genesis 27:1-46 and 28:1-5 confirm that he got two special blessing from their father before he set out from Canaan to Laban's home at Haran of Mesopotamia. Yet, Genesis 28:1-22 says on his way to Laban's place God still thought it necessary to send His angels to him in a dream during a night sleep at Bethel. It was meant to be a sort of reassurance of His presence with Jacob wherever he went like II Samuel 7:8-9 and I Chronicles 17:7-8 confirm that God reiterated to David that He had been with him wherever he went all his life. Psalm 105:12-15 says the same thing about God's covert protection of Abraham and his covenant descendants. That is what Psalm 23:1-5 which is attributed to David meant. When Jacob woke up from that dream, he made special request to heaven for God to send him needed help to prosper while in Laban's place and return with his wealth safely. In fact, Jacob still needed to make a personal oath or promise of what he would do in return if God blessed him and protected him to return safely.

One of the reasons the request for God's help while away was important was that Rebecca's promise to get him back whenever she was convinced that Esau had forgiven him could not be relied upon because she was only human. She might have meant well but like all humans, she had her limitations. And indeed, she could not keep herself alive long enough to bring Jacob back to Canaan. By the time God ordered Jacob to return to Canaan she had been long dead and buried. Also, Rebecca could not do anything to protect Jacob from her brother, Laban's ill-treatment of Jacob because they lived in different nations. Only God has the ability to protect and prosper wherever a man lives on earth.

This emphasizes the fact that it is not enough to get the support of well-wishers and personal survival strategies. I Kings 2:13-15 recounts Adonijah's confession that he lost the battle to occupy his father's throne to his younger half-brother, Solomon solely because Solomon had God's support which he lacked despite the fact that he was the eldest surviving son of their father as well as enjoying the overwhelming support of the majority of the Israelites. I Samuel 16:1-13 suggests that David's eldest brother, Eliab had king-befitting features like Saul had when he was chosen to be king of Israel and David had as well. But Eliab lacked God's support which David had. As a result, on the day God sent Samuel to their father's household to choose a replacement for Saul, David was chosen above Eliab. Human support and possession of required qualities are not enough to obtain greatness.

Furthermore, neither God's promise nor prayer to Him is enough alone. Much as Genesis 25:19-24 confirms that God had promised Jacob greatness before he was born, Genesis 28:10-22 confirms in verses 18-22 that he still needed to make formal request to God for the promised blessing to manifest in the physical. Even then, Genesis 31:38-42 says Jacob still had to add hard work to God's promise and prayers plus the vow of a tenth of the sum total of the wealth that God gives him at the end of his stay at Laban's place. This alludes to the concept of 'Neither Nor' which in this sense means that 'Neither is Enough Alone' – God's promise is not an excuse not to pray to Him, work hard or live stupidly. Jacob combined all sorts that he considered necessary to achieve God's promised help to prosper and return to Canaan wealthy. Part of the other components that he added was 'secrecy and surprises'. He concealed his departure from Laban's employment and hometown of Haran.

Genesis 28:1-5 and 10-22 can be said to mean that it seems like God appeared to Jacob at Bethel to see what Jacob would ask or how he would react to His presence with him. Jacob took advantage of the God's appearance or revelation through His angels in a dream to ask God to be with him during his stay in a strange land until his safe return and richer. By that request he meant that without God's help he could not achieve anything. He suggested that his mother's plans and father's blessings/prayers were not enough to make him prosper and return safely from his uncle's place. By so doing, he gave God His rightful place in his life and affairs. God used that encounter at Bethel to open the door of personal relationship between Him and Jacob for the very first time. God's plan that he would be greater before he was born still required that he had personalized relationship with God during his stay on earth to realize that prime plan. It is like the way that a company's depot manager must stay in touch with the company's headquarters to get regular directives to the manager for the manager to achieve the objective of the company's headquarters.

There is the concept of 'Beyond Parental Projections and Planning – BPPP' which in this case is the fact that after Jacob's parents had planned for him to relocate to Laban's place in order to stay safe from Esau's threat as well as to get a wife, God showed up to give Jacob an opportunity to strike a personal relationship deal with Him. God meant that his parents' projection and plans to bring him back when Esau's anger would have subsided was not enough for Jacob to achieve the goals set for him by his parents while at Laban's place. God knew that his mother would not be alive to bring him back just as his uncle, Laban would not make his stay a sweet experience. Also, considering that Genesis 35:1 confirms that God directed him to return to Bethel where they first met and Jacob made a vow, it meant that God expected Jacob to have returned to Bethel directly to settle immediately he returned from Laban's place rather than go to settle in Shechem as he did upon his return to Canaan.

Genesis 27:46 and 28:1-5 say Isaac's marital mandate was that Jacob went to Laban's household to find a wife only for Genesis 29:1-35, 30:1-24 and 46:1-8 to confirm that he ended up with two wives and two concubines who bore him a total of 13 children including a daughter. Laban, who was his chief host, triggered the events that began the process or journey into polygamy while his beloved wife, Rachel began his journey into concubineage. His original marital projection and plans was distorted by the environment and people among whom he lived and interacted with unavoidably. Laban claimed that it is not their traditions for the older daughter to remain unmarried while the younger gets married just because the older had not gotten a suitor. Then, Laban's household gods were never part of what Jacob went to collect or take back to Canaan but his beloved wife, Rachel took them along to Canaan. While sending him to Laban's place, his parents never considered that Laban would cause Jacob pains during his stay like it happened. Migrants should prepare for any form of ensnaring eventuality rather than assume that everything would work out as planned before leaving home to live abroad.

There is the concept of the sorrows of skipping God's guidance. Genesis 31:1-29 confirms that God decided the time was ripe for him to return to Canaan with his acquired wealth. However, Jacob failed to clarify with God where he should settle upon his return. God had hoped that he would remember to return to Bethel to pay the vow he made there 20 years earlier that he would give God a tenth of whatever amount of wealth that God help him to acquire in that migration journey. If he was wise enough to make a vow to God at Bethel so that he would not return empty-handed he should have been wise enough to ask God where in particular he should settle upon his return. Otherwise, he should have begun with going to Bethel to pay the vow when he was desperate for God's help to return richer 20 years earlier even if he would settle somewhere else. He did not remember to pay the vow that he made immediately he returned.

The factors he considered to arrive at the decision to settle in Shechem remains a mystery. One reason it is strange is that there is no record that he passed through Shechem on his way to Laban's place or that he had a friend who was a native of Shechem. Even if he had passed through Shechem on his way to Laban's place, there is no record that there was any significant occurrence at Shechem that should highlight the reason to settle there. The only place that he had a unique experience on his way to Laban's place was Bethel yet he did not think that it was enough reason to return there since the same God who appeared to him there was the one who asked him to return to Canaan after 20 years stay. The other place where he could have settled was their father's family house since Genesis 32:13 and 33:14-16 confirm that he found out that by the time of his return Esau who he was afraid of had relocated from their traditional family house to the land of Edom.

One of the reasons the subject of where he chose to settle upon his return to Canaan is worth mentioning is that first, the fact that it was while in Shechem that his daughter was raped and his sons' reaction to the rape threatened his life and that of his entire household members and wealth. Second, Genesis 34:23-24 confirms that the ultimate ambition of the king of Shechem and his kinsmen was to dispossess him of the same wealth that he brought from Laban's place. This means that if his sons had not killed all the men of Shechem, including their king and heir-prince who raped his daughter and the Shechemites had succeeded in their plot to take over his wealth, he would have lost everything just as Genesis 31:1-55 can be interpreted to mean that Laban and his sons meant to do to him before he left his place. If that had happened, Jacob would have returned to their traditional family house after the death and burial of their father empty-handed.

One probable reason he did not go straight to Bethel immediately he returned to Canaan could have been that Bethel was uninhabited and he did not want to take on the responsibility of opening it up. Whereas the probable reasons he did not return to their family house were because

(1) their mother who loved him was dead,

(2) their father who did not love him as much as Esau was still alive in the family house,

(3) he did not want to take on the responsibility/duty of caring for a father he never liked,

(4) perhaps, he was even unhappy with their father because he was determined to give the generational blessing to Esau if their mother had not backed him to steal it from him at the expense of Esau,

(5) perhaps, he was suspicious that his father and Esau might have contributed to the death of their before she could fulfill the promise to bring him back to Canaan,

(6) perhaps, he was sad and angry that his father saw Esau's children whereas his own mother never lived to see his own children,

(7) perhaps, he thought that if not for Esau's threats he would not have gone to Laban's place and given Laban the chance to ill-treat him. That would have meant that their father and Esau was responsible for his problems and by so doing absolved himself and their mother of any responsibility for his travails at Laban's place.

Esau had taken on that responsibility of caring for their father even before he left home 20 years earlier. Apparently, as far as he was concerned it is the sole responsibility of the eldest son to fend for parents and he would not lend a helping hand to his brother who he never liked. He forgot that he had children already and was growing old and would soon need them to support him and that it is whatever he sowed into his father's life that he would reap from his own children.

Genesis 32:3, 33:14-16, 35:27-29 and 36:1-8 strongly suggest that it was when Esau noticed that Jacob refused to settle in their family house immediately he returned to Canaan, that he returned to be with their father until his death and burial. It was after their father's burial that Jacob relocated from Bethel to the traditional family house where he left their parents and Esau to go and live with Laban. He joined Esau there – it was lack of enough space for them both that made Esau return to the land of Edom to avoid conflict over space like Genesis 13:1-13 says Abraham and Lot had earlier. His moving to the family house only after the burial of their father suggest that Jacob had purposed in heart that much as he would like to settle in the family house some day, he was not prepared to do so when their father was still there without their mother. If that was his reason, was he reacting to the fact that their father never loved him like their mother did or that their father preferred Esau to him? Did he believe that it is the sole responsibility of older or eldest son to take care of the parent?

It is not a surprise that all his eleven other sons could not fend for him except Joseph who God empowered. Meanwhile, Genesis 15:12-17 and Psalm 105:16-24 confirm that God empowered Joseph to fulfill His plan to take them as Abraham's covenant descendants into Egypt as He had indicated to Abraham much earlier. I Samuel 26:24 can be interpreted to mean that David implied that part of his heart-hidden reasons for sparing Saul's life despite deserving to be killed was so that God would shield him from his enemies as well. He meant that he was investing into his future safety from his enemies when he would have become king of Israel. Along this line, Job 31:21-23 can be said to confirm that Job had a heart-hidden reason for most of the good works that he is known to have engaged in as an affluent and influential member of his community or society. We can call it Job's heart-hidden reward reasons. First, Job 1:1-8 quote God's testimony in verse 8 that –

(1) there is no one on earth as faithful to God as Job,

(2) he is good to his fellow man particularly weak, poor and needy, and

(3) worship God consistently as well as careful not to do anything evil to his fellow man and in God's sight.

Second, Job 29:1-25 can be interpreted to strongly suggest in verses 7-10 that he greatly enjoyed the respect, attention and honour that he got from other influential and powerful citizens of his nation. Verses 11-13 can be said to confirm that he enjoyed the praises of the weak and poor that he assisted in some ways. Verses 14-18 says he was kind to the blind, protected the oppressed from their oppressors as well as acted justly and always with the hope for the reward of long life and dying at home in comfort. This means that he was eager to sustain the life of comfort and convenience that his abundance provided him so long as he lived. Finally, verses 19-25 summed up the considerations that made him to please God and his fellow man in the period preceding his tribulation as follows:

> 19 I was like a tree whose roots always have water and whose branches are wet with dew.

> 20 Everyone was always praising me, and my strength never failed me.

> 21 When I gave advice, people were silent and listened carefully to what I said;

22 they had nothing to add when I had finished. My words sank in like drops of rain;

23 everyone welcomed them just as farmers welcome rain in spring.

24 I smiled on them when they had lost confidence; my cheerful face encouraged them.

25 I took charge and made the decisions; I led them as a king leads his troops, and gave them comfort in their despair. (TEV)

As we can see, he had personal reasons for the kindness to his fellow man which was confessed because of the troubles that befell him despite his concerted efforts that God recognized and praised highly to damn Satan. It should be noted that Job 42:7-10 confirms that God granted his desire to live a long life and die in peace after the period of tribulation.

This is one concept that Jacob did not understand in his dealings with his father whom he got blessing from so he could prosper and be greater than his older brother. He claimed his father's blessing at no cost to him. Genesis 27:1-40 says the meal he took to their father to get his blessing was prepared by their mother. The dress he wore was acquired and owned by Esau. The information that he needed to claim the blessing that their father meant as reward for Esau was provided by their mother. As if that was not enough, their mother volunteered to take on the consequences of deceiving his blind father on his behalf. He was a freebies magnate.

Genesis 37:1-36, 39:1-23, 40:1-23 and 41:1-57 can be safely interpreted to mean that God's prospering presence helped Joseph away from Canaan in Egypt. God's plans for his life was still accomplished despite living abroad and it was his siblings and parents who were back home who can be said to have lacked the same God's prospering presence at the time that Joseph did in Egypt. God's prospering presence made him head of his colleagues wherever he lived and worked in Egypt. He added hard work, honesty and loyalty to God's presence that was available to him. That is, diligence is a necessary addition to God's favour wherever and whatever one does to earn a living.

David enjoyed unprecedented support of God wherever he went. He confessed that God's help enabled him to kill wild animals that threatened him and his father's flock while watching over them in the grazing fields of Bethlehem. I Samuel 18:6-30 includes the fact that Saul as sitting king of Israel dreaded David because of the presence of God with him. I Samuel 18:12-15 can be interpreted to mean that God's transfer of support from Saul to David which made David successful in his endeavors became Saul's worst nightmare from the point that David killed Goliath until Saul died. Saul considered David's killing of Goliath his personal humiliation. Also, he knew that his subjects, the Israelites preferred David to be their king after him rather than any of his sons. He could not live with that humiliation – his sons who were princes would become subject to the son of one of his subjects after him. I Samuel 23:14 confirms that the presence of God with David was the spiritual reason Saul could not kill David. Then, God confirmed the significant role that His presence with David played in David's journey from the status of a commoner to the status of greatness as a ruler in his lifetime about which II Samuel 7:8-9 says:

> 8 "So tell my servant David that I, the Lord Almighty, say to him, '<u>I took you from looking after sheep in the fields and made you the ruler of my people Israel</u>. 9 <u>I have been with you wherever you have gone</u>, and <u>I have defeated all your enemies as you advanced</u>. I will make you as famous as the greatest leaders in the world. (TEV)

I Chronicles 17:7-8 repeats this fact nearly verbatim. On his path of travel from the status of smallness to the status of greatness there were obstructive enemies who God had to cut off for him to reach the status of greatness. The result of reaching the status of greatness is that he would join the council of the world famous of the earth. That is why his name still resonates till date. One sound interpretation of God's message to the Jews carried captive from Jerusalem and Judah to Babylon in Jeremiah 29:4-7 that they should pray to Him for blessing is that much as one should pray to God while at home, it is more important when you are away. Keep in touch with God who sent you to live on earth wherever you live. I Kings 8:33-34, 46-51 and Jeremiah 29:4-10 say:

> 33 "When your people Israel are defeated by their enemies because they have sinned against you, and then when they turn to you and come to this Temple, humbly praying to you for forgiveness, 34 listen to them in heaven. Forgive the sins of your people and bring them back to the land which you gave to their ancestors.
>
> 46 "When your people sin against you—and there is no one who does not sin—and in your anger you let their enemies defeat them and take them as prisoners to some other land, even if that land is far away, 47 listen to your people's prayers. If there in that land they repent and pray to you, confessing how sinful and wicked they have been, hear their prayers, O Lord. 48 If in that land they truly and sincerely repent and pray to you as

they face toward this land which you gave to our ancestors, this city which you have chosen, and this Temple which I have built for you, 49 then listen to their prayers. In your home in heaven hear them and be merciful to them. 50 Forgive all their sins and their rebellion against you, and make their enemies treat them with kindness. 51 They are your own people, whom you brought out of Egypt, that blazing furnace.

4 "The Lord Almighty, the God of Israel, says to all those people whom he allowed Nebuchadnezzar to take away as prisoners from Jerusalem to Babylonia: 5 'Build houses and settle down. Plant gardens and eat what you grow in them. 6 Marry and have children. Then let your children get married, so that they also may have children. You must increase in numbers and not decrease. 7 Work for the good of the cities where I have made you go as prisoners. Pray to me on their behalf, because if they are prosperous, you will be

prosperous too. 8 I, the Lord, the God of Israel, warn you not to let yourselves be deceived by the prophets who live among you or by any others who claim they can predict the future. Do not pay any attention to their dreams. 9 They are telling you lies in my name. I did not send them. I, the Lord Almighty, have spoken.' 10 "The Lord says, 'When Babylonia's seventy years are over, I will show my concern for you and keep my promise to bring you back home. (TEV)

First, II Chronicles 6:24-25 and 36-39 repeats I Kings 8:33-34 and 46-51 above nearly verbatim. Second, God had assured the Israelites since the time that Solomon led them to dedicate the temple in Jerusalem that he would certainly answer their prayers, even those who were carried captive by their enemies because of their sins against God. The case of the Jews carried captive to Babylon fits this prayer point. However, God added another dimension to the original prayer point. He said upon arriving Babylon, they should not start with praying to Him to help them to return to Jerusalem but that they should begin with prayers to Him to bless their captors so that in the process of blessing their captors they too would benefit from His blessing to their captors. This is because they would stay there for at least seventy years.

Going by Solomon's version, he did not expect that God would let the Jews stay under the captivity and control of their enemies and captors for long but in this instance God decided otherwise. Therefore, it is particularly important to confirm God's own plan for one's sojourn in the land of captivity. It is very striking to note that God's message through Jeremiah was not God's response to the prayers of the Israelites who were already in Babylon as captives. Rather it was God who took the initiative to instruct Jeremiah to write to them that they should not be deceived that they would return quickly and therefore focus their prayers to Him on the subject of helping them to return to Jerusalem quickly.

One of the most challenging things about prevailing prayers is recognizing the right point of focus. Some would just pick a verse or some verses of the Bible and start to pray believing that because God would perform His word anyhow, they have prevailed undoubtedly. Much as God would not let His written word go unfulfilled it is also both true and particularly important to understand that not every word of God is ordained for fulfillment in the life of an individual at the same time. And that is what God meant when He sent Jeremiah through the letter in chapter 29 to the Jews in Babylon that much as He would hear their prayer to free them some day, His immediate plan was not to free them but rather for them to live normal lives in Babylonian captivity. It is immensely helpful and refreshingly rewarding when one can recognize what God meant to do for one in the immediate and focus one's prayer utterances and demonstrations on it.

There was when Jacob needed God's help to trace Laban's home in Haran. There was when he needed God's help to prosper him while managing Laban's flock. There was when he needed God's protection from Laban's threats or ill-treatment. Then, there was when he needed God's guidance to return to Canaan and finally, there was when he needed God's protection from Laban who was determined to collect everything that he had gathered during his 20 years stay in Laban's employment. The different stages required different prayer point or focus. Request for increase in wealth is different from the request for protection from one's swindler. At the point when Jacob chose to ask God to protect him from Esau's possible attack, he was not asking for wealth because he already had wealth but he needed protection from attack by Esau who he knew was stronger than him.

Isaiah 60 – 62:1-12 is very striking in this respect when it suggest that after God promised that He would prosper the Jews as the dominant inhabitants of Jerusalem, He still asked the Jews living in Jerusalem to play their part in the process of getting the prosperity that He was determined to implement in Jerusalem. For everything that God determine to do on earth for anyone to enjoy, there is the part that He expects the beneficiary to play in the manner of his contribution. God's plan and promise to an individual does not exempt the man from his assigned productive participatory role and responsibility. If the man who is ill does not submit himself for necessary treatment or take his drugs as prescribed, there is not much that the best physician on earth can do to help such an individual.

Living away from home is not enough reason to forget to pray to God rather it is the more reason to pray to God for His help. Jeremiah 29:5-7 can be summed up as God meant every migrant to live normal life in their host country. That is the summary of the detailed items such as; build houses and settle down, plant gardens and eat what you grow in them, marry and have children, let your children marry and have children to make you grandparents so that you will increase rather than decrease. Also, work for the good of the cities where you live and don't forget to pray to God to bless the land and natives so that you could share in the prosperity that God sends because of your prayers to Him on behalf of the land and its people. The only thing that God did not include is that you should not strive to rule over the natives of the land probably because He had commanded through Moses in Deuteronomy 17:15 that a foreigner should not be allowed to rule over natives. God has a clear plan for whoever He helps to go and live in a strange land.

The other thing worthy of mention is the fact that it is helpful to define one's heart desire from onset. David knew that his stay in the land of the Philistines was going to be short or at least not permanent. Ruth knew that she would remain in Bethlehem in the land of Israel for the rest of her life. Joseph knew that some day the Israelites would return to Canaan and he would like his bones to be carried back to Canaan for what he believed to be befitting burial and preferred burial place. Jacob indicated that he would prefer to be taken back to Canaan to be buried. DDYD means Define and Declare Your Desires to those who are in position to implement them in the case of any eventuality like Jacob and Joseph did appropriately.

8

WISHES DON'T BETTER BEGGARS

This could have as well been titled the worthlessness of wishful thinking or unprofitable wishful thinking. The famous saying "if wishes were horses beggars would ride" means that if desire alone was enough factor to prosper, everyone would prosper or there would be no poor persons who have to beg for alms before they could have something to live on. Proverbs 14:23, 21:25-26 and 24:33-34 can be summed up to mean that wishful thinking without commensurate actions in the manner of hard work leads to poverty. Also, Proverbs 19:8 says learning is like doing oneself favour and it is more favourable when the learner lives according to his learning. Hebrews 4:2 says if God's word is not mixed with enough faith to act on what it says, it would never benefit the hearer. James 2:14-17 says faith without action is dead while James 1:22-23 says hearers must heed what they have heard.

Meanwhile, II Corinthians 3:6 says the letter killeth while it is the spirit that gives life. This does not negate the fact that God's word gives life rather it only means that any man who desires to benefit from the word of God must let God's spirit interpret the word of God to him rather than take God's word literally dogmatically always. Jesus overcame Satan's temptation partly because He knew when to comply with the word of God and when not to. Satan reiterated God's word three times and each time Jesus tore Satan's mischievous use of God's word into shreds. He knew that much as Satan was quoting God's word it was never meant for the purpose that God intended with that word so it would be unprofitable to obey it just because it is God's word. For instance, someone could say God command children to obey their parents but not when a parent tells the child to go and steal for them to live on or engage in prostitution to provide for them. Dogmatism has the capacity to both delight as well as destroy.

For Ruth to benefit from her faith in the God of her late husband, her surviving mother-in-law, Naomi and their Israelite kinsmen, Ruth 2-4 confirms that she took definite steps beyond embracing their God as she lived among them. She did not sit back at home in Bethlehem to wait for her late husband's relatives to provide for her and Naomi rather she went out in search of any job that she could do to earn a decent living under Naomi's guidance. When Ruth went out of their home to glean behind reapers in farmlands soon after settling in Bethlehem, she practically acted in accordance with God's guideline through Moses that farmers should share their produce with the needy when harvesting their produce/crops. Now, the term "share their produce with the needy" should be clarified – how she got her entitled share of the produce of those who farmed before she and Naomi arrived Bethlehem is important and need to be understood. Practically, God meant that the poor are entitled to a share of the rich's wealth even if it is the leftover. God expects the "haves" to provide leftover for the "have-nots" to survive on.

In this respect, Leviticus 19:9-10, 23:22, Deuteronomy 24:19-22, Ruth 2:1-9 and Ecclesiastes 5:11 say:

> 9 When you harvest your fields, do not cut the corn at the edges of the fields, and do not go back to cut the ears of corn that were left. 10 Do not go back through your vineyard to gather the grapes that were missed or to pick up grapes that have been fallen; leave them for poor people and foreigners. I am the Lord your God.

> 22 When you harvest your fields, do not cut the corn at the edges of the fields, and do not go back to cut the ears of corn that were left; leave them for poor people and foreigners. I am the Lord your God.

> 19 When you gather your crops and fail to bring in some of the corn that you have cut, do not go back for it; it is to be left for the foreigners, orphans, and widows, so that the Lord your God will bless you in everything you do. 20 When you

have picked your olives once, do not go back and get those that are left; they are for the foreigners, orphans, and widows. 21 When you have gathered your grapes once, do not go back over the vines a second time; the grapes that are left are for the foreigners, orphans, and widows. 22 Never forget that you were slaves in Egypt; that is why I have given you this command.

1 Naomi had a relative named Boaz, a rich and influential man who belonged to the family of her husband Elimelech. 2 One day Ruth said to Naomi, "Let me go to the fields to gather the grain that the harvest workers leave. I am sure to find someone who will let me work with him." Naomi answered, "Go ahead, daughter." 3 So Ruth went out to the fields and walked behind the workers, picking up the heads of grain which they left. It so happened that she was in a field that belonged to Boaz. 4 Some time later Boaz himself arrived from Bethlehem and greeted the

workers. "The Lord be with you!" he said. "The Lord bless you!" they answered. 5 Boaz asked the man in charge, "Who is that young woman?" 6 The man answered, "She is the foreigner who came back from Moab with Naomi. 7 She asked me to let her follow the workers and gather grain. She has been working since early morning and has just now stopped to rest for a while under the shelter." 8 Then Boaz said to Ruth, "Let me give you some advice. Don't gather grain anywhere except in this field. Work with the women here; 9 watch them to see where they are reaping and stay with them. I have ordered my men not to molest you. And whenever you are thirsty, go and drink from the water jars that they have filled."

11 The richer you are, the more mouths you must feed. All that you gain is the knowledge that you are rich. (TEV)

Our immediate concern is the fact that the needy who are defined as poor people, foreigners, orphans and widows who did not cultivate a farm of their own during the previous planting season to harvest from during the harvest season should be allowed to glean in the farm of the farmers who have just harvested their crops. The point is that the needy must go out to glean rather than expect that the owner of the farm would share the harvest he had brought home with the poor. God meant that even if the poor was too lazy to farm during the preparation of the land, planting, weeding and watering stages of the farming season, he must not be too lazy to go to another man's farm to harvest the leftovers that the farmer left for the poor as God commanded. Therefore, if the poor man still fails to go out to glean in a farmer's farm, if such a poor man starves to death, the farmer cannot be blamed for being unkind to the poor man.

Perhaps, this is part of what Proverbs 19:24 and 26:15 mean when it says there are persons who are too lazy to put food in their own mouth so that they would not starve to death. The farm owner is not under obligation to share part of his main produce which he harvested with the poor. Just as he went to harvest the main produce so also the poor must go to the farm personally to harvest the leftover. God has played His part by giving the commandment. The farmer has played his part by providing leftovers during the harvest. The remaining role that would make God's provision to benefit the poor is for the poor to leave home and visit the farm to harvest whatever the farmer left in the farm. This means that the poor must make some personal efforts for him to survive starvation. God's provision does not include the poor waiting at home for the rich to bring him (the poor) the supplies that he needs to survive starvation. That is the tactical boundary of care, compassion, and kindness. It could be called the poor's mandatory personal participation, the receiver's required responsibility/role, the expectants' expected contributory action or expectants' obligatory role/responsibility. Ruth was looking forward to a second husband after becoming a young childless widow. Ruth 3:1-18 and 4:1-22 tell how she played her part gallantly and never regretted it and left exemplary lesson for successive generations.

This is God's thinnest lifeline strand for the lazy. If anyone fails to take advantage of it or obey this command, then even God cannot help him or her. God meant that there is a limit to which the haves can go to help the have-nots. His command to the haves to help the have-nots does not include the haves doing everything for the have-nots. The have-nots still have a part to play for them to stay alive. It is important to note that Ruth was a stranger in Bethlehem when she went out to glean. If she had not gone out, she might never have had direct access to Boaz who became her husband later. Her obedience to one of God's command solved all her marital problems at the same time, is the meaning. Even the solving of the marital need in her life followed the same pattern of leaving home to catch-up with Boaz privately. She activated God's solution for persons in her peculiar predicament all the way through and never regretted it. She could have been hoping that somehow, she would stumble on a young man who would ask her out or provide for her needs.

This is one reason that lends credence to the fact that God had made provision for any problem that anyone could have on earth where he lives long before the problem erupted. The gleaning solution that God provided for the poor, foreigners, orphans, and widows had been in place since the time of Moses. One of the facts that make Ruth benefiting from the guideline very striking is that it is even though Deuteronomy 23:3-6 says God never meant the Israelites to wish any Moabite well. It means that, by reason of Ruth's Moabite background she was not supposed to benefit from God's good plans for the Israelites. However, when God talked about produce provision for foreigners, He never said all foreigners could benefit from it except Moabites.

Wherever one lives and whatever challenges one faces during his stay on earth, there is God's prior provided solution for personal survival. Exodus 1:8-22 confirms that Moses was born at the time that the oppression of the Israelites began in Egypt. Judges 6 confirms that God allowed the Midianites to oppress the Israelites for seven years and when it was time to use Gideon to free them from the Midianites, God told Gideon to sacrifice a seven years old lamb. This means that the lamb that Gideon was asked to sacrifice was born in the year that the Midianites began to oppress the Israelites. Usually, God provides the solution to every problem along with the manifestation of the problem.

It is called 'the problem's complementary solution' or 'the solution complements the problem'. This means that the problem and its solution are paired by God like the economists would talk about complementary demand. If someone buys a car or any motorized vehicle then he would necessarily need petrol or diesel to power it, tyres and other necessities to run and enjoy the benefits the vehicle was designed to provide for its user. It is like when God paired Esau and Jacob as twin male with contrasting character and personalities. Before the famine years God had provided Joseph in Egypt to sustain Jacob and other members of his household during and beyond the famine years. Before Moses arrived Midian there was Jethro who had seven daughters and needed young men to marry them. Before Jacob arrived Laban's home in Haran, there were two of his daughters who needed suitors and household business for Jacob to do.

Much as God had provided the gleaning solution for the needy to survive, if Ruth did not go out to glean behind reapers but stayed at home like Naomi did, she and Naomi would have starved to death. Whether Ruth knew about God's arrangement for her to glean before she went out to glean or not we are not told. But supposing she knew, it means that she understood that if she failed to take the practical step to go out to glean behind reapers or harvesters she would never benefit from the provision that God made for a migrant like her in Bethlehem. Her action on God's word activated the benefit God meant in that word, admonition, or arrangement that farm owners should leave some of their produce for the needy and migrants to harvest for them to live on. She then went a step further to do whatever was necessary to remarry as a young widow in a strange land. This means that she was determined to live happily among the people where she relocated to settle. Did some of the natives reject her? Yes, of course, but she did not allow it to dampen her zeal to remain among them. Elimelech's closer relative would not have anything to do with her because of their Jewish tradition yet she was contented with the fact that there was a Boaz who cherished her greatly and did not mind her at all.

This is very important considering the way Uriah died in the hands of King David because Uriah failed to recognize when to trust David as a good and God-fearing man that he had always been until that point. II Samuel 11:1-3 confirms the fact that Uriah was a native Hittite who lived as a migrant among the Israelites and made a career in the army of Israel. He married an Israelite and all his bosses, Abishai, Joab and David were Israelites. Meanwhile, in some ways David and Uriah were good and Godly men in their own respects which mean that one righteous man ruined another righteous man. II Samuel 11:10-11 says:

> 10 When David heard that Uriah had not gone home, he asked him, "You have just returned after a long absence; why didn't you go home?" 11 Uriah answered, "The men of Israel and Judah are away at the war, and the Covenant Box is with them; my commander Joab and his officers are camping out in the open. How could I go home, eat and drink, and sleep with my wife. By all

that's sacred, I swear that I could never do such a thing!" (TEV)

Uriah did not know that while he thought that God and his career was more important and tactically at stake, he did not realize that his life was what was really in danger. He did not understand that the battle would be won without his personal contribution or even if he dies. There is when the most urgent threat is to one's life more than the secondary things such as loyalty to the boss, colleagues and job. The Covenant Box was not as threatened as Uriah's life at this point. It is like the series of events that I Kings 21:1-19 recounts led to Naboth's death. He placed priority on the religious ritual of fasting without realizing that it is the preservation of his life that was at stake and that if he failed to protect his life, his loyalty to the religious ritual would cut short his life and would not have another opportunity to participate in future religious ritual of fasting.

The other thing is that II Samuel 11:14-25 can be interpreted to mean that despite Uriah's sacrifice of personal pleasure to prove his loyalty to Joab, Joab still obeyed his boss, David's directive to sacrifice Uriah in that battle even when he needed not be sacrificed before they could win that battle against the Ammonites. Among other important points, this highlights the fact that individuals have a crucial role to play in their personal safety. Uriah's loyalty to God through determination to sacrifice personal pleasure to protect God's Covenant Box, devotion to his boss, warrior colleagues and career in the army of Israel, he still died an avoidable death because he was oblivious of the threat to his life. Uriah determined to sacrifice a good time with his wife to please Joab whereas unknown to Uriah, Joab was eager to do anything to please David including sacrificing Uriah's life. This means that Uriah was loyal to persons who were not ready to reciprocate his loyalty. There is no doubt that Joab might not have known what Uriah did and said to prove his unflinching loyalty to him and the army of Israel, it does not reduce the fact that Joab practically trivialized Uriah's loyalty to the success of the army of Israel under Joab's command.

This is part of the reason the subject of absolute trust in fellow human is a stupid thing to do. If the man you trust absolutely chose to display the human weakness of unreliability you are dead. Apparently, Joab chose to please his boss rather than reciprocate Uriah's loyalty on this occasion and the consequence was the death of Uriah. David decided to cover up his adulterous relationship with Bathsheba rather than prove that he feared God enough to not hurt an innocent man who regarded God and His chosen people highly. David decided to disregard Uriah's unparallel loyalty to God and the victory of the people of Israel. A young man was promised all sorts by an older man who was the head of the organization. Upon that promise the young sacrificed so many personal development opportunities to build up the branch of the organization that he was posted to pioneer and nurture. Fifteen years down the line, when the branch had grown and pioneered several other branches and it was time for the overall head to fulfill his promise to the younger man, he found all sorts of reasons not to and chose to literally give what should have been the younger man's deserved reward to someone else who joined the organization much later. The shortchanged younger man lamented to high heavens and no one seemed concerned that he had been treated unfairly. Those who should sympathize with him could not because they too were looking up to the overall head of the organization to favour them with positions of authority within the organization.

Did the head of the organization offend or treat him unfairly? Probably, but the other angle to their experience is that the younger man failed to understand and heed God's revelation that whoever puts his trust in a fellow human would undoubtedly regret it. Jacob trusted Laban's promise that after seven years servitude he would be allowed to marry Rachel, but Laban failed him. Rebecca trusted that for her sake, her brother, Laban would not hurt her beloved son, Jacob but Laban never lived up to Rebecca's expectation. Did Laban do wrong? Yes, however, he was only being human. A man whose lieutenant turned against shortly after he lost the high profile position of authority was asked by journalist how he felt that one of the closest lieutenants for nearly eight years that he was in power had turned against him by going to his opponents to declare his loyalty, the man just said 'dogs are more loyal than some persons'.

Isaac's treatment of Esau is one of the most preposterous cases of the unreliability of humans in the Holy Bible. Genesis 25:27-28 says Isaac claimed to love Esau a great deal or at least more than Jacob. Genesis 26:34-35, 27:46 and 28:1-9 can be interpreted to mean that apparently Isaac did not like the fact that Esau married Canaanite girls yet, he would not let Esau know so that he would make necessary amends despite giving the impression that he loved Esau. It can also be deduced from Genesis 25:27-28, 27:1-46 and 28:1-9 that while Rebecca worked assiduously for the welfare of Jacob who she preferred to Esau, Isaac did not do likewise for the wellbeing of Esau who he claimed to prefer to Jacob. This is even though they all lived in the same house as household members. Isaac did not learn from Rebecca how to protect the interest of one's beloved from neighbours with devouring mindset and attitude.

One of Esau's saving graces was that he never expected anything in the manner of reward from Isaac. As a result, even when it was obvious that Isaac failed him, rather than blame Isaac, he merely forced Isaac to teach him the solution to the monstrous mistake of Isaac. Genesis 27:1-45 confirms in verses 37-40 that after Isaac's failing of Esau, he would not eagerly remedy the situation until Esau pleaded profusely with him. If he had a genuine sense of responsibility to reward Esau, Esau need not beg or plead with him before he would do anything to help Esau. Now, what he needed to do to remedy the bad situation that he contributed to create was to merely tell Esau the solution – just to open his mouth to speak out the solution yet he must be begged or cajoled, eulogized, pampered and made to feel like deputy-God before he would tell the man or son he claim to love. What if Esau was someone that he never loved? It means that no amount of begging or threat would make him give the solution to remedy the bad situation that he partly created.

First, II Samuel 23:8-39 and I Chronicles 11:10-41 confirm that Uriah belonged to the exclusive club of David's respected warriors. It was like belonging to the elite crop of Israel's warriors during David's reign. Second, his father-in-law, Ammiel was a member of this elite crop of Israel's warriors while his grandfather-in-law, Ahithophel who II Samuel 15:12 and 31, 16:20-23 and 17:1-14 and I Chronicles 27:33-34 confirm as one of Israel's wisest men and David's revered counsellor. Third, II Samuel 11:1-27 and 12:1-25 tell how David stage-managed Uriah's death without Uriah spotting the suspicious red-flags in the series of events leading to his death. Fourth, II Samuel 11:18-19 and I Chronicles 11:20-21 confirm that Abishai was the leader of the elite crop of warriors to which Uriah belonged. Fifth, II Samuel 23:20-23 and I Chronicles 11:22-25 confirm that one Benaiah was in charge of David's personal bodyguards because he was another great warrior.

Sixth, I Chronicles 11:6 and 27:34 confirm that Joab was the COAS. This means that by reason of chain of command, Uriah never reported directly to David rather through Abishai to Joab before David. However despite this obvious fact, II Samuel 11:1-27 says after David failed to go to a battle in which he should have led other Israel's warriors against the Ammonites, he sent to Joab to ask Uriah to come back home in the middle of the battle. Even if this was not the first time David chose to stay at home rather than go to war, it must have been the first time he sent for Uriah to return from the battlefield while idling away at home. Yet, Uriah failed to note the strangeness of the request to return home as sufficient red flag to reflect on and take great caution in his dealings with David. Nehemiah 6:1-13 confirms in verse 10-13 that Nehemiah was able to use the tool of thoughtfulness to spot the red-flag of his detractors' attempt to use someone that he respected a great deal to stop his detractors in their tortuous tracks before they could harm him as they intended. The tool of thoughtfulness is available to all humans.

Individual survival and prosperity is a personal responsibility. It is the reason Genesis 25:19-34, 27:1-46 and Hebrews 12:16-17 can be interpreted to mean that heaven's personnel department blamed Esau rather than Jacob, Rebecca or Isaac who contributed immensely to Esau's loosing his birthright entitlements to Jacob. Genesis 27:37-40, 32:3-8, 33:1-16, 36:1-43, Deuteronomy 2:22-23 and I Chronicles 1:34-54 can be said to mean that the little reprieve that Esau got from Isaac to prosper in life by God's help was because Esau mounted considerable pressure on Isaac. He combined tears and persistent pressure to get Isaac to tell him the solution to his mistake. It means that God lent His support to Esau's implementation of the solution he got from his father only when his desperation to get the solution convinced God that Esau had learnt to value his personal prosperity and success in life. This is part of the reason some claim that anyone's destiny is in his own hands. Proverbs 18:14 says "Being cheerful helps when we are sick, but nothing helps when we give up. (CEV)/14 A good attitude will support you when you are sick, but if you give up, nothing can help. (ERV)" which can be interpreted to mean that if an individual lose hope to live longer no amount of human care and/or spiritual intervention could keep such an individual longer; that is phenomenal revelation. And of course, I Kings 19:13-21 confirms that when Prophet Elijah gave up hope of living, God did not stop rather asked him to go empower his successors.

Personal safety is a personal responsibility of the hard working, honest, loyal and reliable individual. God has His part, but the individual has his own major responsibility for his personal safety. God protected David from Saul and all his other enemies, but David played his own part as well. First, be cautious while working hard, work hard wisely/cautiously, hard work plus personal safety caution or tortuous total trust are the diverse ways the plight of Uriah can be summed up. He failed to be conscious of the fact that his wife was beautiful enough to attract the attention of any other man including the king.

Second, in his hard work, loyalty and devotion to duty, he did not factor in his personal safety – hard workers must make provision for their personal safety is the key point. They must do their work with the consciousness of their personal safety because doing otherwise amounts to foolishness that could be fatal or translate into their committing suicide unknowingly or committing unintended suicide (CUS). Third, God punished David after Uriah's death or for causing Uriah's death rather than caution Uriah to escape David's plot. Abel had died in the hands of Cain before God punished Cain rather than caution Abel to beware of Cain's plot. God meant that everyone should take his personal safety as his personal responsibility much as he could ask God's help to achieve it. No one should be so stupid to say so long as he is loyal to God and His anointed, God would automatically protect him or stop his assailants before he finds out or he is killed by the assailants.

The request did not seem too strange enough for Uriah to ask God what could be amiss. He did not remember the fact that his home in Jerusalem where he had left his beautiful young wife behind to go to the battle was within the proximity of David's palace and that as such David could oversee his wife having her bath in their bathroom from the roof-terrace of his palace. He was too engrossed in playing his part to give the army of Israel victory over the Ammonites to envision the danger around his personal life and prevent it. The thoughts of the battle that they were fighting against the Ammonites had consumed his mind and he did not remember to ask God the reason for such an unusual request from David. Perhaps, he just assumed that David was too righteous to mean any harm by asking him to return home from the battle without realizing that David had already committed the evil of adultery against him before instructing his repatriation from the battlefield. This helps to appreciate the reason Psalm 146:3-4 and Jeremiah 17:5-7 can be said to mean that God admonishes that we should not be so stupid to put our trust in fellow man absolutely. In David's moment of moral vulnerability, Uriah became his victim. Upon arriving the palace in Jerusalem, David got him drunk like Genesis 29:30-38 confirms that Lot's daughter had done to him to get him to do their incestuous bidding without been able to apply good judgment to resist them. Uriah still did not suspect anything even when David kept urging him to go home to his wife after getting him drunk. The only thing he remembered to do right in his drunken state was to insist that it was sacrilegious for him to go home to have good time with his wife while God's Covenant Box and the army of Israel were still been threatened on the battlefield.

Finally, David gave him a letter to Joab with the instruction that he be sacrificed to their enemies. He never opened the letter to find out the content until he delivered it to Joab who did not hesitate to implement the damnable deadly directive. II Samuel 12:1-23 can be safely interpreted to mean that God did not hesitate to punish David for so doing because it was never part of God's plan for Uriah to die that way despite the fact that Uriah was loyal to God and David, God's anointed. That is self-liquidating loyalty. God never meant loyalty to Him to cause the death of anyone hence II Corinthians 3:6 admonishes that everyone who fears God and determined to obey His word should not depend on the word alone without getting clarification from God's spirit on how and when to comply with the written word of God in any particular circumstance.

It is very saddening to say like Uriah, Jonathan's fear of God did not save him from dying with his father even when he feared God more than his father because he did not take the decisive step that should have helped him to outlive his father and accomplish God's plan for him to be next-in-command to David as king of Israel. It can be said that Jonathan lacked the prophecy profiting essential of 'destiny determining decisiveness'. I Samuel 18:1-30 can be interpreted to mean that the more Saul knew that God was with and prospered David to be his successor the more he tried to kill David. That means that Saul hated the man God loved while I Samuel 19:1-24 report that Jonathan made his first effort to discourage his father, Saul from continuing to seek to kill David. Then, I Samuel 20:1-42 confirms that when Jonathan realized that it was impossible to persuade his father to stop attacking David, he rose up to David's defense by demanding that his father explained to everyone his real reason for wanting David dead. This angered his father to threaten his life along with that of David.

I Samuel 23:15-18 strongly suggests that when God saw the extent to which Jonathan was determined to defend David, He made known to Jonathan the fact that he could become the Prime Minister of Israel during David's reign after the death of his father, Saul. However, shockingly, after such monumental delightful destiny discernment, Jonathan opted to return to the same father who tried to kill him for defending David. As a result, I Samuel 28:1-25 and 31:1-13, II Samuel 1:1-27, 2:1-32, 3:1, 4:4 and 5:1-5 and I Chronicles 10:1-14 confirm that Jonathan died along with his father after which David became his father's successor. The fact that Jonathan loved God and His anointed, David as well as risked his life to protect David was not enough to keep him alive without his playing his assigned role. That he found out that God meant that he served as second-in-command to David did not make it happen to his benefit because he failed to be decisive as much as the plan that God had for him required. After confirming that his father was irredeemable, he should have left him alone and go away with the man he understood that God meant him to spend delightful destiny together with.

II Samuel 4:4, 9:1-13, 16:1-4, 19:24-30 and 21:1-14 confirm that Jonathan's son, Mephibosheth determined to show the depth of loyalty that David as his father's covenanted friend rightly deserved but Mephibosheth's David-forced servant, Ziba betrayed and stalled Mephibosheth's effort to show David the deserved loyalty. He was willing to repay David's kindness to him but his physical disability made it expedient to engage the assistance of Ziba but Ziba denied him and used the opportunity to get David to undo Mephibosheth in his favour. If Mephibosheth had another personal aide who could do whatever he wanted without reference to Ziba he might not have been short-changed the way Ziba did. Yet he should have known that Ziba was enjoying his grandfather's estates before David forced him to hand them over to him (Mephibosheth) because of his unforgettable relationship and experience with Jonathan. He should have known that even though David as the sitting king had ordered Ziba to regard him as the new boss, Ziba would exploit any opportunity to undo him and Absalom's rebellion which forced David out of Jerusalem provided Ziba that golden opportunity. The fact that God has used someone to help you is not enough reason to become complacent and not make advance plan just in case a situation arises that makes it difficult for your benefactor to help you or even work against your wellbeing.

Much as God meant David to be king of Israel after Saul it was not until seven and a half years after Saul's death that he eventually began to reign over all of Israel because Saul's die-hard loyal warriors led by Abner defied the wishes of the Israelites to resist David gaining control over the entire nation of Israel that Saul ruled over for 40 years except David's tribe of Judah. The journey through life is like driving a car from one point to another. If the driver fails to turn the steering when necessary as he drives along, he will crash into other vehicles, pedestrians and other objects along the road. He would drive into the bush or off the main road wherever there is a curve or bend because no road is straight. Just as no road is a straight course from the beginning to the end so also life and its endeavours are not straightforward from the beginning to the end. The fact that someone is the only child of a wealthy parent does not mean that the only child would inherit the parent without any challenge. There would be greedy souls who would want to get a share or even all of it at the expense of the only heir. The fact that Abel pleased God and never encouraged Cain to offer what

God adjudged as unacceptable sacrifices did not make Cain to let Abel live to reap the reward of pleasing God.

Genesis 27:1-46 and 28:1-5 can be interpreted to mean that Rebecca had believed that Jacob would be safer with her brother, Laban than with her older son and Jacob's twin brother, Esau. It was as a result that she manipulated their father, Isaac to send Jacob to go live with Laban. However, Genesis 29:1-30, 30:25-43 and 31:1-42 confirm that Laban made life unbearable for Jacob throughout the 20 years that he hosted Jacob. He made Jacob to marry more than one wife. He would not let Jacob have and keep his 20 years' earnings without a fight and God's threat to his life that he let Jacob alone. He would not let Jacob withdraw his services and return to the land of Canaan where he was born without a fight. Things did not play out smoothly for Jacob at Laban's place exactly as Rebecca and Jacob had assumed that they would be when Rebecca proposed Jacob's relocation to Laban's place.

Wishes without personal determination plus God's help from heaven and personal street wisdom do not improve the wellbeing of the wishful thinker. Proverbs 14:23 says while hard workers earn decent living poverty is the lot of persons who talk about great ideas but never step out to work hard in order to realize them. Jacob had to combine God's help with his personal determination by way of hard work and street survival wisdom in the absence of his mother before he could outsmart Laban to prosper and return to Canaan with the wealth he had gathered while with Laban.

Acts 9:1-31 confirms that just because Apostate Saul the native of Tarsus had turned a new leaf to become Apostle Paul and zealous to preach Jesus-centered God of Israel-authored salvation plan for mankind did not make the believers in Christ Jesus who he once led their persecution to readily accept him into their fold. Acts 9:1-31 confirms in verse 30 that their resentment forced him to withdraw to Tarsus where he remained until Acts 11:19-26 confirms that Barnabas went to recall him to join him at Antioch in order to become accepted by Christ's ardent believers and message propagators or preachers. Paul's experience is similar to the lament of ex-convicts who say even when they had served their term and turned a new leaf, employers and other members of society continue to treat them with suspicion and do not like to have them around as employees, tenants or neighbours. Much as they have determined not to break the laws of the land again, law abiding citizens are not so convinced that they would not offend again and they might be their next victim.

Paul had to cleave to Barnabas as the only available lifeline to the body of Christ believers until he was able to carve an image of a genuine convert and God-approved apostle. Galatians 2:6-10 confirms that later on Peter, John and James (PJJ) who served as the leaders of Christians at their headquarters in Jerusalem acknowledged that God ordained him and Barnabas to lead the preaching of Jesus' salvation message to the Gentiles just as PJJ were meant to lead the preaching of the same message to the Jews. The point is that wishful thinking is not enough to become better. Migrants should not assume that their heart-hidden reason for migrating would be achieved automatically without any hitches and hard-work. It would be like someone who got admission into any educational institution who hope to pass and obtain the certificate without any or much academic work.

First, Genesis 47:9, Exodus 6:4, Psalm 119:54, Hebrews 11:13 and I Peter 2:11 can be sensibly interpreted to mean that all humans are pilgrims or migrants on earth just like anyone who migrates from his land of birth to live elsewhere for sometime. Perhaps, the only difference is that earthly migration by all humans is not permanent – all must depart the earth at some point. In fact, Job 14:5, Psalm 39:4 and 139:16 and Acts 17:26 confirm that God had set the length of time and place that everyone would live on earth ever before he or she was born. It is partly as a result that Luke 2:22-38 confirms in verses 34-35 that on the day Jesus was dedicated at the Temple as a child, the same Pa Simeon who God's Spirit prompted to indicate to Jesus' parents the real reason God sent Him to live also told them that Jesus would cause them great grief. Through Pa Simeon, God's Spirit meant that Jesus would not outlive His parent that was fulfilled when John 19:16-27 confirms in verses 25-27 that Jesus' mother, Mary witnessed His death on the cross helplessly. Pa Simeon's revelation to Mary and Joseph was quite comprehensive in the sense that it included both the pleasant and the unpleasant aspect of His life or the experience that the parents would have over Him. He meant that much as Jesus who was the first child of their marriage is the much expected Messiah, they should bear in mind that they would outlive Him and by so doing cause them a great deal of heartache. It is one of the worst nightmares of an average parent to outlive their child.

We used the term an average parent because II Kings 3:26-27, II Chronicles 22:10-12, 28:3 and 33:6 confirm that there were parents who sacrificed their children and grandchildren in order to achieve their horrendous heart desires. Jesus made reference to the painful side of His experiences when Luke 24:26 quotes Him as saying that God the Father planned His sojourn on earth in such a way that He would enter into glory in eternity only after some sufferings. Isaiah 53:1-12, Philippians 2:5-11 and Hebrews 12:2b lend credence to this fact. Bible historians claim that Jesus' earthly migration lasted 33½ years. Matthew 1:17 says there were 42 generations between Abraham and Jesus, 14 generations between Abraham and David and

28 generations between David and Jesus. Meanwhile, Genesis 25:7-10 confirms that Abraham spent 175 years on earth while it can be estimated from II Samuel 5:4-5, I Kings 2:11 and I Chronicles 3:4 and 29:27 that David lived for 70½ years. This means that just as David spent less than half of the number of years that Abraham spent on earth so also Jesus spent less than half the number of years that David spent. Interestingly, Genesis 15:15 and 25:7-8 confirm that just as God meant and assured the number of years that Abraham lived was classified by God as 'a ripe old age' so also I Chronicles 29:26-28 refer to the 70½ years that David lived as equally 'a ripe old age'. This makes what constitutes a ripe old age or how long someone remain a migrant either on earth or wherever he lives on earth to be a relative term depending on how long God meant the individual to live either on earth or what ever location on earth.

While Genesis 12:1-9, 13:1-18 and 24:1-9 can be interpreted to mean that God meant Abraham to be a stay-put migrant in Canaan, Genesis 12:10-20 can be said to mean that Abraham was meant to be a temporary migrant in Egypt just like I Samuel 27-31 and II Samuel 1-2:1-7 can be interpreted to mean that

David was a temporary migrant in the land of the Philistines during the 16 months preceding Saul's death. In the same vein, Ruth 1-4 can be said to mean that (1) Elimelech and his family intended to be temporary or short-stay migrants in the land of Moab while (2) Ruth purposed to be a stay-put migrant in Bethlehem and by extension in the land of Israel.

II Kings 8:1-6 says the woman of Shunem kept strictly to the terms of her temporary migration to the land of the Philistines. Things did not quite work out for Elimelech as he and his two sons did not return from the land of Moab to Bethlehem as he had planned. They left Bethlehem for the land of Moab in order to escape the brunt of the famine in the land of Judah including their hometown of Bethlehem. But before they could learn that the famine in their hometown had abated for them to return three out of the four of them or all the men of the household had died. While JAP is Just-as-Planned, NAP is Not-as-Planned. It takes God's help in addition to other factors to experience just as planned in the matter of migration. While God asked Moses to return to Egypt after spending 40 years in

Midian with Jethro, He asked Jacob to return to Canaan after spending 20 years with Laban.

Genesis 15:13-16, Exodus 12:37-42, Psalm 105:16-29 and Acts 7:2-38 mean that the now famous God of Abraham, Isaac, Jacob, Israel or the Jews and Christians authored the migration of Jacob and members of his household to Egypt with the intent that the stay of the Israelites in Egypt would be as long as 430 years before He would lead them back to the land of Canaan that He meant to be their land of permanent possession. Acts 7:15-16 gives the impression that the generation who Jacob led into Egypt died there and their bodies were returned to Canaan to be buried immediately except that of Joseph which Genesis 47:27-31, 49:29-33 and 50:22-26, Exodus 13:19, Joshua 24:32 and Hebrews 11:22 confirm was kept with the Israelites in Egypt until God empowered and guided Moses to free them before it was taken to Canaan to be buried.

This suggests that there are two types of short stay – the rich woman of Shunem stayed in the land of the Philistines for seven years that the famine endured in the land of Israel. Immediately the famine ended she rushed back to her native town of Shunem to claim her estates unlike the case of Jacob and his sons who did not return to the land of Canaan at the end of the famine that forced him to take the rest of his family to go and join Joseph in Egypt. Genesis 45:4-13 and 47:9 can be said to mean that Jacob was 135 years old when the famine that forced him to go and live in Egypt ended and he spent another 12 years in Egypt before Genesis 47:27-31 and 50:1-14 say he died at 147. Genesis 45:1-28 and 46:1-27 confirm in chapter 46:1-4 that God had given Jacob the hint that he would die with Joseph by his side even before he departed Canaan to join Joseph in Egypt. His long stay in Egypt through his descendants was part of God's plan.

The relocation to and stay in Egypt was Jacob's second migration, the first was when he went to spend 20 years with Laban as his chief host in Haran. While God led him back to Canaan after spending 20 years in Haran, from the onset God implied that he would not return from Egypt to Canaan alive. Genesis 28:1-5 and 10-22 says it was God who took the initiative to contact him on his way to Haran while Genesis

45:21-28 and 46:1-7 say it was Jacob who took the initiative to clarify with God before relocating to Egypt. It suggests that God expects anyone contemplating migration to get His input or opinion. In the case of Jacob's children except the youngest, Benjamin were born in Haran and taken to Canaan from where they went with Jacob to Egypt.

Abraham did not just believe that his son must be his heir rather did everything humanly possible to ensure it. Genesis 15:1-17 can be interpreted to mean that he asked God to play His part just as Genesis 24 can be interpreted to mean that he played his own part by preventing his chief servant, Eliezer a native of Damascus from thwarting his efforts to ensure that his son succeeded him. This means that he did not leave his duty or job of ensuring that Isaac who God gave to succeed him actually transformed into his chief inheritor as God had confirmed to him. He forced Eliezer to accept that Isaac was his next boss after him (Abraham). In Genesis 15, Abraham told God he did not like Eliezer to become his chief inheritor and God assured him that Eliezer would not be. Then, Genesis 16:1-16, 17:1-27, 18:1-15 and 21:1-21 confirm that despite the presence of Ishmael as Abraham's first child, God gave Isaac to serve as Abraham's heir. Despite this fact Genesis 24:1-10 says Eliezer made last minute effort to get Abraham's approval to send Isaac away from Canaan to Abraham's hometown of Mesopotamia so that he would be left alone in Abraham's home in the land of Canaan to take over Abraham wealth. Genesis 21:9-21 and 23:1-20 confirm that Isaac's mother had ensured that Ishmael had been sent away from Abraham's home in Canaan solely to ensure that only Isaac was left as Abraham's biological heir before Sarah died.

It was three years after Sarah's death when Abraham decided to get a wife from among his Mesopotamia relatives for Isaac that Eliezer made his final push to get rid of Isaac from Abraham's home in Canaan. Genesis 24:1-9 confirms that when Eliezer asked if he could take Isaac back to Mesopotamia because of marriage and Abraham said much as he would love Isaac to marry the daughter of one of his Mesopotamia relatives it was not enough reason to take Isaac away from Canaan to Mesopotamia. His reason was that God meant him and Isaac and his descendants through Isaac to be stay-put migrants in

Canaan and as a result, for no reason whatsoever should Isaac be relocated outside of Canaan. Genesis 24:34-41 says Eliezer emphasized the fact that Abraham had given his wealth to Isaac in his discussion with Rebecca and her family when he arrived their home to get Rebecca to accompany him to Canaan to become Isaac's wife.

9

TOLERANCE'S TORTUOUS TRAP

Ruth 1:6-22 confirm in verse 16-17 how Ruth can be said to have invited God into her determination to relocate to the land of Israel and particularly the town of Bethlehem permanently. She said she was not just eager to accompany Naomi to go and live among her people but also embraced their God. It means that she did not behave like Rachel who Genesis 31:1-16 and 30-35 confirms that much as she was ready to accompany Jacob to Canaan in obedience to the command of Jacob's God she was not ready to give up on her father's household/native gods. As a result, she stole her father's household gods to take along to Canaan. I Kings 11:1-8-14 confirms that King Solomon's wives who were all non-Israelites took their natives gods along to Jerusalem to stay put as his wives just like I Kings 16:29-33 confirms that Jezebel took her native god named Baal along to become King Ahab's wife in Samaria in the land of Israel where she stayed put. I Kings 21:1-29 and 22:1-40 and II Kings 9:1-37 confirm that she remained in the land of Israel after the death of Ahab until King Jehu ordered her killing.

Solomon's wives and Jezebel embraced their husbands enough to relocate to live permanently with them but never believed that it was enough reason for them to embrace their husbands' God of Israel. They desired the man that God of Israel has been kind to but not the God who was kind to them. Zechariah 8:20-23 can be interpreted to mean that prosperity is part of what God uses to woo others to join His people to worship Him. Numbers 10:29-32 confirms that Moses tried to use it to convince Hobab to join them. I Samuel 23:15-18 can be interpreted to mean that the prospect of outliving his father and become second-in-command to David on the throne of Israel did not convince Jonathan to abandon his father to remain with David.

However, what Solomon's wives and Jezebel did was like saying "Much as it is obvious that God has been very good to you it is not enough reason for me to join you to regard that God just because I am partaking in the blessings of that God to you". There are persons who crave God's reward but resent personal relationship with Him because of the responsibilities that such relationship demands or would place on them. Genesis 12:1-9 and 18:17-19 can be said to mean that God told Abraham that their relationship has unprecedented rewards that are eternal that is hinged on Abraham and his partaking descendants' obedience. God's promise has a profitable purpose just as it demands the obedient participation of the promise's beneficiary.

Since Numbers 12:1-16 confirms that God punished Miriam for criticizing Moses' marriage to a non-Israelite woman, we can claim that God approved or did not mind much that Moses married a non-Israelite. Exodus 2:11-22, 4:18-26 and 18:1-27 confirm that Moses' wife, Zipporah was the daughter of the chief priest of Midian, Jethro. Yet, there is no record that she lured Moses to join her family to serve the god of Midian for which her father was the chief priest. This is even though Moses lived with them in Midian for 40 years continuously without ever returning to Egypt to his fellow Israelites. In fact, first, Exodus 4:24-26 can be said to mean that God of Israel found Zipporah good enough to serve as a priest to Moses when God wanted to kill Moses on his way back to Egypt to lead the Israelites out of Egypt. Second, Exodus 18:1-27 confirms that Jethro came over to the wilderness to meet Moses while leading the Israelites. Verses 8-12 confirm that during this visit Jethro acknowledged Moses' God of Israel as the greatest God of all and offered sacrifices to Him.

It should be said that neither Jethro nor Moses forced their gods on one another like Jezebel can be said to have forced her native god on her husband and his fellow Israelites in the land of Israel that she came to live and Ahab's wife. Joseph, his boss and benefactor, Pharaoh, his Egyptian officials and subjects as well as Joseph's father-in-law and entire wife's family did not say because he lived among, married one of them and got the position of the highest official in their kingdom he must embrace their religious beliefs before they would let him remain among and reign over them. They let him remain loyal to the God of his ancestors who gave him the wisdom to interpret Pharaoh's dreams and use same wisdom to manage their economy for them during the very critical 14 years of their nation's economy.

Jeremiah 25:1-14 and 27:1-8 confirm that God of Israel ordained Nebuchadnezzar's reign as well as instigated him to carry the Israelites or Jews captive to Babylon where Jeremiah 29:10 confirms that God meant them to remain for 70 years and Daniel 9:1-2 confirms that they did remained there for the 70 years. Jeremiah 39:11-14 confirms that when Nebuchadnezzar had accomplished the capture of Jerusalem and Judah, he acknowledged that God of Israel made it possible. Daniel 2:46-49 confirms that Nebuchadnezzar confessed in verse 47 that God of Israel is the greatest of all gods of the universe. However, there is no record that he joined Daniel and other Jews to worship Him or ordered that the nations of the earth that he ruled over should discard their native gods to worship the God of Israel. Daniel 3:1-30 and 4:1-37 confirm two other instances when Nebuchadnezzar acknowledged God of Israel as the greatest God of all gods yet he still did not consider it enough reason to join the Israelites to worship Him only.

This is one of the vital focuses of the concept of "I Know But Cannot". Nebuchadnezzar did not contest the fact that God of Israel is the greatest of all gods, but he was too addicted to his native gods to switch loyalty. This is the real irony of the story of Ahab and his Israelite subjects: how do you know that you have affinity with the greatest, yet you ditch Him to seek other lesser gods? It does not add up logically. No reasonable individual gives up gold for anything less!

Genesis 41:45-46 confirms that Joseph married Asenath the daughter of the chief or head priest of Egypt. There is no record that she lured Joseph to join her father and family as well as other Egyptians to worship their native gods just because Genesis 41:37-46 and 45:4-9 and Psalm 105:16-22 confirm that Joseph was offered the position of the highest official next only to the king of Egypt. Joseph's and Moses' wives, Asenath and Zipporah respectively can be said to have embraced the God of their husbands unlike Solomon's non-Israelite wives and King Ahab's non-Israelite wife, Jezebel. Also, it means that Solomon and Ahab followed in the footsteps of Adam who Genesis 3:1-24 confirms to have followed his wife's urging to disobey God's command.

Meanwhile, Job 2:9-10 confirms that Job did not heed his wife's ungodly counsel. Job consciously resisted his wife's suggestion that he cursed God and die. That was like urging Job to hang himself – it is very shocking that she knew very well that if he cursed God he would die yet she pressured him to do it. Job 14:7-14 strongly suggests that apparently he refused to curse God and die because tucked away somewhere in Job's heart was the belief that God would yet restore his fortunes and it would be counterproductive if he cursed God and died as she suggested. This is the reason for his refusal to heed her counsel to curse God. He acted on his faith in the ability of God to still turn round his fortunes as well as the fact that God is good and would not let him end his stay on earth on a sad note.

Something else worthy of mention is how God never did anything to suggest that He got angry with Job's wife for such sinister suggestion. Perhaps, God understood that she did it out of frustration as well as the fact that she never understood that

He would yet put an end to their household's troubles and bless them more than ever before. Also important is the fact that as long as Job did not heed her counsel or divorced her for it God left her alone so that punishing her would not cause Job further heartaches. This is important because it means that Job made up for his wife's weakness in God's sight. God was able to regard him enough to forgive her mistake. This is similar to the way God spared the lives of Noah's wife, their three sons and their wives for Noah's sake.

That is how God meant it to be with every household. Jeremiah 15:1-4 and Ezekiel 14:12-21 confirm that there are instances when a man's uprightness would be considered by God to favour and forgive where necessary the misdeeds of his household members. Because Job quickly stopped his wife from going down the path of insulting God because of their predicament, God overlooked her verbal misadventure. It means that Job saved his wife from the punishment that she deserved from God. That is one of the fundamentals of God's purpose for marriage, one partner would save the other from deserved pains. Exodus 4:14a and 24-26 confirms that when God was angry with Moses, it was his wife,

Zipporah that God regarded her efforts to spare Moses' life. It is an integral part of what Ecclesiastes 4:9-12 mean that two are better than one because when one falls the other would help him to rise. Ezekiel 22:30-31 can be interpreted to mean that God is always looking for someone to stand in the gap so that He would not vent the full measure of His anger on the sinner. It can be likened to when Genesis 19:29 says He spared Lot's life because of Abraham, Genesis 6-8 gives the impression that He saved Noah's wife, three sons and their wives because of Noah, and II Samuel 7:1-17, I Kings 1:5-53 and I Chronicles 17:1-15, 22:1-10 and 28:1-7 confirm that He gave Solomon to be king of Israel because David gladdened Him and I Kings 11:1-42 says He spared Solomon of his due punishment because of David. Ezekiel 22:23-31 means that God is always looking for someone to help the weak and oppressed on His behalf.

That is what Adam failed to do for Eve when he found out that she had erred by heeding Satan's deception to disobey God's command to them. That is what Eli failed to do for his sons when he found out that they were doing things that earned them God's anger and punishment. That is what in Christian circles is called standing in the gap for a loved one. The rich woman of Shunem made all the difference in the life of the old man that she married. II Kings 4:7-37 can be said to mean that the man was neither rich nor seemed to have cared about having children in his lifetime but the rich woman provided him her wealth to manage as well as encouraged him to let her cultivate relationship with God's prophet, Elisha which led to their having a son to inherit her wealth. In that sense, she made up for his weakness.

Another thing is what can be called the variation of individual capacity to endure pains or hardship. Job lost his children and wealth as much as his wife who was also the mother of the children that they lost. In fact, Job suffered more than she did because while Job 2:7-8 confirms that sores broke out all over Job's body there is no record that her personal health was affected directly during the period of tribulation. Job 19:1-29 says it was Job that their servants disrespected throughout the period of the tribulation apparently because he could no longer pay their wages during the precarious period. He was the one whom his friends deserted and the three of them that

Job 2:11-13, 8:1-4 and 11:3-6 say came to commiserate with, but chose to blame him and their dead sons for the misfortune that befell them. They never blamed his wife. Job 1:1-5 says it was Job rather than his wife who cared enough to appease God to forgive whatever sins their children might have committed before the children were killed. In that sense, it was Job's effort to prevent misfortune in the household that was really wasted as she never did anything noted to appease God with the hope of preventing any misfortune happening to any of their household members. Yet, she was the one who was angrier or felt more pained and would not reason properly to help restrain her from blaspheming God. That is getting angrier than the most bereaved.

It is similar to when Naomi and Ruth became childless widows – while Naomi blamed her God of Israel for her woes, Ruth a non-Israelite who became Israelite only by marrying one of Naomi's late sons found their common misfortune of childless widowhood the more reason to believe in Naomi's God of Israel. That is not cheap to explain apart from the fact that God helped Ruth to so do. While wealth or abundance made Solomon to err it did not make Job to err with God and man. Some would work hard to earn enough to enjoy luxury while others would try the precarious path of robbery to get resources to afford luxury.

Job's wife would have worsened their predicament with her poor reaction to the already bad situation that they found themselves. She seemed to be blaming Job for not doing enough to make God save them from the misfortune of loosing their children and wealth. She was used to Job doing everything including getting God's covering over them as a family. When only one member of the family does everything for everyone else it can be very difficult for the resourceful individual. II Kings 4:18-37 can be interpreted to mean that it is part of the reason that when their son died, the rich woman of Shunem did not waste her time intimating his father rather she only sent to him to send her the equivalent of the family car to take her to meet Elisha at Mount Camel. If the man's efforts seemed not to have measured up in God's sight why not take over from him and make up for the balance so that God would for the sake of your additional effort turn round your family's fortune rather than tell the man to commit suicide by cursing God.

It is on record that just as Solomon's wives lured him to sin against God of Israel so also Jezebel and her daughters did to Ahab and their husbands, respectively. Job might not have been the king of his nation, but he lived like one, and yet he was able to resist his wife's frustration fuelled outburst to revere God. Meanwhile, it was not any tribulation precipitated heartaches that made Solomon's wives and Jezebel and her daughters to convince their husbands to sin against God. Ahab and Job might have operated 'one-man one-wife' policy but Ahab could not join Job to maintain a policy of 'not even my spouse can make me displease God of all gods who have been my help in life' like David did successfully rather Ahab joined the ensnaring example of Solomon to succumb to his wife's inducement, influence and manipulation to sin against God. We cannot say for sure if Ahab remained with one wife like Job because he feared Jezebel or because he was just contented with one wife like Job inferred in chapter 31:1 that he had never lusted after a young girl or woman in his lifetime. That sounds like the case of Joseph as the Prime Minister of Egypt and Moses as the leader of the Israelites who never married more than a wife despite their exalted position and the associated privileges.

Solomon married 700 wives and went a step further to add 300 concubines – if his greatness and success as king of Israel made him to have intimate relationship with as many as a thousand women it would amount to 'success-syndicated moral bankruptcy'. He had no iota of respect for marital decency. But perhaps, he wanted a woman for every of the thousand bullocks that II Chronicles 1:6 says he offered to God on a single day. Solomon broke all the rules that Deuteronomy 17:14-20 claims that God meant to regulate the conduct of whoever became the king of Israel. Meanwhile, he is the first royal ruler of Israel who God indicated his plan for him to rule over Israel before his mother became one of his father's wives. Samuel who could have been said to have being before him was not a royal ruler but theocratic ruler of Israel. Much as David married more than one wife, only Absalom's mother was not an Israelite and she could not convince David to join her to worship her native gods.

Proverbs 30:7-9 says abject/acute poverty could make an individual steal and bring shame to the name of his God just as overwhelming riches could make an individual conclude that he no longer needs God who helped him to prosper. Then, Deuteronomy 8:7-14 says the prosperous should not forget to revere and worship God who helped them to become prosperous. Job 1-2 means that neither prosperity nor poverty made Job to curse God though his wife thought that he should have cursed God for letting them lose their children and wealth. That is what makes the case of Solomon letting his wives lure him to despise God after God had helped him become the wealthiest man on earth profoundly serious. Solomon is a perfect example of a bad example of men whom God-given greatness made mad and monstrous.

Jethro's grandsons who jumped at Moses' offer that their father, Hobab joined the commonwealth of Israel were not said to have taken any of the gods of Midian along to join the Israelites. That presupposes that they followed in Ruth's footsteps to embrace the God of the Israelites or their cousins, Moses' sons who Exodus 2:21-22, 4:18-20, 18:1-5 and I Chronicles 26:23-28 give their names as Gershom and Eliezer. There is no record that Hobab's sons who went with the Israelites took along the god of their ancestors who their grandfather, Jethro served as chief or head priest to live among the Israelites. In this respect, Numbers 10:29-32 and Judges 4:11 say:

> 29 Moses said to his brother-in-law Hobab son of Jethro the Midianite, "We are about to start out for the place which the Lord said he would give us. He has promised to make Israel prosperous, so come with us, and we will share our prosperity with you." 30 Hobab answered, "No, I am going back to my native land." 31 "Please don't leave us," Moses said. "You know where we can camp in the wilderness, and you can be our guide. 32 If you come with us, we will share with you all the blessings that the Lord gives us."

> 11 In the meantime Heber the Kenite had set up his tent close to Kedesh near the oak-tree at Zanannim. He had moved away from the other

Kenites, the descendants of Hobab, the brother-in-law of Moses. (TEV)

This means that apparently, Hobab's sons heeded Moses pleas to join their cousins, Gershom and Eliezer to leave their native land of Midian behind to join the Israelites and they stayed put. The subject of not taking their Midianite gods along to worship among the Israelites in the land that God allocated to the Israelites is very important considering the damage that Solomon's non-Israelite wives caused to him and the people of Israel over the worship of foreign gods in the land of Israel. Nehemiah 13:26 confirms that though God of Israel loved Solomon greatly but because Solomon loved and indulged his non-Israelite wives God got angry with him. Solomon did not reciprocate God's love till the end of his life. He loved God earlier in life, but prosperity provided pleasure made him derail in his loyalty and love for God. The evil that Solomon's non-Israelite wives did to him is applicable to Jezebel and her daughters. Over a period of 40 years that I Kings 11:41-43 confirms in verse 42 that Solomon ruled over Israel and Judah after his father, the great King David, his non-Israelite wives were able to break down the wall of defense of his loyalty to God of Israel who II Samuel 7:1-17 and I Chronicles 17:1-15, 22:6-10 and 28:1-7 confirm to have sent him to live and rule over Israel and lured him to join them to worship their native gods.

One thing that is common to Hobab's sons and descendants, Ruth, Solomon's wives and Jezebel is that they were all marriage motivated, related or rooted migrants in the land of Israel. However, what is different is that while on the one hand, Hobab's descendants were not known to have imposed the worship of Midianite gods on the religious landscape of the Israelites while in the case of Ruth she openly confessed her embrace of or allegiance to the God of the Israelites which meant that she gave up the gods of her native land of Moab, on the other hand, Solomon's wives and Jezebel used their vantage position of being married to the king of Israel to introduce their native gods on the religious landscape of the nation and people of Israel. In fact, only Solomon's wives introduced their native gods to the Israelites whereas in the case of Jezebel, she forced it down their throat with threats to kill whoever refused to go along with her. Jezebel and her supportive Baal prophets totaled

451 which should not have been enough suffocate the Israelites numerically in the land that God gave to them. Genesis 46:8-27, Exodus 1:1-7,12:37, 38:26b, Numbers 2:32, 11:21 and 14:6 and Acts 7:14-15 give the impression that before the presence of the Israelites began to give the Egyptians serious concerns, the Israelites were nearly five million because they men of war alone were 605,000. It took 430 years for them to multiply from 75 persons to that figure. Even then, the Egyptian rulers and their officials still tamed the Israelites. I Kings 16:29 confirms that Jezebel's husband ruled over Israel for 22 years and within that period she was able to literally make mincemeat of the Israelites in their own God-given land.

I Kings 11:1-8 can be interpreted to mean that Solomon's non-Israelite wives could only make him join them to worship their foreign gods. The reasons Solomon yielded to their pressure or lure is another matter except that the passage includes the fact that he loved foreign women which strongly suggests that he was trying to prove that he loved them so much that he was willing to do just anything to prove his love for them. Meanwhile, Deuteronomy 6:5 and 13:1-11 made it clear that no Israelite should join anybody to worship any other god rather individually they should love and worship God of their ancestors with all their heart, soul and strength. Of course, once he agreed to serve the native god of one of them, he had to do same for all the women. Solomon's wives were sane enough not to kill the prophets and priests of God of Israel in Jerusalem and the land of Israel. However, I Kings 16:29-33, 18:3-4 and 9-13, 19:1-2, 10 and 14 and 21:1-29 confirm that by the time of King Ahab of Israel, his wife Jezebel took the imposition of foreign gods on the religious life of the Israelites to a heinous higher level of abomination. Beyond making her husband, King Ahab and their children join her to worship her native gods in Israel's new capital city of Samaria, she went ahead to kill God of Israel's authentic prophets.

I Kings 19:9-18 confirms that the Israelites who would not join her and Ahab to worship her Baal were so intimidated that Prophet Elijah who was the only visible Prophet of God of Israel did not even know that there were 7000 other worshippers of God of Israel who I Kings 18:3-4 and 13 strongly suggest to have included Obadiah who was the equivalent of the principal staff officer to King Ahab. I Kings 19:13-18 says it took God to inform Elijah that there were 7000 Israelites who had not joined to worship Jezebel's imposed god of Baal. It means that it got to a point that the Israelites were afraid to worship the God of their ancestors in the very land that God gave to them through their ancestors. Obadiah could not discourage his boss, Ahab from letting his wife the queen kill God's prophets and could only protect a total of 100 of them without the knowledge of Jezebel. She became what can be called the queen of religious terror to the Israelites.

I Kings 18:15-40 can be interpreted to mean that she contracted her own prophets to provide her spiritual support. I Kings 21:1-19 confirms that she killed Naboth in order to get his inherited vineyard for Ahab which can be interpreted to be her own way of bribing Ahab to let her continue with her religious atrocities. She would get him some personal benefits so that for the sake of the personal benefits he was deriving he would not do anything to restrain her from the religious atrocities so that the personal benefits would not stop. I Kings 21:25-26 says all the evil things that Ahab did were at the urging of Jezebel just like II Kings

8:16-19 and 25-27 and II Chronicles 21:1-20 and 22:1-6 confirm that all the kings of Judah who were related to Ahab's family were led to sin by either Ahab's daughter or her family members.

There is what we can call 'The Ridiculousness of the Righteous and Reasonable' or 'Righteous and Reasonables/Responsibles' Ridiculous Reasoning and Reaction/Response'. One woman backed by 450 prophets (totaling 451) successfully or victoriously or both drove 7000 righteous men into hiding because perhaps, if you asked the 7000, they would say it is because they want to live in peace with all men. These 7000 made nonsense of the claim by Proverbs 28:1 that the righteous is as bold as a lion while evil doers are supposed to be the timid ones in society. Again, Judges 2:7 confirms that Joshua and his lieutenants ensured that the Israelites did not worship other gods or do anything else to displease the God of their ancestors who guided Moses to lead their ancestors or parents from Egypt to Canaan. We do not know how many lieutenants served as leaders of the Israelites under Joshua. Whatever their number was, they were able to make the rest of the Israelites join them to please God.

This means that the leaders of Israel under Ahab and Solomon did the exact opposite.

God created the position of leadership among humans for the leaders to show and where necessary make them to do the right thing. However or despite this fact, I Kings 21:1-19 confirms that Ahab's lieutenants who in this case were the leading citizens of the city of Jezreel helped him to stage-manage the death of Naboth for Ahab to take over Naboth's inherited vineyard against Naboth's wishes. Malachi 2:5-7 says one of the core duties of the Levitical priests is to (1) give other Israelites example of how to respect and fear the God of their ancestors, (2) teach what is right, (3) give example of how to live in harmony with one another and God of their ancestors, (4) help many others to stop doing evil, (5) teach the true knowledge of God, and (6) reveal God's will to those seeking clarifications from God since they are the true messengers of God. Just as the Levites including the Aaronite priests had religious obligation to the people so also the king and other leaders of the nation had obligation to the people. In the same vein, the people had an obligation to ensure that they are not swayed from what they had known about their relationship with the God of their ancestors from childhood.

Now, if based on their understanding of the loyalty that their God required of them, the Israelites had stood up against Jezebel and her initial efforts to impose the worship of her native god of Baal on them in the land of Israel she would not have gone to the extent of killing any Israelite who would not worship her Baal. Ecclesiastes 8:11-14 can be interpreted to mean that the more you tolerate evil doers the more room you give them to become emboldened to do more evil against the tolerant. The fact that Elijah was the only visible God of Israel's worshipper meant that all other worshippers of God of Israel like him practically abandoned Elijah to face Ahab and Jezebel alone or by himself. That is part of what helps evil doers to flourish in their evil doing. All those who are righteous often keep silent or too scared to confront the wicked to stop them from continuing to torment the entire citizenry. Along this line, Jeremiah 5:29-31 says:

> 29 "But I, the Lord, will punish them for these things; I will take revenge on this nation. 30 A

terrible and shocking thing has happened in the land; 31 prophets speak nothing but lies; priests rule as the prophets command, and my people offer no objections. But what will they do when it all comes to an end?" (TEV)

The point is that as evil as Jezebel was the Israelites have their own share of the blame for whatever evil she was permitted to do among them. They cannot claim that they did not know that their kinsman and king by the name of Ahab had erred when he married a non-Israelite and let her bring her native gods to their God-given land of Israel to worship. I Samuel 2:12-17, 22-36 confirms that the generation of Eli and his sons knew when his sons were doing the wrong thing and some of them went to report Eli's sons to him to correct them. I Samuel 8:1-6 confirms that the leading citizens of Israel in Samuel's generation were courageous enough to point out the misdeeds of Samuel's sons to him. But the generation of Ahab did not even speak up to correct Ahab. Jezebel could not have begin killing any Israelite who refused to worship Baal from the very day she arrived her husband's home and palace. It must have taken some time. II Chronicles 26:16-21 confirms that when King Uzziah erred in religious matters, some priests summed up the courage to challenge him. This is where members of Ahab's generation have their own share of the blame. Wherever and whenever the righteous fails to match the wicked action for action every step of the way the common thing that often happens is that the wicked becomes more emboldened and prevails. Some would say the sane of society should use their good conduct to show evil doers the right way to live. The truth is that the wicked knows that they are doing wrong which means that they know what is right before they just prefer to do evil. It is not because they do not know what is right and would do it only if someone dies in order to show them example before they would stop doing evil. Proverbs 29:27 can be interpreted to mean that the righteous is not under obligation to like the wicked because the wicked have no intention to love the righteous.

It is like trying to excuse Cain's evil of killing Abel by saying he learnt his lessons later on. That is rubbish and complete nonsense. He was older or arrived this world before Abel. First, how did Abel know how to offer the right sacrifices that God adjudged acceptable and Cain did not? They were brought up by the same parents in the same environment. He knew what he was doing when he offered unacceptable sacrifices to God. He knew what he was doing when he conceived the idea of killing Abel. If he did not know that it was wrong, he should not have lured him to the fields away from the eyes of their parents to kill. If he did not know that it was wrong, he should have told Abel the reason he was luring him to the fields. Good people are sacrificed unjustly to appease evil doers under the guise of trying to reform the irredeemable and incorrigible of this wearisome world. Authorities wait until some innocent persons have been killed before accepting that a known evil doer deserve some punishment. It is an unforgivable injustice to the peaceful and well behaved of society. Any punishment of the evil doer after a law-abiding person had been harmed is a worthless and unprofitable punishment because the harm has been done.

Cain knew that affliction is not good for any human before he killed Abel. How do we know? It is very simple – when he heard God's punishment, he said it was too much for him to bear and it would lead to his own death. How is untimely death caused by a fellow human unbearable, yet he did it to his younger brother? He did not mind doing it to his younger brother, neighbour or fellow human but should not be done to him even when he deserved it. Evil doers are the most selfish souls that ever walked the earth, they do not mind hurting others but abhor being hurt for the hurt that they have caused others. Cain is the pioneer of all such persons.

What God meant in Jeremiah 5:30 above is that even if the king and his boot-licking lieutenants are crazy, the people who knew what is right should resist them. II Corinthians 8:1-5 and Revelation 2:1-6 say:

> 1 Our brothers, we want you to know what God's grace has accomplished in the churches in Macedonia. 2 They have been severely tested by the troubles they went through; but their joy was so great that they were extremely generous in their giving, even though they are very poor. 3 I can assure you that they gave as much as they could, and even more than they could. Of their

own free will 4 they begged us and pleaded for the privilege of having a part in helping God's people in Judaea. 5 It was more than we could have hoped for! First they gave themselves to the Lord; and then, by God's will they gave themselves to us as well.

1 To the angel of the church in Ephesus write: "This is the message from the one who holds the seven stars in his right hand and who walks among the seven gold lamp-stands. 2 I know how hard you have done; I know how hard you have worked and how patient you have been. I know that you cannot tolerate evil men and that you have tested those who say they are apostles but are not, and have found out that they are liars. 3 You are patient, you have suffered for my sake, and you have not given up. 4 But this is what I have against you: you do not love me now as you did at first. 5 Think how far you have fallen! Turn from your sins and do what you did at first. If you

don't turn from your sins, I will come to you and take your lamp-stand from its place. 6 But this is what you have in your favour: you hate what the Nicolaitans do, as much as I do. (TEV)

Heaven acknowledged the Macedonia and Ephesus Christians' endurance of sufferings for righteousness sake patiently. The Ephesus Christians did check out some self-styled apostles and confirmed that they were fakes which is like when Acts 17:10-12 says the Berean Christians crosschecked the bible-based authenticity of the preaching claims of Paul and Silas before they believed. Why would some be sensible enough to confirm that some are fake, and Ahab's generation of Israelites would not care that they were being made to worship foreign gods that they should not? Are there contemporary Christians who dare challenge their prophets and bishops for lying to them courageously? They must study and understand the bible to be able to confirm that a pastor or bishop is lying to them and therefore deserve the classification of fake. But our ready excuse is that there is no time to study the bible so whatever our presiding bishops claim we accept whether in agreement with the bible or not.

Interestingly, God did not make the punishment of the liars a priority in the sense that their punishment was not mentioned in the passage rather it is the punishment of the Ephesus Christians for the area that they are not measuring up that God talked about in the passage. The reason is not far fetched. The punishment of the wicked is reserved for eternal damnation. God is more concerned about the righteous because they are His priority. He does not want their sufferings in one area to go unrewarded because of failure to measure up in another area. God is honest enough to indicate the area in which the Ephesus Christians measured up to His expectation and the aspect in which they are yet to and encouraged them to do so, so that they would get their reward because if they failed to, they would miss the reward that they deserved for the area where they measured up as well. It might make God's standard of expectation to be remarkably high but that is what it is. This is where there is no doubt that Ahab's Israelite subjects failed as God's people to play their assigned responsibility to checkmate their king and his household when they erred in the matter of serving the God of their ancestors as expected.

Now, it might be that Ahab was just a liberal minded individual who believed that though he was the symbol of the royal authority in Israel, he should not force anyone including his wife to do anything including his religious faith. He loved her and if she wanted to continue to worship her natives gods in their family home or palace so be it. However, from the first inch of freedom that he gave her she claimed more than comfortable measure and graduated into imposing her own religious beliefs and god on her husband and subjects. This is a pointer to the fact that usually the regrets of liberal lifestyle do not become obvious quickly rather it takes a gradual process over time. God in His infinite wisdom knew this fact, so He warned the Israelites never to intermarry with non-Israelites or worship their gods. Ahab's response to God's threatened punishment for his ungodliness and wickedness which practically peaked when he approved of the killing of Naboth by gladly taking over Naboth's inherited vineyard strongly suggests that Ahab would not have been so evil if he did not marry and bring

Jezebel to live with him in the land of Israel and left her free to worship the gods of her native land. I Kings 21:20-24 and 27-29 confirms that Ahab showed what God regarded as genuine remorse worthy of granting him some reprieve.

Whoever deals reasonably with an unreasonable person will regret it inevitably. Whoever tries to be sane with an insane person will surely regret it. I Kings 1:5-53 and 2:13-25 can be interpreted to mean as follows:

1. Adonijah did not desire his father's throne until he became the eldest surviving son of his father. His ambition to be his father's successor agreed with God's provisional plan for the eldest son of any man in Deuteronomy 21:15-17 just as he was the Israelites' choice.

2. Yet, once he understood that God insisted on Solomon taking over the throne of their father at his expense he agreed to God's will or the reconfiguration that disregarded Deuteronomy 21:15-17 to take away the throne Israel from him without any resistance. This means that he feared God enough to accept His decision

on who succeeded their father. He did not follow in Abner's footstep to resist God's candidate's rule – Abner resisted David's rule after Saul's death even when he knew that God meant David to rule after Saul. Adonijah did not follow in Saul's footsteps to try to kill God's candidate for the throne of Israel so that Saul's preferred successor could remain alive to become the king of Israel. That is, Adonijah did not plot to kill Solomon so that he (Adonijah) could remain alive to succeed David like Judges 8:22-35 and 9:1-57 confirm that Gideon's abominable Abimelech did and ruled for three years before God punished him and his sponsors. II Chronicles 22:10-22 and 23:1-15 say Jezebel's daughter, Athaliah murdered her grandsons to take over her dead son's throne to rule over Judah for seven years before she was punished as she deserved. Adonijah could have killed Solomon and seized their father's throne even if his rule would not last more than three or seven years. But he chose not to be so uncivil with his ambition to be king of Israel. Joab was dastardly enough to do such dirty job for him and he enjoyed Joab's support to be king at Solomon's expense.

3. Solomon's mother was so impressed with Adonijah's respect of God's decision in favor of Solomon that she agreed that Adonijah deserved the compensation that he requested Solomon for giving up the throne of their father for Solomon to occupy.

4. Adonijah believed that Solomon was a reasonable son who would respect his mother's views. It is as a result that Adonijah went to engage his mother to present his desired compensation to Solomon. However,

5. Solomon was not as reasonable and respectful to his mother as any reasonable person would expect, rather than consider the same judgment of his mother to grant Adonijah's requested compensation, he chose to humiliate his mother by ordering the murder of Adonijah in cold blood.

6. By so doing, Solomon turned the head of good judgment, good counsel, the concept of live and let's live upside down. This was his first strategic mistake which he followed up by marrying foreign women who brought their foreign gods to live with him in his palace in Jerusalem.

7. Adonijah's greatest mistake was trying to deal reasonably with a man who had sworn by his own life never to be reasonable so long as he lived. This is part of what Matthew 7:6 says Jesus meant when He admonished that no wise individual should give what is precious to persons who have no value for such valuable. Uriah died because he tried to honor God in the life of a man who was too desperate to remember or consider God's commandment not to shed the blood of an innocent man. II Kings 25:22-26 and Jeremiah 40-42 can be said to mean that Gedaliah died because he chose to be civil with an uncivilized soul by the name of Ishmael. Gedaliah did not die prematurely and violently because he lacked the information and capacity to prevent his

untimely death but because he chose to be civil when he should not. Matthew 10:5-6, 13:53-58 and 15:20 and 26, Mark 6:1-6, Luke 4:16-44 and John 7:1-4 can be said to detail how Jesus dealt with His fellow Jews and even hometown of Nazareth's natives according to His admonition in Matthew 7:6. Much as He claimed that He was sent primarily to bless His fellow Jews, as long as the Jews and particularly His Nazarene kinsmen failed to appreciate the blessings that He meant for them, He never forced it on them. He meant that if the intended recipient of a blessing rejects it whether they did on account of ignorance or sheer stubbornness, do not waste your time trying to force it on them. God give it to some other persons who are desperate for it. There are certain benefits that are too good for certain persons and they are better left to wallow in their sufferings.

There is the angle of the return of religious regret. Earlier, God of Israel dispossessed the original inhabitants of the land of Canaan for the Israelites to possess because the Canaanites would not worship Him. However, we see what seems like the heathen gods staging a sort of come back through the likes of Solomon's wives and Jezebel. It is like the way that II Kings 18:1-8, 21:1-18 and II Chronicles 29:1-36, 30:1-27, 31:1-21 and 33:1-17 confirm that Manasseh restored and added more idols to the ones that his father removed from Jerusalem and Judah.

I Kings 22:51-53 confirms that Ahab's son and successor, King Ahaziah of Israel followed in the footsteps of his father and mother, Jezebel to commit abominations. Then, II Kings 1:2-17 confirms that when Ahaziah thought that he needed to consult God over a problem that he had, rather than consult the God of Israel he opted to consult the priests of the god of the Philistine city of Ekron. In response, God of Israel sent Prophet Elijah to accost his messengers to say it was an insult for him to go and consult a foreign god when God of Israel was available in the land of Israel to consult. Rather than heed Elijah's words from God he determined to capture and punish Elijah. Even when Elijah resisted arrest at the expense of the palace guards sent to capture him, Ahaziah did not give up rather he sent another contingent to get Elijah arrested and brought to his palace. Elijah was not ready to cooperate, so he wasted the lives of the second contingent as well and to prevent further waste of innocent lives, God persuaded Elijah to go with the third contingent whose leader behaved much better. Ahaziah proved that the safety of his servants or palace guards did not worth anything to him.

There is the economic aspect of the failed attempt to consult the god of the Philistines – which is cheaper or cost effective, is it to send your palace officials to go consult one god abroad or get a better service locally? The fact that the local expert knew that you had sent some emissaries abroad for the job that he could do better at no cost to the national treasury despite the fact that he was never present when you sent your officials and none of your officials went to inform the prophet should have made Ahaziah know that Elijah was more capable of solving his problem than the foreign gods that he sent his servants to consult. But of course, the real reason he did not want to hear from Elijah and God of Israel that Elijah represented was that his mother had made him believe that there is nothing good about the God of Israel that his father was supposed to have been brought up to worship. She must have introduced that idea in their household even before Ahaziah was born or grew up into a young adult. He must have witnessed or heard the account of how I Kings 18:3-4 and 13-14 and 19:10-14 confirm that his mother killed prophets and worshippers of God of Israel. He must have known how his mother threatened Elijah for the killing of the prophets of Baal. As a result, he did not see anything wrong with threatening the life of Elijah as God of Israel's prophet.

Strangers do not regard what is sacrosanct to natives no matter how long they have lived among the natives. The fact that natives are liberal and tolerant of strangers does not mean that the strangers would be sensible enough to even reciprocate automatically. Jezebel's mindset is to impose her native gods that she imported into the native land of her husband who hid his stupidity under the guise of liberality and tolerance to accommodate her and her religious faith. She never thought that her husband and his people's tolerance was anything worthy of emulation and reciprocity.

I once had an office assistant in the mid-1990s who would tell me "My boss, the problem is that he or she does not understand that what you know to be awful is so wrong". This often happens when someone had done something that is unforgivably awful and I start to complain bitterly that I cannot understand why someone in his right senses would not know that such a thing is not proper and should not be done. After a while he would literally sum up the courage to say "Sir, please forgive me for what I am about to say just in case you might consider it offensive". And then, he would begin by saying 'you remember when I just got here I was not any better and you found a way to endure me even though it was very tough for me initially until I began to understand your views on some of these things. Just like it seemed to me then, I think that these people do not even understand that they are doing anything awful. I understand it to be awful now but back then it was not because I did not know any better'.

Now, someone might claim that Ahab was tolerant because he had hoped that Jezebel would understand and follow in his path of tolerance but as we know the end of their story, her abominable attitude of religious intolerance never abated until God chose army officer Jehu to put an end to it or complete the process of ending it which God had used Elijah to commence when he got 450 prophets of Baal killed in one full swoop. The reason God began the punishment of the prophets of Baal, Ahab and finally Jezebel was because God had seen that like Eli's sons, Jezebel could not be convinced to change her ways any longer. The reason God used Moses to command in Deuteronomy 17:14-20 that whoever is made the king of Israel must be conversant with the Sacred Books which is the present day Holy Bible was so that the king would have a good understanding of the religious heritage so as to be able to use his royal authority to support the priest and prophets of God of Israel to protect their relationship with Him as the God of their ancestors. This is because the worship of the God of their ancestors was the chief cornerstone of their existence as a nation – their existence as a nation was God's conscious effort. However, Ahab failed in his responsibility to support the priests and prophets of their God to protect the core of their existence as a nation.

Numbers 27:18-23 and Deuteronomy 32:8-11 say the responsibility of the priests and prophets of Israel to their king or ruler were to (1) help the king to confirm and comply with

God's directive on any matter and (2) teach the Israelites in general the laws of God. Yet, Deuteronomy 17:14-20 and Joshua 1:1-8 include the fact that the same king of Israel or whoever occupied this position to rule over the nation by whatever title must still study and meditate on the Bible personally. This admonition that the king studied the bible personally can be interpreted to mean that the king must be conversant with and be convinced enough of God's commandments in order to protect/defend them as well as support the God approved religious leaders in every way necessary like Nehemiah did gloriously as the governor of Judah. We have gone this length to point out the extent to which Ahab failed in his duty as sitting king of Israel for 22 years in the religious life of the Israelites when he allowed his wife to impose her native gods on his subjects, the Israelites.

Ahab's attitude in this respect is an equivalent of 'religious insanity' as well as affection insanity – his tenure typifies "Madmen's Reign". He turned religious tolerance on its head. I Samuel 16:14-23, 18:10-11 and 19:1-10 confirm that Saul was the first insane individual to sit long on the throne of Israel. His aides kept him on the throne even when he was no longer sane enough to continue as king.

Solomon only joined his foreign wives to worship their gods in the land of Israel while Ahab took it to the heinous higher level of not only joining his wife to worship her heathen god in the land of Israel but let her kill God of Israel's worshippers, priests and prophets. Curiously, this tortuous trend had been going on since the time of Jacob when Genesis 31:20-35 and 35:1-5 say his beloved wife, Rachel was the one who took her father's household gods along with Jacob to Canaan. It took God's specific instruction for Jacob to have the guts to get rid of that god. The claim by I Kings 11:1-9 that it was Solomon's beloved foreign wives who brought their native gods to the land of Israel for Solomon to worship just as Genesis 29:1-30, 31:30-35 and 35:1-5 say it was Jacob's beloved wife outside of Canaan who brought the heathen gods that Jacob's household worshipped in Canaan is very curious. Solomon and Ahab allowed loquaciousness because of love. No responsible individual watches his life liquidated for any reason including love for the opposite sex. No one should watch his life liquidated just to prove that he is kind and liberal.

Perhaps, Jacob's experience in this respect contributed to God's command that the Israelites must not marry foreign women so that they would not turn their hearts from the God of their ancestors to worship their wives' native gods. Meanwhile, God gave this command despite the fact that God knew that Joseph's Egyptian wife and Moses' Midian wife never lured them to worship their native gods in their native land where Joseph and Moses were strangers and more so, despite the fact that Joseph and Moses' fathers-in-law were the priests of their native gods. God knew that there would be feeble-minded men like Solomon and Ahab who would readily do their wives' biddings and if such men became king they would watch their heathen wives persecute the Israelites who failed to worship their heathen gods in the land of Israel. God in His infinite wisdom decided that the safest solution was to prevent close relationship between the Israelites and non-Israelites by way of marriage.

Jezebel was practically though discretely on religious expansionist mission when she married Ahab and relocated to the land of Israel but Ahab and his fellow Israelites did not understand her heart-hidden motive accordingly. Just like David prevailed over Uriah because Uriah did not suspect David's monstrous motive and Uriah died cheaply and Genesis 4:1-10 can be said to mean that Abel died cheaply because he did not suspect that Cain had evil intensions so also Jezebel prevailed because the Israelites led by their King Ahab underestimated Jezebel and her monstrous motive. That is why whenever persons who claim to be large-hearted, liberal and tolerant care less about the real intent of strangers, they and their descendants are doomed irreversibly. It is just a matter of time.

Before we continue, Ahab's tolerance policy that allowed his wife to promote her natives gods in his home and domain ended up becoming tortuous tolerance. It can be likened to when Proverbs 29:21 says if anyone let his or her servant do as he or she likes without any restraints all the time, some day the servant would seek to take over the master's or madam's heritage at the expense of their children. There is no doubt that

Ahab's wife is not his slave or servant in the sense of servitude but the fact still remains that the same way that he chose to let her worship her native gods in his household and domain so also she too could have chosen to give up her gods to be with him as a wife just like Moses' wife or Ruth did. Once Zipporah and Ruth agreed to marry their husbands who were not their native kinsmen, they chose to join their husbands to worship their God.

Jezebel was allowed to worship her native god in the land of Israel, yet she would not allow Ahab and his fellow Israelites to worship their own God in the same land of Israel concurrently. It amounts to the fact that she took undue advantage of her husband's liberality. If someone allows you to squat in his house then you start to evict him from what is his own home, it is unforgivable aggression. Often in this world, it is the sane who suffers the most in the hands of the insane of this world because the sane chose to be senselessly sane and operate the policy of 'live and let's live'. All those who are quick to heed the voice of reason usually regret at the end. In most cases, sharing shatters the sharer because of the tripartite evil of greed, deception and presumptuousness. There is a difference between saneness and stupidity. In fact, protecting behavioral boundaries is one of the pillars of saneness. It was Gideon's legitimate and obedient sons who were slaughtered by the illegitimate because he was determined to disobey their father's implied command in Judges 8:22-23 that they (Gideon's sons and descendants) should not seek to rule over Israel after him. Some say life is not fair but the stupidity of those who assume that they are sane, and pontificate moral conscience fuels the unfairness. It is part of the reason that Ecclesiastes 8:11-14 says:

> 11 Why do people commit crimes so readily? Because crime is not punished quickly enough. 12 A sinner may commit a hundred crimes and still live. Oh yes, I know what they say: "If you obey God, everything will be all right, 13 but it will not go well for the wicked. Their life is like a shadow and they will die young, because they do not obey God." 14 But this is nonsense. Look at what happens in the world; sometime righteous men get the punishment of the wicked,

and wicked men get the reward of the righteous.

I say it is useless. (TEV)

Kindness is a double-edged sword in many respects. This is not just about the fact that it cost the kind and benevolent on the one hand just as it benefits and gladdens the beneficiaries and God who authored and admonishes it on the other. There are those who can be classed as buccaneer beneficiaries who do not see anything wrong or evil in killing benefactors to take over their wealth completely. King Saul engaged Ziba to manage his estates and gave Ziba so much freedom that Ziba took over Saul's estates after Saul's death at the expense of Saul's surviving son, Ishbosheth, daughters, Merab and Michal and grandchildren that included Mephibosheth. Some of the greatest challenges of managing kindness and benevolence are (1) reciprocity and (2) restraining the beneficiaries from becoming greedy to the extent of undoing their benefactor in order to take total control of their benefactor's wealth that he is God-fearing enough to share with them.

Proverbs 17:2 and 29:19 and 21 and Matthew 21:33-39 can be said to mean that it is the reason God admonishes the rich to be kind to their servants cautiously. The rich should not hide under the guise of kindness to give room for their beneficiary to undo them and their children who are entitled to inherit them. It means be kind but do not allow your beneficiaries to cut you down or off for their own benefit at your expense. Ecclesiastes 8:11-14, Jeremiah 5:30-31, Matthew 27:15-26, Mark 15:6-15, Luke 23:13-25 and John 18:28-40 and 19:1-16 can be said to mean that evil doers protect themselves more than good people try to protect themselves. There were more people who supported Saul against David an innocent and good man while only Jonathan defended David from Saul. Just as envy pitched Saul against David so also it pitched the Pharisees against Jesus. Only Nicodemus and Joseph of Arimathaea could stand up for Jesus while all the other Pharisees did not. Genesis 37:1-36 confirms that among Joseph's ten older brothers only two, Reuben and Judah stood up to protect him.

The claim in Amos 3:3 that two cannot travel together unless they have agreement can be said to mean that under normal circumstances, two people should have or cultivate consistent relationship only if they have a common ground, views and opinions. Also, it means that it is not helpful and advisable for persons who do not have a common objective to collaborate. As a result, Proverbs 22:10 can be interpreted to mean that rather than waste your precious time and effort to argue with someone that you do not agree with on many fronts it is better that you part ways with him or her so you can have your peace. This means that there are actions God expects man to take to enable him enjoy peace during his stay on earth. Genesis 16:1-16 and 21:9-20 can be interpreted to mean that when Sarah discovered that despite giving the extraordinary privilege to her maid to share her husband with her was not appreciated by Hagar, she drew on her legitimate authority in her husband's household to oust Hagar. Interestingly, Genesis 21:9-13 can be interpreted to mean that God approved Sarah's demand by way of asking her husband to accept and implement her decision over Hagar. Coincidentally, Genesis 13:1-13 confirms that Abraham had done something similar to his unappreciative nephew, Lot. If a visitor denigrates his host's treasure he deserves to be shown the doorway by the host. There are things that God's admonition that we strive to live in peace with all men does not cover or include.

Hagar's case is very striking in the sense that Genesis 16:1-16 says the same God who approved that she and her son could be sent away also ordered Hagar to return to Abraham's household just before Ishmael was born. Hagar left of her own accord earlier when she concluded that she could no longer bear the pains of the punishment by Sarah. But when Sarah made the demand some years after Hagar had returned to their household God agreed that it was the right time to let Hagar leave their household finally. It is not part of God's plan for a host to endure a stranger with intolerable character and conduct beyond what the host can tolerate.

As advisable, commendable and delightful as it is to be nice to fellow human, if the beneficiary of one's niceness would not appreciate it for whatever reason, God do not expect that benevolent should continue to waste his niceness efforts on such beneficiary. Even God does not and it is as a result that

He did not spare the sons of Eli. That is what I Samuel 2:22-36 can be interpreted to mean when it says He took away the privilege of the Aaronite priesthood that He gave to Eli's sons as descendants of Aaron who He appointed the High Priest lineage of Israel forever. It is not for strangers to dictate how natives should live their lives, it is an abomination in the principles and practices of the concept of migration management.

Just as they say respect is reciprocal so also reward is reciprocal, or kindness is reciprocal even if it would not be at the same level or equally. II Samuel 7:1-29 and I Chronicles 17:1-27 confirm that David reciprocated God's kindness as much as he could and it gladdened God enough to reward David for being so thoughtful. II Samuel 9:1-13 and 21:1-14 can be reasonably interpreted to mean that David reciprocated Jonathan's kindness just as II Samuel 17:27-29 and 19:31-29 and I Kings 2:7 confirm that he did not forget to reward Barzillai's kindness through their children after the death of Jonathan and Barzillai.

Natives should not be punished or abused to appease, traumatized to thrill, or frustrated to make migrants feel welcomed. Some say strangers should be protected from the abuse of natives without regard for the other side of the coin; how the natives should be reciprocated. Matthew 6:24 and Luke 16:13 say no man can serve God of heaven and mammon equally concurrently just as no one can show equal affection for two women at the same time. In the same way no one can please strangers and natives equally at the same time therefore, while pleasing strangers, people in authority are inevitably hurting and displeasing natives just as pleasing natives would be at the expense of strangers. Finding the balance is a challenge. It is like when Leviticus 20:22-23 and Ezekiel 11:12 imply that worshipping other gods displeases God of Israel automatically. Jeremiah 2:36 says by shifting their loyalty to other gods, the Israelites cheapened themselves because Deuteronomy 32:8-9 says while God assigned other spirits to serve as god to other nations He assigned Himself to serve as the God of the Israelites. Meanwhile, Exodus 18:9-11, Deuteronomy 10:17, Joshua 22:22, Psalm 136:2 and Daniel 2:47 and 11:36b confirm that He is the greatest of all gods. Jeremiah 2:11 confirms that it is not common for a people to change the god that they grew up accepting as the god of their ancestors and it is for this reason that God of Israel was greatly surprised that the Israelites could quickly accept other gods as His replacement.

There is the curious concept of liquidating love license or regrettable love reason. There is no doubt that Jesus showed the greatest love for others by dying for them, but it was never in vain. God the Father gave Him a greater reward for so doing. When it was said that Ahab sinned against God and did a lot of evil at the urging of Jezebel it typifies spouse sponsored wickedness. In the case of Ahab's Jezebel, I Kings 21:25-26, II Chronicles 18:1, 21:1-4, 22:1-4, 10-12 and Proverbs 29:21 say:

> 25 There was no one else who had devoted himself so completely to doing wrong in the Lord's sight as Ahab—all at the urging of his wife Jezebel. 26 He committed the most shameful sins by worshiping idols, as the Amorites had done, whom the Lord had driven out of the land as the people of Israel advanced.

1 When King Jehoshaphat of Judah became rich and famous, he arranged a marriage between a member of his family and the family of King Ahab of Israel.

1 Jehoshaphat died and was buried in the royal tombs in David's City and his son Jehoram succeeded him as king. 2 Jehoram son of King Jehoshaphat of Judah had six brothers: Azariah, Jehiel, Zechariah, Azariahu, Michael, and Shephatiah. 3 Their father gave them large amounts of gold, silver, and other valuable possessions, and placed each one in charge of one of the fortified cities of Judah. But because Jehoram was the oldest, Jehoshaphat made him his successor. 4 When Jehoram was in firm control of the kingdom, he had all his brothers killed, and also some Israelite officials.

1 Some Arabs had led a raid and killed all of King Jehoram's sons except Ahaziah, the youngest. So

now the people of Jerusalem made Ahaziah king as his father's successor. 2-3 Ahaziah became king at the age of twenty-two, and he ruled in Jerusalem for one year. Ahaziah also followed the example of King Ahab's family, since his mother Athaliah—the daughter of King Ahab and granddaughter of King Omri of Israel—gave him advice that led him into evil. 4 He sinned against the Lord, because after his father's death other members of King Ahab's family became his advisers, and they led to his downfall. 10 As soon as King Ahaziah's mother Athaliah learned of her son's murder, she gave orders for all the members of the royal family of Judah to be killed. 11 Ahaziah had a half sister, Jehosheba, who was married to a priest named Jehoiada. She secretly rescued one of Ahaziah's sons, Joash, took him away from the other princes who were about to be murdered and hid him and a nurse in a bedroom at the Temple. By keeping him hidden, she saved him from death at the hands of Athaliah. 12 For six years he remained there in hiding, while Athaliah ruled as queen.

21 If you give your servants everything they want from childhood on, some day they will take over everything you own. (TEV)

Apparently, Athaliah saw her mother manipulate her father to do all sorts of evil and concluded that it was the norm. Ecclesiastes 5:8b, Micah 3:9 and Habakkuk 1:4 confirm that there are persons who pervert the cause of justice. So, she made her husband kill his brothers without any deserving reason. Her husband did not know that some day after his death Athaliah would kill his grandsons to enable her take over his throne upon the death of his son and successor. If Jehoram had resisted Athaliah's encouragement to kill his brothers she would have understood that she could not do the kind of evil that her mother, Jezebel made her father do while Athaliah was growing up in the palace of Israel. When Jezebel was hurting the feelings of God of Israel, Ahab did not care because she seemed not to hurt him directly or in the immediate. However, we see Jezebel's daughter taking the art of evil doing that she learnt from her mother to the next notorious level by slaughtering her grandsons that were Ahab's great grandsons through her. It is like standing by while an evil doer hurts a neighbour, some day the evil doer would make the person who kept silent and watched from afar the next victim.

Let us note that the kingdom of Israel as ruled over by Eli, Samuel, Saul, David and Solomon broke up into the kingdom of Judah with the capital city at Jerusalem and kingdom of Israel with the capital city at Samaria since the reign of Rehoboam over Judah and Jeroboam over Israel. I Kings 22:51-53 confirms that Ahab's son became king of Israel after the death of Ahab. It means that just as Ahab's family was ruling over the kingdom of Israel in Samaria so also, they were ruling over the kingdom of Judah in Jerusalem via their daughter who was married to Jehoshaphat's son and successor as the king of Judah. When traced further backwards to I Kings 16:29-33 when Ahab acted as if he could not find any Israelite young woman to marry to be the queen of the kingdom of Israel and went to get a wife from the family of King Ethbaal of Sidon, it means that the Ethbaal ruling house of Sidon was ruling the kingdoms of Israel and Judah concurrently after the death of Ahab and Jehoshaphat.

Meanwhile, Deuteronomy 17:14-20 confirms in verse 15 that through Moses, God had commanded that (1) whoever would be king of Israel must be approved by their God and (2) such an individual must be an Israelite who must be able to read and meditate or study the Sacred Books containing God's commandments, (3) Numbers 27:18-23 says the king of Israel and by extension Judah must be guided by God only, which can be interpreted to mean that even if he would be anyone's stooge on the throne of Israel, he must be the stooge of God of Abraham, Isaac, Jacob and Israel only, not that of the ruling house of any other nation or country. However, once Ahab broke God's command in Deuteronomy 7:1-4 to not marry girls from other nations, he inadvertently opened the door of the kingdom of Israel for the foreigner to rule over them as God's chosen and special people.

I Kings 16:29 confirms that Ahab ruled for 22 years while I Kings 22:39-40 and 51 confirms that his son and successor,

Ahaziah ruled for two years. Then, II Kings 1:17 and 3:1 confirm that Ahaziah was succeeded by his brother, Joram who ruled over Israel for 12 years. Then, II Kings 8:16-18 says:

> 16 In the fifth year of the reign of Joram son of Ahab as king of Israel, Jehoram son of Jehoshaphat became king of Judah 17 at the age of thirty-two, and he ruled in Jerusalem for eight years. 18 His wife was Ahab's daughter, and like the family of Ahab he followed the evil ways of the kings of Israel. He sinned against the Lord. (TEV)

This means that 36 years after Ahab married Jezebel, she began to influence the king of Judah in addition to that of Israel via her daughter who was married to the king of Judah. Just as Ahab erred by getting his wife from outside Israel so also King Jehoshaphat erred by arranging marriage between his heir prince and the daughter of Ahab by Jezebel, Athaliah. It is a case of mistaken marriage hurting their heritage horribly – Ahab and Jehoshaphat must have arranged this marriage because they wanted to have relationship with a royal king colleague which can be interpreted as the manifestation of part of what I John 2:16 refers to as pride of life. It is like when II Samuel 12:1-25 and I Kings 7:1-12 say Solomon felt that his father's palace in Jerusalem where he was conceived and born was not befitting for him as king and he built the one that he considered much better and befitting of him. Ahab did not care that he did not share the same heritage and religious beliefs with the king and people of Sidon when he went to get a wife from his household just as Jehoshaphat cared less about the fact that Ahab and his family were not loyal to the God of their ancestors as expected of an Israelite. II Chronicles 19:1-3 confirms that God of Israel sent Prophet Jehu son of Hanani to reprimand Jehoshaphat for making alliance with Ahab and Jezebel. Ahab and Jehoshaphat can be said to have committed a monumental marital mistake by so doing.

Ahab became a victim of tolerance or torn into shreds by tolerance, liquidated by liberality, conquered, and caged by compromise, punctured, and pained by permissiveness, obliterated by openness, lambasted by large-heartedness as well as abused by alliance. It would have been better for him if he had married an Israelite commoner rather than the way he went to marry a non-Israelite probably because she was a princess. The claim in Proverbs 29:21 that no sensible master should give room under the guise of kindness and fair-play for his servant to shortchange him and his children mean that every nice master must or let us say should be strategic in his dealings with his servants just as natives should in their dealings with strangers. He should crosscheck the likely heart-hidden intent of his servant's utterances and actions. Abraham teaches an outstanding lesson in this regard when Genesis 15:1-4 and 24:1-10, 64-65 say:

> 1 After this, Abram had a vision and heard the Lord say to him, "Do not be afraid, Abram. I will shield you from danger and give you a great reward." 2 But Abram answered, "Sovereign Lord, what good will your reward do me, since I have no children? My only heir is Eliezer of Damascus. 3 You have given me no children, and one of my slaves will inherit my property." 4 Then he heard the Lord speaking to him again: "This slave

Eliezer will not inherit your property; your own son will be your heir."

1 Abraham was now very old, and the Lord had blessed him in everything he did. 2 He said to his oldest servant, who was in charge of all that he had, "Place your hand between my thighs and make a vow. 3 I want you to make a vow in the name of the Lord, the God of heaven and earth, that you will not choose a wife for my son from the people here in Canaan. 4 You must go back to the country where I was born and get a wife for my son Isaac from among my relatives." 5 But the servant asked, "What if the young woman will not leave home to come with me to this land? Shall I send your son back to the land you came from?" 6 Abraham answered, "Make sure that you don't send my son back there! 7 The Lord, the God of heaven, brought me from the home of my father and from the land of my relatives, and he solemnly promised me that he would give this land to my

descendants. He will send his angel before you, so that you can get a wife there for my son. 8 If the young woman is not willing to come with you, you will be free from this promise. But you must not under any circumstances take my son back there." 9 So the servant put his hand between the thighs of Abraham, his master, and made a vow to do what Abraham had asked. 10 The servant, who was in charge of Abraham's property, took ten of his master's camels and went to the city where Nahor had lived in northern Mesopotamia. 64 When Rebecca saw Isaac, she got down from her camel 65 and asked Abraham's servant, "Who is that man walking toward us in the field?" "He is my master," the servant answered. So she took her scarf and covered her face. (TEV)

Abraham had taken Lot along to Canaan as a substitute heir in case he never had his own child to inherit him. However, Genesis 13:1-13 recounts how Lot zealously left him behind to settle in Sodom. Then, the passage above says in the absence of

Lot and any other biological relative of Abraham, he told God that Eliezer who was the son of one of his slaves was the available likely heir to his wealth. Why would a rich man worry that one of his servants would transform into his child to inherit him? Why does he feel helpless, unable to stop the slave or domestic servant? Why would such a thought cross his mind in the first place? The reason is that he had observed that the servant was already behaving like the potential heir in the absence of his master's son or relative and he could not stop the slave because even if he used his authority to try to stop the servant, there was no son to replace the servant. Numbers 27:1-11 says Zelophehad's daughters followed in Abraham's footsteps to ask Moses to ask God to let them inherit their father since he died without a son to inherit him. Numbers 36:1-13 says God did not just approve their request but made it a law for the Israelites to live with forever.

That is a classic example of the concept of "Lack Lamed", "Lack made Lamb", "Lack Lambed", Lack Looped or Compelled Compromise, Cooperation and Collaboration" or "Lack Cheapened" – it means that because of lack he had to endure what he abhorred necessarily. Proverbs 18:23 says the poor pleads where the rich speaks boldly or courageously like Genesis 47:27-31 and 49:29-33 confirm that the same request which Jacob pleaded with Joseph to do for him, he shouted it down on Joseph's older brothers. The obvious reason was that Joseph was the most illustrious son of his family at the time. Genesis 15:1-17-detailed encounter between God and Abraham was before the birth of Ishmael, Abraham's first child ever when he was 86 years old. Then, Isaac who God meant to be his chief heir was born 14 years later or when he was 100 years old. This means that Eliezer witnessed the births of and watched Ishmael and Isaac grow up, Ishmael and his mother sent away, and Isaac attained the age of 40 when he was sent to get a wife for him. Eliezer had manifested the character and conduct of an ambitious servant seeking transformation into chief inheritor of Abraham much earlier hence Abraham voiced his opposition to it before Ishmael was born.

Abraham had realized this inordinate ambition of his for over 50 years before he was been sent to get Isaac a wife from among Abraham's relatives back in Mesopotamia. That is why when he tried to clarify with Abraham if he could take Isaac back to Mesopotamia, in case the girl would not come over to live with Isaac as a wife in Canaan Abraham forbade such relocation of Isaac away from Canaan. Abraham saw through Eliezer's game-plan. If Abraham had said he could return to take Isaac to Mesopotamia on the ground that the girl refused to come over to Canaan, Eliezer would simply go to Mesopotamia, spend some days without even looking for Abraham's relatives and return to Canaan to say he could not find any girl who agreed to come over to Canaan to marry Isaac. Therefore, Isaac should follow him to Mesopotamia to remain with the girl. That way, Eliezer would return to Canaan to take over Abraham's wealth which had been his greatest ambition for more than five decades. Abraham double crossed and stopped Eliezer in his tortuous track to take over his wealth even when he had gotten Isaac from God to serve as his heir.

What Eliezer tried to do to Abraham before he stopped Eliezer is what migrant could do to natives if the natives fail to deal strategically with migrants. Pharaoh dealt honestly with Joseph in the fairest manner possible. He placed higher emphasis on Joseph's excellent performance above his non-Egyptian background by appointing Joseph as his second-in-command to exercise authority over everyone else in his kingdom because Joseph was the only one who could interpret his dreams. However, such fair treatment did not stop Joseph from making slaves of the Egyptians when the Egyptians were most vulnerable economically. Only Joseph can tell if he enslaved the Egyptians to punish them for despising his Hebrew background. If it is, then it is a pointer to us that even if natives treat strangers fairly it would still not prevent the best of the strangers to repay the natives with evil because there was an instance when natives suggested that they despised strangers.

10

THE OBNOXIOUSNESS OF OVERSTAY

During house dedication I would pray that God should sanctify and abide in the house through His presence such that His peace, joy, and protection would be abundant to the inhabitants. Therefore, even if there is trouble everywhere else the occupants would be safe therein. This does not mean that it is every time that the owner or occupants should remain at home and never go out. Despite the fact that Genesis 18:14, Jeremiah 32:27 and Luke 1:37 confirm that God of Israel can do all things or that there is nothing impossible for Him to do, I Corinthians 6:18 says one of His recommended key solutions to the temptation to fornication is that the individual being tempted should flee from the environment that is breeding the temptation or the reach of the tempter. Now, this solution can be applied to the temptation of adultery as well.

So long as the Egyptian officials who were determined to kill Moses were still alive, the land of Egypt became the deadliest place for him. His best option was to relocate to Midian where he spent the next 40 years of his life even when he would still return to Egypt to spearhead the deliverance of his fellow Israelites from Egyptian bondage under God's supervision. Haven been brought up in the palace of Egypt as heir-prince, he understood that if he lived a day longer, he might not outlive his assailants and return to help his fellow Israelites 40 years later. It is a case of 'escape to outlive and return to rule and reign appropriately'. It is like the old saying that he who fights and run away lives to fight another day.

There is no doubt that Moses' escape extended the oppression and sufferings of the Israelites for extra 40 years considering that Exodus 1:8-22 and 2:1-25 confirm that their oppression started around the time Moses was born. Moses must have borne the pains of the suffering of the Israelites during the 40 years that he was away and could not protect them from their oppressors. Both he and the Israelites had to live with the oppression for the 40 years that it took for the Egyptian officials who wanted him dead remained in charge of the royal authority of Egypt. If he had not escaped when he did he would have been dead and not be able to help them 40 years later.

Much as God meant Moses to lead the Israelites out of Egypt it is striking that He did not quicken the death of Moses' assailants in order to get Moses to return to help the Israelites rather He let them die of natural causes over a 40-year period or let them live out the number of the years, months and days that Job 14:5, Psalm 39:4 and 139:16 and Acts 17:26 can be said to mean that He had assigned to them from the foundations of the world. This means that sometimes, God's solution for His chosen is to wait in hiding patiently until His appointed time. This agrees with Psalm 110:1, Matthew 22:44 and Hebrews 1:13b that say God's beloved should wait at His feet until He had put all his enemies under his footstool.

I Kings 11:14-25 recounts that Hadad escaped to Egypt until the death of David and his COAS, Joab and returned to his country of Edom to take over the throne of his ancestors as the only surviving prince of Edom. I Kings 11:28-42 and 12:1-23 recount how Jeroboam escaped to Egypt until after Solomon's death before he returned to become one of Solomon's successors to the throne of Israel while Solomon's son, Rehoboam ruled over the tribal kingdom of Judah concurrently. II Chronicles 22:10-12 and 23:1-15 confirm that the priest Jehoiada and his wife, Jehosheba hid Joash inside the temple in Jerusalem for seven years before leading rebellion against Joash's paternal grandmother, Queen Athaliah who had killed Joash's older brothers and took over their father's throne upon the death of their father seven years earlier.

Again, Acts 9:26-30 confirms that when the Greek-speaking Jews tried to kill Paul for converting from Judaism to Christianity, the Christians helped him to escape their threat to his life and he returned to his hometown of Tarsus where he remained until Acts 11:19-23 says Barnabas went to recall him to join him and other believers to preach the Gospel of Jesus at Antioch until

God indicated in Acts 13:1-3 that He meant Barnabas and Paul to serve as apostolic partners to the Gentiles. Also, Acts 12:1-24 confirms that when Peter had been rescued from Herod's beheading, he went into hiding until God orchestrated Herod's death. As a result Peter was able to return to lead the Christians from Jerusalem side-by-side with John.

In the same vein, much as God meant David to become king of Israel after King Saul, as long as Saul determined to kill him because of envy, the land of Israel became the wrong place for David to remain as long as Saul was still serving as the sitting king of Israel. As a result, David relocated to the land of the Philistines 16 months before Saul died in battle, coincidentally against the Philistines. David's delightful destiny pair, Jonathan who failed to join David to hide from his father who was determined to kill them both did not outlive his father because he opted to remain in the land of Israel. There is no doubt that Moses' delightful destiny pair, Aaron remained in Egypt during Moses' stay away but he was never the target of the Egyptian king and officials who wanted Moses dead without accomplishing God's plan for his stay on earth.

Now, II Samuel 5:6-12 and I Chronicles 11:4-8 confirm that when David built his palace in Jerusalem, he built a stronghold, fortress, or bunker to ensure his personal safety therein. Then, II Samuel 5:17-25 confirms that he hid inside this bunker to feel safe enough and concentrate to consult the God of Israel when the Philistines tried to capture him upon learning that he had been made the king of Israel in addition to Judah. Yet, II Samuel 11:1-27 and 12:1-23 can be interpreted to mean that King David became a victim of "Regrettable Remain" at his home/palace in Jerusalem in the sense that because he chose to remain there rather than go to the battle against the Ammonites as expected of him, he found himself in the environment in which he was tempted into committing twin evil of adultery and murder against Uriah. In his desperation to cover up the evil of impregnating Uriah's wife he used the Ammonites to kill Uriah in battle. Though he was at home, he stayed where he should not be and caused serious problems for himself, his household members, and the entire nation of Israel. The fact that the palace was his home did not make it safe for him at the time that he should have been physically present leading the warriors of Israel to defeat the army of Ammon with the support of God of Israel.

This means that there is when a man's house is the right place for him to be and there is when it is the wrong place to be. Saul's threats made the land of Israel the wrong place for David to be and it is as a result that I Samuel 27:1-12 confirms that David relocated to live among the Philistines for the 16 months preceding Saul's death. If he had refused to relocate, he might have been sorry for himself. I Samuel 19:11-24 says Saul's daughter, Michal told her husband, David that if he fails to escape from their home, he would be sorry for himself for staying put that night. The passage goes further to say that after God prevented Saul's efforts to capture David in Samuel's home at Ramah, David left Samuel's place for good. Michal meant that "My husband, if you stay put here because it's your home, you would be dead by morning" or "You stay you die".

The fact that David was anointed three different times did not make him escape the consequences of staying where he should not be at a point in time. The fact that he was considered as

God's beloved did not save him from the consequences of his own abode's overstay. All the misfortunes that II Samuel 13 – 20 catalogue to have happened to David's household members in particular and the people of Israel in general was authored by the singular mistake of staying at home because they were punishments for killing Uriah to have his wife. If he never killed Uriah, Amnon would not have raped his daughter, Tamah and Absalom would not have killed Amnon for so doing. Absalom would not have led rebellion that forced David out of his throne and palace in Jerusalem, the same palace where he committed adultery with Uriah's wife. Several thousands of Israelite warriors would not have died along with Absalom on the same day. The battle to quell Absalom's rebellion would never have taken place and David would not have had reason to replace Joab with Amasa and, Joab would not have had any reason to kill Amasa. David sourced the sorrow that befell the land of Israel from the rape of his daughter in II Samuel 13 to the killing of Sheba in II Samuel 20. The other significant part of the punishment for the killing of Uriah was that violence would never cease from occurring in his lineage.

The other point worthy of note is the likely reasons for overstaying. Did David remain in his palace against kings' spring season battlefield practices or norms because he was afraid of going to battle or he felt that he had capable warriors to win the battle without his personal participation? There must be a reason. He had built what he adjudged as a beautiful palace that provided him great comfort and convenience unlike in the past when he lived in caves and wilderness. The pleasure that became available to him in the palace could have lured his heart from the hazards of the battlefield. He might have thought that he had suffered a great deal since he joined Saul's royal service until he got to the point when II Samuel 5:11-12 and I Chronicles 14:1-2 confirm that King Hiram of Tyre provided him the materials and expertise to build a beautiful and befitting palace in Jerusalem. Interestingly, II Samuel 7:1-29 and I Chronicles 17:1-27 confirm that the beauty of his palace prompted him to consider building a temple for the sole purpose of the worship of the God of his ancestors who graciously made him king of Israel and Judah despite the fact that he was the youngest child of his father's household.

Whatever was David's probable reason for not going to the battlefield; whether it was to enjoy the comfort of his palace or the benefit of having competent warriors who could win battles without his personal participation, it turned out to be one of the most unwise decisions that he ever took during his lifetime. This highlights the fact that it is highly unprofitable to overstay for any reason whatsoever. Only God can rightly instruct an individual on the best time and seasons that anyone should spend wherever one lives because as Ecclesiastes 3:1-15 and Acts 17:24-26 can be said to strongly suggest or practically mean, He is the supreme chief-in-charge of times and seasons.

The death of Elimelech and his two sons, Mahlon and Chilion in the land of Moab started with his decision to take his household along to a foreign land to escape the temporary famine in his native land of Bethlehem. Usually, famine is a temporary experience. The one that Genesis 12:10-20 claim forced Abraham to relocate from Canaan to Egypt even though God had confirmed that He meant him to settle in Canaan eventually abated. The one that Genesis 26:1-33 says nearly forced Isaac to relocate to the land of Egypt before God said he should remain in the land of the Philistines abated eventually just as the one that Genesis 41-50 confirm to have led to Jacob's relocating with his family to join Joseph in Egypt where Jacob spent the final 17 years of his life abated after seven years. II Kings 8:1-6 confirms that the famine of the time of the rich woman of Shunem lasted for seven years. I Kings 17:1-5 and 18:1-2 confirm that the one that God can be said to have used Prophet Elijah to author in the land of Israel during the reign of King Ahab lasted for between two to three years. II Samuel 21:1-14 confirms that the one caused by King Saul's unjust attack on the Gibeonites during David's reign lasted for three years. Then, Acts 11:27-30 confirms that there was a famine when Claudius was the Emperor of the Roman Empire.

Ruth 1:1-21 can be said to mean that Elimelech refused to stay put in Bethlehem during the famine like many other Bethlehemites did. Consequently, only his wife, Naomi and the wife of Mahlon, Ruth a native of Moab returned to Bethlehem only after Naomi learnt that the famine had abated and furthermore, God of their ancestors had prospered the people of Bethlehem and the rest of Israel greatly. This suggests that

Elimelech left the impression that unless there is prosperity no location is worth staying. It is this belief that he left for his wife and two sons that might have made them continue to stay in Moab even after Elimelech's death until Mahlon and Chilion died without leaving a child behind. And even after the death of Mahlon and Chilion, Naomi still did not return until she learnt that God had prospered her native land. This highlights the subject of the economic factor or consideration determining migration. The longer Naomi delayed her relocation from Moab where her husband should not have taken her and their two sons in the first place, the more the misfortune of death of the male members of her household.

If she had taken her two sons and returned immediately after the death of their father, she might not have lost the two sons. It was a case of overstay enhanced obliteration of male members of the family. Economic benefit should not be the only consideration in relocation. There is no doubt that anyone can die anywhere he or she lives but it is quite strange that all the men died where they relocated. The people of Bethlehem who were surprised to see her return an incredibly sad individual might not have relocated elsewhere during the famine that her husband used as an excuse to relocate to the land of Moab. II Kings 8:1-6 gives the impression that the rich woman of Shunem rushed back to her hometown immediately the seven years of the famine ended because she had her estates to claim back. The claim in Ruth 4:1-5 that the closer relative should buy over Elimelech's field or estate from Naomi as well as marry Ruth meant that Elimelech had an estate that he left behind to relocate to the land of Moab because of famine. This means that Elimelech was not so poor that he did not own an estate among his people in Bethlehem. He just decided not to remain in his hometown where he had his own farmland to go and live where he did not have his own farmland because of temporary famine. He should not have gone outside Bethlehem not to talk of overstaying outside of it.

The rich woman of Shunem would not have gone outside the land of Israel if not for Elisha's counsel. This claim is based on the fact that II Kings 4:11-17 confirms in verse 13 that she once told Elisha that she was very contented with her life in her hometown and have no need of anything from anyone including Elisha as God's prophet. Until the subject of an heir to inherit her wealth was indicated she did not need any material thing from anyone. Again, II Kings 8:1-6 includes the fact that when she returned to the land of Israel seven years after the famine some persons had farmed her estates and the king of Israel had to order that the proceeds of her estate be given to her in full measure. It means that many of her people remained in the land of Israel during the seven years that she went to live among the Philistines in obedience to Elisha's counsel. Of course, all the Israelites could never have relocated outside the land of Israel because of seven years' famine. It means that because she had her wealth to return to in the land of Israel, she never spent a day longer than the seven years that Elisha had indicated to her to live away. If she had overstayed, she might never have met Elisha's servant, Gehazi talking to the king of Israel about her experiences with Elisha and particularly how Elisha had restored her son to life before Elisha died. Our focus will not allow us to dabble into the subject of a man of God who is able to use God's power at his disposal to resurrect a dead man or child but he himself still died of an ailment as was the case of Elisha or Jesus who brought Lazarus to life after been dead and buried for four days while he himself was killed by His assailants.

It was Abraham's famine forced relocation to the land of Egypt that led to the availability of Hagar who Sarah converted into Abraham's concubine that led to the conception and birth of Ishmael which in turn led to all the accompanying consequences. If Abraham never went to Egypt to escape famine in Canaan, there might never have been all that the Bible makes us to understand about the regrettable role of Hagar and her son in Abraham's household till date. Abraham and Elimelech can be said to have engaged in regrettable relocation that should never have happened in the first place. Let us remember that like in the case of Elimelech, when Abraham left Canaan for Egypt because of famine there must have been Canaanites who remained in their native land rather than relocating because of the famine. Most famine forced relocating natives forget that there are many of their colleagues who are not relocating, and they would not starve to death because of the famine by the time they would return if ever they return home. If the rich woman of Shunem never returned home after the seven years she would have lost her estates to the persons who took them over to farm in her absence and it would not have been the fault of the illegal occupiers or God but herself who failed to return to get back her estates.

Acts 9:1-19 specifies in verse 15-16 that God of Israel indicated from the very beginning of Apostle Paul's conversion from Judaism to Christianity that He foreordained him to serve as an apostle primarily to the Gentiles and secondarily to the Jews. There was an instance when God told Paul that he had overstayed among the Jews and should relocate to work among the Gentiles appropriately. The use of 'appropriately' means that if he continued to work as an apostle among the Jews just because of his Jewish background when he should have gone to work among the Gentiles then his stay and work among the Jews at such a time was inappropriate even when he was doing the very work that God foreordained him to do during his stay on earth. Along this line, Genesis 28:10-22, 31:1-55, 33:18-20, 34:1-31 and 35:1-5 can be said to mean that Jacob's settlement in Shechem rather than going straight to Bethel to pay the vow he made to God on his way to Laban's place 20 years earlier was inappropriate. Even the altar that Genesis 33:20 says he built to God of his ancestors at Shechem was inappropriate because that is not the place that God had expected him to settle upon his return from Laban's place. For this reason, God said he should leave Shechem to go and settle in Bethel and not forget to pay the vow that he made there 20 years earlier without been compelled. In the case of Apostle Paul, Acts 9:10-20 and 22:17-20 say:

> 10 There was a believer in Damascus named Ananias. He had a vision, in which the Lord said to him, "Ananias!" "Here I am, Lord," he answered. 11 The Lord said to him, "Get ready and go to Straight Street, and at the house of Judas ask for a man from Tarsus named Saul. He is praying, 12 and in a vision he has seen a man named Ananias come in and place his hands on him so that he might see again." 13 Ananias answered, "Lord, many people have told me about this man and about all the terrible things he has done to your people in Jerusalem. 14 And he has

come to Damascus with authority from the chief priests to arrest all who worship you." 15 The Lord said to him, "Go, because I have chosen him to serve me, to make my name known to Gentiles and kings and to the people of Israel. 16 And I myself will show him all that he must suffer for my sake." 17 So Ananias went, entered the house where Saul was, and placed his hands on him. "Brother Saul," he said, "the Lord has sent me—Jesus himself, who appeared to you on the road as you were coming here. He sent me so that you might see again and be filled with the Holy Spirit." 18 At once something like fish scales fell from Saul's eyes, and he was able to see again. He stood up and was baptized; 19 and after he had eaten, his strength came back. Saul stayed for a few days with the believers in Damascus. 20 He went straight to the synagogues and began to preach that Jesus was the Son of God.

17 "I went back to Jerusalem, and while I was praying in the Temple, I had a vision, 18 in which I saw the Lord, as he said to me, 'Hurry and leave Jerusalem quickly, because the people here will not accept your witness about me.' 19 'Lord,' I answered, 'they know very well that I went to the synagogues and arrested and beat those who believe in you. 20 And when your witness Stephen was put to death, I myself was there, approving of his murder and taking care of the cloaks of his murderers.' (TEV)

While Elimelech experienced regrettable relocation, it can be claimed that God meant that if Paul stayed any longer in Jerusalem, he would have experienced what we can call regrettable remain. This means that remaining against God's directive causes regret just as relocating against God's directive causes regret. Irrespective of the circumstances God should instruct the final decision to either relocate or remain. The passage above includes the fact that much as God's original plan include Paul's preaching among the Jews the core people, he should work among were the Gentiles therefore, he should not spend much time among the Jews. In any case, there were Jews living among the Gentiles among whom he worked even though the Jews in the land of the Gentiles were few just as the Gentiles in the land of the Jews that Peter and John were meant to work primarily among were few. What God really meant was that Paul was to work in the land of the Gentiles to preach to the majority Gentiles and the few Jews living among them.

I Samuel 27:1-12, 29:1-11, 30:1-29 and II Samuel 1:1-27 and 2:1-7 say King Saul of Israel's threats forced David to relocate from the land of Israel to live among the Philistines with King Achish as his chief host. After Saul's death, David asked God what he should do and God asked him to return to the territory of Judah and specifically to Judah's capital city of Hebron. When he got there the elders of Judah anointed him to become the king of Judah. David did this because he had known that God meant him to be king after the death of Saul. He did not waste time in asking God to indicate what his next action should be after the death of Saul. This means that he did not stay a day longer in the land of the Philistines. In fact, there is no indication that he went to formally notify his chief host, Achish before he relocated to Hebron. He gave the reason he left the land of Israel to live among the Philistines but not the reason he left Philistine to return to Israel.

11

Be Focused

As we know the famous story, Genesis 11:27-31, 12:1-9, Acts 7:1-4 and Hebrews 11:8-9 confirm that God led Abraham to relocate to Canaan with the plan that Abraham would claim the land for his future generations. It is important to note that he never lost focus of the reason he went there just as he did not divulge it to the original inhabitants for any reason whatsoever. Genesis 17:1-27, 18:1-15, 21:1-21, 22:1-19 and 24:1-10 confirm that apparently because Abraham was conscious of the fact that God meant his descendants through Isaac to inherit the land of Canaan, when Eliezer talked about the possibility of taking Isaac back to Mesopotamia under the guise of getting a wife, Abraham forbade it. Genesis 24:8b says rather, he prayed that God would guide Eliezer to get the girl who would be willing to come over to become Isaac's wife without seeing Isaac personally.

Abraham understood that God's command for him to relocate to Canaan and the choice of Isaac as the carrier of the covenant meant that relocating out of Canaan back to Mesopotamia was out of it for him and Isaac. He ensured that God's plans dictated what he did or did not do, what he approved for implementation or did not approve for implementation. When he met famine in Canaan, he went to Egypt and when he left Egypt, he returned to Canaan rather than return to his hometown of Ur in Mesopotamia of the Chaldees. He never considered relocating outside of Canaan. He knew his bounds and operated within it throughout.

Abraham did not engage himself in striving to become ruler of any locality in Canaan. He did not say because he had some friends among them who had a lot of respect for him, it was enough reason for him to seek to become a ruler of a portion of their territory. There are things that some foreigners involve themselves in that instigate natives to resent them. If a stranger dabbles into seeking positions that natives could not afford to seek and get, it is natural that the natives would resent the implied factor that a stranger came over to rule over them just because he became richer than them in their native land.

DDT means Don't Taunt the Troubled while DTAT means Don't Taunt the Already Troubled. DTF means Don't Trample the Fallen – not only by action but by words of mockery. Much as there is no attempt to necessarily lend support to Saul's attack of David, however, the functional truth is that Saul determined to kill David because David's killing of Goliath resulted in David stealing attention of his subjects, the Israelites from him as the sitting king of Israel. This has a deeper implication. When Saul would be made king of Israel probably nearly three decades before David killed Goliath, I Samuel 8:1-22 confirms in verse 20 that the Israelites whose demand for a king led to Saul's emergence as king of Israel, emphasized that their desired king would lead them to their battles to defeat their enemies. And accordingly, I Samuel 10:17-27 and 11:1-12 confirm that until Saul led the warriors of Israel to defeat the Ammonites the Israelites did not accept Saul as a worthy individual to rule over them. Furthermore, I Samuel 14:47-48 confirms that he led them to defeat their enemies heroically earlier in his reign. And that is what really made the failure to defeat Goliath and the Philistines later very humiliating for him.

It meant that he had begun to suffer the shame of failure to live up to the expectation of the Israelites who used to look up to him to lead the defeat of their enemies. By extension, he had lost the respect of his subjects. Therefore, even without the women of Israel exalting David above Saul as the sitting king of Israel, Saul was already traumatized by his inability to live up to the expectation of his subjects. That is what makes the women's elevation of David above him in their celebration being equivalent to adding insult to injury. It amounted to passing a vote of no confidence in Saul as the king of Israel formally and publicly. I Samuel 21:10-11 confirms that the celebration song of the women of Israel was well known to the Philistines or beyond the territory of Israel. This means that non-Israelites were aware that the Israelites did not respect Saul as their king any longer. It gave the impression that Saul was clinging to power unworthily. That is an integral part of the concept of "Success-Syndicated Sorrows", "Success-spilled/splashed Sorrows", "Success Rainbow" or "Success Sting/Spike". Success has both bitterness and sweetness. David's success saddened Saul while it sweetened the Israelites. While Jacob's love might have gladdened Joseph it saddened Joseph's older brothers. Goliath's family, friends and admirers could never have been glad or celebrated when David killed him while the women of Israel were celebrating.

David's killing of Goliath because Saul wasted the opportunity of the preceding 40 days and nights was more than an embarrassment for Saul. In addition to that embarrassment/shame is the realization that by that feat, the Israelites preferred David to be their king after him rather than his son, Jonathan, or any other son of his. Saul understood the devastating impact of David killing Goliath on his family and the attendant frustration was too painful for him to respond properly. Until David emerged on the national fame scene of Israel Saul considered the throne of Israel as his personal exclusive territory and David's killing of Goliath opened the door for David to sort of flagrantly encroach on his exclusive royal territory.

Accordingly, when a resident stranger transforms into ruler over the natives, it is viewed in like manner by the native. David came from the class of the downtrodden to steal the attention of Saul's subjects from him under the guise that David achieved one feat that Saul could not.

Apparently because he was conscious that he was a migrant, Abraham focused on his personal prosperity and did not dabble into the leadership tussles among the natives. He did not try to build and live in the best house in Canaan to prove that he had the backing of the greatest God of the universe. The benefit of God's prosperous and protective presence that Abraham enjoyed would have prompted some to become proud, arrogant and determine to prove some precarious and punitive points. The way God punished Pharaoh because he took Abraham's wife based on the half-truth that Abraham told him about Sarah being only his half-sister and not also his wife, Abraham could have said that he would not leave Egypt as Pharaoh ordered his officials to get him out of his domain. He could have defied Pharaoh's expulsion order to stay put in Egypt believing that

God would continue to punish Pharaoh and his household if Pharaoh punished him for refusing to leave Egypt.

Genesis 20:1-18 includes the fact that God instructed King Abimelech to get Abraham to pray for him and his household members to stop the punishment for taking Abraham's wife based on the half-truth that Abraham told Abimelech and his palace officials. First, Abraham could have asked for more payments of damages from Abimelech before offering prayers for God to heal Abimelech's household members. Secondly, he could have demanded that Abimelech appoint him as Abimelech's second-in-command equivalent of the position that Genesis 41:1-57 confirms that Pharaoh gave Joseph in Egypt in addition to the damages Abraham was paid. Rather, he was contented with whatever he was given as damages and prayed to God for Abimelech. If all migrants follow in Abraham's example in the matter of reasonable conduct among natives, the tension between migrants and natives would reduce considerably. Throughout the 100 years that he spent in Canaan before he died and was buried there, there is no record that he broke any laws of the land or the Canaanites.

First, I Samuel 17:1-58 specifies in verse 26-27 that when David first caught sight of and heard Goliath's boast his first question was what his reward from the king after he would have killed Goliath. By do so doing, he gave the impression that he was desperate for great reward for his services. Second, however, there is no record in I Samuel 27:1-12 to suggest that when he went to hide from Saul's threats to his life with King Achish of the Philistines he demanded a great reward from Achish to serve as Goliath's replacement. The way I Samuel 27:1-12 and 29:1-11 say Achish claim to have trusted David, if David had asked to be appointed as second-in-command to Achish on the throne of the Philistines in order to accept to serve as his loyal warrior like late Goliath, Achish would have agreed. Achish never thought that David only came over to his domain to escape Saul's threats to his life. He was elated to engage David to replace Goliath as his greatest warrior even though David killed Goliath.

The point is that David did not say that just because Achish seemed prepared to give him whatever he wanted as reward he would demand to be second-in-command to Achish as king of the Philistines. The reason we can claim or speculate is that

David knew that his mission in Achish's domain was to escape from and survive Saul so that he could return to the land of Israel to become king as I Samuel 16:1-13 confirms that God meant and revealed through Samuel that he ruled over Israel after Saul. I Samuel 3:8-20 and 5:1-3 and I Chronicles 11:1-3 attest to the fact that indeed, David outlived Saul and became king of Israel as God planned.

Apostle Paul knew his limits and remained within them as an apostle called, ordained, and ordered/commissioned by God to work mostly among the Gentiles or foreigners. He knew the difference between his God-assigned role and that of the likes of Peter and his apostolic teammates. He emphasized the difference between his role and that of the other apostles as well. He focused on his God-assigned territory. I Corinthians 3:1-16 and II Corinthians 10:13-16 confirm that Paul did not just understand his God-set boundaries and remained within it, he went a step further to write about it to the very people whom

God sent him to as his apostolic 'catchment area population'. II Timothy 2:4 says:

> 4 A soldier on active service wants to please his commanding officer and so does not get mixed up in the affairs of civilian life. (TEV)

David's commendable conduct of not getting involved in how the kingdom of the Philistines was ruled over by Achish is the kind of insight that Paul meant in the above passage, which was part of his letter to his disciple, Timothy. The point is that this is the kind of attitude that strangers should adopt while living among strangers. There is no doubt that Joseph became the second-in-command of the king of Egypt but that was because the king believed that he needed Joseph to steer the ship of his administration or regime in the next critical 14 years of his nation. David understood the plan of God for his life which was to serve as the king of Israel rather than high official in the palace of the Philistines. He knew why he went to live among them and remained within it. Now, it should be noted that David did not have to ask God formally before remaining within the limits of his self-set boundaries during his stay among the Philistines. Greed for what we do not deserve is one of the greatest sources of sorrow and sadness in the world. It can be inferred from Deuteronomy 17:14-15 that God of the universe meant natives to be ruled by one of their own rather than a foreigner. Therefore, any migrant who hides under any reason to seek to rule over natives against the wishes of the natives is courting avoidable trouble. Just as R&D means Research and Development there is also D & DR which means Define or Discover and Determine to Remain – migrant should confirm their boundaries among natives and remain within it rather than break their boundaries and begin to blame or blackmail natives as been intolerant of strangers.

It is not only rulers who are respected. The 70 elders God approved for Moses to appoint to support him to lead the Israelites in the wilderness were respected by the people before Moses chose them to lead along with him. What can be called National Council of Leading Citizens (NCLC) is made up of leaders in different spheres of life rather than only the national leaders. The council of leading citizens of any nation is made up of persons who have succeeded in their chosen fields of human endeavour. II Kings 25:8-12 and Jeremiah 52:12-16 give the impression that they include persons who have earned enough to own their own estates as well as palace officials and skilled persons. Isaiah 3:1-3 and Ezekiel 22:23-29 say they include the heroes, soldiers, judges, prophets, priests, fortune-tellers, statesmen, military and civilian leaders, politicians, government officials and the wealthy. Then, I Chronicles 25:4-6 and Job 29:5-10 say persons who are gifted enough to render service to the king in some form are included as well as those who make decisions in the cities that make up a nation. Numbers 11:16-17 says God told Moses to appoint already recognized leaders of Israel into his council of ministers. Even God in heaven knows that these men were regarded as deserving leading citizens of Israel by other Israelites or commoners. Amos 6:1 says they are the leading Israelites to whom the Israelite commoners' approach to solve their problems – they give hope to the masses of the nation.

Genesis 23:1-16 can be interpreted to mean that though Abraham was not the ruler of the land of the Hittite or governor of one of their districts, the notable citizens among the Hittites considered him a respectable resident in their community. The point is that Abraham did not say the fact that God sent him to take over the land was enough reason for him to seek to be among the rulers of the people immediately. If he had tried to, the Hittites would quickly suspect that he had an ulterior motive but by increasing his possessions, he was ultimately regarded as a great leader among them. When Genesis 17:15 quotes God as saying that there would be king among his descendants through Sarah Abraham understood correctly that God did not mean him to rule personally rather that royal rulership would be among his descendants. In fact, Genesis 25:1-10 and 26:1-5 can be interpreted to mean that there were wealth that Abraham deserved from God because of his obedience to God that God delayed its delivery until after the death of Abraham and gave or delivered it to Isaac because Isaac was Abraham's covenant child and chief inheritor or heir.

The choice child and the others mean Abraham's Isaac and his other children by other women; Sarah, Hagar and Keturah. Genesis 23:3-4 says Abraham still referred to himself as a stranger in Canaan when he went to negotiate for a parcel of land to use as his family's burial ground with the natives. This is very significant when we consider that Genesis 12:1-9, 17:15-17 and 21:1-5 confirm that Abraham had spent the previous 62 years of his life among the Canaanites when he still referred to himself as a stranger in Canaan. He said as long as he was a stranger or migrant he must pay for the land that he needed in the land of Canaan. One sensible interpretation is that he chose not to live in the illusion that there was no difference between him and his native friends and allies even when the friends tried to sell that "dummy" to him. Abraham understood or was conscious of the undeniable truth that he did not own any inherited land in Canaan like his native allies. He was aware that unlike his native friends his father, Terah was not buried in Canaan rather he was buried back in his ancestral hometown in Haran of Mesopotamia. He was conscious of the fact that he was referred to as a Hebrew by the locals because he crossed over the River Euphrates to settle among them. How could the same people who nicknamed you a migration-implied name tell you that you are one of them and you do not know that they are only cajoling or flattering you? Perhaps, because Abraham was quite old, 137 years old, it was easy for him to be honest to himself about his real status in Canaan.

As to how we arrived at the claim that Abraham had spent 62 years in Canaan, Genesis 12:1-9 confirms that he was 75 years old when he entered Canaan while Genesis 17:15-19 confirms that he was ten years older than Sarah therefore, when he was 75 years old Sarah was 65 years old. This means that when she died at 127, Abraham was 137 years old. When 75 is deducted from 137 we have 62 years. That is how we arrived at the claim that even after spending 62 years in Canaan Abraham still reiterated the fact that he was conscious that he is a stranger in Canaan. There is no doubt that he had spent a brief period in Egypt before he returned to Canaan and some time in the land of the Philistines with King Abimelech at Gerar of the Philistines. Genesis 21:22-34 says:

> 22 At that time Abimelech went with Phicol, the commander of his army, and said to Abraham, "God is with you in everything you do. 23 So make

a vow here in the presence of God that you will not deceive me, my children, or my descendants. I have been loyal to you, so promise that you will also be loyal to me and to this country in which you are living." 24 Abraham said, "I promise." 25 Abraham complained to Abimelech about a well which the servants of Abimelech had seized. 26 Abimelech said, "I don't know who did this. You didn't tell me about it, and this is the first I have heard of it." 27 Then Abraham gave some sheep and cattle to Abimelech, and the two of them made an agreement. 28 Abraham separated seven lambs from his flock, 29 and Abimelech asked him, "Why did you do that?" 30 Abraham answered, "Accept these seven lambs. By doing this, you admit that I am the one who dug this well." 31 And so the place was called Beersheba, because it was there that the two of them made a vow. 32 After they had made this agreement at Beersheba, Abimelech and Phicol went back to

Philistia. 33 Then Abraham planted a tamarisk tree in Beersheba and worshiped the Lord, the Everlasting God. 34 Abraham lived in Philistia for a long time. (TEV)

While the king of his host community honoured God in the life of migrant Abraham, verse 24-25 says the king's officials hurt him, without the king's approval and hearing about it. The meaning in contemporary times is that the government representing the king can make all the laws in this world to make migrants feel at home or welcomed yet, there would still be some natives who will continue to remind the migrants that they are not natives and cannot live freely like natives. Again, we see Abraham paying for his stay in the land of the Philistines. It is very striking that the passage says it was after making formal payment to the king that he is said to have lived among the Philistines for a long time. Until then, he could not enjoy respite among the Philistines.

Part of the crucial counsel here is that rather than any migrant spending a great deal of his time and effort seeking equal rights and treatment with natives they should channel their effort and time to what they can do to better their lives. It is worthy to note that Abraham never went out of his way to report to Abimelech that his officials were oppressing him in any way because he was a migrant even though it was apparent that it was part of the reason that they did. Abraham endured the unfair treatment of King Abimelech's officials until when Abimelech told Abraham that he and his fellow Philistines had been very fair in their dealings with Abraham. That was when Abraham thought it was the right moment to put the records straight before signing up to the peace agreement that Abimelech proposed. The peace agreement that Abimelech proposed can be likened to what in contemporary time is regarded as citizenship approval for Abraham as a settled migrant in the country. It would enable Abraham to enjoy full citizen's rights in the land of the Philistines.

Abraham meant that just because the law of the land approves that migrants should be treated fairly should not become the reason for migrants to spend all their time and effort shouting from the rooftop that natives are oppressing them. Any migrant who do such a thing is only wasting the precious time and effort that he should have spent to achieve tangible gains. Genesis 26 says Abraham's second son and chief inheritor, Isaac who experienced similar persecution from the same Philistines provided us another kind of solution to such resentful natives by relocating from the reach of the unfriendly persecutors rather than waste any time to force the authorities to punish his oppressors. The attitude of Abraham and Isaac strongly suggests that it is next to sheer waste of time to engage in a running battle with natives over fair or unfair treatment as a migrant. Abraham reinforced the concept of ignoring the inevitables. If one does not ignore the inevitables he would not amount to much in life. In any case, if you were living in your native land there is no assurance that your kinsmen and even relatives and siblings would not make your life hell on earth. After all, Saul was a fellow Israelite when he made life hell for David to the extent that David was forced to migrate to the land of the Philistines until Saul died. When migrants claim that they are been victimized by some natives, it is not always only because they are migrants. If such migrants are honest, they would agree that there are natives who are constantly at one another's throat just as there are migrants who are at another migrants' throat constantly. That is, there are natives attacking natives and migrants attacking migrants in the same country.

A pastor got into trouble with a pastor colleague on what was obviously a case of envy and jealousy probably because the victim held two positions at the same time in their denomination. One position at a local branch of their denomination and the second position which commanded considerable influence and respect was at the national headquarters. The antagonistic pastor held position only at another local branch of their denomination. Whether curiously or coincidentally or both, this antagonistic pastor happened to speak the same native language/mother-tongue as his victim. It was one of the reasons that he told me the story. Majority of the pastors in his denomination were from other tribes and, according to him, he seems to have had far better relationship with these other pastors from other tribes than this one with whom we speak the same native language. That is why it is sheer self-deception belonging to any nativity association.

If someone would hate you not even sibling-hood would stop them otherwise, Cain would not have killed Abel, Joseph's older brothers would not have threatened his life, Jacob's maternal uncle would not have treated him badly while Joseph's non-Israelite masters were fairer and kinder to him in Egypt just as Moses' non-Israelite father-in-law was kinder to him than Jacob's uncle turned father-in-law was to Jacob. It is blackmail of natives when migrants accuse them of racism over every little disagreement when the migrants know deep down in their hearts that they left home because their own people wanted to kill them. Some would seek asylum on the ground that they are fleeing threat to their lives in their native land. Then, after being granted the asylum they begin to say some natives are treating them unfairly on account of racial discrimination. How do you have the guts to say your hosts are discriminating against you, the same people who provided you a safe haven from your own kinsmen who you claimed tried to kill you. It does not add up. It is either you lied earlier that your kinsmen tried to kill you in order to get asylum to live in that country falsely or you are just trying to blackmail the natives who's authorities were humane enough to consider your claims favorably and granted you asylum.

On the part of natives, the time and effort being spent persecuting strangers or migrants, they should invest it in productive endeavour to prosper their life and family members. Imagine Isaac's experience with the Philistines, while they filled the wells he dug in their locality, Isaac continued to dig new ones. The more they wasted his efforts the more he dug new ones until he dug outside their territory and they lost the right or native authority and control to cover his wells. There is no doubt that they wasted some of Isaac's efforts but at the end while Isaac had a well or wells it was the Philistines who did not have. The efforts and time that they invested in covering up Isaac's dug wells they should have spent to dig their own wells so that just as Isaac had his own wells, they too would have had their own wells. It was the same thing with the efforts and time that they invested in covering up Abraham's well. It is like people who spend a lot of effort and time to plan and steal from their neighbours. It is the most unwise thing to do because the effort that goes into stealing and covering up the act so that one would not be caught would give more gains when spent on legitimate means of getting one's heart desire.

There are rulers who support the atrocities that their officials commit just as there are rulers who do not even known that their officials are committing atrocities. Abimelech did not know about the atrocities that his officials were committing against Abraham. Ecclesiastes 5:8-9 confirms that there are atrocities that the ruler approves for his officials to perpetuate on the populace or subjects because he and his officials benefit from it. Genesis 41:53-57 and 47:13-26 simply mean that Pharaoh approved that his appointed most powerful official, Joseph son of Jacob should make a mince meat of his subjects during the worst five years of the seven-year famine. It says when Pharaoh was told that Joseph was introducing some sadistic measures to manage the economy of the nation rather than investigate and order Joseph to let his policies have human face, he ordered them to return to do whatever Joseph instructed them to do. Genesis 47:13-14 can be said to mean that the most likely reason that Pharaoh ordered the Egyptians to return to comply with

Joseph's policies was that Joseph was taking all the mega profits to the safe of Pharaoh in the palace.

When lieutenants want to oppress the populace, they know how to compromise their boss' conscience – give the boss personal profit. Esther 3:8-11 says when Haman needed his boss, the Emperor's approval to deal decisively with the Jews because of what he saw as Mordecai's insolence, he told the Emperor that if he gave his approval he would enrich the Emperor greatly. Once the Emperor heard that he would gain personally, he approved without asking for details. As a result, the Emperor signed away the life of his beloved queen who was a Jew and Mordecai's cousin. Lieutenants know how to use money to extract authority from their boss to deal wickedly and recklessly with the subjects or desperate clients. Philippians 3:19b says there are persons who's god is their belly or personal benefit and gain. In like manner, while lieutenants treat their boss as their gods the boss treat reward, gain and personal benefit as their god. It is part of the reason Zephaniah 1:9 says there are lieutenants who go as far as killing vulnerable subjects to fill their boss' home with ill-gotten wealth. It can be called Rulers Regard Reward

Regrettably or Rulers' Regrettable Regard/Request for Reward/ Revenue. Rulers regard reward to the extent that it causes regret is the point. Along this line, Nehemiah 5:14-18 says:

> 14 During all the twelve years that I was governor of the land of Judah, from the twentieth year that Artaxerxes was emperor until his thirty-second year, neither my relatives nor I ate the food I was entitled to have as governor. 15 Every governor who had been in office before me had been a burden to the people and had demanded forty silver coins a day for food and wine. Even their servants had oppressed the people. But I acted differently, because I honored God. 16 I put all my energy into rebuilding the wall and did not acquire any property. Everyone who worked for me joined in the rebuilding. 17 I regularly fed at my table a hundred and fifty of the Jewish people and their leaders, besides all the people who came to me from the surrounding nations. 18 Every day I served one beef, six of the best sheep, and many

chickens, and every ten days I provided a fresh supply of wine. But I knew what heavy burdens the people had to bear, and so I did not claim the allowance that the governor is entitled to. (TEV)

Supposing the governors before Nehemiah had ruled for a total of 120 years, considering that God original duration for the Babylonian captivity was 70 years and by the time of Nehemiah it was long past 70 years. Daniel 9:1-3 confirms that the 70 years was completed during the first year of the reign of Darius the Mede over Babylon. Daniel 5:1-30 tells how Darius succeeded the son of King Nebuchadnezzar of Babylon. It means that for more than 70 years the governors of Judah watched their lieutenants oppress the poor who are usually in the majority in the nation or region. Nehemiah made a conscious effort to prevent such experience during the 12 years that he served as governor.

There is no assurance that Nehemiah's successors followed in his exemplary style of working for the wellbeing of the poor and weak subjects. The weak Jews enjoyed 12 years of relief which can be adjudged to be less than enough compensation for 70 or more years of suffering in the hands of their rulers and their lieutenants. If the relief period would not be more it should at least be equal to the years of suffering like Psalm 90:15-17 says Moses, the man of God pleaded with God to give as much happiness. Along this line, Judges 3:12-14 and 30 confirms that after God used Othniel to free the Israelites from 18-year long sufferings or oppression in the hands of King Eglon of Moab they enjoyed 80-year period of peace or freedom from foreign oppression. This means that for every year that they were oppressed God compensated them with four years and four months of peace.

Furthermore, Judges 4:1-3 and 5:31b confirms that after God let King Jabin oppress the Israelites for 20 years, He used Barak and Deborah to free the Israelites and they enjoyed peace for 40 years or two years of peace for every one year of suffering. Then, Judges 6:1 and 8:28 say after using the Midianites to punish the Israelites for seven years, God empowered Gideon to free the Israelites from the oppression of the Midianites and the Israelites enjoyed a 40-year period of peace. Judges 9:22 and 10:1-5 say

Gideon's 40-year peaceful reign was followed by Abimelech's three years rule, Tola's 20-year reign and Jair's 22-year rule. This is a total of 85 years of peace after freeing the Israelites from Midianites' 7-year oppression. This means that for every one year that the Israelites suffered when God put them at the mercy of the Midianites God let them enjoy 12 years and one month of peace after He had used Gideon to free them from the Midianites.

Judges 10:6-8 says when the Israelites offended again, God let them be oppressed by the Philistines and Moabites for 18 years before sending Jephthah to free them and enjoyed peace under Jephthah's rule for six years. Judges 12:7-15 says Jephthah's six years was followed by Ibzah's 7-year rule, Elon's 10-year rule and Abdon's 8-year rule (6+7+10+8=31÷18=1.7) which means that for every one year of oppression God let the Israelites enjoy a year and seven months of peace.

One of the key points in the foregoing is that people of God run into trouble because they dabble into the realm of greatness that God meant for their descendants rather than themselves personally. We know the famous story of David in this respect. Once God said that his son would take the credit for building the Temple, the idea of which he conceived, David did not struggle with God's decision on it. God accused him of shedding too much human blood in his lifetime and very interestingly, David did not turn round to accuse God of being the one who sent him to live as a warrior and, in fact, helped him to shed the blood for which God now adjudged him guilty and disqualified from taking credit for building the Temple. If David had, he would have followed in Adam's footsteps when he implied in his defense that if God had not given him a wife, he would not have agreed with her to disobey God.

It is important to note that God, who is Spirit commanded Abraham's migration to live as a stranger among the Canaanites which means that there was a spiritual undertone to his relocation or migrant status in Canaan. It can be said to stress the importance of the need for spiritual guidance in migration. Genesis 15:1-17, Psalm 105:16-25 and Acts 7:1-35 confirm that the Israelites' sojourn in Egypt which Genesis 37, 39-50 and Exodus 1-15 can be said to detail had spiritual undertone as well. Genesis 26:1-6 can be said to mean that Isaac's stay in Gerar during famine had spiritual undertone considering that God of Israel ordered him to remain there. Jeremiah 29:1-11 says God meant the Jews' migrant status in Babylon to endure for 70 years. Ruth 1:1-22 can be said to mean that when Elimelech relocated without God's guidance he and his sons did return to Bethlehem while II Kings 8:1-6 can be said to confirm that the rich woman of Shunem relocated by necessary and rewarding spiritual guidance and never regretted it. While God authored the Jews' 70-year Babylonian captivity it was Ruth who invited the same God of the universe into her determination to relocate from her native land of Moab to the land of Israel as permanent resident.

Abraham did not divulge what God told him about his sojourn in Canaan to his hosts but took strategic steps towards it by paying the full price for a landed property or estate so that his future generations can lay claim to a part of the land in Canaan. He acquired land and built a house which his descendants could relate to as their ancestral home in Canaan. He dug wells just as he acquired servants in Canaan. On the part of host nations or natives, they should be concerned about the spiritual undertone of migrants' relocation. Just as the Canaanites were not aware of the spiritual undertone to Abraham's presence in their territory so also the Egyptians were not aware of the spiritual undertone to the relocation of the Israelites to their nation or country. It was beyond the seeming economic reason that was known to the Egyptians. The Canaanites did not know that some 500 years later Abraham through his descendants would take over their land from the natives' descendants. The Egyptians did not know that 430 years later the Israelites would carry away their nation's wealth.

This can be called "Migrants' Monstrous Metamorphoses", "Migrants' Malignant Metamorphosis" or "Migrants' Tortuous Transformation". This damage is more than the immediate common crime of stealing by migrants. In the case of the Egyptians, the first evil that one of them by the name of Joseph did was to enslave the Egyptians to their king. Until Joseph became the manager of their economy, it was not their custom for their king to get part of their land and its produce. It was Joseph who hid under the guise of famine to force that policy down their throat. Genesis 47:13-26 concludes in verse 26 that when the famine ended, he never deemed it fit to reverse the precarious policy. In a way, it is some sort of 'migrant manufactured' pain on natives. God did not say Joseph should ensure the Egyptians were enslaved to their king during the period of his greatness in Egypt.

Then, in addition to the pain that Joseph caused the Egyptians while he served as their Prime Minister much later, there was also the misfortune of the Israelites or Joseph's people taking away their wealth. The same way Joseph caused them pain economically so also his people who outlived him caused them pain economically. So, what did the Egyptians gain from Joseph and his fellow migrants? By enslaving the Egyptian commoners to their king, Joseph took away the confidence of the average Egyptian. He widened the gap between the king and the people wealth wise. Joseph's attitude as governor or public officer/administrator typifies government officials' attitude to the populace – they exploit every opportunity to lord themselves and their employer or boss over the people. This is what Ezekiel 22:25 and 27 mean when it says "The leaders are like lions roaring over the animals they have killed. They kill the people, take all the money and property they can get, and by their murders leave many widows. The government officials are like wolves tearing apart the animals they have killed. They commit murder to get rich. (TEV)" Nothing has changed.

The other significant point that their story proves is that both the generation that arrived and the generation born in the land would never love the natives in the real sense. Because of Joseph's Prime Minister position, the generation of Israelites who arrived were fed free while the Egyptians who grew the grains during the years of bumper harvest paid for the same grain. There is no mention that Joseph gave discount to Egyptians when selling the grains to them. It means that Joseph ensured that the Egyptians paid the same price as the non-Egyptians who Genesis 47:53-57 says travelled from other parts of the world to buy grains from Joseph. Of course, since he was not an Egyptian originally he was more loyal to non-Egyptians than to the Egyptians or the best he could do was to treat the Egyptians and non-Egyptians equally without regard for the fact that the Egyptians produced the grain he stored and resold. God knew that a migrant can never work for the good of the natives genuinely hence He used Moses to say in Deuteronomy 17:14-15 that natives should never allow a foreigner to rule over them. It would be unreasonable for anyone to say that it was God who manipulated the circumstances that forced Pharaoh to make Joseph the Prime Minister of Egypt. The reason is simple.

When God made him to appoint Joseph, God gave him the wisdom to leave a safety belt or leverage of authority. God did not manipulate him to surrender his authority completely to Joseph. However, throughout the period that Joseph ruled over Pharaoh's fellow Egyptians on behalf of Pharaoh there is no record that Pharaoh made it a duty to check on Joseph's conduct and particularly as it pertained to the treatment of his fellow Egyptians. Genesis 47:14 can be interpreted to mean that as long as Joseph was bringing him money in his palace daily he did not care about the wellbeing of his own people enough to go out to visit and hear about their feelings. Genesis 41:53-57 says once the Egyptians by-passed Joseph to go and talk to him to help them and without finding out the reason for their concern, he told them to return to obey whatever Joseph instructed them to do. What can the people do when one of their own who had the authority to curb Joseph's or a foreigner's excesses says they must return to obey 'whatever' the foreigner tells them to do? Their kinsman put them at the mercy of a migrant. Most natives who insist that migrants must be allowed to have a field day do so for their own selfish reason. The reason it was easy for Boaz to embrace Ruth more than any other Bethlehemite was that Boaz's mother, Rahab was originally from the city of Jericho. What Elimelech's closer relative did in rejecting Ruth was partly because he was an undiluted Israelite unlike Boaz.

It is like what Solomon's heathen and foreign wives did to him, Ahab's non-Israelite wife, Jezebel did to him, and their daughters did to their husbands who were kings of Judah. This is what we can call the "Sojourner's Strangeness" or "Sojourner's Strange Style". Solomon's non-Israelite wives like Jezebel and her daughters sunk their husbands spiritually in the sense that they made their husbands to lose their cordial relationship with God of their ancestors. Pharaoh granted faulty freedom to migrant Joseph who he used to make mincemeat of Pharaoh's kinsmen, the Egyptians just like King Ahab let Jezebel to do to his fellow Israelites who were his subjects.

There is a concept that can be summed up as "God's ... Does Not Mean ...". Even though God was with Joseph and would make him great in Egypt, Joseph still suffered earlier. One key point is that the fact that God sent you to live anywhere, His presence is with you there as well as even provided you with a powerful benefactor who is a native does not mean that you will be 100% trouble free. It only means that no matter the challenges you would overcome with His help partly because of the aims and objectives that He meant to use you to achieve in that foreign land. Genesis 12:1-20 and 20:1-13 say much as God guided Abraham to migrate to the land of Canaan, Abraham still met famine there, he could not trust that the natives feared God enough to not hurt him over his beautiful wife. Genesis 20:1-13 and 21:22-34 can be interpreted to mean that despite the fact that God had threatened King Abimelech, his officials and subjects to beware of Abraham and his household otherwise He would punish them if they hurt him and members of his household yet Abimelech's officials still made efforts to afflict Abraham by covering up the wells he dug. There are disobedience dogmas who the threats of punishment spur them to continue in disobedient acts.

Genesis 26:1-6 and 12-33 confirms that though it was God who asked Isaac to live in Gerar among the Philistines, they still persecuted him because they are envious of the miraculous prosperity that God engineered and established in his life within a short period. God's undeniable help and blessing anywhere is a double-edged sword. It would make some people respect and revere you while it would make others resent and persecute you. Isaac engaged or practiced DTD – Deter The Distraction, Defeat The Distractions or Dispel The Distractions to delight yourself by achieving your aims and objectives. It is like saying drown the distractions to deliver your delight. DDT means Delighted Despite the Troubles or MMM which means Manage the Mess Marvelously or Muzzle the Mess Maker.

It is like David's killing of Goliath, while it earned him fame, respect and honour among the majority of the Israelites and in fact, endeared him to the heart of King Saul's eldest son and preferred heir, Jonathan, it offended Saul as sitting king of Israel so much that he determined to kill David. While some Israelites revered David for it, there were some who loathed David and in fact, reported David's presence in their locality to Saul so that Saul could come over to kill David in their locality. I Samuel 25:2-42 says while Abigail revered David, her husband, Nabal despised David so much that even God could not help punishing Nabal fatally. Also, I Samuel 21:1-10 and 22:6-19 say while the priest Ahimelech respected David greatly, Ziba supported Saul against David and whoever had any affiliation with David. Genesis 28:10-23, 29:1-35, 30:1-43 and 31:1-42 can be interpreted to mean that though God accompanied Jacob to live in Haran as a stranger, he still experienced all sorts of troubles in the hands of his chief host, maternal uncle, fathers-in-law and employer, Laban. Despite his troubles, God protected and helped him prevail over Laban by the end of his 20 years stay.

Another important issue about a migrant being focused is the subject of setting goals and targets early enough or upon arrival. It can be summed up as 'Define Purpose, Plan and Pursue to achieve it in earnest'. The reason this is important is that like any effort to achieve in life, there would be distractions. There would be all sorts of things that would attempt to distract you from achieving and ending well. All such distractions must be stopped. Imagine the magnitude of embarrassment if Jacob had returned from Laban's place empty-handed while his brother, Esau had become so wealthy that he could afford to reject Jacob's gifts. The fact that God personally ensured that Jacob did not return from Laban's place empty-handed can be used as a basis to say it is not necessarily carnality and worldliness for anyone who went to live abroad to ensure that he or she has wealth to show for his or her stay away from his own people for a long while. God takes note of whether a migrant returned empty-handed or full, particularly anyone that claims to be a child of God by reason of the God-initiated Abrahamic covenant.

In a way, Esau was a stranger in Canaan considering that we are told that fundamentally, God assigned the hill-country of the Edomites to him and his descendants. While Esau was a stranger in Canaan where he was born, his twin brother, Jacob was a stranger outside Canaan. Therefore, we can argue without fear of controversy that God ensured that while Esau lived in his spiritual foreign land, he earned enough wealth to take away to establish his own kingdom in Edom by the time Jacob returned to the land of Canaan, their traditional family house and compound. Meanwhile, this is the same Esau whom Malachi 1:2-3 and Romans 9:13 confirm that God said He did not love as much as He loved Jacob and his descendants. This can be said to mean that even persons whom God do not like just like Esau, God do not expect them to go to a foreign land and return to settle in their native land without bringing back something tangible and enviable to show as their admirable achievement during their sojourn. Nehemiah 1-13 can be said to mean that Nehemiah returned from Suza with the clout and resources to rebuild Jerusalem and restore the values that distinguished his fellow Jews from all other nations of the world. It is only for the sake of niceties that we shall not say that it is both disgusting and disgracing for a sojourner abroad to return home without something to better the lot of the kinsmen he or she left behind.

Ezra and Nehemiah can be said to have led their fellow Jewish migrants back to their native land to add value to the life of their fellow Jews who were back home in Jerusalem and Judah. Along this line, Genesis 28-33 confirms that when Jacob returned to Canaan after 20 years migration, he was able to afford to pay for an estate where he built his own home to settle. Genesis 34:23-24 says he had great wealth that the king and men of Shechem coveted. Also, Luke 19:12-15 says:

> 12 ... There was once a man of high rank who was going to a country far away to be made king, after which he planned to come back home. 14 Now, his countrymen hated him, and so they sent messengers after him to say, 'we don't want this man to be our king.' 15 The man was made king and came back ... (TEV)

This man had a specific objective when he left home. He knew or determined to return an empowered and greater member of his native community. He was so focused that those who did not want him to prosper as he desired by the time he returned failed in their bid. The rest of the story says he equally made some arrangement for his return. Just as this man left his servants to tend his business at home while he was away, II Samuel 15:16 and 16:22 confirm that David left ten of his concubines to take care of his palace in his absence. It means that David was sure that somehow, he would quell Absalom's rebellion and return to rule in Jerusalem. Genesis 28:10-22 confirms that Jacob asked God to help him to return to Canaan prosperous.

As much as possible it is unacceptable and probably unforgiveable for a sojourner abroad to return not far richer and better than most of his peers that he left behind at home. This is a profoundly serious matter. Genesis 24:34-61 recounts the famous story of the time when Abraham's chief servant, Eliezer recounted the magnitude of his boss's wealth since he left the relatives in Mesopotamia to live in Canaan. His boss's brother, Nahor and his household members were so elated that Rebecca was eager to leave the family behind to become Isaac's wife in Canaan where she was going for the very first time in her life. There is no record that she ever returned to visit the parents, siblings, relatives, and other acquaintances that she left behind to marry

Isaac. This strongly suggests that she was excited about the foreign land where she was taken to marry that she never desired to even pay a flying visit to her parents and place of birth.

Abraham did not return to settle in Haran or Mesopotamia with the wealth that God gave him in his land of sojourn or lived as a resident migrant but when his relatives would hear about how he was doing it was that those of them at home seemed not richer or that in fact, he was richer than them. He could not have attained that level of greatness if he were fighting one battle after another over fair or unfair treatment by his hosts in Canaan. Once he left home or while in Canaan the children, he never had at home were born to him. The wealth he took from Haran to Canaan increased astronomically. Much as he gave up his entitled/inheritable estates in his ancestral home, he was able to acquire estates in Canaan where he went to live as a migrant.

Genesis 28-31 can be said to mean that Rebecca's son, Jacob had the capacity to prosper more than her brother, Laban's children. Let us remember that Rebecca was a marriage-motivated migrant away from their native land of Haran or Mesopotamia where her brother remained and raised his family. Genesis 32-33 and 36 confirm that Rebecca's children, Esau, and Jacob were so prosperous that they had to live apart from each other. Rebecca's Jacob made Laban and his family richer during his 20-year stay. He was so beneficial that when he determined to return to Canaan, Laban did not want him to leave. Because of Jacob's prosperity prowess Laban's daughters preferred to return to Canaan with Jacob rather than remain with Laban and their brothers. Since he had the secret that prospered Laban's family, it is logical to say after he returned to Canaan Laban's family's fortune dwindled. The point is that Rebecca who left home to become a migrant eventually became better than the family members she left behind at their family's native land.

Migrants should strive to return richer, stronger, wiser, and rewardingly. Genesis 29:1-16 gives the impression that until Jacob arrived in Laban's household and business it seemed that it was Laban's daughter, Rachel who served as his household business manager. Only God can tell what his sons were doing at home while their sister managed their father's flock. More importantly, it was Jacob who came from Canaan where their father's sister had gone to settle as a marital migrant who put an end to that practice when he took over that job and turned round the fortunes of the business noticeably within the first month of his employment. When migrants or their children return home to the migrant's native land, they must introduce better ways of doing things that would produce overwhelmingly refreshing results.

In this respect, it was Samuel who returned from Shiloh to his hometown of Ramah who made Ramah relevant nationally because he operated from there as the ruler of the nation of Israel. There is too much at stake for any migrant to have the time for frivolities where he lives as migrant. Much is expected from them and their children whenever they return home whether on short visit or resettlement after many years abroad. The relevant concept here is "They Are Waiting" or "They Are Expectant". It was migrant Moses in Midian who God found worthy to free the Israelites from their Egyptian oppressors. Moses and his generation of Israelites were born and bred in Egypt. He happened to be the only one who lived abroad for as long as 40 years. Rather than engage any of the Israelites who never left Egypt God chose to go all the way to the land of Midian where Moses was a migrant to recruit him to return to help the Israelites who were back home in Egypt who could not help themselves or God could not find anyone suitable among them to use to free them from their oppressors.

It was Ezra and Nehemiah who lived abroad who returned to add value to the lives of their fellow Jews back in their native land of Judah. The case of Ezra and Nehemiah is very striking in the sense that though they lived away from their native land they seemed more committed to the wellbeing of their native land and home-based kinsmen. It was Ezra who was not at home who spent his time to study the sacred books and religious life of the Jews more than the Jews who remained or lived in Jerusalem and other parts of Judah. It is like saying though Ezra lived abroad he was committed to their ancestral heritage more than the Jews who lived at home. That is very unusual. What were the people at home doing while a live-away kinsman was acquainting himself with their heritage? Now, Ezra and Nehemiah were part of the captivity migrants or those who were taken away to live as migrants against their wish. Their parents or great grandparents were carried captive and they were probably born abroad. Yet, they were committed to their ancestral heritage more than those who were fortunate to have remained at home. Those left at home were overwhelmed by the poverty-pummeled/plated/paneled plight. This is confirmed when Nehemiah 1:1-4 says:

> 1 This is the account of what Nehemiah son of Hacaliah accomplished. In the month of Kislev in the twentieth year that Artaxerxes was emperor of Persia, I Nehemiah, was in Suza, the capital city. 2 Hanani, one of my brothers, arrived from Judah with a group of other men, and I asked them about Jerusalem and about our fellow-Jews who had returned from exile in Babylonia. 3 They told me that those who had survived and were back in the homeland were in great difficulty and that the foreigners who lived near by looked down on them. They also told me that the walls of Jerusalem were broken down and that the gates

had not been restored since the time they were burnt. 4 When I heard all this, I sat down and wept. For several days I mourned and did not eat. I prayed to God. (TEV)

Do you see the essential matters arising from the above passage? It says some who had returned home without the necessary capacity to solve the problems that they met in their native land were living with depression. We can claim that it is as a result that Nehemiah ensured that he returned with what he required to make positive impact. If he was not good enough in his catering profession to the extent of working for the Emperor, he could not have gotten the approval of the emperor to return to help his native land and kinsmen living there. Before we continue, it is part of the reason we admonish in this chapter that migrants should focus on how they can empower themselves so that, if necessary, they could be in position to return home to help their people who cannot help themselves. It is noteworthy that there were returnee migrants who could not do anything except to join those who never left home to bear the shame and frustration of the despising of non-Jews who lived around them. It is not enough to be fortunate to survive in a foreign land and return home alive, it is expedient to be in the position to add value to the lives of those at home upon your return home. Nehemiah 1:5-11 and 2:1-20 tell how Nehemiah got the approval of the Emperor to return to Jerusalem to solve the problem that the Jews were facing that was of concern to him. Nehemiah 8:1-12 confirms how Nehemiah involved Ezra in making the Jews do the right thing in compliance with their ancestral and religious heritage in Jerusalem. Of course, Ezra 1:1-11 and Nehemiah 1:1-11 and 2:1-20 confirm the fact that Ezra and Nehemiah were Jewish migrants who returned to their native land of Jerusalem and Judah to improve the wellbeing of their ancestral home a great deal. After the rebuilding of the walls and gates of the city of Jerusalem which seemed the primary concern of Nehemiah, he went further to improve on other things in the lives of the Jews in Jerusalem and Judah.

Genesis 11:27-32 suggests that when Abraham, his father and the rest of his father's family members set out from Mesopotamia to go and live in Haran where his father died, there is no record that Abraham owned any wealth of his own. His father led the family delegation that left Mesopotamia to Haran. However, Genesis 12:1-5 says after the death and burial of his father, Terah, Abraham left the remaining members of his father's family behind in Haran with the wealth that he had acquired in Haran while he lived there. This means that he arrived Haran with next-to-nothing tangible and left with something significant. Exodus 2:11-25 confirms that Moses arrived the land of Midian an equivalent of a homeless refugee fleeing death threats with no possessions despite being the heir prince of Egypt. Exodus 3:1-10 and Acts 7:23-34 confirm that Moses spent 40 years in Midian before God ordered him to return to Egypt to lead the freedom of the Israelites from the oppression of their Egyptian hosts and manpower heist masters. Exodus 4:18-20 confirms in verse 20 that when Moses set out to leave Midian, there is no mention of the wealth that he had acquired during his 40-year stay. He had no material possessions that he took back to Egypt. Verse 20 says:

> 20 So Moses took his wife and his sons, put them on a donkey, and set out with them for Egypt,

carrying the walking stick that God had told him to take. (TEV)

This is contrary to what Genesis 12:5 says of Abraham's experience when he obeyed God to leave Haran for Canaan. It is contrary to what Genesis 31:1, 14-16, 31 and 38-43, 32:3-5 and 13-16, 33:1-8 and 34:23 say of Jacob's departure from Haran to Canaan at God's command. It is contrary to what Genesis 36:1-19 and 31-39 says of Esau's final departure from Canaan to his God-assigned permanent possession territory of the hill-country of Edom. It is contrary to what Genesis 46:1-7 confirms in verse 6 that Jacob and his sons took the possessions that they owned in Canaan along to go and join Joseph and his household in Egypt where Genesis 37:27-31 confirms that Jacob spent his last 17 of a total of 147 years that he lived. The only thing that Moses can boast of that he took back to Egypt apart from his wife, two sons and the donkey that they rode was his shepherd staff turned God-empowered miracle working rod.

Along this line, there is what Yoruba people of West Africa call "Adebiyi" and "Adegoke" in this respect. It is like saying "arrive small or insignificant" and "depart great and mighty". The thought behind both terms which some bear as names is that an individual arrived with nothing or little and departed or returned home with much. This is the battle that God had to support Jacob to win by the time he left Laban's place after 20 years to Laban's great sorrow. Genesis 31:4-18, 22-29 and 32:9-10 illustrates this about Jacob's sojourn when it say:

> 4 So Jacob told Rachel and Leah to meet him in the field where he kept his flocks of sheep and goats. 5 He said to them, "I have seen that your father is angry with me. He was always friendly with me in the past, but now he is not. 6 You both know that I have worked as hard as I could for your father. 7 But he cheated me. He has changed my pay ten times. But during all this time, God protected me from all of Laban's tricks. 8 "At one time Laban said, 'You can keep all the goats with spots. This will be your pay.' After he said this, all the animals gave birth to spotted goats, so they were all mine. But then Laban said, 'I will keep

the spotted goats. You can have all the striped goats. That will be your pay.' After he said this, all the animals gave birth to striped goats. 9 So God has taken the animals away from your father and has given them to me. 10 "I had a dream during the time when the animals were mating. I saw that the only male goats that were mating were the ones with stripes and spots. 11 The angel of God spoke to me in that dream. The angel said, 'Jacob!' "I answered, 'Yes!' 12 "The angel said, 'Look, only the striped and spotted goats are mating. I am causing this to happen. I have seen all the wrong things Laban has been doing to you. I am doing this so that you can have all the new baby goats. 13 I am the God who came to you at Bethel, and there you made an altar, poured olive oil on it, and made a promise to me. Now I want you to be ready to go back to the country where you were born.'" 14 Rachel and Leah answered Jacob, "Our father has nothing to give us when he dies. 15 He treated us like strangers. He sold us to you, and then he spent all the money that should have been ours. 16 God took all this wealth from our father, and now it belongs to us and our children. So you should do whatever God told you to do." 17 So Jacob prepared for the trip. He put his children and his wives on camels. 18 Then they began traveling back to the land of Canaan, where his father lived. All the flocks of animals that Jacob owned walked ahead of them. He carried everything with him that he had gotten while he lived in Paddan Aram. 22 Three days later Laban learned that Jacob had run away. 23 So he gathered his men together and began to chase Jacob. After seven days Laban found Jacob near the hill country of Gilead. 24 That night God came to Laban in a dream and said, "Be careful! Be careful of every word you say to Jacob." 25 The next morning Laban caught Jacob. Jacob had set up his camp on the mountain, so Laban and all his men set up their camp in the hill country of Gilead. 26 Laban said to Jacob, "Why did you trick me? Why did you take my daughters like they were women you captured during war? 27 Why did you run away without telling me? If you had told me, I would have given you a party. There would have been singing and dancing with music. 28 You didn't even let me kiss my grandchildren and my daughters goodbye. You were very foolish to do this! 29 I have the power to really hurt you. But last night the God of your father came to me in a dream. He warned me not to hurt you in any way.

9 Then Jacob said, "God of my father Abraham! God of my father Isaac! Lord, you told me to come back to my country and to my family. You said that you would do good to me. 10 You have been very kind to me. You did many good things for me. The first time I traveled across the Jordan River, I owned nothing—only my walking stick.

But now I own enough things to have two full groups. (ERV)

9 Then Jacob prayed: You, Lord, are the God who was worshiped by my grandfather Abraham and by my father Isaac. You told me to return home to my family, and you promised to be with me and make me successful. 10 I don't deserve all the good things you have done for me, your servant. When I first crossed the Jordan, I had only my walking stick, but now I have two large groups of people and animals. (CEV)

Genesis 32:9-10 above is Jacob's reference to this aspect of his life's experiences and perhaps, the most essential summary of his stay in Laban's household. Bearing in mind that it is forbidden even according to God's mandate for mankind on earth to go abroad and return without much to show for the successes and achievements while there, it is vital for anyone relocating abroad to focus on how he or she would not return empty-handed. This is very vital as countless cases have shown that when some persons travel abroad, they engage in resource-wasting pleasures and activities and by the time they would realize that they had been wasting their lifetime, they would have spent 10 to 15 or even 20 years without anything worthwhile to show and earn the respect of those they left behind at home. One of the results would be that such persons find it difficult to return to where they came from or even visit because each time they see what some of the persons they left behind have achieved, they burn with great regret. This simply means that even God do not want anyone to relocate abroad without the aspiration to return far better than he was when he left; none should live away aimlessly. Whoever returns without any substance to show for his stay should not complain when those he met back home ridicule him as a result. This is the reason Naomi said she was better regarded as the most sorrowful soul in Bethlehem by the time she returned from Moab. In her case, it was even worse because even if she would not bring anything more or much, she should not have returned depleted like the way she left with three other members of her household and returned without any of them but only a younger lady, her daughter-in-law.

When Saul went in search of his father's donkey even when he did not find them, he still did not return home empty because he returned with the anointing to be king and the Spirit of God that enabled him to prophesy. In fact, he returned with something more valuable than the donkeys he went to look for. David returned from the battlefield where his father sent him to give food to his brothers with the fame of having killed Goliath. It is unacceptable to return home without something to prove that you have been focused and dutiful wherever you have been. Wise people do not go anywhere without an objective to achieve before returning home. Whoever is setting out should realize that it is just natural for those back home to expect or anticipate that you will not return empty-handed. If anyone returns home with nothing, he or she must not be surprised that he is being despised and disrespected. Not even on account of age should such expect to be respected because such a person who returns empty-handed has broken the fundamental rule of living far away before returning home to relatives and acquaintances.

Genesis 31:14-16 above can be interpreted to mean that while Laban squandered his income including the one that Genesis

31:38-42 imply that he extorted from Jacob by reducing Jacob's wages every two years of the 20 years that Jacob was in his employment, Jacob saved every bit of his own share of the profit. He knew that it would be the most shameful thing if he returned to Canaan without anything tangible for the 20 years he spent. He was not sure that his brother was not as wealthy, and he did not want anyone to use his brother as a yardstick to say he had wasted the years he spent away from home. Genesis 33:1-9 and 36:1-8 confirm that Jacob was not any richer than Esau by the end of the 20 years. In fact, Genesis 32:1-6 and 33:16-20 can be said to mean that while Jacob went to buy an estate in Shechem to settle upon his return from Laban's place, Esau already founded the hill-country of Edom by claiming it from the original inhabitants – a fact which Genesis 36:31-39 and Deuteronomy 2:12 and 22 confirm was made possible by the same God of their ancestors. As we all know, God knows and sees everything, therefore He knew that Esau had become very wealthy back home in Canaan and it would be a shame even to God who had professed His preference for Jacob above Esau to see Jacob return not wealthier than or as wealthy as

Esau. God's decision to prefer and support Jacob to become greater than Esau would be in question. It would seem like God lack the ability to establish His plan for Jacob. That is the reason God did everything possible to ensure that Jacob did not return home to become a shame when his fortune was compared to that of his sibling, God-rejected or unloved Esau.

The other notable point is the fact that Genesis 31:14-16 and 43-44 confirms that Laban's daughters dumped him to stick to, and follow Jacob to Canaan. It is a shame on Laban though it favoured Jacob because if Laban was prudent with his share of the profit to become equally wealthy or even wealthier than Jacob, perhaps, convincing them to follow him as their husband and the father of their children might have been difficult for Jacob. The real issue is that it is like Proverbs 14:24 and 19:4 and 6-7 say, the wealthy would attract followership inevitably. Meanwhile, Proverbs 14:23 says hard work contributes to becoming wealthy. Proverbs 18:23 says the poor man pleads where the rich man speaks with confidence which is near being rude. Genesis 47:27-31 says when Jacob would request Joseph to take his body back to Canaan for burial, he begged him, only for Genesis 49:29-33 to say when he would present the same request to his other children, 92% of who were older than Joseph, he practically shouted it down on them. The obvious reason was that Joseph's greatness towered exceedingly high above that of his older sons. Genesis 50:15-21 confirms that indeed it was Joseph who had the clout to lead the delegation that took Jacob's body back to Canaan with great pomp and pageantry to give him grand burial. This means that those who returned from abroad without anything will be ignored and rejected by their relatives. There will be no one to cheer and celebrate their return to settle at home. Only if they return with wealth would the relatives and old friends come around as we all like to be loved and commended by others.

All migrants must understand what can be considered as the mindset of the people they left behind at home. Those at home believe that if you are not prospering where you are among strangers who are mostly hostile to you, commonsense dictates that you return home immediately. Therefore, so long as you remain overseas, then you are doing well more than them otherwise it is foolish to endure natives' hostilities and notoriety when there is no worthwhile benefit. And this is the heart-hidden reason that makes people at home believe that their overseas dwelling relatives and children must provide for them from the gains which made them decide to continue to live among strangers. This is one reason that sojourners abroad must work extra hard and be fervent in prayers to get God's help to succeed, achieve and return home deserving great respect and honour from their home-based people by reason of their achievements brought back for everyone to join them to enjoy in diverse forms, including employment provision.

If overseas based persons returned richer than home based people, those at home can give the excuse that their predicament is because they did not have the chance to travel abroad but, and dearly beloved, this is a brutal but, if a returnee from many years of sojourn abroad is not richer he or she has provided enough reason to be tortured with ridicule, resentment and rejection until his dying day. It is believed that only those who remained at home all their lives have acceptable reasons to remain poor or unsuccessful while those who live abroad have only and all the reasons to be richer so if they are not, they are better dead.

One of the greatest misfortunes of the migrant or sojourner is to be mocked and taunted by the natives of their land of sojourn. There was a point when the Jewish exiles in Babylon lamented that their Babylonian captors taunted them to sing their Zionist songs to entertain them by the rivers of Babylon. This means that these forced strangers were being humiliated by natives of their land of sojourn. In this and other respects, II Kings 25:8-12, Psalm 137:1-9 and Ezekiel 11:14-16 say:

> 8 On the seventh day of the fifth month of the nineteenth year of King Nebuchadnezzar of Babylonia, Nebuzaradan, adviser to the king and commander of his army, entered Jerusalem. 9 He burned down the Temple, the palace, and the houses of all the important people in Jerusalem, 10 and his soldiers tore down the city walls. 11 Then Nebuzaradan took away to Babylonia the people who were left in the city, the remaining skilled workers, and those who had deserted to the Babylonians. 12 But he left in Judah some of

the poorest people, who owned no property, and put them to work in the vineyards and fields.

1 By the rivers of Babylon we sat down; there we wept when we remembered Zion. 2 On the willows near by we hung up our harps. 3 Those who captured us told us to sing; they told us to entertain them: "Sing us a song about Zion." 4 How can we sing a song to the Lord in a foreign land? 5 May I never be able to play the harp again if I forget you, Jerusalem! 6 May I never be able to sing again if I do not remember you, if I do not think of you as my greatest joy! 7 Remember, Lord, what the Edomites did the day Jerusalem was captured. Remember how they kept saying, "Tear it down to the ground!" 8 Babylon, you will be destroyed. Happy are those who pay you back for what you have done to us—9 who take your babies and smash them against a rock.

14 The Lord spoke to me. 15 "Mortal man," he said, "the people who live in Jerusalem are talking about you and those of your nation who are in exile. They say, 'The exiles are too far away to worship the Lord. He has given us possession of the land.' 16 "Now tell your fellow exiles what I am saying. I am the one who sent them to live in far-off nations and scattered them in other countries. Yet, for the time being I will be present with them in the lands where they have gone. (TEV)

Jeremiah 52:12-16 repeats II Kings 25:8-12 above that says the captors carried away only achievers and left behind the poorest Jews who owned no tangible possessions. This means that in the absence of the owners of houses, buildings and other estate structures, farmlands and flock, the poorest took over their estates and other possessions. As a result, they did not wish that the original owners ever returned to reclaim them and by so doing dispossess them of the wealth that they had been enjoying since the owners were carried away to Babylon. They did not want the experience of the rich woman of Shunem who II Kings 8:1-6 says rushed back from the land of Philistia after seven years as Elisha advised her to compel the king to order those who took over her estates to return them to her with all the yields that they gained on her land in her absence. Her estate hijackers did not think that they stole her land to use in her absence. They were going to resist the return of the land and the proceeds that is why the woman went to the king to use his royal authority to compel them to return her estates and the yield during the seven years she was away. Yet, on the side of her land grabbers, the implication is that the people who took over her estates lost all the gains that they thought that they had made in her absence. God's promise to be with the Jews living in the foreign land of Babylon in Ezekiel 11:16 above is similar to the way Genesis 28:10-22 confirms that God assured Jacob that He would be with him throughout his stay at Laban's place and bring him back to the land of Canaan. Genesis 31:10-13, 22-24, 29 and 38-42 confirms that God fulfilled this promise to Jacob. Genesis 39-41 confirms that God was with Joseph in the land of Egypt and as a result, he prospered greatly.

The double dilemma of the migrant is revealed in the above passage. Just as they are enduring taunting abroad so also those at home are plotting their misfortune that they would never return. The home-based relatives are working hard to ensure that even if the migrant decides to return home, there would be nothing treasurable for him to return to. That is where or why the migrant needs God like no man's business if there is such a thing. The migrant needs God a million times over. Imagine what would have been the sad state of Jacob if he had returned to Canaan empty-handed as Laban meant after Jacob had spent 20 years in his employment. Esau had taken over their father's business and managed it to enrich himself. Meanwhile, Jacob's chief host away from Canaan where he could not call home country swindled him of his due wages year in year out. Though he was God's designed heir of their father, Jacob would have been one of the most shameful members of his generation if God had not helped him to earn enough to return from Laban's place wealthy. It is the reason that migrants must seek God's help as much as they work harder where they live otherwise they would end up the most miserable of all souls who ever lived by the end of their sojourn in foreign land.

Jeremiah 29:1-7's account of God's counsel to migrant Jews in Babylon is very outstanding in the matter of the need for migrants to mind their business to focus on their social, professional and economic prosperity more than anything else. God says they should focus on their spiritual lives by way of offering prayers to Him to prosper their host community so that they would be in-turn prosper to have enough to live on and build their own houses or own their own homes among their hosts. They should marry and have children and grandchildren. God meant that they should not squander their earnings on frivolities for any reason whatsoever. It can be said that God expected them to live as responsible citizens of wherever that they live away from Jerusalem, Judah, and the rest of the land of Israel. By telling them not to be deceived by the fake prophets who claim that they would not live there for long, God can be said to mean that migrants should not listen to persons who try to discourage them from working for the good of the land in which they are migrants. Also, God practically set goals, aims and objectives for the migrant Jews. By so doing, He meant that every migrant should set goals for his or her sojourn or that no migrant should live aimlessly in his or her land of sojourn.

12

Mind Your Business

One of the common challenges that strangers face in their land of sojourn is noticing what they consider as inappropriate behaviour and ways of life by the natives. The mere fact that their customs, traditions and way of life is different from what you are used to where you were born and bred does not mean that everything, they are doing is totally wrong. Even if it is so in your opinion, remember that it is your opinion and you do not have the right to impose it on them. Whatever is your personal opinion is, is actually your personal business which you should treat as such. Restrain yourself from the temptation to want to impose your beliefs on others, worst still, forcefully.

It is like the fact that missionaries who take the gospel of Jesus Christ to places where the worship of God through Christ Jesus is unknown and unheard of are forbidden from imposing it on their audience. They do not get there to force the people to accept the message, rather, they persuade them by providing them with what they lack to have the chance to introduce their message to them. They find a willing native to take them into confidence and sell your ideas to the native to present to his kinsmen while the missionary remains in the background to provide necessary back up to the cooperating native rather than emphasize the points of difference openly in order to get personal recognition. In most cases, no matter how good what a stranger has to say, the fact that it is coming from a stranger would be the very reason the natives would reject it and resent the strangers for daring to want to change their ways of life.

Quoting Jesus, Matthew 7:6 says (1) if you are sure that what you have to offer is really precious, valuable and beneficial you don't have to force it on anyone (2) don't be so desperate to help others to the extent of offering what you know to be valuable and helpful to persons who are yet to appreciate the value or what you have to offer even when you are sure that it would help them a great deal therefore, (3) use your valuable to help only those that would appreciate it and thank you for it. Apparently, it is as a result that when Jesus sent out the apostolic disciples to preach on His behalf, Matthew 10:5-15, Mark 6:6b-13 and Luke 9:1-6 confirm that His guideline included the fact that if their intended beneficiaries of His salvation message give the impression that they are not interested in the message, the disciples should not waste their time and effort trying to persuade such uninterested persons. They should leave such persons alone and move on to the next persons until they find anyone who is willing to hear and heed the message. In this respect, Luke 9:1-6 says:

> 1 Jesus called the twelve disciples together and gave them power and authority to drive out all demons and to cure diseases. 2 Then he sent them out to preach the Kingdom of God and to heal the sick … 4 Wherever you are welcomed, stay in the same house until you leave that town; 5 wherever people don't welcome you, leave that town and

shake the dust off your feet as a warning to them.

6 The disciples left and travelled through all the villages, preaching the Good News and healing people everywhere. (TEV)

We believe that they did as they were told since there is no record in the synoptic gospels that Jesus queried them upon their return for not complying with the guidelines, He gave them. We can say Jesus never meant anyone to get acrimonious with anyone because he is eager to make them accept the message of Jesus-centered salvation to mankind. Whoever does is not representing Jesus and God of Israel appropriately. When applied, it means that just as Jesus-sent missionaries should not force His salvation message on anyone so also it is not for migrants to force their beliefs on their hosts. Any migrant who is so uncomfortable with the lifestyle of the hosts should relocate either back home or anywhere else rather than insist on staying put to change the ways of life of the natives. It amounts to courting trouble that God never intended and therefore, have not provided the grace or capacity to solve or live with.

Along this line, Acts 16:6-10 says God guided Paul to leave Troas and go to Macedonia to preach Jesus-centered salvation message rather than go into the province of Bithynia. Then, Acts 18:1-11 says after Paul left Athens for Corinth, God appeared to him to instruct that he remained in Corinth for a while because there were many in Corinth who would embrace the gospel of Christ. Acts 19:21-22, 22:17-21 and 23:10-11 say Paul left Ephesus to Jerusalem where God commanded him to leave Jerusalem to go and continue to work among the Gentiles in Rome. Acts 22:17-18 says God asserted that the Jews in Jerusalem would not accept Paul's message yet, Acts 23:11 says God affirmed that Paul had given his witness about Him to the people in Jerusalem. That provokes the question of which is the case, the same people that God said would not heed Paul's message about Him had had enough of it from Paul. God meant that Paul should concern himself with mentioning His salvation plan through Jesus the Christ to his hearers and it is left for God to decide to help the hearers to heed the message or not.

I Corinthians 3:6-8 can be interpreted to mean that because God is the one who determines who heeds and does not heed His message, His messenger should be content with whatever role God chose to use him to play in the delivery if the message and leave the outcome for God to determine. It is like what happened between Prophet Jeremiah and the members of his generation that God sent him to try to convince the heed God's warnings so they could escape the planned Babylonian captivity. Jeremiah 1:1-19 says right at the point of commissioning Jeremiah, God said the people would not heed his warnings. God meant that Jeremiah should just play his assigned part or role and not concern himself with what the members of his generation does with the message. It means that the messenger's concern should be to deliver the message and nothing more.

It is not part of his responsibility to ensure that his hearers heed the message that he delivered. Exodus 3:7-10 and 18-20 confirms that while commissioning Moses at the foot of Mount Sinai also known as Mount Horeb, God said though He was sending Moses to Pharaoh to let go of the Israelites, Pharaoh would not readily approve the request. Exodus 3:21-22 confirms that God told Moses that He would convince the Egyptians to give up their treasures for the Israelites to take away when they leave Egypt. Only for Exodus 4:21-23 to say God said He would harden the heart of the King of Egypt to resist the freedom of the Israelites so that God would have the reason to perform miracles before Pharaoh would let go of the Israelites.

God told Moses that he should go tell Pharaoh to let the Israelites leave Egypt though Pharaoh would not readily let go of the Israelites. God's core concern was never making the Egyptians to join the Israelites to worship Him but to let the Israelites sort of hibernate and increase numerically during their 430-year stay in Egypt. Exodus 4:21-23 and 9:16 can be interpreted to mean that the second core reason was to perform several miracles to free them and by so doing spread His fame across the earth for many generations to come. As a result, it would have amounted to engaging in an impossible task if the Israelites had tried to convert the Egyptians. Migrants should focus on their motive for migrating more than trying to make their hosts to embrace their own lifestyle. That is how the subject of God's real reason for His messengers concerns the need for migrants to mind their business in their land of sojourn.

Again, Daniel 3:1-30 tells the story of Shadrach, Meshach, and Abednego's refusal to join others to engage in the idolatry that King Nebuchadnezzar forced on all the inhabitants of the earth. Much as Shadrach, Meshach, and Abednego (SMA) were resolute never to worship Nebuchadnezzar's idolatrous statue there is no record that they tried to force any other to join them to disregard Nebuchadnezzar's idolatrous directives. Much as they will not join others to worship a man-made statute they will not force or even convince anyone else to join them to take the same stance. They meant that they would mind their business just as the others have done by not forcing them to join them to worship the statute. It is a personal choice.

Also, Daniel 4:1-49 tells the story of Daniel's admonition to Nebuchadnezzar to heed God's warning to him through a dream to restrain himself from pride and arrogance and show kindness to the poor in his kingdom. There is no record that Daniel went beyond the boundaries of admonition to try to compel Nebuchadnezzar to heed his counsel just because he was representing the greatest God who Jeremiah 25:1-14 and 27:1-8 confirm gave Nebuchadnezzar the privilege to rule over the earth on His behalf. Once he told Nebuchadnezzar what might happen if he failed to heed his counsel, Daniel stopped at that and left Nebuchadnezzar to decide what to do with his counsel. When Nebuchadnezzar rejected his counsel, Daniel kept his cool for the next 12 months until the said punishment was triggered against Nebuchadnezzar. This means that like SMA, Daniel did not force his beliefs and counsel on others who were not willing to accept them just as he did not allow any to force their beliefs on him while he lived as a captive in Babylon.

Meanwhile, II Samuel 16:15-23 and 17:1-23 can be said to mean that when Ahithophel realized that his valuable counsel was rejected he chose to end his own life because he considered it insulting for Absalom to discountenance his counsel. On the contrary, I Kings 11:28-40 and 14:1-20 can be interpreted to mean that when Prophet Ahijah saw that King Jeroboam had cared less about him after becoming king of Israel, Ahijah kept his cool until Jeroboam got into trouble that was beyond his ability to solve and was forced to seek Ahijah's help once more. If the counselee chose to despise good or life saving counsel, it is not for the counsellor to want the counselee dead or the counsellor kill himself rather the counsellor should wait patiently and watch the counselee suffer the consequences of rejecting good counsel. I Kings 22:1-40 and II Chronicles 18:2-34 say the worst that Prophet Micaiah did was to tell King Ahab that if he ever returned from the battle then Ahab and his fake prophets should not regard him (Micaiah) as true prophet of God of Israel. He never forced Ahab to heed his counsel. Micaiah endured Ahab and his precarious prophets' persecution until Ahab died in the battlefield.

Genesis 19:3-11 confirms in verse 4-9 that the men of Sodom told Lot that as long as he was a migrant among them, he could not educate them on the right thing to do. Verse 14 says his would-be sons-in-law did not take him serious when he tried to save them from the destruction of their city of Sodom. Their rejection of Lot's help to them is ridiculous because Genesis 14:1-16 and 21-24 say God had helped Abraham to save them and their nation from their captors earlier. Strangers should understand that sometimes, natives have God-given basis to resent the attempt of a stranger changing their traditions and customs. In this respect, Deuteronomy 32:8-9 and Acts 17:24-26 say:

> 8 The Most High assigned nations their lands; he determined where peoples should live. He assigned to each nation a heavenly being, 9 but Jacob's descendants he chose for himself.

> 24 God, who made the world and everything in it, is Lord of heaven and earth … it is he himself who gives life and breath and everything else to everyone. 26 From one man he created all races of mankind and made them live throughout the whole earth. He himself fixed beforehand the exact times and the limits of the places where they would live. (TEV)

Verse 8 says God assigned land to the nationals living in the countries or nations of the earth. The God who made the heaven and the earth assigned the land that indigenes you went to live among, possibly by God's leading. He gave them the gods they are serving therein and considering that Job 1:6-7, 2:1 and Daniel 10:11-13, 20-21 say:

> 6 When the day came for the heavenly beings to appear before the Lord, Satan was there among them. 7 The Lord asked him, "What have you been doing?" Satan answered, "I have been walking here and there, roaming around the earth."

> 1 When the day came for the heavenly beings to appear before the Lord again, Satan was there among them.

> 11 The angel said to me, "Daniel, God loves you. Stand up and listen carefully to what I am going to say. I have been sent to you." When he had said this, I stood up, still trembling. 12 Then he said, "Daniel, don't be afraid. God has heard your prayers ever since the first day you decided to humble yourself in order to gain understanding. I have come in answer to your prayer. 13 The

angel prince of the kingdom of Persia opposed me for twenty-one days. Then Michael, one of the chief angels, came to help me, because I had been left there alone in Persia. 20-21 He said, "Do you know why I came to you? It is to reveal to you what is written in the Book of Truth. Now I have to go back and fight the guardian angel of Persia. After that the guardian angel of Greece will appear. There is no one to help me except Michael, Israel's guardian angel. (TEV)

We can see that the natives of every land are subject to influence of their assigned guardian angel. Therefore, when you attack their lifestyle that their guardian angel has laid down for them through their ancestors, even if the individuals are convinced, the guardian angel would instigate them to resist you because he is envious that you are trying to free such persons from his control and manipulation. You have gone to his territory to challenge him. This is the reason Daniel 10:11-14, 20-21 says the guardian angel of Persia resisted the angel sent to Daniel. These territorial guardian angels report to God almighty directly, that is why Job 1:6-7 and 2:1 above say in the time of Job they attended meeting with God on two occasions. It is like whenever God called for a meeting they attended they are in the same arch-angel status with Satan hence, we are told that Satan attended those meetings where God chose to use Satan to prove Job's loyalty to Himself before promoting him to the next level of greatness.

Also important is the fact that there are some natives who are so proud that they hate to hear that a stranger has come to tell them to renounce their traditional ways of life and embrace a new one which he or she has brought to them in their own homeland. A man went from his home country to live in America and dared to say that the gun and the accompanying gun-crime culture is not good enough for human existence and should be controlled by the government. Among the many who were spear-heading this crusade to reduce wastage of human lives, it was this non-American that some stood up against and insisted that must be deported to where he came from. As far as these natives were concerned, so long as he remained a stranger among them, he lacked the right to tell them the culture they inherited was not the best.

Naturally, we believe that gun is used against an enemy therefore, if there is love, no one should use gun against his fellow man. Since many are using it against persons who had never done anything that suggests that they are enemies, controlling how people get access to guns and use it against innocent persons should be considered a sensible suggestion. But the natives say even if that is the most sensible thing to do, it is not normal and acceptable for a non-native to have enough courage to speak out such admonition. What natives would do and get away with, if non-natives do just ten percent of such, they would suffer heavily for it. Therefore, non-natives should be careful with what they talk about and do with regard to the character and conduct of their hosts. The mindset propelling natives against non-natives is "this is where God assigned to us and we can do whatever we like in it, if you are not pleased, remember that you migrated here to live among us and if you are not pleased with how we do things simply return to where God assigned to you through your ancestors and do what you claim to be good and the best for you over there. To come over to squat with us and hope to impose the ideas you cherish in your own place on us is simply unacceptable, intolerable and unforgivable."

In tertiary institutions' hostel accommodation, the concept of legitimate room occupants who paid the required fees based on proper allocation and their squatting friends gives us a good idea of this subject. No matter how long a squatter has lived in the room, when serious issues are to be discussed about space in the room, the squatter have no strong opinion that would be taken seriously. Disrespectfully speaking, a squatter has no right to claim where he is squatting or living. He or she has no strong opinion to make or the original owners are not bound by his ideas, opinions, or claims. Whatever he or she enjoys is at the prerogative of the hosts.

These days, some migrants hide under the guise of activism to join local activists to attack government policies and locals over whatever they consider inappropriate in their host community. A university don joined other activist in the country of his wife where he and the wife lived and earned their living to attack government policies and actions. Finally, the government decided to deal with him, and he was deported along with his wife or his wife had to leave along with him. Much as he was supposed to be a citizen by marriage, so long as he would not remain within his approved limits, he was sent back to his country of birth. Whether it is a God given right for natives to resent an immigrant who engages in 'intrusive activities' is another matter; whether it is based on the fact that God assigned lands to the different nations on earth is another matter altogether.

"Fallow Ground for Fellow Group" is an integral part of that broad revelational understanding but with regard to Deuteronomy 32:8, it means "God-assigned Land for Fellow Humans" and under the concept of minding your own business, it is unacceptable to interfere with or intrude into the chosen lifestyle of persons assigned their own portion. Deuteronomy 2:2-25 recounts God's insistence to the Israelites never to make the slightest attempt to claim the portion of lands He had assigned to the descendants of Lot comprising of the Ammonites and Moabites, as well as Esau's descendants, the Edomites.

There is this concept of "Natives and Neighbours" on the one hand and "Natives and Non-natives" on the other hand. The natives of a nation or country can be regarded as those to whom God assigned their acclaimed and occupied territory through their ancestors. God gave them the ability to take possession and dictate what happens and is prohibited within that particular territory. Their neighbours are those to whom God assigned the nearest portion of land to control as well. It is like allotted plots of land in an estate. The earth is God's estate which He assigns to the sons of men to occupy according to His pleasure. That is why II Chronicles 16:9, Jeremiah 32:18-20 and Zechariah 4:10 say His eyes travels or roves to and fro the earth to note what we do to recompense.

Now, a citizen or native of one territory can migrate to another territory outside his native land of birth to live and make his living. Such a migrant is a non-native resident of the country of sojourn. The immigrant must understand his responsibility to 'do as a Roman during his stay in Rome' otherwise he would have himself to blame if he exceeds his limits as a sojourner. Even natives have their assigned quarters as we know that the different tribes of Israel had their assigned portion when they took over the land of Canaan according to God's plan for them as covenant descendants of Abraham, God's exclusive friend.

Numbers 27:1-11 says Zelophehad's daughters based their request to God through Moses on this idea. Much as David ruled Israel on God's behalf, it is on record that he never went outside his tribe of Judah to set up his throne either as king of Judah initially or as the king over the entire nation of Israel later. II Samuel 2:1-7 and 5:1-13 and I Chronicles 11:1-9 and 14:1-3 confirm that earlier his throne was established or sited at Hebron the headquarter city of the tribe of Judah and later, in Jerusalem, one of the cities of the territory assigned to his tribe of Judah through Moses and claimed during the leadership of his successor, Joshua. I Samuel 10:17-26, 11:4-7, 13:1-2 and 15:34 can be interpreted to mean that King Saul operated from his hometown of Gibeah throughout the 40 years that Acts 13:20-22 says he ruled and reigned over Israel.

I Samuel 1:1-2 and 19-28, 2:18-21, 3:19-21, 7:15-17, 9:1-17 and 19:18-24 confirm that long after his predecessor, Eli's death,

Samuel moved his operational headquarters from Shiloh where Eli had nurtured him to his hometown of Naioth of Ramah in the territory of his tribe of Benjamin. This is part of the reason Samuel later relocated from Shiloh where he was bred to his father's hometown of Ramah to site his leadership headquarters over the nation of Israel. I Samuel 7:15-17 confirms that Samuel merely travelled round designated administrative headquarters to judge cases for the Israelites. This is also part of the reason Amos 1:1-2 and 7:10-17 say the Priest Amaziah abhorred the Prophet Amos coming from his hometown of Tekoa in the territory of Judah to preach against evil in Bethel which Judges 1:22-26 confirms to be one of the cities in the territory of the tribe of Ephraim and Manasseh where Amaziah was presiding as the leading religious man under the guise that God sent him to speak against the evil going on there.

Jeremiah 6:1 confirms that Tekoa is a town far south of Judah. II Chronicles 11:1-6 confirms that after the breakup of the northern tribal kingdom of Israel from the southern tribal kingdom of Judah, Tekoa was one of the cities of Judah that King Rehoboam, son of Solomon who ruled over the tribal kingdom of Judah from Jerusalem fortified. Therefore, even when Amos was speaking on God's behalf, Amaziah played the card of God-assigned territory to insist that Amos, a native of Tekoa or from the tribe of Judah should return to the territory God assigned to his Judean ancestors to speak on God's behalf rather than come over to his own God-assigned territory of Ephraim and Manasseh the descendants of Joseph, the eleventh son of Jacob also known as Israel to make any claim that God of their ancestors sent him to them. Meanwhile, I Kings 11:26-41 and Amos 7:10 confirm that King Jeroboam of Israel who worshipped at Bethel was from the tribe of Ephraim/Manasseh or of the same tribe and tribal region as the priest Amaziah. This means that just as nations try to protect their territorial enclave from the interference of a non-native, so also tribes within the same nation or country try to protect their tribal territories from any non-tribal-native.

This case is very striking because I Kings 12:25-33 and 13:1-10 claim that God was angry and determined to punish King Jeroboam for setting up illegal or irreligious place of worship at Bethel and appointing irreligious priests to preside over them.

Even when God sent Amos to condemn the idolatry, Amaziah stood up against him on account that he could not come from his assigned territory of Judah to claim that what they were doing in their own God-assigned territory of the descendants of Joseph was unacceptable. So we read in Amos 7:10-17 that Amaziah told Amos to return, remain and try to influence what was done in his own God assigned territory of Judah, beginning from his hometown of Tekoa, as much as his fellow people of Judah allows him to tell them what to do or not to do.

This territorial rivalry between natives and strangers can be said to be part of the reason that I Kings 13:1-32 confirms that the old prophet at Bethel deceived to destroy the young prophet that God sent from Judah to confront and condemn King Jeroboam over his idolatry on His behalf. This might be part of the reason God told the young prophet from Judah to return from Bethel quickly. Surely God sent him there to condemn Jeroboam's idolatry, but with the specific warnings never to fall to the temptation to wait after accomplishing the assignment. God understood that He sent this young prophet to another prophet's traditional territory and as long as he is not within his traditionally assigned territory by heaven, it was very dangerous for him to spend longer time than was carved out for him to operate therein to accomplish the assignment. If he did not get out on time, the prophet originally assigned to operate in that territory would find a way to devour him against God's will for him.

It can be called "Tortuousness of Territorial Trespass" or "Territorial Trespass Tortuous". It is a very volatile activity to engage in. Going to challenge the authority of rulers of non-assigned territory is highly injurious. One of the lessons from the story of the young prophet from Judah in I Kings 13:1-32 is that if you must go to operate in a strange territory and survive, then such an individual must adhere strictly to the specific guidelines attached to the assignment. Every assignment has appropriate operational/implementation guidelines. Matthew 10:5-14, Mark 6:6b-13 and Luke 9:1-6 confirm that Jesus gave what He considered as relevant operational guidelines to His apostolic disciples while sending them out. The young prophet from Judah was told never to eat any food or waste any time once the assignment was accomplished. It was his failure to keep to the 'no food, no fellowship and felicitation' instruction that wasted his life. 'Don't feast, don't fellowship' means do not rest and do not delay because the window of time given to accomplish the task and escape from the attack of the original powers assigned the authority to determine what goes on in that territory where you are a stranger would have lapsed and the territorial controllers would have the right to exert their authority against you.

It is the reason God did not prevent David from escaping from the land of Israel to outlive Saul so he could become king of Israel after Saul. God had planned that if Saul were still alive, he would remain king and therefore, had authority to determine what happens and who lived in the territory of Israel. Even when God was done with his dynasty the punishment did not include inability to determine who lived in the territory of the kingdom of Israel if he still lived. The fact that he had become insane did not rob him of the authority to control his kingdom. It is the reason God waited for Moses' Egyptian official assailants to die naturally over a period of 40 years before ordering Moses to return to the land of Egypt to lead the freedom of the Israelites.

Exodus 18:1-27 is very striking in this respect. The background to it is that Exodus 2:1-24, 3:1-22 and 4:1-31 say Moses came in contact with Jethro who became his benefactor, chief host, employer and father-n-law when Moses needed refuge from his assailants. Moses spent 40 years with Jethro before returning to Egypt in obedience to God's directive. Then, Exodus 18:1-27 says sometime after Moses had gone away Jethro had reason to visit him where he was leading or presiding over the Israelites in the wilderness. The wilderness was not far from Jethro's hometown of Midian because Exodus 3:1-12 says God told Moses that He would help him to free the Israelites from Egypt and bring them to the same Mount Sinai where He commissioned Moses to enable the Israelites to worship Him. It means that Mount Sinai was between Jethro's hometown of Midian and Egypt.

Now, first, Exodus 2:11-22, 3:1, 6:28-30, 7:1-7 and 18:1 and Acts 7:23-35 confirm that Moses was between 40 and 80 years old when he lived and worked for his father-in-law, Jethro who was the priest of Midian just like Genesis 41:45-46 confirms that Joseph's father-in-law was the priest of Egypt. Meanwhile,

Psalm 105:16-25 give them impression that while Joseph led the Israelites into Egypt, Moses took them out and that it was God who used both of them to play their different role in the history of the Israelites. Joseph who took them into Egypt was born outside Egypt while Moses who took them out was born inside Egypt. Then, Exodus 18:9-12, 27 confirms that

> "9 When Jethro heard all this, he was happy 10 and said, "Praise the LORD, who saved you from the king and the people of Egypt! Praise the LORD, who saved his people from slavery! 11 Now I know that the LORD is greater than all the gods, because he did this when the Egyptians treated the Israelites with such contempt." 12 Then Jethro brought an offering to be burned whole and other sacrifices to be offered to God; and Aaron and all the leaders of Israel went with him to eat the sacred meal as an act of worship. 27 Then Moses said good-bye to Jethro, and Jethro went back home. (TEV)

It is noteworthy that after indirectly admitting that the God of his son-in-law was greater than the god that he was serving as national chief priest he still left Moses or his son-in-law and his greater God to return home rather than remain with the son-in-law and join the son-in-law to worship the greatest God continually. Do you see why God cannot afford to forgive Christians who claim to believe in and worship Him yet, go to seek other gods under the cover of the night? Those who know that He is the greatest God still return to worship the lesser gods of their ancestors and God of Israel expects the same thing from those that claim that they believe in and worship Him. God expects those that are associated with Him to be equally loyal to Him alone like those worshipping heathen gods remain loyal to their heathen gods. Jeremiah 2:11 says God of Israel once lamented that though other nationals do not readily change their gods the Israelites does shamelessly.

There is no doubt that most would say is 'what an insult', that a father-in-law abandons his ancestor's gods to join his son-in-law to worship the God of the son-in-law's ancestors. That is an abomination – that is part of what I John 2:16 refer to as pride of life and arrogance engineered categorized abomination. Genesis 3:1-7 can be interpreted to mean that the seed of pride of life was sown into mankind by Satan through Adam and Eve in the Garden of Eden. Jethro did not want to become a laughingstock, so he chose to return home. He meant that 'I know that you worship the greatest God but the circumstances surrounding my relationship with you will not allow me to respond positively or appropriately to my realization about your God by joining you to worship Him for the rest of my life'. That is the kind of thing that forms the core of the concept of "I Know But Cannot". Exodus 18:13-26 says Jethro even went further to suggest an idea to Moses about how to administer justice among the Israelites and the special people of the greatest God but did not think that it was still enough reason for him to join them. It is not like he did not see any sign that he would not be accorded due respect if he joined the Israelites if he never returned to his hometown of Midian.

In the matter of been accorded the respect that he deserved, Exodus 18:7 says when Moses went out to welcome him into the camp of the Israelites, he bowed low to show Jethro respect despite the fact that Moses was the leader of the Israelites. Verse 12 says Moses mobilized all his lieutenants to show Jethro respect yet, he could not resist the temptation to return to his native land of Midian. Then, Numbers 10:24-32 and Judges 1:16, 4:11 say:

> 24 and Abidan son of Gideoni was in command of the tribe of Benjamin. 25 Finally, those under the banner of the division led by the tribe of Dan, serving as the rear guard of all the divisions, would start out, company by company, with Ahiezer son of Ammishaddai in command. 26 Pagiel son of Ochran was in command of the tribe of Asher, 27 and Ahira son of Enan was in command of the tribe of Naphtali. 28 This, then, was the order of march, company by company, whenever the Israelites broke camp and set out. 29 Moses said to his brother-in-law Hobab son of Jethro the Midianite, "We are about to start out for the place which the Lord said he would give us. He has promised to make Israel prosperous, so come

with us, and we will share our prosperity with you." 30 Hobab answered, "No, I am going back to my native land." 31 "Please don't leave us," Moses said. "You know where we can camp in the wilderness, and you can be our guide. 32 If you come with us, we will share with you all the blessings that the Lord gives us."

16 The descendants of Moses' father-in-law, the Kenite, went on with the people of Judah from Jericho, the city of palm trees, into the barren country south of Arad in Judah. There they settled among the Amalekites.

11 In the meantime Heber the Kenite had set up his tent close to Kedesh near the oak tree at Zaanannim. He had moved away from the other Kenites, the descendants of Hobab, the brother-in-law of Moses. (TEV)

This means that while Jethro and his son, Hobab returned to their native Midian, some other family members remained with Moses' wife, Zipporah and their two sons. How Jethro continued to serve as the priest of their Midianite native gods despite knowing or realizing that there is a greater God is another matter that we shall not be able to deal with because of lack of any details. Zipporah's nephews and nieces, i.e. her brother, Hobab's descendants thought that even if their grandfather and father would not take advantage of the privilege that Moses presented them, they would because of their aunt, Zipporah. Now, it could be that Hobab's children and their cousins, Zipporah's two sons had grown up together to become best of friends. Their young age might have helped them to turn their back on their father, grandfather and their ancestral homeland and gods to join the God of their cousins' father who their grandfather had openly acknowledged to their hearing as being greater than the gods that they knew while growing up in Midian.

Exodus 18:1-12 confirms that Jethro acknowledged God of Israel as been greater than all other gods. With regards to minding one's business, Moses did not use the decision of Hobab's children to insist on convincing Jethro and Hobab to join them. Once Hobab declared his determination to return to Midian even when his sons would remain with Moses and his sons, Moses let go of the subject. He did not insult Hobab by insinuating that his sons were behaving better by accepting his offer that they joined the Israelites. The other issue is the fact that Hobab who was offered rejected while his sons who were not offered directly embraced the offer. That is what Isaiah 65:1-6, Matthew 13:53-58 and 22:1-10, Mark 6:1-13 and Luke 4:16-44 and 14:16-24 mean when it tells how God feels bad when those He meant to help fail to embrace His help and Jesus view on how to react to or treat those that trivialize the salvation offer that He has for them.

One striking point that can be safely interpreted from Genesis 12:10-20 is the fact that one would have thought that since Pharaoh found out that Abraham had a God that is superior to his native gods because Abraham's God was able to undermine his natives gods that Pharaoh relied on to threaten him in his own domain, Pharaoh would consider it as enough reason to give up his native gods to join Abraham to worship Abraham's greater God. The story says Pharaoh never did, no matter how reasonable and logical that it sounded. In like manner, I Samuel 4:11, 5:1-12, 6:1-21 and 7:1-2 can be safely interpreted to mean that even when the Philistines knew that the God of Israel is undoubtedly greater than their natives gods, they still did not think it was enough reason for them to abandon their own god to join the Israelites to worship their God. Genesis 20:1-13, 21:22-24 and 26:1-6 and 12-31 is very unique in this respect when it can be interpreted to mean that despite knowing that the God of Abraham and his son, Isaac are greater than his natives gods, King Abimelech along with his Philistine officials and subjects did not think it was wise for them to desert their native gods to join Abraham and Isaac to serve their greater God. The fact that they acknowledge to Abraham and to Isaac after the death of Abraham that they worshipped the greater God meant that they had several decades to think over the subject of Abraham and Isaac having greater God and as a result they should join them to worship Him or remain loyal to their native gods and they opted to remain loyal to their native gods.

Genesis 29:31-35, 30:1-43 and 31:1-55 say (1) though Laban knew that the God that sponsored his nephew, Jacob was greater he still preferred his household gods. He would not agree that Jacob or any member of his family took away his household gods. (2) Also, his daughter, Rachel knew that her husband, Jacob's God was greater yet still stole one of her father's gods to take along with her to Canaan where she hoped to enjoy the blessings of God of her husband alongside the children that she bore him. Whether it is one of the reasons that God let her die shortly after they arrived Canaan is another matter.

Acts 13:4-12 says when the governor of the island of Paphos experienced the power of God of Israel, he readily rejected the magician who used lesser spiritual power to embrace the God of Israel that Barnabas and Paul presented to him. However, Acts 16:16-24 says when some sorcerers realized that the God of Israel had rubbished the spiritual power they relied on for commercial success they opted to attack God of Israel's representatives, Paul, Silas and Timothy who God used to make this show of His superiority to happen.

Migrants should live their lives according to their native customs and traditions within the confines of the laws of the land where they are strangers but leave the natives alone to decide how best to react to their strange ways of life. If the natives chose to embrace your imported way of life, then thank God but if not just mind your own business rather than try to persuade natives to embrace your way of life. Proverbs 17:27 and 20:15 say:

> 27 Those who are sure of themselves do not talk all the time. People who stay calm have real insight.
>
> 15 If you know what you are talking about, you have something more valuable than gold or jewels.
> (TEV)

This is similar to Jesus' admonition that no one should give his valuables to persons who would not appreciate or His counsel to the disciples that they should not waste their time trying to make some unwilling persons not to accept His salvation message. Daniel did not argue with the Babylonians over any issue throughout his 70-year stay in the palace of their king. When his wisdom and understanding was to be tested or compared to that of other palace officials after three years of preparation or training, it was his performance that proved that he was wiser. Much as he continued to depend on the God of his ancestors that He was used to before arriving Babylon, he did not try to convince anyone to join him to worship his God. He did not go out of his way to advertise his wisdom and understanding unless when the need arose. When the need arose when Nebuchadnezzar had dream that he forgot and threatened the lives of his wise men that included Daniel that was when Daniel sought God's help and went to solve the ridiculous riddle by asking audience with Nebuchadnezzar. Daniel 4 says when he interpreted Nebuchadnezzar's dream a second time, it was because he was formally asked to do it rather than jump out to offer help without been asked. When Nebuchadnezzar did not heed his counsel, he never forced Nebuchadnezzar to. He waited until Nebuchadnezzar suffered the consequences of disregarding his counsel.

13

Reduce Friction with Your Native Neigbhors

In the first place, there are too many good things to do in life than to have time to engage in endless acrimony. Second, it is always impossible to live in peace with everyone. Genesis 25:19-34 confirms that twin brothers by the name of Esau and Jacob began their disagreement while in the womb. Perhaps, the most shocking point is that this disagreement lingered practically forever. Genesis 16:1-16 says Sarah's persecution forced Hagar away before God sent her back to Sarah's home while Genesis 21:9-21 says the same God approved that Hagar and her son be sent away as Sarah demanded. This can be interpreted to mean that part of God's solution to constant conflict between relatives or siblings is that they live apart just like marital mates who would not live together in peace with their husband/wife should part ways. Proverbs 22:10 can be said to lend credence to this fact when it says getting rid of a conceited person stops arguments, quarreling or name calling. Genesis 13:1-18 says when Abraham adopted this solution in his dealings with his nephew, Lot God impliedly approved.

Then, Genesis 36:1-8 can be said to mean that Esau did not even wait for another round of arguments to break out before he left their traditional family home for Jacob to go and settle in the land of Edom. He probably understood that he had never enjoyed living side-by-side with Jacob since they were kids or so long as he could remember despite being twin brothers. Genesis 25:29-34 and 27:1-41 can be interpreted to mean that apparently, Esau had not forgotten the loss of birthright to Jacob and the loss of their father's special blessing to the same Jacob. It is as a result that he thought that it was best to live apart in their old age after the death of their father. Genesis 25:26 says their father was 60 years old when they were born while Genesis 35:27-28 confirms that their father died when he was 180 years old which means that they were 120 years old when their father died and they were left alone to share their family house with their household members and servants. Despite being twin brothers, they still had to live apart to be happy. Interestingly, God had a hand in their living apart or gladly gave Esau and his descendants their own land in the land of Edom which means that God ordained that they must live apart to be happy citizens of the earth. This means that if they had insisted on living together, they would never have experienced peace and happiness during their stay on earth.

GASS means God Approved Separation Solution which sums up Abraham's separation from Lot, Ishmael from his relatives and Esau from Jacob. When it became expedient, David parted ways with Jonathan and his sister, Michal for David to outlive Saul who was determined to kill David if David remained within the territory of Israel. God did not object to David's separation from Jonathan and Michal if such separation would contribute to the fulfillment of God's plan that David became king of Israel after Saul. To avoid constant argument or avoidable arguments, Acts 13:1-3 and 15:36-41 and Galatians 2:6-10 confirm that Barnabas and Paul separated despite the fact that they were very much aware that God meant them to work together as apostles primarily to the Gentiles.

RRSS means Reasonable and Responsible Separation Solution which means that the individual can reason and respond to prevent plausible/probable problems accurately. It is one of the marks of the highest sense of maturity. Esau was able to calculate correctly that considering the space available to them and their possession, there is every tendency for them or their servants to clash over space like Genesis 13:1-18 says their grandfather, Abraham and his nephew, Lot so decided that it was better to leave the family home for his younger brother, his family, servants and other possessions in peace. What Abraham did for Lot by initiating their peaceful separation was what Esau did by choosing to leave the family house for Jacob.

There is the concept of GOOSS which means God Ordained and Ordered Separation Solution which is like GASS. If Abel had lived apart from Cain and as a result Cain never knew about the fact that God accepted Abel's sacrifices while He rejected that of Cain, perhaps, Abel would not have died in the hands of

Cain the way Genesis 4:1-8 confirms. There are persons who live through life with envy-molded mindset, attitude, and lifestyle. They see everything from the prism of envy and jealousy. It is best to live far away from such persons as much as possible.

It is very striking that Genesis 11:27-31, 12:1-19 and 24:1-67 can be said to mean that Abraham left Haran behind for Nahor and his descendants to claim for their permanent possession at God's directive or instance only for Genesis 13:1-18 to say the same Abraham activated Lot's departure to Sodom. Then, it was Esau who followed in Abraham's footsteps to leave the land of Canaan for Jacob and his household members. It can be said to mean that Esau ensured that his final separation from Jacob was not acrimonious like Genesis 29 – 31 says of Jacob's final separation from their maternal uncle, Laban. One other thing worthy of note is the fact that it was Esau who Genesis 25:27-28 suggests to be closer or enjoyed a closer relationship with Isaac who opted for a peaceful separation or never did anything to hurt Jacob whereas it was Jacob who enjoyed closer relationship with their mother who initiated troubles with Esau on two occasions. Coincidentally, even when Jacob went to live with their maternal uncle, they had acrimonious relationship. As a result, it can be argued that while Esau learnt peaceful means of separating from relatives when it becomes expedient from the father and grandfather, Jacob learnt acrimonious relationship with relatives from their mother and her relatives.

Oppression obstructs focus just as conflict cripple concentration and squabbles slows success. When the oppression of the Israelites became unbearable for them, God empowered and encouraged Moses to go and set them free so they would be free to serve Him without the distractions of oppression and suffering. Do you get the point, part of the reason God encourage separation or parting of ways with conflict causing relatives or neighbors is so that the peaceful person can concentrate on serving Him rather than be constantly distracted by the troublesome regrettable relatives. It is the reason that God did not object to David's relocating from the land of Israel to the land of the Philistines in the last 16 months of Saul's reign over Israel. Ordinarily, God provided David to lead the victories of the army of Israel during the last years of Saul's reign. However, envy and jealousy would not allow Saul to let David be and God agreed that it was better for David to leave the army of Israel rather than remain and continue to run from pillar to post because of Saul's threats.

The claim that God approved of David's migration from the land of Israel under Saul's control during Saul's final 16 months is based on the fact that there is no record that when David decided to migrate God discouraged him from going to hide from Saul with the king of the Philistines, Achish. Now, I Samuel 23:13-14 confirms that God intervened from heaven to protect David from Saul's threats yet David still had to go away from Saul's physical reach as if to suggest that no one should say because God is protecting him, he should remain within the reach of his enemies or a regrettable assailant relative. God's protection is not enough reason to disregard personal safety precautions or measures. God abhors household conflicts and wars. Micah 2:8, 7:5-6, Matthew 10:36 and John 18:35 say:

> 8 The Lord replies, "You attack my people like enemies. Men return from battle, thinking they are safe at home, but there you are, waiting to steal the coats off their backs.

5 Don't believe your neighbour or trust your friend. Be careful what you say even to your wife. 6 In these times sons treat their fathers like fools, daughters oppose their mothers, and young women quarrel with their mothers-in-law; a man's worst enemies are the members of his own family.

36 A man's worst enemies will be the members of his own family.

35 Pilate replied, "Do you think I am a Jew? It was your own people and the chief priests who handed you over to me. What have you done?" (TEV)

It is absurd for a man to be safer with strangers and enemies than relatives is one core point in the above passage. Jesus' own people handed Him over to a non-Jew to condemn for them to kill. Acts 18:12-17 says a non-Jew by the name of Governor Gallio did not allow the Jews to use him against Paul like they had used Pilate to achieve their obnoxious objective against Jesus earlier. In order to understand the above passage further, it would help to remember that Genesis 4:1-16 can be interpreted to mean that part of the reason Cain killed Abel easily was because Abel never imagined that his older brother would harm him in the fields away from the presence of their parents at home. Genesis 25:28-34 and 27:1-47 can be interpreted to mean that Jacob short-changed Esau twice because Esau never imagined that his only brother, Jacob could undo him right at home. On the day that Jacob stole birthright from Esau, Genesis 25:29-34 says Esau had gone to the field all day long hunting. He was not killed or injured by wild animals or mistakenly shot by other hunters in the wild only to get home and his only brother stole his birthright from him.

When the same sibling would short-change him over generational blessing from their father, Genesis 27:1-41 says he went out to hunt to bring back game to make their father happy as their father requested. While he was away, their mother instigated Jacob to deceive their father to steal the blessing. I Samuel 17 – 31 can be interpreted to mean that what a lion, a bear, and the Philistine enemies could not do to David in the grazing fields of Bethlehem and in battle at the valley of Elah, Saul determined to do to him. I Samuel 18:6-27 and 19:1-24 confirm that right in his palace, Saul tried to kill David because of envy and jealousy. In fact, I Samuel 17:34-37 and 45-51 and 23:14 can be interpreted to mean that just as God had to make conscious effort to save David from being killed by wild animals and Goliath so also God had to shield David from being killed by King Saul. II Samuel 2:12-32, 3:20-39, 17:25, 18:1-16 and 19:13 and 20:1-10 and I Kings 2:5-7 confirm that one of the reasons David could not forgive Joab for killing Abner and Amasa was because he killed them during a time of peace for the killings that they caused during a time of war. We can go on and on in this respect.

Genesis 26:12-25 says in his bid to avoid trouble, Isaac moved away from his hosts, the Philistines. Genesis 26:1-33 explains natives' arrogance in their dealings with non-natives living among them. This is about what to expect from them – their notorious nature. I Samuel 27:1-12 confirms that David lived away from his host community, covered his track when he committed crime and went to renew his allegiance to his chief host at regular intervals. If he did not go to the chief host at regular intervals, he would have given room for the chief host to suspect him and send spies to check whatever he was doing away from his presence. Living away from his host indigenes is like the way Joseph said his siblings settled in the region of Goshen in order to reduce friction between them and the Egyptians who despised an average Hebrew that they were. Joseph did not want a situation where his relatives would have to be clashing with the Egyptians and he would have to be settling dispute frequently.

Genesis 43:23, 45:4-20, 46:31-34 and 47:1-6 can be said to mean that because Joseph was aware that residing in the region of Goshen, away from the regular Egyptians' core or concentrated neighbourhood, agreed with his benefactor and chief host/boss, Pharaoh who made him the first Prime Minister in human history. This means that it is important to find out what your chief host approves for you in the land where you are a stranger because as long as you do what he suggests or pleases him, he would stand up to defend you even if his fellow natives try to attack, or make life miserable for you among them. Whatever you know that the host expects from you, do your level best to do it, otherwise in your moment of trouble, you will not find anybody to assist you to overcome. Second, he knew that the Egyptians despised his fellow Hebrews and as a result, constant contact between the Egyptians and his relatives would stoke tensions. To reduce such tensions, he decided that they should live apart from the Egyptians with his boss' approval. Judges 4:11 and 11:6 confirm that after settling down among the Israelites in Canaan, one of Moses' brother-in-law, Hobab's descendants felt that he could no longer live beside his fellow descendants of Hobab. Judges 4:11-23 confirms that it was his wife by the name of Jael who killed Sisera the army commander of the army of King Jabin of the Canaanites who had his throne in the city of Hazor. Heber could not continue to live beside his fellow Kenites. Rather than continue to live beside his sources of sorrow and sickening siblings he thought that life was too short for him to spend part of it beside sorrow spewing souls just because they were his siblings or relatives.

There is an important lesson to learn from the story of Abraham and the Hittites in Genesis 23:1-16 when it says the leading citizens of the place where he lived considered him a great man who deserved their respect. Part of the implication of this is that, even if the commoners wanted to make trouble with him for any reason, he had the leading citizens who could call the commoners who are their fellow natives to order in the event of Abraham clashing with them. This is a survival strategy that sojourners should adapt to their advantage. The other important angle to the case of Abraham here is that while we are told that he had friends, there is no record that he had enemies or that he clashed with some of the natives for any reason whatsoever. This means that he did his level best to be at peace with all men. The time that some spend making troubles with their neighbours for whatever reason, Abraham chose to spend his to ensure that he lived in peace with all men. The only time he had to go to war with his friends was not because he had a personal bone of contention with the enemies. It was only on account of Lot who lived among the Sodomites who led him to war. When he had a disagreement with Lot because of space, it was their servants who quarreled rather than Abraham with Lot and we are told that Abraham's solution was to make peaceful separation. We can argue that it was partly to avoid conflict that he gave up his wife on two occasions to his hosts before God forced them to return her to him. Because he was a stranger and did not know their character, he readily concluded that they did not fear God and dealt with them from that perspective until he was sure that God had shown Himself to them personally.

This presupposes that anyone who is led to a new location by God or who is forced to a new location by circumstances of life should deal with the natives from the premise that they are not godly. That mindset will help the stranger to deal carefully with them. It is like the concept that for safety reason, every wise driver on the road should drive with caution as if every other driver is a mad man. Way back in tertiary institution, a course-mate would say, every person is a criminal until he or she proves himself or herself otherwise. What manner of upbringing makes an individual to believe that every other person is a criminal until he can prove from interactions with the person that he or she is not a criminal? We merely need this thought to help us understand that it is wise for a foreigner to be very circumspect while dealing with his hosts.

Abraham can be said to have adopted it when Genesis 12:10-20 and 20:1-18 say more than once, he told his wife to claim to be his sister rather than his wife so that the natives in the strange land they were about to enter would not kill him and take her to be their wife because he was not sure that they respect God so much as to let a man keep his beautiful wife. The concept of 'Fifty-Fifty Chance' in this respect means that there is fifty-fifty chance that the natives might like or not like the migrant. Some would embrace while some would resent the migrant. In fact, this concept is applicable to all and in all respects. There are siblings who get along and those who do not so long as they live. There are parents and children who get along very well and those who do not. There are neighbours who get along and those who never do. Migrants should be conscious that there are natives who will not like them no matter how much they behave nicely just as there are those that would like them no matter what they do wrong. That is a natural law of life. Genesis

20:10-11, Esther 2:20, Jeremiah 1:1-10, 17-19, Matthew 10:1, 16, Luke 10:1, 3 and Acts 9:15-16 say:

> 10 Why did you do it?" 11 Abraham answered, "I thought that there would be no one here who has reverence for God and that they would kill me to get my wife.

> 20 As for Esther, she had still not let it be known that she was Jewish. Mordecai had told her not to tell anyone, and she obeyed him in this, just as she had obeyed him when she was a little girl under his care.

> 1 This book is the account of what was said by Jeremiah son of Hilkiah, one of the priests of the town of Anathoth in the territory of Benjamin. 2 The Lord spoke to Jeremiah in the thirteenth year that Josiah son of Amon was king of Judah, 3 and he spoke to him again when Josiah's son Jehoiakim was king. After that, the Lord spoke to him many times, until the eleventh year of

the reign of Zedekiah son of Josiah. In the fifth month of that year the people of Jerusalem were taken into exile. 4 The Lord said to me, 5 "I chose you before I gave you life, and before you were born I selected you to be a prophet to the nations." ... the Lord said to me, "Do not say that you are too young, but go to the people I send you to, and tell them everything I command you to say. 8 Do not be afraid of them, for I will be with you to protect you. I, the Lord, have spoken!" 9 Then the Lord reached out, touched my lips, and said to me, "Listen, I am giving you the words you must speak. 10 Today I give you authority over nations and kingdoms to uproot and to pull down, to destroy and to overthrow, to build and to plant." 17 Get ready, Jeremiah; go and tell them everything I command you to say. Do not be afraid of them now, or I will make you even more afraid when you are with them. 18-19 Listen, <u>Jeremiah! Everyone in this land—the</u>

kings of Judah, the officials, the priests, and the people—will be against you. But today I am giving you the strength to resist them; you will be like a fortified city, an iron pillar, and a bronze wall. They will not defeat you, for I will be with you to protect you. I, the Lord, have spoken."

1 Jesus called his twelve disciples together and gave them authority to drive out evil spirits and to heal every disease and every sickness. 16 "Listen! I am sending you out just like sheep to a pack of wolves. You must be as cautious as snakes and as gentle as doves.

1 After this the Lord chose another seventy-two men and sent them out two by two, to go ahead of him to every town and place where he himself was about to go. 3 Go! I am sending you like lambs among wolves.

15 The Lord said to him, "Go, because I have chosen him to serve me, to make my name known

to Gentiles and kings and to the people of Israel.

16 And I myself will show him <u>all that he must suffer for my sake</u>." (TEV)

Jeremiah 1:18-19 above can be interpreted to mean that if you live where everyone is against you, part of what you need is resilience and God's help to succeed in your endeavours and prosper despite their opposition and attacks. Then, Matthew 10:16 says such persons should deal cautiously among his haters and persecutors. That means the ready solution should not be to run away. God knows that you are under attack and He is ready to help you to prosper despite their attack, therefore, determine to delight yourself despite their abominable activities. Alternatively, it could be said to mean that when it becomes expedient to live among haters and persecutors, you must always conduct yourself cautiously. You must not give your haters any room to find fault with your character and conduct. Live within the ambits of the law or legitimacy. Jeremiah 1:8 can be said to mean that God knew that Jeremiah would need protection from his persecutors, so He promised to provide the necessary protection.

God knew that Jeremiah was going to be persecuted because of speaking for Him or on His behalf yet, He did not think it was enough reason to remove such persons so that they would not be alive to afflict Jeremiah. God decided to let the persecutors live on to do their evil deeds against Jeremiah but help Jeremiah to continue to do his work despite their persecution. John 13-18 can be said to mean that at the end of Jesus' seeming valedictory speech to the 12 apostolic disciples which chapter 17 says He concluded with a prayer to God the Father for the disciples and then chapter 18 recounts His prayer at the Garden of Gethsemane for three hours followed by His arrest and kangaroo trial. John 16:1-3 quotes Jesus as telling the disciples that they would be persecuted for believing in Him and propagating His message. Only for Him to say in John 17:9-15 that much as He pleads with God the Father to help the disciples to live with the troubles that they must suffer for His sake God should not take them out of the world to end their sufferings. Jesus meant that pleasant promises of the Christian faith represent the assets while the sufferings represent the liabilities that any Christian should determine to accept along with the assets. He had reiterated the troubles that the disciples would suffer while sending them out to preach on His behalf earlier when Matthew 10:16 and Luke 10:3 say He indicated that they would be like vulnerable sheep amongst wolves in the midst of the people that they would share His salvation message with. That is the way that migrants or strangers should determine to survive among their hosts. Despite knowing that they would be like endangered species, Jesus did not ask God to stop their persecutors from persecuting them.

God's claim about the things that Paul must suffer for His name sake is very striking considering that Jesus made similar claim about Himself in Luke 24:26 which is indirectly reiterated in Isaiah 53:10-11, Philippians 2:5-11 and Hebrews 12:2b that it seemed mandatory for Him to suffer in some ways before he would enter into greatness and glory. Joel 2:25-27 can be said to make veiled reference to this fact in general terms. Esther 2:21-23, 3:1-15, 4:1-17 and 6:1-13 can be said to mean that Mordecai did not get the due reward for saving the life of the Emperor Ahasuerus until his life had been threatened by Haman which forced Mordecai and his fellow Jews to abstain from food and drink for three consecutive days. It is part of the concept of 'No Threat No Triumph No Thrill'.

Based on the above passage we can say 'Like Abraham like Mordecai to Esther, God to Jeremiah, Jesus to His disciples and God to Paul'. Since the time of Abel's death in the hands of his older brother good people have always been among the most endangered species in every generation of this wearisome world. Meanwhile, Abel and Cain are the first sibling ever in human history. The Ever Endangered Good People of the Earth means that good people who are reasonable, recognize and revere the sanctity of human life, restrain themselves from seeking to have what belong to others, peace-loving with commendable character and conduct are the most threatened members of any society. They are perpetually at the mercy of criminals and the rulers particularly the law enforcement officers and the so-called criminal justice system.

Much as God sent Abraham to live among the Canaanites and Philistines, Abraham admitted that he was like a lamb amid wolves in the places (Canaanites, Egyptians, and Philistines) he migrated. It is as a result that Genesis 12:10-20 and 20:1-18 say he conspired with Sarah to lie about their marital relationship to Pharaoh of Egypt and Abimelech of the Philistines. Then, Jeremiah 1:1-10 and 17-19 and Matthew 1:17 can be said to confirm that 28 generations beyond Abraham, God told Jeremiah that he would live like a sheep among wolves in his generation while at home among his fellow Israelites. Finally, Matthew 1:17 and 10:1-2 and 16 and Luke 10:1-3 confirm that 14 generations after Jeremiah, Jesus said the same thing in plain language to His disciples. Shortly after the death, burial, resurrection and ascension to heaven of Jesus, Acts 9:15-16 can be interpreted to mean that God said the same thing about His plan for Paul as an apostle mostly to the Gentiles.

It is like David's confession in Psalm 23:1-6 that God set a table of pleasure for him to enjoy during his lifetime but in the presence of his enemies. Perhaps, he also meant that the pleasure of the greatness that God ordained for him to enjoy would incite many to attack him. Meanwhile, Psalm 16:1-11 quotes David to have said in verse 6 that God had made his lifelong experience a pleasant one. II Samuel 4:9 quotes David to have confessed that

God saved him from all dangers or his enemies. This means that despite the troubles that he suffered in life as a man made great by God he still believed that God had been very good to him in his lifetime. This can be said to mean that he looked at the positive side of his lifelong experiences more than what should be the negative side. This is the attitude that migrants should have towards their hosts.

Let us borrow a leaf from the story of Jesus' disciples who Acts 1:1-17, 3:1, 4:13, 19 and 23, 15:6-8 and 19-20 and Galatians 2:6 and 8-9 strongly suggest were led by Peter, John and James in Jerusalem. Acts 3:1-26 and 4:1-31 tell the persecution of the disciples and their response of asking God for both boldness and power to perform miracles despite the heinous activities of their haters and persecutors. That is very instructive. Asking God to give them the capacity to continue to operate in the face of hate and persecution meant that they were determined never to back down or succumb to the intimidation of their persecutors. They could have blamed God for not stopping their persecutors from attacking them. Rather they determined to disregard or endure the pains of the persecution to work for

God gladly. This agrees with John 17:9-15-detailed prayer of Jesus that God should protect the disciples from their attackers rather than taking the disciples out of the world.

Along this line, II Kings 24:18-20 and 25:1-26, Jeremiah 25:1-14, 27:1-8, 29:1-32, 39:1-1-14, 40:1-6 and 52:1-30 and Daniel 1:1-21 say though God of Israel or their ancestors let them be carried captive, DSMA still humbled themselves and submitted to His decision to let them live as captives in Babylon to seek His help in Babylon. They did not seek God's help to return to Jerusalem, that is, end their stay in captivity before the 70 years that God had decided that they would remain in the Babylonian captivity. Rather, they asked God's help for them to prosper while in Babylon. Their attitude was something like "we know that we are in a strange land as you planned even before we were born but we believe that you can still make us prosperous as much as we would have been if we were at home in Jerusalem." They meant that they wanted God to make them great where God sent them to live as much as they would have been great, powerful, and influential back home in Jerusalem as princes of Judah. When translated into contemporary times, it means that someone who had qualified as a professional in his home country migrating to another country working hard and seeking God's help so that he could practice as a respected and prosperous professional in the country where he is a migrant. As princes of Judah in Jerusalem they knew that they were supposed to oversee the affairs of their nation and they still wanted to remain in charge of the affairs of the empire of Babylon during their stay there. Once they had the opportunity to enter the royal service in the palace of Babylon, they ensured that they performed excellently to enable them to remain relevant and respected by their bosses who ruled over the Babylonian Empire. Daniel 2:1-49, 3:1-30, 4:1-37, 5:1-30 and 6:1-28 can be summed up as follows:

- DSMA remained faithful, loyal, and devoted to God of their ancestors throughout their stay in Babylon. This means that they did not blame and were never angry with God for letting them be carried captive.

- God reciprocated appropriately so long as they remained there.

- They did their assigned royal duties so well that successive rulers or regimes retained them to continue to serve in the palace. This means that they were competent and dutiful at their jobs.

- They asked God's help whenever they deemed fit like Daniel 3:1-30 affirms that they never thought that just because they were competent at their jobs, they no longer needed God of their ancestors in their lives again. Whatever they achieved and became they continued to believe that it was by God's help and as a result remained loyal to Him.

All migrants should learn from Jesus' disciples and DSMA.

The other important point is that Acts 5:17-42 says in verse 41 that the disciples were happy that God let them suffer persecution in the hands of their haters. That is no doubt phenomenal. The natural human reaction to persecution is to blame either the persecutors or whoever was in position to prevent it but failed. Jeremiah 15:10-23 and 16:1-9 say when Prophet Jeremiah's persecution got to its peak, he blamed God for not doing anything to stop it. This is even though Jeremiah 1:1-11 and 17-19 confirms that God had given him prior notice that he would be persecuted severely on the day God commissioned him formally as a prophet. Apparently because Jesus had forewarned Peter and other disciples in Matthew 24:9-14, Mark 13:9-13 and Luke 21:12-19 that they would be persecuted for His sake, when it began to happen, Acts 5:41 says rather than being sad or blame God, Peter and others were glad that God considered them worthy to suffer persecution for His name sake. When applied, it is helpful for migrants to hope for the worst so that they can cope with whatever natives do to them. They should follow in the example of Apostle Peter and others to seek ways to survive such persecutions and still achieve their aims and objectives where they live. One of the banes of blamers is that the blamer misses the rewarding part of the experience. When Jeremiah blamed God he forgot that God had informed him earlier. He forgot that members of his generation were his problem rather than God; your attackers are your own relatives yet you chose to blame God or someone else. Relatives should protect from other attackers not for them to become the attackers.

Let us not digress into the subject of the fact that Abraham's claim in Genesis 20:10-20 that he was afraid he could be killed because of his wife confirms that man killing another man over contention for a beautiful woman has been going on since the time of Abraham or even before he was born. He must have grown up to know that there are places and people where the strong kill the weak or natives kill strangers to take their wives. And we know that II Samuel 11:1-27 and Matthew 1:17 confirm that David did it to Uriah 14 generations later. Dearly beloved, do not you think that this a good point to offer prayer to God to have mercy on humans. Should someone kill another man like himself because of his wife when he could get another woman who is still a virgin to marry?

First, it is mostly armed robbers who seek another's acquired possessions by force or illegally rather than spend time and effort to obtain theirs legitimately. No sane individual takes pride in seizing another's possession against the wish of the owner. That is why robbers can never boast of their stock in trade. Second, another man's wife is not better than a colleague's leftover. There is no pride in settling for a colleague's leftover under any circumstance. So, why prefer another person's leftover when you can get a fresh food to yourself without sharing it with any other. It is not necessarily my opinion because II Samuel 12:7-12 says:

> 7 "You are that man," Nathan said to David. "And this is what the Lord God of Israel says: 'I made you king of Israel and rescued you from Saul. 8 I gave you his kingdom and his wives; I made you king over Israel and Judah. If this had not been enough, I would have given you twice as much. 9 Why, then, have you disobeyed my commands? Why did you do this evil thing? You had Uriah killed in battle; you let the Ammonites kill him, and then you took his wife! 10 Now, in every generation some of your descendants will die a violent death because you have disobeyed me and have taken Uriah's wife. 11 I swear to you that

I will cause someone from your own family to bring trouble on you. You will see it when I take your wives from you and give them to another man; and he will have intercourse with them in broad daylight. 12 You sinned in secret, but I will make this happen in broad daylight for all Israel to see.'" (TEV)

Meanwhile, I Samuel 24:14 and 26:20b confirm that David told Saul that it was debasing for him as sitting king of Israel to abandon his legitimate royal duties to concentrate on cutting short David's life only for II Samuel 11:1-27 to say the same David practically stooped low to take the wife of one of his officers. He committed both adultery and murder against one of his finest officers because of a woman. Unfortunately, his son and successor, Solomon killed his older half-brother, Adonijah because of David's leftover youngest wife, Abishag after David's death. Coincidentally, Genesis 16:1-16 says Abraham had condescended to have a child by his wife's maid, Hagar 14 generations earlier. Unfortunately, Abraham's and David's condescend caused long lasting consequences. Some sorts of consequential condescend. There is no doubt that sometimes you condescend to conquer but, in these cases, it was catastrophic condescend.

One way to interpret the passage above is that God meant that He gave the throne of Israel and all the accompanying benefits and privileges without David asking for it. II Samuel 7:8-9 and I Chronicles 17:7-8 confirm that God reiterated this fact when He sent Prophet Nathan to respond to David's determination to build a Temple of worship to show his appreciation for God's favour and kindness in choosing him from among his father's sons to be king of Israel on behalf of his tribe of Judah. David attested to this fact when he confessed in I Chronicles 28:4 that though he was the youngest among his father's children it pleased God to choose him to be king of Israel. It is part of what he meant in Psalm 16:5-6 when he partly said that the lines have fallen to him in pleasant places. We know the famous story in I Samuel 16:1-13 which says that his father did not want him to participate in the anointing ceremony by Samuel for reasons best known to his father alone. Even Samuel had thought that his eldest brother, Eliab was fit enough to be anointed but God insisted until David was called back from the grazing fields.

God said if he wanted more women added to his already over bloated harem of queens, He would have allowed him to multiply them so long as none of the new women was any other man's wife. We say it is over bloated harem of queens because I Samuel 14:49-50 and II Samuel 21:1-14 strongly suggest that his predecessor, King Saul had one wife by the name of Ahinoam and one concubine by the name of Rizpah. Both bore Saul a total of six sons and two daughters – Rizpah had two sons for him while Ahinoam bore him two daughters and four sons. God said because David took another man's wife rather than getting an unmarried woman, he would suffer severe punishment – his descendants would share in it. God meant something like 'You Can, Yet Must Not' or 'You Can, However …' which in this case means that much as David could take more wives, none of them must be another's wife or at the expense of any other man like him. He must not hurt any other to make himself happy with any woman. Every God's approval has a boundary that the beneficiary must remain within otherwise he would suffer the punishment of the same God who gave the approval. That is why in this life, caution is crucial, commendable, and key. God's reason is that if David saddened others to make himself happy over a woman it would give basis for those that God never helped to become great on earth to say God's chosen is not godlier than them. That would mean that God was not fair to them compared to David. There is an implied obligation on God's favoured persons to behave better than non-God favoured individuals.

I Samuel 25:2-43, 30:1-5, II Samuel 2:2-4, 3:2-5 and II Chronicles 3:1-4 confirm that he had five wives who bore him children during the seven and a half years that he ruled over Judah from their tribal capital city of Hebron. Among the women was Abigail, Nabal's widow. God never blamed him for marrying Nabal's widow because he never contributed to Nabal's death in order to marry her though he nearly contributed to it. Then, II Samuel 5:13-15 and I Chronicles 3:5-9 and 14:3-7 say after becoming king of Israel in addition to Judah and moving his throne to the city of Jerusalem he got more wives and concubines who bore him more children.

Matthew 14:1-12 and Mark 6:14-29 say John the Baptist died by beheading because he rebuked Herod for marrying or taking over his brother, Philip's wife, Herodias while Philip was still very much alive. Luke 3:1-3-20 opens with the fact that when John the Baptist began his sacred assignment, Tiberias was the Emperor of the Roman Empire, Pontius Pilate was the governor of Judaea, Herod was the ruler of Galilee while his brother or sibling, Philip was the ruler of the territory of Iturea and Trachonitis; Lysanias was ruler of Abilene, while Annas and Caiaphas were high priests in the Temple in Jerusalem. Two brothers who were rulers or prominent personalities had issues over a woman. It is interesting that Matthew 14:1-12 and Mark 6:14-29 say Philip did not make trouble with Herod over the stealing of his wife. It was John the Baptist who made some trouble with Herod over stealing Philip's wife.

How it concerns our case is that David took the wife of one of his officers or subordinates. In fact, II Samuel 23:8-39 confirms in verses 18-19, 34 and 39 that Uriah's immediate boss or supervisor was Abishai who's immediate boss or supervisor was Joab who's superior or boss was David. I Chronicles 11:10-47 confirm the same fact in verses 20-21 and 41 just as II Samuel 8:15-18 and I Chronicles 11:4-6 and 27:34b confirm that Joab was COAS of David's army of Israel. It means that David stooped down three levels of authority structure to kill his subordinate to have his wife for keeps. God meant that David should have been contented with what He had given him rather than become greedy for what his fellow man owned. Esther 2:1-18 says when the Emperor of Persia wanted another queen, he ordered for virgins to be found for him. I Kings 1:1-4 says when it became necessary to get David another woman in his old age, a young woman or virgin by the name of Abishag was found for him. That is what God meant that he should have done rather than kill a man in order to take over his wife.

Genesis 35:22 and 49:1-4 is the story of Reuben having intercourse with his father's concubine and his father placing a curse on him and his descendants as punishment. I Chronicles 5:1-2 says it is as a result that he lost the respect and honour that the eldest son deserved among his siblings and it was transferred to Joseph the eldest son of Reuben's step-mother, Rachel. Deuteronomy 33:1-6 says by the time of Moses the precarious predicament of the descendants of Reuben was so bad that when Moses was pronouncing his final blessings on the twelve tribes, he had to plead with God not to let the tribe of Reuben go into extinct. It is not just that they were not producing prosperous persons, but they were not even increasing in number like other tribes of Israel. This was all because their pioneer ancestor, Reuben opted for his father's leftover woman rather than look for a fresh young woman to marry. But let us leave that train of thought for now.

For Abraham to believe that he could be killed in order to take his wife and he never had such fear back home means that he could not vouch for the character of the people in the place he chose to sojourn and that is very relevant to us all. It is stupid and suicidal to assume that the place you have gone to sojourn is not different from where you are coming from. Also, as Abraham projected about taking his wife, she was taken indeed until God forced them to return her. Each time he perceived that she would be taken, she was taken from him. It appears like his spirit-man told him what to expect each time and that is a pointer to us that amid strangers, it is safer to be sensitive to your inner voice. When a thought flows into your heart, do not brush it aside fast, meditate on it, ask yourself why such a thought should come to you at that point, is it a message from the spiritual realm to guide you to survive the environment and situation? I Samuel 18:1-5, 19:1-24, 20:1-43, 23:15-18 and 31:1-13 can be interpreted to mean that because Jonathan ignored his inner voice he died prematurely without accomplishing God's plan for his life alongside David as his divine destiny partner like Barnabas and Paul were.

We are spirit, soul and body and our spirit inhabits our body to operate on earth, when anything dangerous is about to harm us, the spirit would sound an alarm to the soul to pass on to the body to take precautionary steps to avoid the looming danger. That is what King Saul meant when I Samuel 28:15 quote him as lamenting to Samuel that God had stopped speaking to him either by prophets or by dreams. Genesis 37:1-11 says God revealed His planned future fortune to Joseph through two dreams. Genesis 41:1-36 confirms that God did the same thing for Pharaoh of Egypt just as Daniel 4:1-37 says He did for Nebuchadnezzar.

It is interesting to note that it was not that Abraham heard from some natives that they were fond of taking beautiful wives of strangers in their nation. He did not go to ask anyone before he could draw that conclusion and correctly too. Abraham was a prophet to himself in the sense of being able to foresee what could happen to him in the immediate future and wherever God led him, and he took measures to prevent it. God did not appear to him in a vision to tell him that the people in Egypt or Gerar could take his wife because of her beauty, he just thought about it and he was correct. This suggests that he was exercising his senses correctly which means that though God led him to Canaan, he did not stop to use his senses where necessary. When God came to talk to him specifically on any issue, he heeded but if not, he used his God-given sense and the experiences he had gathered and learnt from the things that he heard from others, including elders. Strange land is not a place to deal presumptuously that everybody is God-fearing like yourself just because you are. Abraham never took another man's wife, but it was not enough reason for him to assume that there were no other men who could not kill to take another's wife.

14

STRATEGIC PURCHASE OF LOYALTY

The general belief is that God gave Joseph the wisdom with which he interpreted Pharaoh's dreams for which reason Pharaoh appointed him to supervise his nobles. Joseph attested to this claim when Genesis 41:15-16-32 says he told Pharaoh that it is God who gives wisdom to give correct interpretation to dreams. If he were not able to interpret the dreams, Pharaoh would not have found reason to appoint him the Prime Minister and supervisor of all the older officials and nobles he met in the palace of Egypt. Therefore, his ability to do what others could not do made Pharaoh to prefer him to serve as his second-in-command which is like using his dream-interpreting ability to win the preference of the big boss, Pharaoh.

Genesis 47:13-26 confirms that afterwards, Joseph used this position to convert the land of the Egyptians to that of Pharaoh and Genesis 41:53-57 confirms that as a result, when the people went to complain to Pharaoh to tell Joseph to be kinder to them, he told them to return to do whatever Joseph instructed them because doing Joseph's instructions benefited Pharaoh personally. Now, Joseph's brief/schedule of duty or terms of reference as the Prime Minister outlined by Genesis 41:33-44 did not say he must take the land and proceeds of the land of the citizens for Pharaoh, but he added it when he realized that he needed to do something more to make Pharaoh continue to retain him in that exalted position which Genesis 45:4-12 strongly suggests that he became obsessed with and spoke highly of it when he told his brothers glowingly about his greatness and power in the land of Egypt. He told them to go back to Canaan to bring their father along with them to Egypt to see how great and powerful he had become.

Repaying his benefactor and boss at the expense of the subjects can be said to mean that Joseph understood that it is one thing to attain the position of the Prime Minister, and another to keep it for long or so long as one lived or loved to. Having got the position on merit by reason of the fact that he was the only one who was able to interpret the king's dreams, Joseph needed to do something more to encourage the king to retain him in the position as long as they both lived. Despite the fact that God made the king to look favorably on him, he still had to do something personally or exclusively beneficial to the king to convince him that he was not just doing God's will in favour of Joseph without him getting any personal benefit. Since Joseph remained in that position for the rest of his life after appeasing the king of Egypt, we can as well say that if he had not appeased the king, he might not have kept the position long after the 14 years that were most critical to the sustenance of the economy of Egypt.

In other words, Joseph went the extra mile to please the native who God used to make his stay in the strange land of Egypt a pleasant experience. It can be summed up as "Benefiting Benefactor Benefits" or "Repaying Helper Rewards". II Samuel 17:1-36 and 23:1-7 and I Chronicles 17:1-27 and 28:1-4 can be interpreted to mean that God rewarded David for determining to build a place of worship as a proof of his appreciation that God made him king of Israel though he was the youngest child of his father. His father's vision for him was to be a shepherd in the grazing fields of his hometown of Bethlehem only for God to take him far beyond that social status to make him the king of Israel. Joseph knew that he began his sojourn in Egypt as domestic servant and prisoner before Pharaoh freed him from prison and made him the most powerful official in his kingdom.

When Exodus 1:1-16 says until long after Joseph's reign and death, the Egyptians did not torture Joseph's kinsmen, the Hebrews/Israelites, it was not just because God favoured Joseph, it was partly because Joseph used the position to appease the most powerful Egyptian, Pharaoh. He understood that to survive among strangers, it is expedient to do something extra to make them happy. If you claim that God gave you a position and do not need any man to help you keep it, be rest assured that the sons of men would make life most miserable for you while occupying the position. It can be claimed that one of Samuel's greatest undoing was that while he did everything possible to please God as the leader of Israel, he did not care about doing things to make the leading citizens of Israel feel regarded and honoured by him as the national leader. It is the real heart-hidden reason the leading citizens of Israel hid under the guise that his sons were not as honest as he had been as their leader.

The rejection of his sons as his successor made him sorrowful in his retirement after Saul had been made king in place of his sons as the national leader. When God said He was unhappy just as Samuel was, that his sons were not allowed to rule Israel after him, surely it was encouraging but as we know the story, it did not stop God from granting the request of the leading citizens of Israel to provide them a royal ruler who replaced Samuel's sons as his successor. This means that God's support for Samuel did not stop the frustration that attended the rejection of his sons, and therefore, Samuel still died with that heartache. It was part of the reason that Samuel stage-managed the sad end of Saul just before he died, and even after.

Pharaoh must have been glad that Joseph never made him regret appointing and giving him what can be tagged 'sweeping powers' to govern the nation on his behalf. He must have been most glad that Joseph used the delegated authority to enrich him and to have a stronger hold on his subjects. So long as you please those they call the 'powers that be' in the environment and territory, they would lend support to your position and status among them. There are persons that much of the citizens respect and accept whatever they say whether rightly or wrongly and if you get the support of such persons, most of the people would do your bidding. I Samuel 27:1-12 can be said to mean that once King Achish decided to host David in his kingdom, his officials and subjects, including the wife and relatives of Goliath whom I Samuel 17:1-58 confirms that David killed had no choice than to allow David live among them. I Samuel 8:1-22 can be said to mean that once the acceptable leaders of Israel rose from their national conference and concluded that they did not want Samuel's sons to lead their nation after him, it was taken that the entire populace rejected the reign of Samuel's sons whereas it is very possible that there were some commoners who did not think that Samuel's sons should not lead them after him.

The saying that the voice of the people is the voice of God can be reframed to be the voice of the leading citizens is taken as the voice of the entire citizens. Amos 6:1b can be interpreted to mean that the commoners seek the help of their leading citizens. Isaiah 3:1-3 gives the impression that the commoners hinge their hope and confidence on the leading citizens. Nehemiah 5:1-5 can be interpreted to mean that the commoners are economically dependent on the rich leading citizens of the nation or society. Some of the people are too wretched for their voice to ever be heard and accepted. Ecclesiastes 9:13-16 confirms that even if a poor or wretched man has the wisdom that could benefit the entire nation the leading citizens would not accept and adopt the man's wisdom to save the entire nation. The word 'wretched' could really be replaced with the word 'remote' in which case, it would be that their voice is too remote from where decisions that are binding on the entire populace could or should be heard.

Their opinion can be taken for granted or is naturally subsumed into that of the prominent and popular. It is part of the reason Numbers 11:16-17 says God's opinion or directive to Moses was that whoever that he would appoint to serve as his lieutenant must be persons who are already respected and honoured as worthy leader by the people. It explains why II Samuel 2-3:1-20 says until Abner agreed that David could become king of the entire 12 tribes of Israel, it did not happen despite the fact that the Israelites, including members of Saul and Abner's tribe of Benjamin had been itching for David to rule over them immediately after Saul's death, seven and a half years earlier.

As powerful as Samuel was, he was a stranger to the politics of human survival. He knew only one aspect of surviving in the position of greatness and glamour which was pleasing God. This is vital because, God made all humans and would consider the other people when taking sides with persons who please Him. He understood that the leading Israelites who held a national conference behind Samuel and came up with the damning verdict that Samuel hated were his (Samuel's) fellow descendants of His beloved friend, Abraham. Much as He did not like the way Samuel's feelings had been hurt, yet, He did not want to force His views on the people who had said what Samuel did not like because numerically speaking, they were in the majority.

Also, God realized that it was easier for Him to tell Samuel to endure the hurt than convince the protesting Israelites to drop that idea and stop hurting Samuel. These Israelites meant that much as Samuel had pleased God, God should understand that Samuel had not pleased them as persons who had become so successful in their different fields of endeavour to earn the respect of the poor Israelites who now considered them as the leading citizens of the nation.

The fact that all of them could hold meeting behind Samuel without any of them going behind the majority to report their plan to reject his sons becoming his successor meant that he had no good rapport with those leading citizens of the nation he had led since he was only a youth. That is not good enough. Sure, he was the most religious person in his generation of Israelites but to have distanced himself from the other leading citizens because of that 'holier than thou' mindset led to his feelings being hurt when he should sit back in retirement and be happy with the way he had lived his life. The tone with which he spoke against Saul from the world of the dead in I Samuel 28:15-20 speaks of one of the greatest men of God who ever lived who was still angry with someone who offended him while still on earth even in the world of the dead. It strongly suggests that the events that led to the rejection of his sons had not left his heart or that the hurt that attended the rejection of his sons as his successor never healed for the rest of his lifetime. This fact makes Genesis 4:8-10, I Samuel 28:15-20 and Revelation 6:9-11 to have something in common – the righteous who suffered in the hands of the wicked while on earth seeking the punishment of the wicked from the world of the dead. Jeremiah 11:18-23 and 18:18-23 say Prophet Jeremiah sought the punishment of his attackers in his lifetime. He did not wait for them to kill him before asking God to deal decisively with them like Abel did.

There is the subject of 'Ruined by Regrettable Respect Request' or 'Ruinous Regrettable Respect Request' with regards to Saul's regrettable relationship with Samuel as Saul's benefactor. I Samuel 15:30-31 says Saul as sitting king of Israel after admitting that he had sinned against God demanded respect from his predecessor as well as benefactor – the man that God used to make him king when he least expected and who had not sinned against God to show him respect/honour in the presence of his officials and officers. The palace officials and army officers he was able to appoint only because Samuel obeyed God to appoint him king of Israel. I Kings 19:15-23 confirms that when Prophet Elijah refused to obey God to go anoint Hazael as king of Syria and Jehu as king of Israel, God did not reprimand him. It means that it was great favour that Samuel did for Saul when he obeyed God and anointed Saul as his successor at the expense of his sons even though Samuel was unhappy that his sons were replaced as his successor.

Saul disregarded this fact to demand respect from Samuel in the presence of his officials and officers. He tried to use Samuel to prove to his officials and officers that he had become so great that even his predecessor gives him considerable respect. But this is the real reason we went into Saul's great mistake of demanding respect from Samuel. I Samuel 28:14-15 says this same King Saul bowed low to the ground to show Samuel respect when he thought that he needed Samuel's help. The Samuel you humiliated before your appointed officials and officers or publicly, you now went to him in private to show respect because you are desperate and you expect him to regard your respect and help you in your time of need. That is the height of stupidity and self-deception. Samuel saw it as his chance to tear him into shreds.

I Samuel 19:1-24 says Saul had disrespected God and Samuel earlier over David. First, he failed to honour God when he disregarded the oath that he took in God's name to refrain from hunting down David. Second, he disrespected Samuel when he learnt that David had gone to seek refuge at Samuel's place, rather than let David be, because of the respect that he had for Samuel who God used to make him king, he made four attempts to capture David there and stopped only after God's spirit humiliated him all day long and learnt that David had left Samuel's place because of his determination to still come over to capture him to kill at Samuel's home. It meant that he could not spare David's life for neither God's sake nor Samuel's sake. Meanwhile, I Samuel 24:1-22 and 26:1-25 confirm that David spared his life on two occasions because David honored God.

Fundamentally, just as Joseph was a stranger not only in Egypt but to the office of the Prime Minister of Egypt so also Saul and his tribe of Benjamin were strangers to the throne of Israel. Genesis 49:1-28(8-12) and I Chronicles 5:1-2 and 28:4 confirm that God assigned the royal rulership of Israel to David and his tribe of Judah. That is why it can be safely claimed that just as Joseph became the Prime Minister of Egypt by God's special arrangement so also Saul became king of Israel by God's special arrangement. Then, you can readily guess why we linked the two stories – while Joseph pleased the powerful men that God used to make him great in the strangest of places, Saul failed to do likewise even when Joseph's example was available for him to learn from. Joseph thought Pharaoh was one of those who he must not offend in order for him to continue to enjoy the position that God ordained for him whereas Saul did not think or believe that he was better off offending his officials and officers to please Samuel rather than otherwise if he desired to retain the throne for long. I Samuel 13:5-14, 15:30-31 and 28:14-15 say:

> 5 The Philistines assembled to fight the Israelites; they had thirty thousand war chariots, six thousand cavalry troops, and as many soldiers

as there are grains of sand on the seashore. They went to Michmash, east of Bethaven, and camped there. 6 Then they launched a strong attack against the Israelites, putting them in a desperate situation. Some of the Israelites hid in caves and holes or among the rocks or in pits and wells; 7 others crossed the Jordan River into the territories of Gad and Gilead. Saul was still at Gilgal, and the people with him were trembling with fear. 8 He waited seven days for Samuel, as Samuel had instructed him to do, but Samuel still had not come to Gilgal. The people began to desert Saul, 9 so he said to them, "Bring me the burnt sacrifices and the fellowship sacrifices." He offered a burnt sacrifice, 10 and just as he was finishing, Samuel arrived. Saul went out to meet him and welcome him, 11 but Samuel said, "What have you done?" Saul answered, "The people were deserting me, and you had not come when you said you would; besides that, the Philistines are gathering at Michmash. 12 So I thought, 'The Philistines are going to attack me here in Gilgal, and I have not tried to win the Lord's favor.' So I felt I had to offer a sacrifice." 13 "That was a foolish thing to do," Samuel answered. "You have not obeyed the command the Lord your God gave you. If you had obeyed, he would have let you and your descendants rule over Israel forever. 14 But now your rule will not continue. Because you have disobeyed him, the Lord will find the kind of man he wants and make him ruler of his people."

30 "I have sinned," Saul replied. "But at least show me respect in front of the leaders of my people and all of Israel. Go back with me so that I can worship the Lord your God." 31 So Samuel went back with him, and Saul worshiped the Lord.

14 "What does it look like?" he asked. "It's an old man coming up," she answered. "He is wearing a

cloak." Then Saul knew that it was Samuel, and he bowed to the ground in respect. 15 Samuel said to Saul, "Why have you disturbed me? Why did you make me come back?" Saul answered, "I am in great trouble! The Philistines are at war with me, and God has abandoned me. He doesn't answer me any more, either by prophets or by dreams. And so I have called you, for you to tell me what I must do." (TEV)

Can you see the stupidity in Saul's respect misadventure in the above passage? When he thought that he was the greatest thing that ever happened to the nation of Israel, he asked his benefactor and predecessor to show him respect in the presence of his officials however, when he realized, many years later, that he was nobody worthy of any respect, he went to bow down to the same man that he once asked to show him respect. Even if he got the respect when he demanded it what use was it when he had to go and return it, so to speak. Samuel did not ask him to bow low to worship before what he did later. By consulting a dead man and bowing low to the ground to worship the dead man, he violated Leviticus 20:6-based God's command that forbade the consultation of the spirit of the dead. I Chronicles 10:13-14 can be said to mean that it is the reason God let Saul die in that battle against the Philistines. Deuteronomy 34:1-6 can be interpreted to mean that one of the reasons God concealed Moses' burial site from the Israelites is because God knew that considering the miracles He used Moses to perform the Israelites were likely to go to worship at his graveyard.

Whoever demands respect from the person that he should respect has ruined himself by reason of demanding respect from him. Whether the time-gap be long or short, he is doomed by the mere opening of his mouth to demand it whether he was shown the respect demanded or not. It is like a smashed egg, you can never put it back again, you can not say 'I am sorry, I recall my demand for respect from you' unless he decides to be extra merciful. Some would quip, what was he thinking placing such a demand on Samuel who I Samuel 8-11 can be said to have single-handedly made him king of Israel or great as God instructed. Was he 'high' on any substance? Proverbs 21:14 can be summed as 'Gift Pacifies' that is if someone is angry with you, giving him gift secretly should pacify such an offended individual however, the passage above says Samuel could not be appeased because Saul came to show him respect in secret. Samuel wanted the respect from Saul when he was still alive not when he had died and the Israelites can no longer be conscious that even though Saul had succeeded him it had not diminished the respect that he enjoyed from them since he was a youth. One of the most unfortunate rulers are those whose predecessor(s) are not just alive but still around within the nation because those predecessors would still want to flex their influence. Samuel knew that if he moved against Saul, God regarded him highly enough to support his determination to undo Saul and he did not shy away from using that advantage over Saul. The worst thing was that Saul knew next to nothing about God's ways, methods, and tactics.

Usurping Samuel's role to offer sacrifice was the first time and way that Saul disrespected Samuel as his benefactor. I Samuel 13 – 14:1-46 confirms that the battle was won without Samuel's proper sacrifice which means God never commanded that sacrifice before He would give Israel's army led by Saul victory over the Philistines. God understood that Samuel ordered Saul to wait for him to offer the sacrifices just to prove if Saul would respect him (Samuel) enough to wait for him no matter the pressure that Saul was under. Saul confirmed Samuel's feelings that Saul no longer had high regard for him again once he led the defeat of the Ammonites to become fully accepted by the Israelites since I Samuel 11:1-15. It is part of the reason I Samuel 15:1 says before Samuel would tell Saul God's assignment in the next verse 2-3, he first reminded Saul not to forget that he was the one who God used to make him king rather than his appointed officials and officers. But unfortunately for Saul, he did not comprehend the "Oldies' Manner of Speech". In fact, apart from disobeying God's instruction through Samuel in I Samuel 15:1-35, Saul committed two other grievous evils against Samuel as follows:

(i) Verses 24-27 says he tore Samuel's dress while

(ii) Verses 25 and 30-31 say he demanded respect from Samuel in the presence of his officials and officers.

Samuel was not only his predecessor, benefactor and God's prophet and priest, he was older than Saul. Would Saul ask his father, Kish to show him respect in any form in the presence of his officials and officers just because he was the sitting king of Israel? What Joseph did in favour of Pharaoh, there is no assurance that Pharaoh's sons would have done any better if Pharaoh had appointed any of his sons to that position. Saul displayed unforgivable ignorance when verses 24-31 says while Samuel talked about his loss of the throne of Israel, Saul was more concerned about

(1) Been shown respect in the presence of his officials and officers.

(2) Going to worship the Lord without any focus – he did not go to the presence of God in the place of worship to ask for God's forgiveness that was most crucial for him at this point. He admitted that he had sinned yet no mention of his desire for God's forgiveness as if to say Samuel's respect in the presence of his officials and officers was more important to him than asking God's

forgiveness or appeasement of God who he had sinned against.

(3) It is an abomination in God's sight for a sinner whether self-confessed or not to demand respect or expect a holier individual, non-sinner or God's pleaser to show him respect no matter how great and powerful the sinner. God regarded Samuel so highly that when Samuel felt offended God felt unhappy as well.

Psalm 99:6, Jeremiah 15:1 and Ezekiel 14:12-14 and 19-20 can be described as God's signed and sealed certificate and testimonial of the high premium that God placed on Samuel as a righteous man of an impeccable repute in God's sight or rating. Job 1:1-22, 2:1-10, 8:1-7, 11:1-6 and 42:7-10 can be said to mean that when Job's three friends implied that they were holier than him in God's sight, God debunked their curious claim and indirectly disgraced them by asking them to regard Job as being holy enough to serve as HP to them and therefore, they should provide sacrifice materials for Job to offer sacrifices to Him on their behalf so that Job would pray to Him so He would forgive their sin of claiming to be speaking for Him against Job when He never sent them to blame Job and his sons for the misfortune that He allowed Satan to do to them.

Someone could claim that Saul could not have retained the throne of Israel to pass on to his sons and descendants because God never meant it for his tribe of Benjamin originally. Therefore, David was able to retain it and pass it on to his son, Solomon, and descendants because God meant it for his tribe of Judah originally. I Samuel 17:1-58, 18:1-30, 19:1-24, 20:1-42, 21:1-15, 22:1-23, 23:1-29, 24:1-22, 26:1-25, 27:1-12, 28:1-25, 29:1-11, 30:1-29 and 31:1-13 and I Chronicles 10-14 can be interpreted to mean that if Saul had tolerated David or joined his reasonable and God fearing eldest son and preferred heir, Jonathan to accept David as God preferred, chosen and anointed successor to him (Saul), he (Saul) would not have died fighting the Philistines as it happened. He would not have found himself in the desperate situation that forced him to go to the witch of Endor to seek spiritual guidance from already dead and buried Samuel, an abominable act which angered God to decree that he and his sons died 24 hours after. He should have respected the oath that I Samuel 19:1-6 confirms that Jonathan made him to take in God's name never to attack David again. Jonathan reminded him that David was one of his benefactors. He should have condoned David as a strategic ally that he needed rather than an enemy that must die because of envy and jealousy. As the most prominent member of the tribe of Judah in his regime, Saul should have pampered David to sustain his stay on the throne. Genesis 39:1-6, 19-23, 41:37-41 and I Samuel 18:6-16, 28-30 say:

> 1 Now the Ishmaelites had taken Joseph to Egypt and sold him to Potiphar, one of the king's officers, who was the captain of the palace guard. 2 The Lord was with Joseph and made him successful. He lived in the house of his Egyptian master, 3 who saw that the Lord was with Joseph and had made him successful in everything he did. 4 Potiphar was pleased with him and made him his personal servant; so he put him in charge of his house and everything he owned. 5 From then on, because of Joseph the Lord blessed the

household of the Egyptian and everything that he had in his house and in his fields. 6 Potiphar turned over everything he had to the care of Joseph and did not concern himself with anything except the food he ate. Joseph was well-built and good-looking,

19 Joseph's master was furious 20 and had Joseph arrested and put in the prison where the king's prisoners were kept, and there he stayed. 21 But the Lord was with Joseph and blessed him, so that the jailer was pleased with him. 22 He put Joseph in charge of all the other prisoners and made him responsible for everything that was done in the prison. 23 The jailer did not have to look after anything for which Joseph was responsible, because the Lord was with Joseph and made him succeed in everything he did.

37 The king and his officials approved this plan, 38 and he said to them, "We will never find a

better man than Joseph, a man who has God's spirit in him." 39 The king said to Joseph, "God has shown you all this, so it is obvious that you have greater wisdom and insight than anyone else. 40 I will put you in charge of my country, and all my people will obey your orders. Your authority will be second only to mine. 41 I now appoint you governor over all Egypt."

6 As David was returning after killing Goliath and as the soldiers were coming back home, women from every town in Israel came out to meet King Saul. They were singing joyful songs, dancing, and playing tambourines and lyres. 7 In their celebration the women sang, "Saul has killed thousands, but David tens of thousands." 8 Saul did not like this, and he became very angry. He said, "For David they claim tens of thousands, but only thousands for me. They will be making him king next!" 9 And so he was jealous and suspicious of David from that day on. 10 The next

day an evil spirit from God suddenly took control of Saul, and he raved in his house like a madman. David was playing the harp, as he did every day, and Saul was holding a spear. 11 "I'll pin him to the wall," Saul said to himself, and he threw the spear at him twice; but David dodged each time. 12 Saul was afraid of David because the Lord was with David but had abandoned him. 13 So Saul sent him away and put him in command of a thousand men. David led his men in battle 14 and was successful in all he did, because the Lord was with him. 15 Saul noticed David's success and became even more afraid of him. 16 But everyone in Israel and Judah loved David because he was such a successful leader. 28 Saul realized clearly that the Lord was with David and also that his daughter Michal loved him. 29 So he became even more afraid of David and was his enemy as long as he lived. 30 The Philistine armies would come and fight, but in every battle David was more successful than any of Saul's other officers.

As a result David became very famous. (TEV)

There is no doubt that the reason we read this passage is obvious. Potiphar, the prison superintendent and Pharaoh teach that whenever you find that someone has God's help to do what no other can do the wise and profitable thing to do is to appoint such a person to the position of authority so you can benefit more from God because of him. How Saul did not find this out to follow is known to him alone. Daniel 6:1-3 says it is the reason that Darius determined to promote Daniel to the office of the Prime Minister to the Babylonian Empire after he became king of Babylon at the expense of Nebuchadnezzar's son and successor, Belshazzar. The difference between Pharaoh and Saul is that while Pharaoh disregarded Joseph's despicable Hebrew background to get the best out of Joseph who God sponsored, Saul an Israelite failed to maximize God provided David to save him from the shame of not been able to lead the army of Israel to secure victory over the enemies of Israel particularly the Philistines in the later years of his reign. Pharaoh believed that he needed Joseph as much as Joseph needed him, so he gave Joseph free hand to administer his kingdom. Consider the magnitude of evil that Saul did to himself in this respect. Pharaoh had only one man who had God's spirit and presence or support and got the best out of him. Saul had Samuel and David yet threw both of them away because (1) he was desperate for ruinous respect in the presence of his appointed officials and officers in the case of Samuel and (2) he was jealous in the case of David. It is very unfortunate to say God could not help Saul in the circumstance because he chose to fear his officers rather than God who made him king when he least expected.

The other issue is the subject of Saul typifying (i) they that the gods wants to destroy they first make mad, (ii) buccaneer beneficiaries. Saul was obsessed with respect from everyone including those he should not demand respect from. In any case, respect is better earned than extorted because extorted respect does not reward like earned version. Then, he damned the persons God used to benefit him at different times and in different ways as well as those that could benefit him. Apart from Samuel and David who he had benefited from, he defied his bodyguards' discouragement to kill God's authentic priests somewhat unjustly. The killing of the priests was against the law of natural justice because it was never true that (1) David was against Saul and (2) that the priests were supporting David to undermine Saul as king of Israel. He could have used the priest he killed to clarify God's counsel rather going to consult Samuel in the world of the dead via the witch of Endor. Let us consider simple logic or commonsense. The David who killed the Goliath that Saul could not kill went to consult the priest Abimelech to consult God for him.

Should Saul not go to that priest who consults God for a greater warrior to consult God for him so he could get God's help to be able to conquer the enemies that the greater warrior can conquer by God's help? First, I Samuel 17:1-58 and 18:30 say apart from defeating the Philistines on the day he killed Goliath, David led the defeat of the Philistines several other times afterwards during the period that he served as officer in the army of Israel with Saul as king. Second, I Samuel 18:12-16 and 28-29 confirms that Saul was conscious of the fact that God was no longer with him but was with David and that as a result he feared or revered David. Therefore, third, if the man you revere goes to a man of God for spiritual support does commonsense not that you should go to the same man of God to help you rather than continue to attack the man that you revere a great deal?

Since you are the king of the nation who I Samuel 8:10-19 confirms that God gave the uncommon privilege to enrich yourself at the expense of your subjects, it should follow that you should have more resources to give to the priest than David would have since you had implied in I Samuel 9:1-11 that it is not right to go to the man of God without a gift. In fact, I Samuel 21:1-10 strongly suggest that rather than give to the man of God, David was collecting sustenance from the man of God whenever he went to visit the man of God to consult God for him. Something was fundamentally wrong with Saul spiritually to have disregarded the most logical line of action that any reasonable individual would take in the circumstance. He should have done everything to secure and enjoy the support of Samuel, David and the priests and prophets of God as long as he remained the king of Israel or throughout the 40 years that he served as the king of Israel.

15

REWARDING SELF-INTEGRATION

When Pharaoh appointed Joseph as the Prime Minister of Egypt on merit, Genesis 41:1-57 confirms in verses 37-46 that he went further to give him an Egyptian wife. It would have been counter-productive for Joseph to say it was an abomination for him to marry a non-Hebrew wife and if part of the condition for occupying the exalted position of the Prime Minister is marrying a native, he would not take the position. Meanwhile, we can argue that Pharaoh made him marry his fellow Egyptian in order to silence those who might resent Joseph's occupation of that exalted position on account that there was no proof that he even liked them as Egyptians. This is because if he liked them, he should have married one of their daughters since he was not married before he met the king who appointed him as the Prime Minister. Another benefit of marrying one of the natives is that even if there is persecution for being a non-native, one's native spouse and his or her family would do everything possible to save and protect one in order to make one's native spouse happy. Someone told me the story of his business exploits in a foreign country. He took his younger brother to head his business in that country, got him a wife from among the people there and once she got pregnant for him, they gave reason to ship her to his home country. From that point, the younger brother visits home to impregnate her and returns to the foreign country base. When I asked his reason, he said it was obvious that as long as the girl's family was conscious that their daughter and her children were living in his own country, they would not do anything injurious to them and their interest in their country so that they would not retaliate by harming their own daughter and their grandchildren. For him, it was business survival strategy in a foreign land.

As we know the famous story of Rahab, Joshua 2:1-24 and 6:22-24 confirm that she started relevance in life as a harlot among her natives in Jericho but upon taking her relatives to join the commonwealth of the Israel, Matthew 1:1-17 can be interpreted to confirm in verse 4-6 that she became famous for marrying probably one of the Israelites and spies who Joshua had sent to Jericho and she hosted by the name of Salmon, a member of the tribe of Judah. This means that she chose to integrate herself into the Israelites by marrying one of them rather than merely continuing as a harlot. Also, Uriah was a Hittite when he joined the Israelites and their army and married Bathsheba the daughter of one of Israelite-native officers. Joining the army of Israel meant he was committed to the Israelites' fortune to the extent of killing any other nationals considered as enemies by the Israelites and their rulers. Then he took a further step to take one of their daughters to be his wife rather than go back to his Hittite country to get a wife. It was like he ceded his Hittite nativity to cleave to the acquired nativity. His case is very important considering that God told the Israelites who were carried captive to Babylon that as long as they lived there, they had a responsibility to work for the good of the land they found themselves. Therefore, we can say that Uriah was determined to work for the good of the land of Israel where he relocated to. This is completely opposite to what David did during the period that I Samuel 27:1-12 confirms that he lived among the Philistines.

Not only that, Moses married the daughter of a leading citizen of Midian during the forty years he spent there. He accepted employment from this same father-in-law, Jethro which can be said to fully integrate him into Midian even when he did not join them to serve their gods even though Jethro served as the priest of Midian. Getting married to one of them means that you believe that they are good enough to be your flesh and blood. Moses was homeless when he got to Midian such that marrying Jethro's daughter and taking up job with him gave Moses a roof over his head. Here was someone who was being groomed to become the king of Egypt before he transformed into a homeless wanderer in Midian. He had to give up his ego and take up a job with his wife's father to survive in the immediate. He did not flaunt his Egyptian royal heritage in the strange land but humbled himself to do whatever was necessary to survive even when he would return to Egypt by God's leading to become greater than the king and the people of Egypt because Exodus 11:3 confirms that when he returned 40 years later, the Egyptians considered him a very great man.

It is important to remind ourselves that the case of Elimelech relocating to Moab in order to escape famine in Bethlehem, his place of birth and home of his ancestors, lends further credence to this fact when it says his two sons married Moabite girls. One important line of thought is that if the natives are good enough for you to live among them, then they should be good enough to be your spouse. It is not right to nurse this heart-hidden resentment that you can never marry any of them yet remain among them to reap from the prosperity of their nation. A lady's mother was very fond of her own natives while she lived among another tribe completely. When her surviving first daughter was to get married, her first surviving son who was born after the daughter suggested that their mother should allow her to marry from among the natives of the land where they resided. This woman shut the son up, saying he was too young to know or be able to tell her what was right or wrong. Then, the daughter missed marrying the first man who was their mother's kinsman. Out of frustration, she settled for another of mummy's kinsman who was not as well-to-do as the first man she missed marrying. As the years progressed, the fortune of this daughter's husband became so bad that she could not afford more than the equivalent of US$1.50 as support to the mother annually. By this time, this woman was incredibly old and needed the support of the children to survive because she was not getting any pension or government support. It was then that she realized that her insistence on her daughter marrying their native was not the best idea.

Let us understand something incredibly significant about the mystery behind the magic-wand nature of marital affinity with natives by foreigners. There is the concept of "For the Sake of …". So long as Joseph remained the Prime Minister of Egypt, the Egyptians did not consider afflicting the Hebrews even though the Egyptians were brought up to despise Hebrews. So long as Pharaoh liked and supported Joseph on the throne even when he claimed the land or practically enslaved the people to Pharaoh, the Egyptians had no choice than to abide by whatever Joseph did to them. So long as Joseph's economic policies made

Pharaoh richer and stronger than the ordinary Egyptian, he told them to return to do Joseph's bidding. Isaiah 22:20-24 says when God elevates an individual to a position that he influences several thousands and even millions, such an elevated individual would become a source of honour to his relatives. For the sake of his affiliation with Jesus, Acts 5:13 says the rulers of the Jews were compelled to respect Apostle Peter and others who were unlearned individuals. For the sake of Mordecai and Esther as the Prime Minister and Queen of the Persian Empire, their Jewish kinsmen were revered throughout the Persian Empire. Now, there are countless other of such examples in the Holy Scriptures but more important is the fact that in the same way, for the sake of an immigrant's native spouse, the generality of the natives will naturally treat the immigrant kindly or more kindly.

Along this line, Genesis 12:10-20 and 20:1-18 say for the sake of Sarah whom the Pharaoh of Egypt and Abimelech of the Philistines married at different times because Abraham did not tell them that she was his wife as well, they treated Abraham more kindly. It is a natural thing for natives to waive some stringent rules against foreigners for any foreigner who marries their native or vice versa. If a native marries a foreigner, they would for the sake of the foreigner-spouse treat his or her relatives living among them kindlier. This is not bribery to get marital benefit or to compromise but just a natural human way of basing attitude toward others on benefit which is "Benefit-based Attitude to Others" or "Benefit based Beamed Attitude" which means that the attitude that man beams toward his fellow man is usually predicated on the benefits gained, being enjoyed or anticipated.

Resentment for non-natives is another natural phenomenon of life in every generation and any clime. This is part of what really happens in this matter. It is inevitable that we all have issues wherever we live at any time. And when we have issues, it is natural for us to seek solution and mostly, through fellow humans. However, if you are married to a native, when you have your challenges and the authorities try to make things difficult for you, it would be the responsibility of your spouse to go to his or her own people to say, 'look, though he or she is supposed to be a stranger, he or she is my spouse and treating him or her like a typical stranger would affect my happiness therefore, consider my happiness and joy and treat him or her kindly like you would do me as a native and/or in order to make me happy'. We know that famous story when Esther 8:1-2 says once King Ahasuerus, the Emperor of the Persian Empire learnt that his current Queen, Esther was Mordecai's relative, he favoured Mordecai with determination. This case is important to us in this respect because, there are two reasons that Ahasuerus favoured Mordecai. The first reason was to reward Mordecai for saving his life earlier while the second reason was because Mordecai was related to his wife and Queen.

Another angle to this case is that the story includes the fact that, in my thinking, Mordecai exposed the plot to kill King Ahasuerus because his younger relative, Esther was married to him. He knew that there was no assurance that if Ahasuerus was killed and another Persian emerged as the king of the Persian Empire, he would retain Esther as the reigning queen, also, Esther would be very sad that the man who loved her had died and Mordecai would have to cope with the challenge of making her happy. He preferred the man who loved and made his relative the Queen of the Empire to remain in power and position of authority than for someone whose disposition to his relative he could not be sure of, to emerge. So, it is an endless chain of consideration or continuous circle of considerations.

While living in his hometown of Mesopotamia, Genesis 20:11-13 confirms that Abraham married his half-younger sister, Sarai, whom Genesis 17:15-16 confirms that God renamed Sarah in Canaan where God sent him to live without returning to his parents' hometown again. He never returned to Mesopotamia to take the two other women that Genesis 16:1-16 and 25:1-6 confirm bore him children. Genesis 16:1-16 confirms that Hagar who bore his first son, Ishmael was an Egyptian by birth while Genesis 25:1-6 suggests that Keturah must have been a Canaanite, though her nativity was not documented just as we are not told that he sent his chief servant back to his native land of Mesopotamia to get Keturah to become his wife after the death of Sarah. Genesis 12:1-9, 24:1-10, 23:1-20 and 25:8-10 confirm that God guided him to live among the Canaanites for the rest of his life and he died and was buried therein. If they were good enough to become his neighbours because God commanded him to live among them, then they should be good enough to be his spouse in the meantime. Furthermore, Numbers 12:1-16 tells us the famous story of Miriam criticizing Moses' marriage to a non-Hebrew/Israelite wife without regard for the fact that Moses spent forty years in the native land of his wife, Zipporah and because he became due for marriage during those years, he married her. Numbers 12 says God punished Miriam for daring to criticize Moses' Midian wife partly because God thought Moses did the right thing by marrying a native of Midian where he found suitable to survive when he needed it. His life was threatened by the Egyptians among whom he was born. To survive, he escaped to Midian and they cooperated to preserve his life.

Exodus 2:11-22 can be interpreted to mean that Moses was practically homeless in Midian before he met Jethro's daughters who mentioned their rewarding encounter with Moses. Based on their report, Jethro invited him to live in his family house. He was unmarried while he had seven daughters still in his home tending his flock which meant that the daughters were unmarried otherwise, they would have been in their husbands' homes. How should he have turned down such an offer? Exodus 3:1 gives the impression that upon joining Jethro's family and marrying one of his daughters, Moses took up the job of his father-in-law's shepherd man. What other choice did he have in the circumstance? It seemed that the only thing he did not do was joining his father-in-law and his family members to worship their native gods because his father-in-law was the chief priest of the nation. Moses' was circumstantially under obligation to marry his host and benefactor's daughter and take up whatever job he had for him. He was afraid for his life so could never have returned to Egypt to get an Israelite girl to be his wife. Curiously, the critics of his marriage or wife's background are his older siblings who never went looking for him throughout the 40 years that he was AWOL as they say it in military circles. If they cared so much about the background of the wife that he married, they should have gone to look for him and take an Israelite girl to be his wife wherever he was hiding from the Egyptian authorities. He left Egypt at 40, were they expecting him to wait until whenever he returned before he would marry an Israelite girl? It would have meant that he would have married at 80 because that was when he returned to where he could find an Israelite girl to marry.

As at the time of attacking Moses on account of the non-Israelite or Hebrew background of his wife the only basis that his bitter siblings turned critic has was that Genesis 24:1-10 says Abraham insisted that Isaac's wife must be his relative. Meanwhile, Genesis 27:1-46 and 28:1-5 and 10-22 confirm that Rebecca manipulated Isaac to send Jacob to go to her brother's place to marry one of his daughters for a reason other than keeping to the tradition. Then, her brother treated Jacob worse than Esau who she thought she was protecting Jacob from. In fact, Genesis 25:1-7 confirms that Abraham himself had children by other women apart from his half-sister who he married. How terrible it would have been if Joseph's father and brothers had said because Joseph married an Egyptian, they could not join him in Egypt – they would have starved to death. Dogmas can be very unrealistic – even when God understood that Moses did the realistic thing by marrying Zipporah in the circumstance that he found himself in Midian, disgusting dogmas thought that they knew more than God. Perhaps, Miriam and Aaron believed that no matter the circumstance, until Moses could find an Israelite girl, he must not marry otherwise he should remain a celibate so long as he lived. Defending Moses' marriage to a foreigner or non-Israelite suggests that God's view is that it is the circumstance that dictates that an Israelite could marry a non-Israelite.

This provides the basis for the concept of the fact that "the people God found suitable to preserve your life when you are most vulnerable are good enough for you to marry or collaborate with maritally. It is in line with Deuteronomy 21:10-14-based God's admonition that the Israelites could marry any prisoner of war or war captive who lived among them. The women prisoners of war are strangers in the land of Israel, yet God says they are fit to be married by the Israelites. The wisdom here is that the mere fact that they are in a strange land do not mean that they should not fulfill Genesis 1:27-28 reiterated God's commission to all humans to multiply and fill the earth. God does not care who you marry as long as you would populate the earth to fulfill His desire that the entire earth be filled by humans so that there would be enough hands for Him to replenish the earth in each generation. This is one of the fundamental reasons Jeremiah 29:4-7 says God commanded the Jews who He allowed the great King Nebuchadnezzar to carry captive to Babylon to marry and bear children while there. One of the reasons foreigners loathe marrying any of the natives available to them is superiority complex, age held biases and ignorance of God's plan and opinion in this respect. Without being told, the natives know that the reason a foreigner is refusing to consummate intimate relationship with any of their kinsmen is unpleasant, so they vent their displeasure on that stranger.

It would be partly foolish to assume that this is a full-proof solution to resentment by natives. There are instances when another native of the opposite sex is interested in your native spouse who is his or her kinsman. It is one of the most dangerous situations to find oneself. If a man is interested in amoral affairs with the native woman you married or a native woman is interested in the native man you married, in all honesty, it would take the help of God for you to escape the deadly trap. If your spouse is not an assertive personality, he or she could be easily swayed by the native who is making the supposed amoral advances. We cannot say but it could be that part of the reason Bathsheba readily settled for David was that her original husband was not a Jew like herself and David was a fellow Jew or Israelite. Surely, the fact that David was the sitting king and was highly respected by all must be part of the reasons she preferred him, but the fellow-native factor might have been part of it also.

On the face value, Deuteronomy 7:1-6 is a sort of contradiction of Deuteronomy 21:10-14. Moses wrote the Bible books of Genesis divided into 50 chapters, Exodus divided into 40 chapters, Leviticus broken into 27 chapters, Numbers have 36 chapters while Deuteronomy is made up of 34 chapters. However, he could not have written the 34th chapter because it is the account of how he died, and God buried him secretly. Also, Deuteronomy 1-33 is the summary of his leadership and what he did in the final months leading to his death. Deuteronomy 31:14-21 reports God's final instructions to him while chapter 32:1-44 tells his personal victory song to celebrate his 40-year long leadership while verses 45-52 was his final instructions to his successor who had been his Personal Assistant, Joshua son of Nun. He used chapters 33:1-29 to give his final blessings to the tribes of Israel as he deemed fit. Quoting him, Deuteronomy 7:1-6 and 21:10-14 say:

> 1 "The Lord your God will bring you into the land that you are going to occupy, and he will drive many nations out of it. As you advance, he will drive out seven nations larger and more powerful than you: the Hittites, the Girgashites, the Amorites, the Canaanites, the Perizzites, the Hivites, and the Jebusites. 2 When the Lord your God places these people in your power and you defeat them, you must put them all to death. Do not make an alliance with them or show them any mercy. 3 Do not marry any of them, and do not let your children marry any of them, 4 because then they would lead your children away from the Lord to worship other gods. If that happens, the Lord will be angry with you and destroy you at once. 5 So then, tear down their altars, break their sacred stone pillars in pieces, cut down their

symbols of the goddess Asherah, and burn their idols. 6 Do this because you belong to the Lord your God. From all the peoples on earth he chose you to be his own special people.

10 "When the Lord your God gives you victory in battle and you take prisoners, 11 you may see among them a beautiful woman that you like and want to marry. 12 Take her to your home, where she will shave her head, cut her fingernails, 13 and change her clothes. She is to stay in your home and mourn for her parents for a month; after that, you may marry her. 14 Later, if you no longer want her, you are to let her go free. Since you forced her to have intercourse with you, you cannot treat her as a slave and sell her. (TEV)

Could and did God contradict Himself on the same issue of marriage to non-Israelite by an Israelite or give the approval concerning war captives because of the case of Moses who He used to hand down this marital prescription? Before we continue, let us remind ourselves that the same King David son of Jesse whom I Samuel 15:27-28 and I Kings 14:7-8 can be said to confirm that God delighted in greatly is confirmed by II Samuel 2:2-5(3), 13:37-38 and I Chronicles 3:1-4 to have married a non-Israelite who bore him Absalom and his sister, Tamah. This means that –

(1) Abraham had children by non-Israelite,

(2) Joseph and Moses married non-Israelites and God tolerated it

(3) David married a non-Israelite and God did not consider it enough reason not to make the covenant of eternal dynasty with him or use him as a yardstick to measure the obedience and loyalty of all others that He made ruler of Israel and Judah after him.

(4) Consider this irony – God preferred David to Saul by the end of their 40-year long reign each, yet Saul married an Israelite girl and the only concubine that he had was also an Israelite. He did not marry many wives, or a

non-Israelite like David is known to have done. That should shake the mindset of holier than thous to its very foundations if they are realistic.

Now, the passage above provides the explanation to what God-like contradiction on the face value is. God made all humans to live on earth so does not show favouritism or discriminate. God does not have permanent favourite but permanent principles and preference. Ezekiel 18:1-32 attests to this fact. Deuteronomy 7:3-4 above gives the core reason God forbade the Israelites from marrying non-Israelites in his domain. It is because of joining the foreign wives to serve other gods rather than because the non-Israelites are less humans to the Israelites. Therefore, what God meant in Deuteronomy 21:10-14 is that the girls who are taken to the land of Israel to live among the Israelites who will not manipulate her Israelite husband to stop worshipping God of Israel can be married by an Israelite man who likes her enough to make her his wife. Matthew 1:1-6 can be said to mean that it is the reason God let us understand that among the matriarchs of His ordained mankind's Messiah was non-Abraham's descendants such as Judah's daughter-in-law, Tamar, the onetime harlot and native of Jericho, Rahab and a Moabite, Ruth.

Now, there is no record that Zipporah or her family members tried to make Moses join them to worship their gods rather than put his hope in the God of his ancestors. The fact that Job 1:1 and 42:1-17, Jeremiah 15:1 and Ezekiel 14:12-14 and 19-20 say God of Israel regarded a man from the Far East so highly that He put his level of righteousness on the same level with the likes of Noah, Moses, Samuel and Daniel confirm that God of Israel does not discriminate against whoever worships Him genuinely. Isaiah 56:1-8 attests to this fact just like Jeremiah 12:14-17, Ezekiel 47:21-23, Matthew 22:1-10, John 10:11-16, Acts 9:15-16 and 10:1-35, Romans 10:5-13 and Galatians 2:7-10 can be said to do as well. Furthermore, Jeremiah 38:1-13 and 39:15-18 confirm that God promised a reward to a non-Israelite by the name of Ebedmelech who helped to reduce the sufferings of His prophet Jeremiah in the horrendous hands of his fellow Israelites. However, Jeremiah 1:1-3 and 11:18-23 confirm that God agreed that just as Jeremiah have requested, He would surely punish his hometown kinsmen who wanted him dead. Jeremiah was a prophet whose father, Hilkiah was a native of the priestly town of Anathoth which I Kings 2:26-27 confirms that the Priest Abiathar hailed from. It means that it was Jeremiah's fellow descendants of Aaronite priests who wanted him dead and he decided to ask God to punish them with death. Therefore, Jeremiah 1:1-3, 11:18-23, 38:1-13 and 39:15-18 means that —

(a) A helpful foreigner is better than a destructive relative

(b) A foreigner should get what his actions deserve just as a relative or fellow native should get what his actions deserve as well

(c) God believes it and approves of it

(d) God did not say because Ebedmelech was not an Israelite his kindness to Jeremiah should be trivialized and go unrewarded or that the natives of Anathoth plotting against Jeremiah should escape their due punishment because they were priests and prophets descended from Aaron just like Jeremiah. Also, Jeremiah 20:1-6, 26:1-24,

28:1-17 and 29:1-24-32 can be said to confirm that God did not spare other Israelites who undermined His efforts through Jeremiah to prevent the Babylonian captivity. It is a case of spike the sinner and spare the saint irrespective of their background.

16

Self-saving Secrecy

There is the concept of "Too Deep to Discuss" and just as it suggests, everyone has past experiences that cannot or should not be discussed with every Tom, Dick and Harry of this wearisome world. There is no record that Abraham told his Canaanite allies that God told him that their land of Canaan would belong to him and his descendants forever. There is no record that Jacob told Laban, his family or daughters who became Jacob's wives the true circumstance surrounding his relocation to their home. The claim that his mother sent him to get a wife from among Laban's daughters is not the real reason he left Canaan to live with them.

Genesis 25:24-34, 27:1-46, 28:1-5 and 10-22 and 35:1 say the truth is that his offensive dealings with his twin-brother, Esau and the threat of Esau forced him to relocate to Laban's household and he never mentioned it to them. Genesis 32:1-32 and 33:1-20 confirm that even when he was returning twenty years later and was about to meet Esau, he became jittery and still did not tell his wives his reason for being afraid to meet his only sibling in the whole wide world. So that he would not be tempted to expose this secret to his wives and children, when he had to seek God's help to find Esau's favour, Genesis 32:1-32 says he sent his wives and children across the River Jabbok and remained behind to pray alone at night so that he would not forget himself in the process of fervent prayers and speak out the sin he committed against his brother which forced him to go over to Laban's place.

It can be said that he did not hide if from God only because it is impossible to hide anything from Him otherwise, he would have. And in fact, he was so careful never to consciously mention to God that it was because he offended Esau hence, he ran away earlier. He started by reminding God not to forget that (in

Genesis 31:10-13) He directed him to return to Canaan and should protect him and his family from Esau's possible attack.

Also, there is no record that throughout the forty years that Moses lived in Midian, he got so intoxicated with love for Zipporah that he mentioned that he came to live in her country of Midian because he killed an Egyptian for which the Egyptian officials tried to kill him. As long as Jethro forgot to ask why he left Egypt to live among them before giving his daughter to be his wife and offering him a job and abode, Moses wisely chose to keep silent. There is no point talking about something you are never asked so that someone would not use the very information you volunteered out of honesty or for whatever reason, against you. When people want to be mischievous, there is nothing they cannot turn around to screw you up. If you provide more than required information, it could be used against you by anyone, particularly sworn detractors.

There is no record that Joseph told Pharaoh or any Egyptian official about the fact that he came to Egypt because his siblings sold him there unjustly. If he had, the Egyptians might have used it to taunt his relatives and even deride Joseph when he took undue advantage of them during the worst seasons of the seven years' famine and collected their land and part of its proceeds for his boss, Pharaoh. No matter how pleased you are with your hosts, there are certain things about your past that you should not divulge. Otherwise when you disagree with them, they would use such information against you.

It is not likely that the young Levite from Judah made his desire and preparedness to take up any better job known to his employer, Micah. Judges 17:3-17 and 18:1-31 can be interpreted to mean that as long as Micah's offer was the only one he could get, he did his job dutifully and by the time a better offer came along he did not consult Micah before he left which is similar to the way Genesis 31:1-55 confirms that Jacob concealed his departure from Laban. There must be certain information that should be kept only between you and God who led you to where you went to live. Even if you married a native, being your spouse is still not enough reason to divulge such information to him or her. Like we said, there is information that Moses never told his wife about the real reason he relocated from Egypt to her hometown of Midian where they spent the first forty years of their marriage in the home of her father.

Exodus 4:18-26 says Moses' wife, Zipporah found out 40 years later while they were on their way back to Egypt already. In fact, she never got the full information. She only exclaimed or confessed that she just found out that Moses was a husband of blood, but she had no full detail. There were facts about Jacob's activities in Canaan that he never divulged to Rachel just because he loved her greatly to the extent that he served 14 years just to marry her. Genesis 29:1-30, 30:25-34 and 31:38-42 confirm that Laban never divulged the spiritual information that he had about Jacob until he was under duress to keep Jacob in his business. It means that he concealed the reason he continued to reduce Jacob's wages to enrich himself at Jacob's expense. Genesis 29:31-35 and 30:1-2 can be interpreted to mean that Jacob did not tell Rachel who gives children and therefore, she should ask for a child of her own until she threatened suicide. Jacob was very frugal with such vital information to the same Rachel that he claimed to love her more than any other woman. Genesis 27:36-40 confirms that Jacob's father, Isaac did not reveal the solution to Esau's problem until Esau put pressure on Isaac. This is even though Genesis 25:27-28 claim that Isaac loved Esau more than Jacob.

It can be called the concept of "Not Without Pressure - NWP" or "Unless Pressured Up". There are persons who would not do what they know to be right except they are pressured to. Genesis 29:1-30 and 30:25-34 confirm that Laban did not agree to give Jacob his due reward until Jacob threatened to withdraw his services from Laban's employment. It is nearly like saying the wicked do not do the right thing unless they are under pressure to do so or the righteous do not do evil unless they are under pressure. Psalm 125:3 says if the wicked is allowed to rule over the righteous for too long, the righteous might be tempted to join the wicked to do evil therefore, God should do everything within His power to prevent the wicked from ruling over the righteous. Then, Proverbs 30:7-9 includes the fact that abject poverty could make a righteous man steal to eat and become a source of shame to God therefore, God should be kind enough to not let the righteous become poor to the point of stealing to eat.

There were truths that Joseph never told his Egyptian wife, Asenath though he spent the last 80 years of his life with her in Egypt. Love is not enough reason to divulge certain information and whoever does would suffer like Judges 16:4-31 says Samson did in the hands of Delilah and those who hired her to afflict him. Genesis 29:1-30 and 30:25-28 can be interpreted to mean that it was the information Laban found out about Jacob that made him to undo Jacob. There is no doubt that Jacob never divulged the information to Laban, but once he found out that God prospered his business because of Jacob he shortchanged Jacob so that Jacob would never save enough from his earnings to have the confidence to return to Canaan. Of course, most host and employers hate to let go of a useful migrant or employee. I Samuel 27:12 says King Achish readily employed David because he had hoped that David would serve him till death. Meanwhile, Matthew 1:17 gives the impression that between Jacob/Laban and David/Achish there was a gap of at least 11 generation. The point is that it is the norm no matter the generation.

David did not divulge the fact that he hated the Philistines and would never do anything to favour them when he took up the job of the greatest warrior in the land of the Philistines from their king, Achish throughout the sixteen months that I Samuel 27:1-12 confirms that he lived among them. Natives must realize that foreigners will tell them only the information that they know would convince the natives to let them live among them. They will never tell the truths about their past that could make the natives refuse them entry and stay in their nation. Immigrant managers must not stop keeping an eye on foreigners in their midst no matter how long they have stayed. It is shocking that Moses' Midian hosts never found out that he was a murderer throughout the forty years that Acts 7:23-35 confirms that he lived among them. He could have been overwhelmed with anger and killed their daughter or any other member of their family. This is not to say 'once a criminal always a criminal' but it is profitable to know the dangerous things that the individual migrant has the tendency to do so that the natives would know how to monitor his activities and reduce the likelihood of his or her afflicting their own people. Usually, there is always a reason, and it may not be pleasant, why people migrate. Abraham migrated to Canaan because God led him to take over the place for his descendants and anyhow we look at his reason for coming to live among the Canaanites, the fact that God initiated it did not make the reason to favour the Canaanites. Tactically, Abraham's relocation, to and presence, among the Canaanites was to the detriment of the Canaanites. It has no other reasonable interpretation. It is only on the part of Abraham and his covenant descendants that it was reasonable and rewarding. When Moses went to live among the Midianites it was not because he liked them rather it was only because he needed a haven from the punishment due to him for killing an Egyptian. Even when he was not eager to return to Egypt, God came to lead him back. Let us note that Abraham who arrived Canaan to stay put was to take over the land from the Canaanites which was injurious to them.

David did not benefit the Philistines even when they allowed him to escape Saul's sword. He did great damage to them and took extraordinary measures to conceal it and escape due punishment. He did not live among them because he loved them but for his personal benefit only. Joseph's acclaimed help to the Egyptians during famine is contestable considering that Genesis

47:13-26 says he enforced a decree that made the Egyptians to cede part of their land and income to their ruler forever. Verse 26 includes the fact that Joseph refused to abrogate the inhuman decree even after the famine had ended making the ensnaring economic policy needless, if ever it was needful. It can be likened to the way Genesis 25:27-34 says Esau was said to have taken a meal in exchange for permanent loss of his birthright to Jacob. Natives have a responsibility to ensure that migrants do not do more damage than delight by the end of their stay among them. Judges 18:1-31 confirms that the natives of Laish suffered because of their uncontrolled border policy or visitor-liberal immigration policy.

17

Migrants' Investment Mindset (MIM)

Migrants' mindset, be it corporate body or individuals, is to take more than they give or that they give to get more like every investor. Even God have the motive of personal benefit for His migration motivation. He had His own reason for getting Abraham to Canaan and Joseph to Egypt. It was because He had not given up on His plans to use Moses to lead the Israelites out of Egypt that He watched Moses escape to Midian to stay for 40 years before asking him to return to Egypt to lead the Israelites out on their way to Canaan.

Abraham went to Canaan to take over their land, went to Egypt for personal survival because he met famine in Canaan. Isaac went to live in Gerar during famine to survive rather than add anything tangible to the lives of the natives of Gerar. Christians are quick to say the natives of Gerar persecuted Isaac because of envy that he prospered more than them during famine. That is just an aspect of what happened. The other aspect is the fact that it is most likely that Isaac had no friend among them and never shared his famous hundred-fold bumper harvest with any of them. If he was generous with his huge harvest at such a time, the beneficiaries would have prevailed on their kinsmen not to persecute Isaac to the extent that he was forced to relocate away from them.

Now, leaving their territory meant that he took the wealth that he gathered in their God-assigned location from them to enjoy elsewhere. This is the basis for my claim that hurt is the heart-hidden motive of some migrants and strangers wherever they live. Migrant's mission is marvellous to them alone but miserable to their hosts. It has been like that since the time that God led Abraham to live as a stranger among the Canaanites.

Please, do not misquote me to say it means that God authored it, thus supports migrants hurting their host communities or nations. I do not have the capacity to discuss such claim.

Whenever people seem to lament that foreign investors are engaged in something awful, it should amuse any thoughtful person. What do they mean that a foreign national came to invest in their economy for their benefit? God forbid, not even God can convince any foreign national to work for the wellbeing of where they came solely to make profit to take back to their country to enjoy not to seek profit. Let us get the point clear here. Someone could rush to conclude that it amounts to insulting God to suggest that He cannot convince someone to do His bidding or the right thing. The fact that there is nothing God cannot do, does not mean that God would impose His will or counsel on anyone. Heeding God's opinion is a choice that every man consciously decides to do. God gave man the choice power or will power—whatever anyone chose to call it, and He does not force anyone to comply with His directive. Whenever He does force anyone to do His bidding it is usually a sign of a bad omen for the individual concerned because it would amount to an unforgivable evil in God's sight. God would force the person to do His will and dispense with such an individual shortly after because He prefers that the individual personally decides to do His bidding without having to force him. It is a complex issue. God's pattern is to give enough reasons to convince anyone to do His bidding but would still leave the individual to choose to do His bidding personally based on the reasons He had provided. It is the reason that Exodus 3:1-22 and 4:1-31 include the fact that when Moses remained unconvinced that God could use him to free the Israelites from Egyptian bondage by all the proofs he had been given, the story say God was so angry with him that He wanted to kill him on his way from Midian to Egypt.

Evangelism is one of the major things that God uses migration to achieve. He told Abraham in Genesis 15:12-17 about the captivity of his descendants in the future only for Exodus 9:16 to quote God claiming that the reason He led Abraham's descendants, the Israelites to live in Egypt for 430 years was to spread His fame across the globe which still resonates till date. He chose Nebuchadnezzar to rule the earth on His behalf only to send Daniel to Nebuchadnezzar's palace in Babylon through the now famous Jews' 70-year Babylonian captivity to provide Nebuchadnezzar His guidance from heaven. God used the presence of DSMA to reveal Himself to Nebuchadnezzar who He made the greatest on earth at the time.

The fact that God made Joseph great in Egypt did not make him to work for their wellbeing on long term basis. The choice to do good with the privilege of the office of Prime Minister that he occupied was his. The fact that David had been anointed and the Spirit of God had been upon him from the day he was anointed by Samuel did not make him to work for the wellbeing of the Philistines who were kind enough to host him to escape Saul's threats to his life. The godliest and holiest migrant will still not work for the genuine wellbeing of the host nation. The only thing I cannot be too sure to say in this respect is that God never meant any migrant to work for the wellbeing of the host nation genuinely. It seems, and it is only perhaps, God never gave man the capacity to work genuinely for the wellbeing of any country where he or she sojourns. This is a principle and an understanding that should guide managers of migrants in all nations of the world and in all generations or until the second coming of Jesus. Every effort of foreigners to work for and help the natives is mere window dressing under the guise of CSR – corporate social responsibility. One of the most painful things to compel foreign investors to do is to pay tax to the host nation's government. Every acclaimed CSR effort by foreign investors is mere propaganda. Business venture is not about benevolence since human history record began. Acts 9:36-42 and 10:1-4 confirm that Dorcas and Cornelius spent their hard-earned income on the poor. That is different from when Genesis 41:1-57 says when Pharaoh found out that famine would accompany bumper harvest, he approved for his newly appointed Prime Minister, Joseph to spend his money to build storage facilities at strategic locations throughout the length and breadth of Egypt and bought up all the excess harvest from the subjects to store up. When the famine started, Genesis 41:53-57 and 47:13-16 say they sold to the Egyptians at the highest price and made slaves of them.

18

IGNORING THE INEVITABLES

Joseph suffered double injustice in the home of Potiphar his first Egyptian master when Potiphar's wife blackmailed him, and Potiphar sent him to jail without giving him the slightest chance to state his own side of the accusation story. He was punished by being sent to jail for doing the right thing. Interestingly, and this is very interesting, when Joseph had become the most powerful official in the palace of Egypt where Potiphar was the chief security officer, there is no record that Joseph cared enough to consider punishing Potiphar and his wife for the evil done to him earlier. It is not everything natives can go to court to seek redress for that non-natives would equally go to court and secure justice partly because most of the persons presiding in such courts of law are natives and their first instinct is never to punish their fellow native because of a foreigner who they kindly gave the privilege to live among them.

There is no doubt that God's admonition is that natives should treat strangers equally, but the reality is that it does not happen that way most of the times. Exodus 22:21-24, 23:9, Leviticus 19:33-34 and Deuteronomy 24:17-18 and 27:19 admonish that natives should be kind to foreigners. Ruth warmed herself into the hearts of the people of Bethlehem. This means that in addition or despite God's admonition, Ruth went the extra mile to encourage the people of Bethlehem to accept her to integrate into their community. It can be called "God's Command Plus" which means God's command plus your effort produces the desired delightful experience among strangers.

Genesis 26 tells us the story of the Philistines resenting Isaac simply because during famine when they suffered poor harvest and the attendant hunger, Isaac, a non-native prospered greatly and became very great or greater than them all. Not even their king sitting on the throne could resist the temptation to envy Isaac at this time. It was so bad that he joined his nobles and subjects to force Isaac to relocate outside their territory. Basically, it is unacceptable to natives for a non-native to prosper more than them in their own native land. They consider it an abomination that must not be tolerated. It is not common to find natives who are large-hearted enough to accommodate a foreigner leading them in prosperity in their own native land.

Therefore, when a foreigner begins to prosper more than his hosts, he should expect persecution and the onus is on him to endure most of what they do to him or share part of his gains with some of the natives so that his beneficiaries would be encouraged to protect him from the onslaught of their kinsmen, and if the attacks becomes unbearable, follow in the footsteps of Isaac's who left the wells the Philistines covered up to dig new ones until they left him alone. There is no record that Isaac took up his case against the native Philistines to the king to adjudicate because in any case, even the king took sides with his subjects and kinsmen.

One of the logical questions from Isaac's experience with the Philistines is why did the Philistines not opt to ask Isaac the secret of his prosperity during famine rather than choose to persecute him? If your neighbor prospers greatly under the most unusual circumstance the wise thing to do is to approach him in humility to ask or even plead with him to show you the secret of his prosperity or success so that you could copy it to prosper personally. However, the functional fact is that natives can never become humble to the extent of asking a stranger the secret of his success in their own God-given domain. They see it as insult to their sense of national pride, nativity and indigeneship. Some of them who are very arrogant would prefer to starve to death rather than ask for help of any kind from a stranger. It was after Isaac had relocated outside their territory that the king, his adviser and his army commander came to seek peace treaty with him that he used the opportunity to ask the king of what use was his visit to him since they did not allow him to live among them. In this respect, Genesis 21:22-33 and 26:26-33 say:

> 22 At that time Abimelech went with Phicol, the commander of his army, and said to Abraham,

"God is with you in everything you do. 23 So make a vow here in the presence of God that you will not deceive me, my children, or my descendants. I have been loyal to you, so promise that you will also be loyal to me and to this country in which you are living." 24 Abraham said, "I promise." 25 Abraham complained to Abimelech about a well which the servants of Abimelech had seized. 26 Abimelech said, "I don't know who did this. You didn't tell me about it, and this is the first I have heard of it." 27 Then Abraham gave some sheep and cattle to Abimelech, and the two of them made an agreement. 28 Abraham separated seven lambs from his flock, 29 and Abimelech asked him, "Why did you do that?" 30 Abraham answered, "Accept these seven lambs. By doing this, you admit that I am the one who dug this well." 31 And so the place was called Beersheba, because it was there that the two of them made a vow. 32 After they had made this agreement at

Beersheba, Abimelech and Phicol went back to Philistia. 33 Then Abraham planted a tamarisk tree in Beersheba and worshiped the Lord, the Everlasting God.

26 Abimelech came from Gerar with Ahuzzath his adviser and Phicol the commander of his army to see Isaac. 27 So Isaac asked, "Why have you now come to see me, when you were so unfriendly to me before and made me leave your country?" 28 They answered, "Now we know that the Lord is with you, and we think that there should be a solemn agreement between us. We want you to promise 29 that you will not harm us, just as we did not harm you. We were kind to you and let you go peacefully. Now it is clear that the Lord has blessed you." 30 Isaac prepared a feast for them, and they ate and drank. 31 Early next morning each man made his promise and sealed it with a vow. Isaac said good-bye to them, and they parted as friends. 32 On that day Isaac's servants

came and told him about the well which they had dug. They said, "We have found water." 33 He named the well "Vow." That is how the city of Beersheba got its name. (TEV)

The first poignant point to note is Abimelech going to seek peace agreement with Isaac after forcing Isaac outside of his native domain. It reminds of the concept of "I Know But Cannot" – King Abimelech can be said to have meant that 'I know that under the law of natural justice you do not deserve to have been forced out of my domain however, as long as you are a stranger who came to live among us and prospered at a time that we the natives could not we cannot afford to let you continue to live among us. We cannot humble ourselves to ask you the secret of your success among us yet we cannot watch you prosper among us because we fear that if we let you remain among as some day you could become powerful enough to rule over us and it is an abomination for a stranger to rule over us. It would be unforgivable if we wait until you become powerful enough to rule over us. Much as there is no written law that forbade you from prospering among us there is an implied obligation on us as natives to prevent a migrant from becoming so powerful that he could rule over us in our own land.

Also, Abimelech said Isaac should not forget that they allowed him to leave in peace – he meant that 'let us remind you of what we did right since you are emphasizing what you believe that we did wrong to you'. He meant that even if they were wrong to have forced Isaac out because of envy and jealousy, there is the good thing that they did which was that they did not retrieve the wealth that Isaac acquired while living among them from him before sending him away. Isaac should not forget to mention what they did right while talking about whatever he believed that they did wrong to him. In any case, Isaac cannot deny that he prospered while living among them and that they did not threaten to take away the wealth that he acquired while living among them like Genesis 31:1-46 claim that Laban tried to do to Jacob before God prevailed on Laban to let Jacob return with the wealth that he had saved during his stay. Natives consider it a great gesture if they allow migrants to repatriate their savings to their native country without hassles.

Second, let us consider other poignant points – (1) they tolerated Abraham, but not Isaac, (2) because they tolerated Abraham we are told that he lived among them for a long time whereas Isaac who they did not tolerate left them behind or relocated outside their locality, (3) even Abraham that they tolerated they seized his well, (4) maybe, the king of his host community compelled his people to return Abraham's well upon learning of the seizure but it is not indicated that he instructed them to do so. This means that the most tolerant natives would still do certain things to hurt strangers, (5) it is very striking that they (the king, his officials and subjects) recognized that God was with and helping the stranger yet they attacked him. That provokes the logical question of what if they knew that God was not with the stranger what magnitude of evil would they have done to him? Recognizing God's support to the stranger suggest that they were godly to some extent which provokes the question of what if they were not godly at all what gravity of evil would they have done to the stranger among them? Now, this is the same king who Genesis 20:1-18 confirms that God threatened over Abraham and his wife and he warned his subjects or kinsmen-subjects not to afflict Abraham in the least manner. In fact, Genesis 20:14-18 and 26:6-11 say:

> 14 Then Abimelech gave Sarah back to Abraham, and at the same time he gave him sheep, cattle, and slaves. 15 He said to Abraham, "Here is my whole land; live anywhere you like." 16 He said to Sarah, "I am giving your brother a thousand pieces of silver as proof to all who are with you that you are innocent; everyone will know that you have done no wrong." 17-18 Because of what had happened to Sarah, Abraham's wife, the Lord had made it impossible for any woman in Abimelech's palace to have children. So Abraham prayed for Abimelech, and God healed him. He also healed his wife and his slave women, so that they could have children.
>
> 6 So Isaac lived at Gerar. 7 When the men there asked about his wife, he said that she was his sister. He would not admit that she was his wife,

because he was afraid that the men there would kill him to get Rebecca, who was very beautiful. 8 When Isaac had been there for some time, King Abimelech looked down from his window and saw Isaac and Rebecca making love. 9 Abimelech sent for Isaac and said, "So she is your wife! Why did you say she was your sister?" He answered, "I thought I would be killed if I said she was my wife." 10 "What have you done to us?" Abimelech said. "One of my men might easily have slept with your wife, and you would have been responsible for our guilt." 11 Abimelech warned all the people: "Anyone who mistreats this man or his wife will be put to death." (TEV)

First, God made Abraham to act as high priest for Abimelech and his household members. Second, the king approved that Abraham could live anywhere in the land. Despite what we can call in contemporary times as a nationally approved legislation that legitimized the stay of the foreigner, Genesis 21:25-26 still says some of the king's officials or lieutenants still seized Abraham's wells. God's presence with Abraham and the legislation was still not enough to convince and/or compel some of the hard-line non-native haters to stop hunting down strangers living among them. Do you see the root of hatred for foreigners and how long it has been going on in human history? Perhaps, the connection between Genesis 29:17-18 and 21:25-26 is that some of the palace officials who witnessed the punishment of their boss' household members with barrenness by God because Abraham deceived their boss to mistakenly take his wife to add to his queens were unforgivably upset by the experience. Their possible logic was that –

(1) they were living in their God-given land when Abraham came to live among them. They never sent for him to come over to work for them or do them any favours,

(2) he was the one who lied that his wife was his younger sister,

(3) God did not take the fact that he failed to tell them the whole truth when He decided to punish their boss and his household members for the mistake,

(4) Meanwhile, immediately he found out the truth he obeyed God and returned his wife with generous damages and instant formal approval to let Abraham stay among them for as long as he liked.

(5) Yet, God says Abraham who lied about his wife was still holy enough to serve as high priest to their king and boss and his household members. It amounted to subjecting their king and boss and by extension all of them who are subject to the king to Abraham – they could not accept to live with the understanding that the stranger that they kindly allowed to live among them was superior to them. But perhaps more importantly, they failed to understand that God used Abraham to try to point their attention to Himself by so doing. This case points out the challenges that accompany the undeniable presence of God in the life of any man. It would make the proud to hate and attack the man enjoying God's prospering presence in an unprecedented scale. God meant His immense support to the readily despicable persons to call the attention of

the proud to Himself but in most cases, the proud would opt to attack the God's presence beneficiary.

(6) King Abimelech's approval (an equivalent of government legislation or home office approved citizenship in contemporary times) that Abraham lived freely and unhurt among them did not go down well with some of his officials so they disobeyed his decree to seize Abraham's wells and by so doing hurt him despite the subsisting laws. If King Abimelech did not punish the officials who disobeyed his order that Abraham be left alone to enjoy equal rights with natives he merely proved that it was not logical to punish a native because of any stranger for any reason whatsoever and it can be said that Abraham lived with it that way since Genesis 21:33 emphasized the fact that after reporting the maltreatment by the king's officials he went ahead to live among them for a long time.

(7) The king might not have punished his erring officials but let us assume that he did not allow any of them to hunt

down Abraham any further hence Abraham remained in their midst for a long time.

(8) Genesis 26:12-25 says until Isaac relocated out of the land of Philistia, the natives did not stop putting the pressure of persecution on him. It means that the natives' purpose of putting the pressure of persecution on the stranger is to force the stranger out of their land or territory. Genesis 26:26-29 says when told that it was not necessary to visit him considering that he was forced out of their country their response was that he should not forget that they let him leave their country with the wealth that he gathered while living among them was an act of kindness to him by them. This is the king and his apparently two highest officials (the chief adviser and COAS) responding to Isaac's claim that they should not have visited him after they forced him out of their country. They meant that Isaac should not forget that they could have killed him or dispossessed him of the wealth that he made in their country and sent him away empty-handed but they decided to be nice to him by letting him leave with the

wealth that he acquired from their land. And let it be said, dearly beloved, these guys knew what they were talking about because we know the famous story of Laban and his sons against Jacob in this respect. Genesis 29:1-30 and 31:1-44 confirm that Laban still laid claim to Jacob's wealth despite the fact that they were supposed to be part of Jacob's savings from his earnings during the 20 years that he remained in Laban's employment. In fact, he went further to even lay claim to Jacob's wives and the children that Jacob's wives bore him. If not for God's intervention Laban and his sons would not have allowed Jacob to take his wives and children back to Canaan. That is what King Abimelech of the Philistines and his two highest officials were telling Isaac that they did not wait for God to threaten them before they let Isaac take away the wealth that he acquired during the period that he spent in their land. This is the real workings of the mind of natives over or against strangers. Now, to be very honest, Abimelech and his officials and people should be given credit for this considering that Isaac was a total stranger to them whereas Laban was supposed to have been Jacob's maternal uncle. Natives do not believe that you should cart away the wealth that you got in their land. It was even worst that Isaac did not marry their daughter whereas Jacob married Laban's daughters and fathered his grandchildren. He confessed that the only reason he was letting Jacob take his wives and daughters away was because he had noticed that his daughters and grandchildren by the daughters were not ready to remain with him.

(9) Natives believe dogmatically that strangers must spend whatever they earn in their land rather than carry it away. The case of Isaac is very striking in a sense in this respect. Genesis 26:1-6 and 12-13 says Isaac's multiple fold prosperity during famine in the land of the Philistines was based on three key factors,

(a) God's plan to reward him for the obedience of his late father, Abraham,

(b) Isaac's obedience to God's command to remain in Gerar during the famine rather than going down to Egypt,

(c) Cultivating crops during drought because he had faith in God's ability to bless him irrespective of the climatic circumstances.

However, the Philistines cared less about the essential factors that made him prosper. The only factor that they focused on was just that he prospered in their land. If he had obeyed God to live anywhere else and cultivated, he would have still prospered but that was not important to them. Their treatment of Isaac in this respect highlights the fact that it is not enough for someone to say God sent me to live in that land where I am a stranger, they must understand that the natives would not stop envying them. It is just natural. It means that the fact that natives are convinced that God is with you does not mean that they would spare you of envy engineered persecution. As far as they are concerned you and God cannot put them to shame in their own land that they inherited from their ancestors.

In this thoughtful story of Isaac's experience among the Philistines, there is no mention that God punished the Philistines for persecuting and driving Isaac away from the land He had allocated to them through their ancestors. Also noteworthy is that the Philistines did not deem it fit to seek the secret of prospering during general famine from Isaac. But the mindset of an average native is that it is an insult to seek help from a stranger in his own native land. Natives believe it must not be said that a foreigner came over to teach them prosperity strategies in their own home. This is one reason we must salute the humility and courage of someone like Pharaoh who admitted that since his native wise men could not interpret his dreams, 'foreigner Joseph' who was able to do it should become the boss of his fellow native Egyptian wise men who were serving in his palace. But like we said earlier, it was part of his effort to indigenize Joseph as an Egyptian that he made him marry an Egyptian so that Joseph could be classified as an Egyptian by marriage. Ecclesiastes 9:13-16 says:

13 There is something else I saw, a good example of how wisdom is regarded in this world. 14 There was a little town without many people in it. A powerful king attacked it. He surrounded it and prepared to break through the walls. 15 Someone lived there who was poor, but so clever that he could have saved the town. But no one thought about him. 16 I have always said that wisdom is better than strength, but no one thinks of the poor as wise or pays any attention to what they say. (TEV)

That is what can be called Self-demeaning and destructive dignity driven dealings or dealership. Refusal to accept needed help because of pride and arrogance. Genesis 41:1-57 and 47:13-26 confirm that Pharaoh was wiser than that just as John 3:1-2 confirms that Nicodemus was far wiser than that when it says that he went to Jesus to resolve his salvation at night. John 7:45-52 says his Pharisee colleagues were busy insisting that Nazareth was too insignificant to produce the saviour that God promised them through Moses. Once he noticed that his colleagues would not heed his views because of Jesus' acclaimed hometown, Nicodemus left them alone to their fate and went secretly to secure his own salvation or place in eternity.

There is general problem of superiority complex between natives and non-natives living among them. Natives believe they have the God-given right to be the best and above non-natives living among them in their native land. It can be called "Nativity Superiority Complex". They believe that even if a foreigner living among them becomes greater than them, such foreigner must still relate to them in a manner that clearly proves that they are still superior to him as long as he lives and thrives among them. They like the foreigner to regularly remember that it was in their land that he prospered and must show gratitude to them who allowed him to prosper among them.

It is common for us to talk about 'holier than thou' mentality but this time, we are talking about 'natives better than non-native neighbours' mentality and mannerisms. Natives believe that the best foreigner among them remains subject to the worst native so long as the foreigner lives among them. To this end, Exodus 1:1-22 tells us the story of a Pharaoh who said in verses 8-22 that it was a punishable crime for the Israelites who remained strangers in their land long after the death of Joseph to increase in population more than the Egyptians. One would have thought that if you feel strongly about someone's increased birth rate, you would only need to ask your children to marry early and have more children to catch up with the strangers rather than device measures to stop them from having more children. Verses 18-19 and 22 say even when he was told that God was responsible for their high birth rate he resorted to killing the new born male Israelites rather than ask how he could get God to do the same for his Egyptian kinsmen. This Pharaoh's response to the realization of the high birth rate by the Israelites is the natural way that natives respond to the success and prosperity of non-natives living among them. It is unacceptable for a foreigner to prosper above the natives and natives believe they have the right to stop the success of such foreigners in any way they deem fit. This is partly what can be called "Resentment Wrapped Reasoning and Response/Reaction".

The 'superior than thou' sensibilities have sunk many against God's plan for their lives. It was the problem that Saul had with David from the point when David killed Goliath. There is the abominable 'holier than thou' as well as 'superior than thou'. While holier than thous believe that they are better behaved than their peers the superior than thou assume that they have something that their neighbour does not have and when they realize belatedly that in actual fact, their neighbour is better than them, they practically go crazy. In Nigeria they call it 'I take this one pass my neighbour'. It takes different forms. Someone could think that at least I am better than my neighbour who does not have the electricity generator that I have and puts on to generate electricity when there is power outage from the national grid. It could be that at least I have a car which my neighbour does not have or I am a landlord while my neighbour is a tenant. Some would think at least I have a child while my neighbour is childless. Some would be conscious of the fact that they have money while their neighbour is poor without regard for the fact that perhaps, their poor neighbour has peace of mind that they lack. Ecclesiastes 4:4 exposes the intent of the heart of such persons by saying the heart-hidden reason many work extra hard sometimes to breaking point is because they want to be seen to be more successful than their neighbour.

I Samuel 16:1-23 and 17:1-58 confirm that before David killed Goliath, David had begun to serve as Saul's armour bearer or at least one of them. If David did not accompany him to this battle as his armor bearer then someone else did. In any case, before the birth and emergence of David in Saul's palace, someone must have been serving as Saul's armour bearer in the many battles that he led the army of Israel to fight and win in the past. Since, Acts 13:21 confirms that Saul ruled over Israel for a total of 40 years and I Samuel 31:1-13, II Samuel 1:1-27, 2:1-11 and 5:4-5, I Kings 2:11 and I Chronicles 3:4 and 29:26-27 confirm that David began his 40-year reign only after the death of Saul when he was 30 years old, it means that David was born in the eleventh year of Saul's 40-year rule. Meanwhile, I Samuel 11:1-11 and 14:47-48 confirm that Saul led the defeat of the armies of the enemy nations of Israel. These victories were before he could no longer lead the army and either Jonathan or

David had to lend him a helping hand. That is why we said he had other armour bearers before David was ever born and grew up to the age of killing Goliath or before God sent Samuel to anoint him as Saul's successor designate at his father's home in Bethlehem. But probably because Saul thought that David was not experienced enough in battlefield, he did not take him to the battle against the Philistines at the valley of Elah.

It was 40 days and nights later that David's father sent him to the battlefield where he met Goliath's boast which provoked him to confront and conquer Goliath to lead the defeat of the Philistine army. Impliedly, it was a thorough humiliation to Saul because it made David a greater Israelite when as the sitting king of Israel, he (Saul) was supposed to be the greatest warrior in the nation. The women of Israel added to the heart-hidden pain and shame when in their victory celebration song, they elevated David above Saul. Even when Saul knew that God was behind David's achievement rather than seek God's help to reclaim his glory and glamour as the capable warrior king of Israel that God helped him to be in the past or earlier in his reign, he resorted to the persecution of David throughout the rest of his reign.

Consider the words traded between Abraham and the king of Sodom the only time that they ever had dealings. Genesis 13:1-3 says Abraham's nephew went to live in Sodom. Then, Genesis 14:1-16 and 21-24 says when the Sodomites were carried captive, Abraham went to rescue them for Lot's sake. The king of Sodom decided to repay Abraham for his assistance only for Abraham to claim that so that the king of Sodom would not go about announcing to whoever cared to listen that he made him (Abraham) rich, he would not accept the king of Sodom's reward for his assistance. This is the same Abraham who Genesis 12:10-20 and 20:1-16 confirm to have collected the bride price and damages on his wife on two occasions from the kings of Egypt and Philistines respectively who married his wife because he made false declaration about their relationship to them. The cardinal point is that envy and jealousy-engineered persecution of migrants by natives is natural and migrants should not waste all their efforts on fighting it. When native leaders shout from the rooftop that they do not approve of their kinsmen subjects persecuting migrant it is a mere face-saving stunt and nothing more.

19

NEEDFULNESS NULLIFIES NEGATIVITY

This could have been titled "Relevance Reduces, Restrains, Restricts/Removes Resentment", "Proof Prevents Persecution" or "Resourcefulness Restrains Resenters". It is indisputable to claim that so long as Joseph was useful in Egypt where a Hebrew like him was highly resented, the Egyptians were forced to suspend their traditional resentment for Hebrews in their dealings with Joseph. The admonition is that whoever wants to prosper in a foreign land must make himself or herself highly relevant or rewardingly relevant and useful to the natives' benefit. So long as Joseph's presence prospered Potiphar, he appointed Joseph the leader of his household servants who might have included Egyptians and other natives who had been serving him before Joseph arrived in his household. Usefulness nearly naturally helps a foreigner to triumph over natives in the battle of resentment of foreigners by natives.

The contents of I Samuel 17:1-58, 18:17-27, 21:10-15 and 27:1-12 can be described as a bundle of contradictions. First, I Samuel 17:26, 36 confirms that David disdained the Philistines when he claimed that it was an unforgivable insult for Goliath a Philistine to mesmerize the army of Israel. Second, I Samuel 18:17-27 confirms that he gleefully killed 200 Philistines to get their foreskins to give to Saul as bride price payment to marry Saul's daughter, Michal. Saul had asked for 100 and he provided 200. Third, I Samuel 21:10-15 claimed that during the first meeting of David and Goliath's King Achish, after David had killed Goliath, Achish did not want to have anything to do with him mostly because David feigned insanity. However, shockingly, fourthly, I Samuel 27:1-12 says the same King Achish turned round to employ David alongside his warriors, a total of 600 men who had wives and children. He employed David to replace his greatest warrior, Goliath who David killed to become famous as the greatest warrior in the land of Israel. It means that after directing his officials to take an assumed insane David away from his presence he sent some of his officials to go and find out if the same David who he knew killed Goliath had gone mad or not. It was after the confirmation that David was sane that he began to look forward to having David to work for him. When David became gravely concerned for his personal safety within the territory of Israel surprisingly he opted to go and hide in Achish's kingdom rather than with the king of Moab who I Samuel 22:1-4 confirms that he left his father and brothers with to protect them for him. If his father and family were safe with the king of Moab away from Saul's Israel domain/territory, why did he conclude that he would be safer in Goliath's hometown of Gath and with their King Achish?

Therefore, it is logical to say that he knew that Achish was eager to engage him to replace Goliath who he killed. It can be said that Achish concluded that killing Goliath meant that David was a greater warrior than dead Goliath and he was eager to employ the greatest warrior available to win his battles for him. He cared less about the collateral damage that David did to his army of the Philistines in the recent past. David's competence as a warrior was enough reason to overlook his past affliction to his Philistine kingdom. Competence covers the multitude of resentment that natives have for a foreigner. They do it to maximize the benefit that they could get from the competent foreigner. Many times people shout from the rooftop that natives despise and denigrate foreigners among them as we said in the last chapter, Exodus 22:21-24, 23:9, Leviticus 19:33-34 and Deuteronomy 24:17-18 and 27:19 confirm that God do not approve of it. Also, most nations have legislations discouraging it. However, it is still commonplace.

It is not something that legislation can enforce because it is nearly natural for natives to despise strangers. One of the most helpful solutions is to encourage and possibly help migrants to get down to work hard to be productive. Practically, productivity pays or profits a great deal in this respect. Acceptance and respect are some of the things that cannot be legislated or enforced by legislation. You cannot force people to like, accept and embrace any other. They are better and easier earned than enforced. Boaz regarded Ruth very highly once he learnt about all the moral support that she gave to Naomi after the death of her husband and two sons. Apparently, Naomi and her husband, Elimelech were known to Boaz personally before they relocated to Ruth's land of birth, Moab. Because Ruth showed great loyalty to Naomi, he gladly embraced her. Even then, Ruth 2:11 and 4:1-12 confirm that Elimelech's closer relative still had a reason not to desire Ruth for marriage. The closer relative practically defied or disregarded God's command that put an obligation on him to marry Ruth in Deuteronomy 25:5-10 and the popularized commendable character and conduct of Ruth reported in Ruth 2:11 and 4:15 to still reject Ruth. There are natives who's resentment for foreigners cannot be changed no matter how you try. They would neither regard God's view and admonition, government's view or legislation nor the views of fellow natives on it. Yet, there would be natives who would regard the usefulness of foreigners and embrace them. Supposing Ruth did not step out to work in the fields she would not have met someone like Boaz who would go the whole hog to be kind to her. That she took the initiative to go and glean behind the reapers meant that she was a hard-working individual. The women she met harvesting Boaz's fields were not better than her.

The other significant point in the claim in Ruth 2 that she went out to glean meant that she obeyed the God-given command that was the law regarding a foreigner like her in Bethlehem or anywhere else in the land of Israel. Non-Israelite have the right to glean in the land of Israel behind farm reapers. It means that when she arrived in a foreign land she found out their laws as they pertained to her and operated within them in order to earn a decent living rather than going about asking for handouts from her late husband's people in the land that she now lived. Sustenance is a common cause of friction among family members. If you can fend for yourself it is most likely that your family members would respect you but otherwise you would soon have problems with them. Also, the story of Ruth teaches us that forging stronger collaboration with the natives earns regard and respect for your quintessence qualities. It was Boaz who Naomi and Ruth had reason to believe valued and respected Ruth greatly that they agreed that they should have a permanent cordial relationship with through Ruth getting married to him rather than the closer relative who had never shown any sign that he cared about the wellbeing of Ruth. The events that followed proved that they were right.

The other important fact from the case of Ruth as a stranger in Bethlehem is the fact that before she met Boaz the news had spread about her activities. It was great that it was the news of her good deeds that spread. The core point is that if she was engaged in any unprintable things or activities that is how it would have spread and she would have met resentment and rejection from natives partly because of her inappropriate and unacceptable character and conduct. Natives do not just monitor the character and conduct of foreigners in their midst, they faithfully, frantically and perhaps, fanatically circulate the report among their fellow natives as quickly as they hear or observe it. Part of the reason is that the natives are determined to prevent their kinsmen from being hurt by some foreigners who when things get bad would return to wherever they came from. Natives are conscious of the fact that they have no other place to call their home therefore, would not let those who have another place they can call home to afflict them in their home where they cannot readily run away from. It is not like Laban's sons did not know that their two sisters confessed that their father squandered most of the wealth that they should have inherited from him before they started claiming that Jacob had swindled their father of his wealth. Much as their father had his own fault, they knew that all the wealth that their cousin turned brother-in-law, Jacob had acquired he would take away to Canaan which Jacob regarded as his real home. And Genesis 31:1-55 says they were right because not long after Jacob took everything and disappeared into thin air.

Genesis 45:16-20 confirms that when Pharaoh learnt that Joseph's brothers could come over to stay in Egypt or his kingdom, his spontaneous response was that they should come over to keep his flocks, which he knew to be their area of specialization. Meanwhile, there is no indication in Genesis 45:4-15 that Joseph indicated his desire to get a job for his brothers as Pharaoh's shepherds. Pharaoh said they should be fed from the royal treasury meanwhile Genesis 41:53-57 and 47:13-26 confirm that he told his fellow Egyptians to go back to comply with Joseph's policy to subjugate and impoverish them. We can as well claim that if Joseph's brothers or father's household members did not have any skill that he needed; he might not have readily approved their coming to live in his kingdom with joy. In this respect, Genesis 43:32 confirms that the Egyptians had no regard for Joseph's Hebrew background on account of their shepherding profession. However, Genesis 45:16-20, 46:28-34 and 47:1-6 say the king and ruler of Egypt that goes by the title of Pharaoh eagerly looked forward to Joseph's siblings joining him to serve him as shepherds of his flock while Joseph continued as the Prime Minister of Egypt. This means that at least the king of Egypt had flock and needed the services of competent shepherds. Yet, the all-time-relevant implication of this thought is that whoever is eager to live as a foreigner should equip himself with at least a skill with which he could contribute to the host nation or community. Considering this example, perhaps, natives have God's approval to refuse anyone without relevant skills to contribute to the benefit of their nation, entry into their country to live. This is more so because Jeremiah 29:4-7 confirms that God's admonition to any migrant in a foreign land is that he contributes to the economy of that country. Exemplifying this further, II Kings 25:8-12, Proverbs 26:10 and Jeremiah 52:12-16 say:

> 8 On the seventh day of the fifth month of the nineteenth year of King Nebuchadnezzar of Babylonia, Nebuzaradan, adviser to the king and commander of his army, entered Jerusalem. 9 He burned down the Temple, the palace, and the houses of all the important people in Jerusalem, 10 and his soldiers tore down the city walls. 11 Then Nebuzaradan took away to Babylonia the people who were left in the city, the remaining skilled workmen, and those who had deserted to the Babylonians. 12 But he left in Judah some of the poorest people, who owned no property, and put them to work in the vineyards and fields.

> 10 An employer who hires any fool that comes along is only hurting everybody concerned.

> 12 On the tenth day of the fifth month of the nineteenth year of King Nebuchadnezzar of

Babylonia, Nebuzaradan, adviser to the king and commander of his army, entered Jerusalem. 13 He burned down the Temple, the palace, and the houses of all the important people in Jerusalem; 14 and his soldiers tore down the city walls. 15 Then Nebuzaradan took away to Babylonia the people who were left in the city, the remaining skilled workmen, and those who had deserted to the Babylonians. 16 But he left in Judah some of the poorest people, who owned no property, and he put them to work in the vineyards and fields. (TEV)

We are not told the reason that II Kings 25:8-12 and Jeremiah 52:12-16 repeat the same story but for the sake of this discourse, let us speculate that it is because the story is very vital to heaven and earth or God and mankind at the same time. But perhaps, more importantly relevant to our focus is the fact that the passage gives sufficient basis for one to claim without fear of contradiction that generally, the unskilled is not fit to be tolerated because he or she is a bundle of affliction to all and sundry. A fool in this context is someone who claims that he wants to work but do not know anything about the work to be done, not passionate to learn and worst still not determined to endure the rigors that the job requires to be productive or contribute to the achievement of the objective of the work. In one word or statement do not hire anyone who cannot be useful to the achievement of the objective of the work to be done. That is the guideline that God gave in Deuteronomy 20:5-9, Judges 7:1-8 which I Samuel 30:9 and 21-25 which can be said to mean that David followed. Excuse or exclude the unuseful or useless is the point. If they want to be engaged or involved, they should go and refurbish themselves with a skill to become useful and employable. The unuseful are not desirable or not to be desired. Therefore, only the useful are desirable is something that foreigners should not forget. Now, the natives already have their own fellow natives who are useless that they must fend for therefore, they do not want to add some foreign useless persons to the ones that they are already coping with. We have jumped a step which is the fact that the unskilled is unfit for employment or somewhat an unviable personality. It is like when Proverbs 10:26, 14:20, 18:9 and 19:4, 6-7 say:

> 26 Never get a lazy man to do something for you; he will be as irritating as vinegar on your teeth or smoke in your eyes.
>
> 20 No one, not even is neighbour, like a poor man, but the rich have many friends.
>
> 9 A lazy person is as bad as someone who is destructive.
>
> 4 Rich people are always finding new friends, but the poor cannot keep the few they have. 6 Everyone tries to gain the favour of important people; everyone claims the friendship of those who give out favours. 7 Even the brothers of a poor man have no use for him; no wonder he has no friends. No matter how hard he tries, he cannot win any. (TEV)

This can be safely interpreted to mean that just as it is senseless to condone a destroyer so also it would be ridiculous to blame natives who abhor the unskilled because even God's word counsel against it. The earlier passage says the Babylonians took away only the skilled Jews to their country which means that the poor who were left behind to do mostly menial and non-skilled required jobs became so poor that they could not own any property because they were unskilled individuals. It seems that the Babylonians started to carry the most skilled or specialists and when they came down to the regular unskilled persons, they stopped their decision on who was worthy to be carried captive. They did not want to spend their nation's resources on transporting persons without any useful skills that would benefit their nation. They have enough unskilled Babylonian natives at home than to add some other foreigners to their curious class of citizens. They are persons not worthy of any classification among the respectable inhabitants of the country or community as the case might be. This points to the fact that the law of life and this world is that it is unacceptable to be unskilled as well as to live as an unskilled individual. Unfortunately, there is no proviso or caveat that unless the unskilled person is your relative or child either. Meanwhile, Ephesians 4:28, I Thessalonians 4:11 and II Thessalonians 3:6-12 say:

> 28 The man who used to rob must stop robbing and start working, in order to earn an honest living for himself and to be able to help the poor.
>
> 11 Make it your aim to live a quiet life, to mind your own business, and to earn your own living, just as we told you before.
>
> 6 Our brothers, we command you in the name of our Lord Jesus Christ to keep away from all brothers who are living a lazy life and who do not follow the instructions that we gave them. 7 You yourselves know very well that you should do just what we did. We were not lazy when we were with you. 8 We did not accept anyone's support without paying for it. Instead, we worked and toiled; we kept working day and night so as not to be an expense to any of you. 9 We did this,

not because we do not have the right to demand our support; we did it to be an example for you to follow. 10 While we were with you, we used to tell you, "Whoever refuses to work is not allowed to eat." 11 We say this because we hear that there are some people among you who live lazy lives and who do nothing except meddle in other people's business. 12 In the name of the Lord Jesus Christ we command these people and warn them to lead orderly lives and work to earn their own living. (TEV)

We are told that whoever does not work should not eat and we know that the resultant starvation would lead to death which makes us to say whoever is unskilled and therefore, unemployable is tactically not fit to live. This means that even God recognizes viability and respect of the viable persons above non-viable ones. Therefore, natives preferring the viable to the unviable have not sinned in the sight of God. This lends credence to the fact that it is the responsibility of migrants to make themselves viable and thereby, contribute to the economy of their host countries or communities. Along this line, Leviticus 19:9-10 and 23:22, Deuteronomy 24:19-22 and Ruth 1:1-22 and 2:1-23 can be interpreted to mean that Ruth gives a good example for us to follow. Before she relocated from her native Moab to live among the Jews in Bethlehem, the Jews or Israelites had a God approved tradition that strangers or non-natives would glean behind reapers or harvester in the land of Israel. Whether this custom was equally practiced in Moab we are not told but she found it out to be in force in Bethlehem and complied with it. She complied with the law of the land she went to live to survive. She did not have to break the laws of the land to survive. Naomi was Ruth's chief host and the way she supported Naomi quickly spread among the natives and contributed to her finding favour.

Also important is the fact that she went out to work hard gleaning behind reapers. One reason this is important is the fact that she did not wait for Naomi to fend for her which can be interpreted to mean that she ensured that she was an asset to the sustenance of her chief host rather than a liability. Naomi was too distraught to look after herself talk more about looking after another person. She left Bethlehem with husband and two sons and returned with neither of them. As a woman she was very ashamed of how her life had turned out. Her peers she left behind were doing well by the time she returned with Ruth. Rather than encourage Ruth it was Ruth who took on the responsibility of encouraging her. When Ruth found out that staying at home would not put food on their table, she came up with the idea of going to glean behind reapers which their Jewish traditions allowed her to do as a stranger. Ruth 2:1-23, 3:1-18 and 4:1-17 and Matthew 1:1-17 confirm that it brought the turn around that the lives of Ruth and Naomi needed at the time and forever.

The other point worthy of note in the above passage is the fact that the writer, Apostle Paul said that he did two jobs at the same time. Just as he did what we famously call sacred service so also, he engaged in secular job to provide for his personal needs along with his colleagues engaged in rendering the sacred service because they recognized that it was what God meant them to do at that time of their life. They were not so carried away with the idea of full-time sacred service to the extent that they failed to engage in secular job to provide for their personal needs. In the same vein, I Kings 19:13-21 confirms that Elisha was a successful agriculturist before God recalled or conscripted him to serve as the prophet after Elijah, just as II Kings 9:1-37 confirms that Jehu was a professional soldier who had done so well that he was already a commander in the army of Israel when God redeployed or conscripted him to serve as the king of Israel. Amos 1:1 and 7:10-17 confirm that Amos was a successful farmer when God commissioned him to serve as a prophet at some point in his life to the nation of Israel. Luke 5:1-11 confirms that Peter was a certified fisherman, even when he was not formally educated. Most of Jesus' full-time disciples were gainfully employed before He called them to serve as His apostolic disciples.

From the foregoing, it is not out of place to say mankind's universal constitution frowns and even prohibits any unviable individual from living on earth unless such an individual is determined to add viability value to him or herself so he or she could join others to contribute to improve the standard of living of humanity. This is not the point to quote fundamental human right to live, and in any case, for every right there is a responsibility, duty, and obligation on the part of the right beneficiary. The world or earth has no room for persons who have nothing to contribute to its wellbeing no matter how small. The dictum is "Not Useful Not Wanted" or "The Unuseful Unwanted" by mankind and the world. Put in another way, "Usefulness Partly Justifies Acceptance".

Someone lamented to me that his mother sounded unhappy with his situation and that he was both confused and unhappy with it to the extent he was beginning to resent talking with her on phone or visiting her. When I asked what he thought could be wrong he said she seemed to compare him with his younger siblings. I asked his age and he said nearly 36. So, I said your mother have not done anything wrong rather she is just doing the normal thing. You graduated before your half siblings, yet they have steady career jobs that you lack. They are married with children just like you are. Your mother is hoping after hope that you too would be successful to the extent that you would visit her in your own car with your family like the children of her marital mate are doing already. How do you assume that your mother has no expectation from you? She had spent her younger years to nurture you and now she is eager to exhibit your success as part of what she spent her life to achieve to her peers who have their children who are successful to show for how well they spent their active years. Now you want me as a pastor to say your mother is asking for too much. The way I understand life, it would be unjust for me to blame her for having such expectation from you. Ruth 4:13-17, Proverbs 23:22, Jeremiah 31:15-17 and I Timothy 5:4, 16 say:

> 13 So Boaz took Ruth home as his wife. The Lord blessed her, and she became pregnant and had a son. 14 The women said to Naomi, "Praise the Lord! He has given you a grandson today to take care of you. May the boy become famous in Israel! 15 Your daughter-in-law loves you, and has done more for you than seven sons. And now she has given you a grandson, who will bring new life to you and give you security in your old age." 16 Naomi took the child, held him close, and took care of him. 17 The women of the neighborhood named the boy Obed. They told everyone, "A

son has been born to Naomi!" Obed became the father of Jesse, who was the father of David.

22 Listen to your father; without him you would not exist. When your mother is old, show her your appreciation.

15 The Lord says, "A sound is heard in Ramah, the sound of bitter weeping. Rachel is crying for her children, they are gone, and she refuses to be comforted. 16 Stop your crying and wipe away your tears. All that you have done for your children will not go unrewarded; they will return from the enemy's land. 17 There is hope for your future; your children will come back home. I, the Lord, have spoken.

4 But if a widow has children or grandchildren, they should learn first to carry out their religious duties towards their own family and in this way repay their parents and grandparents, because that is what pleases God. 16 But if any Christian

woman has widows in her family, she must take care of them and not put the burden on the church, so that it may take care of the widows who are all alone. (TEV)

This mother was not talking about material reward from this son of hers rather she was asking for the prestige of being a mother to a successful respectable member of society. It would be ungodly for anyone to say she was asking for too much. Jesse would have been unknown if not for David. Meanwhile, David was his youngest child. Social status-wise, Jesse had two children: David and the others. Even parents prefer their productive child to the unproductive.

20

ENGAGE IN LEGITIMATE ENDEAVOURS

Fundamentally, all human endeavours do one of two things at any point in time – it endears on the positive side or it ensnares on the negative side. Human effort could be legitimate or illegitimate just like intimate relationship with the opposite sex. 'Employer' Laban cheated his 'employee' Jacob, but later Jacob took Laban's role to cheat to gain more than Laban as a way of recouping what he had lost to him. That talks about doing illegitimate things during legitimate endeavor. This leads to the subject of doing legitimate job ethically rather than otherwise. Manufacturers of household items could engage in non-payment of correct tax to relevant government authorities or circumventing due duties on the imported raw materials, machinery and their spare parts for the production process and profit making.

They could lower the standard of their products and yet make false claims on the packaging of the items they push into the market for the consuming public. This is where the subject of illegitimacy in income earning endeavours is very vast and impossible to exhaust. As respectable and honorable as wealth and prosperity/success or achievement, **the way that wealth and the likes are obtained matters to God and good people anywhere anytime.** It is part of the reason that Leviticus 19:13, 35-36, Deuteronomy 24:14-15, 25:13-16, Job 31:13-28, Proverbs 16:11, 20:10, 13, Jeremiah 22:13, Ezekiel 45:10, Malachi 3:5 and James 5:1-6 say:

> 13 "Do not rob or take advantage of anyone. Do not hold back the wages of someone you have hired, not even for one night. 35 "Do not cheat anyone by using false measures of length, weight, or quantity. 36 Use honest scales, honest weights,

and honest measures. I am the Lord your God, and I brought you out of Egypt.

14 "Do not cheat poor and needy hired servants, whether they are Israelites or foreigners living in one of your towns. 15 Each day before sunset pay them for that day's work; they need the money and have counted on getting it. If you do not pay them, they will cry out against you to the Lord, and you will be guilty of sin.

13-14 "Do not cheat when you use weights and measures. 15 Use true and honest weights and measures, so that you may live a long time in the land that the Lord your God is giving you. 16 The Lord hates people who cheat.

13 When any of my servants complained against me, I would listen and treat them fairly. 14 If I did not, how could I then face God? What could I say when God came to judge me? 15 The same God who created me created my servants also. 16 I

have never refused to help the poor; never have I let widows live in despair 17 or let orphans go hungry while I ate. 18 All my life I have taken care of them. 19 When I found someone in need, too poor to buy clothes, 20 I would give him clothing made of wool that had come from my own flock of sheep. Then he would praise me with all his heart. 21 If I have ever cheated an orphan, knowing I could win in court, 22 then may my arms be broken; may they be torn from my shoulders. 23 Because I fear God's punishment, I could never do such a thing. 24 I have never trusted in riches 25 or taken pride in my wealth. 26 I have never worshiped the sun in its brightness or the moon in all its beauty. 27 I have not been led astray to honor them by kissing my hand in reverence to them. 28 Such a sin should be punished by death; it denies Almighty God.

11 The Lord wants weights and measures to be honest and every sale to be fair.

10 The Lord hates people who use dishonest weights and measures. 13 If you spend your time sleeping, you will be poor. Keep busy and you will have plenty to eat.

13 Doomed is the one who builds his house by injustice and enlarges it by dishonest; <u>who makes his people work for nothing and does not pay their wages</u>.

10 "Everyone must use honest weights and measures:

5 The Lord Almighty says, "I will appear among you to judge, and I will testify at once against those who practice magic, against adulterers, against those who give false testimony, <u>those who cheat employees out of their wages</u>, and <u>those who take advantage of</u> widows, orphans, and <u>foreigners</u>—against all who do not respect me.

1 And now, you rich people, listen to me! Weep and wail over the miseries that are coming upon you! 2 Your riches have rotted away, and your clothes have been eaten by moths. 3 Your gold and silver are covered with rust, and this rust will be a witness against you and will eat up your flesh like fire. You have piled up riches in these last days. 4 <u>You have not paid any wages to those who work in your fields. Listen to their complaints! The cries of those who gather in your crops have reached the ears of God</u>, the Lord Almighty. 5 Your life here on earth has been full of luxury and pleasure. You have made yourselves fat for the day of slaughter. 6 You have condemned and murdered innocent people, and they do not resist you. (TEV)

God approves that the investor should profit from his efforts but not at the expense of his employees or distributors. In every generation and locality, there are bad natives looking for anyone including strangers to use to achieve their objectives by any means including obnoxious ones. That is partly what Pharaoh succeeded in using Joseph to achieve even if it was not intentionally. King Saul was glad to have Doeg support him to destroy the priest, Ahimelech and his relatives and their families and possessions when his Israelite bodyguards would not obey him to kill the priests. Something worthy of note is the fact that there is no indication that after using Doeg to destroy them, Saul kept the promise that he made to whoever supported him against David or David's supporters. I Samuel 22:6-23 started with Saul claiming that he had more gifts for whoever supported him against David yet there is no record of how he rewarded Doeg for giving him information about Ahimelech consulting God for David or killing God's priests. One would have expected that Saul would reward Doeg generously to encourage others to continue to supply him information about David's affiliates in his kingdom. He never did because perhaps, Doeg was a non-Israelite or migrant.

There have been stories of native employers who shortchange their non-native employees and when such employees want to get their dues the native employer would connive with immigration or homeland security officials to deport such migrant employees. Only God can reclaim the entitlement of such migrants. Yet, part of the solution is for migrants to get legitimate employment. When Saul did not reward Doeg for leaking Elimelech's relationship with David, there is no record that Doeg was able to remind Saul to fulfill his promise to him for giving him information about David. Zephaniah 1:9 can be interpreted to mean that there are employers who look for employees who could steal and kill to enrich them while Proverbs 30:14 can be interpreted to mean that there are employers who do not mind if their employees oppress the poor and weak as long as they enrich them. One of the sound interpretations that can be given to I Samuel 22:6-19 is that Doeg was Saul's employee who Saul hood-winked to leak information about his enemy or rival and kill his perceived enemy's supporter or ally. If we consider the position of the royal ruler of Israel as the trade or business that Saul was engaged in and David was Saul's abhorred competitor for the throne of Israel, then we can say Saul used his employer influence or advantage over Doeg to make Doeg join him to seek the death of his competitor and his supporters or customers. When I Samuel 21:7 and 22:16-19 say:

> 7 Saul's chief herdsman, Doeg, who was from Edom, happened to be there that day, because he had to fulfil a religious obligation.
>
> 16 The king said, "Ahimelech, you and all your relatives must die." 17 Then he said to the guards standing near him, "Kill the Lord's priests! They conspired with David and did not tell me that he had run away, even though they knew it all along." But the guards refused to lift a hand to kill the Lord's priests. 18 So Saul said to Doeg, "You kill them!"—and Doeg killed them all. On that day he killed eighty-five priests who were qualified to carry the ephod. 19 Saul also had all the other inhabitants of Nob, the city of priests, put to death: men and women, children and babies, cattle, donkeys, and sheep—they were all killed. (TEV)

It means that while Saul's employee in the position of bodyguards saw what we can call religious conscience reason not to do what they believed to be wrong, his other employee in the position of chief herdsman who was not an Israelite like the bodyguards did not care about such religious conscience reason. Meanwhile, this same Doeg was religious enough to go and pay a vow in the very place of worship where Elimelech presided as high priest. There would be times when your boss wants to do his dirty jobs and the point is you must seek not to please him rather than please God. Jonathan might not have done enough to stay alive and fulfill God's plan that he served as second-in-command to David on the throne of Israel but one thing that we cannot take away from Jonathan is that he never joined his father to seek to harm David. Not even when his father touted the throne of Israel as Jonathan's reward if only, he supported him to kill David. That is one truth that can be safely deduced from I Samuel 18:1-30, 19:1-24, 20:1-42, 23:1-18 and 31:1-13 and I Chronicles 10:1-12.

Saul never punished his bodyguards because he understood that they acted according to their culture but as for Doeg who was brought up with another culture he did not understand the fundamental reason his fellow Saul's employees found it difficult to obey the boss in this instance. Natives who are in position to employ their fellow humans knows that there are odd things their fellow natives would not do no matter the amount he pays them so they would look for foreigners to employ for the purpose of doing such dirty deals. The point is that even if Doeg would get into trouble with God or Ahimelech's surviving son after Saul's death, it did not matter to Saul. That is part of what the migrant employee must not forget when his native employer is looking for who would help him to deal treacherously.

Imagine what would have been the fate of Doeg if David had decided to avenge the death of Ahimelech and his priestly relatives, relatives, and possessions, Doeg would have been finished literally. That is when he would have realized that it was wrong for him to do what Saul's bodyguards refused to do. He might have thought that he should do anything to please his boss who gave him the privilege to serve as his chief herdsman when there are uncountable professional herdsmen of Israelite origin that his boss could have appointed in his stead. All things being equal, no one should consider immediate gain alone rather should be strategic in whatever he or she does. Yet, it is more important for the migrant employee. The migrant employee must not consider the benefit from his current employer alone otherwise he might not be able to survive the backlash of pleasing the boss by engaging in dirty deals.

The story of Solomon lends great credence to the subject of employers using their employees to do all sorts including the most bizarre. As the king of Israel, he was in position to appoint all sorts of officials. As a result, it was very much in order that he did appoint officials to help him to run in kingdom or regime. However, morally speaking, listing his appointed officials, I Kings 4:1-19 can be interpreted to mean that he appointed two fundamental classes of officials to run his kingdom. Socially speaking, he appointed both the commendable and the condemnable classes of officials. Commendable were to do what can be called legitimate tasks and the condemnable to do the condemnable and damnable duties. Verses 1-6 lists the commendable while the remaining verses 7-19, 22-23 and 27-28 say the other officials did the dirty job for him.

A count of the palace officials suggests that he appointed 12 officials to do legitimate duties and 12 to do the dirty job. Here is a man who God meant to rule even before he was born. That can be interpreted to mean that he was doing the job that God designed for him to do during his stay on earth. Despite living according to God's plan for him on earth he still found persons and time to do things that did not help his subjects who can equally be described as clients or inhabitants that his job or business impacted directly. The damnable appointees or employees were meant to extort from his subjects to provide for his prodigal lifestyle. This is someone who took over the throne of Israel from his father who I Chronicles 14:1-2 and 18:14 confirm ensured that the subjects were never oppressed. His father never collected anything from the Israelites for himself. It means that he did not learn the example of extorting from the subjects to sustain lavish lifestyle from his father.

The governors that he appointed to extort from the Israelites to sustain his lavish lifestyle were Israelites yet never thought that it was inappropriate to put such a burden on the subject or their fellow Israelites. It means that there are persons who by nature do not care who are hurt as long as they please their boss or they live lavishly, luxuriously and prodigally. They can be described as Solomon's sickening disciples or Solomon's scandalous disciples. It was not like Solomon did not have personal source of income or legitimate sources of income. He was supposed to be richer than his subjects probably even put together. Despite been richer he still stole from the subjects who are not as rich. That is the real evil in it – to legitimize stealing from poorer persons under the guise of new royal order during your regime and administration. I Kings 4:20-28 says:

> 20 The people of Judah and Israel were as numerous as the grains of sand on the seashore; they ate and drank, and were happy. 21 Solomon's kingdom included all the nations from the Euphrates River to Philistia and the Egyptian border. They paid him taxes and were subject to him all his life. 22 The supplies Solomon needed each day were 150 bushels of fine flour and 300 bushels of meal; 23 10 stall-fed cattle, 20 pasture-fed cattle, and 100 sheep, besides deer, gazelles,

roebucks, and poultry. 24 Solomon ruled over all the land west of the Euphrates River, from Tiphsah on the Euphrates as far west as the city of Gaza. All the kings west of the Euphrates were subject to him, and he was at peace with all the neighboring countries. 25 As long as he lived, the people throughout Judah and Israel lived in safety, each family with its own grapevines and fig trees. 26 Solomon had forty thousand stalls for his chariot horses and twelve thousand cavalry horses. 27 His twelve governors, each one in the month assigned to him, supplied the food King Solomon needed for himself and for all who ate in the palace; they always supplied everything needed. 28 Each governor also supplied his share of barley and straw, where it was needed, for the chariot horses and the work animals. (TEV)

First, God can prosper a nation and its people, yet their rulers could make life miserable for them by their oppressive laws even when God ordained such a ruler and his appointed lieutenants.

By reason of prosperity the Israelites were happy but because of the oppressive extortion of their God-given king or ruler by the name of Solomon son of David and his predecessor the Israelites were unhappy. What Solomon did when he took from his less rich subjects to sustain his lavish lifestyle can be said to typify how the rich and strong or prosperous and powerful become greedy for the wealth of those that are not as rich as they are. Though he was richer he still wanted part of the wealth of the people who are not as rich as himself. I used to tell my bank's employees that it is not right for them to collect any charge on my account because their bank declare billions as profit every year and I can't even boast of millions as income or profit. They laugh it off but that is exactly what Solomon did to the Israelites. It is unforgivable to collect from the poor when you are rich.

Someone once said that one of the worst bible passages in his estimation is when Matthew 25:28-30 and Luke 19:24-26 say in part that the little that the poor have would be taken from them and given to those that have more than the poor. The part of the parable that led Jesus to that conclusion meant punishment for the poor. Therefore, the point is that God never meant or made Solomon king of Israel so that he would be punishment to the people of Israel. Only a ruler who has decided that he would be a curse rather than a blessing to the subject would hide under the conclusion of that parable to say even Jesus said the rich would get what belongs to the poor therefore, it is appropriate for the rich to be greedy for what belongs to persons who are poorer than them.

There is a difference between providing services that people need and collecting reasonable price from them to enjoy the services or product and going all out to over charge in order to get mega profits to pay for your hyper luxurious lifestyle while the larger populace live in squalor. One of the reasons the interpretation we have given to the above passage is important is that I Kings 12:1-20 confirms that this oppressive lifestyle of Solomon during his 40-year reign was partly responsible for the break-up of the kingdom of Israel after his death. It is like the misdeeds and sins of Kings Hezekiah and his son and successor, Manasseh laid the foundation for the 70-year

Babylonian captivity during the generation of Jeremiah, Daniel, Ezekiel, and others.

There is a difference between God making you great for a purpose and you using that God given privilege of greatness to benefit the lives of members of your generation and immediate environment. I Samuel 8:10-19, 9:1-27, 10:1-27 and 11:1-13 confirm that God approved that Saul could extort from the Israelites during his reign yet there is no record that he did in the flagrant way that Solomon did even when there is no record that God meant Solomon to oppress the people. The other shocking thing is that this is the same Solomon who started by asking for God's wisdom to rule the Israelites fairly turning round to oppress the same Israelites that he seemed to have made their wellbeing his top priority initially.

It is not enough to do legitimate job, it is important to work hard at it and prosper rather than remain at what is famously referred to as the underdog performance success level perpetually. Outstanding success would earn the respect of all and sundry like it favoured Daniel in the palace of Babylon. It favoured

Joseph in Egypt when he was able to interpret Pharaoh's dreams which others could not. Do legitimate job and outstandingly too to enjoy in foreign land more than others.

Joseph accepted and did only legitimate jobs so long as he lived in Egypt and when his brothers joined him, they engaged in the legitimate job the king who had the final authority in the land of Egypt gave them. There is no record that they engaged in any untoward duty or activities which contradicted the laws of the land. Even when Potiphar's wife tried to lure Joseph to do evil, he resisted it till the end. Throughout Moses' 40-year stay in Midian, he never did anything adjudged illegal. Once Joseph and Moses married the natives of where they lived, there is no record that they considered marrying an additional wife. All the women Jacob married in Padan-Aram of Mesopotamia, outside his place of birth, Canaan, were forced on him by his chief hosts, maternal uncle turned employer and fathers-in-law, otherwise his original intention was to marry only Rachel which means one wife. His case is useful here considering that while he married Leah because of her father's manipulation, Leah and Rachel made him marry their maids.

On the other hand, Genesis 26:34-35, 27:41-46 and 28:6-9 say while his twin brother, Esau was back home in Canaan, he married many wives at will. The confidence which Esau had to marry one woman after another, Jacob could not muster such courage to marry one woman after another but made do with the ones he was given in addition to the only one he loved, Rachel. The relevance of this point is that if a foreigner decides to move from one woman to another in a foreign land, any or some of them could plot the harm of such foreigner on account that he could not come from his place of birth to break her heart in her own native land. Therefore, much as it is beneficial for a foreigner to marry among his hosts, he should not do anything to offend such natives otherwise they could make life miserable for him. This is part of the reason many foreigners languish in jail in the land of their sojourn because they had offended natives who would naturally have upper hand in the courts.

Genesis 38:1-30 can be interpreted to mean that when the natives of Adullam saw that Judah who came to live among them tried to undermine one of their own, his daughter-in-law, Tamar, they helped her to trap him with pregnancy and he had no choice than to treat her fairly. The story starts with the fact that he relocated away from other family members to go and live among the people of Adullam. There he married a native who bore him three sons. He got Tamar to be wife to his eldest son who God killed because he sinned. He asked her to marry his second son who equally sinned and God killed him as well. Because his third son was still young, he asked Tamar to return to her parents until the surviving son was old enough to marry her. But because he was afraid of losing the third son, he would not recall Tamar even when the surviving son was old enough to have her. The natives thought that it was not fair on Tamar. Her mother-in-law who was a native like Tamar was dead, if she were alive maybe she would have prevailed on her husband, Judah to fulfill his promise to Tamar. It was one of the natives who provided Tamar with the information that she needed to force Judah to restore her to his home. Any foreigner who tries to ill-treat any native should prepare for a stiff resistance. It is better not to contemplate it.

21

WORK FOR THE GOOD OF THE LAND

God meant that all foreigners have a responsibility to work for the good of the land of their residence so that by so doing, they would benefit from His blessing on the land. This is serious because it presupposes that whoever fails to work for the good of his host community will not benefit from God's blessing on the land. This means that to eat the good of the land as God promised, the individual must work for the good of the land just as God prescribes. Much as God blessed Laban's business because of Jacob who was a stranger and employee in the business, it was because Jacob worked for the benefit of Laban's business that he gained from God's blessings on Laban's business that he managed. The other important angle is that when God saw that Laban would not allow Jacob to get his dues, God made Jacob to gain more than Laban based on the renewed remuneration agreement Jacob reached with Laban. Also, when the Egyptians did not allow the Israelites to get their due wages, God made the Egyptians to give their dues from the many years of labour in the land of Egypt when they were to leave Egypt. It can be summed up as the concept of "Balance the Books" or "Balancing the Books" – bless those God meant to bless you, bless your God ordained and ordered beneficiaries or beautify your benefactors.

Genesis 37:12-36 and 39:1-23 confirm that away from Canaan in Egypt God blessed Joseph's bosses because of his presence in their employment. The bosses responded by rewarding him with promotion. Their favourable response made God to bless them the more. God did not say because Joseph was forced to be a slave or serve them against his wish, He would not bless his bosses. In any case, it was his brothers who sold him into Egypt to live as a slave so it would be wrong to punish his Egyptian masters who did not invade his home in Canaan, capture and took him away captive. God blessed Joseph's masters in Egypt to encourage them to be kind to Joseph to reduce the impact of the pains of the unfair treatment by his older brothers. When God would make this concept of His intention for all strangers plainer, He made it a direct instruction to the Jews that He contracted King Nebuchadnezzar to carry captive to Babylon.

Jeremiah 15:1-4 confirms that the Babylonian 70-year captivity was devised and implemented by God because of the sins of King Hezekiah's son and successor, monstrous Manasseh. This means that even the 70-year Babylonian captivity was supposed to be punishment that He implemented for the sins of Manasseh. Since they were serving punishment in Babylon God decided that they must subdue their resentment for their captors/oppressors and pray to Him to bless them and their land so that they would share in the blessing that He rains down on their oppressors in response to their prayers to Him on the behalf of their oppressors. In this respect, Jeremiah 29:4-7, 10-14 says:

> 4 "The Lord Almighty, the God of Israel, says to all those people whom he allowed

Nebuchadnezzar to take away as prisoners from Jerusalem to Babylonia: 5 'Build houses and settle down. Plant gardens and eat what you grow in them. 6 Marry and have children. Then let your children get married, so that they also may have children. You must increase in numbers and not decrease. 7 Work for the good of the cities where I have made you go as prisoners. Pray to me on their behalf, because if they are prosperous, you will be prosperous too. 10 The Lord says, 'When Babylon's seventy years are over, I will show my concern for you and keep my promise to bring you back home. 11 I alone know the plans I have for you, plans to bring you prosperity and not disaster, plans to bring about the future you hope for. 12 Then you will call to me. You will come and pray to me, and I will answer you. 13 You will seek me, and you will find me because you will seek me with all your heart. 14 Yes, I say, you will find me, and I will restore you to your land. I will gather you from every country and from every place to which I have scattered you, and I will bring you back to the land from which I had sent you away into exile. I, the Lord have spoken." (TEV)

This passage means that God's commandment is that foreigners should work for the good of the land where they live. You might think that you would not stay in the land for long but end up staying for a long time. Apparently, these Jews did not want to work hard and do the good things that natives were doing for them to enjoy the land of Babylon so God sent the Prophet Jeremiah to them to join the natives to work hard and earn enough to build houses and plant vineyards. God meant that the Jews should get over the frustration and bitterness that the Babylonians did the evil of carrying them captive. The Jews should not see themselves as strangers who should not care about the wellbeing of their captors and their native land. They should see the strange land as their home during their stay.

Look at it this way, if a migrant says because he is in a strange land, he would not care about its wellbeing, what if he stays there for long with that unprofitable mindset, he would have wasted those years not achieving anything tangible and realize at the end that he has wasted some decades of the number of years that God meant for him to stay on earth. Therefore, whether one is at home of birth or not, set goals and pray to God to help you to achieve them. Pray to God for blessing like you would do if you were at your land of birth. God meant that the Jews should not blame the Babylonians for their precarious plight because in any case, II Kings 18:1-37, 19:1-37, 20:1-19, 21:1-18, 23:24-27 and 24:1-4 and Isaiah 38:1-22 and 39:1-8 confirm that Hezekiah and Manasseh had provoked God to plan the Babylonian captivity for implementation during the generation of Prophets Daniel, Ezekiel and Jeremiah. Also, Jeremiah 34:8-22 confirms that God's final window of opportunity to escape the Babylonian captivity was wasted or missed by the king, his officials and the nobles of Jerusalem and Judah. Since they have justified their going into captivity, the only thing that God can do for them to cope while they are there is to bless the land of captivity for their sake but they have to prove their obedience and loyalty to God which would prove that they deserve God's help in captivity by overcoming their bitterness to pray to God to bless their captors and the land.

God meant that wherever He let any man live is a stage or phase of his life and he must spend the time there to prepare for the next location or phase. He must give a good account of himself while there. He said He would bring them back and He does not want them to return without children who would take over their native land. Imagine if Joseph did not marry and have children while in Egypt there would have been no tribe of Ephraim and Manasseh. Imagine if Moses did not marry and have children or his two sons while in Midian there would have been no mention of his descendants serving as Levitical priests in I Chronicles 26:24-28. That is what God meant in Jeremiah 29:6 when He says that they should marry to have children and the children should marry and have children so that the Jews would increase rather than decrease. The subject of increase in population and prosperity of God's people is important to Him. It is so important that even when He is compelled to punish them, He kept their population increase and personal prosperity in sharp focus. There is no place that He allows a man to live on earth that He is not willing and even eager to bless the individual but such an individual must get beyond sentiments of blaming the natives and pray to God for them and their land so that as God responds to the prayers of the foreigner to bless the land the foreigner would benefit personally.

Also, Jeremiah 29:4-7 means that there are locations God will prosper because the inhabitants who are not necessarily natives pray to Him to bless the land and its people. Genesis 30:25-28 and 39:1-6 confirm that God blessed Laban and Potiphar because of the presence of Jacob and his son, Joseph, respectively. This means that there are God prospering presence carriers whose presence changes the prosperity template of their environment. It is like when I Samuel 17:1-58 confirms that David's entry into the battlefield changed the template of the battle in favour of the Israel's army. Until he arrived or showed up the Philistines had the upper hand but once he entered the wind of victory blew against the Philistines. Now, God did not wait for Jacob and Joseph to make formal prayers to Him before He decided to bless Laban or Potiphar. Once they began working for Laban and Potiphar, God began to bless their employers. But in the case of the Jews in Babylon, God said they needed to pray to Him to bless their host land and people. It should be said that Genesis 31:38-42 and 39:1-6 and Jeremiah 29:4-7 confirm that Jacob, Joseph and the Jews had to work hard during their stay in the employment of their respective foreign employers in their native lands.

Blessing Laban because of Jacob, Potiphar because of Joseph and Babylon because of the Jews' prayer to Him fulfills God's promise to their grandfather, great grandfather and ancestors, Abraham in Genesis 12:1-3 when He declared to Abraham in verse 2-3 that 'I will give you many descendants, and they will become a great nation. I will bless you so that you will be a blessing. I will bless those who bless you and but will curse those who curse you. And through you I will bless all the nations.'- TEV. Jacob was God's channel of blessing to Laban; Joseph was to Potiphar and all his other Egyptian masters and the Jews to the Babylonians during the 70-year long captivity. It is as a result that Daniel 1:1-17, 2:1-49 confirm that DSMA were of great benefit to the kings of Babylon during this period.

Another way to view this admonition of God is the belief that the whole earth is His constituency. Therefore, wherever He sends any man to live at any time, such a man should see it as his God-assigned hometown to live well and make the best out of life. Let us consider the logic this way; God meant DSMA to spend seventy years in Babylon, if they decided not to do anything with their lives because they would yet return to Jerusalem, even if they returned after that period, they would not be less than 90 years old. What would they have the strength to do and achieve again in Jerusalem at such an old age? Therefore, while they yet have strength to work hard and achieve, they should just do so not minding if it is in a strange land or their native land. In any case, just as one is a stranger in a strange land so also are strangers living in and contributing to the development and wellbeing of one's native land. Now, the ratio of such cross-border stranger contribution to nations, countries and societies may not be equal just as there is nothing equal in this life. It is the responsibility of the leaders of each country to ensure that strangers contributing to the development of their country outnumber that of their natives living as strangers and contributing to the development of other nations of the world.

First, Matthew 23:37-39 and 13:34-35 can be interpreted to mean that Jesus inferred that any nation or group of people who resents, persecutes, rejects and kills God-sent prophets to them would not have and enjoy God's solution until they repent of their evil ways to embrace God's messengers and prophets sent to them. He symbolizes God's salvation and solution to the Jews making His claim that they would not see Him again until they learn to embrace God-sent prophet to mean that they will not enjoy the benefits of God's planned help to them in full until their attitude to God's prophet changes. Lot was the prophet that God sent to the people of Sodom to help them but because they said as a foreigner they could not listen to his counsel, God had to punish them as their wickedness deserved. Then, there is the unbearable shadow of shame that the story of Ebedmelech's efforts to save Jeremiah from King Zedekiah and his precarious palace officials connotes. It took Ebedmelech who was a non-Israelite to make Zedekiah realize that it was awful for him to give approval to his palace officials who were Israelites like himself and Jeremiah to stop the slow death process that Zedekiah approved for his officials to subject Jeremiah to. It was Saul's son, Jonathan who tried to discourage him from killing David. While Saul's bodyguards would not obey him to kill God's priests, a non-Israelite by the name of Doeg did gleefully. Second, while Ebedmelech stood up for what is right in the foreign land where he lived Doeg did the opposite.

Proverbs 14:34 says righteousness exalts a nation while sin or unrighteousness is a reproach that hinders the exaltation of any nation or group of people. Proverbs 30:14, Ecclesiastes 3:16, Isaiah 5:8-30, 56:9-12, Jeremiah 7:1-34, 8:10, 21:11-12, 22:1-5, 23:1-6 and 9-40, Ezekiel 13:1-23, 22:23-29, 33:23-29, 34:1-10, Micah 3:11, Habakkuk 2:5-17, Zephaniah 3:1-4, Zechariah 3:1-10, Malachi 2:1-17 and 3:1-12 list some of the evils that constitute sin and unrighteousness that could hinder the prosperity of any nation.

Genesis 19:1-29 says Lot tried to help the natives of Sodom to repent of their evil ways to no avail. He was a stranger among them and in fact, they told him that it is an integral part of the reason that they can never take his counsel seriously. In like manner, it was Ebedmelech who as not a Jew who persuaded the king to not continue to agree with his royal advisers to kill Jeremiah gradually. Just as God saved Lot from the destruction of Sodom so also God promised a reward to Ebedmelech for saving Jeremiah from the hands of Jeremiah's fellow Jews in Jerusalem. Furthermore, Jeremiah 38:1-13 and 39:15-18 say:

> 1 Shephatiah son of Mattan, Gedaliah son of Pashhur, Jehucal son of Shelemiah, and Pashhur son of Malchiah heard that I was telling the people that 2 the Lord had said, "Whoever stays on in the city will die in war or of starvation or disease. But whoever goes out and surrenders to the Babylonians will not be killed; he will at least escape with his life." 3 I was also telling them that the Lord had said, "I am going to give the city to the Babylonian army, and they will

capture it." 4 Then the officials went to the king and said, "This man must be put to death. By talking like this he is making the soldiers in the city lose their courage, and he is doing the same thing to everyone else left in the city. He is not trying to help the people; he only wants to hurt them." 5 King Zedekiah answered, "Very well, then, do what you want to with him; I can't stop you." 6 So they took me and let me down by ropes into Prince Malchiah's well, which was in the palace courtyard. There was no water in the well, only mud, and I sank down in it. 7 However, Ebedmelech the Sudanese, a eunuch who worked in the royal palace, heard that they had put me in the well. At that time the king was holding court at the Benjamin Gate. 8 So Ebedmelech went there and said to the king, 9 "Your Majesty, what these men have done is wrong. They have put Jeremiah in the well, where he is sure to die of starvation, since there is no more food in the city." 10 Then the king ordered Ebedmelech to take with him three men and to pull me out of the well before I died. 11 So Ebedmelech went with the men to the palace storeroom and got some worn-out clothing which he let down to me by ropes. 12 He told me to put the rags under my arms, so that the ropes wouldn't hurt me. I did this, 13 and they pulled me up out of the well. After that I was kept in the courtyard.

15 While I was still imprisoned in the palace courtyard, the Lord told me 16 to tell Ebedmelech the Sudanese that the Lord Almighty, the God of Israel, had said, "Just as I said I would, I am going to bring upon this city destruction and not prosperity. And when this happens, you will be there to see it. 17 But I, the Lord, will protect you, and you will not be handed over to the men you are afraid of. 18 I will keep you safe, and you will not be put to death. You will escape with your

life because you have put your trust in me. I, the Lord, have spoken." (TEV)

Ebedmelech played the role that DSMA played in the palace of Nebuchadnezzar, king of Babylon. Ebedmelech used his privileged position in a foreign land to work for justice and fairness as well as save the life of a man of God despite being a foreigner. This case introduces the dimension of a foreigner having the clout to save a native from trouble and even death. Since God gave him the privilege to serve and advise the king of the foreign land where he lived, he ensured that God's prophet was saved from dying unjustly and it is very striking that God rewarded him for it. God did not say that just because he is a foreigner, the good he did for the benefit of a native did not deserve a reward. This is part of what I call 'God delight delighters' irrespective of their background and where they live. If you deliver others from destruction, God will deliver you as well when necessary.

It is very irritating to read that this king dreaded his nobles, counselors, or friends who we assume he appointed and even if he inherited them from his predecessors, they are either ready to work with him submissively or he dismisses them from his royal service. It exemplifies captured captains or captive captains. It is a case of a king who has been held hostage in his palace by his lieutenants. Advisers do not have the right to force the advisee to accept and adopt their advice. Considering that Jeremiah 38:14-28 says:

> 14 On another occasion King Zedekiah had me brought to him at the third entrance to the Temple, and he said, "I am going to ask you a question, and I want you to tell me the whole truth." 15 I answered, "If I tell you the truth, you will put me to death, and if I give you advice, you won't pay any attention." 16 So King Zedekiah promised me in secret, "I swear by the living God, the God who gave us life, that I will not put you to death or hand you over to the men who want to kill you." 17 Then I told Zedekiah that the Lord Almighty, the God of Israel, had said, "If you surrender to the king of Babylonia's officers,

your life will be spared, and this city will not be burned down. Both you and your family will be spared. 18 But if you do not surrender, then this city will be handed over to the Babylonians, who will burn it down, and you will not escape from them." 19 But the king answered, "<u>I am afraid of our countrymen who have deserted to the Babylonians. I may be handed over to them and tortured</u>." 20 I said, "You will not be handed over to them. I beg you to obey the Lord's message; then all will go well with you, and your life will be spared. 21 But the Lord has shown me in a vision what will happen if you refuse to surrender. 22 In it I saw all the women left in Judah's royal palace being led out to the king of Babylonia's officers. Listen to what they were saying as they went: 'The king's best friends misled him, they overruled him. And now that his feet have sunk in the mud, his friends have left him.' " 23 Then I added, "All your women and children will be taken out to the Babylonians, and you yourself will not escape from them. You will be taken prisoner by the king of Babylonia, and this city will be burned to the ground." 24 Zedekiah replied, "Don't let anyone know about this conversation, and your life will not be in danger. 25 If the officials hear that I have talked with you, they will come and ask you what we said. They will promise not to put you to death if you tell them everything. 26 Just tell them you were begging me not to send you back to prison to die there." 27 Then all the officials came and questioned me, and I told them exactly what the king had told me to say. There was nothing else they could do, because no one had overheard the conversation. 28 And I was kept in the palace courtyard until the day Jerusalem was captured. (TEV)

The Unreported Most Fearful of the Earth sums up King Zedekiah in the above passage. He made God's prophet to lie because he was afraid of his officials. And it is a common feature to all rulers. I Samuel 15:1-24 and 28:15-18 confirm that the reason King Saul lost the throne was because he feared his men and decided to disobey God. He did not hide this reason from Samuel. It was not that he thought that the suggestion of his men was right rather because he was afraid of them. Genesis 12:10-20 can be safely interpreted to mean that the king of Egypt was afraid to keep someone who he could not treat shabbily in his kingdom so sent Abraham away. He did not want the continued stay of Abraham to increase the number of subjects who had the support of God of the universe that he could not control. The longer Abraham remained in his domain the more likelihood that some of his fellow Egyptians would befriend Abraham and join him to worship his God and if that happens then the subjects that had remained loyal to him since he became king might start questioning his actions because of the confidence that the God of Abraham would protect them from his punishment.

This curious king dreaded even his subjects who had defected to the enemy's side. Second, he is said to have allowed his friends and counselors to deceive him. Even though he sought the counsel of God through the man of God, he told the man of God to lie about the core content of their conversation. It is shameful that a foreigner did not dread him to the extent of not telling him the truth about the inappropriate treatment of Jeremiah, yet he was afraid of the officials he appointed to high positions. What manner of king was he? In this respect, he seemed to have taken after King Saul who disregarded God's command through His prophet Samuel to heed the counter suggestions of his warriors and God could not forgive him for that. The king has God's backing, yet he could not use that royal authority to compel his appointed nobles to do the right thing while a stranger who should be afraid that his counsel would not be regarded had the courage to tell him the right thing to do. This foreigner did so well that God rewarded him for so doing. This means that the king was a worse person at home while Ebedmelech was a better abroad.

22

United Voice/Front

Before we talk about Joseph and his brothers as fellow sojourners speaking with common voice for their benefit, let us lay the background of the commonness of conspirators or conspirators' curious commonness generally. It is very striking that Pharaoh and Joseph spoke with one voice over the matter of taking good care of Joseph's family members so that Joseph would be happy to continue to work for the benefit of Pharaoh. Then, Joseph and his brothers spoke with one voice to get Pharaoh to approve a way of ensuring that Joseph's brothers enjoyed their stay in Egypt. It made Joseph the interface between Pharaoh and his brothers. Unfortunately for the Egyptians, they spoke with one voice to be slaves to Pharaoh so long as Joseph gave them something to live on during the worst years of the famine. If they had jointly asked to be fed without payment because they produced the grains that were stored, the king would have been forced to approve because he still needed the Egyptians to rule over to feel great because Genesis 14:21, I Samuel 18:6-9, 19:1-7, Proverbs 14:28, Matthew 14:3-5 and Acts 12:1-5 say:

> 21 The king of Sodom said to Abram, "Keep the loot, but give me back all my people."

> 6 As David was returning after killing Goliath and as the soldiers were coming back home, women from every town in Israel came out to meet King Saul. They were singing joyful songs, dancing and playing tambourines and lyre. 7 In their celebration the women sang, "Saul has killed thousands, but David tens of thousands." 8 Saul did not like this, and he became very angry. He said, "For David they claim tens of thousands, but only thousands for me. They will be making

him king next!" 9 And so he was jealous and suspicious of David from that day on.

1 Saul told his son Jonathan and all his officials that he planned to kill David. But Jonathan was very fond of David, 2 and so he said to him "May father is trying to kill you. Please be careful tomorrow morning; hide in some secret place and stay there. 3 I will go and stand by my father in the field where you are hiding, and I will speak to him about you. If I find out anything, I will let you know." 4 Jonathan praised David to Saul and said, "Sir, don't do wrong to your servant David. He has never done you any wrong; on the contrary, everything he has done has bee a great help to you. 5 He risked his life when he killed Goliath, and the Lord won a great victory for Israel. When you saw it, you were glad. Why, then, do you now want to do wrong to an innocent man and kill David for no reason at all?" 6 Saul was convinced by what Jonathan said so he made

a vow in the Lord's name that he would not kill David. 7 So Jonathan called David and told him everything; then he took him back to Saul, and David served the king as he had before.

28 A king's greatness depends on how many people he rules; without them he is nothing.

3 For Herod had earlier ordered John's arrest, and he had him chained and put in prison. He had done this because of Herodias, his brother, Philip's wife. 4 For some time John the Baptist had told Herod, "It isn't right for you to be married to Herodias!" 5 Herod wanted to kill him, but he was afraid of the Jewish people, because they considered John to be a prophet.

1 About this time King Herod began to persecute some members of the church. 2 He had James, the brother of John, put to death by the sword. 3 When he saw that this pleased the Jews, he went on to arrest Peter. (This happened during

the time of the Festival of Unleavened Bread.) 4 After his arrest Peter was put in jail, where he was handed over to be guarded by four groups of four soldiers each. Herod planned to put him on trial in public after Passover. 5 So Peter was kept in jail, but the people of the church were praying earnestly to God for him. (TEV)

The list of proofs from the bible that the king needs the people than they need him is numerous. It is the reason the same Jewish rulers who John 9:22 and 34 says were determined to expel whoever believed in Jesus from the Temple in Jerusalem and their synagogues scattered all over the land of Judah still went ahead to do everything to get Jesus killed because He was stealing the attention and loyalty of the people from them. They were not satisfied with expelling whoever believed in Jesus from the Temple and synagogues because if they continued with that policy while Jesus continued unhindered they would have an empty Temple and synagogues during their services and that would spell doom for their ego and sustenance. King Saul could not live with the thought of loosing the loyalty of his subjects to David or someone else. He determined to kill David and whoever he believed supported David like I Samuel 22:6-23 confirms that he did to the priest Ahimelech and his fellow priests, their families, and possessions. John 11:45-54 and 12:9-11 confirm that the High Priests and Pharisees determined to kill Jesus and Lazarus for the same reason. They prove that rulers cannot afford to lose their subjects or their loyalty. This is what the Egyptians did not know and exploit to their advantage during the famine. All that they needed to have done would have been to unite and speak with one voice that either the king ordered Joseph to feed them from the royal treasury without asking them for payment otherwise they would relocate or never be loyal to him again. Moreover, they could have proposed that the king should loan them grains during the worst years of the famine and when it would have ended they would repay him instalmentally over a period of 10 years without losing part of their land or yield to the king.

So long as the Jewish people loved Herod persecuting the followers of Jesus, he was ready to do it. That is like buying the loyalty of the Jewish people at any cost, including human lives. Do you see why rulers behave like mad men? They can sacrifice their own people to achieve their objective so long as there would be majority of their subjects who love them for so doing. I Samuel 19:1-6 says it is not like Saul did not know that David helped him by killing Goliath. Much as he knew he was supposed to remain indebted to David for the rest of his reign, but he concluded that so long as the help that David rendered was an equivalent of 'hurting help', 'humiliating help' or 'annoying assistance' because it enabled David to steal the attention, praise, respect and loyalty of the people from him made David deserve death in his hands. The other thing from the story of the king of Sodom's offer to Abraham is why rulers do not mind if their subjects are poor as along as he rules over them. It gives us an insight into why rulers would approve for implementation of ideas that would impoverish their subjects so long as they rule over the people. Rulers do not care what foreign investors do to keep their citizens and subjects poor so long as they remain in power. In fact, the poorer their people are the better because that way the subjects would not have the courage to question their actions and inactions. They run a policy of keep them poor to keep them subservient perpetually. It is only in theory that rulers are supposed to work for the wellbeing of their citizens or subjects. In practice, the wellbeing of their citizens is none of their business. They pretend to care about the wellbeing of the citizens only when their position is threatened by reason of outrage by the populace consequent upon glaring ineptitude that cost the lives of some of the poor.

Jonathan's efforts did not yield the desired results because practically envy and jealousy do not have any iota of regard for commonsense and logical reasoning. Someone who has become a slave to envy and jealousy can never understand logical argument. I Samuel 19:9-24, 20:1-42, 22:6-23, 23:1-29, 24:1-22, 26:1-24, 27:1-12 and 31:1-13 confirm that Saul still spent the rest of his life seeking to kill David despite swearing to an oath in God's name that he would never hunt down David again. Envy and jealousy is like a cancer in the soul of its victims. Saul proved that the envious don't regard even God of Israel, maker of the universe. This is despite the fact that I Samuel 9:1-27 and 10:1-27 say God of Israel showed him great favour by making him the king of Israel when he least expected. Yet, I Samuel

18:12-15, 28-30 says the more he was convinced that God was with David the more he determined to kill David.

It is self-injurious to oppose your benefactor's decision – it is even worse if you are opposing the extension of the same favour that he extended to you earlier to another individual. How can your son prove to be wiser than you on an issue, yet you will not heed his voice of reason? That is the work of envy and jealousy. It is like all the good deeds of Jesus; all the help that He rendered to the Jews did not make any meaning to the Jewish religious rulers so long as they were gripped by envy and jealousy. Here was a younger man solving the problems that had been with you and your people for so long, rather than celebrate Him for solving those problems they were preoccupied with the fact that He stole attention of the people from them. 'The People Their Prime Problem' means that the greatest problem that rulers have is their people or subjects. What the people think and talk about them or any other around them particularly in their domain is of killer concern to them.

Furthermore, about the ruler dreading the people more, there is the story of Pilate during the trial of Jesus. First, Matthew 27:18, Mark 15:10 and John 12:17-18 confirm that he knew very well that they brought Jesus to him to condemn for them to crucify because of envy and jealousy. In fact, John 12:17-19 says:

> 17 The people who had been with Jesus when he called Jesus out of the grave and raise him from death had reported what had happened. 18 That was why the crowd met him-because they heard that he had performed this miracle. 19 The Pharisees then said to one another, "You see, we are not succeeding at all! Look, the whole world is following him!" (TEV)

As far as the traditional Jewish religious rulers are concerned, the High Priests and Pharisees saw that they were losing the loyalty of the people and they considered it an unforgivable offence on the part of Jesus. Without the Jewish people the High Priests and Pharisees were irrelevant, and they could not standby and watch someone they considered as one young man do that to them. Some of them had spent all their lives to become High Priests or be accepted into the council of the Pharisees and one 'little boy' has decided to take the most valuable benefit of the position that they occupied just because He could perform miracles that they could not and teach the knowledge of God in a way that they could never. For them, it was no longer a matter of doing God's work for the benefit of the people but what becomes of their relevance and respect if Jesus continued the way He was going.

Second, Matthew 27:22-26 confirms in verse 24 that it was for the fear that the Jewish crowd of commoners instigated by the Jewish religious rulers could riot that Pilate agreed to their demand that Jesus be condemned for them to crucify even when he knew that Jesus was innocent. It means that rather than spend his time and effort to educate the crowd about the real reason that their religious rulers were instigating them to demand the killing of Jesus he chose to let them have their way. As a ruler and judge, he does not want to be queried by his boss for not been able to keep the peace of his domain. If there was a riot, his boss might not care to confirm the root cause before blaming him for incompetence. That sounds like personal survival reason or letting the wicked have their way so that he have his wish of continuing as the ruler of Judah under the Roman Empire.

Third, John 19:12-16 can be interpreted to mean that the Jews understood that Pilate was eager to keep his job at any cost, so they played the card to their maximum advantage. Verse 12 says they threatened that if he failed to condemn Jesus for them to kill it would mean that he is not loyal to his boss, the Emperor who gave him the chance to be governor of Judah. The story continued that once he heard this threat, he quickly mounted his judgment seat to do the bidding of the real criminals who wanted an innocent man killed unjustly. Tactically, they held Pilate's conscience hostage and he succumbed to their satanic demand and blackmail. This is part of what the Egyptians failed to do during the famine, they failed to employ their leverage over their king and his appointed official. They readily caved into the desperation to survive and personally offered to be slaves to the king and Joseph so long as they were given grains to stay alive. Offering to be slave so long as they remained alive is not different from the way Jacob negotiated with Laban that he would serve for 14 years to marry Rachel. His twin brother, Esau never served any would be parents'-in-law to marry his wives so where did Jacob get that idea from, only he and God who knows all things have the answer. Also, it is like when the Gibeonites did not mind remaining slaves to the Israelites so long as they were not destroyed by the army of Israel led by Joshua.

There is a unique lesson from the story of Joseph, his siblings and their families in Egypt and the Jews in the Persian Empire during the reign of Mordecai as the Prime Minister and his younger cousin, Esther as the Queen. They spoke with one voice and acted in unison. Genesis 45:9-11, 16-20, 46:31-34, 47:1-6 give the account thus:

> 9 "Now hurry back to my father and tell him that this is what his son Joseph says: 'God has made me ruler of all Egypt; come to me without delay. 10 You can live in the region of Goshen, where you can be near me — you, your children, your

grandchildren, your sheep, your goats, your cattle, and everything else that you have. 11 If you are in Goshen, I can take care of you. There will still be five years of famine; and I do not want you, your family, and your livestock to starve.' " 16 When the news reached the palace that Joseph's brothers had come, the king and his officials were pleased. 17 He said to Joseph, "Tell your brothers to load their animals and to return to the land of Canaan. 18 Let them get their father and their families and come back here. I will give them the best land in Egypt, and they will have more than enough to live on. 19 Tell them also to take wagons with them from Egypt for their wives and small children and to bring their father with them. 20 They are not to worry about leaving their possessions behind; the best in the whole land of Egypt will be theirs."

31 Then Joseph said to his brothers and the rest of his father's family, "I must go and tell the king

that my brothers and all my father's family, who were living in Canaan, have come to me. 32 I will tell him that you are shepherds and take care of livestock and that you have brought your flocks and herds and everything else that belongs to you. 33 When the king calls for you and asks what your occupation is, 34 be sure to tell him that you have taken care of livestock all your lives, just as your ancestors did. In this way he will let you live in the region of Goshen." Joseph said this because Egyptians will have nothing to do with shepherds.

1 So Joseph took five of his brothers and went to the king. He told him, "My father and my brothers have come from Canaan with their flocks, their herds, and all that they own. They are now in the region of Goshen." 2 He then presented his brothers to the king. 3 The king asked them, "What is your occupation?" "We are shepherds, sir, just as our ancestors were," they answered. 4

"We have come to live in this country, because in the land of Canaan the famine is so severe that there is no pasture for our flocks. Please give us permission to live in the region of Goshen." 5 The king said to Joseph, "Now that your father and your brothers have arrived, 6 the land of Egypt is theirs. Let them settle in the region of Goshen, the best part of the land. And if there are any capable men among them, put them in charge of my own livestock." (TEV)

Let us note the fact that Joseph instructed his brothers on arrival in Egypt to request from his boss and benefactor, Pharaoh to live near him so that he could take good care of them. Let us remember that this was never part of the mandate he was given by the king of Egypt when he was made the Prime Minister of the empire in Genesis 41:1-57. There was no mention of bringing his kinsmen so that he would provide for them lavishly. This subject of providing for them gives any reasonable thinker more concern when we remember that during this time that he was taking good care of his kinsmen from the nation's treasury under his care, he was not equally kind to the Egyptians from whom he collected the resources before the arrival of his kinsmen. Instead, Genesis 47:13-26 confirms that he made life miserable for the Egyptians who worked during the years of bumper harvest to provide the same grains he used to provide for his kinsmen in their own land of Egypt.

The pathetic point is that if given the chance, foreigners would use the resources of the natives to fend for their fellow foreigner kinsmen at the expense of the natives. This is one fundamental justification for the claim that 'this world is wicked' which means man deals wickedly with his fellow man without batting an eyelid. Man is inherently wicked or wicked by default. Joseph did not consider that his kinsmen did not contribute anything to the resources he was using to provide for them. It can be called "Feeding Fellow Kinsmen-Foreigners with Natives' Resources to the Regret of the Natives". That does not go down well with commonsense and logic. To say that it is against the fundamental principle of human equality is to say the least. Jeremiah 17:9 says the heart of man is desperately wicked and cannot be fathomed.

As saintly as Joseph was reputed to be, he could not afford to be fair when he was faced with the challenge of balancing fair dealing between his kinsmen and the Egyptians who were kind enough to accommodate him when his own kinsmen sold him into slavery. One thing that cannot be taken away from the Egyptians is the fact that they dealt very fairly with Joseph because all his bosses proved that they were fair and just. First, when Potiphar saw that Joseph merited promotion, he did not consider his despiteful Hebrew background but promoted him as deserved.

Genesis 39:7-20 can be interpreted to mean that the only time Potiphar could not tolerate him was when his wife lied and stirred up sentiments to blackmail Joseph and he sent him to jail without giving Joseph the chance to defend himself. And Potiphar can be excused considering that Proverbs 6:34-35 confirms that one of the wisdoms that God taught mankind through Solomon later is that a man is not angrier than when he finds out that another man is taking his place to enjoy intimate relationship with his wife. Also, Genesis 39:21-23 says when Joseph arrived in prison, the superintendent gave him what he deserved by promoting him to the position of the head of all prisoners.

Again, Genesis 41:1-57 and 45:4-11 and Psalm 105:16-22 confirm that when he interpreted Pharaoh's dreams, Joseph was made the head of all the palace officials who could not interpret the dreams before he was called for to do it. This means that during this time, most Egyptian masters were very fair persons who gave reward to whom it was due without discrimination on any ground. However, for someone who had enjoyed tremendous fair treatment from his hosts, it is unbelievable and unacceptable that he dealt treacherously with many of the natives when they were most vulnerable.

It is interesting that the passage above equally says Joseph told his siblings what to request from his boss when he took them to him to present their request. This is what many do under the name of "Association of Nigerians in America", "Association of Ghanaians in Britain" or Association of South Africans in China or Russia" as the case might be. From the example of Joseph and his brothers in Egypt, the singular aim and objective of such groupings is to maximize their benefits from the host community. It is not to work for the benefit of the host nation. Generally, Genesis 47:20-26 is interpreted to mean that Joseph saved the Egyptians from dying during famine, but he also used the opportunity of their vulnerability to enslave them to their ruler which was never part of their culture until 'foreigner Joseph' served as the Prime Minister with autocratic powers. Therefore, while members of Joseph's well-wishers and fan club would hail him for saving the lives of the Egyptians non-members of that club would hide under the guise of objectivity to say he made the Egyptians to pay a very high price before he agreed to keep them alive. He did something like 'I will save you to remain slaves' or 'I will save you so long as you agree to remain my boss' slaves'.

Now, you will have to permit me this once to run riot with reasoning here though I might do it again. What Joseph did when he insisted that the Egyptians must give up part of their lands and proceeds for the king before he could give them food to live on during famine is basically forcing a vulnerable individual to part with what he would not normally part with if he was not vulnerable. It is not different from forced slavery of the vulnerable, having sex with a woman because she is desperate to get one's help and these days, we call it abuse of power and position of authority. But more importantly is the fact that when natives give authoritative power to a foreigner, they have only given such foreigner permission to introduce strange ideas, policies and practices into their native land and culture. Until Joseph's premiership, it was never part of the culture of the Egyptians that their king would control part of their land and get part of the proceeds of their land. Therefore, Joseph saved them from dying at the expense of their future generation as that policy was never repealed after the seven years' famine such that the future generation that never experienced the famine continued to pay the price.

An Egyptian who was born and bred at home could never have subjugated his fellow natives to the king just because the king gave him the privilege to serve as the Prime Minister. Such native Egyptian Prime Minister would respect the culture he grew up in and would lack the courage to change it. In this respect, an example that readily comes to mind is when I Samuel 21:7

and 22:9-10 and 16-19 say Saul's bodyguards did not care if he would punish them for disobeying his command because they just could not see themselves breaking the culture of revering God's priests because of God. This is one of the saddening influences of strangers on their host communities. They would hijack the slightest opportunity to impose their strange ideas on the people of the host communities by emphasizing the benefits of their actions.

Once Joseph discovered that his boss was enjoying the benefit of subjugating the subjects who were the king's kinsmen by the stranger he appointed, Joseph went all out to push the Egyptians about. Meanwhile, he was not doing the same thing to his fellow Hebrews who were living in Egypt with him. From this case, we can safely say that the best foreigner's kindness to natives is laden with pains and agony even long after the foreigners would have departed. Typical example in modern times is that no country that was colonized has recovered from the damage the colonial master's interference has done to their national psyche. It is a permanent damage; the acclaimed independence of the colonies from their colonial masters has not repaired the damage several decades after.

There is what can be called "Foreigners Fatal Friendship" or "Foreigners' Frustration-filled Friendship" and "Foreigners Consequential Kindness". There is a thin line between strange ideas and strangulating ideas in this life and strange ideas are usually imported from other places and forced on the people or natives by powerful personalities in their society. People who have travelled to other nations return to introduce the ideas which they believe they enjoyed the benefit while living in the strange land. Let us remember what we read earlier in Genesis 41:33-57 and 47:13-26 in which chapter 47 verse 25 says the Egyptians claimed that Joseph saved them while they were glad to be Pharaoh's slaves. Nobody in his right senses and not in his worst moments of life would accept to be a slave to someone he or she was not previously a slave. Surely, it is better to remain alive and be a slave than dead but it is unforgivable that the same Egyptians who produced the grains while there was bumper harvest, and sold them at rock-bottom price to Joseph were made to repurchase the same grains at the highest price possible. Only God knows where Joseph learnt the idea of monopolistic exploitation which he used against the Egyptians during the worst years of the famine, the management of which was the reason he was appointed the Prime Minister of Egypt.

If he had been kind enough to give grains to the Egyptians as part of the king's duty to sustain the subjects during their most vulnerable moments, the subjects would have been forever grateful and enjoyed the benefits of having a ruler. Joseph merely made the people believe that he helped them when thoughtfulness reveals that he merely took adverse and abominable advantage of them when they were most vulnerable. He should have been satisfied with the profit which Genesis 41:57 and 47:14-15 strongly suggest that he made from selling part of the grains he stored for the king to non-Egyptians that came over to buy from them. That profit would have been enough to cover the cost of constructing the storage facilities and serve as the return on the effort made. In any case, it was the subjects who were used as labourers to build the storage facilities. Joseph and Pharaoh and his sons and relatives could not have engaged in the building of the storage facilities personally.

Genesis 41:37-57 and 47:13-26 typify what can be called the "Economics of Vanquishing and Voiding the Vulnerables", "Foreigners and Natives' Conspiracy to Consume the Native Commoners" or the "Abominable Alliance to Abuse the Natives". Pharaoh as native Egyptian and king of the Egypt found an ally in foreigner Joseph to undermine vulnerable Egyptians in a space of 14 years. In contemporary times, money mongering investors traverse the globe in search of natural resources to exploit and make profit by finding locals to share their profit with and work against the entire populace.

Genesis 41:45-53 and 45:4-9-11 can be said to mean that Joseph had served Pharaoh for nine years before his father and family came to join him in Egypt. Therefore, he used his nine years' experience of working with the king to tell them what best to tell the king to get the most beneficial answer from the king. Also, he wanted his brothers or fellow Hebrews to avoid clashing with the natives through frequent interaction. There is no doubt that one of the reasons that the king was eager to hire his brothers was because his experience with Joseph convinced him that his brothers would follow in his example to work for his good while working for him. Joseph believed that as the earliest Hebrew to live in Egypt for long, it was his responsibility to fend for Hebrews and use his wealth of experience among the Egyptians to guide his fellow Hebrews to settle in Egypt smoothly or without much hassles. He told them to give tailored response to any questions by the king. He had an idea of what the king would ask and what they should say in response.

His mode of operation was like 'tell the natives what they like to hear so that they would let you have what you need to enjoy your stay among them'. That is the concept that Joseph taught mankind. It is helpful to new arrivals to learn from the experience of their kinsmen who had been around and integrated in their land of sojourn. Joseph's brothers did not doubt Joseph's suggestions to them on what to say and not to say. They could have said because they were unkind to him earlier perhaps, he would deceive them to offend the king to punish them for him for the evil that they did to him in the past. Joseph quickly forgave them so that they could join him to enjoy the best that the land of Egypt could offer them. Cooperation among foreigners is crucial for them to maximize the benefit that they can get where they live as foreigners. There is no record that Joseph involved his wife, Asenath who was a native in all that he did to get the best deal for his father, brothers, and their families. Foreigners need one of them who have clout to work for their wellbeing in their land of sojourn like the Hebrews had Joseph in Egypt, the Jews had Mordecai and Esther as well as Nehemiah and Ezra in the Persian Empire. Also important is the fact that Joseph's father and older brothers did not think that because they were older than Joseph, they could not comply with his suggestions of what best to say to the king. The king did not despise Joseph's interpretation of his dreams which is the solution to the looming famine on account of Joseph's younger age. Sentiment sabotages survival strategies if allowed.

23

Maintaining Self-saving Spirituality (MSS)

Sometime in 1989, in my search for job as a young graduate and, I filed application for employment with a fledgling company with beautiful premises at the time. It was also at a time when I became serious with hearing God personally. God's Spirit told me to not literally waste my time seeking employment there. Honestly, I never understood the reason. They were producing consumable item that was in high demand which meant or suggests that the company have enough reason to prosper. By 2016 the premises of this company was still overgrown by tall grasses. In fact, it never survived the first five years meanwhile other companies in the same product line continue to prosper. I never asked the spiritual reason why it would never survive as I understood what the spirit of God meant later. God knew that the company was moribund from inception. That instruction led to my discontinuing to seek employment with them.

There is what can be called 'lack of spiritual insight instigated, induced and precipitated injurious ignorance'. Genesis 13:1-13, 14:1-16, 18:20-33 and 19:1-38 can be interpreted to mean that if Lot had known that divine judgment on Sodom was imminent and worst still, he would not be able to escape with his wealth just before the destruction of Sodom he would not have relocated there when he decided to leave Abraham behind in Canaan. Lot just looked at the physical greenery of Sodom and chose to pitch his tent among them without confirming God's plan. Genesis 41:1-57 and 47:13-26 say God revealed an imminent economic emergency to the king of Egypt. Majority of the other Egyptians who would be affected did not know anything. The distressing part is that because they were ignorant of that fact, their king and his domesticated foreign ally, Joseph took advantage of them. If only their farmers had followed in the footsteps of Rebecca and her brother Laban who Genesis

25:19-24 and 30:25-28 confirm that when they had what they considered as strange experiences they engaged in spiritual consultation to know the reason and implication.

During the bumper harvest season that lasted seven years, the Egyptians should have consulted to know why and how else it could impact on their lives. They would have been told that it would have a permanent consequence of losing part of their land and its produce to the king forever if they failed to plan ahead so that they would not need to ask the king's chief official, Joseph for help during the famine. They just assumed that everything was fine and things would continue like that forever. Since their history, their king had never appointed any individual to the office of next-in-command to him. He had never ordered storage facilities to be built across the regions of the empire. Then, one day he did not just appoint a foreigner in the position of highest official next-in-command to him, he approved that this official supervised the building of storage facilities throughout the cities and towns of the kingdom and they did not think it was enough reason for them to seek clarification. Even if they will not go to the king or his appointed official to get clarifications, they should seek their own clarifications spiritually as to how what the king has ordered his official to do would impact on them, their children and descendants.

The king is not an idiot, he is not what they call 'money-missed-road' in Nigeria, someone who does not know what to do with money and would squander it on some unprofitable venture. He is an articulate individual, well educated and an intellectual. We know this because Acts 7:22 confirms that while being prepared to ascend the throne of Egypt, Moses was educated. If an intelligent or wise man is doing something new, it is worth finding out what his ultimate target or objective is. Even if the Egyptians would find a way to sniff information from the palace. There must have been some regular Egyptians who had personal relationship with persons working in the palace of the king. They should have put their ears to the ground to find out the motive behind the new move of their king. They did not find out physically or spiritually and the consequence according to Genesis 47:13-26 is that they became slaves to their king forever. Even after the famine had abated, the king and his chief enslavement official never reversed the enslavement decree that they hid under the famine predicament to impose on them. II Kings 8:1-6 confirms that the rich woman of Shunem did not suffer the consequences of famine because she had someone who had spiritual insight to tell her what to do in advance. Acts 11:27-31 says those who had prior information about the famine during the time of Apostle Paul did not use it to afflict the uninformed populace. The leaders who found out persuaded the haves to contribute to support the have-nots to reduce the injurious impact of the famine on the have-nots. Every problem in this life has the pleasant and unpleasant solutions. The choice of solution depends on the persons in position to decide and implement the solution.

Daniel was of high spiritual standing throughout his stay in Babylon where he could be described as having spent a special captive status. Daniel 1:1-21 and 6:10 say he started his journey to greatness in Babylon by depending solely on God in words and deeds as well as prayerfully. Daniel 2:1-49 says when the big boss, Nebuchadnezzar made one of the most unreasonable requests ever, DSMA did not try to tutor Nebuchadnezzar that such request was too unreasonable rather they turned to God for the solution that only God could provide from heaven. This was when Nebuchadnezzar insisted that he must be reminded of his own dream and told its meaning at the same time. Genesis 41:1-36 says Pharaoh of Egypt did not make such an unreasonable request. Rather he remembered and told his dreams for his wise men to tell him their meaning and when they could not, he sent for Joseph whom God helped to give correct meaning which Pharaoh used Joseph to implement. One sound interpretation from Daniel 1:1-21 is that God gave uncommon wisdom to DSMA to dazzle Nebuchadnezzar and other wise men in the palace because they did not join other palace officials to participate in the royal meals meant for them. God of heaven and earth also known as God of Abraham, Isaac, Jacob, and Israel whom they determined to honour by rejecting the meals because such meals had been dedicated to the gods of Babylon rewarded their loyalty to Him.

The spiritual exercise that DSMA engaged in for three years is like the 40 days and nights that Jesus spent in the wilderness without food and any drink, including water after which He received empowerment from heaven. First, Jesus can be described as a stranger in this world like Hebrews 11:13 and I Peter 2:11 confirm that all humans are pilgrims on earth. Second, though He had to operate in His earthly native land of Israel controlled by the Romans at that time, He still needed to engage in special spiritual exercise when it was time for Him to commence and complete the real reason He was sent by God the Father to live on earth as a human being. This tells us that whether at home or abroad, whoever desires to prosper and to accomplish God's plan for his life, have need of spiritual support and must device his God assigned method to keep in touch with God in heaven while he lives and operates on earth. If someone requires God's support to be successful and great in his hometown, then he needs spectacular spiritual support to do same in a strange land.

The use of the term 'personalized spiritual method of contacting God while on earth' is deliberate. Genesis 12:1-9 can be said to tell it all as well as lay the foundation for this incontrovertible claim. It says Abraham left his place of birth and parent's ancestral home to live as a stranger in Canaan in obedience to God's command or directive and instructions or both. Then, it went further to say once God indicated that he had arrived the place where He wanted him to live and claim for himself and his descendants, Abraham built a personal altar through which he could be contacting God whenever necessary. Genesis 28:10-22 and 35:1-15 confirm that God took time to establish personal relationship with Jacob at Bethel and much later, God directed Jacob to return to Bethel to continue to relate with Him from there. In like manner, Genesis 33:18-20 says when Jacob returned from Laban's place at Haran of Mesopotamia to settle in Shechem of Canaan where he had been born and bred, he built an altar to God of Israel who made a personal covenant with him at Bethel when he was leaving Canaan twenty years earlier. Perhaps, and this is just perhaps, if he had gone directly to Bethel where he met with God and had built his first personal altar to God upon his return from Laban's place, his daughter would not have been raped and his sons would not have caused the mayhem they caused which forced him to leave Shechem as Genesis 34:1-31 and 35:1-7-15 report that he experienced.

Genesis 12:1-9, 13:14-18, 22:9, 26:23-25, 33:20, 35:7 confirm that just as Abraham built an altar to God, so also his covenant son, Isaac was said to have personally done and Jacob followed suit. Despite the fact that Genesis 17:1-27, 18:1-15, 21:1-14, 22:1-19, 24:1-10, 25:1-11 and 19-26, 26:1-6 and 17-25, 28:1-5 and 10-22, 31:10-13 and 32:9 confirm that they were operating under the same covenant, the son and grandson had to build personal altars which could be part of the reason we talk about the God of Abraham, Isaac and Jacob. Interestingly, they did not build in the same place but in different parts of the land of Canaan that God meant for them to possess from the original inhabitants. This is one of the integral reasons we are often reminded that parents' religiousness will not save the children who are adults. Individuals must seek and sustain personal spiritual support wherever he or she lives on earth. Joseph was not reported to have built the kind of altar his great grandfather, grandfather and father built to maintain necessary sustaining relationship with God in Egypt. He only needed to refer to God and refrain from doing anything that God could frown at in his lifestyle and daily activities. Even when David did not live away from home most of his lifetime, he considered God as the prime factor in his actions and reactions. In addition, he had priests and prophets through whom he consulted God regularly. He did so well in this respect that I Kings 14:7-8 says God confirmed that one of the things that endeared David to His heart is that David would never do anything without confirming His views and it is whatever He approved that David did.

Daniel was so addicted to talking to God in Babylon that Daniel 6:1-28 confirms that even his detractors hijacked it to try to afflict him. Just as man eats thrice daily, Daniel formed a lifestyle of talking to the Lord thrice daily for as long as he lived and operated in the palace of Babylon. His case is very striking in a sense. He could be said to have been carried captive to Babylon because God instigated and empowered Nebuchadnezzar to so do. That could be enough reason for some to say it is not necessary to regard the same God who allowed their oppressors to overcome them. If Daniel determined to please and maintain responsible relationship with God in Babylon where he was a captive, then it is most likely that he was not one of those who committed the sins that angered God so much that Jeremiah 25:1-8-11 and 27:4-8 confirm that He employed, contracted or engaged Nebuchadnezzar to carry them captive. However, Daniel and his Hebrew friends thought God's approval of captivity for them along with the real sinners was not enough reason for them to refuse to serve and please Him in their captivity. They seemed to have thought that whether at home or away, they still needed to connect with God to survive in life. In fact, staying connected with the God of Israel is an integral part of His plan for man on earth. In this respect, during the dedication of the Temple by Solomon, I Kings 8:22-61 and II Chronicles 6:12-42 confirm in verse 46-50 and 36-39 respectively, I Kings 8:62-66 and II Chronicles 7:1 confirm that God agreed to regard and answer the prayers of His people irrespective of the land where they live. As we used to joke in secondary school with the term 'head or tail' in this case we would have said, "head or tail, man needs God". Wherever you are, God is a necessity. Jonah 2:1-10 confirms that God heard and honoured Jonah's prayer from the belly of a whale in the deepest part of the sea.

Practically, DSMA continued to be conscious of the God in whom they had believed while they started life at home when they arrived in the strange land. They determined never to serve the gods of the strange land and they never regretted it. They might not have made any conscious effort to make their hosts join them serve their God and they too never joined them just because they were living among them either. They remained faithful to the God of heaven and earth that their parents taught them to believe in. They were like the Rechabites who Jeremiah 35:1-19 confirms never joined most of the Israelites to serve other gods or imbibe their lifestyle which was contrary to the teachings of their ancestor and father. Exodus 24:1-18 and 32:1-30 confirm that the Levites never joined other Israelites to sin against God while Moses was on Mount Sinai meeting with God. Just as Joseph remained loyal to the godly practices he was taught by his father while he was growing up before he arrived Egypt, Queen Esther was said to have remained obedient to the teachings of Mordecai since she was a child even when she had become the Queen of the Persian Empire in Suza. This was part of what sustained Esther in the palace of Persia.

24

FUNCTIONAL FACTS

It would be rare to find a native who would support or take sides with a foreigner against a fellow native unless such native is benefiting from the foreigner more than the fellow natives at home. Foreigners should not expect a native to support him against another native therefore, before a foreigner decides to take a native to the court of the country he or she is sojourning, he or she should think twice. God knows that it is natural for anyone to oppress foreigners, hence He admonishes (in Exodus 22:21 and 23:9, Leviticus 19:33-34 and Deuteronomy 24:17-22 and 27:19) that natives should not cheat foreigners living among them. Even in the acclaimed self-styled civilized and fairest societies, there is discrete discrimination against foreigners by natives. The native authorities would stage-manage fairness when the dispute between the native and foreigner is politicized to embarrass them and antagonize their claim of the fairest society on earth.

One of the best bets of strangers is to do something more than the ordinary, like doing the things that natives would not volunteer to do for their fellow natives. For instance, Exodus 2:15-22 can be interpreted to mean that it was because Moses went out of his way to help Jethro's daughters to water his flock that he was invited to live with them and he eventually become his son-in-law as well as business manager for the rest of the 40 years that he lived in their land or country. The story has it that Jethro was pleasantly surprised that they returned from the watering of the flock earlier than usual. It means that no young man had ever done it for them until Moses did. Maybe the job of helping ladies serving as shepherd is resented by the young men of Midian. It is as a result that when Moses did not mind that he was supposed to be heir to the throne of Egypt once he found himself in Midian he went out of his way to help, and it touched the heart of the beneficiary, Jethro to host him for so long as he decided to stay among them.

This leads to something else regarding functional fact about foreigners' sojourn and it is that foreigners cannot afford to be lazy or lackluster where natives are. What they call social welfare support to the needy in advanced nations of the world are not meant for non-natives. That is the reality. Where non-traditional natives get it, they must understand it is regarded as a privilege in the hearts of the traditional natives even when they never mention it. For the non-traditional natives who became natives by naturalization or by being born there by their migrant parents, the traditional natives consider them as imputed, intrusive, and pest-infested or pest-infesting like-natives. They regret the laws that give others entitlement to what they consider their exclusive rights in the native land that God assigned to them or that they grew up to know that they inherited from their ancestors and parents. It can be called transnational border migrant natives as heart-hidden unwanted pest-like personalities in the estimation of the traditional natives. Even when the law of the land permits the migrant native to become the ruler of the land, if ever he becomes so by God's sponsorship, the traditional natives would vent their frustration by criticizing him when it is obvious that there is no concrete reason.

Also, like in the case of Moses' hard work and decision to do the job that natives would not do naturally paved the way for him to have a place of abode, wife and permanent job, the famous story of Ruth the Moabites surviving in Bethlehem was because she went the extra mile to show loyalty to the native of Bethlehem, Naomi. She followed Naomi from her place of birth to Bethlehem to live as supposed stranger which endeared her to Boaz, the women of Bethlehem and other people who reported her support to Naomi to Boaz. For the women of Bethlehem and Boaz to appreciate her supportive loyalty to Naomi, it suggests that such level of loyalty is not common among the young women of Bethlehem. Therefore, she went the extra mile to support her mother-in-law. When Boaz said he had expected her to seek remarriage with younger men, it simply means that the practice for the young childless widows of Bethlehem was to seek remarriage with a younger man rather than much older men like Boaz at the time. Also, it was not the common practice of the young women of Bethlehem to go out of what they considered the norm to ask a man to marry them. She did those things that were not commonly done by the young women of Bethlehem to survive because she understood that she was not on the same fundamental human rights pedestal with the traditional native young women of Bethlehem.

Whether the traditional natives should be blamed for their resentful attitude to the migrant natives or not, I do not have a strong view but would state what I know from the Holy Scriptures for individuals to decide what is right or wrong. In this respect, Leviticus 19:9-10, Deuteronomy 17:14-15, 24:17-22 and 32:8-9 say:

> 9 "When you harvest the crops of your land, do not harvest the grain along the edges of your fields, and do not pick up what the harvesters drop. 10 It is the same with your grape crop—do not strip every last bunch of grapes from the vines, and do not pick up the grapes that fall to the ground. Leave them for the poor and the foreigners living among you. I am the Lord your God.

14 "You are about to enter the land the Lord your God is giving you. When you take it over and settle there, you may think, 'We should select a king to rule over us like the other nations around us.' 15 If this happens, be sure to select as king the man the Lord your God chooses. You must appoint a fellow Israelite; he may not be a foreigner. (NLT)

14 "When you arrive in the land the Lord your God will give you, and have conquered it, and begin to think, 'We ought to have a king like the other nations around us'- 15 be sure that you select as king the man the Lord your God shall choose. He must be an Israelite, not a foreigner.

17 "Justice must be given to migrants and orphans, and you must never accept a widow's garment in pledge of her debt. 18 Always remember that you were slaves in Egypt and that the Lord your God rescued you; that is why I have given you this

command. 19 If, when reaping your harvest, you forget to bring in a sheaf from the field, don't go back after it. Leave it for the migrants, orphans, and widows; then the Lord your God will bless and prosper all you do. 20 When you beat the olives from your olive trees, don't go over the boughs twice; leave anything remaining for the migrants, orphans, and widows. 21 It is the same for the grapes in your vineyard; don't glean the vines after they are picked, but leave what's left for those in need. 22 Remember that you were slaves in the land of Egypt-that is why I am giving you this command. (TLB)

8 The Most High assigned nations their lands; he determined where peoples should live. He assigned to each nation a heavenly being, 9 but Jacob's descendants he chose for himself. (TEV)

8 that God Most High gave land to every nation. He assigned a guardian angel to each of them, 9 but the Lord himself takes care of Israel. (CEV)

As we can see, we have mixed two fundamental ideas together herein. First, the law of gleaning classifies the strangers and poor traditional natives in the land as belonging to the same level of people who the productive and prosperous should care for or allow to enjoy free benefits to enable them survive. God commands that the productive who becomes prosperous should give some margin in their output for the benefit of the poorest and foreigners. This is what the rich societies of modern times converted into welfare benefits for the poor who are struggling to stay alive.

Second, God said through Moses that He assigned lands to different peoples to claim as their native land. They have the God given right to decide what should be done therein. And as natural selfish humans, equally sharing with others is strange to us. This is objectively speaking now. When we live as strangers, we would like to be treated fairly but if the case is reversed, most of such people who desire fair treatment as strangers would not readily agree to treat strangers fairly as they desired while living as strangers elsewhere. We know that very well from the story of Nehemiah who was the wine steward to the Emperor. He asked God to give him favour before his boss to get permission to return home to help his people. His boss approved everything he needed but when he got back, he was never kind to the natives of neighbouring nations who tried to dictate what happened in his native land.

Third, God said natives should not allow a non-native to be their ruler and this is serious because the kind of non-native is not defined in detail. This is the loophole that those we have been referring to as traditional natives as different from migrant natives have been exploiting to resent the emergence of migrant natives becoming their ruler. Judges 17:5-13 says one Micah a member of the tribe of Ephraim deposed his own son as his household head priest for a foreigner or someone who is not his son to take the position for personal reasons. Though this was at a household level, it could have some relevance to what national leaders would allow to happen. Pharaoh created the position of Prime Minister for a foreigner, Joseph to control his officials in his palace who were supposed to be traditional natives and much older than Joseph because he thought that the nation and therefore, natives needed Joseph's services which any of his fellow Egyptian natives who were officials could not render the way Joseph could. Therefore, the discretion of the king makers and the prevailing circumstances is a factor in the decision of who becomes ruler or powerful official to exercise supervisory control over other native officials. II Kings 18:13-37, 19:1-2 and Isaiah 22:15-24, 36:1-22, 37:1-2 can be said to confirm that while Hezekiah was king of Judah in Jerusalem, his most powerful official was Shebna, an Israelite/Jew. When God punished Shebna with the loss of his position in the palace of Jerusalem, God chose another Jew by the name of Hilkiah to replace Shebna rather than use a non-Jew to replace Shebna. It is important to note that God was careful enough to ensure that Shebna was replaced by another Jew. Meanwhile, their boss, King Hezekiah was a bonafide Jew and prince of Judah.

Fourth, another implication of what we read in the above passages is that non-traditional natives should not expect that the traditional natives would ever allow them to rise beyond certain positions in their native land. Even in the case of Joseph's emergence as the chief official in the palace of Egypt, though he knew the solution that his boss, Pharaoh the king did not know (more knowledgeable than his boss) but the highest position he could be allowed to ascend and occupy is next-in-command to the king and no more. The fact that Pharaoh did not know how to solve the problem of his dreams until Joseph showed up does not mean that Joseph could take his position because it was an abomination for the non-native to rule over the natives. Even the oppression that Joseph inflicted on the people of Egypt was not necessarily to his personal benefit but that of his Egyptian boss. Some would complain that when it comes to deserved promotion to certain level in the foreign country they went to serve, they were denied and someone not as experienced and competent was made their boss because they were not traditional natives. The point is that even God knows that it is normal for traditional natives to be unkind to non-traditional natives when it comes to such matters. So, in some ways, the traditional natives have not done anything unusual.

Daniel 5:1-30 says when God allowed a non-native to succeed native in Babylon, it was divine punishment. It takes us back to Isaiah 22:15-24 that says when God would replace an offensive most powerful official in the palace of Judah, He chose his fellow Jew rather than a non-Jew. Therefore, only in the case of extreme punishment would God use a non-native to replace a native as a ruler of a nation or a non-native becomes the most powerful individual over natives. II Samuel 7:23-24, II Kings 16:3, 17:8 and 21:2, I Chronicles 17:21-22 and II Chronicles 28:3b can be interpreted to mean that when God used the descendants of Abraham to control or rule over the Canaanites and their land, it was to punish the Canaanites for serving gods other than Him who created the universe. Punishing a people by making a migrant their ruler can be classified as extreme punishment by God of Israel.

Jeremiah 38:1-13 and 39:15-18 can be interpreted to mean that much as God determined to reward Ebedmelech's help to His authentic prophet Jeremiah, God did not say the reward should include promoting Ebedmelech a Sudanese to rule Judah when the Jews would have been carried away captive. That is, God did not make Ebedmelech to rule over the poorest Jews who were left to tend the land of Judah. Instead, Jeremiah 40:1-16 and 41:1-18 can be interpreted to mean that even when he would not remain governor for long, God can be said to have used Nebuchadnezzar to make Gedaliah the governor of Judah. II Kings 25:22-23, II Chronicles 34:8-15 and Jeremiah 39:1-14, 40:5-7 give the impression that Gedaliah's grandfather, Shaphan was the court secretary of Judah during the reign of King Josiah. In fact, Gedaliah's father, Ahikam served as a high official in the palace of Judah alongside his father, Shaphan during the reign of Josiah.

Daniel 4:1-37 can be said to mean that much as God of Israel punished Nebuchadnezzar, He did not use Daniel to rule Babylon during the seven years that Nebuchadnezzar served his punishment living in the wild – the natural habitat of animals. This is even though Daniel 2:1-49 confirms in verse 46 that Nebuchadnezzar bowed to the ground before Daniel which can be interpreted to mean that Daniel was greater than Nebuchadnezzar. If Daniel had claimed that God who punished Nebuchadnezzar had asked him to rule in Nebuchadnezzar's absence the other palace officials would not have argued with Daniel, but he never did because Daniel knew that God never meant him to rule until Nebuchadnezzar acknowledged God, and God restored him to his throne.

II Samuel 8:5-6, 14, I Kings 11:14-21 and I Chronicles 18:5-6, 12-13 say that King David set up garrisons (military bases) in the overseas territories that he conquered during his reign. The surviving royal family members escaped into exile until after the death of David and his COAS, Joab. II Kings 23:29-34 and II Chronicles 35:20-24, 36:1-5 confirm that when King Neco of Egypt decided who became king of Judah in Jerusalem, he made one of the princes of Judah king and asked him to pay him tribute. Neco did not deem it fit to make an Egyptian the king of Judah just because he had the chance to determine who ruled over Judah.

Fifth, something very fundamental in the above passages is the dimension that Deuteronomy 24:18 and 22 can be said to introduce when it says God commanded that natives should be kind to foreigners living among them because the natives should not forget that they were once slaves to some people. For instance, there was a time that what is today known as Britain or UK was controlled by the king of France just as Britain once controlled America and other commonwealth countries. There is no nation that had never been previously under the control of other nations and God who allowed it at that time says He did it so that the subsequent generations that would enjoy the independence would as a result treat foreigners kindly. You might notice that the tone of this paragraph did not give the impression that the above passages were meant for just the Israelites. Rather, it is meant for all mankind because Deuteronomy 32:8-9 and Acts 17:26 say the God associated with the Israelites who gave this command is the one who gave other nations their territorial borders, therefore, the laws He gave to the Israelites are actually meant for the human race to obey. He merely passed it through Moses to the Israelites and subsequently to the entire human race to obey or live by for their own benefit during their sojourn on earth. This is not in doubt because Psalms 105:7 says:

7 The Lord is our God; his commands are for all the world. (TEV)

7 He is the Lord our God. His laws are for all the world. (NCV)

This is understandable considering the fact that Deuteronomy 32:8-9 says He made and assigned guardian angels or archangels to supervise the non-Israelites that He assigned other parts of the land to live as their nations or territorial defined border locations. Those assigned guardian angels which the natives of the localities worship as their native gods handed over to them by their ancestors through their parents in every generation contribute to dictate what is regarded as customs and traditions of the people of the nation or locality. It would be insulting if laws and commandments of God who made and assigned those angels would not be applicable in those territories and restricted only to the Israelites through whom He gave the laws or to whom He gave the laws directly. It is in order to enable mankind identify Him as different from other gods that He chose to direct the affairs of the lives of the Israelites, the descendants of His chosen personal friend, Abraham, his son, Isaac and grandson, Jacob with whom He pioneered the name Israel which is the root of the term 'Israelites'. Sorry we went into this to make us appreciate the fact that God's commandment for natives to be kind to strangers who are living among them is meant to be a universal law to humans.

Sixth and finally in this segment, Deuteronomy 24:17 mentions the need for true justice for foreigners like it should be given to the poor who are traditional natives. God knows that it is not in the nature of the rulers of nations to let the poor and foreigners get justice so He says, much as it seem difficult for the human nature that the strong deal fairly with the weak of the society, that is what they must do to prove their regard and respect for Him. He meant that whenever heartless human nature wants to tempt them to maltreat the poor and foreigners, they should remember His opinion given in the form of commandment and restrain themselves and treat them fairly and kindly. The reason we have to present this aspect this way is to let foreigners understand that the same way that the strong tend to oppress the poor who are their fellow natives, so also they like to treat foreigners. This will prepare the mind of foreigners for the worst wherever they live and plan for how long they would stay before they return home and when they return, they must not give the bad treatment they got from natives where they sojourned to the foreigners in their native land because God commands fair treatment for them.

Rulers care less about the background of the competent that they need their services like the case of Joseph in Egypt, Moses in Egypt before he fell out with them when he attained the age of 40, David in Ziklag, Daniel in Babylon, Nehemiah and Ezra in the Persian Empire. Darius' determined to promote Daniel so that he and his subjects could benefit more from the Daniel's excellent services. He cared less about Daniel's stranger or captive status in Babylon. Jethro did not regard Moses 'non-Midian' background when he invited him home to live with, work for and marry one of his daughters by the name of Zipporah.

There is what can be called Moses' Lifelong Stranger Experience. Genesis 15:12-16 says God promised that his generation of Abraham's covenant descendants would be strangers in Egypt or foreign land. Then, Genesis 46:8-11 and Exodus 6:14-20 confirm that Moses' great-great grandfather, Jacob, great grandfather, Levi and grandfather, Kohath went to join Joseph and his family in Egypt in fulfillment of God's revealed plan in Genesis 45:4-20, 46:1-34 and 47:1-12. Exodus 2:1-25 imply that Moses was born in the Israelite exclusive region of Goshen in Egypt but brought up in the palace of Egypt in preparation to become the next Pharaoh of Egypt. As a result, he can be said to have grown up in the strange environment of the palace rather than among his fellow Hebrews or Israelites. By age 40 he was forced to go and live among the Midianites. By age 80 he returned to Egypt to lead the Israelites out of Egypt. Then, Numbers 10:29-32 says Moses admitted that he was not quite familiar with the desert that he led the Israelites through as they travelled from Egypt to Canaan. From being a stranger in Egypt, palace, and Midian he ended up as a stranger in the wilderness. In fact, he was a stranger to the Israelites in the matter of values, spirituality, character, and conduct. He was the strangest of the strangers that the Israelites were in Egypt. His burial was a strange one as no one knew his burial place just as no human participated in it. He is one of the strangest fathers and husbands who ever lived.

Nehemiah and Mordecai were more concerned about the wellbeing of their fellow Jews than the natives of the land where they lived as migrants. Most migrants divide their loyalty between their ancestral land of birth and the new location where they are living as resident migrants. It is like an adopted child or child surrogacy – they are torn between their parents who conceived and bore them and the parents who contracted their birth parents and took them over to nurture into maturity. Genesis 24 can be interpreted to mean that even when Abraham knew that he would never return to Mesopotamia again, he still insisted that his covenant child, and God approved chief inheritor, Isaac's wife was from among his relatives who were not living in Canaan where God ordered him to live. It is the reason Genesis 21:9-22 says that Hagar returned to her native land of Egypt to get a wife for her son, Ishmael even when she would not return to remain, die and be buried in Egypt.

25

NATIVES RIGHT TO SUSPECT/ RESENT STRANGERS (NRSRS)

I Samuel 27:1-12 confirm that David did not go to live in the land of Philistia because he loved them and desired to add any value to them rather it was for his personal safety. Worst still, he deceived their king and harmed the vulnerable among them, including the most vulnerable women and children. The sixteen months he lived among them, was a curse rather than a blessing to the Philistines. In order to sustain his large number of dependants, he killed and maimed the natives, wiping out everyone so that none would escape to report his atrocities to the king who was kind enough to host him to escape from the sword of his own King Saul. He determined not to harm Saul who wanted him dead but killed his hosts to stay alive. This means that he preferred his life-threatening kinsman to stay alive than for his non-kinsmen hosts to be alive. This means that he had no regard for the non-kinsmen even if they wished him well more than his kinsmen and most foreigners feel that way towards natives of where they are taking refuge from the threat of their kinsmen in their hometown or country. The ounce of loyalty that David had to his Philistine host was stage-managed or fake like most rulers or politicians have fake loyalty and commitment to the wellbeing of their subjects.

As I Samuel 27:1-12 recounts the story of the Philistines' regret of King Achish giving David and his followers "faulty full freedom" to do whatever they liked in his domain outside his close supervision, so also Judges 18:1-31 reports another most pathetic story of the evil of letting foreigners have all the freedom in the host nations. The Danites were looking for where to take over from the original occupants when they arrived Laish and the natives of the land allowed them to roam through their land undisturbed because they were never used to suspecting and quizzing strangers in their midst. The Danite spies returned to bring their warriors to overrun the land, killed everyone and took over their land. It would have been much better for the Laishites to suspect and stop the Danite spies from completing their assignment than the way they allowed them to complete their first visit and return to destroy them afterwards. If Satan knew that God created him like other angels, yet led rebellion against God in heaven, then it is advisable for anyone to suspect the other person including natives suspecting every foreigner until that foreigner proves him or herself otherwise. Therefore, no amount is too much to expend in protecting one's territory. It was part of territorial protection that God sent rebellious arch-angel Satan who used to oversee worship right in His presence out of His heavenly abode. Whoever tries to get rid of troublemaker around his or her territory is taking after God in whose image and likeness he or she was made originally.

Genesis 49:16-17 says the Danites' lives are controlled by the spirit of armed robbers who believe that the best way to have the resources to enjoy life with is to collect other people's resources forcefully. It is like when Proverbs 30:14 says there are people who see nothing wrong in making their living by taking cruel advantage of the poor and needy – it is the only way that they love to make their living. Such people will not repent if they relocate to a foreign land. They would look for loopholes in the strange land that they are living to undo the poor and needy. The hoodlum lifestyle that God's spirit prompted to indicate about the Danites is what they displayed several generations later when they invaded the land of the Laishites and took over their land. When other tribes of Israel were claiming their land the Danites did not try to claim their own portion. They waited for the natives of Laish to build their kingdom before going to destroy them and rebuild it to their taste. Genesis 16:12, 21:9-14 and 49:16-17 can be interpreted to mean that God's views, counsel and admonition is that no peace-loving person should retain a trouble-maker as his neighbor even if the trouble maker is a relative. Genesis 13:1-18 can be interpreted to mean that God had used Abraham to lend credence to this fact. It is for the benefit of natives to treat trouble-throttling strangers accordingly.

Now whether God would forgive whoever fails to protect his or her territory only God can readily say but each can ask God's plan for him or her over an unpleasant individual threatening his or her territory. Genesis 21:9-14 confirms in verse 12-13 that when Sarah demanded the expulsion of hurting Hagar from Sarah's marital or matrimonial territory, God readily agreed with her and as a result, Hagar and her son were sent away instantly. Similarly, Genesis 26:12-25 confirms that when the Philistines forced Isaac out of their territory, though it was because of envy and jealousy, there is no record that God punished them for it. When God punished the Philistines at other times it was not partly because they protected their territory by sending Isaac away even when he was God's covenant carrying child of Abraham. In this world, there are always people who want to take over what you have. Majority of foreigners do not have the interest of their host community at heart but go to other nations in search of whatever they can get from the foreign land they are visiting.

Judges 17:5-13 and 18:1-31 report the story of the young Levite from Judah whom Micah employed on generous terms and at the expense of his own son but when this expatriate employee got a job offer from the Danites, he betrayed Micah and left with them leaving Micah with nothing tangible. This means that he remained loyal to Micah only because he had no alternative or choice. Micah's son was less likely to have betrayed him to his enemies like that young Levite from Bethlehem of Judah did to him. The risk of trusting a foreigner is higher when compared to that of trusting a native who have no other land away from yours. Another example is when Joshua 2:1-24 and 6:22-24 say Joshua's spies went to the city of Jericho to find ways to take over their land or do harm to the natives. This is the reason the king, nobles and people of Jericho made concerted efforts to capture these spies, except that one of them by the name of Rahab betrayed them for her own personal benefit. Joshua's spies meant great harm for the people of Jericho that they visited. Even strangers seeking greener pastures in other countries are seeking to take the jobs the natives could have done and are therefore, inimical to the benefit of the natives except for the tax that such foreigners pay. The migrants that could be tolerated are those experts invited by the leadership of the nation to help solve problems that no native could solve.

Again, Genesis 12:1-9, 23:1-20, 24:1-10 and 25:7-10 mean that Abraham relocated to Canaan with the heart-hidden motive of getting the land for himself and his descendants. He agreed with God that there was nothing wrong with taking over the land of the Canaanites. In fact, it can be said that he was so eager to get the land of the Canaanites for himself and his descendants that he obeyed God from that point until He died. God confirmed in Genesis 18:17-19 that He had seen inside the heart of Abraham that he was not only eager to obey but that he would tutor his children to do likewise. Man likes to take over what belongs to others and this is the reason natives are constantly thinking any visiting stranger have an ulterior motive to take over their God-assigned land. Despite the fact that Genesis 14:13-16 and 21-24 and 23:1-20 confirm that Abraham had friends among the Canaanites, there is no record that he loved them to the extent of telling them what he knew to be God's motive for sending him to live among them. Foreigners, no matter how godly, never divulge their real reason for sojourning where they are, and it would be foolhardy for natives to trust them.

Jacob went to Laban's home because he needed a haven from the threat of his brother who he had offended. It was never because he deliberately desired to contribute to his uncle's prosperity. When he left Laban, he never had pity on the old man. He sucked him dry and left him empty because Laban had cheated him earlier. He left unceremoniously. As for Moses, Exodus 2:11-22 and 4:18-19 confirm that he went to Midian because he needed to escape from the punishment due to him for killing an Egyptian even though he killed the Egyptian in defense of his fellow Israelite despite the fact that the Egyptians were magnanimous enough to offer him their throne regardless of the fact that he was not a traditional native Egyptian. Furthermore, Moses did not divulge the fact that he was a murderer to his host family in Midian. Thus, they endangered their own lives by hosting a 'registered murderer'. If they had offended him, he could have killed any of them like he had done to the Egyptian.

Moreover, it is difficult to prove that a foreigner would not work against his host country if there is a dispute between his native country and the host country. Exodus 1:8-11 confirms that this was the reason the Egyptians suspected the Israelites and oppressed them after the death of Joseph. Esther 10:1-3 confirms that Mordecai worked for the wellbeing of the Jews more than anyone else when he was made the Prime Minister in place of Haman. Esther 2:19-23 confirms that his first achievement before becoming the Prime Minister was saving the life of the Emperor so that his younger cousin, Queen Esther did not become a young widow. The second achievement that he was reputed to have used his office of the Prime Minister to achieve was to work for the interest of his kinsmen, the Jews. There was nothing else recorded that he achieved for the Empire and other races throughout his reign.

II Kings 8:1-6 says the rich woman of Shunem went to the land of Philistia for her personal survival rather than to contribute to the development of the land of Philistia and the natives. Most natives view strangers and sojourners from this point of view. And in all honesty, it is not far from the truth. Most migrants do so for personal survival reasons more than for the desire to benefit their host community. Man is travelling from creation to eternity through the earth and God says man should improve on the earth before he departs into eternity and it is proper for sojourners to contribute to the wellbeing of wherever they have reason to live until they return to their homestead.

Lot had the opportunity to save some Sodomites and opened that door for only the two suitors of his two daughters. Lot had become one of the leading citizens of Sodom when the angels came to talk about imminent destruction and the opportunity to save whoever Lot considered important to his heart. We believe he was among the leading citizens because the angels met him at the city centre or square where the leaders met to decide cases. Yet, when given the opportunity to save some lives, he did not have friends among his fellow leaders to extend the invitation and once his daughters' suitors turned down the offer he never approached any other friend to make the offer. This means that when sojourners have the chance to help the citizens, they never take it to heart to help them like they would do to their loved ones.

From the foregoing, foreigners need to be monitored because the loss that can be suffered from their activities by the host communities can be colossal. This means that it is very much for natives to scrutinize the activities of non-natives constantly to ensure that they are not doing anything that is inimical to the interest of the host community. Yet, we must remember to mention the other side of this issue. Often, the officials of the native authorities who engage in such scrutiny on behalf of the native authority allow their personal prejudices to overtly-affect their sense of fairness in the discharge of their duty. Some incriminate the migrants on account of envy or retaliatory mission because they had bad experience with strangers at home or as a stranger in another nation. To balance the art of dealing with strangers without bias but solely to protect the interest of the nation is a delicate task.

Much as some migrants work for the interest of their native country and fellow kinsmen migrants, there is the case of the likes of DSMA who worked for the progress of Babylon throughout the 70 years that they served in the palace of Babylon. This means that there are exceptional cases or instances when some migrants are completely loyal to the wellbeing and prosperity of their new nation. They are less concerned about the plight of their ancestral homeland. Because of Moses' bad experience with his fellow Israelites in Egypt when they damned him despite risking his life to protect them upon attaining age 40, he was reluctant to return to Egypt to help the Israelites 40 years later. His reluctance to return to Egypt dragged on until it offended God. It was like he was done with the Israelites in his heart and willing to remain in Midian for the rest of his life. Correctly discovering the well-meaning migrants from the buccaneers is a very tasking job for native authorities in charge of this assignment.

26

MIGRATION MOTIVE/ REASONS FOR MIGRATION

Life is a mix bag of everything and anything. Absalom and Ahithophel had different reasons for wanting David dead. The reason Ittai and his fellow Philistines joined David was different from the reason some Israelite warriors and army commanders joined David while Saul was still the sitting king of Israel. The reason Jethro employed Moses is different from the reason Achish employed David. The circumstances surrounding Jacob's sojourn in Laban's place is different from the circumstances that led to Joseph's sojourn in Egypt. The reason Joseph went to Egypt differed to the reason his father, brothers and their families joined him in Egypt. Let us consider some of the reason that makes people migrate to settle in places other than their land of nativity.

A. *Economic Consideration* –

Reason for migration includes economic consideration as exemplified by the cases of Elimelech, the rich woman of Shunem, and Jacob to Egypt. Ruth 1:1-22 says it was economic consideration that compelled Elimelech to relocate from Bethlehem with his wife and children to Moab during famine in Israel and never made it back with his sons except his wife and daughter-in-law, Ruth a Moabite. His wife, Naomi decided to return to Bethlehem only when she learnt that the economy of Bethlehem had improved. II Kings 8:1-6 says the rich woman of Shunem heeded Prophet Elisha's counsel to relocate from Shunem to the land of Philistia to escape the brunt of the seven years famine and she returned after the seven years Elisha said the famine would endure. These are examples of famine-forced migration or relocation. There is no record that the rich woman of Shunem waited for any form of calamity to befall her in Philistia before she returned to Shunem. She kept to the terms of the counsel she was given and returned on time. However, this adds another dimension compared with the story of Elimelech's relocation and inability to return. There is no record that he relocated based on spiritual guidance by any man of God. There is no doubt that he was not the only person who made logical reasoning and conclusion to relocate to another land because of famine or economic consideration.

Genesis 12:1-20 says Abraham complied with God's directive to relocate to Canaan but because he met famine in Canaan, he relocated to Egypt that was not experiencing famine. There is no record that God directed him to go down to Egypt though when his wife was taken by the king of Egypt, God forced the king to return her to him. As a result, the king of Egypt ordered his officials to drive him out of Egypt and he returned to Canaan. Genesis 26:1-34 says during Isaac's generation's famine, he considered going down to Egypt to survive but God restrained him to remain in Gerar of the Philistines where God blessed his efforts and he became so rich that the Philistines persecuted him because of envy and jealousy. King Abimelech of the Philistines also joined his subjects to drive Isaac out of their territorial domain.

Another very important story in this subject of combining spiritual guidance with physical circumstances or God-instructed with circumstances-instigated/induced to decide migration option is that of Jacob; Genesis 41 – 46 confirms that much as Jacob had all the physical reasons to relocate to Egypt, Genesis 45:1-28 and 46:1-6 confirm that he took time and effort to confirm from God if it was appropriate for him to relocate. The story says God gave him the necessary approval before he went with the rest of the family to join Joseph and his wife and two sons in Egypt. His first reason to jump at the chance to relocate was the discovery that his beloved son, Joseph who was believed to be dead was still alive and in fact had become the most important, powerful, and influential official in Egypt. Second, there was famine in Canaan like the rest of the then known world and he needed the food available in Egypt to survive the famine with his entire family. Third, Joseph had sent enough wagons to make their journey to Egypt smooth. Despite all these, Jacob did not jump at the invitation to go to Egypt without consulting and confirming God's approval because he believed that God's approval was important to his prosperity, joy and happiness wherever he lived at any point in time during the total number of years that Genesis 6:3, Job 14:5, Psalm 39:4, 90:10 and 139:16 and Acts 17:26 confirm that God meant for him to live on earth like all humans.

Also, it is possible that he had learnt that much as his grandfather, Abraham went to Egypt to escape famine without getting formal approval from God, when his father, Isaac tried to go to Egypt to escape famine in the land of Canaan, God disapprove. He had not forgotten that his mother's solution to escaping the punishment he deserved from Esau was filled with pains and that only God's help saved him from been killed by his mother's brother and his sons. His sad end in Shechem was still very fresh in his mind – if he had known that he would leave Shechem on such a sad note, he would never have gone there to settle rather he would have returned to Bethel upon his God-enabled safe return from his monstrous maternal uncle's place. By age 130 he had known that circumstances are not enough to relocate without clarification from God who knows the end from the beginning.

If those who relocated to a foreign land without God's consent suffered casualty, even Abraham, God's friend who went to Egypt because of famine lost his wife and was driven back unceremoniously while those that confirmed God's will like Jacob returned gloriously just as God restrained Isaac from going down to Egypt, then, it is a reason to conclude that any wise individual would confirm God's will before determining to go and live as a stranger anywhere under the sun. This means that God's backing to survive and prosper in a foreign land is crucial and most important. If Isaac had chosen to go down to Egypt just because his father had gone to Egypt during the famine of his father's generation, God would not have blessed his efforts or labour like He did when he obeyed, remained in Gerar and worked hard. This means that God blessed him because he remained where God chose for him. Therefore, consideration of only physical reasons and failure to obey God's command to be where He had commanded would deny the disobedient of His support to prosper wherever else one decides to live.

Genesis 12:10-20 can be interpreted to mean that because Abraham went down to Egypt without God's approval and lied which made his chief host do what caused him great pain and he was forced to compel Abraham to get out of his domain. As a result, we can say the admiration which the king of Egypt had for him was short-lived and in principle, that is what happens to anyone who travels to become a stranger in a land that God did not approve for him or her and lie to the hurt of the natives. Genesis 26:12-34 can be interpreted to mean that God's powered prosperity equally compels natives to be hostile to foreigners. It gets to a point when natives can no longer endure the presence of a foreigner who prospers far more than them particularly if most of the natives are struggling to make ends meet. Isaac prospered during famine when the Philistines were struggling to make ends meet. They were angry that their God-given land was yielding bumper harvest for Isaac while it was not doing the same thing for them.

Non-God approved strangers would discover that even if they find favour with the hosts, it would be short-lived as something would soon go wrong to turn them into hostile hosts. To this end, Genesis 27:1-46 confirms in verse 41-46 that because Rebecca encouraged Jacob to cheat Esau a second time, Esau threatened Jacob. When Rebecca found out about Esau's plan to punish Jacob after the death of their father, she manipulated Isaac to send Jacob away to her brother's place from Esau's reach. Considering Abraham's view in Genesis 24:1-10 and God's plan that Jacob would succeed Isaac like God had chosen Isaac to be Abraham's chief inheritor or heir in Genesis 25:19-24, Jacob was not supposed to have gone to Laban's place or anywhere outside the land of Canaan. But because Isaac could not follow in his father's footsteps to prevent it, Genesis 28:1-5 and 10-22 can be interpreted to mean that God was forced to lend His credence to Jacob's relocation outside of Canaan by blessing Jacob on his way to Laban's place at Bethel. Like Deuteronomy 7:7-8 and Ezekiel 36:16-38 say God helped the Israelites because of His own plans, God accompanied Jacob to Laban's place only because of His great plans that He had decided to use Jacob to achieve even before Jacob was ever born.

It is also important to note that Genesis 27:1-46 means that Rebecca authored Jacob's sojourn in the home of her brother back in her own place of nativity rather than God. She was a master manipulator who started manifesting her manipulative skills by making Jacob cheat her other son, Esau, and when she learnt of the plot of Esau to get back at Jacob, she manipulated her husband to send Jacob away. She did not consult God to know if Jacob would be safe with her brother like Genesis 25:19-24 says she went to ask God for clarifications when she discovered something strange about their pregnancy. She just assumed that her brother would not harm her son for her sake. It turned out that she overrated the loyalty she expected from her brother.

God's conscious promise to help Jacob while living as a stranger in Laban's home should interest us considering that Genesis 31:1-42 confirms that Laban was unkind to Jacob throughout his stay. God had seen that Jacob's mother was channeling his life in the wrong direction but so long as Jacob allowed her to still remain in the position to do so, verse 15 of Genesis 28:10-22 can be said to mean that God went the extra mile to support Jacob wherever he went.

There is what we can call the "Mundane Minded". Genesis 26:34-35 confirms that Jacob's twin brother got two wives for himself when they attained the age of 40. Yet, Jacob remained unmarried or could not get any young woman to agree to marry him rather he waited until their mother decided that it was time for him to go get a wife from some faraway place – that is not different from their mother baby-sitting him on marital matters or serious decision making at 40 when his peers were deciding and implementing ideas about their lives. There is nothing respectable about that. That is why we said Jacob allowed his mother to decide when, where and who he could marry. Jacob lacked the confidence to face life outside family circles. While Esau went outside their family to marry, he remained at home. When their mother suggested that he went to their maternal uncle to get a wife he did not mind or in fact, jumped at the offer even when he would have to travel thousands of kilometers away from home. Before he could detach from his parents' family was when he went to settle in Shechem with his own family even then he still had two of his cousins, Leah, and

Rachel as his wives. He could not have the confidence to face life without family surrounding him.

More importantly, anyone who is going anywhere needs God's support as much or perhaps more than he needs God's support at home. One of the points is that your kinsmen would protect you against strangers at home and there are fewer strangers in your home country. This means that with the support of your kinsmen, strangers are supposed to be at your mercy at home. But when you are out in a strange land, there are more strangers than your kinsmen and they would overwhelm you readily. This is part of the reason that when Laban cheated Jacob in Haran which was Laban's home base where Jacob was a stranger, Jacob could not do anything except for heavenly help. If God does not support and protect you in a strange land, you can never get enough help to overcome the natives and prosper appropriately.

Second, Genesis 31:1-55 confirms in verse 10-21 that after 20 years at Laban's place, Jacob did not leave Laban's place until God had confirmed that he should leave. Earlier, his mother made him to offend his brother and escape the brother's planned punishment. Then, his mother's brother caused him pains for the 20 years he lived and worked for him. He was afraid that his brother might still attack him if he returned home so he endured his uncle's tortuous treatment. Then, God said he could return home. Genesis 35:1-5 confirms that God led him out of Shechem to Bethel. Genesis 45:4-28 and 46:1-6 say he consciously confirmed God's approval before he went to join Joseph in Egypt. It is important to note that with age, experience and in the absence of his mother, Rebecca, Jacob had learnt that it was not proper to relocate without God's approval, so even when he was desperate to see Joseph, he started his desire to meet Joseph with confirming God's approval. In the matter of following proper procedures to do things, irrespective of the pressure under which we are, Ecclesiastes 8:5-7 says:

> 5 He who keeps a royal command experiences no trouble, for a wise heart knows the proper time and procedure. 6 For there is a proper time and procedure for every delight, when a man's trouble is heavy upon him. 7 If no one knows what will

happen, who can tell him when it will happen? (NASB)

5 If you obey the king, you will stay out of trouble. So be smart and learn what to do and when to do it. 6 Life is hard, but there is a time and a place for everything, 7 though no one can tell the future. (CEV)

5 As long as you obey his commands, you are safe, and a wise man knows how and when to do it. 6 There is a right time and a right way to do everything, but we know so little! 7 None of us knows what is going to happen, and there is no one to tell us. (TEV)

This is what can be called "Profitable Proper Procedure and Timing" or "Profitability of Proper Procedure and Timing/Timeliness". Timeliness is part of proper procedure. Proverbs 15:23 says getting the right word for the right occasion is gratifying and it is part of proper procedure. The admonition in the above passage is that no matter the pressure we feel, we must not forget to follow proper and most profitable procedure. And for intending migrants, it is proper and profitable to confirm God's approval in addition to meeting the migration requirements.

In the story of Jacob suffering while working for Laban, we would notice that Rebecca who initiated the idea could not protect Jacob from her brother's oppression rather, it was God who was able to ensure that Jacob never returned to Canaan empty-handed. This is one reason that it is important for anyone to get God's approval so that the aim and objective of going abroad to make a living is achieved. Rebecca assumed that all things being equal, her brother would be kind to her son, but it turned out otherwise. In fact, she should have known that her brother could not have behaved better than her who caused pain to her own son, Esau because she preferred Jacob. If she could support Jacob to undo Esau her son, then she should have known that her own brother could equally undo her son but the wicked never understand that the evil they do to others could be done to them. She did not think that by helping Jacob to undo Esau, she was sowing a seed of evil that Jacob was bound to reap in the future and anyone could be used to make him reap the seed of evil earlier sown to his benefit. If a man persuades and supports another to relocate, such a man cannot help and ensure that the migrant succeeds, prospers, and attains his set goals and objectives in his land of sojourn. Only God can help a man to achieve his heart desires wherever he goes to live and strive to survive.

Third, Genesis 28:10-16 and 46:1-7 say just like God told Jacob about the outcome of his sojourn in Laban's home, so also God told him the would-be outcome of his sojourn in Egypt to the extent that God told Jacob ahead of time that Joseph would be beside him when he dies. The main significance of this is that God has the capacity to tell the end of any man's sojourn in a foreign land from the very beginning. First, Isaiah 41:4 says He determines the course of human history. He initiates and completes ideas that make history. Second, Genesis 31:1-55, 32:9-10 and 22, 33:1-3, 13 and 18-20, 47:27-31, 49:33 and 50:1-14 confirm that God fulfilled the promises He made to Jacob when he went to Laban's place as well as to Egypt where he spent the 20 and 17 years respectively. Third, Genesis 25:5-11 gives the impression that Isaac took over the family house of his father after his father's death and burial. He had left the bulk of his wealth for Isaac. Then, Genesis 26:1-33 says sometime later there was famine in Canaan and Isaac thought that his best option was to relocate to Egypt but God said he should not go beyond the land of the Philistines and particularly Gerar. Judges 16:5, 23 and 27 and I Samuel 29:2 confirm that there are a total of five Philistines nations with their different capital cities and God specified Gerar in particular. Also, God indicated the reason He would bless Isaac there to be the obedience of his late father.

God does not just have the capacity to make a man's sojourn in a foreign land successful, He has the capacity to make the man take his acquired success in a foreign land back home to become established in greatness and great honour. He can tell the man necessary details about what he would experience wherever he goes. God said Isaac did not need to go to Egypt to survive during famine and when he stayed in Gerar where God chose for him at such time of his life, Genesis 26:1-6 and 12-13 confirms that he prospered and became very great and powerful. This further means that there is a place where God has assigned prosperity and greatness for everyone at any point in time. Of course, this agrees with the claim in Acts 17:26 that from the very foundations of the world or at creation, God of Israel had decided where and when we would live during our stay on earth. It explains why Genesis 17:1-26 and 18:1-15 give the impression that Abraham was living at the Sacred Trees of Mamre when God visited in the form of three men to talk about the imminent conception and birth of Isaac. Then, Genesis 20:1-18 and 21:22-34 say he left the Sacred Trees of Mamre to live in Gerar and remained there for an exceedingly long time. Perhaps, it was while there that Genesis 22:1-19 says God tested him by asking him to go offer up Isaac on Mount Moriah. Then, Genesis 23:1-20 opens with the fact that he was living in Hebron when Sarah died while verse 17 says the burial site he bought was located at eastern side of Mamre which suggests that he returned to the place he once lived at Mamre where Isaac was born. This means that Abraham relocated to different parts of the land of Canaan which God commanded.

The subject of God's blessing for an individual per place per time made it possible for Esau who remained in the family house to prosper during the twenty years Jacob lived away from their traditional home in Canaan. He lived in the same family house that Abraham and Isaac lived. Because they carried God's covenanted blessing, the environment was supernaturally charged, filled and overflowing with God's prospering presence such that even when he was not supposed to be the covenant-carrying child in his generation he still prospered. Staying where God's presence inhabited in a spectacular manner made it possible for Esau to earn enough to build his own country in Edom and readily left for Jacob to take over after their father died and was buried.

Genesis 31:38-42, 32:13-21 and 33:8-9 confirm that the many gifts Jacob gave to buy Esau's favour were not regarded by Esau because according to Esau, he was so rich that he did not need to collect them. It is like when Genesis 14:1-16 and 21-24 confirms that Abraham rejected what the king of Sodom considered the worthy reward due to Abraham for helping to rescue him and his subjects from their captors. Furthermore,

Genesis 32:1-3 confirms that when Jacob tried to contact Esau upon his return from their maternal uncle's place, he sent his servants to Esau at Edom rather than where their father lived in Canaan and Jacob left Esau and their two parents 20 years earlier. Again, Genesis 33:16 confirms that after receiving Jacob into the land of Canaan formally, Esau returned to his country of Edom. But rather than go straight to take over their father's place immediately upon his return from Laban's place, Genesis 33:18-20 confirms that Jacob chose to go and settle in Shechem. Apparently, when Esau found out that Jacob had not gone to take his rightful place in their father's home, he returned to be with their father in Canaan. It is as a result that Genesis 35:27-29 and 36:1-8 say after the death and burial of their father, only then Jacob came over with his family and possessions to formally take over their father's home. Because there was not enough space, Esau left with his large family and wealth finally for his newly founded country of Edom.

Interestingly, Deuteronomy 2:12 and 22 confirms that God helped him to claim it from the original Edom inhabitants. This means that according to God's plan for them as children of the same parents, Esau was supposed to be a temporary dweller in Canaan. He was supposed to live there until adulthood and relocate to the land of the Edomites which was assigned to him and his descendants for a permanent possession by God before he was born. Meanwhile, though Canaan was meant to be Jacob's permanent home, he allowed his mother to relocate him outside the place and in his absence, his brother, Esau had to run the family house and their father's business to enrich himself.

Proverbs 17:2 says 'a wise servant will rule over a disgraceful son, and will share the inheritance as one of the brothers'-NIV. In this case, it is the hardworking son who God did not love and bless that took the place of the God-preferred and blessed son to prosper while preferred and blessed went away to suffer before he could manifest the blessing and belatedly too. It is like the famous proverbial prodigal son who's father's servants were enjoying in the employment and household of his father while he was suffering in a foreign land because he chose to do the unthinkable of claiming his inheritance while his father was still very much alive. Genesis 32:3, 6 and 33:1 say by the time

Jacob returned from Laban's place, Esau was wealthy enough to have 400 men in his entourage whenever he travelled. Even their grandfather, Abraham could not maintain more than 317 warriors at a time. Jacob was afraid upon learning that Esau could afford to travel with 400 men at a go because he never had such number of servants by the time he returned from Haran. He knew that physically he could not match Esau if there was trouble or confrontation. Esau typifies a man who is not in the good books of God but very smart when it comes to survival in the things of this world while Jacob is the opposite. It is the sadistic reason Jesus alluded to the fact in Luke 16:1-8 that non-Christians as we would like to put it, are wiser than Christians.

Genesis 25:27-28 says Esau started life as a hunter and was successful. Genesis 26:34-35 confirms that it enabled him to afford two wives. Genesis 25:27-28 and 27:1-4 confirm that he had enough gains to share with their father. Then, Genesis 27:15 confirms that he acquired expensive clothing as part of his gains which he kept with their mother. Genesis 28:6-9 says he could afford to marry more wives just to please his father before Jacob ever left home to their maternal uncle's place to start to work to earn personal income at all. Therefore, when Genesis 36:6 says when he was leaving Canaan finally, he had a lot of livestock among his possessions, it means that he took over their father's livestock after Jacob's departure from Canaan to their uncle's place. It means that he took to hunting earlier because he believed that Jacob as their God-ordained chief inheritor would take over their father's livestock like Genesis 25:6-11 confirms that their grandfather, Abraham had done for their father, Isaac. Their grandfather was 160 years old when they were born and died when they were 15 years old. Therefore, they were old enough as teenagers to understand that their grandfather gave gifts to his other sons and sent them and their mother, Keturah away for their father to inherit him without stress. It was from their father's livestock that Genesis 27:5-14 and 17-25 says Jacob slaughtered the two fat young goats that their mother cooked and gave to him to get the blessing that their father meant for Esau. So long as God never meant Esau and his descendants to possess Canaan permanently, he could be described as home-grown stranger. And there are many strangers in their own homeland of birth. Their God assigned prosperity location is outside where they were born and bred. Joseph was born in Haran also known as Padan Aram, bred in Shechem and Bethel of Canaan and lived great in Egypt.

B. *Self-exile for Personal Safety* –

Another reason people migrate is what can be described as personal safety prompted self-exile. To this end, Genesis 35:1 says:

> 35 God said to Jacob, "Go to Bethel at once, and live there. Build an altar there to me, the God who appeared to you when you were running away from your brother Esau." (TEV)

Without any attempt to digress, the above passage means that God did not forget the circumstance that led to His first personal encounter with Jacob at Bethel. He reminded Jacob that it was while Jacob was running away from his brother, Esau who threatened his life for cheating him on two occasions. We shall not delve into the details of what can be considered "Like Jacob like Moses" in the matter of escaping from one's place of birth and breeding into adulthood to escape punishment due for wrongdoing. I Samuel 18:1-30, 19:1-24, 20:1-42, 21:1-15, 22:1-23, 23:1-29, 24:1-22, 26:1-25 and 27:1-12 say King Saul's repeated threats forced David to escape from his land of birth and upbringing not because he committed any offence deserving any form of punishment rather because of envy and jealousy.

I Kings 11:28-40 says Jeroboam's life was threatened by King Solomon because of God's favour to be chosen as prospective successor to the throne of Israel and this threat forced Jeroboam to relocate to the land of Egypt to preserve his life and returned only after the death of Solomon. Jeroboam can be said to have followed in David's footsteps in this respect. Jeremiah 26:20-23 says when the life of Prophet Uriah, son of Shemaiah from Kiriath Jearim was threatened because he reprimanded King Jehoiakim of Judah on God's behalf, he escaped to Egypt but King Jehoiakim got him repatriated to Judah and killed. Jacob did not lose his life at Laban's place but lost some of his reward for hard work as Laban dealt treacherously with him because of greed for gain and prodigality.

Judges 9:1-57 confirms that Gideon's youngest son, Jotham went to hide to outlive his father's only son out of wedlock, Abimelech who had massacred his other sane legitimate sons in order to succeed Gideon as the ruler of Israel. Jotham prophesied the sad end of Abimelech's reign before he ran into hiding. Numbers 21:16 and Judges 9:1-21 give the impression that Jotham went to hide in a place called Beer where their ancestors who left Egypt led by Moses had asked God for water to drink in the wilderness. There is no record that Jotham returned throughout or after Abimelech's three-year reign.

I Kings 11:15-24 says one Hadad, the only surviving prince of Edom had been taken by his father's royal servants to hide in Egypt when David and Joab conquered Edom. Hadad grew up in Egypt and when he learnt that David and Joab had died, he returned to Edom to rule as king. Also, II Chronicles 22:10-12 and 23:1-15 tell how Joash was hidden in the Temple in Jerusalem for seven years before his paternal grandmother, Athaliah was punished for the killing of Joash's older brothers and Joash was made king of Judah in Jerusalem.

Moses relocated to Midian to preserve his life and Exodus 2:1-25, 3:1-22, 4:1-31, 6:13 and 26-27 and Acts 7:23-35 confirm that after 40 years, God restored him to Egypt to pursue and accomplish the reason God sent him to live on earth. In the same vein, I Samuel 27:1-12 and 31:1-13, II Samuel 2:1-7 and 5:1-5 and I Chronicles 10:1-14, 11:1-3 and 14:1-2 confirm that David relocated to Gath to outlive his chief assailant, King Saul and returned to rule after Saul according to God's plan and purpose. In this respect, we can talk about "Like Moses like David and Jeroboam". They were persons who escaped from their land of birth to outlive their assailants and returned to accomplish the very plan of God for which their lives were previously threatened. Coincidentally, there is no record that each of them consulted God before they set out to sojourn in a foreign land. Yet, since they returned to rule and lead according to God's will and plan, we can say God approved of their decision to relocate when they did.

Some measure of credit should go to a mere mortal who is able to take decisions that God approves of even when he did not formally consult God before taking and implementing such decisions. It is very much like when Numbers 27:1-11 and 36:1-13 say fortunately for the daughters of Zelophehad, their request to be allowed to inherit their father who never had any son was agreeable to God. This is important considering that Isaiah 55:8-9 confirms that God's thoughts and plans are too advanced for mere mortals to comprehend and fathom without consciously consulting God.

How did Esau know that God meant the land of the Edomites for him and his descendants to claim and possess permanently? That is a suffocating fact that should worry Jacob and his descendants who were supposed to enjoy God's favour more than Esau and his descendants. It is very embarrassing that Genesis 36:31-39 and I Chronicles 1:43-54 say long before there were kings in Israel Esau's descendants, the Edomites already had their established kingdoms ruled over by their own kings. It means that just as Esau prospered before Jacob so also Esau's descendants prospered before Jacob's descendants. There is no record that Esau had problems at home in Canaan while he transformed from a hunter into a shepherd like Jacob suffered in Haran in the hands of their uncle, Laban. If you stay where you should not, you become liable, prone, and susceptible to suffer what you could have avoided.

Genesis 13:1-13, 19:1-38 and Ruth 1:1-22 can be interpreted to mean that Lot and Elimelech's decision to relocate without God's approval or guidance or both led to a sad end for them. Lot lost his wealth that gave him the confidence to leave Abraham behind in Canaan to go and settle in Sodom to the divine judgment on Sodom. He was only able to escape with his life and two daughters. Elimelech and his two sons died in Moab where he relocated with his wife and two sons because of famine in Bethlehem. When the famine ended only his wife returned. This means that Lot and Elimelech's conjecture that they could survive in a foreign land did not get God's support to survive there.

God did not think it was necessary to stop David from leaving the land of Israel to the land of the Philistines to escape the threats of King Saul. He still searched out Moses in Midian to return to accomplish divine purpose in Egypt after forty years even though Moses did not ask His consent before going to live in Midian. Meanwhile, there is no record that God led Elimelech back to Bethlehem before he died in the land of Moab where he had gone without asking and getting His profitable and protective obligatory consent.

C. *Divine Guidance/Direction* –

Genesis 12:1-9 and Acts 7:1-10 confirm that Abraham left his place of birth to spend the rest of his life in Canaan mostly because God commanded him to do so. He spent the last 100 years of the total of 175 years he lived in Canaan in obedience to God's directive. He had no relative in Canaan just as he was not desperate for a job when he went to live there. He was not a young man when he did, just as he did not go there to get a wife or because he had met a Canaanite girl in his hometown who said she would remain his lover only if he accompanied her to settle in Canaan. Also, Genesis 15:12-17 confirms that before Isaac was born God had revealed that Isaac's son and heir, Jacob would take his family to live in Egypt as strangers for a total of four generation which Exodus 12:40-42 confirms turned out to be 430 years. Genesis 15:13-14 and Exodus 3:21-22, 11:1-2 and

12:35-36 confirm that God fulfilled His promise that He would help the Israelites to leave Egypt with the movable wealth of Egypt. Then, Genesis 36:1-6 confirms that Jacob went to Egypt because God confirmed that it was His will for him to take the rest of his family to join Joseph therein because it agreed with the plan He had revealed to Abraham that his covenant descendants would be enslaved in a strange land for 400 years.

Genesis 37:1-36 and 45:4-9 and Psalms 105:16-24 say though Joseph's brothers sold him to Egypt to serve as a slave because of envy, God stage-managed Joseph's advance arrival in Egypt. This is in order to preserve Abraham's covenant descendants during the great famine of Jacob and his sons' generation, and in order to fulfill the plan of God for Abraham's covenant descendants to live in Egypt before He would bring them back to take over Canaan for their permanent possession. Likewise, Acts 19:21-22, 20:22-24, 21:10-14, 22:17-21 and 23:10-11 say God authored Paul's relocation to Rome. This is a spiritual factor responsible for relocation which turns an individual into a stranger in the place God sent him or her to live. All the people that God of Israel sent as religious missionaries can be said to belong to this category.

D. *Professional/Career Pursuit* –

There is the economic concept of mobility of labor which says skilled citizens move from one locality to another to use their skills to earn a living while contributing to the national development. Much as God meant Jacob to lead his household into Egypt which we can say gave spiritual undertone to his spending the last 17 years of the 147 that he lived in Egypt, there is the economic and employment undertone or angle to their relocation. They went to survive the famine of their generation just as upon their arrival in Egypt they were employed by Joseph's boss, Pharaoh, the king of Egypt. This means that in Egypt, Joseph's brothers got the privilege of serving as shepherds to a king for the very first and only time in their professional practice and career. They had been self-employed shepherds like their ancestors and father until this point in their lives. Again, about the sojourn of the young Levite from Bethlehem of Judah outside his place of birth in Israel, Judges 17:1-13 says:

1 There was once a man named Micah, who lived in the hill country of Ephraim. 2 He told his mother, "When someone stole those eleven hundred pieces of silver from you, you put a curse on the robber. I heard you do it. Look, I have the money. I am the one who took it." His mother said, "May the Lord bless you, my son!" 3 He gave the money back to his mother, and she said, "To keep the curse from falling on my son, I myself am solemnly dedicating the silver to the Lord. It will be used to make a wooden idol covered with silver. So now I will give the pieces of silver back to you." 4 Then he gave them back to his mother. She took two hundred of the pieces of silver and gave them to a metalworker, who made an idol, carving it from wood and covering it with the silver. It was placed in Micah's house. 5 This man Micah had his own place of worship. He made

some idols and an ephod, and appointed one of his sons as his priest. 6 There was no king in Israel at that time; everyone did whatever he wanted. 7 At that same time there was a young Levite who had been living in the town of Bethlehem in Judah. 8 He left Bethlehem to find another place to live. While he was traveling, he came to Micah's house in the hill country of Ephraim. 9 Micah asked him, "Where do you come from?" He answered, "I am a Levite from Bethlehem in Judah. I am looking for a place to live." 10 Micah said, "Stay with me. Be my adviser and priest, and I will give you ten pieces of silver a year, some clothes, and your food." 11 The young Levite agreed to stay with Micah and became like a son to him. 12 Micah appointed him as his priest, and he lived in Micah's home. 13 Micah said, "Now that I have a Levite as my priest, I know that the Lord will make things go well for me." (TEV)

Apparently because Micah feared the consequences of stealing his mother's money to become wealthy, he desperately desired to appease God to escape the punishment for his misdeeds. Thus, he dethroned his son to appoint the young Levite from Judah as his household high priest. On his part, the young Levite from Judah had his Levitical right to serve as a priest of the God of their ancestors and maker of the universe to mediate between God and his fellow Israelite or man as the kind of skill he had to earn his living and contribute to national development. When he could not find a job in his place of birth, he migrated to another part of the country in search of means of livelihood what is also called greener pastures. He got a job with Micah on a seemingly generous remuneration package. Micah relieved his son of the prestigious position of his household priest and replaced him with this young Levite from Judah. This is migration for personal survival reason and appropriate national redistribution of human capital.

The young Levite was born and bred where there were surplus skilled Levites whereas Micah's hometown was suffering from insufficient number of required skilled Levites to mediate between them and God of Israel, the maker of the universe. This young man accepted Micah's offer without asking for more. He needed everything Micah offered him just as Moses readily embraced Jethro's offer to marry his daughter and become his household's business manager when Moses arrived in Midian. If the young Levite had rejected Micah's job offer and sought employment in similar position with any of Micah's kinsman, it is possible that if such second potential employer was an acquaintance of Micah, he could decide against employing the young man as a result.

Like Moses and this young Levite, it is on record that when David arrived King Achish's domain, he readily accepted Achish's offer of employment. The reason the subject of accepting whatever job one is offered in a strange land is worthy of note is that there are no relatives and other acquaintances (the bank of family and friends) to support one until the stranger gets the job or employment of his choice. The job is the only physical lifeline of the stranger therefore he must accept it without hesitation. In the case of David, it was impossible for family and friends to help out for even a day because he had 400 men with their own households in addition to his own household and the priest Abiathar and his household to fend for when he arrived in Gath of the Philistines to seek refuge with their king. Moses did not consider his royal status before he left Egypt when he took up the ego-bruising job of his father-in-law's chief shepherd. This job provided him accommodation, a set of people he could trust that they loved him like his blood-bonded relatives would. Even if Moses, the young Levite from Judah or David had any challenge in the strange land they found themselves, their employer would intervene with their kinsmen to help them. This is the benefit of getting a job immediately upon arriving a strange land. We shall not digress into the subject of "Employment as an Enhancer and Enabler" or "Employment as Enhancer of Diverse Benefits" at this point but suffice to say an employable individual is an acceptable and respectable individual migrant. When someone is employable, the employer would go the extra mile to remove all the encumbrances that would deny him the services of such an individual.

Let us close his case by saying again that Judges 18:1-31 recounts that this young Levite from Judah left Micah's employment to take up the job of the high priest of the tribe of Dan who treated Micah as an enemy when they forcefully collected Micah's household gods. They decapitated Micah's religious life and strength to establish their own religious institution against Micah's consent. The young Levite took up that new position at Micah's expense without regard for the way he started working for Micah because he agreed with the Danites that it was better for him to serve as the high priest of an entire tribe than remain the high priest of an individual household. He took the wealth of experience garnered at Micah's employment to serve the entire tribe of Dan just like Joseph took his experience as human and material resource manager in Potiphar's household to serve as the human and material resource manager in prison which he in turn took to serve as the human and material resource manager of the entire nation of Egypt later on. Employees desire to attain higher position of service is a key reason people migrate from one place to another. The term expatriates refer to persons who relocate from one country to another to contribute to the national development of the country they migrated to and in turn get mouth-watering reward for their services. To this end, the young Levite left his native land of Judah to Micah's place of birth to render service and later left Micah's place for the region of the Danites where he must have worked till old age and retired.

When David relocated to the land of the Philistines to keep safe from King Saul, he took up the job of army commander with King Achish of the Philistines. When Moses relocated to the land of Midian to keep safe from the Egyptian officials who wanted him dead, he took up the job of looking after his father's-in-law flock throughout his stay. Judges 10:1-11 can be interpreted to mean that when family inheritance-fueled feud following the death of his father forced Jephthah to relocate from his father's hometown of Gilead to live in his maternal hometown of Tob, he engaged himself in the business of leading a gang of worthless men. Jephthah found the job of guiding worthless and hopeless men where he went to live against his wish or out of frustration from rejection by his father's legitimate sons. By engaging himself in this unpaid job he equipped himself with soldiering skills to the extent that the people of Israel and particularly their leaders heard of his soldiering leadership skills. As a result, when the nation of Israel needed someone that God could use or support to free them from the oppression of the Ammonites, they contacted this same erstwhile rejected Jephthah. As a result, Jephthah emerged the ruler of Israel after leading the defeat of the Ammonites. It makes his migration to and the way that he spent his time and life in Tob to be one of the best things that ever happened to him. He laid the foundation for his greatness in Tob. Those that forced him to migrate become subject to him upon his return.

E. *Marital Consideration/Loyalty to Spouse* –

This is about marriage motivated migration. Genesis 38:1 and 12 can be safely interpreted to mean that Tamar stuck to Judah's family maritally even after the death of Judah's two sons that she married one after the other. The famous story of Ruth in chapters 1 – 4 say she stuck to her husband's family even after his death until she followed her mother-in-law, Naomi back to Bethlehem where she married their relative, Boaz as a result of which she is listed among the matriarchs of mankind's Messiah, Jesus Christ of Nazareth. Zipporah migrated from her native land of birth, Midian to Egypt onward to Canaan when God directed her husband and father of their two sons to return to Egypt to lead the freedom of the Israelites from the famous Egyptian bondage. Let us be reminded that though Asenath, an Egyptian, married Joseph, a Hebrew in her homeland of Egypt, she did not need to relocate to Joseph's native land of Canaan till she died. Jacob's wives, Leah and Rachel spent the first 13 years of their marriage in their place of birth before they had to follow him to his homeland of Canaan where Genesis 35:16-21 and 49:29-33 confirm that they died and were buried. This is how Genesis 31:4-18 gives the account of Leah and Rachel's determination to accompany Jacob to Canaan:

> 4 So Jacob sent word to Rachel and Leah to meet him in the field where his flocks were. 5 He said to them, "I have noticed that your father is not as friendly toward me as he used to be; but my father's God has been with me. 6 You both know that I have worked for your father with all my strength. 7 Yet he has cheated me and changed my wages ten times. But God did not

let him harm me. 8 Whenever Laban said, 'The speckled goats shall be your wages,' all the flocks produced speckled young. When he said, 'The striped goats shall be your wages,' all the flocks produced striped young. 9 God has taken flocks away from your father and given them to me. 10 "During the breeding season I had a dream, and I saw that the male goats that were mating were striped, spotted, and speckled. 11 The angel of God spoke to me in the dream and said, 'Jacob!' 'Yes,' I answered. 12 'Look,' he continued, 'all the male goats that are mating are striped, spotted, and speckled. I am making this happen because I have seen all that Laban is doing to you. 13 I am the God who appeared to you at Bethel, where you dedicated a stone as a memorial by pouring olive oil on it and where you made a vow to me. Now get ready and go back to the land where you were born.' " 14 Rachel and Leah answered Jacob, "There is nothing left for us to inherit from our father. 15 He treats us like foreigners. He sold us, and now he has spent all the money he was paid for us. 16 All this wealth which God has taken from our father belongs to us and to our children. Do whatever God has told you." 17-18 So Jacob got ready to go back to his father in the land of Canaan. He put his children and his wives on the camels, and drove all his flocks ahead of him, with everything that he had gotten in Mesopotamia. (TEV)

Let us make our first concern the fact that verses 13-16 say Jacob's wives confessed/confirmed that as long as they had nothing personally profitable to benefit from their father, they were determined to travel with their husband to where he came from to sojourn in their own land of birth. They meant that 'if your native land, kinsmen, even parents and relatives will not benefit you, there is nothing wrong with dumping such location and unprofitable people for another profitable location'. Also, children's inheritance is enough reason for any woman to relocate to be with her children wherever their father's heritage is located. Despite being their father, so long as Laban would not benefit them like their husband would, they rejected him to cleave and move away with their husband. Genesis 12:1-3 says God's promise to Abraham while asking him to relocate from his land of birth included blessing as if to say God had concluded that the blessing He meant for Abraham was not in his birthplace but in a foreign land. Also, God is not against relocating because of greater chances of better life or that He could help anyone who desires to relocate to enjoy better quality of life. This highlights what we can call the "reward of relocation" or "Rewarding Relocation" and the fact that reward, profitability, and benefit is an integral reason that even God would encourage relocation. Yet, there is something else important that comes to mind from the case of Jacob's twenty years' sojourn in the household and business of Laban away from where Jacob was born and bred in Canaan.

Genesis 32:9-10 reports Jacob's confession that when he was leaving Canaan for Haran (detailed in Genesis 28:1-5 and 10-22) the most valuable thing he had was just the blessing of his father and God which cannot be seen with the naked eyes.

However, during his 20-year stay in Haran and through hardwork and God's help and protection, he converted this spiritual grace or blessing into visible material blessings of wives, children, servants, flock, and other material things. It is very striking that he could not achieve the same material blessings in Canaan where he was born and bred, and God meant for him and his descendants to possess permanently. While Jacob had God's prospering capability that helps a man to get great gain from the work of his hands, Laban owned the flocks that Jacob needed to work on to increase the wealth for Laban as his employer and himself through his due wages. Therefore, one important point worthy of note is that a migrant must carry the backing of God's prospering presence to the foreign land he is going to live for him to work there and prosper accordingly. He or she must be sure of God's prospering presence in his life while there. DSMA prospered in Babylon by the same support of the Lord God who supported Abraham in Canaan and Egypt, recovered his wife for him in Philistia and Egypt, prospered Isaac in Gerar to the envy of the Philistines, prospered the Israelites in Egypt, made Esther and Mordecai to become Queen and Prime Minister of the Persian Empire, respectively; and guided the steps of Ruth to the fields of Boaz initially and helped her to marry Boaz later.

27

YOUTHFUL ADVENTURE/ PEER PRESSURE

Just as there are accidental inventions and inventors, unplanned pregnancies, and unintended consequences so also there are unplanned migration. It was to escape threat of Esau that Jacob left Canaan for Haran of Mesopotamia. It was not like Jacob planned that he would leave home to Laban's place to make a living. There are persons who migrate because their lover has travelled abroad and he or she is desperate to be with such lover. Judah travelled out to live away from home because he had a friend from that foreign country. In this respect, Genesis 38:1-5, 12, 20-23 says:

Surviving Among Strangers

1 About that time Judah left his brothers and went to stay with a man named Hirah, who was from the town of Adullam. 2 There Judah met a young Canaanite woman whose father was named Shua. He married her, 3 and she bore him a son, whom he named Er. 4 She became pregnant again and bore another son and named him Onan. 5 Again she had a son and named him Shelah. Judah was at Achzib when the boy was born. 12 After some time Judah's wife died. When he had finished the time of mourning, he and his friend Hirah of Adullam went to Timnah, where his sheep were being sheared. 20 Judah sent his friend Hirah to take the goat and get back from the woman the articles he had pledged, but Hirah could not find her. 21 He asked some men at Enaim, "Where is the prostitute who was here by the road?" "There has never been a prostitute here," they answered. 22 He returned to Judah and said, "I couldn't find her. The men of the place said that there

had never been a prostitute there." 23 Judah said, "Let her keep the things. We don't want people to laugh at us. I did try to pay her, but you couldn't find her." (TEV)

This means that Judah made a friend outside his brothers and followed this friend by the name of Hirah to live in Hirah's native land of Adullam. Genesis 38:2-11 confirms that Judah married in Adullam, had three sons, and got a girl named Tamar to marry his eldest son, Er. It means that Judah lived in Adullam for quite a while. Then verse 12 above confirms that he prospered in Adullam. He had flock that was sheared just like I Samuel 25:2-7 says of Nabal. Then, verse 20-23 says his friend and chief host so to speak was so trustworthy that he could share his secrets with him. He was not ashamed that Hirah knew that he had intercourse with a prostitute or a presumed prostitute. He did not want any other person to know but was comfortable with Hirah been aware. It means that he regarded Hirah like one of his siblings throughout his stay in Adullam. Also, Genesis 38:13, 24 and II Samuel 18:10-15 say:

13 Someone told Tamar that her father-in-law was going to Timnah to shear his sheep. 24 About three months later someone told Judah, "Your daughter-in-law Tamar has been acting like a whore, and now she is pregnant." Judah ordered, "Take her out and burn her to death."

10 One of David's men saw him and reported to Joab, "Sir, I saw Absalom hanging in an oak tree!" 11 Joab answered, "If you saw him, why didn't you kill him on the spot? I myself would have given you ten pieces of silver and a belt." 12 But the man answered, "Even if you gave me a thousand pieces of silver, I wouldn't lift a finger against the king's son. We all heard the king command you and Abishai and Ittai, 'For my sake don't harm the young man Absalom.' 13 But if I had disobeyed the king and killed Absalom, the king would have heard about it—he hears about everything—and you would not have defended me." 14 "I'm not going to waste any more time

with you," Joab said. He took three spears and plunged them into Absalom's chest while he was still alive, hanging in the oak tree. 15 Then ten of Joab's soldiers closed in on Absalom and finished killing him. (TEV)

Among the 3,000 warriors who II Samuel 15:13-23 and 18:1-3 claim that accompanied David out of Jerusalem during Absalom's rebellion, II Samuel 18:10, 15 above says there were some of them who were loyal to David and some others who were loyal to Joab. Of course, we can deduce from II Samuel 15:18-22 that there were some 600 Philistine warriors who were loyal to their leader and fellow Philistine, Ittai among the 3,000. This means that while David was killing the Philistines to live on their wealth or possessions in I Samuel 27:1-12 these Philistines warriors led by David were involved. In fact, I Samuel 22:1-4, 27:2-7-14 and 30:9-10 and 21-25 strongly suggest that they were the men with David when his Ziklag camp was raided and their family members were carried away captive by the Amalekite raiders. If they were the ones with David in Ziklag for the 16 months that he remained there then there is serious food for thought. It would mean that though Ittai and his fellow Philistines knew that their leader, David who was an Israelite was leading them to destroy their fellow Philistines to provide them and their families food and clothes to live on or sustain them, they did not care because they benefited from the havoc that David was leading them to cause to their fellow Philistines.

Yet, there is another dimension to this fact. I Samuel 27:7-12 says:

> 7 David lived in Philistia for sixteen months. 8 During that time David and his men would attack the people of Geshur, Girzi, and Amalek, who had been living in the region a very long time. He would raid their land as far as Shur, all the way down to Egypt, 9 killing all the men and women and taking the sheep, cattle, donkeys, camels, and even the clothes. Then he would come back to Achish, 10 who would ask him, "Where did you go on a raid this time?" and David would tell him that he had gone to the

southern part of Judah or to the territory of the clan of Jerahmeel or to the territory where the Kenites lived. 11 David would kill everyone, men and women, so that no one could go back to Gath and report what he and his men had really done. This is what David did the whole time he lived in Philistia. 12 But Achish trusted David and said to himself, "He is hated so much by his own people the Israelites that he will have to serve me all his life." (TEV)

Verse 8 says David attacked the people of Geshur, Girzi, Amalek whereas we know from II Samuel 3:3, 13:37-38 and I Chronicles 3:1 confirm that the people of Geshur had their own king and in fact, David's son, Absalom's mother was the princess of Geshur. Therefore, to talk about the people of Geshur not surviving to report David's nefarious activities to King Achish of the Philistines suggests that the Geshurites, Girzites and Amalekites who David killed were original natives of Geshur, Girzi and Amalek who had settled in Achish's Philistine territory. If that be the case, then it means that Ittai and his fellow Philistines who joined David to destroy them in order to have something to live on with their family members did so because they believed that they were not original Philistines like them after all, therefore it is still okay to join their non-Philistine leader to destroy them. That is a serious matter because it lends credence to the value that natives place on non-natives no matter how long the non-natives have been around. Even if the current non-natives are the fourth generation, in order words, their great grandparents, grandparents and parents were born in the land, the original natives still view them as foreigners. Ittai and his fellow 600 Philistine followers of David have not forgotten that the Philistines with foreign ancestral roots are true Philistines like them.

The other thing worth pointing out from the above passage is the fact that usually, when foreigners would do havoc to natives or undermine the interest of their host countries, they often find an ally among the natives. Ittai knew that David was not truthful to their king, Achish but they never betrayed David to Achish. Their reason is that Achish did not care about their personal wellbeing like David did. Foreigners can rarely defraud their land of sojourn without the collaboration of natives. And the natives do collaborate with the fraudulent foreigners because they believe that they are not getting a fair share of their national wealth. Again, I Samuel 27:5-6 says:

> 5 David said to Achish, "If you are my friend, let me have a small town to live in. There is no need, sir, for me to live with you in the capital city." 6 So Achish gave him the town of Ziklag, and for this reason Ziklag has belonged to the kings of Judah ever since. (TEV)

Before someone would blame Ittai and his fellow Philistines and loyalists for supporting 'foreigner David' to undermine their own people such an individual should understand I Samuel 27:5-12 above from the angle of what Achish did wrong on his own part. If he had the interest of his citizens at heart indeed, why would he let the same David who had killed Goliath a native of Gath, the capital city where Achish's throne was located or established and let him go and live away from his constant monitoring. This is the same David who I Samuel

21:10-15 says once feigned madness and he asked his officials to take away from his presence. It is part of the weakness of his rulership that led to the poverty and indebtedness that I Samuel 22:1-4 and II Samuel 15:17-20 say forced Ittai and others to join David as their leader. I Samuel 29:1-11 confirms that Achish's fellow Philistine leaders were able to know even without further facts apart from the killing of Goliath that there is nothing that they as Philistines could ever do to win the loyalty of David genuinely. This points us to the fact that whenever the leadership or ruler of any nation is failing its citizens there would be foreigners who would come over to take undue advantage of the weak national administration structure to undermine the nation. It would not have mattered if it were not happening in contemporary times.

Meanwhile, I Chronicles 12:1-22 confirms that while David was living in Ziklag in the land of the Philistines as King Achish of the Philistines' engaged army commander, some Israelite warriors deserted their sitting King Saul of Israel to join David. The Philistine warriors had joined David before the Israelite warriors decided that the right thing to do was to leave

Saul behind to join David. The reason the Israelite warriors left the land of Israel to join David in the Philistine town of Ziklag was, according to them in I Chronicles 12:16-18, because they had noticed that God no longer supported Saul but He is now with David. Their desertion is serious because unlike I Samuel 22:4 says of Ittai and his fellow Philistines, the Israelite warriors were gainfully employed as commanders and soldiers in the army of Israel. Apparently, there was no national border control of movement as we know it today, so it was easy for them to cross from the territory of Israel into that of the Philistines to join David. I Chronicles 12:21 confirms that the Israelite warriors and their officers who deserted Saul to join David were appointed officers by David in which case David made them feel that they had not lost their officer position by deserting Saul to join him. In any case, some of them might have even joined Saul's army of Israel and appointed officers before David killed Goliath but subsequently withdrew his services because of Saul's relentless threats to David's life.

Recognizing that God supported David against Saul can be interpreted to mean that these Israelites were sure that this same David would become king after Saul and by that time they would become officers in the army of Israel that they deserted to join David while Saul was still alive and sitting king. I Chronicles 12:22 says "Almost every day new men joined David's forces, so that his army was soon enormous. - TEV" This means that even if David wanted to launch an attack to overthrow King Saul, he had enough men and officers to prevail with God's support that he enjoyed more than Saul did. When Achish employed him and gave him Ziklag to live with his men, he had only 600 however, over time, the officers and warriors under David's command had become enormous that should in fact constitute a threat to Achish and his army of the Philistine.

It is important to note that just like Judah considered Hirah a reliable friend that he could accompany to his hometown to live among his own people of Adullam, so we see David regarding Achish a friend to shield him from the threats of Saul. Just as Judah found Hirah a friend to conceal his shame so also David found Ittai and his fellow Philistines as die-hard loyalists to conceal the atrocities that he committed in their land of Philistia. We can call them laudable local allies.

28

NOTORIOUS NATIVITY NATURE/ MENTALITY OR MONSTROUS NATIVITY MINDSET

Native's notoriety is nearly natural and inevitable in practical terms. King Saul ruled Israel for forty years while David ruled after him for the same number of years. While Saul operated his throne from his hometown of Gibeah, David operated from his own tribal headquarter of Hebron for the initial seven and a half years before relocating to Jerusalem also in his tribal region for the remaining 33 years. Neither of them thought it was proper to locate their throne and national headquarters in any other tribe of the nation for the sake of fostering national unity. It was like Saul and David thought or concluded that when God made them rulers of their nation in their lifetime, it was their right to plant the throne in their respective tribal region.

Samuel was trained to be the national leader at Shiloh by Eli only for I Samuel 1:1-2, 7:15-17, 8:1-4, 9:5-18, 15:34 and 19:18-24 to say he relocated his administrative headquarters to his hometown of Ramah in the hill country of Ephraim when he had gathered enough clout to hold sessions from wherever he decided or preferred. If rulers operate from a centralized location in their nation rather than from their own tribal region or hometown, it will contribute to foster cooperation and oneness among the citizens within the same nation or who traditionally make up the nation. Again, while King Saul made his cousin, Abner the head of the army of Israel during his reign, David made his own nephew, Joab, the head of the army of Israel during his own reign.

Consider another version of nativity nonsense that we all engage in discretely. Genesis 16:1-2 and 21:21 say because she was an Egyptian, Hagar got an Egyptian girl to marry her son and only child, Ishmael. When she was sent away with Ishmael, she did not take him back to her native land of Egypt rather Genesis 21:14-20 concludes with the fact that she chose to remain in the wilderness of Paran which is nearer where his father and other members of his family lived. But verse 21 says when it was time for her son to marry, she returned to her native land to get his wife. She could not trust that a non-Egyptian like herself was good enough to be the wife of her son, not even a girl from his father's hometown. Why would the man or woman be good enough to be your spouse but his or her kinsmen are not good enough to be spouse to the child you had with him or her? Genesis 25:27-28 and 27:46 can be interpreted to mean that Rebecca insisted that her beloved son, Jacob must marry from her family while Genesis 28:6-9 says in order to please his father, Esau went to marry his father's niece or Esau's paternal cousin.

One reason it would be unfair to blame Hagar, Rebecca or Esau in this respect is that Genesis 24:1-10 confirms that even Abraham said because Isaac was his covenant child, he must not marry a non-relative. As a result, he sent his chief servant, Eliezer to go to get a wife from among his relatives in the same Mesopotamia. Meanwhile, he confessed in the same Genesis

24:1-10 (3-4, 7) that he knew that God never meant him and his covenant son and descendants to return there. Unfortunately for him, the fact that Genesis 24:11-67 confirms that Isaac married his relative did not stop that relative turned wife by the name of Rebecca from manipulating Isaac to send Abraham's covenant grandson, Jacob back to the same hometown of Mesopotamia that Abraham claimed that neither Isaac nor his covenant son and descendants should not return to for any reason.

How can you say Isaac should not return there yet he must marry a girl from there because they are your relatives – what is the assurance that the relative-wife would not manipulate the same Isaac to return there after your death? In our short-sightedness we contradict ourselves and promote what we think that we are trying to prevent. We disguise our disdain for others discretely. Many are disdainfully delightfuls – they appear to be the most delightful of the earth, yet they conceal their disdain for their fellow humans including those that they seem to be kind to. Much as Isaac did not return to Mesopotamia, Genesis 27:46 and 28:1-5 and 10-22 confirm that he was made to send the carrier of the very sacred covenant that Abraham thought was the very reason Isaac should not return to his original hometown back there.

There are two significant fallouts from Jacob's sojourn in Mesopotamia. First, if not for God's merciful intervention on Jacob's behalf, Laban would not have allowed Jacob to return to Canaan and what would have become of the covenant. Second, it is very curious that Genesis 31:32 and 35:1-3 say:

> 32 But if you find that anyone here has your gods, he will be put to death. Here, with our men as witnesses, look for anything that belongs to you and take what is yours." Jacob did not know that Rachel had stolen Laban's gods.

> 1 God said to Jacob, "Go to Bethel at once, and live there. Build an altar there to me, the God who appeared to you when you were running away from your brother Esau." 2 So Jacob said to his family and to all who were with him, "Get rid of the foreign gods that you have; purify yourselves and put on clean clothes. 3 We are going to leave

here and go to Bethel, where I will build an altar to the God who helped me in the time of my trouble and who has been with me everywhere I have gone." (TEV)

Genesis 31:30-35 and 43-55 tells the full story of how Rachel who Genesis 29:1-31 and 48:5-7 say Jacob loved unreservedly to the extent that not even God could ignore it stole and took the gods that God meant Abraham to have left behind in Mesopotamia to the land of Canaan. There is no doubt that part of the reason Genesis 12:1-3 say God asked Abraham to leave his people behind to go and settle in Canaan was so that Abraham and his descendants would worship Him alone rather than continue to worship the gods of his ancestors.

Genesis 18:17-19 confirms that God made this abundantly clear before Isaac was born. It is the reason He used Moses and all the prophets to repeat to the Israelites that they must not serve any other god beside Him. However, and this is an horrendous version of however, we can sensibly insinuate from the above passage that because Abraham sent his servant to go and get a wife from among his own relatives in his hometown, and the wife that was brought as a result of that insistence sent his covenant grandson back to his hometown, part of the consequence is that the covenant grandson brought back the gods of his ancestors to the land of Canaan where God never meant him or any of his descendants to worship any other god including the gods of Abraham's ancestors. It is like what II Chronicles 18:1-34, 19:1-3, 21:1-20 and 22:1-12 say King Jehoshaphat did to his sons and grandsons.

First, Numbers 27:15-23 includes the fact that whoever serves as the ruler of the nation should have the priest of God who's duty is to confirm God's will for the king to comply with in whatever he does as the ruler of the nation or over his fellow humans. Acts 7:35 confirms that Moses had a God-sent angel that served this purpose for him throughout the 40 years that he led the Israelites. Nevertheless, I Kings 22:1-37 and II Chronicles 18:1-34 say without asking God's approval King Jehoshaphat who II Chronicles 17:1-19 and 20:1-32 confirm had pleased God in all other ways chose to get a wife from among the daughters of King Ahab and Queen Jezebel of Israel despite knowing that they were God certified sinners and evil doers. Second, II Chronicles 21:1-4 says Jehoshaphat's son and successor, Jehoram who had married Ahab's daughter killed his brothers for no reason whatsoever. Third, II Chronicles 22:10-12 says when Jehoshaphat's grandson, Ahaziah who had succeeded Jehoshaphat's son and successor died, Ahab's daughter who Jehoshaphat made the wife to his successor killed Jehoshaphat's great grandsons and took over Jehoshaphat's throne in Jerusalem. This is the very throne that II Samuel 7:12-13 and 16 and I Chronicles 17:11-12 and 14 confirm that God promised Jehoshaphat's ancestor, David that his descendant would occupy forever.

In this respect, Rachel was like Solomon's non-Israelite wives who I Kings 11:1-9 says took their native gods along to be with him in Jerusalem. As a result, they were able to make him join them to worship those gods to the disgust and anger of the God of Israel. It can be said that it is as a result that Exodus 34:10-17 and Deuteronomy 7:1-4 quote God and Moses admonishing the Israelites as follows:

10 The Lord said to Moses, "I now make a covenant with the people of Israel. In their presence I will do great things such as have never been done anywhere on earth among any of the nations. All the people will see what great things I, the Lord, can do, because I am going to do an awesome thing for you. 11 Obey the laws that I am giving you today. I will drive out the Amorites, the Canaanites, the Hittites, the Perizzites, the Hivites, and the Jebusites, as you advance. 12 Do not make any treaties with the people of the country into which you are going, because this could be a fatal trap for you. 13 Instead, tear down their altars, destroy their sacred pillars, and cut down their symbols of the goddess Asherah. 14 "Do not worship any other god, because I, the Lord, tolerate no rivals. 15 Do not make any treaties with the people of the country, because when they worship their pagan gods and sacrifice to them, they will invite you to join them, and you

will be tempted to eat the food they offer to their gods. 16 Your sons might marry those foreign women, who would lead them to be unfaithful to me and to worship their pagan gods. 17 "Do not make gods of metal and worship them.

1 "The Lord your God will bring you into the land that you are going to occupy, and he will drive many nations out of it. As you advance, he will drive out seven nations larger and more powerful than you: the Hittites, the Girgashites, the Amorites, the Canaanites, the Perizzites, the Hivites, and the Jebusites. 2 When the Lord your God places these people in your power and you defeat them, you must put them all to death. Do not make an alliance with them or show them any mercy. 3 Do not marry any of them, and do not let your children marry any of them, 4 because then they would lead your children away from the Lord to worship other gods. If that happens,

the Lord will be angry with you and destroy you at once. (TEV)

Abraham should not have insisted that Isaac's wife must be one of his relatives because he assumed that she would not make him to serve the gods of his ancestors that God of the universe had forbidden him and his covenant child and descendants from worshipping.

Exodus 33:1-3 says after the ensnaring events in the previous chapter 32:1-35 in which the Israelites made the golden calf idol to worship as the god that brought them out of Egyptian bondage and oppression that had endured for 430 years, God of their ancestor said His personal presence would not travel with them again rather an angel would accompany them. However, in the case of Jacob's travel to Laban's place where he ended up spending 20 years before returning to the land of Canaan, Genesis 28:10-19 and 32:1-2 say:

> 10 Jacob left Beersheba and started toward Haran.
> 11 At sunset he came to a holy place and camped there. He lay down to sleep, resting his head on

a stone. 12 He dreamed that he saw a stairway reaching from earth to heaven, with angels going up and coming down on it. 13 And there was the Lord standing beside him. "I am the Lord, the God of Abraham and Isaac," he said. "I will give to you and to your descendants this land on which you are lying. 14 They will be as numerous as the specks of dust on the earth. They will extend their territory in all directions, and through you and your descendants I will bless all the nations. 15 Remember, I will be with you and protect you wherever you go, and I will bring you back to this land. I will not leave you until I have done all that I have promised you. 16 Jacob woke up and said, "The Lord is here! He is in this place, and I didn't know it!" 17 He was afraid and said, "What a terrifying place this is! It must be the house of God; it must be the gate that opens into heaven. 18 Jacob got up early next morning, took the stone that was under his head, and set it up as a memorial. Then he poured olive oil on it to dedicate it to God. 19 He named the place Bethel. (The town there was once known as Luz.)

1 As Jacob went on his way, some angels met him. 2 When he saw them, he said, "This is God's camp"; so he named the place Mahanaim. (TEV)

Verse 15 above quotes God as saying He would accompany Jacob wherever he goes which included his journey to Laban's place. This is like what II Samuel 7:8-9 and I Chronicles 17:7-8 confirm that God told David that He had been with him everywhere he had gone in his lifelong journey. Then, verses 12-13a say while God's angels were ascending and descending on a ladder that reached from heaven to earth the Lord stood beside Jacob to tell him His plans for the journey that Jacob was making to Laban's place. Genesis 31:10-13 says Jacob claimed to have had another dream at the end of his stay at Laban's place in which God's angel explained to him what God had been doing to his benefit throughout the 20 years he had lived with and worked for Laban and that it was the right time for him to return to Canaan. God sent that angel to speak to him in that dream rather than see many angels ascending and descending a ladder like he experienced at the place that he named Bethel at the exit border of the land of Canaan. The next time Jacob would have encounter with angels was when he entered the territory of Canaan on his return journey. Therefore, verses 17 and 1-2 above mean that Jacob left his God assigned home and place of peace and prosperity to another person's God-assigned location of peace and prosperity. It is partly as a result that he endured sufferings and pains that he would never have endured in Canaan which God foreordained to be his permanent place of rest, peace, and prosperity.

When his mother was stage-managing his departure to her brother's place she did not know that it would take the grace of God for him to survive there and return alive and prosperous. Proverbs 14:12 and 16:25 say:

> 12 What you think is the right road may lead to death.

25 What you think is the right road may lead to death. (TEV)

12 There is a way which seems right to a man and appears straight before him, but at the end of it is the way of death.

25 There is a way that seems right to a man and appears straight before him, but at the end of it is the way of death. (AMP)

Abraham did not know that getting a wife from among his relatives would lead to his covenant grandson going back to his hometown and one of the covenant grandson's wives would bring the gods of his ancestors to the land of Canaan. He assumed that the same way that he never allowed his wife to make him to do anything that God never approved so also the covenant son that she bore him would follow in his footsteps never to allow the relative wife that he got for him to make him do anything that God never approved. He did not understand that God is more interested in an individual's attitude towards Him more than where the individual originates from. So long as Joseph's and Moses' wives did not lure them to join their own Egyptian and Midianite peoples respectively to serve their Egyptian and Midianite native gods, God of Israel as we know Him now never cared whether they were Israelites or not.

This means that even Abraham the father of the Christian faith had the mentality of 'my people are trustworthy more than your people'. Further still, Genesis 12:17-20, 26:6-11, 16-33 say:

> 17 But because the king had taken Sarai, the Lord sent terrible diseases on him and on the people of his palace. 18 Then the king sent for Abram and asked him, "What have you done to me? Why didn't you tell me that she was your wife? 19 Why did you say that she was your sister, and let me take her as my wife? Here is your wife; take her and get out!" 20 The king gave orders to his men, so they took Abram and put him out of the country, together with his wife and everything he owned.

6 So Isaac lived at Gerar. 7 When the men there asked about his wife, he said that she was his sister. He would not admit that she was his wife, because he was afraid that the men there would kill him to get Rebecca, who was very beautiful. 8 When Isaac had been there for some time, King Abimelech looked down from his window and saw Isaac and Rebecca making love. 9 Abimelech sent for Isaac and said, "So she is your wife! Why did you say she was your sister?" He answered, "I thought I would be killed if I said she was my wife." 10 "What have you done to us?" Abimelech said. "One of my men might easily have slept with your wife, and you would have been responsible for our guilt." 11 Abimelech warned all the people: "Anyone who mistreats this man or his wife will be put to death."

16 Then Abimelech said to Isaac, "Leave our country. You have become more powerful than we are." 17 So Isaac left and set up his camp in

Gerar Valley, where he stayed for some time. 18 He dug once again the wells which had been dug during the time of Abraham and which the Philistines had stopped up after Abraham's death. Isaac gave the wells the same names that his father had given them. 19 Isaac's servants dug a well in the valley and found water. 20 The shepherds of Gerar quarreled with Isaac's shepherds and said, "This water belongs to us." So Isaac named the well "Quarrel." 21 Isaac's servants dug another well, and there was a quarrel about that one also, so he named it "Enmity." 22 He moved away from there and dug another well. There was no dispute about this one, so he named it "Freedom." He said, "Now the Lord has given us freedom to live in the land, and we will be prosperous here." 23 Isaac left and went to Beersheba. 24 That night the Lord appeared to him and said, "I am the God of your father Abraham. Do not be afraid; I am with you. I will bless you and give you many descendants because of my promise to my servant Abraham." 25 Isaac built an altar there and worshiped the Lord. Then he set up his camp there, and his servants dug another well. 26 Abimelech came from Gerar with Ahuzzath his adviser and Phicol the commander of his army to see Isaac. 27 So Isaac asked, "Why have you now come to see me, when you were so unfriendly to me before and made me leave your country?" 28 They answered, "Now we know that the Lord is with you, and we think that there should be a solemn agreement between us. We want you to promise 29 that you will not harm us, just as we did not harm you. We were kind to you and let you go peacefully. Now it is clear that the Lord has blessed you." 30 Isaac prepared a feast for them, and they ate and drank. 31 Early next morning each man made his promise and sealed it with a vow. Isaac said good-bye to them, and they parted as friends. 32 On that day Isaac's servants came and told him about the well which they had dug. They said, "We have found water." 33 He named the well "Vow." That is how the city of Beersheba got its name. (TEV)

It is very striking that once the king of Egypt found that he could not have the wife of the stranger in his kingdom, he sent him and his wife away. Even when he knew that the stranger had a greater God, he did not consider it important to join the stranger to worship and serve such powerful God who protected His worshipper and would not allow anyone to do anything harmful to him. This means that natives cannot humble themselves to the extent of joining any stranger or migrant to do anything that the stranger suggests no matter how rewarding. When Abimelech and his people knew that Isaac had the support of the same great God who had helped his father, Abraham, rather than join him to worship the great God he decided to drive Isaac away from his domain, although he later went to make alliance with him. Natives consider it insulting to seem to be subject to any foreigner in their domain. This is part of the reason we are not sure if the Pharaoh who oppressed the Israelites after the reign and death of Joseph as the Prime Minister of Egypt did so because he was sad to remember that Joseph was said to have enslaved the Egyptians during his reign as the Prime Minister.

It seems that natives do believe that it is because their nation is better that other nationals choose to spend their resources to come over to live among them. They believe that if their nation was not better, such persons would not bother to come and live with them. Sometimes, it seems that they are right in the sense that Elimelech took his wife and two sons to relocate to Moab because there was famine in his hometown of Bethlehem and nation of Israel and going to Moab meant that the economy of Moab was better in the immediate. The rich woman of Shunem went to the land of Philistia because there was famine in the land of Israel. Moses went to Midian because his life was not safe in Egypt. Just as Pharaoh made Abraham leave his country so also Abimelech made Isaac leave his country except that Pharaoh never went to make peace with Abraham later like Abimelech later went to make peace with Isaac. It is very striking to observe that Abimelech joined his subjects or Philistine kinsmen to drive Isaac away only for him to go behind his people to make peace agreement with Isaac. He could have as well used his royal authority to stop his people from oppressing or persecuting Isaac in the first instance.

Genesis 12:10-16, 20:1-11 and 26:6-7 can be said to mean that Abraham and Isaac believed that non-natives of Mesopotamia men do kill the husbands of beautiful woman so that they could have such beautiful woman for themselves. That is nothing short of holier than thou mindset. Isaac was not born when Abraham claimed that Egyptian men kill non-Egyptian to have their wives. In fact, Genesis 12:1-16 confirms that Abraham was 75 years old when he did while Genesis 21:1-8 confirms that Isaac was born when Abraham was 100 years old while Genesis 24:1-67 says Abraham was 140 years old when Isaac married his wife. Then, Genesis 25:1-11 confirms that Isaac was 75 years old when Abraham died and Genesis 26:1-7 suggests that it was some years after Abraham's death when Isaac followed in Abraham's footsteps to give the impression that only men from their hometown of Mesopotamia who are Godly enough to refrain from killing other men to have their beautiful wives.

Genesis 43:23 confirms that Egyptians despised the Hebrews because the Hebrews are predominantly shepherds. The Hebrews were not engaged in any criminal activity just as the Egyptians do eat meat from animals reared by the professional shepherds. What is the logic in consuming a product yet despise the producers of the product? If you eat a product so you would not starve to death or give your body nutrient that it needs, why still despise the producer of such products? It does not make sense.

29

Home-based Immigrants or Native Stranger/ Strangers at Home

Genesis 30:22-25 confirms that Joseph was born in Haran and partly bred there and partly at Canaan only for Genesis 37 and 39-50 to imply that God assigned his delightful destiny and adult life to be spent in Egypt but his body returned to Canaan for burial long after his death. As an individual, he was a stranger in Canaan, and it was such that the teenage years he spent in Canaan were filled with persecution and associated sorrows. Even when his father made concerted efforts to make life pleasant for him, his older siblings made life miserable for him. It was like though he could claim to be a Canaanite because his father lived there but God did not assign comfort and convenience for him in Canaan. As a result, and for the sake of his father's love alone, his ten older brothers abhorred him even to death.

This aspect of Joseph's life experience represents persons whose God-assigned greatness and glory while on earth is meant to be harnessed and enjoyed outside their land of birth even when they might have been born and bred in their parent's traditional hometown. The success or achievement of such persons is greatest when they live and operate outside their hometown. David was born and bred in Bethlehem of Judah, when he would become famous, it was when he led the defeat of Goliath in the battle fought in the region of Judah before Saul's persecution drove him from one part of Israel to another. However, when he would become king according to God's plan, it was in Hebron, the headquarters of his tribe of Judah. After becoming the king of other tribes of Israel in addition to Judah, he made Jerusalem in the region of Judah his capital city. He enjoyed his throne in Jerusalem for the last 33 years where he died and was buried.

There is the subject of the stranger at the scene, God sponsored delightful difference maker stranger at the scene or the stranger strong and great native like when I Samuel 9:1-27, 10:1-27 and 11:1-12 confirm that after Saul had been anointed king of Israel, when the Ammonites threatened the people of Jabesh Gilead, Saul was the only Israelite who had the confidence to lead the defeat of the Ammonites. The Delightfully Different or The Delightful Difference Maker. I Samuel 13:1-23 and 14:1-46 confirm that Jonathan was the only stranger among the Israelite warriors in the battle against the Philistines. I Samuel 17:1-58 confirms that David was the only Israelites who could confront and kill Goliath after mesmerizing the Israelite warriors in the preceding 40 days and nights before David arrived at the battlefield. Moses was the stranger among the Israelites in the matter of freeing the Israelites from Egyptians. God empowered him to think, talk and act differently to free the Israelites. Joseph was the different and stranger personality among the sons of Jacob. Genesis 37:1-2 says he was the one who recognized that the character and conduct of some of his older brothers were less than appropriate and reported same to their father.

Verses 3-24 confirm that even when he knew that his older brothers hated him, he still shared his God-given dreams with them and in fact, gladly took food to them to prove that he did not hate them in return or repaid their evil with good.

Genesis 35:22 and 39:1-20 can be interpreted to mean that while his eldest brother readily committed incest, he would not have his boss' wife who threw herself at him. Then, Genesis 37:12-36, 39:6-20 and 45:1-28 confirm that while his older brothers concealed the truth of what happened to him on the day he went to give food to them for 22 years Joseph concealed the real truth of what transpired between him and Potiphar's wife probably to avoid creating room for Potiphar to distrust his wife as she deserved. Genesis 39:9 says part of the reason he did not agree to his master's wife's advances was because he feared God something that his brothers did not care about. Genesis 45:4-9 and 50:15-21 confirm that when he should have punished his older brothers for the evil that they did to him earlier he considered God's overall plans for them as a family and forgave them freely. Even his brotherhood of wickedness older siblings knew surely that they deserved whatever punishment he decided to implement on them.

Then, there is the subject of the other personal caustic cost of greatness. I Samuel 22:16-23 recounts the personal cost that the priest Abiathar suffered to become the priest using the ephod to guide David. Esther lost her own parents and was nurtured by her older cousin, Mordecai whose strict guidance prepared her for the position of the Queen of the Persian Empire in her adult life. Haman paid the high price that led to Mordecai becoming the Prime Minister of the Persian Empire. Ruth lost her first and young husband and left her family and kinsmen behind in Moab to sojourn as a stranger in Bethlehem to become married to Boaz and as a result she is listed among the matriarchs of mankind's Messiah.

In another development, Queen Esther, and her older/father-figure cousin who became the Prime Minister of the Persian Empire became relevant outside their native nation of Israel. They and the great Apostle Paul hailed from the same Israelite tribe of Benjamin and God assigned Paul's apostolic relevance outside the land of Israel as well. Now, we cannot say if this is part of the root cause of the problem that King Saul had when he was made king of Israel outside his hometown but returned home to establish his throne and rule Israel from his hometown. Most of the prominent members of the tribe of Benjamin became powerful away from home and Saul who did not operate outside his tribal part of Benjamin did not end well or gloriously.

Moses was born and bred in Egypt though he never thought of himself as an Egyptian but an Israelite foreigner in Egypt. True to his feelings, he became famous for the role he played in leading the Israelites out of Egypt to enable them take possession of Canaan which God assigned to them. Likewise, though Esau was born and bred in Canaan, he was always at home and never became established or enjoyed rest in life until he founded his own nation in the famous hill-country of Edom. Upon taking over the land of Edom from the original owners by God's help, there is no record that he continued to live the restless lifestyle he was previously famous for. Therefore, he was restless as a young man because God's spirit kept nudging him that he had not arrived where God meant for him to possess permanently in life.

That is "Arise to Arrive and Accomplish" which is self-explanatory. It is an admonition to rise and run to God's designated location of greatness and glory for you. It took Esau the first 120 years to take permanent possession of the land of Edom which Genesis 33:1-17, 36:1-43, Deuteronomy 2:12 and 22 and I Chronicles 1:34-54 implied that God assigned to him and his descendants. Genesis 35:27-28 and 36:1-8 confirm that it was after his father had died at the age of 180 that Jacob had the courage to move in to take over their traditional family house in Canaan from him. Genesis 32:1-3, 33:16, 35:27-29 and 36:1-43 can be safely interpreted to mean that encouraged by the fact that he had established his own kingdom in the hill country of Edom, Esau readily left Canaan when they found out that the family estate at Canaan was too small to accommodate their wealth.

Again, it is important to note that Esau had built Edom for himself and his descendants before Jacob returned from Laban's home after twenty years' sojourn but never moved to Edom to live permanently until their father had died and they had given him a befitting burial, and Jacob arrived from Bethel to formally take possession of the family house in Canaan. Our focus will not permit us to dabble into the subject of "Esau and His Father" in detail but it is partly because of the fact that he stayed glued to his father as long as the old man lived and the fact that he ensured that he spent the period to identify and claim the land which God meant for him. Even after claiming the land, Esau remained with his father until he died before he relocated to where God meant for him and his descendants. He maximized the cordial relationship he enjoyed with his father. Fortunately for him, his mother who never wished him well in life left him and his father behind early enough for him to achieve greatness as God meant for him.

However, it is important to note that though God did not ordain the land of Canaan for him as permanent possession, he lived in Canaan while he went to claim the land of Edom victoriously by God's help and return to continue in Canaan because he did not want to leave his father in the hands of the servants without him being present to ensure that his father was well taken care of. This is important because Jacob whom God meant to take over the land of Canaan from their father was never there to protect the father in his most vulnerable years of old age. In fact, Jacob never did anything to the personal benefit of their father like Esau did for which we can claim that God rewarded him accordingly. Only God's will and plan before they were born made Jacob to get the land of Canaan from their father, who got it from their grandfather for the same reason.

It is vital to note that Esau was smart enough to plan for his own future and that of his children and by extension descendants while taking care of his beloved father. He did not put his own life on hold because he must support his father who Genesis 25:27-28 says preferred him only because of what his father benefited from him. Genesis 32:1-3, 33:1, 3-4, 8-9, 16 say:

> 1 As Jacob went on his way, some angels met him.
> 2 When he saw them, he said, "This is God's camp"; so he named the place Mahanaim. 3 Jacob

sent messengers ahead of him to his brother Esau in the country of Edom.

1 Jacob saw Esau coming with his four hundred men, so he divided the children among Leah, Rachel, and the two concubines. 3 Jacob went ahead of them and bowed down to the ground seven times as he approached his brother. 4 But Esau ran to meet him, threw his arms around him, and kissed him. They were both crying. 8 Esau asked, "What about that other group I met? What did that mean?" Jacob answered, "It was to gain your favor." 9 But Esau said, "I have enough, my brother; keep what you have." 16 So that day Esau started on his way back to Edom. (TEV)

This means that by the time Jacob returned from Laban's place after 20 years, Esau had his own place in Edom and in fact, Jacob was very much aware of that fact hence he is said to have sent his servants there to inform Esau of his return to Canaan.

He did not prepare to battle Jacob for the permanent possession of the family house where Jacob left him behind to go to their maternal uncle's place. Some home-based relatives would stay put in the traditional family house and establish themselves in such a way that their relatives or siblings who travelled abroad would never return to lay claim to any part of the family house that they left to travel abroad. Esau prepared to give up the family house in case, Jacob returned to want to claim it. Esau understood the implication of the kind of father he had. He knew that his father lacked the will power to help him obtain anything. He knew that his father's acclaimed love or preference for him was motivated solely by only what he could offer his father and therefore, his father did not love him to the extent of wanting to do anything for his personal benefit. He knew that just to give him blessing with the words of his mouth, his father could not do it easily, he had to force his father to teach him what he needed to do to survive in life.

The claim by Genesis 27:37-40 that Isaac did not tell Esau the solution to the loss of blessing to Jacob until Esau put pressure on Isaac is an unprecedented indictment of Isaac.

What explanation do you have for waiting for the son that you claim to love to put pressure on you before you will tell him the solution that he needed to succeed for the rest of his lifetime? In such circumstances, the sensible question is what if the individual were not your acclaimed beloved son or daughter what you would have done. It means that no matter the pressure put on you, you will never reveal the solution he needed to him. Esau understood the weakness of his father and worked hard to survive despite it. If you are helping someone who has nothing to offer you in return, it is for your own benefit to ensure that you do not liquidate yourself because of the assistance that you are rendering to him. There are persons who do not have the nature to be of help to anyone including those that benefit them the most. Isaac was not a poor man or someone who lacked the grace of God to be of help to who ever he decides to help but he just lacks the necessary guts, management skills and relevant abilities to be of help to even those that he knows deserved some reward from him. How can a father, the head of the household not be able to implement an idea as simple as giving blessing to his beloved son without giving room for someone to hijack it?

In the first place, he should not have made the subject of pronouncing blessing on Esau a hide and seek game or affair. There is no secret about his preference for Esau and their mother's preference for Jacob. Since he had the blessing to be given out and had decided that he had enough reasons to give it to Esau, he merely needed to call Esau in the presence of everyone, ask him to kneel in front him and go ahead to pronounce the blessing. Afterwards tell Esau to go get his favourite meal to celebrate the event and whoever is not comfortable with what he has just done can as well go ahead to lick his wounds. What use is having the asset of authority and you cannot use it appropriately when you deem fit? You should not have the authority in the first place. It would be ridiculous for anyone to think that he should not have used his God-given authority as he deemed fit. Whoever says so has a weak argument because those who did not have it ended up manipulating him to give it to the persons, he never meant it for. That is the real problem; if you fail to use it those who do not deserve it would hijack it against your wish so your attempt to be decent causes permanent pain to those who do not deserve such pain.

Someone might think how the story of Isaac's failings and Esau's survival strategy in the circumstances that he found himself and his mother and sibling concern surviving among strangers, it is quite simple. Strangers must make provision for the family members that they left behind. Not all left behind relatives and family members would behave sensibly like Esau who ensured that before his sibling who travelled abroad returned, he too had established himself. There are strangers who see themselves as the God-sent saviour to the economic survival misfortune of the relatives that they left behind at home. They fail to plan for their personal survival upon their return home. Esau understood that he was no better than a stranger in Canaan where he was born on the same day with Jacob. He knew that one day he would have to leave the family house for Jacob because by reason of God's plan and their father's inability to bless him above Jacob, he would have to relocate to where God meant for him. So, while taking care of his aged father in the absence of Jacob and their mother he made provision for himself by preparing a personal abode in the hill country of Edom. Edom is home and Canaan is his strange land refers to no other but Esau.

On the other hand, I Samuel 27:1-12 confirms in verse 7 that the period that David ever spent outside his nation of Israel was 16 months which he lived in the land of the Philistines as King Achish's guest while the total number of years the rich woman of Shunem ever lived outside her place of birth was seven years that her Prophet Elisha stipulated she should live outside. This is in sharp contrast to someone like Abraham and Joseph who spent longer part or percentage of their lifetime outside where they were born originally. Genesis 37:1-36 and 39:1-29, 40:1-26 and 41:1-57 strongly suggest that Joseph spent 93 of the 110 years he lived outside Canaan even when he would request that his body be returned to Canaan to be buried. Exodus 2:1-24, 3:1-22 and 4:1-31, Deuteronomy 31:1-2, 32:45-52 and 34:1-8 and 10-12 and Acts 7:17-36 can be interpreted to mean that Moses spent 40 years in Egypt where he was born but could not claim as his permanent home, spent another 40 years in Midian before spending the last 40 years in the wilderness between Egypt and Canaan and finally died at the age of 120 without stepping into Canaan in his lifetime though Deuteronomy 32:48-52 and 34:1-8 and 10-12 confirm that he only saw it from afar. He was assumed to have been buried in the periphery of Canaan. Apparently, he did not like the strange land he lived just as he never had the privilege to live and enjoy the homeland he cherished. This is in contrast to the experience of Nehemiah who lived in the Persian Empire but cherished his native land of Jerusalem and got the privilege to go over there to contribute meaningfully to the development of the place that he regarded highly because his ancestors were buried there. Nehemiah took considerable pride in his land of nativity and was able to do something about it by God's help, the support of his boss in the foreign land he lived and natives back home.

Nehemiah's case introduces the dimension that migrants could get the support of their powerful hosts to return home to improve the lives of their kinsmen they left behind at home. It was the misfortune of captivity that transported Nehemiah from his cherished homeland to become a foreigner in Suza, the capital city of the Persian Empire. There he had the privilege of working for the Emperor whose favour he sought and got by God's help and returned home to improve the wellbeing of his kinsmen. His cherished hometown was part of the empire his boss ruled and the support his boss commanded was provided for him when he arrived home and he used it to help his people powerfully and profitably. He was a needed native in foreign land. This means that his native land needed him while he lived in the foreign land. The fact that living abroad enabled him to work directly for the Emperor did not make Nehemiah to lose the consciousness of his roots. This is nativity allegiance in foreign land. There are persons whose interest in their native land literally dies once they have spent some years in the foreign land they find themselves. Even when Abraham had left home, he was still finding reasons to get in touch with home like when he insisted that Isaac's wife must be brought from his kinsmen at home. Joseph's reaction when he saw his brothers in Egypt suggests that he had always been eager to meet with them and particularly their father who left a strong impression of love, care and comfort on his heart when he was young.

The story of Nehemiah's return home to be of help to his fellow natives highlights another matter altogether. First, Nehemiah 2:17-19 says some natives of Judah's neighbouring nations did not want Nehemiah and other willing Jews to do anything to improve the rating of the Jews as Nehemiah determined to. Second, Nehemiah 4:1-23 details their efforts to prevent the project that Nehemiah believed would add value and respect to the lives of his fellow Jews in Jerusalem and beyond and how they overcame the opposition. Third, the most heart breaking aspect of the story is that Nehemiah 6:1-19 indicates that (1) even prominent Jews were among those who joined hands with the non-Jews to work against the completion of the project, (2) there were Jews who took up the responsibility of extracting Nehemiah's opinion of the enemies of his efforts to take to the enemies as well as bring their views to Nehemiah. That means that rather than join other Jews to contribute to the national project that would benefit them and others they chose to be tail bearers between persons that they knew did not like one another. How can a God approved project be going on and there would some of God's own people who cannot consider how they can be part of it rather they determined to spend their time and energy on unprofitable tale-bearing? To say the Jews who dedicated themselves to serve as such inglorious intermediaries between Nehemiah and his detractors are tortuous tale bearers is an understatement. There is profitable and unprofitable tale bearing in this world just as there are good news bringers (messengers of joy and happiness) on the one hand and bad news bringers (messengers of sorrow and sadness) on the other hand. It is good to talk about Jesus' mission on earth to as many as possible rather than talk about how deep some persons resent one another.

The Jews at home did not think that it was their responsibility to do anything to improve the rating of the Jews in the eyes of their neighbouring nations. Then, someone by the name of Nehemiah returned from abroad to do something tangible about it for the benefit of all Jews both at home and abroad yet, you still find some Jews not thinking that it was an idea good enough for them to support. It does not add up. But more importantly, it teaches us that there are natives who are so comfortable with the sickening status quo that they would do anything to stop whoever determines to change the status quo for the better. Nehemiah 6:1-19 says:

1 Sanballat, Tobiah, Geshem, and the rest of our enemies heard that we had finished building the wall and that there were no gaps left in it, although we still had not set up the gates in the gateways. 2 So Sanballat and Geshem sent me a message, suggesting that I meet with them in one of the villages in the Plain of Ono. This was a trick of theirs to try to harm me. 3 I sent messengers to say to them, "I am doing important work and can't go down there. I am not going to let the work stop just to go and see you." 4 They sent me the same message four times, and each time I sent them the same reply. 5 Then Sanballat sent one of his servants to me with a fifth message, this one in the form of an unsealed letter. 6 It read: "Geshem tells me that a rumor is going around among the neighboring peoples that you and the Jewish people intend to revolt and that this is why you are rebuilding the wall. He also says you plan to make yourself king 7 and that you have arranged

for some prophets to proclaim in Jerusalem that you are the king of Judah. His Majesty is certain to hear about this, so I suggest that you and I meet to talk the situation over." 8 I sent a reply to him: "Nothing of what you are saying is true. You have made it all up yourself." 9 They were trying to frighten us into stopping work. I prayed, "But now, God, make me strong!" 10 About this time I went to visit Shemaiah, the son of Delaiah and grandson of Mehetabel, who was unable to leave his house. He said to me, "You and I must go and hide together in the Holy Place of the Temple and lock the doors, because they are coming to kill you. Any night now they will come to kill you." 11 I answered, "I'm not the kind of person that runs and hides. Do you think I would try to save my life by hiding in the Temple? I won't do it. 12 When I thought it over, I realized that God had not spoken to Shemaiah, but that Tobiah and Sanballat had bribed him to give me this warning. 13 They hired him to frighten me into sinning, so that they could ruin my reputation and humiliate me.

14 I prayed, "God, remember what Tobiah and Sanballat have done and punish them. Remember that woman Noadiah and all the other prophets who tried to frighten me."

15 After fifty-two days of work the entire wall was finished on the twenty-fifth day of the month of Elul. 16 When our enemies in the surrounding nations heard this, they realized that they had lost face, since everyone knew that the work had been done with God's help. 17 During all this time the Jewish leaders had been in correspondence with Tobiah. 18 Many people in Judah were on his side because of his Jewish father-in-law, Shecaniah son of Arah. In addition, his son Jehohanan had married the daughter of Meshullam son of Berechiah. 19 People would talk in front of me

about all the good deeds Tobiah had done and would tell him everything I said. And he kept sending me letters to try to frighten me. (TEV)

There are natives who prefer that foreigners treat them despitefully because of some benefits that they are getting from such oppressive foreigners in their own land. The story of Nehemiah is very striking in some respects, he did not have problems with his boss in the foreign land where he lived rather it was at home that he had issues or opposition to the idea that he believed would improve the lives of his fellow Jews at home. If the project was never started and completed because some Jews joined forces with the formidable force of the strangers and the Jews despising of the Jews continued unabated, how is that supposed to be the fault of God or the individual that God empowered to come over to help the people? That question is very vital because some think that God is not doing enough to help the weak and poor of society or condoning evil on earth. Nehemiah got all that he needed to get the project started and completed before he returned. The only thing that he needed from his fellow Jews was cooperation to concentrate on the project, rather than render that cooperation zealously some chose to join with the enemies of the improvement on the wellbeing of the Jews to hinder the project. Even some leading Jewish citizens joined forces with the opposition to the project. How could there be a section of leading citizens of any nation be satisfied with the despising of their own people to the extent that they do not want anyone to do something to stop it? It is stressful to think about – more than disheartening. Whoever is not zealous about the wellbeing of his own people is not fit to be considered a leading citizen among his people because the primary purpose of leadership is to add value to the lives of the commoners, any and every other thing is an addition or secondary. God who made the earth and put humans there to live established the position of leadership for this primary reason to add value to the lives of the weak. It is as a result that we say leaders lighten the burden of the less privileged of society.

30

Do Not Flaunt Your Success and Affluence

This could have been titled Flaunting Success and Affluence Afflicts. So long as Laban and his sons saw that Jacob had become richer than them, Genesis 31:1-29 can be said to confirm that they hated him for it. Experience has shown that natives are readily envious, jealous and would seek to afflict any stranger who comes over to prosper more than them. As we said earlier, Genesis 26:1-33 confirms that the Philistines hated Isaac for prospering more than them during famine. If Isaac were a fellow native who prospered greatly during famine, they would not have minded and would have even celebrated him greatly. Great prosperity does not earn a foreigner the same level of respect, honour and praises that it earns a native because of envy and jealousy by the natives who are in the majority in the environment where the stranger prospered. This gives rise to what can be called the "Offensive Affluence Obstructing Deserved Influence". Affluence and influence are supposed to go together but is not always the case for a fortunate and God-favoured foreigner. It is not only ill-gotten affluence that produces influence that is offensive rather there are legitimate affluence and influence that offends depending on several factors which may include the beneficiary's background in relation to where he lives and/or who he is involved with, either as recipient or watcher.

As we all know, when you are prosperous, even your relatives would be filled with envy and jealousy for the basic reason that you are proving that they are lazy, unwise, and unproductive. Therefore, we should expect that it would be worst when you are among natives where you are a stranger. When you drive a better car, live in a better house, and enjoy what is luxury by the standard of the locality, you are courting serious trouble. These days, people claim that they are contributing to the economy of their host societies and as a result the natives should be grateful to them rather than envy and hate them for their success, sorry, such persons can say that to the marines. Man is not designed to reason, cherish, and reward a foreigner who came over to make money and lord it over them by enjoying a higher standard of living that the natives cannot attain in their own land. The dual politics of prosperity and migration do not allow it.

I Samuel 17:1-58 can be interpreted to mean that because Eliab understood that if his baby brother, David killed Goliath who he and others could not in the previous 40 days and nights, it would be interpreted to mean that he is incapable of achieving in his chosen profession of soldiering – it was as a result of that heart hidden reason that he tried to discourage David from making an attempt at killing Goliath. If a professor fails to solve a problem in his field of study and any of his students does, the professor's sense of failure would be worsened than if his senior professor colleague solved the same problem.

There are persons who would not see anything wrong with Eliab's reaction to David on the day because they believe that David was really insulting his older siblings by standing up to say he could solve the problem that his older brothers led by Eliab could not. This is particularly so because this was not the first time that he had put his older brothers to shame. There are successes that carry along with them the sense of shame. If an amateur solves a problem that a certified professional could not, it rubs the grease or powder of shame on the face of the experienced professional, sometimes permanently. David started when I Samuel 16:1-13 recounts that when the revered mighty man of God, Samuel visited their home to anoint someone who would rule their nation after the sitting King Saul, they were side-tracked to anoint David which means that though they were older, he was a better person to be king than any of them. As if that was not enough, I Samuel 16:14-23 says when the sitting king thought that he needed one of their father's son to serve in his palace, it was this same David who was chosen above them. Meanwhile, I Samuel 17:12-25 confirms that before David arrived at the battlefield their current king had said to their hearing that whoever killed Goliath would get a great reward, become the king's son-in-law as well as exempt his father and his household members from paying of taxes. Eliab and his likes could not live with the shameful implication or reality of David's unhindered speedy travel to prominence beside them. And just as Eliab feared, once David killed Goliath, he became a household name in addition to becoming an officer in Saul-led army of Israel while Eliab, Abinadab and Shammah remained without any rank in the same army of Israel.

Genesis 37:1-36 says for daring to suggest that he would be greater or that they would be subject to him, Joseph's older brothers threatened his life. His case is stressful in this respect because he had not even become greater than them. He did not even make the claim in plain language rather he only told them about the dreams that he had and they quickly interpreted it to mean that he would be greater and they would be subject to him. To worsen it, verses 10-11 say even his father who claimed to love him more than his older brothers scolded him for having such dreams. Can you imagine been blamed for having a dream as if any can conjure the kind of dreams that favor him during his sleep all by herself at the expense of others. If they had said he made up the dreams – they did not believe that he really had any such dreams it would make sense but to blame him for having any dream is ridiculous. The fact that they believed that Joseph's claim that he had dreams meant that Joseph was an honest person who says only what happened. They could not doubt the fact that he had the dreams that he claimed that he had but they could not reason further if God gave him the dream and if God did why would God make such decision over them.

If his father were to have learnt anything good from his mother, Rebecca, since he considered Joseph's dreams to be strange, he should have followed in his mother's footsteps in Genesis 25:19-24 to go and ask God for clarification. When his mother had what she understood to be a strange experience with her pregnancy, she went to find out its meaning from God rather than blame her husband who impregnated her. Genesis 37:1-11 is very striking – verse 3 says Jacob claimed to love Joseph more than his other children. Verse 4 says because of his loquacious love or precarious and pain prompting preference for Joseph, Joseph's ten older brothers hated Joseph. That means that the one point of good that Jacob did for Joseph caused Joseph ten points of pains. The benefit from such show of love is not worth it for the reaper or beneficiary. It would have been better if Jacob did not show greater love for Joseph.

In the consumption benefit concept of marginal utility in basic economic concept of opportunity cost or cost-benefit-analysis (CBA) meant that Joseph would have been better off without Jacob's so-called love. Bearing in mind that Jacob provoked his older brothers to detest him, verses 5-9 say the older brothers persecuted him even more for his dreams that they concluded demeaned them compared to Joseph. Their persecution of someone that they never liked seemed understandable than when verses 10-11 recount that his father who claimed to love him scolded him upon learning of the dreams. Scolding him for the dreams meant that he did not like the meaning of the dreams. If the man who claimed to love him did not like the implications of the dream why blame his haters for persecuting him for the same dreams?

Some practically put their lives on hold mourning endlessly over the fact that someone did not show them the depth of love that they think they desired or deserved or both from such a person. They do not realize that they are better off without the love of such a person. If your parent abandoned you before you could recognize him or her yet you still grew up to know the difference between right and wrong and you could afford to live on your own by God's help, it means that you are better off in life without such a parent. It would be a waste of your time to lament that you never enjoyed his or her parental love. The only pain is when such a parent wants a relationship with you because he or she thinks that she needs you in his or her old age. Esther did not enjoy the love of her parents while growing up before she lived a delightful life. She did not put her life on hold because of the absence of her parents since she was a child. She lived her life with those who God provided to play the role of loving parents in her life.

It is not so sensible to lock-down your life because of past bad experience. If your parent failed to be there for you when he or she should, the shame should be on that irresponsible individual rather than for you to stop living delightfully. God made the world in a diverse manner. We have mountains, valleys, deserts, and green pastures. It is not helpful to insist that your life must be picture perfect with that of your friend in the matter of experience. If your friend had his parents from childhood until adult age it is not enough reason to kill yourself because your parents were not there for you as a growing child. Live your life the way that God has allowed it to play out. It is not helpful to insist that one must experience everything good that a companion experienced. God never designed the same pattern for two people. The commonest example is the story of Esau and Jacob, though they were twin brothers God meant their lifelong experience to be different. Their demeanour was completely opposite. It is helpful to understand the way God patterned one's life and be contented with it.

Genesis 25:25-28 confirms that Jacob stayed at home while his twin brother, Esau went out frequently when they grew up. A grown man stayed at home while his peer went out to work hard to earn a living. As a rich man's wife, their mother stayed home which means that Jacob stayed home with their mother more than his brother. So, what did Jacob learn from their mother during those years that he engaged in the self-employment of fulltime idleness and idle talks with his mother? How did his discussions with his mother never digressed to the fact that when his mother had strange experience with their pregnancy she went to find out the meaning from God who readily gave her the vital information she needed about their diverse destinies? That is how he failed to take the initiative to ask God what he should do when Laban tormented him in Haran for 20 years. He waited until God took the initiative to come to his aid as if he were forbidden from taking the initiative to consult God.

If he had consulted God about the implications of Joseph's dreams, he would have found out that he and the rest of his family members would need Joseph's greatness during the last 17 years of his life. Jacob and his older sons would have known that they would not be able to stop God's plan to make Joseph greater than them. Therefore, their best bet was to woo Joseph's favour in advance by being kind to him in the present rather than be angrier at him over the dreams. Even if we excuse his older sons who were younger, Jacob who was not less than 90 years at the time should have behaved or reacted much better to the realization that Joseph would be greater than the rest of them. God meant success, achievement, prosperity, and greatness to benefit mankind but 'the sickening souls among the sons of men' have turned it into a sustained source of sadness, sorrow, and a nightmare for themselves because of greed, envy, and jealousy. Once they can suspect that their neighbor is going to be successful and great, they would start to do anything and everything humanly possible to work against him and his imminent greatness. If a man could scold his beloved son for suggesting that he would be greater than he and other family members, what would such a man do to any of his unloved sons who makes similar claim? What manner of father does not wish his son to be greater than him or her? What if he or she was Jesse who became relevant and respected because of his youngest son, David – what would he have done? It is one of the sickening signs of parenting failures to let your children realize that you love one of them more than the others or you are not pleased that he or she is greater than you are. It is parental and family-life abomination that should be condemned in its entirety wherever and whenever it is practiced. It is against the ethics of parenting and family life.

A lawyer concealed his success and prosperity from his wife and relatives for many years. By the time he would reveal his real worth to his wife, he had built a house for his wife, himself, and each of their children. His wife wept for joy on the day he took her to the house that he had built in her name. His wisdom was that once he found out that his wife and most of his relatives loved to party and spend even the money, they have not earned he did not waste his time and effort to dissuade them. He left them to fool themselves believing and living as if the greatest good thing anyone could do with his life is to spend all that he had earned to host lavish parties. He left them alone to concentrate on his focus which was to lay a strong economic base for their children and enough to live on in their old age as husband and wife. So long as he did, his wife and relatives assumed that he was not making enough money as a legal practitioner. When his wife and relatives have chosen not to plan for a better future he decided to and his wife honoured him for the rest of his lifetime for been smarter not necessarily academically but in basic wisdom for laudable living. That is where Jacob failed his older sons. If he had found out and known that it was part of God's plans for them, he should have educated the older children on why they should embrace the plans for Joseph's greatness rather than opposing it.

Jacob and his older sons could not live with the thought that someone that they were older than was designated to be greater than them. To wake up one morning to suddenly realize that someone you had always believed that you are better than is actually better and greater than you are is capable of causing an incurable migraine to the delusional who had always believed that he was a better man. Jacob and his older sons woke up to realize that the Joseph they had always believe to be their subordinate on account of age was poised to be greater than them socially and that they could not do anything to stop the train of Joseph's greatness that had left the station on its way to put them at his mercy. That is one of any man's greatest nightmare to suddenly realize that the man who used to be his subordinate is bound to become his superior and that it would remain like that for the rest of their lives. It is a killer thought. When Ahithophel realized that David would return to exercise royal authority over him, he opted to take his own life rather than wait to witness it. It was the heartache that Saul could not live with when David killed Goliath and realized that David was on his steady journey to becoming the next king of Israel. Killing the Goliath that he could not kill, David practically emptied every sense of self-worth that Saul had since he became the king of Israel. He could not live with the fact that the same David who arrived in his palace to serve as his private musician had suddenly been elevated to the same pedestal of fame as himself even when he was supposed to still be the sitting king of Israel. And that in fact, the women of Israel considered David to be a greater warrior than he. We can go on and on. The same Solomon who promoted Jeroboam on merit tried to kill him once he found out that even God who chose him above Adonijah and his other older brothers had also chosen Jeroboam to share his throne with his son after him. In most cases, no superior likes his subordinate to become his equal or rise above the position that the superior believes that the subordinate deserves, or the superior had ear-marked for the subordinate.

This is one heart-hidden hurting secret about a stranger coming over to make more money or become richer than the natives within a few years of stay. If a stranger implement an idea that the natives never knew could spin money for them to become prosperous, it is a tactical proof that the natives are not smart enough to have known about his strange idea that is a money spinner. They would wish that they knew that idea and had used it to make money before he ever arrived to live among them. Also, they know that the stranger made the money from their own people rather than from his own people. Surely, the stranger might have brought money from his home country to invest in the idea that he foresaw that it would give him profit to become rich but in all honesty he has only used his initial investment brought from his home to gain money from their own people. This is the aspect that is unacceptable to the natives.

Now, there is another angle to the matter, natives' ruling class might show enough maturity to conceal their resentment of the stranger's success, but they will not do much to restrain their non-ruling class kinsmen from afflicting the stranger. The common experience is that members of their security forces would zealously arrest and dangle all sorts of false allegations against foreigners who are doing well. The truth is that security operatives are among the less privileged natives and therefore, harbor bitterness or grudge against foreigners who operate businesses that have made them richer than the average native citizen.

When the foreigner arrived with his money to invest, he was not living a luxurious lifestyle because he knew his mission which is; to invest and make profit. However, when he has invested and made money, the natives do not even know, care or have quickly forgotten that he came with his money to invest earlier. They see only the fact that when he arrived, he was squatting with his fellow foreigner and suddenly he has become wealthy before their very eyes while they continue to wallow in poverty. This stranger has joined the class of their very rich when they thought that he was not better than them on his arrival a while earlier. Foreign investors must understand this fact and minimize or moderate their display of their business and investment success through their improved standard of living. This is part of the heart-hidden reason that some persons earning their living abroad repatriate at least half of their income home to invest so that whenever the natives' hostilities become unbearable, they can readily tidy up their sojourn and return home where they would be celebrated for returning home richer than they left and establish business to provide employment for their kinsmen.

It is sad to report this personal experience, but it would help to drive home the point. Several years ago, a colleague visited me to seek a personal loan, and in all honesty, the Spirit of God warned that I should not lend him, but he would not take his leave for nearly three hours. Because of the way he was lamenting his predicament, human sentiment took the better part of me and I went inside the bedroom to pick my cheque book from the drawer and issued the cheque for the amount of money he was asking or claim to have needed. Curiously, he spent another hour giving reasons I could have had the said amount in the bank to issue him a cheque. It was only then it dawned on me that the Spirit of God knew that if I gave him the money, he would be filled with envy that I had the amount he did not have and had to be running from one friend to the other asking for assistance. I learnt my lessons, but it was very bitter. Over the years, I realized that this acquaintance was overwhelmed with envy and pettiness of "my farm is bigger than yours".

There are persons whose greatest problem in life is comparing themselves against their neighbor in their interpersonal relationships. They are ever eager to tell you the latest thing they have done, and you have not done. If they find out that you have done something they have not done, they will not mind borrowing money from the Devil himself to get it so that it would not be on record that you have something that they do not have or that makes you to look better than them. It is the same with people who think that their tribe or race is better than yours. Most of the time, if they cannot acquire what you have, they would resort to destroying yours to erase the fact that you have something that they think makes you to be better than them. While preaching a pastor told us the story of one of his friends whose half brother organized car thieves to steal his car because he was the only child of their father who owned a car of his own at the time. When Proverbs 27:4 and Ecclesiastes 4:4 say:

> 4 An angry person is dangerous, but a jealous person is even worse.

> 4 Then I realized that we work and do wonderful things just because we are jealous of others… (CEV)

> 4 I realized the reason people work hard and try to succeed: They are jealous of each other. … (NCV)

> 4 Then I observed that the basic motive for success is the driving force of envy and jealousy! … (TLB)

> 4 I have also learned why people work so hard to succeed: it is because they envy the things their neighbors have… (TEV)

> 4 Then I thought, "Why do people work so hard?" I saw people try to succeed and be better than other people. They do this because they are

jealous. They don't want other people to have more than they have… (ERV)

We can see why most wealthy entrepreneurs reply to the question of when they would be content with what they have and therefore, stop investing to add to their current wealth they would say just a little more. One of the heart-hidden driving forces is that they do not want their wealthy colleague to be said to be wealthier. It is even worst with the yearly publication of the list of the wealthiest in the world, continent, and countries. Man is addicted to comparing and the craving to improve to be seen to be better than one's neighbors. On the side of the migrant, it could be that he worked extra hard to prove to the natives that they are lazy or unwise or both. Even if he worked extra hard to succeed because he considered the money he brought to invest as his lifeline, the natives do not know his heart-hidden reason so they readily conclude that he meant it to slight them. Like we said earlier, the natives have done what they considered their best and did not measure up to the foreigner or migrant investor and envy would constrain them to want to deport the migrant and take over his business or even his wife. Once they have degenerated to the low level of attacking the migrant, envy will not allow them to stop until they have succeeded anyhow and if the migrant is not careful, he could lose his life along with his investments.

One of the commonly overlooked reason foreigners prosper more than natives is the subject of ego or pride. While foreigners do not mind doing just any job no matter how dirty as long as it gives them income to live on, a native would not do just anything to survive. A typical stranger would do any kind of job as long as it earns him income whereas most natives would not do certain jobs because it is not dignifying for them to be seen by their childhood peers doing such seemingly demeaning jobs just because they must have something to live on. While the natives are waiting to get what they consider as dignifying jobs strangers do not have any childhood colleagues around to be ashamed of seeing them doing such menial jobs that sometimes gives good income because of scarcity of persons who are willing to take up such jobs. The result is that the stranger ends up better off economically while the natives are worse off.

A university graduate who had been selling palm oil to support himself as an undergraduate went into fulltime selling of palm oil upon his graduation because he could not readily find office work or the proverbial white-collar job. One day a lady who was his classmate in the university met him with his work clothes delivering palm oil supplies to customers and would not even acknowledge his greetings. She was working as a contract staff with a bank. The young man said he understood why she was cold towards him, but he cared less because his profit was equivalent of a General Manager's salary the last time, he checked newspaper adverts for vacancies. He had 12 employees and was already building his own house. Then a journalist who had passion for young graduates engaging in self-employment rather than spending years looking for office work did a story on this young man that was published in a national daily. In a follow-up story the young man said after the first story was published his old university mates began to contact him and when next he ran into this same lady, she was friendlier. The sales of palm oil used to be small trade done mostly by housewives or homemakers at neighbourhood level, but this young man decided to engage in it in another dimension. He supplied to food canteen operators. His work wears would be stained with the palm oil while loading and offloading them from his delivery van but he cared less about who saw him wearing palm oil dirtied clothes while on duty as long as he made his money to meet his needs and ambitions.

The Holy Bible gives the impression that Jacob's maternal cousins and Laban's sons could not work day and night on Laban's flock like Jacob did and as a result, by the end of 20 years Jacob became so rich with savings from his earnings that not only Laban but his sons became envious of Jacob. In this respect, Genesis 31:1-4, 36-44 says:

> 1 Jacob heard that Laban's sons were saying, "Jacob has taken everything that belonged to our father. He got all his wealth from what our father owned." 2 He also saw that Laban was no longer as friendly as he had been earlier. 3 Then the Lord said to him, "Go back to the land of your fathers and to your relatives. I will be with

you." 4 So Jacob sent word to Rachel and Leah to meet him in the field where his flocks were. 36 Then Jacob lost his temper. "What crime have I committed?" he asked angrily. "What law have I broken that gives you the right to hunt me down? 37 Now that you have searched through all my belongings, what household article have you found that belongs to you? Put it out here where your men and mine can see it, and let them decide which one of us is right. 38 I have been with you now for twenty years; your sheep and your goats have not failed to reproduce, and I have not eaten any rams from your flocks. 39 Whenever a sheep was killed by wild animals, I always bore the loss myself. I didn't take it to you to show that it was not my fault. You demanded that I make good anything that was stolen during the day or during the night. 40 Many times I suffered from the heat during the day and from the cold at night. I was not able to sleep. 41 It was like that for the whole twenty years I was with you. For fourteen years I worked to win your two daughters—and six years for your flocks. And even then, you changed my wages ten times. 42 If the God of my fathers, the God of Abraham and Isaac, had not been with me, you would have already sent me away empty-handed. But God has seen my trouble and the work I have done, and last night he gave his judgment." 43 Laban answered Jacob, "These young women are my daughters; their children belong to me, and these flocks are mine. In fact, everything you see here belongs to me. But since I can do nothing to keep my daughters and their children, 44 I am ready to make an agreement with you. Let us make a pile of stones to remind us of our agreement." (TEV)

Laban's sons were men like Jacob therefore, why would Jacob work out his ass on their father's business and they did not? What else were they doing with their time that their cousin who came from a distant land took their rightful place in their father's business to prosper more than them and even their father? Out of frustration that their stranger cousin had become richer than them under their noses over the period of 20 years they resorted to blaming Jacob for taking over their father's wealth. It is helpful to note that the fact that Jacob was their cousin did not make them overlook the fact that Jacob had become richer than them in their own land. Jacob came from his land of birth of Canaan while Laban's sons were in their land of birth of Haran. They knew that Jacob was taking the wealth that he had made in their homeland back to Canaan which means that they would not have the chance to share in the wealth. The fact that their sisters and the children that they bore for Jacob would enjoy part of the wealth did not assuage either Laban or his sons.

When Proverbs 17:2 says 'a wise servant will rule over a disgraceful son, and will share the inheritance as one of the brothers'-NIV; 'a wise servant will rule over the master's disgraceful son and will share the inheritance of the master's children'-NLT; and 'a shrewd servant will gain authority over a master's worthless son and receive a part of the inheritance'-TEV; it includes a son who chooses to be idle while his father's servant is working hard on his father's business. At the end, the servant would be an expert on the father's business and the son would be at the mercy of the servant in the absence of his father and pioneer of the business. Genesis 31:1-41 says while Laban and his sons placed emphasis on the fact that Jacob's wealth came out of Laban's wealth that Jacob managed, Jacob placed emphasis on the fact that Laban's wealth increased because he toiled day and night managing Laban's initial wealth. Something very significant is that just as Jacob could not say that Laban owned the initial wealth so also Laban and his sons could not deny the fact that Jacob worked hard to increase Laban's wealth part of which had gone to Jacob as due wages. Commonsense says if Laban's sons had worked on their father's wealth, they would have earned the wages that Jacob earned before they would inherit their father's share as their deserved inheritance in the absence of their father. Therefore, by not taking their rightful place to manage their father's initial wealth they shortchanged themselves and their father just as by not making his sons to work on his wealth or letting his sister's son replace his sons in his business, Laban shortchanged himself and his sons.

Another significant issue that could be easily overlooked is that of whether the natives would share in the benefits of the wealth that the stranger amassed in their native land. Genesis 31:10-16 confirms that as long as Laban's daughters were going back to Canaan to share in the wealth that Jacob gathered in their native land of Haran, the daughters did not really mind that Jacob was taking away the wealth that he got while working for their father. But their brothers who could not afford to leave their native land of Haran behind to accompany them to Canaan to share in the wealth of Jacob they did not like that Jacob was carting away the wealth he got while working for their father. Personal benefit is an issue in the affairs of life or this world.

There is no doubt that Jacob stole from Esau because it was obvious that Esau was richer than or doing better than Jacob. Genesis 25:27-34 recounts the first time that he stole from Esau. The story says Esau did not just lead an outdoor lifestyle but that he earned enough to bring back home for their father to enjoy part of the proceeds of his activities away from home. This means that he prospered from his legitimate efforts. It seemed that at a point Jacob concluded that it was because he was the older or that birthright of being the older was the source of his prosperity so decided to claim it from Esau. Fortunately for Jacob and unfortunately for Esau, Jacob succeeded in getting the birthright from Esau. Genesis 26:34-35 can be interpreted to mean that as a result of his prosperity from his hard work away from home, Esau was able to afford two wives by age 40 while Jacob could not. Again, Genesis 27:15 can be interpreted to mean that in fact, Esau could afford expensive clothes as well. There was no such report about Jacob most likely because he remained at home all the time rather than go out to spend his life to do something tangible and profitable. Genesis 27:1-46 can be interpreted to mean that Esau prospered so much that not only Jacob was envious of his success but even their mother joined Jacob to envy Esau enough to plot to hurt Esau for so doing. She did because she thought that Esau never considered it appropriate to share prosperity from his hard work with her but with only their father. Let us not delve into the subject of Esau's decision to favour only his father with part of his proceeds and whether by so doing, he unknowingly infuriated and therefore, instigated and provoked their mother to determine to work against him.

Yet, this case teaches us that if you share your earnings with some, those that are hurt by the fact that you excluded them from the list of those that you chose to favour with your prosperity would do everything within their power to work against you. That is what Genesis 31:1-16 confirms that Laban's daughters, Leah, and Rachel did to him. They were unanimous about the fact that as long as Laban did not share his wealth with them, they would desert him to stick to Jacob who they believe would share his wealth with them because of the children that they bore him. Their case lends credence to the concept of "Give/Gladden Otherwise Grieve" or "Share Otherwise Shock" which simply means share with others otherwise they would shock you with attacks. If you think that just because you earned your wealth from hard work and God's help you will not share with any other or share with some and leave out others in the spreading of the benefit of your earnings, be rest assured that there are persons who would not stop until they have caused you great pain for excluding them from the enjoyment of your earnings.

The example of the family of Isaac and Laban above are meant to teach us that it is not only natives who treat strangers who prosper around them harshly. Parents do as typified by Rebecca against Esau did just as siblings do, typified by Jacob against Esau. Also, children do against parents as typified by Laban's daughters against him when Jacob determined to return to Canaan with all the wealth that he had gathered while living with and working for Laban. Cousins who feel short-changed in the sharing of supposed family wealth resent the gainers. It is part of the battle of resentment and acrimony between gainers and losers in the process of sharing resources. Whoever feels discriminated against in the process of sharing resources and their benefits never forgive the sharers and beneficiaries.

We have said marrying a native would help reduce the resentment of the prospering stranger, but it is just a factor. If the prosperous stranger marries a native but fails to curtail his display of affluence, he will still find tangible number of the natives resenting him or her to an unbearable level. In general terms, it can be called "Not Enough Reason" which in this case means that marriage to a native is not enough reason to engage in 'show off' of wealth otherwise the stranger would reap regret. So, it is one reason that strangers must engage in "Manifest Majesty Moderately", "Marvellous Moderate Mannerisms" or "Marvellous Moderate Majesty Manifestation Mannerisms". This means that the stranger who prospers greatly must necessarily constrain himself to behave far better than the native who prospers at the same level making the non-native to act as the precautious prosperous or cautious captain of industry.

This is about ensnaring exhibitionism. Even when you do not exhibit your success and progress you will be attacked not to mention if you do. As a result, it could be said that faulty flaunting fractures and frustrates. This means that keeping laudable low profile profits a great deal. It is one thing to do well and another to determine that others must recognize that one is doing well. The danger of making others to recognize that one is doing well is that it could and does instigate/coerce envy and jealousy slaves of this world to attack the personal success exhibitionists. The indigenous people of Urhobo would say if there is an argument between the rich and the poor if the rich man is wise and loves his life, he would seek peace with the poor man quickly because it is the rich man who have good life to enjoy and therefore would suffer the most if the disagreement results into injurious conflict. Their wisdom is that the successful and prosperous should tread cautiously because he is enjoying pleasantness in the land of the living.

The subject, factor or consideration of what can be called "Same Source Solidarity" or "Similarity/Sameness Solidarity" is very vital for the stranger because natives believe strongly that what their fellow native has the right to enjoy, the non-native lacks the right and even privilege to enjoy in their native land. Sameness means that we are the same and should tolerate each other's idiosyncrasies more than those of any other source that is not the same with us. It is played out in the story of Moses when Exodus 2:11-13 says Moses killed an Egyptian for oppressing his fellow Israelite only to employ mere words of mouth to dissuade another Israelite from oppressing a fellow Israelite despite the fact that Moses was supposed to have been brought up to be the Egyptian king-in-waiting. Nativity or same source solidarity is so strong a factor that people could sacrifice anything to prove and protect it.

A newspaper reported a very sad story of a son who killed his widowed mother's lover because the randy man came into their home to have sex with his mother to the extent of impregnating her and his sister about the same time. This boy had warned the man to stay off their detached home premises and his mother several times to no avail. Apparently, this man and his mother were so engrossed in the enjoyment of their night rounds of sex that they did not heed the warnings to stop. This boy's friend who narrated the issues that the boy mentioned as his source of annoyance before he killed the man and went into hiding included the fact that every night this man came to engage the mother in their house, the noise she made while they were engrossed in sex disturbed the young man from sleeping. This same noise might be part of the reason the daughter fell to the lure that led to the man impregnating her as well. As horrifying as the end of this story was, what we know is that if this boy's father were to be the one handling his mother at night like this stranger of a man was doing to her, the boy would not have minded. If his father was caught up in the incest of impregnating his sister while his mother was carrying his baby, this boy might not have killed his father either, like he killed this man after a careful planning.

One of the issues that came up when I discussed it with another pastor is that the spirit of the dead father stirred the boy to kill this man who dared to come into the house he built and left on earth for his widow and children to live to somewhat abuse his wife and daughter just because they were vulnerable. If he must have intimate relationship with this widow, why come over to the premises that the late husband left behind for them to live in with the feeling of safety or being shielded from molestation? He could not even afford to take her to his own apartment outside that premises. Even if he was a tenant in the late husband's house, it is wrong to have her right there. The abomination of engaging a mother and her daughter in sex and impregnating them incurred greater punishment for the stranger than it would have incurred for the woman's husband if he had impregnated their daughter. If the dead man's younger brother had done it, his punishment might not have been as devastating as the one doled out to this stranger who came into the house to do it and suffered capital punishment.

This highlights what can be called tortuous territorial trespassing. Deuteronomy 32:8-9 which we read earlier gives the impression that there is a heaven-imposed and therefore, spiritually-set boundary which the spirit-man of natives recognize and determined to take charge over – it is like the subject of professional territorial boundaries. Doctors do not like lawyers to take decisions in their medical field just as lawyers would not let architects take decisions over legal matters. All humans like to protect any territory that they considered exclusive to them. In the story of the conflict between the old prophet at Bethel and the young prophet that God sent from Judah to King Jeroboam of Israel, it is for the sake of exclusive territorial control that the old prophet at Bethel deceived the young prophet from Judah to his sudden death. This is also tantamount to natives' resentment of migrants.

31

THE VICTIMIZATION OF NATIVES

Sometimes migrants are unfair to their hosts. Genesis 37:1-36 says Joseph's older brothers sold him into slavery unjustly while Genesis 39:1-20 says Joseph's Egyptian boss, Potiphar sent him to prison for an offence that he did not commit and without giving him the chance to defend himself. Imprisonment without fair trial is inappropriate, and worst still, of an innocent man. It would have been very unfair on Potiphar, if Joseph blamed him for sending him to jail more than he would blame his older brothers who sold him into slavery in Egypt. If not for his older brothers who sold him to the Ishmaelites who in turn sold him to Egypt, Potiphar would not have had any contact with him and there would have been no reason for Potiphar to jail him. Genesis 37:1-36 includes the fact that on the day Joseph made extra effort to take food to his sickening older brothers their conscience was so twisted or dead that they still made attempt to murder him even when they would still sit down to eat the food that he took to them. Whereas, Genesis 39:1-6 says when Potiphar recognized that Joseph's presence favored him, his reaction was to reward Joseph. It means that Joseph's brothers did not think that the fact that he was their loving, caring and kind younger brother was enough reason to refrain themselves from hurting him. If they hurt him as their younger brother and brought them food, do they expect a total stranger to save him from their onslaught? It would have been wrong for Jesus to blame Pilate a non-Jew more than Jesus' fellow Jews who forced Pilate to condemn Jesus for them to kill.

Genesis 37:1-36, 40:14-15, 41:50-52 and 42:21-23 can be said to mean that Joseph seemed to have grouped the affliction of his older brothers while he was still in Canaan and that of his false imprisonment by Potiphar as being at the same level of wickedness or man's inhumanity to man in his estimation. Yet, it would be unfair to Potiphar if the record is not set straight by emphasizing that his brothers did not fear God enough to reward the kindness of Joseph to them like Potiphar repaid Joseph's help earlier before his wife lied to him about Joseph. Genesis 39:1-6 confirms that Potiphar consciously rewarded Joseph's usefulness and help to his fortunes while Genesis 37:1-36 says rather than reward Joseph for doing more than instructed by their father to take food to them in Shechem they chose to afflict Joseph. Their father said he should take food to them in Shechem. When he did not meet them in Shechem, he went further to Dothan to search them out. Rather than reward his efforts to ensure that they got what their father sent to them, they chose to punish him because they had understood that it seemed that God meant him to be greater than them.

Doeg is the only non-Israelite who is noted to have been appointed high official by King Saul during the 40 years that Acts 13:21 confirms that he ruled over Israel. I Samuel 21:1-9 says Doeg was present during what turned out to be David's final meeting with the priest Elimelech. While Deuteronomy 2:22 confirms that the Edomites were Esau's descendants I Samuel 21:7 confirms that Doeg was an Edomite who King

Saul of Israel considered to be skilled enough to serve as his chief herdsman. He was religious enough to go and fulfill a religious obligation the same way that I Samuel 1:1-28 and 2:1-21 can be said to mean that Samuel's parents went to Shiloh annually to fulfill religious obligation or Luke 2:41-52 confirms that Jesus accompanied His parents and other family members to travel from their hometown of Nazareth to Jerusalem annually to fulfill religious obligation to the Lord.

However, I Samuel 22:6-19 confirms that Doeg's religiousity or religious loyalty, devotion and commitment did not make him to revere God to the extent of following in the example of Saul's bodyguards who verses 16-19 confirm that they refused to obey Saul to kill God's authentic priests because they hallowed God. Despite the fact that Doeg did not revere God in the life of the priests, the abominable nature of his action in this respect is not as bad and unforgivable as that of Saul who was an authentic Israelite who had enjoyed God's great favour by reason of the fact that among all the young men of his generation, God sent Samuel to choose him to be king of Israel when he least expected. If Saul who had the same upbringing that taught reverence for Aaronite priests because of God of their ancestors like his bodyguards did not think he should join his bodyguards to spare God's authentic priests, their household members and possessions why should anyone beginning with Saul's fellow Israelites blame Doeg who was never brought up to reverence Saul's God of Israel for failing to join Saul's bodyguards to reverence Aaronite priests because of the God of their ancestors and of all gods. It would be very unfair to blame Doeg and Saul equally or even more than Saul though there is no doubt that he committed sacrilege. After all, first, I Samuel 9:6-11 confirms that there was a time that Saul knew that it was not appropriate to go and consult a man of God for spiritual guidance without taking a gift to him. Second, I Samuel 24:1-19 and 26:1-21 confirm that even when his actions made him to deserve capital punishment David convinced his men to spare his life on two occasions partly because God once anointed him. If Doeg put up the defense of ignorance of Genesis 12:10-20 and 20:1-18 and Psalm 105:12-15 based God's implied command of touch not my anointed and do my prophet no harm, Saul as a bonifide

Israelite cannot make the same claim and he would be believed by any reasonable and objective individual.

Furthermore, Jeremiah 38:1-13 and 39:15-18 say Jeremiah's Jewish kinsmen led by King Zedekiah and his palace officials dropped Jeremiah into a mud-filled well to die from pneumonia and it took a non-Jewish palace official by the name of Ebedmelech a Sudanese to convince King Zedekiah to let him get Jeremiah out before it was too late. Meanwhile, Jeremiah 38:1-6 and 14-28 confirms that this same King Zedekiah who approved that God's authentic prophet, Jeremiah could be killed sought Jeremiah's help after Ebedmelech had saved Jeremiah from dying in the muddy well. Dearly beloved, it would be ungodly to say Ebedmelech was not a better man than King Zedekiah and his fellow Jewish officials who wanted Jeremiah dead just because Ebedmelech was not a Jew like Jeremiah, Zedekiah, and his obnoxious palace officials. Jeremiah 39:1-10 and 15-18 confirms that while God allowed Zedekiah and his Jewish palace officials to be carried away captive, God promised to reward Ebedmelech for saving Jeremiah's life. There are migrants who blame the natives of their land of sojourn for maltreatment as if they got a better treatment from their kinsmen before they relocated to live among the natives who they are blaming for ill-treating them.

Exodus 1:8-24 says Pharaoh threatened Moses along with members of his generation of Israelite male babies. In fact, the other members of his generation of newly born were massacred and only he seemed to have survived. Exodus 2:1-25 says when Moses tried to help the Israelites, they rejected him and his help. Acts 7:35 makes the excuse of ignorance for the Israelites when it says that it was because they did not know that God meant to use Moses to save them from their Egyptian oppressors. The Egyptian officials who wanted Moses dead had the reason of punishing him for killing one of them but what about the Israelites who rejected Moses. The Israelites' rejection of Moses was as bad as the Egyptian officials who wanted him dead because it left Moses with no choice than to escape to the land of Midian.

Most of the inhabitants of Anathoth were priests of God or that Anathoth was a priestly town. Jeremiah 1:1-3, 29:27 and

32:6-9 confirm that the Prophet Jeremiah hailed from this same Anathoth. However, Jeremiah 11:18-23 says:

> 18 The Lord informed me of the plots that my enemies were making against me. 19 I was like a trusting lamb taken out to be killed, and I did not know that it was against me that they were planning evil things. They were saying, "Let's chop down the tree while it is still healthy; let's kill him so that no one will remember him any more." 20 Then I prayed, "Almighty Lord, you are a just judge; you test people's thoughts and feelings. I have placed my cause in your hands; so let me watch you take revenge on these people." 21 The people of Anathoth wanted me killed, and they told me that they would kill me if I kept on proclaiming the Lord's message. 22 So the Lord Almighty said, "I will punish them! Their young men will be killed in war; their children will die of starvation. 23 I have set a time for bringing

disaster on the people of Anathoth, and when that time comes, none of them will survive." (TEV)

Someone could say that it is not proper for God's prophet to ask God to avenge him of his hometown kinsmen when they were authentic priests and prophets like himself. Such an individual should remember that God approved that He would implement the punishment at the appropriate time. It means that God agreed that they deserved to be punished as Jeremiah requested. If God agreed, then who are we to still blame Jeremiah? Yet, the other serious issue which is the real reason we read the passage is to determine who deserved greater blame, if ever Jeremiah deserved any at all. If Jeremiah's fellow Aaronite priests as well as his hometown relatives did not care that it should not be said that they plot the killing of God's authentic prophet what makes them to deserve the consideration and compassion of Jeremiah who they determined to kill? The priestly natives of Anathoth should be too busy with their religious duties to engage in the plot to kill anyone beginning with a fellow prophet. If every other person supposed to hallow them as God's authentic priest because of their reverence for God under the concept of 'touch not my anointed and do my prophet no harm' yet they themselves did not consider or care about that concept that God meant to be in their favour to determine to kill one of their own, then they ceased to deserve to enjoy the benefit of that God-ordained concept.

Again, Jeremiah 26:1-24 says in contemporary times equivalent of politicians and top government functionaries saved a prophet of God from been killed by his fellow prophets, pastors, and Christians. The royal palace officials who saved Jeremiah was led by one Ahikam son of Shaphan. II Kings 22:1-14 and II Chronicles 34:1-20 confirm that Ahikam and his father Shaphan had began to serve in the royal palace of Judah since the reign of King Josiah. Then, Jeremiah 38:1-6 says at a later date some palace officials said Jeremiah should be killed and that is when verses 7-13 say it was Ebedmelech the Sudanese who saved Jeremiah from been killed or left to die in a muddy well. It is important to note that when the politicians and high ranking government officials wanted to kill him, his fellow prophets and priests or pastors did not come to his rescue. This then is the point, it would be very unfair to blame the politicians and top government functionaries for trying to kill Jeremiah more than his fellow prophets, priests and pastors who had tried to kill him and it was the politicians who saved him from them.

I Samuel 2:12-17 and 22-36, 3:1-18 and 4:1-22 confirm that in God's reaction to Eli's sons, Hophni and Phinehas' disrespect for Him at Shiloh, He reversed His supposed eternal promises to Eli and his sons as descendants of Aaron and all his descendants forever. In this respect, I Samuel 2:27-30 and Jeremiah 7:31, 19:5 and 32:35 can be interpreted to mean that when a man crosses certain boundaries, God is forced to reserve His promise to such a man. When Solomon crossed the boundaries of disobedience God did not hesitate to punish him. When David did in his dastardly dealings with Uriah, God reacted in like manner. It is part of the reason Matthew 23:34-35 and Luke 13:34-35 say Jesus implied that it cannot be well with whosoever that resents, rejects and attacks whoever God sent to help him. Jesus was referring to what can be described as the punishment due to Jerusalem, the traditional capital city of the Jews. This is despite the fact that Matthew 10:5-7 and 15:24 and 26 quote Him as saying that He is sent mostly to the Jews more than the Gentiles or non-Jews. Then, Jeremiah 18:18-23, 20:10 and Hebrews 13:17 say:

18 Then the people said, "Let's do something about Jeremiah! There will always be priests to instruct us, the wise to give us counsel, and prophets to proclaim God's message. Let's bring charges against him and stop listening to what he says." 19 So I prayed, "Lord, hear what I am saying and listen to what my enemies are saying about me. 20 Is evil the payment for good? Yet they have dug a pit for me to fall in. Remember how I came to you and spoke on their behalf, so that you would not deal with them in anger. 21 But now, Lord, let their children starve to death; let them be killed in war. Let the women lose their husbands and children; let the men die of disease and the young men be killed in battle. 22 Send a mob to plunder their homes without warning; make them cry out in terror. They have dug a pit for me to fall in and have set traps to catch

me. 23 But, Lord, you know all their plots to kill me. Do not forgive their evil or pardon their sin. Throw them down in defeat and deal with them while you are angry."

10 I hear everybody whispering, "Terror is everywhere! So let's report him to the authorities!" Even my close friends wait for my downfall. "Perhaps he can be tricked," they say; "then we can catch him and get revenge."

17 Obey your leaders and follow their orders. They watch over your souls without resting, since they must give to God an account of their service. If you obey them, they will do their work gladly; if not, they will do it with sadness, and that would be of no help to you. (TEV)

Jeremiah 18:20 above implies that initially, Jeremiah did not want any calamity to happen to his fellow Jews but they pushed him beyond his human limits of patience and endurance and by so doing they forced him to pray to God against them.

The people's claim in verse 18 means that it is not like they did not know that they needed God's message and guidance. They impliedly confessed that much as they needed God's help through their fellow human who they regard as a prophet, it should not be Jeremiah who was not telling them what they want to hear. Also worthy of note is the fact that it is very possible that the other persons who they preferred were not even praying to God to show them mercy like Jeremiah was doing. Of course, the other persons who they preferred to serve as intermediary between them and God were not God's authentic prophet to them at the time like Jeremiah.

Then, on the part of Jeremiah, one of the worst evil that they could do to him was to reject him as the genuine source through whom they could hear from God because Jeremiah 1:1-19 says serving as an intermediary between them and God in the office of a prophet is the core mandate of God for Jeremiah. It means that if he did not serve as an intermediary between them and God it would have impact on him in eternity because he would miss his deserved reward in eternity for failing to fulfill his earthly mandate. He would have lived and died as a man who wasted his stay on earth. Jeremiah 32:1-25 confirms that for the sake of his lifelong mandate and mission God asked Jeremiah to practically waste his little or only savings by buying an estate in the same territory of Israel that God was about to hand over to foreign invaders and Jeremiah would be carried along with his fellow Israelites away into captivity.

Furthermore, Jeremiah 15:10-21 and 16:1-9 say for the sake of this same sacred assignment, God practically meant that Jeremiah must give up social life experiences including marriage and pleasure. It includes the fact that the Israelites frustrated Jeremiah to the point that his complaints to God angered God to the point of threatening to punish Jeremiah severely. Some of these points are worth being pointed out so that we can appreciate why Jeremiah turned round to ask God to punish his fellow Anathothites and Israelites. Jeremiah 5:30-31, Micah 2:6, 11, Romans 1:28 and II Timothy 4:3-5 say:

> 30 A terrible and shocking thing has happened in the land: 31 prophets speak nothing but lies; priests rule as the prophets command, and my

people offer no objections. But what will they do when it all comes to an end?"

6 The people preach at me and say, "Don't preach at us. Don't preach about all that. God is not going to disgrace us. 11 "These people want the kind of prophet who goes around full of lies and deceit and says, 'I prophesy that wine and liquor will flow for you.'

28 Because those people refuse to keep in mind the true knowledge about God, he has given them over to corrupted minds, so that they do the things that they should not do.

3 The time will come when people will not listen to sound doctrine, but will follow their own desires and will collect for themselves more and more teachers who will tell them what they are itching to hear. 4 They will turn away from listening to the truth and give their attention to legends. 5 But you keep control of yourself in all

circumstances; endure suffering, do the work of a preacher of the Good News, and perform your whole duty as a servant of God. (TEV)

First, this is one of the greatest dilemmas of genuine men of God - the people who God sent them to do not want to hear God's message through them. It is like a salesman who takes the product of a company to a population who does not want to buy any of the company's products for whatever reason. It would be very frustrating for the salesman. Look at what they did to Jeremiah at some point. Jeremiah 42:1-22, 43:1-12 and 44:1-30 say the remnant Jews in Jerusalem went to ask Jeremiah to clarify from God what God would want them to do. Jeremiah did their bidding by asking God and got a clear message from God for them. However, when Jeremiah relayed God's message to them, they refused to comply. That is very strange.

The logical question should be why ask for God's will for you when you will not comply with it? They visited Jeremiah to ask God's plan for them, they went home to wait for the answer. When Jeremiah had God's response, he contacted them to come over to hear it. Yet, they would not comply with it. So, why did they come to ask, wait for an answer, and return to hear the answer? They should have as well gone ahead to do whatever they preferred rather than pretend that they valued God's directive or opinion or both. Perhaps, they knew what they wanted to do but merely wanted God to rubber-stamp it for them and when God said what they did not intend to do, they threw God's opinion into the trash can.

One of the things that make the trivialization of God's response through Jeremiah very painful is the fact that they had more than enough proof that Jeremiah was God's authentic prophet to them. Jeremiah had warned about the Babylonian captivity and told them what they could do to avert it. They witnessed the consequences of rejecting Jeremiah's warnings or actually, God's warnings through Jeremiah. Any thoughtful person would readily conclude that it is as a result that they approached Jeremiah to seek God's counsel to comply with after their fellow Jews had been carried captive.

Surviving Among Strangers

The other shameful fact is that Jeremiah 39:1-14 and 40:1-6 say King Nebuchadnezzar of Babylon and his COAS, Nebuzaradan believed in Jeremiah as God of Israel's authentic prophet. Nebuchadnezzar and Nebuzaradan believed so much in Jeremiah's authenticity as God of Israel's prophet that they freed Jeremiah from the prison that Jeremiah's Jewish kinsman and king put him in for speaking God's mind to them. How does that make anyone feel when a total stranger saves you from being killed by your own brother, sister, relative or kinsman? Honestly, only God can tell. Jeremiah 39:1-14 says after Nebuchadnezzar and his Babylonian army overran Jerusalem, captured their king and officials, they freed Jeremiah from prison where Jeremiah 37:11-16 says he had been kept by King Zedekiah of Judah and his officials.

A woman's older sister who was equally married was seeking adulterous affair with her husband who was very wealthy. When she found out and caught the older sister with her husband, in anger she told her husband that he is free to date any other woman but not her older sister. She did not know what to do to her older sister. She had been spying on the older sister since she got wind of the fact that she was seeking after her husband. The older sister frequently visited their home but she never thought anything of her frequent visit until her husband's younger brother told her that her husband had lamented to him that her older sister was pestering him for a relationship and his wife does not seem to have the capacity to cope with the information if he told her. The point is does the woman want her husband to flirt with other women? Not at all however, considering that her older sister chose to have an affair with her husband who was gracious enough to use his younger brother to inform her, she preferred that her husband had affair with a total stranger rather than with her older sister who was doing whatever she could to get him for herself. She meant that there are things that should not even be heard that was done by a relative to hurt someone.

The other significant point is that Jeremiah 37:17-21, 38:1-28 and 39:1-14 say during the time that Jeremiah was imprisoned in the palace of Judah, the same King Zedekiah who approved his imprisonment was still consulting Jeremiah to find out what God says. It is ridiculous – you imprisoned or punish a man for speaking the mind of God which does not agree with what you want to hear yet you continue to ask him to tell you what God would have you do. It does not add up. It makes the king seem like a very confused and conflicted individual – perhaps, he was hoping that at some point Jeremiah would claim that God has spoken what he (the king) wants or prefer to hear. God is not in the business of telling anyone what he wants to hear rather He tells any man what the man needs to hear. Nebuchadnezzar deserved Jeremiah's prayer more than his fellow Jews who punished him for telling them what God meant them to hear. I Samuel 17:1-58 and 27:1-12 can be interpreted to mean that Achish shielded David from Saul's life-threatening attacks even though David saved Saul from the shame of Achish's Goliath's threats, shame, and humiliation. Saul should be the one protecting David from Achish not the other way round as it turned out to be.

Judges 13:1-25 says God sent Samson to begin the process of freeing the Israelites from the oppression of the Philistines only for Judges 15:9-19 to say Samson's fellow Israelites and the chief beneficiaries of the real reason God sent Samson to live on earth bound and handed him over to the same Philistines to kill or harm in any way that the Philistines were able to. Someone could say that it was because they did not know that God meant Samson to save them from the oppression of the Philistines or that they were afraid of the Philistines. That is a very weak excuse because whatever happens they should be eager to join whoever was determined to risk his life to free them from their oppressors. But perhaps more importantly is the fact that it would be very unfair for anyone to blame the Philistines for whatever they did to Samson more than his own people who bound and handed him over to the Philistines. If your relative invited a non-relative to steal from or harm you in any way, you should blame your relative rather than the non-relative.

In this respect, II Samuel 16:5-14 says David told his nephews, Joab and Abishai that the attack by his son, Absalom was worse than whatever a non-family member did to afflict him, Shimei who was the relative of King Saul, David's predecessor who never wanted David to be his successor did to him. David was only been honest with himself on this matter. It is very unfair to emphasize only what non-relatives have done to afflict you when your relatives are not any better than those non-relatives in their dealings with you. David meant that he was very much aware that there must have been Saul's relatives who still believed that he was the reason Saul lost the throne of Israel. In which case, he was not surprised that any of Saul's relatives was gloating over his misfortune led by his son who he gave the chance to live as a prince of their nation to find reason to wish him dead was more precarious. If a non-beneficiary claim not to care about you or even resent you, it can be understood but for a beneficiary to join a non-beneficiary to hate you is shocking, ridiculous, and unforgivable.

II Samuel 9:1-13, 16:1-4 and 19:24-30 can be interpreted to mean that it is the reason David queried why Mephibosheth did not show the level of concern over his plight until Mephibosheth told David about Ziba's lies about him. II Samuel 21:1-9 and 22:6-23 quote David as saying that he was not surprised that Doeg did the evil and sacrilege that he committed. I Samuel 22:1-4 and II Samuel 15:13-22 confirm that David was surprised that Ittai and his fellow Philistines showed him the level of loyalty that he never expected from non-Israelites. This means that David knew what different persons could do for his benefit or against him in view of the kind of relationship between them. David was someone who was always honest with himself. Most people are not. The gospel truth is that if your brother is unkind to you yet you are shameless enough to try to claim kindness as a right from a total stranger, you are not honest with yourself and very unfair to the total strangers.

There is one very cantercarious example in this respect that we must mention no matter how aching it might be to the heart. Matthew 27:15-26, Mark 15:6-15, Luke 23:13-25 and John 18:39-40 and 19:1-16 recount the battle of wits that Pilate fought against Jesus' Jewish kinsmen over whether Jesus should be freed or condemned to die by hanging unjustly. There is no doubt that Pilate lost the battle and approved Jesus' unjust killing. Matthew 27:19 confirms that Pilate's wife persuaded him to either free Jesus or at least not to have anything to do with condemning an innocent man who in this case was Jesus to death. But more important to us here is that John 18:33-36 says:

33 Pilate went back into the palace and called Jesus. "Are you the king of the Jews?" he asked him. 34 Jesus answered, "Does this question come from you or have others told you about me?" 35 Pilate replied, "Do you think I am a Jew? It was your own people and the chief priests who handed you over to me. What have you done?" 36 Jesus said, "My kingdom does not belong to this world; if my kingdom belonged to this world, my followers would fight to keep me from being handed over to the Jewish authorities. No, my kingdom does not belong here!" (TEV)

With every sense of responsibility and reverence, one inevitable interpretation is that Jesus had no response to the question that Pilate put to Him. Pilate meant that Jesus should not forget that His fellow Jews were the only reason he (Pilate) had opportunity to preside over His fate so it would be very unfair for Jesus to make it look like he was bad and evil like His fellow Jews. No matter how wise you are, when a non-relative reminds you not to forget that if not for your relatives he would not have been able to get at you, you can never have any tangible response to such regrettable reminder. In boxing context, it is called technical knockout – a strategic defeat. It is not just that you are suffering the pains of the evil that they did to you but also that you have to live with the heartache of the fact that it is those who should protect you from such pains who are actually responsible for your affliction. It is an integral part of the concept of "unexpected attack by unexpected enemy at an unexpected way, place and time".

Pilate meant that before you blame an external enemy, oppressor or resenter start with your own relative who betrayed you to the non-relative attacker. Pilate's remark or reminder meant that as good a man as Jesus was, it is incredibly sad to note that He had regrettable relatives who He cannot deny as being His relatives. Such fact could be hijacked by His detractors to ridicule Him that if He were such a redeemer why He was not able to redeem His regrettable relative of their curious character and conduct. It is a case of regrettable relatives causes grief to a good man or regrettable relatives causing a respectable man regret. Living with regrettable relatives is one of the worst evils that can happen to any respectable man on earth.

John 18:35 above concludes with Pilate's question to Jesus, "What have you done?" That question provokes another question, 'what could make a relative hand over his relative to a supposed stranger to afflict?' That is a question for unrepentant regrettable relatives. Deuteronomy 13:6-9 and 21:18-21 tell two of the instances when God counseled that relatives should be the first to cast the stone of death on an unrepentant evil doer. But Jesus never did evil rather Acts 10:38 includes the fact that He went about doing good to the relief of the pained and suffering. Therefore, the question should be 'what could make relatives hand over one of them who a good man is – caring, considerate, kind, solving problems in the lives of everyone without charging for his services. He is the first man to procure God's miracle working power to help those who needed God's help yet, go the extra mile to provide those who He had helped to be fed when they were hungry. What would make a relative insist that his relative be harmed by a stranger who knows and confirms that the victim does not deserve to be harmed? It is the regrettable relatives who should be asked rather than any other persons answering for them or speculating possible reasons. There is no doubt that Ecclesiastes 4:4 says people work hard because of envy or the determination to be seen to be better than their neighbour. That still makes some sense because they are working hard to become successful and prosperous in some legitimate endeavours. What about those who devoted their time and effort to engage in the ungodly endeavour of attacking their relative who is well known for helping the poor and weak of society as well as solving problems that had defied solution for a long time?

It is the reason Jesus never forgave Judas Iscariot for betraying Him to His Jewish authorities' assailants. Judas Iscariot had been with Jesus for three and a half years as a full-time apostolic disciple like the other eleven led by Peter, John, and James. He was the treasurer of what can be called 'Jesus Preaching Group' (JPG) or Jesus Eternal Word Preaching and Miracle Performing Group/Ministries (JEWPMPGM). It was not like Jesus discriminated against Judas while giving the title of Apostles to the twelve full-time disciples. Rather, Jesus appointed him the treasurer only for John 12:1-6 to say he stole from the purse. He stole from the purse that he kept for the group – an evil which Jesus overlooked. Yet, Matthew 26:14-16, Mark 14:10-11 and Luke 22:3-6 say he took a sickening and self-sinking step further to betray Jesus to His assailants in order to make some money for himself. He added betrayal for profit to the evil of stealing from the group's purse that he kept. Jesus must have thought that if after fending for Judas Iscariot in the preceding three and a half years he still finds a reason to betray Him to His assailants then Judas did not deserve His forgiveness.

Matthew 26:20-25, Mark 14:17-21 and Luke 22:21-23 can be interpreted to mean that when He talked about Judas' betrayal just before it happened there is no record that He indicated that He wished that Judas never did it like Luke 22:31-34 confirms that when He spoke about Peter's imminent denial He included the fact that He had prayed for Peter. He meant that He did not want Peter's denial to lead to Peter's damnation. In fact, Matthew 26:24, Mark 14:20-21 and Luke 22:22 confirm that He did not wish Judas well for so doing unlike when Luke 22:31-34 and 39-46 confirm that apart from praying for Peter,

He took Peter along to the Garden of Gethsemane to pray further for himself. John 21:1-19 confirms that when Peter failed the test of his faith and went back to fishing Jesus followed Peter to the Lake of Tiberias to recall him to the work of preaching. Meanwhile, Matthew 27:3-10 does not indicate that Jesus made any effort to rescue Judas from suffering the punishment due for his betrayal. The difference between Judas' evil and Peter's denial is that Judas set out to do His betrayal consciously while Peter was a victim of spiritual weakness. Any beneficiary who thinks he still has reason to work against his benefactor deserves the worst punishment.

First, John 6:1-15 says some Jews believed that Jesus should become their king. Then, Acts 1:6-9 can be safely interpreted to mean that on account of Jewish patriotism, Jesus' eleven apostolic disciples led by Peter sought Jesus' help to free the Jews from the control or rule of the Romans of their days. In fact, John 18:28-40 and 19:1-16 give the impression that even Pilate addressed Jesus as the king of the Jews as if to lend credence to the fact that Jesus was worthy to be the king of the Jews. If that be the case, Pilate can be said to have meant that the

Jews did not need any foreigner to rule over them because they have a competent kinsman to rule over them in his judgement. However, first, it is that same worthy kinsman that they forced Pilate to approve for them to kill. Acts 12:1-5 says sometimes after Jesus' death, resurrection and ascension to heaven, some Jews were glad when King Herod who was not a Jew killed their fellow Jew by the name of James because he was a disciple of Jesus. This means that while some Jews as well as Pilate believed that one of them, who in this case is Jesus could save them from foreign rule, some other Jews preferred the foreigner's rule over them for as long as the foreigner approve for them to kill any of their Jewish kinsman who they hate for some sinister reasons. Let us not forget that during Jesus' sham trial, Matthew 27:15-26, Mark 15:6-15, Luke 23:13-25 and John 18:28-40 and 19:1-16 can be interpreted to mean that –

(a) while Pilate a non-Jew believed that Jesus did not deserve to die, the Jewish religious authorities believed otherwise,

(b) the Jews led by their rulers insisted that a certified criminal who had being properly tried and sentenced to death be left to live among them and continue to afflict the populace while Jesus who was a good man be killed in his place, and

(c) the Jewish authorities who can also be described as the Jewish leaders of thought or the leading citizens of the Jews, just like those that I Samuel 8:1-22 says went to Samuel to ask for a king, meant that they preferred foreign rulers who allowed them to hurt their kinsmen rather than enjoy the respect, honour and dignity of being ruled by a fellow Jew.

As a result, it would be very ridiculous for Paul or any other Jew living as a migrant among the Gentiles to say their native hosts are discriminating against him. As unacceptable as discrimination in any form and by whosoever is, the one by a supposed relative is worse than that by a non-relative. Acts 12:1-5 includes the fact that it was the Jews' joyous response to the killing of James who was a Jew that encouraged Herod to arrest another Jew, Apostle Peter. Logical thinking would mean that if the Jews did not celebrate the killing of James which meant that they approved of it, Herod would not have determined go ahead to plot Peter's killing as well. Matthew 14:5 says Herod could not kill John the Baptist as quickly as he would have loved to because he was afraid of the reaction of the Jews. In like manner, Matthew 27:19-24 and Mark 15:8-15 say it was to prevent riot precipitating offence by the Jews that Pilate approved for the Jews to go and kill Jesus by hanging rather than because Jesus deserved to be killed. This means that the Jews had the power to determine who the persons in position of authority could kill or set free. It is as a result that Acts 12:1-5 is very ridiculous and scandalous when it can be said to mean that in order to win the support of the Jews all that the foreigner king needed to do was to kill one of them.

They (the Jews) did not demand that the king appoint one of them as a high official in his palace. They did not ask that the king should reduce their taxes so that they could have more money to spend on their family needs rather they asked the king should cut off the head of some of them who they disagreed with. They did not ask Herod to follow in the example of the Roman officer who Luke 7:1-5 says built a synagogue of worship for the Jews to build them a synagogue of worship or fund the repair work on their Temple of worship in Jerusalem. This generation of Jews chose to use their ability to influence decision-makers or determine the fate of others to hurt their fellow Jews who they did not like. Do you know persons who use their God-given power or privilege in life to hurt others deliberately, to hurt innocent persons, hurt persons who have difference of opinion or religious leaning? Do you know persons who rejoice in the hurt and regret of their relatives? Do you know persons who use their religious learnings ruin/liquidate others? It would not have mattered to us if persons with such monstrous mindset no longer exist on earth.

Acts 12:6-24 confirms that it took God's intervention from heaven using his angel to free Peter from Herod's sword. It amounted to God saving a Jew from a non-Jewish as well as his fellow Jewish co-conspirators and sadistic supporters. It would be wrong to blame Herod more than the Jews who approved that he killed Peter because Peter was as unsafe in the hands of Jeremiah's fellow Jews as he is unsafe in the hands of a non-Jew. If a man is not safe abroad as well as at home where else under the sun is he supposed to live? His own people want him dead as much as strangers want him dead.

Second, Acts 18:12-17 confirms that when Gallio who was not a Jew was appointed the governor of Achaia by the Roman Emperor, Apostle Paul's Jewish kinsmen sued him to Gallio's court to condemn for them to kill like Matthew 27:15-26, Mark 15:6-15, Luke 23:13-25 and John 18:28-40 and 19:1-16 confirm that they had used Pilate to secure the Emperor's approval to kill Jesus earlier. There are two issues here – the first is that they could not kill Paul without the approval of the Roman Emperor's appointed representative just like John 18:28-31 confirms that the Jewish authorities implied to Pilate that the only reason they came to get his approval to kill or before they could kill Jesus was that they could not do it without the Emperor's or His representative's approval. It means that they were afraid to offend the Emperor, but they were not afraid to offend the God of their ancestors and the universe who Paul was ordained and ordered to represent to the Gentiles. It was easier for them to disregard God's command in Exodus 23:7 that forbade them from putting an innocent man to death than to disregard the Emperor's approval. Meanwhile, this is addition to the fact that they lied to get the Emperor's approval. It is striking that they remembered to restrain themselves from offending the Emperor, but they did not regard the traditional brotherhood bond between them and their victim and as a result restrain themselves from harming one of their own. Acts 18:18 says it was only after Gallio refused to grant Paul's fellow Jews request to kill him that they left him alone to share the Gospel among the natives of Corinth. The other issue is that indeed Gallio was fed up with the Jews. He must have been aware of how they had killed Jesus and encouraged Herod to kill James, killed Stephen and tried to kill Peter. Gallio proves that when a people become famous for the wrong reason such as afflicting relatives and killing kinsmen relentlessly other responsible people do not like to have anything to do with them.

Third, Acts 9:1-2 and 26-31 says Paul was commissioned from Jerusalem by the Jewish religious authorities to go and persecute Jews who were Jesus' believers, disciples and propagators in Damascus. However, when Paul returned to Jerusalem as a converted disciple and propagator of Jesus the same Jewish authorities tried to kill him. This threat forced Paul to retreat to his hometown of Tarsus to stay safe. Then, the Jewish authorities stopped hunting him. However, Acts 18:12-18, 21:1-40, 22:1-30, 23:1-35 and 24:1-23 can be interpreted to mean that when next Paul's presence and preaching in Jerusalem offended them, the Jewish authorities were no longer content with forcing Paul out of their supposed territory rather they accompanied him to the Corinthian region of the Gentiles to seek to afflict him. If Gallio had approved the Jews' request to persecute Paul, what moral right does Paul or a Jew in his predicament have to claim that Gallio was discriminating against him because he was not a native Gentile or Corinthian? If his fellow Jews had killed him earlier as Acts 9:26-31 confirms that they tried to, Paul would not have been alive to appear before Governors Gallio and Felix to be tried as Acts 18:12-18 and 24:1-27 confirm.

The other issue is that Gallio's response meant that the Jews and their reason for wanting Paul dead were not worth his attention and time. When kinsmen start fighting one another, they belittle themselves in the sight of non-kinsmen. God used Gallio to reveal how persons who should not fight one another belittle themselves in the sight others when they resort to fight one another dirty and deadly. Part of the core point is that you cannot belittle yourselves by attacking your own people and then you return to say someone else is not respecting you. Also, it means that if your own kinsmen ill-treat you, do you expect that those you went to seek refuge in their place would invent some reasons to respect you. Your kinsmen did not value your life or your worth among them why should non-relatives be obliged to value your life and respect you? There is not much to respect in you because they know that your own people do not value your own life. It may hurt those who do not like to face the truth of their situation, but it is the truth of life. Someone may never be comfortable with this fact, but it does not reduce the fact that it is the truth of life.

Look at it this way, when Rebecca was to become Isaac's wife, Genesis 24:1-67 confirms that Eliezer went to get her from Nahor's family in Haran; Isaac never left home before she was brought to him. However, when Rebecca's son, Jacob would get wife he was sent to Haran rather than a servant going to get a wife from among Laban's daughters. The result was that

Laban trampled down on Jacob throughout the 20 years he lived and worked for Laban. Laban witnessed Rebecca leaving Haran to go and become Isaac's wife in Canaan. As a result, he knew that something was seriously wrong for her son to come over personally to marry a wife in his household. And indeed, it was the troubles between Jacob and Esau that forced Jacob to go to Laban's place hiding under the guise that he was there to get a wife.

Fourth, Acts 22:24-30 and 23:12-35 confirm that when the Jews conspired to kill Paul in Jerusalem at another time, it was a non-Jew, a Roman army commander who saved Paul from their precarious plot. It is very important to note that this army commander's loyalty to saving Paul's life was based on the solidarity of being a Roman citizen just like Paul. Meanwhile, the Jews who were Paul's kinsmen in addition to worshipping the same God of their ancestors before becoming Roman citizens by birth believed that Paul was better dead. Acts 24:1-10 says after the army commander saved Paul from his fellow Jews in Jerusalem, the Jewish authorities followed Paul to Caesarea to accuse him before Governor Felix. Acts 17:1-10 says it was the

Jews living in the Gentile region or city of Thessalonica who attacked Paul who was their Jewish kinsman rather than the Thessalonians who were Gentiles.

This is why the subject of natives being guilty of any form of discrimination against migrant is utter nonsense. Any form of discrimination by whoever is ungodly and unacceptable however, it is equally evil and unacceptable to emphasize only the discrimination perpetuated by non-kinsmen while de-emphasizing the discrimination perpetuated by kinsmen. It is a disguised form of witch-hunt of natives, an attempt to blackmail and intimidate them and therefore, against the law of natural justice as well. There are kinsmen who do worst things to the man who claims that he is suffering racism or homophobic rubbish. Why is the ill-treatment by non-kinsman worst than the one perpetuated by kinsman? Commonly, it is politicians who resort to tribal or religious card or sentiment in their ever-disgusting desperation to win election. It does not make sense when a man who ran away from his family house because of all sorts of attacks by family members start shouting from the rooftop that the natives of where he went to live in hiding from his horrendous household enemies are oppressing him. What about the household attacks that forced him to go and live abroad? How often does he talk about his household attacks? It would have been ridiculous for Paul to say that some Gentiles were attacking him while working among the Gentiles when his fellow Jews attacked him in Jerusalem so much so that God said He could no longer guarantee his safety in Jerusalem and as a result he should leave to go and live and work among the Gentiles.

One of the core reasons we must tell ourselves life-saving truth is that God is not going to come down to do what we should do for ourselves. He would not use angels to do what we should do by ourselves for our own benefit. We have to help ourselves and helping ourselves starts from telling one's self the truth. Whoever cannot afford to be honest with himself can never help himself just as he can never be helped by even God. There are many that even God of Israel cannot help despite the fact that He is all powerful and can do all things. Anyone who is not honest with himself cannot be helped by God or benefit from God's help.

32

MAGNIFICENT MIGRATION MANAGEMENT

Jeremiah 15:1 and Ezekiel 14:12-14 and 19-20 can be interpreted to mean that God of Israel rated Job's holiness, godliness and righteousness or uprightness to be at the same level or height as that of Noah who Genesis 6:1-8 confirms that he was the only man or individual with whom God was pleased in his generation. And it was for his sake that God spared the lives of his wife, their three sons and their wives. Moses, about whom Numbers 12:1-8 says God confirmed to be the meekest or humblest man on earth in his generation and God spoke with him face-to-face belonged to this club. Deuteronomy 34:1-8 and 10-12 can be said to mean that he was the greatest Israelite in his generation just as Psalm 103:7

confirms that while he showed His ways to Moses He showed only His miracles to Moses' fellow Israelites. He used Moses to prove His power through the performance of miracles to the admiration of the Israelites of Moses' generation.

Samuel who Psalm 99:6b confirm that God regarded highly in his lifetime belonged to this group or club of the holiest of holy men who ever lived. I Samuel 3:19-21 confirms that he was the sole authoritative voice of God in his dispensation after his predecessor, Eli's death. I Samuel 7:1-14 says during his reign over Israel the only war that was fought was won by his offering sacrifices to God. The army of Israel could not go into the battle without asking for his prayer assistance and God honoured his prayer by giving the Israelites the needed victory over the Philistines. Verses 5-13 confirm that with this one defeat all Israelites' territories that the Philistines had been controlling were returned to the Israelites without exception. Verse 15 says Samuel ruled Israel so long as he lived.

Meanwhile, Samuel seemed the only high priest or the leading priest and prophet of Israel who never depended on the Covenant

Box in the Tent of the Lord's Presence or the ephod to hear God to guide the Israelites. He served as the priest who offered sacrifices to God for the benefit of the people of Israel, and the prophet who spoke the mind of God for the people to obey as well as served as the judge of the people unlike the case of Joshua about whom Numbers 27:15-23 says God said while Joshua would be the national leader he would be guided by the high priest using the ephod to confirm God's will and instructions. Moses and Samuel were all-in-one leaders of Israel under God's direct guidance and supervision. They combined the office of the chief justice, High Priest, and leading prophet. There was no other priest or prophet of high repute in Israel during their reign. Their relevance towered above all other religious leaders in the nation despite the fact that during the time of Samuel there were supposed to be Aaronite priests and prophets in the priestly cities that Numbers 35:1-8 and Joshua 21:1-42 confirm that they were assigned to the Aaronite and Levitical priests.

I Samuel 2:22-36 says in verses 27-36 that God used a nameless prophet to tell Eli the long term punishment that He had decided against Eli's descendants because of the sins of his two sons and his complicity by way of condoning their sins or not doing enough to stop his sons' sinfulness. Then, I Samuel 3:1-18 says God used inexperienced young Samuel to notify Eli of the immediate punishment for the sins of his sons. From that point until the anointing of Saul when Samuel was already very old, there is no record of any other priest or prophet who God used to do anything noteworthy. Rather, the religious life and experiences of the Israelites revolved solely around Samuel either while he still operated from Shiloh or had relocated his operational headquarters to his hometown of Ramah.

Finally, there is Daniel who despite being a captive in Babylon, Daniel 1:1-21 and 2:1-49 confirm that Nebuchadnezzar who Daniel 2:36 and 5:18-19 confirm as the greatest king and individual on earth in his lifetime yet, Daniel 2:46-47 says Nebuchadnezzar bowed low with his head touching the ground to worship Daniel and offered sacrifices to Daniel. Daniel 6:1-18 confirms that in his stead several thousands of nobles and their household members were destroyed. Daniel 7 – 12 confirms that God revealed the events of the end of the age to him. This introduction is to enable us appreciate the caliber of Job so that we can understand that his example is worthy of noting and emulating where necessary. Job 1:1-22 and 2:1-23 can be interpreted to mean that God trusted him enough to use Satan to test him and prove Satan wrong. Job 42:7-10 can be said to mean that God considered him holy enough to serve as the high priest to his friends. Job 31:33-34 says he did not excuse his sin like Genesis 3:1-17 says Adam tried to blame God as facilitating his disobedience by claiming or implying that if God never gave him a wife he would not have disobeyed God's command. Job 31:1-32 can be summed up as follows: –

(1) wealth did not make him to insult God of Israel who made him prosperous and great

(2) had respect for his fellow man just as he honoured God

(3) had nothing to hide in his life

(4) fought injustice

(5) exhibited high moral standard

Job 2:9-10 says in the worst moment of his tribulation he did not heed his wife's counsel to curse God like Genesis 3:1-7 says Adam heeded his wife's counsel to disobey and displease God. The reason we went into all these about Job is the fact that Job 1:1-5, 29:11-24 and 31:13-15 confirm that just as he was kind to non-members of his household so also he was to his sons and daughters. This means that Job ensured that he did not care for non-family members at the expense of his sons and daughters.

Job cared for his children just as he cared for the poor, needy, strangers, widows and the fatherless. This means that much as he was kind to non-members of his household, he never did it at the expense of his household members. We are not told how his family members or wife and children would have reacted if he had helped non-family members at their expense. However, when Jacob mismanaged his preference for his beloved Joseph to stir the resentment of his other children, they did not spare Joseph of their anger. Jacob's older sons did not care that Jacob was much around or Joseph was their younger half brother, they vented their anger on him. They might have known that God authored the dream that meant that God had chosen him to become greater than them in their adult lifetime, but they did not fear God to the extent of not attacking Joseph. Liking or disliking someone cannot be legislated successfully or to achieve the desired result. To get natives to accept and live side-by-side with migrants, leaders, rulers, or government officials who desire to see it happen must learn to manage the relationship between natives and migrants reasonably well.

With regards to proof that Jacob mismanaged his preference for Joseph it began when Genesis 32:1-12 and 33:1-3 say when he was afraid that Esau was coming to attack and destroy him and his household members he arranged his family members in such a way that proved that he did not mind if Esau killed all other family members and Joseph is spared. Even then at this point his sons did not vent their anger on Joseph. And as if that was still not provocation enough, Genesis 37:1-4 says Jacob went ahead to provide Joseph with a special dress – a coat of many colors which Jacob never made for any of Joseph's older brothers in the past or while getting it for Joseph. It was at this point that they could no longer contain or conceal their disgust and decided to afflict Joseph. The other issue that angered his older sons was that while he left them for their mother to teach the difference between good and evil because he was working hard to become wealthy. Then, when he was retired from hard work, he spent quality time to teach Joseph as a growing child the difference between right and wrong. As a result, Genesis 37:1-4 includes the fact that Joseph was able to point out the inappropriate behaviour of his older brothers. Even if the older brothers agree that they were behaving badly they could not stop because they had been brought up like that whereas Joseph's better behaviour was both indictment and insult to them that their younger brother was better behaved.

I Chronicles 14:1-2 and 18:14 confirm that David ensured that the Israelites or his subjects were treated fairly yet, we get the impression from II Samuel 13:27 and 29 that his sons had their own mule and could afford to host feast fit for a king. That is like following in Job's pattern or it was Job who followed in his footsteps depending on who lived before the other to ensure that he did not take care of non-family members at the expense and envy of family members. Whoever treats family members and non-family members equally or worst still, less kindly to non-family is remotely responsible for family members' resentment of non-family members in his household.

Genesis 20:1-18 says King Abimelech's Philistines recognized Abraham as God of the universe's untouchable representative on earth in the sense that they knew that God threatened Abimelech for taking his wife, Sarah by mistake – a mistake consciously caused by Abraham. They must have known that Isaac was Abraham's son by Sarah. Genesis 21:1-8 and 22-34 strongly suggest that Isaac was conceived and born while Abraham was living among the Philistines in Abimelech's domain. Yet, Genesis 20:1-18 and 21:22-34 can be interpreted to mean that despite them knowing that God of the universe was with Abraham and that Abimelech approved of Abraham living among them, chapter 21:25-26 confirms that Abimelech's palace officials still practically oppressed Abraham by blocking one of the wells that Abraham dug. Then, Genesis 21:9-21, 25:1-11 and 26:1-33 simply mean that despite knowing Isaac to be Abraham's only son around them and that God of the universe was with him like He had been with Abraham they still went ahead to persecute Isaac while he lived among them after the death of Abraham and Sarah. Genesis 21:25-16 and 26:16-22 confirm that just as the Philistines blocked Abraham's dug wells so also, they blocked Isaac's dug wells in their land or Abimelech's domain.

First, Genesis 20:1-18 and 26:26-29 can be interpreted to mean that Abimelech and his fellow Philistine subjects acknowledged that God was with Abraham and Isaac. Second, the understanding that God protected father and son made the Philistines to apparently defy Abimelech to persecute Abraham and Isaac by way of blocking their wells. The more they knew that God forbade them or anyone else from oppressing Abraham and Isaac the more it angered them to oppress them both. Third, there is no record that Abimelech took any punitive measures against his officials and subjects who defied his directives to block Abraham's and Isaac's dug wells. Four, it seemed that Abimelech knew that his officials and subjects might never refrain from hurting non-natives living among them when he warned them in Genesis 26:6-11 never to hurt Isaac. Five, there are unrepentant rebels among natives who would care less about

God and the authorities' threats of punishment to still persecute migrants.

There is no record in Genesis 21:25-26 that Abimelech did anything to investigate Abraham's claim that some of his officials and/or subjects had blocked the wells that he dug and possibly punish such supposed erring natives/subjects. It was like Abimelech thought that defying his directives was not enough reason to punish any of his fellow natives because of any non-native living among them. Again, he did not think that oppression of a non-native by a native was worth investigating for the purpose of punishing the perpetrator. The Philistines in Abraham's generation or times blocked a well while those in Isaac's generation blocked several of Isaac's dug wells. This is even though Isaac was born in the land of the Philistines or Philistia. Furthermore, this is even though God who created the earth led Abraham to live among them and the fact that He was with father and son to protect them was not in doubt. In line with Revelations 2:7a, 11a, 17a and 29 and 3:6, 13 and 22, let those who have ears not only listen but find it convenient to heed what Abraham and Isaac's experiences teach mankind in all generations. One reason this is particularly important is that Hebrews 4:2 says knowing without doing does not benefit anyone, the hearer or knowledgeable.

Even after King Abimelech of the Philistines in Gerar legislated or ordered that none of his officials or native Philistines should harm Isaac, they still defied his order to attack Isaac repeatedly. As the sitting king, Abimelech had the recognized authority to give order to his officials and subjects on any matter within the territory of his kingdom. This made his order concerning Isaac to be legitimate, yet, despite giving legitimate order, his kinsmen officials and subjects still attacked Isaac behind him or without his knowledge. That is why we say no government regulation or law can ever make natives to like any migrant. Therefore, convincing natives by way of giving them realistic and rewarding reasons to let migrants live beside them is the most result-oriented way to manage migrants. The reward of migrants living in the land should be repeated and reiterated constantly like commercial concerns remind consumers of their brands through advertisements constantly.

Legislating punishment for discrimination against migrants emboldens some natives to harm strangers more than discourage them from harming migrants. So long as natives do not understand the benefit of migrants living among them, they will consider any legislation that prescribes punishment for discrimination against migrants as a tool by government officials to force their personal views on them. Persons in position of authority in nations must understand that majority of their native subjects do not share in their belief of commonness or sameness of all nationals on earth. If you want others to accept your personal beliefs, you must do a lot of marketing of your ideas to them and give time for them to comprehend and accept them. If you try to force your kinsmen to accept your beliefs, they will make things difficult for you.

Publicizing migrants' contribution partly persuades natives that migrants are beneficial to them and as a result should be allowed to live side-by-side with them. The appointment of Joseph to the exalted office of the Prime Minister of the Egyptian kingdom was partly because he was able to solve a problem that all the wise men of Egypt could not solve for their king. And the king was careful to remind the wise men and nobles serving in his palace that for the fact that no other person could interpret his dreams,

Joseph who did should be appointed to manage the solution to the problem that the dream indicated was imminent. Joseph's ability to interpret his dreams provided him the opportunity or confidence to say Joseph should be appointed to become the boss of the officials and the subjects. This means that migrants have a responsibility to give basis to government officials to encourage the general native populace to join the government officials to accommodate them (migrants) readily.

Joseph's promotion by Potiphar and the prison superintendent was based on his usefulness. Moses' acceptance by Jethro and members of his household was based on his usefulness which can be called benefit-based acceptance (BA) or the acceptance's benefit barometer (ABB). It is not totally right to demonize natives who do not readily accept strangers in their midst without considering that without usefulness or benefit it is nearly natural to resent the unprofitable. In any case, the determination to promote so-called artificial intelligence is meant to get rid of unuseful human beings from production process and workplace as much as possible in order to eliminate labour union demands and the attendant industrial disputes, delays and hiccups by employers.

Author's Other Published Titles

1. There is Time for Everything … Including Action

2. The Almighty Knows and Cares Very Much for You

3. For The Joy Ahead

4. Only When Men Need You

5. Money Does Not Answer All Things

6. Issues Money Cannot Solve

7. Nothing New Under The Sun - I

8. Aiding and Abetting Evil - I

9. Not Enough Reason

10. God's Two-way Trial-Testing

11. You Need A Personal Pastor In Addition To Your Pulpit Pastor

12. Focus On God In Church

13. Regrettable Relatives

14. How To Prevent Divorce

15. The Qualified Queens

16. How To Prevent Untimely Death

17. God Preferred Personalities

18. Why Your Prayer may Seem not to be Working

19. Leaving Laudable Legacies

20. Profiting From Prophecy

21. The Most Marvellous Marriage Ever

22. The Most Important Prayer Point

23. The Best Time to Pray

24. Questions For God

25. Ahithophel (Humbly Mind Your Business)

26. Had They Known/Now That We Know

27. They Might Have Lived Longer

28. Barack Obama Must Not Fail

29. Abraham's Saner Solution

30. Dual Lifestylists

31. Their Mindsets

32. Hurting Happiness

33. I Know, But Cannot

34. All Humans Are Hebrews

35. The Undoing of the Ungodly

36. Why God Approved and Allowed

37. Pointless Persecutors

38. God-Authored Cabal Concept

39. Special SOS

40. The Many Unforgivable Sins of Jesus of Nazareth

41. God-Recommended Enslavement

42. Real Reasons Rulers Resist Replacement

43. God Authored and Approved Brain Drain

44. All Humans are Helpless

45. Prayer Plus

46. Exemplary Esau

47. Until You Rebel

48. Nigeria Needs Nehemiah

49. This Stage-managed Life and World

50. Why You Must Abhor Poverty

51. Securing Strength to Prevail Through Fasting and Praying

52. The Best Time to Pray

53. Tamar, Tamarites and Judah-like Tamar

54. Save Us to Serve You

55. Governor Nehemiah's Grand Style

56. Moses' Double Standard Dealership

57. Just Like Daddy & Mummy

58. Between Honourables and Hooligans

59. Winning Workplace Wars

60. Why The Righteous Suffer

61. Your Time for Total Recovery

62. Soaring Higher By …

63. SABENA – Such A Bad Experience Never Again

64. The Called and the Co-opted in Christian service

In press

65. Bright, Beautiful & Beckoning, But …

66. The Boss is not Always Right

67. Essential Reminders to the Great and Mighty, Volumes I, II, III, IV, V, VI & VII

68. Prophecy Oh Prophecy, Volumes I, II & III

69. Now is Your time to Press Forward in Life

70. Marks of Maturity

71. My Fantastic Father, Marvellous Mother and Respectable Relatives

72. The Effect of the Event/Experience

www.ingramcontent.com/pod-product-compliance
Lightning Source LLC
Chambersburg PA
CBHW022006120526
44592CB00032B/94